ACCA

Advanced Audit and Assurance – International (AAA – INT) Practice & Revision Kit

BPP Learning Media is an **ACCA Approved Content Provider** for the ACCA qualification. This means we work closely with ACCA to ensure our products fully prepare you for your ACCA exams.

In this Practice & Revision Kit, which has been reviewed by the **ACCA examining team**, we:

- Discuss the **best strategies** for revising and taking your ACCA exams
- Ensure you are well **prepared** for your exam
- Provide you with **lots of great guidance** on tackling questions
- Provide you with **four** mock exams

For exams in September 2019, December 2019, March 2020 and June 2020

Thirteenth edition 2019

ISBN 9781 5097 2458 1
(Previous ISBN 9781 5097 1674 6)
e-ISBN 9781 5097 2450 5

Cataloguing-in-Publication Data

A catalogue record for this book is available
from the British Library

Published by

BPP Learning Media Ltd
BPP House, Aldine Place
142–144 Uxbridge Road
London W12 8AA

www.bpp.com/learningmedia

Printed in the United Kingdom

Your learning materials, published by BPP Learning Media Ltd, are
printed on paper obtained from traceable sustainable sources.

Contents

Review form

Finding questions

Question index

The headings in this checklist/index indicate the main topics of questions, but questions are expected to cover several different topics.

Questions set under the previous syllabus, P7, are included because their style and content are very similar to that of the current AAA exam. The questions have been amended to reflect the current exam.

BPP LEARNING

*Need a group one for plang. D.

PT1

Reporting Q in 3 Mock Q's is v. good per examiner webinar

Part E: Completion, review and reporting	Marks	Time allocation Mins	Page number Question	Answer
47 Rope (P7 Sep/Dec 16) (amended)	25	49	73	390
48 Kandinsky (P7 Sep/Dec 15)	25	49	74	396
49 Butler (P7 6/11) (amended)	25	49	76	403
50 Yew (P7 12/11) (amended)	25	49	78	408
51 Fern (P7 Mar/Jun 17) (amended)	25	49	79	412
52 Boston (P7 Mar/Jun 16) (amended)	25	49	80	419
53 Coram (Sep 18)	25	49	81	424
54 Dexter (P7 12/08)	20	39	83	431
55 Willis (P7 12/10) (amended)	25	49	84	435
56 Newman (P7 12/10) (amended)	25	49	85	440
57 Marr (P7 6/14) (amended)	25	49	87	445
58 Pluto (P7 6/09) (amended)	25	49	88	449
59 Burford (P7 12/13)	20	39	89	454
60 Basking (P7 Sep/Dec 17)	20	39	90	458
61 Hopper (P7 Sep/Dec 15) (amended)	25	49	91	462
62 Darren (P7 6/15)	20	39	92	468
63 Chester & Co (P7 12/13) (amended)	25	49	93	473

Part F: Other assignments				
64 Leopard (P7 Sep/Dec 17)	20	39	95	478
65 Apricot and Lychee (P7 12/09) (amended)	25	49	96	484
66 Mizzen (P7 12/13)	25	49	97	489
67 Titian (P7 Sep/Dec 15) (amended)	25	49	99	496
68 Jacob (P7 6/11) (amended)	25	49	100	502
69 Crocus	25	49	101	507
70 Jansen (Sep 18)	25	49	102	511

Mock exam 1

Mock exam 2 (ACCA 2018 Specimen exam)

Mock exam 3 (March/June 18 exam) (amended)

Mock exam 4 (December 18 exam)

Topic index

Listed below are the key AAA syllabus topics and the numbers of the questions in this Kit covering those topics. We have also included a reference to the relevant Chapter of the BPP AAA Workbook, the companion to the BPP AAA Practice and Revision Kit, in case you wish to revise the information on the topic you have covered.

If you need to concentrate your practice and revision on certain topics or if you want to attempt all available questions that refer to a particular subject, you will find this index useful.

Syllabus topic	Question numbers	Workbook chapter
A1: International regulatory frameworks for audit and assurance services	ME1 Q1	1
A2: Money laundering	1(a), 4(c), 10(c), 11(a)	1
A3: Laws and regulations	22(b), 35(b)	1
B1: Code of Ethics for Professional Accountants	1(b), 2(b), 3, 4(b), 5, 6, 7(c)–(d), 8(b), 9, 10(a), 11(b)–(c), 12(b), 15(a)–(b), 21(d), 25(d), 27(b), 30(a), 33(d), 36(a), 39(d), 40(d), 43(d), 46(b)–(c), 47(c), 51(a), 53(b), 55(c), 57(b), 60(b), 61(d), 63(a)–(b), 67(b), 69(c)	2
B2: Fraud and error	24(a), 25(a), 69(b)	3
B3: Professional liability	13(a)	3
C1: Quality control (firm-wide)	9, 10(b), 14(c), 45(a), 58(c)	4
C2: Advertising, tendering and obtaining professional work and fees	7(c), 12, 17(a), 39(d)	5
C3: Professional appointments	2(a), 15(a)–(b), 34(d)	5
D1: Planning, materiality and assessing the risk of material misstatement	7(a), 17(b)–(c), 20(a), 21(b), 25(b), 26(a), 27(a), 28(a), 30(a), 31(a)–(b), 32(a), 33(a)–(c), 34(a)–(c), 39(a)–(b), 40(b), 41(a), 43(a)–(b)	6
D2: Evidence and testing considerations	26(b), 27(a), 34(a), 40(a), 60(a)	7
D3: Audit procedures and evidence evaluation	7(b), 13(b), 17(b) and (d), 19, 21(c), 22(a), 23, 25(c), 28(b), 29(a), 30(b), 31(c), 32(c), 33(d), 34(e), 35(a), 36(b), 37(a), 39(c), 41(b), 42(a), 43(c), 44(a), 51(b), 53(a), 60(b), 67(b)	8
D4: Using the work of others	20(b), 28(c)	7
D5: Group audits	15(c), 18, 21(a), 32(b), 34(c), 40(c), 47, 61(b)	9
E1: Subsequent events and going concern	18(b), 47(a)–(b), 48(a), 49, 50(a), 52(a), 54, 59, 65(c)	10
E2: Completion and final review	21(c), 24(b), 29(b), 37, 38(a), 45, 46(c), 50(b)–(c), 53(a), 58(b)–(c), 61(c), 70(b)	10

Syllabus topic	Question numbers	Workbook chapter
E3: Auditor's reports	1(c), 14(c), 47(d), 49(b), 51(c), 52(c), 53(a), 54(c), 55(a), 56(c), 57(a), 58(b), 59(b), 60(c), 61(a)–(c), 62, 63(c)	11
E4: Reports to those charged with governance and management	19, 37(b), 52(b), 55(c), 60(a)	11
F1: Audit-related and assurance services	8(a), 66(c)	12
F2: Specific assignments	36(c), 43(b), 64(a)–(b), 65, 66(a), 67(a),(c), 68(a)–(b), 69, 70(a)	12, 13, 14
F3: The audit of social, environmental and integrated reporting	6(d), 41(c), 56(a)–(b)	15
F4: The audit of performance information (pre-determined objectives) in the public sector	20(c), 44(b)–(c), 48(b)	15
F5: Reporting on other assignments	64(b), 68(c)	12
G1: Professional and ethical developments	4(a), 50(a)	1, 2
G2: Other current issues	38(b), 57(c)	16

The exam

Computer-based exams

With effect from the March 2020 sitting, ACCA have commenced the launch of computer-based exams (CBEs) for this exam with the aim of rolling out into all markets internationally over a short period. Paper-based examinations (PBE) will be run in parallel while the CBEs are phased in. BPP materials have been designed to support you, whichever exam option you choose. For more information on these changes and when they will be implemented, please visit the ACCA website.

Approach to examining the syllabus

If you are preparing to sit AAA you should pay particular attention to the following in order to maximise your chances of success. The following is taken from a recent AAA examining team's report.

'In order to pass this exam, candidates are required to **apply the principles and rules** from their earlier studies to more complex scenarios and demonstrate their ability to handle different situations which may arise in audit and related services. In addition, candidates are expected to develop a **broader knowledge of audit services** and practice management. Candidates should also keep abreast of **current developments** and challenges in the field of both auditing and financial reporting to allow them to demonstrate the ability to handle these challenges in the context of auditing financial statements and as areas they may need to brief clients on.

'This **combination of learned knowledge and its application** to complex situations requires candidates to be able to go beyond the topics as covered in text books and be able to react to the scenarios described in the requirement. Study through question practice and following developments in the field through the media, and through IFAC and IAASB will be crucial in taking the learned knowledge from earlier parts of the qualification and converting it into a demonstrable ability to provide audit and advisory services to clients.

'AAA also tests candidates' **ability to tailor their answer to the context in which the requirement is written**. Often the audience of the requirement will dictate the pitch and depth of the answer along with its focus. Failure to take into account such matters will often lead to **time pressures** in the exam as candidates lose time by detailing knowledge that is not relevant to the requirement. This is particularly noticeable in question 1 which is set at the planning stage of an audit and is addressed to the senior members of the audit team, meaning an explanation of the audit risk model is not appropriate. Candidates should allow themselves time to focus on the requirement that is set before they begin their answers. **It would be useful for candidates to visualise delivering the requirement verbally to the report recipient and therefore imagining how a partner in a firm, already qualified and experienced, would react to listening to the answer**.'

Format of the exam

		Number of marks
Section A:	One compulsory question	50
Section B:	Two compulsory questions (25 marks each)	50
		100

The **time allowed** for this exam is 3 hours and 15 minutes.

The examination is constructed in two sections. Questions in both sections will be largely discursive. However, candidates will be expected, for example, to be able to assess materiality and calculate relevant ratios where appropriate.

BPP LEARNING

Question format

The format of questions in AAA is slightly different between Section A and Section B. Section A questions will feature scenarios, with simple requirements such as 'Respond to the partner's request', or 'Draft the briefing notes as requested'. You will have to work out for yourself what you need to include in your answer. Section B questions will feature requirements akin to those in your previous ACCA exams.

For sittings from September 2019 onwards, all questions are set as at the fictitious date of 1 July 20X5.

As AAA is a Strategic Professional exam, **4 professional level marks** will be awarded. Some of these should be easy to obtain. The examining team has stated that some marks may be available for presenting your answer in the form of a letter, presentation, email, report or briefing notes. You may also be able to obtain marks for the style and layout of your answer.

Reports should always have an appropriate title. They should be **formally written**, with an **introductory paragraph** setting out the aims of the report. You should use **short paragraphs** and **appropriate headings**, with a summary of findings as a **conclusion**.

Memoranda and **Briefing notes** should have the following four things at the beginning:

From:	Name of author
To:	Name of recipient
Date:	1 July 20X5
Subject:	………

Letters should be addressed appropriately to the correct person and be dated. They should have a short introductory paragraph, a conclusion and should be in a formal writing style. Letters beginning with 'Dear Sir/Madam' should end with 'Yours faithfully'.

Analysis of past exam sittings

The table below provides details of when each element of the syllabus has been examined in the ten most recent sittings and the question number and section in which each element was examined.

Since September 2016, the ACCA has been issuing two exams each year, after the December and June exam sessions. These exams are compiled from questions selected from the two preceding sessions eg in December 2017, the sample questions were compiled from September 2017 and December 2017 exams.

A specimen exam was also issued for the change in question format for 2018/19, but this has not been included in the analysis below.

Covered in Workbook Chapter		Dec 2018 (AAA)	Sept 2018 (AAA)	Mar/ Jun 2018 (P7)	Sep/ Dec 2017 (P7)	Mar/ Jun 2017 (P7)	Sep/ Dec 2016 (P7)	Mar/ Jun 2016 (P7)	Sep/ Dec 2015 (P7)	June 2015 (P7)	Dec 2014 (P7)	June 2014 (P7)
	REGULATORY ENVIRONMENT											
1	International regulatory frameworks for audit and assurance services						5(a)					
1	Money laundering	3(a)		2(a)				3(b)				2(b)
1	Laws and regulations									2(b)		
	PROFESSIONAL AND ETHICAL CONSIDERATIONS											
2	Codes of ethics for professional accountants	3(b)	1(d), 2(b), 3(b)	2(a)	3(b), 4	3(a)	4, 5(a)	1(c), 4(b)	4	3(a), 4	1(d), 4(b)	4
3	Fraud and error	1						3(a)				
3	Professional liability											
	QUALITY CONTROL AND PRACTICE MANAGEMENT											
4	Quality control		3(b)	3	4	2		2(a)	5(c)	4	5(a)	3(b)
5	Advertising, tendering, obtaining professional work and fees										4(a)	
5	Professional appointments	1									4(a)	
	ASSIGNMENTS											
6, 7, 8	The audit of historical financial information including: (i) Planning, materiality and assessing the risk of misstatement (ii) Evidence	1	1	1, 4	1, 2	1, 4	1, 2, 3	1, 2(b), 3(b), 5(a)	1	1, 2(a), 3(b), 5(a)–(b)	1(a)–(c), 2, 3(a), 5(b)	1, 3, 4
9	Group audits			1(b), 4	1(c)				5(b)			

BPP LEARNING

IMPORTANT! The table above gives a broad idea of how frequently major topics in the syllabus are examined. It should not be used to question spot and predict for example that Topic X will not be examined because it came up two sittings ago. The examining team's reports indicate that the examining team is well aware some students try to question spot. The examining team avoid predictable patterns and may, for example, examine the same topic two sittings in a row.

BPP LEARNING

Syllabus and Study Guide

The complete AAA syllabus and study guide can be found by visiting the exam resource finder on the ACCA website.

Examinable documents

Knowledge of new examinable regulations issued by 31 August will be examinable in examination sessions being held in the following exam year. Documents may be examinable even if the effective date is in the future. This means that all regulations issued by 31 August 2018 will be examinable in the September 2019 to June 2020 examinations.

The accounting knowledge that is assumed for AAA is the same as that examined in Strategic Business Reporting (SBR). Therefore, candidates studying for AAA should refer to the Accounting Standards listed under SBR.

Note. AAA will only expect knowledge of accounting standards and financial reporting standards from SBR. Knowledge of exposure drafts and discussion papers will not be expected.

AUDIT

International

Knowledge of new examinable regulations issued by 31 August will be examinable in examination sessions being held in the following exam year. Documents may be examinable even if the effective date is in the future. This means that all regulations issued by 31 August 2018 will be examinable in the September 2019 to June 2020 examinations.

The study guide offers more detailed guidance on the depth and level at which the examinable documents should be examined. The study guide should therefore be read in conjunction with the examinable documents list.

Accounting Standards

Advanced Audit and Assurance (AAA)

The accounting knowledge that is assumed for Advanced Audit and Assurance is the same as that examined in Strategic Business Reporting (SBR). Therefore, candidates studying for AAA should refer to the IFRS Standards listed under SBR.

N.B. AAA will only expect knowledge of accounting standards and financial reporting standards from SBR. Knowledge of exposure drafts and discussion papers will not be expected.

	Title
	International Standards on Auditing (ISAs)
	Glossary of Terms
	International Framework for Assurance Engagements
	Preface to the International Quality Control, Auditing, Review, Other Assurance and Related Services Pronouncements
ISA 200	Overall Objectives of the Independent Auditor and the Conduct of an Audit in Accordance with ISAs
ISA 210	Agreeing the Terms of Audit Engagements
ISA 220	Quality Control for an Audit of Financial Statements
ISA 230	Audit Documentation

BPP
LEARNING

	Title
International Standards on Auditing (ISAs)	
ISA 240	The Auditor's Responsibilities Relating to Fraud in an Audit of Financial Statements
ISA 250 (Revised)	Consideration of Laws and Regulations in an Audit of Financial Statements
ISA 260 (Revised)	Communication with Those Charged with Governance
ISA 265	Communicating Deficiencies in Internal Control to Those Charged with Governance and Management
ISA 300	Planning an Audit of Financial Statements
International Standards on Auditing (ISAs)	
ISA 315 (Revised)	Identifying and Assessing the Risks of Material Misstatement through Understanding the Entity and Its Environment
ISA 320	Materiality in Planning and Performing an Audit
ISA 330	The Auditor's Responses to Assessed Risks
ISA 402	Audit Considerations Relating to an Entity Using a Service Organisation
ISA 450	Evaluation of Misstatements Identified during the Audit
ISA 500	Audit Evidence
ISA 501	Audit Evidence – Specific Considerations for Selected Items
ISA 505	External Confirmations
ISA 510	Initial Audit Engagements – Opening Balances
ISA 520	Analytical Procedures
ISA 530	Audit Sampling
ISA 540	Auditing Accounting Estimates, Including Fair Value Accounting Estimates, and Related Disclosures
ISA 550	Related Parties
ISA 560	Subsequent Events
ISA 570 (Revised)	Going Concern
ISA 580	Written Representations
ISA 600	Special Considerations - Audits of Group Financial Statements (Including the Work of Component Auditors)
ISA 610 (Revised 2013)	Using the Work of Internal Auditors
ISA 620	Using the Work of an Auditor's Expert
ISA 700 (Revised)	Forming an Opinion and Reporting on Financial Statements

International Standards on Auditing (ISAs)	
ISA 701	Communicating Key Audit Matters in the Independent Auditor's Report
ISA 705 (Revised)	Modifications to the Opinion in the Independent Auditor's Report
ISA 706 (Revised)	Emphasis of Matter Paragraphs and Other Matter Paragraphs in the Independent Auditor's Report
ISA 710	Comparative Information – Corresponding Figures and Comparative Financial Statements
ISA 720 (Revised)	The Auditor's Responsibilities Relating to Other Information
International Standards on Assurance Engagements (ISAEs)	
ISAE 3000 (Revised)	Assurance Engagements other than Audits or Reviews of Historical Financial Information
ISAE 3400	The Examination of Prospective Financial Information
ISAE 3402	Assurance Reports on Controls at a Service Organisation
ISAE 3420	Assurance Engagements to Report on the Compilation of Pro Forma Financial Information Included in a Prospectus
International Auditing Practice Notes	
IAPN 1000	Special considerations in auditing financial instruments
International Standards on Quality Control (ISQCs)	
ISQC 1	Quality Control for Firms that Perform Audits and Reviews of Financial Statements, and Other Assurance and Related Services Engagements
International Standards on Related Services (ISRSs)	
ISRS 4400	Engagements to Perform Agreed-Upon Procedures Regarding Financial Information
ISRS 4410 (Revised)	Compilation Engagements
International Standards on Review Engagements (ISREs)	
ISRE 2400 (Revised)	Engagements to Review Historical Financial Statements
ISRE 2410	Review of Interim Financial Information Performed by the Independent Auditor of the Entity
Exposure Drafts (EDs)	
	IAASB – Proposed International Standard on Auditing 315 (Revised) Identifying and Assessing the Risks of Material Misstatement
	IAASB – Proposed International Standard on Auditing 540 (Revised) Auditing Accounting Estimates and Related Disclosures
	IESBA – Proposed Application Material Relating to Professional Skepticism and Professional Judgment

BPP
LEARNING

Ethical Guidelines		
	ACCA's Code of Ethics and Conduct (July 2018)	
	IESBA's International Code of Ethics for Professional Accountants (Revised August 2018)	
Other documents – Corporate Governance		
	The UK Corporate Governance Code as an example of a code of best practice (Revised July 2018)	
	FRC Guidance on Audit Committees (Revised April 2016) as an example of guidance on best practice in relation to audit committees	
Other documents - IAASB		
	Towards Enhanced Professional Skepticism (August 2017)	
	The New Auditor's Report – Questions and Answers (November 2016)	
	Exploring the Increasing Use of Technology in the Audit with a Focus on Data Analytics (September 2016)	
	Feedback Statement – Exploring the Growing Use of Technology in the Audit with a Focus on Data Analytics (January 2018)	
	Determining and Communicating Key Audit Matters (July 2016)	
	More Informative Auditor's Reports – What Audit Committees and Finance Executives Need to Know (March 2016)	
	IAASB A Framework for Audit Quality: Key Elements that Create an Environment for Audit Quality (February 2014)	
	IAASB Practice Alert Challenges in Auditing Fair Value Accounting Estimates in the Current Market Environment (October 2008)	
	IAASB Staff Questions & Answers - Applying ISQC1 Proportionately with the Nature and Size of a Firm (October 2012)	
	IAASB Practice Alert Audit Considerations in Respect of Going Concern in the Current Economic Environment (January 2009)	
	IAASB Applying ISAs Proportionately with the Size and Complexity of an Entity (August 2009)	
	IAASB XBRL : The Emerging Landscape (January 2010)	
	IAASB Auditor Considerations Regarding Significant Unusual or Highly Complex Transactions (September 2010)	
	IAASB Questions and Answers Professional Scepticism in an Audit of Financial Statements (February 2012)	
	IAASB Integrated Reporting Working Group: Supporting Credibility and Trust in Emerging Forms of External Reporting: Ten Key Challenges for Assurance Engagements (January 2018)	

Other documents – IESBA and ACCA	
	NOCLAR overview (January 2018)
	Ethical Considerations Relating to Audit Fee Setting in the Context of Downward Fee Pressure (January 2016)
	ACCA's Anti-money Laundering Guidance for the Accountancy Profession

Note. Topics of exposure drafts are examinable to the extent that relevant articles about them are published in *student accountant*.

Helping you with your revision

BPP Learning Media – Approved Content Partner

As an ACCA **Approved Content Provider**, BPP Learning Media gives you the **opportunity** to use revision materials reviewed by the ACCA examining team. By incorporating the ACCA examining team's comments and suggestions regarding the depth and breadth of syllabus coverage, the BPP Learning Media Practice & Revision Kit provides excellent, **ACCA-approved** support for your revision.

These materials are reviewed by the ACCA examining team. The objective of the review is to ensure that the material properly covers the syllabus and study guide outcomes, used by the examining team in setting the exams, in the appropriate breadth and depth. The review does not ensure that every eventuality, combination or application of examinable topics is addressed by the ACCA Approved Content. Nor does the review comprise a detailed technical check of the content as the Approved Content Provider has its own quality assurance processes in place in this respect.

The structure of this Practice & Revision Kit

This Practice & Revision Kit is divided into sections which correspond to the different parts of the AAA syllabus. There are also four mock exams which provide sufficient **opportunity to refine your knowledge and skills as part of your final exam preparations.**

Question practice

Question practice under timed conditions is absolutely vital. We strongly advise you to create a revision study plan which focuses on question practice. This is so that you can get used to the pressures of answering exam questions in limited time, develop proficiency in the Specific AAA skills and the Exam success skills. Ideally, you should aim to cover all questions in this Kit, and very importantly, all four mock exams.

Selecting questions

To help you plan your revision, we have provided a full **topic index** which maps the questions to topics in the syllabus (see p v).

Making the most of question practice

At BPP Learning Media we realise that you need more than just questions and model answers to get the most from your question practice.

- Our **Top tips**, included for certain questions, provide essential advice on tackling questions, presenting answers and the key points that answers need to include.

- We show you how you can pick up **Easy marks** on some questions, as we know that picking up all readily available marks often can make the difference between passing and failing.

- We include **marking guides** to show you what the examining team rewards.

Attempting mock exams

This Kit has four mock exams, including the ACCA Specimen Exam, which provide practice at coping with the pressures of the exam day. We strongly recommend that you attempt them under exam conditions. All the mock exams reflect the question styles and syllabus coverage of the exam.

Topics to revise

AAA is a challenging higher-level exam consisting of one compulsory question in Section A (worth 50 marks) and a further two compulsory questions in Section B (worth a total of 50 marks).

Section A will comprise a Case Study, worth 50 marks, set at the planning stage of the audit, for a single company, a group of companies or potentially several audit clients. Candidates will be

provided with exhibits which include detailed information. This will vary between examinations, but is likely to include extracts of financial information, strategic, operational and other relevant financial information for a client business, as well as extracts from audit working papers, including results of analytical procedures.

Candidates will be required to address a range of requirements, from syllabus Sections A, B, C and D, thereby tackling a real-world situation where candidates may have to address a range of issues simultaneously in relation to planning, risk assessment, evidence gathering and ethical and professional considerations.

Four professional marks will be available in Section A and will be awarded based on the level of professionalism with which a candidate's answer is presented, including the structure and clarity of the answer provided.

Section B will contain two compulsory 25-mark questions, with each being predominately based around a short scenario.

One question will always come from syllabus Section E, and consequently candidates should be prepared to answer a question relating to completion, review and reporting. There are a number of formats this question could adopt, including, but not limited to, requiring candidates to assess going concern, the impact of subsequent events, evaluating identified misstatements and the corresponding effect on the auditor's report. Candidates may also be asked to critique an auditor's report or report which is to be provided to management or those charged with governance.

The other Section B question can be drawn from any other syllabus section, including A, B, C, D and F.

Current issues. Syllabus Section G on current issues may be examined in Section A or B as appropriate. Current issues is unlikely to form the basis of any question on its own but instead will be incorporated into the Case Study or either of the Section B questions dependent on question content and the topical issues affecting the profession at the time of writing.

We **strongly advise** that you do not selectively revise certain topics – there are no optional questions for AAA, so there is nowhere to hide if a difficult topic is examined. Selective revision will limit the number of questions you can answer and hence reduce your chances of passing.

BPP
LEARNING

Essential skills areas

There are three areas you should develop in order to achieve exam success in Advanced Audit and Assurance (AAA). These are:

(1)   Knowledge application
(2)   Specific Advanced Audit and Assurance skills
(3)   Exam success skills

At the revision and final exam preparation phases **these should be developed together as part of a comprehensive study plan of focused question practice**.

Take some time to revisit the Specific **Advanced Audit and Assurance skills** and **Exam success skills**. These are shown in the diagram below and followed by tutorial guidance of how to apply them.

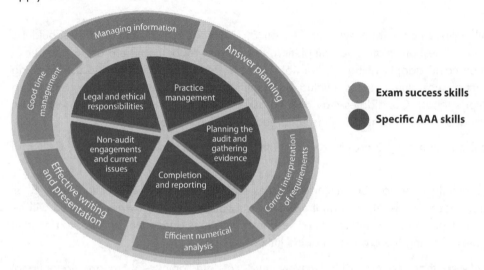

Specific Advanced Audit and Assurance skills

These are the skills specific to AAA that we think you need to develop in order to pass the exam.

In the BPP Advanced Audit and Assurance Workbook, there are five **Skills Checkpoints** which define each skill and show how it is applied in answering a question. A brief summary of each skill is given below.

Skill 1: Legal and ethical responsibilities

The AAA exam will always test the application of your knowledge of this area. Candidates tend to remember enough to be able to identify when something's not right in a scenario – however, explaining why something is not right and how the firm should respond appears to be more challenging. You therefore need to be able to develop an approach that will assist you, both in advance of the exam and on the day itself.

While the context and complexity of scenarios testing legal and ethical responsibilities may be different to those you would have seen in the Audit and Assurance exam, the knowledge that you require for AAA should not be new to you – it is therefore important that you refresh your memory using the technical knowledge presented in this Workbook before you attempt more exam standard questions.

A step-by-step technique for applying these techniques is outlined below.

STEP 1   Think about the requirement and consider all the tasks that you are being asked to undertake.

STEP 2 Read the scenario and identify all the areas of legal and/or ethical concern that you can.

STEP 3 For each of the areas that you have identified, list the reasons why you think they may be of concern to you.

STEP 4 Add suitable responses to each of the matters listed and their reasons.

STEP 5 Write your answer.

Skills Checkpoint 1 covers this technique in detail through application to a preparation question.

Skill 2: Practice management

This area of the syllabus could either be tested in a discrete, stand-alone way or as part of a larger question testing professional issues in general – practice management includes both quality control as well as tendering, fees and acceptance so these could be combined too. There is sometimes even a cross-over with ethical issues as well, so questions on this topic could vary and you need to be prepared.

Answering questions related to practice management do require some learned knowledge to inform your approach – this will also help you identify areas of the scenario that may not look quite right and which will need some further investigation. The AAA skills and exam success skills in this checkpoint help you to develop an approach that you can apply throughout the rest of your studies.

A step-by-step technique for applying these techniques is outlined below.

STEP 1 Isolate the verbs and confirm what the requirement is looking for.

STEP 2 For theory-based requirements, consider whether there is a list that can be used to help you create your answer.

STEP 3 For application-based requirements, what information do you need to focus on?

STEP 4 Create an approach that takes Steps 1, 2 and 3 into account.

STEP 5 Write your answer.

Skills Checkpoint 2 covers this technique in detail through application to an exam-standard question.

Skill 3: Planning the audit and gathering evidence

Question 1 in the exam will be a 50-mark scenario question with a number of requirements that should test some, if not all, the following:

* Risks (audit risks, risks of material misstatement or business risks)
* Other planning issues
* Audit procedures and evidence required to verify specific parts of the scenario
* Ethical and professional points related to the scenario

In this skills checkpoint, we go through an audit risk question, showing you how to use the scenario to draw up a detailed answer. We also show you all of the exam success skills as they relate to Question 1 so you can start to practise them as part of your home study.

BPP LEARNING

A step-by-step technique for applying these techniques is outlined below.

STEP 1 Confirm the requirement (such as defining audit risk) by reference to the verb the marks and the timing.

STEP 2 Annotate the scenario with ideas of audit risks.

STEP 3 Perform analytical procedures on the data supplied (including conclusions).

STEP 4 Create an answer plan that takes Steps 1, 2 and 3 into account.

STEP 5 Write your answer.

Skills Checkpoint 3 covers this technique in detail through application to an exam-standard question.

Skill 4: Completion and reporting

The ACCA has confirmed that one of the 25-mark questions will always come from syllabus section E, and consequently candidates should be prepared to answer a question relating to completion, review and reporting. As a result, this skills checkpoint will cover some of the topics most likely to be seen in these types of questions and the skills required to produce great answers.

Questions on completion and reporting tend to go well together – when you consider issues such as going concern, subsequent events and the evaluation of the auditor's findings, inevitably they will need to considered in the context of the auditor's report and any other communication that might be necessary..

A step-by-step technique for applying these techniques is outlined below.

STEP 1 Determine which parts of the syllabus the requirement is testing.

STEP 2 Actively read the scenario to identify the key issues.

STEP 3 Consider the implications of the issues identified in Step 2 for the auditor's opinion (both cause and extent).

STEP 4 Consider whether there are any additional impacts on the auditor's report from the issues identified in Step 2.

STEP 5 Write your answer.

Skills Checkpoint 4 covers this technique in detail through application to an exam-standard question.

Skill 5: Non-audit engagements and current issues

Remember that although this is an audit exam, the words '...and Assurance' are also in the title. The syllabus contains a number of non-audit elements that you could be tested on, so this checkpoint will consider how you can prepare for these if required. Part F of the syllabus covers these subjects.

The AAA examining team also periodically publishes technical articles on subjects deemed to be of interest to candidates: in some cases, they may recommend exam techniques for syllabus topics that have been poorly answered in previous exam sittings; in others, they may relate to current issues which the examining team want candidates to be aware of.

Traditionally, whenever a technical article is published, the content is often examined within the next couple of sittings, so keeping up to date with these technical articles is essential. You will find references to relevant technical articles with the 'Further reading' sections of the workbook.

A step-by-step technique for applying these techniques is outlined below.

STEP 1   Think about the question and list all the things that you will need to do.

STEP 2   Read the scenario and identify all the areas that are relevant to producing an answer.

STEP 3   Is there any other technical knowledge that will help you to produce and answer?

STEP 4   Draw up an answer plan based on your outputs from Steps 1, 2 and 3.

STEP 5   Write your answer.

Skills Checkpoint 5 covers this technique in detail through application to an exam-standard question.

Exam success skills

Passing the AAA exam requires more than applying syllabus knowledge and demonstrating the specific AAA skills; it also requires the development of excellent exam technique through question practice.

We consider the following six skills to be vital for exam success. These skills were introduced in the BPP Workbook and you can revisit the Skills Checkpoints in the BPP Workbook for tutorial guidance of how to apply each of the six Exam success skills in your question practice and in the exam.

Aim to consider your performance in all six Exam success skills during your revision stage question practice and reflect on your particular strengths and weaker areas which you can then work on.

Exam success skill 1

Managing information

Questions in the exam will present you with a lot of information. The skill is how you handle this information to make the best use of your time. The key is determining how you will approach the exam and then actively reading the questions.

Advice on developing managing information

Approach

The exam is 3 hours 15 minutes long. There is no designated 'reading' time at the start of the exam, however, one approach that can work well is to start the exam by spending 10–15 minutes carefully reading through all of the questions to familiarise yourself with the exam paper.

Once you feel familiar with the exam paper consider the order in which you will attempt the questions; always attempt them in your order of preference. For example, you may want to leave to last the question you consider to be the most difficult.

If you do take this approach, remember to adjust the time available for each question appropriately – see Exam success skill 6: Good time management.

If you find that this approach doesn't work for you, don't worry – you can develop your own technique.

Active reading

You must take an active approach to reading each question. Focus on the requirement first, underlining key verbs such as 'prepare', 'comment', 'explain', 'discuss', to ensure you answer the question properly. Then read the rest of the question, underlining and annotating important and relevant information, and making notes of any relevant technical information you think you will need.

Exam success skill 2

Correct interpretation of the requirements

The active verb used often dictates the approach that written answers should take (eg 'explain', 'discuss', 'evaluate'). It is important you identify and use the verb to define your approach. The correct interpretation of the requirements skill means correctly producing only what is being asked for by a requirement. Anything not required will not earn marks.

Advice on developing correct interpretation of the requirements

This skill can be developed by analysing question requirements and applying this process:

Step 1   **Read the requirement**

Firstly, read the requirement a couple of times slowly and carefully and highlight the active verbs. Use the active verbs to define what you plan to do. Make sure you identify any sub-requirements.

Step 2   **Read the rest of the question**

By reading the requirement first, you will have an idea of what you are looking out for as you read through the case overview and exhibits. This is a great time saver and means you don't end up having to read the whole question in full twice. You should do this in an active way – see Exam success skill 1: Managing Information.

Step 3   **Read the requirement again**

Read the requirement again to remind yourself of the exact wording before starting your written answer. This will capture any misinterpretation of the requirements or any missed requirements entirely. This should become a habit in your approach and, with repeated practice, you will find the focus, relevance and depth of your answer plan will improve.

Exam success skill 3

Answer planning: Priorities, structure and logic

This skill requires the planning of the key aspects of an answer which accurately and completely responds to the requirement.

Advice on developing Answer planning: Priorities, structure and logic

Everyone will have a preferred style for an answer plan. For example, it may be a mind map, bullet-pointed lists or simply annotating the question paper. Choose the approach that you feel most comfortable with, or, if you are not sure, try out different approaches for different questions until you have found your preferred style.

For a discussion question, annotating the question paper is likely to be insufficient. It would be better to draw up a separate answer plan in the format of your choosing (eg a mind map or bullet-pointed lists). For a risk question, you should annotate the scenario noting which areas present the type of risk being examined and explain why.

Exam success skill 4

Efficient numerical analysis

This skill aims to maximise the marks awarded by making clear to the marker the process of arriving at your answer. This is achieved by laying out an answer such that, even if you make a few errors, you can still get some credit for your calculations. It is vital that you do not lose marks purely because the marker cannot follow what you have done.

Advice on developing efficient numerical analysis

This skill can be developed by applying the following process:

Step 1   **Explain your workings where relevant**

Materiality calculations or other forms of analytical procedure should have a brief explanation of their purpose so the examining team can understand what your calculations are trying to tell them.

Step 2   **Show your workings**

Keep your workings as clear and simple as possible and ensure they are cross-referenced to the main part of your answer. Where it helps, provide brief narrative explanations to help the marker understand the steps in the calculation. This means that if a mistake is made you should not lose any subsequent marks for follow-on calculations.

Step 3   **Keep moving!**

It is important to remember that, in an exam situation, it is difficult to get every number 100% correct. The key is therefore ensuring you do not spend too long on any single calculation. If you are struggling with a solution then make a sensible assumption, state it and move on.

Exam success skill 5

Effective writing and presentation

Written answers should be presented so that the marker can clearly see the points you are making, presented in the format specified in the question. The skill is to provide efficient written answers with sufficient breadth of points that answer the question, in the right depth, in the time available.

Advice on developing Effective writing and presentation

Step 1   **Use headings**

Using the headings and sub-headings from your answer plan will give your answer structure, order and logic. This will ensure your answer links back to the requirement and is clearly signposted, making it easier for the marker to understand the different points you are making. Underlining your headings will also help the marker.

Step 2   **Write your answer in short, but full, sentences**

Use short, punchy sentences with the aim that every sentence should say something different and generate marks. Write in full sentences, ensuring your style is professional.

Step 3   **Do your calculations first and explanation second**

Questions often ask for an explanation with suitable calculations, such as materiality. The best approach is to prepare the calculation first but present it on the bottom half of the page of your answer, or on the next page. Then add the explanation before the calculation. Performing the calculation first should enable you to explain what you have done.

 BPP
LEARNING

Good time management

This skill means planning your time across all the requirements so that all tasks have been attempted at the end of the 3 hours 15 minutes available and actively checking on time during your exam. This is so that you can flex your approach and prioritise requirements which, in your judgment, will generate the maximum marks in the available time remaining.

Advice on developing Good time management

The exam is 3 hours 15 minutes long, which translates to 1.95 minutes per mark. Therefore a 10-mark requirement should be allocated a maximum of 20 minutes to complete your answer before you move on to the next task. At the beginning of a question, work out the amount of time you should be spending on each requirement and write the finishing time next to each requirement on your exam paper. If you take the approach of spending 10–15 minutes reading and planning at the start of the exam, adjust the time allocated to each question accordingly; eg if you allocate 15 minutes to reading, then you will have 3 hours remaining, which is 1.8 minutes per mark.

Keep an eye on the clock

Aim to attempt all requirements, but be ready to be ruthless and move on if your answer is not going as planned. The challenge for many is sticking to planned timings. Be aware this is difficult to achieve in the early stages of your studies and be ready to let this skill develop over time.

If you find yourself running short on time and know that a full answer is not possible in the time you have, consider recreating your plan in overview form and then add key terms and details as time allows. Remember, some marks may be available, for example, simply stating a conclusion which you don't have time to justify in full.

Revising AAA

Topics to revise

AAA is a challenging higher-level exam consisting of one compulsory question in Section A (worth 50 marks) and a further two compulsory questions in Section B (worth a total of 50 marks).

Section A will comprise a Case Study, worth 50 marks, set at the planning stage of the audit, for a single company, a group of companies or potentially several audit clients. Candidates will be provided with exhibits which include detailed information. This will vary between examinations, but is likely to include extracts of financial information, strategic, operational and other relevant financial information for a client business, as well as extracts from audit working papers, including results of analytical procedures.

Candidates will be required to address a range of requirements, from syllabus Sections A, B, C and D, thereby tackling a real-world situation where candidates may have to address a range of issues simultaneously in relation to planning, risk assessment, evidence gathering and ethical and professional considerations.

Four professional marks will be available in Section A and will be awarded based on the level of professionalism with which a candidate's answer is presented, including the structure and clarity of the answer provided.

Section B will contain two compulsory 25-mark questions, with each being predominately based around a short scenario.

One question will always come from syllabus Section E, and consequently candidates should be prepared to answer a question relating to completion, review and reporting. There are a number of formats this question could adopt, including, but not limited to, requiring candidates to assess going concern, the impact of subsequent events, evaluating identified misstatements and the corresponding effect on the auditor's report. Candidates may also be asked to critique an auditor's report or report which is to be provided to management or those charged with governance.

The other Section B question can be drawn from any other syllabus section, including A, B, C, D and F.

Current issues. Syllabus Section G on current issues may be examined in Section A or B as appropriate. Current issues is unlikely to form the basis of any question on its own but instead will be incorporated into the Case Study or either of the Section B questions dependent on question content and the topical issues affecting the profession at the time of writing.

We **strongly advise** that you do not selectively revise certain topics – there are no optional questions for AAA, so there is nowhere to hide if a difficult topic is examined. Selective revision will limit the number of questions you can answer and hence reduce your chances of passing.

Question practice

You should use the Passcards and any brief notes you have to revise the syllabus, but you mustn't spend all your revision time passively reading. **Question practice is vital;** doing as many questions as you can in full will help develop your ability to analyse scenarios and produce relevant discussion and recommendations.

Make sure you leave enough time in your revision schedule to practise Section A questions, as these questions are compulsory in the exam. The scenarios and requirements of Section A questions are more complex and will integrate several parts of the syllabus, so practice is essential. Also ensure that you attempt all four mock exams under exam conditions.

BPP
LEARNING

Passing the AAA exam

Displaying the right qualities and avoiding weaknesses

The following are examples of things to avoid – and note our comments about action to take in each case.

Failure to complete the exam	This problem can be avoided by ensuring that you have a very disciplined exam technique and that you set times in which to answer questions and, when that time is over, you move on to the next question. Lots of practice at answering questions in timed conditions will help you to discipline yourself in this way. Remember, it is easier to get marks at the outset of answering a question (when all the marks are still available) than to get the last few remaining marks for a question (when you have made all the easy points and are struggling with the most difficult aspects of the question).
Not reading the question	We recommend that you read each question more than once. Try to force yourself to read slowly as well. Although the exam is time-limited, reading the question properly is a good investment.
Lack of comprehension and analytical skills	These are higher level skills which you have to learn at this level and the best way to enhance them is to practise as many questions as you can. In addition, once you have completed your own answer, you should always work through the suggested answer referring back to the question so that you can see the links that have been made.
Lack of lower-level assumed knowledge	You should endeavour not to commence your AAA studies until you have completed your AA studies. It is not possible to pass AAA unless you have a very firm understanding of basic auditing theory. The same goes for SBR; it is important that you retain your knowledge of corporate reporting from SBR, and that you are up to date with the latest standards and developments.
Lack of awareness of current issues	You should ensure that you keep up to date with current issues in the auditing and business world, by reading examining team articles as a minimum, but preferably by keeping an eye on the accountancy press throughout your studies.
Failure to respond in a practical/ commercial way	The answer to this problem is to practise lots of questions, read other people's answers to questions in this Kit and on the ACCA website and to try and think about how you would respond in practice if it were one of your clients.
Lack of relevant practical experience	You may not be able to do anything about this if you are not employed in a relevant field. However, if you can, do. For example, if you can discuss with your managers the necessity of getting relevant experience and they are able to meet that need, try and obtain as much relevant experience as you can. If not, the best you can do is follow the advice for the previous point, which should stand you in good stead.
Inability to reach a conclusion/make a decision	You must get into the habit of drawing conclusions where the requirement is to do so. Again, practise questions where this is required, and, when reading questions note whether you are required to draw a conclusion or make a decision.
Poor exam technique/time allocation	This point links to the first point made above. There is a great deal of guidance concerning exam technique in this kit. Read it and put it into practice.

Choosing which questions to answer first

We recommend that you spend time at the beginning of your exam carefully reading through all of the questions in the exam, and each of their requirements. Once you feel familiar with your exam we then recommend that you attempt the Section A question first, ensuring that you spend adequate time reading and planning before you begin to write up your answer. Comments from examining teams of other syllabuses that have similar exam formats suggest that students appear less time-pressured if they do the big question first.

During the second half of the exam, you should then put Section A aside and concentrate on the two Section B questions.

Our recommendations are not inflexible though. If you really think the Section A question looks a lot harder than the Section B questions, then do those first, but **DON'T run over time on them.** You must leave yourself plenty of time to tackle the Section A question. When you come back to it, once you have had time to reflect, you should be able to generate more ideas and might find that the question is not as bad as it looks.

Remember also that small overruns of time during the first half of the exam can add up to you being very short of time towards the end.

Tackling questions

You'll improve your chances by following a step-by-step approach to Section A scenarios along the following lines.

Step 1 **Read the background**

Usually the first couple of paragraphs will give some background on the company and what it is aiming to achieve. By reading this carefully you will be better equipped to relate your answers to the organisation as much as possible.

Step 2 **Read the requirements**

There is no point reading the detailed information in the question until you know what it is going to be used for. Don't panic if some of the requirements look challenging – identify the elements you are able to do and look for links between requirements, as well as possible indications of the syllabus areas the question is covering.

Step 3 **Identify the action verbs**

These convey the level of skill you need to exhibit and also the structure your answer should have. A lower-level verb such as define will require a more descriptive answer; a higher-level verb such as evaluate will require a more applied, critical answer. It should be stressed that higher-level requirements and verbs are likely to be most significant in this exam.

Action verbs that are likely to be frequently used in this exam are listed below, together with their intellectual levels and guidance on their meaning.

Intellectual level		
1	**Define**	Give the meaning of
1	**Explain**	Make an idea clear. Show logically how a concept is developed. Give the reason for an event
1	**Identify**	Recognise or select
1	**Describe**	Give a detailed account or key features. List characteristics, qualities and parts
2	**Compare**	Examine two or more things to identify similarities and differences
2	**Analyse**	Break into separate parts and discuss, examine, or interpret each part
3	**Evaluate**	Determine the scenario in the light of the arguments for and against
3	**Assess**	To judge the worth, importance, evaluate or estimate the nature, quality, ability, extent, or significance
3	**Discuss**	Consider and debate/argue about the pros and cons of an issue. Examine in detail by using arguments in favour or against
3	**Criticise**	Present the weaknesses/problems; evaluate comparative worth. Don't explain the situation. Instead, analyse it
3	**Recommend**	Advise the appropriate actions to pursue in terms the recipient will understand

Also make sure you identify all the action verbs; some question parts may have more than one.

Step 4   **Identify what each part of the question requires**

Think about what frameworks or theories you could choose if the question doesn't specify which one to use.

When planning, you will need to make sure that you aren't reproducing the same material in more than one part of the question.

Also you're likely to come across part questions with two requirements that may be at different levels; a part question may for example ask you to explain X and discuss Y. You must ensure that you fulfil both requirements and that your discussion of Y shows greater depth than your explanation of X (for example by identifying problems with Y or putting the case for and against Y).

Step 5   **Check the mark allocation to each part**

This shows you the depth anticipated and helps allocate time.

Step 6   **Read the whole scenario through, highlighting key data**

Put points under headings related to requirements (eg by noting in the margin to what part of the question the scenario detail relates).

Step 7   **Consider the consequences of the points you've identified**

Remember that you will often have to provide recommendations based on the information you've been given. Consider that you may have to criticise the code, framework or model that you've been told to use. You may also have to bring in wider issues or viewpoints, for example the views of different stakeholders.

Step 8   **Write a brief plan**

Your plans should be produced within your answer book.

Make sure you identify all the requirements of the question in your plan – each requirement may have sub-requirements that must also be addressed. If there are professional marks available, highlight in your plan where these may be gained (such as preparing a report).

Step 9   **Write the answer**

Make every effort to present your answer clearly. The Specimen exam and exams set so far indicate that the examining team will be looking for you to make a number of clear points. The best way to demonstrate what you're doing is to put points into separate paragraphs with clear headers.

Discussion questions

Remember that **depth of discussion** will be important. Discussions will often consist of paragraphs containing 2–3 sentences. Each paragraph should:

- **Make a point**

- **Explain the point** (you must demonstrate why the point is important)

- **Illustrate the point** (with material or analysis from the scenario, perhaps an example from real-life)

In this exam a number of requirement verbs will expect you to express a viewpoint or opinion, for example construct an argument, criticise, evaluate. When expressing an opinion, you need to provide:

BPP LEARNING

- **What the question wants.** For instance, if you are asked to criticise something, don't spend time discussing its advantages. In addition if a scenario provides a lot of information about a situation, and you are (say) asked to assess that situation in the light of good practice, your assessment is unlikely to be favourable.

- **Evidence** from theory or the scenario – again we stress that the majority of marks in most questions will be given for applying your knowledge to the scenario.

Gaining the easy marks

Knowledge of the core topics that we list under topics to revise should present you with some easy marks. The Specimen exam suggests that there will be some marks available on certain part questions for definitions, explanations or descriptions that don't have to be related to the scenario. However don't assume that you can ignore all the scenarios and still pass!

As AAA is a Strategic Professional exam, **four professional marks** will be awarded. Some of these should be easy to obtain. The examining team has stated that some marks may be available for presenting your answer in the form of a letter, presentation, email, report or briefing notes. You may also be able to obtain marks for the style and layout of your answer.

Reports should always have an appropriate title. They should be **formally written**, with an **introductory paragraph** setting out the aims of the report. You should use **short paragraphs** and **appropriate headings**, with a summary of findings as a conclusion.

Memoranda and briefing notes should have the following information at the beginning:

From:	**Name of author**
To:	**Name of recipient**
Date:	**1 July 20X5**
Subject:	**Subject**

The language can be **less formal** than a report but the content should still have an **introduction** and **conclusion**, and be divided into small paragraphs with appropriate headings.

Letters should be addressed appropriately to the correct person and be dated. They should have a short introductory paragraph, a conclusion and should be in a formally writing style. Letters beginning with 'Dear Sir/Madam' should end with 'Yours faithfully'.

Exam information

Computer-based exams

With effect from the March 2020 sitting, ACCA have commenced the launch of computer-based exams (CBEs) for this exam with the aim of rolling out into all markets internationally over a short period. Paper-based examinations (PBE) will be run in parallel while the CBEs are phased in. BPP materials have been designed to support you, whichever exam option you choose. For more information on these changes and when they will be implemented, please visit the ACCA website.

Format of the exam

		Number of marks
Section A:	One compulsory question	50
Section B:	Two compulsory questions (25 marks each)	50
		100

Time allowed: 3 hours and 15 minutes.

The examination is constructed in two sections. Questions in both sections will be largely discursive. However, candidates will be expected, for example, to be able to assess materiality and calculate relevant ratios where appropriate.

Question format

The format of questions in AAA differs slightly between Section A and Section B. Section A questions will feature scenarios, with simple requirements such as 'Respond to the partner's request', or 'Draft the briefing notes as requested'. You will have to work out for yourself what you need to include in your answer, using the breakdown of the mark allocation which will be included within the scenario. Section B questions will feature requirements akin to those in your previous ACCA exams. For sittings from September 2019 onwards, all questions are set as at the fictitious date of 1 July 20X5.

Examining team's general comments

If you are preparing to sit AAA you should pay particular attention to the following in order to maximise your chances of success. The following is taken from a recent AAA report by the examining team.

'In order to pass this exam, candidates are required to **apply the principles and rules** from their earlier studies to more complex scenarios and demonstrate their ability to handle different situations which may arise in audit and related services. In addition, candidates are expected to develop a **broader knowledge of audit services** and practice management. Candidates should also keep abreast of **current developments** and challenges in the field of both auditing and financial reporting to allow them to demonstrate the ability to handle these challenges in the context of auditing financial statements and as areas they may need to brief clients on.

'This **combination of learned knowledge and its application** to complex situations requires candidates to be able to go beyond the topics as covered in text books and be able to react to the scenarios described in the requirement. Study through question practice and following developments in the field through the media, and through IFAC and IAASB will be crucial in taking the learned knowledge from earlier parts of the qualification and converting it into a demonstrable ability to provide audit and advisory services to clients.

'AAA also tests candidates' **ability to tailor their answer to the context in which the requirement is written**. Often the audience of the requirement will dictate the pitch and depth of the answer along with its focus. Failure to take into account such matters will often lead to **time pressures** in the exam as candidates lose time by detailing knowledge that is not relevant to the

BPP
LEARNING

requirement. This is particularly noticeable in Question 1 which is set at the planning stage of an audit and is addressed to the senior members of the audit team, meaning an explanation of the audit risk model is not appropriate. Candidates should allow themselves time to focus on the requirement that is set before they begin their answers. **It would be useful for candidates to visualise delivering the requirement verbally to the report recipient and therefore imagining how a partner in a firm, already qualified and experienced, would react to listening to the answer**.'

Examinable documents

AUDIT

International

Knowledge of new examinable regulations issued by 31 August will be examinable in examination sessions being held in the following exam year. Documents may be examinable even if the effective date is in the future. This means that all regulations issued by 31 August 2018 will be examinable in the September 2019 to June 2020 examinations.

The study guide offers more detailed guidance on the depth and level at which the examinable documents should be examined. The study guide should therefore be read in conjunction with the examinable documents list.

Accounting Standards

Audit and Assurance (AA)

The accounting knowledge that is assumed for Audit and Assurance is the same as that examined in Fundamentals in Financial Accounting (FFA). Therefore, candidates studying for this exam should refer to the IFRS Standards listed under FFA.

Advanced Audit and Assurance (AAA)

The accounting knowledge that is assumed for Advanced Audit and Assurance is the same as that examined in Strategic Business Reporting (SBR). Therefore, candidates studying for AAA should refer to the IFRS Standards listed under SBR.

N.B. AAA will only expect knowledge of accounting standards and financial reporting standards from SBR. Knowledge of exposure drafts and discussion papers will not be expected.

	Title
	International Standards on Auditing (ISAs)
	Glossary of Terms
	International Framework for Assurance Engagements
	Preface to the International Quality Control, Auditing, Review, Other Assurance and Related Services Pronouncements
ISA 200	Overall Objectives of the Independent Auditor and the Conduct of an Audit in Accordance with ISAs
ISA 210	Agreeing the Terms of Audit Engagements
ISA 220	Quality Control for an Audit of Financial Statements
ISA 230	Audit Documentation
ISA 240	The Auditor's Responsibilities Relating to Fraud in an Audit of Financial Statements
ISA 250 (Revised)	Consideration of Laws and Regulations in an Audit of Financial Statements
ISA 260 (Revised)	Communication with Those Charged with Governance
ISA 265	Communicating Deficiencies in Internal Control to Those Charged with Governance and Management
ISA 300	Planning an Audit of Financial Statements

BPP
LEARNING

International Standards on Auditing (ISAs)	
ISA 315 (Revised)	Identifying and Assessing the Risks of Material Misstatement through Understanding the Entity and Its Environment
ISA 320	Materiality in Planning and Performing an Audit
ISA 330	The Auditor's Responses to Assessed Risks
ISA 402	Audit Considerations Relating to an Entity Using a Service Organisation
ISA 450	Evaluation of Misstatements Identified during the Audit
ISA 500	Audit Evidence
ISA 501	Audit Evidence – Specific Considerations for Selected Items
ISA 505	External Confirmations
ISA 510	Initial Audit Engagements – Opening Balances
ISA 520	Analytical Procedures
ISA 530	Audit Sampling
ISA 540	Auditing Accounting Estimates, Including Fair Value Accounting Estimates, and Related Disclosures
ISA 550	Related Parties
ISA 560	Subsequent Events
ISA 570 (Revised)	Going Concern
ISA 580	Written Representations
ISA 600	Special Considerations - Audits of Group Financial Statements (Including the Work of Component Auditors)
ISA 610 (Revised 2013)	Using the Work of Internal Auditors
ISA 620	Using the Work of an Auditor's Expert
ISA 700 (Revised)	Forming an Opinion and Reporting on Financial Statements
ISA 701	Communicating Key Audit Matters in the Independent Auditor's Report
ISA 705 (Revised)	Modifications to the Opinion in the Independent Auditor's Report
ISA 706 (Revised)	Emphasis of Matter Paragraphs and Other Matter Paragraphs in the Independent Auditor's Report
ISA 710	Comparative Information – Corresponding Figures and Comparative Financial Statements
ISA 720 (Revised)	The Auditor's Responsibilities Relating to Other Information

	International Standards on Assurance Engagements (ISAEs)
ISAE 3000 (Revised)	Assurance Engagements other than Audits or Reviews of Historical Financial Information
ISAE 3400	The Examination of Prospective Financial Information
ISAE 3402	Assurance Reports on Controls at a Service Organisation
ISAE 3420	Assurance Engagements to Report on the Compilation of Pro Forma Financial Information Included in a Prospectus
	International Auditing Practice Notes
IAPN 1000	Special considerations in auditing financial instruments
	International Standards on Quality Control (ISQCs)
ISQC 1	Quality Control for Firms that Perform Audits and Reviews of Financial Statements, and Other Assurance and Related Services Engagements
	International Standards on Related Services (ISRSs)
ISRS 4400	Engagements to Perform Agreed-Upon Procedures Regarding Financial Information
ISRS 4410 (Revised)	Compilation Engagements
	International Standards on Review Engagements (ISREs)
ISRE 2400 (Revised)	Engagements to Review Historical Financial Statements
ISRE 2410	Review of Interim Financial Information Performed by the Independent Auditor of the Entity
	Exposure Drafts (EDs)
	IAASB – Proposed International Standard on Auditing 315 (Revised) Identifying and Assessing the Risks of Material Misstatement
	IAASB – Proposed International Standard on Auditing 540 (Revised) Auditing Accounting Estimates and Related Disclosures
	IESBA – Proposed Application Material Relating to Professional Skepticism and Professional Judgment
	Ethical Guidelines
	ACCA's Code of Ethics and Conduct (July 2018)
	IESBA's International Code of Ethics for Professional Accountants (Revised August 2018)
	Other documents – Corporate Governance
	The UK Corporate Governance Code as an example of a code of best practice (Revised July 2018)
	FRC Guidance on Audit Committees (Revised April 2016) as an example of guidance on best practice in relation to audit committees

	Other documents - IAASB
	Towards Enhanced Professional Skepticism (August 2017)
	The New Auditor's Report – Questions and Answers (November 2016)
	Exploring the Increasing Use of Technology in the Audit with a Focus on Data Analytics (September 2016)
	Feedback Statement – Exploring the Growing Use of Technology in the Audit with a Focus on Data Analytics (January 2018)
	Determining and Communicating Key Audit Matters (July 2016)
	More Informative Auditor's Reports – What Audit Committees and Finance Executives Need to Know (March 2016)
	IAASB A Framework for Audit Quality: Key Elements that Create an Environment for Audit Quality (February 2014)
	IAASB Practice Alert Challenges in Auditing Fair Value Accounting Estimates in the Current Market Environment (October 2008)
	IAASB Staff Questions & Answers - Applying ISQC1 Proportionately with the Nature and Size of a Firm (October 2012)
	IAASB Practice Alert Audit Considerations in Respect of Going Concern in the Current Economic Environment (January 2009)
	IAASB Applying ISAs Proportionately with the Size and Complexity of an Entity (August 2009)
	IAASB XBRL : The Emerging Landscape (January 2010)
	IAASB Auditor Considerations Regarding Significant Unusual or Highly Complex Transactions (September 2010)
	IAASB Questions and Answers Professional Scepticism in an Audit of Financial Statements (February 2012)
	IAASB Integrated Reporting Working Group: Supporting Credibility and Trust in Emerging Forms of External Reporting: Ten Key Challenges for Assurance Engagements (January 2018)
	Other documents – IESBA and ACCA
	NOCLAR overview (January 2018)
	Ethical Considerations Relating to Audit Fee Setting in the Context of Downward Fee Pressure (January 2016)
	ACCA's Anti-money Laundering Guidance for the Accountancy Profession

Note. Topics of exposure drafts are examinable to the extent that relevant articles about them are published in *student accountant*.

Analysis of past exams

The table below provides details of when each element of the syllabus has been examined in the ten most recent sittings and the question number and section in which each element was examined.

Since September 2016, the ACCA has been issuing two exams each year, after the December and June exam sessions. These exams are compiled from questions selected from the two preceding sessions eg in December 2017, the sample questions were compiled from September 2017 and December 2017 exams.

A specimen exam was also issued for the change in question format for 2018/19, but this has not been included in the analysis below.

Covered in Workbook Chapter		Dec 2018 (AAA)	Sept 2018 (AAA)	Mar/ Jun 2018 (P7)	Sep/ Dec 2017 (P7)	Mar/ Jun 2017 (P7)	Sep/ Dec 2016 (P7)	Mar/ Jun 2016 (P7)	Sep/ Dec 2015 (P7)	June 2015 (P7)	Dec 2014 (P7)
	REGULATORY ENVIRONMENT										
1	International regulatory frameworks for audit and assurance services						5(a)				
1	Money laundering	3(a)		2(a)				3(b)			
1	Laws and regulations									2(b)	
	PROFESSIONAL AND ETHICAL CONSIDERATIONS										
2	Codes of ethics for professional accountants	3(b)	1(d), 2(b), 3(b)	2(a)	3(b), 4	3(a)	4, 5(a)	1(c), 4(b)	4	3(a), 4	1(d), 4(b)
3	Fraud and error	1(e)						3(a)			
3	Professional liability										
	QUALITY CONTROL AND PRACTICE MANAGEMENT										
4	Quality control		3(b)	3	4	2		2(a)	5(c)	4	5(a)
5	Advertising, tendering, obtaining professional work and fees										4(a)
5	Professional appointments	1(d)									4(a)
	ASSIGNMENTS										
6, 7, 8	The audit of historical financial information including: (i) Planning, materiality and assessing the risk of misstatement (ii) Evidence	1(a)–(c)	1	1, 4	1, 2	1, 4	1, 2, 3	1, 2(b), 3(b), 5(a)	1	1, 2(a), 3(b), 5(a)–(b)	1(a)–(c), 2, 3(a), 5(b)

Covered in Workbook Chapter		Dec 2018 (AAA)	Sept 2018 (AAA)	Mar/Jun 2018 (P7)	Sep/Dec 2017 (P7)	Mar/Jun 2017 (P7)	Sep/Dec 2016 (P7)	Mar/Jun 2016 (P7)	Sep/Dec 2015 (P7)	June 2015 (P7)	Dec 2014 (P7)
9	Group audits			1(b), 4	1(c)				5(b)		
	COMPLETION, REVIEW AND REPORTING										
10	Completion	2(a)–(b)	2(a)		5(a)	2	3		2(a)		
11	Auditor's reports	2(c)	2(a)	5	5(b)	5(a)	5(b)	5(b)	5(a)–(b)	5	
11	Communications to management			3			2				
11	Other reports										
	OTHER ASSIGNMENTS										
12	Audit-related services	1(e)			3(a)				3		
12	Assurance services							4(a)			
13	Prospective financial information		3(a)	2(b)		5(b)					
14	Forensic audits									3(c)	
15	Social and environmental auditing										3(b)
15	Public sector audit of performance information					3(b)–(c)			2(b)		
	CURRENT ISSUES AND DEVELOPMENTS										
1, 2, 3	Professional, ethical and corporate governance										
16	Other current issues										

IMPORTANT!

The table above gives a broad idea of how frequently major topics in the syllabus are examined. It should not be used to question spot and predict for example that Topic X will not be examined because it came up two sittings ago. The examining team's reports indicate that the examining team is well aware some students try to question spot. The examining team avoid predictable patterns and may, for example, examine the same topic two sittings in a row.

Additional information

The study guide provides more detailed guidance on the syllabus and can be found by visiting the exam resources finder on the ACCA website: www.accaglobal.com/uk/en/student/exam-support-resources.html

Useful websites

The websites below provide additional sources of information of relevance to your studies for *AAA Advanced Audit and Assurance.*

- www.accaglobal.com

  ACCA's website. The students' section of the website is invaluable for detailed information about the qualification, past issues of Student Accountant (including technical articles) and even interviews with the examining team.

- www.bpp.com

  Our website provides information about BPP products and services, with a link to the ACCA website.

- www.ft.com

  This website provides information about current international business. You can search for information and articles on specific industry groups as well as individual companies.

- www.ifac.org

  This site has links to the IAASB and the IESBA, for up-to-date information on auditing issues.

- www.ifrs.org

  The IASB website features all of the latest IFRSs, as well as news on current developments in corporate reporting.

BPP LEARNING

Question Bank

REGULATORY ENVIRONMENT AND PROFESSIONAL AND ETHICAL CONSIDERATIONS

Questions 1 to 8 cover Regulatory environment and Professional and ethical considerations, the subjects of Parts A and B of the BPP Workbook for AAA.

1 Lark (P7 6/12) (amended)   49 mins

(a)   You are a manager in Lark & Co, responsible for the audit of Heron Co, an owner-managed business which operates a chain of bars and restaurants. This is your firm's first year auditing the client and the audit for the year ended 31 March 20X2 is underway. The audit senior sends a note for your attention:

'When I was auditing revenue I noticed something strange. Heron Co's revenue, which is almost entirely cash-based, is recognised at $5.5 million in the draft financial statements. However, the accounting system shows that till receipts for cash paid by customers amount to only $3.5 million. This seemed odd, so I questioned Ava Gull, the financial controller about this. She said that Jack Heron, the company's owner, deals with cash receipts and posts journals dealing with cash and revenue. Ava asked Jack the reason for these journals but he refused to give an explanation.

'While auditing cash, I noticed a payment of $2 million made by electronic transfer from the company's bank account to an overseas financial institution. The bank statement showed that the transfer was authorised by Jack Heron, but no other documentation regarding the transfer was available.

'Alarmed by the size of this transaction, and the lack of evidence to support it, I questioned Jack Heron, asking him about the source of cash receipts and the reason for electronic transfer. He would not give any answers and became quite aggressive.'

Required

(i)   Discuss the implications of the circumstances described in the audit senior's note; and

(6 marks)

(ii)   Explain the nature of any reporting that should take place by the audit senior.

(3 marks)

(b)   You are also responsible for the audit of Coot Co, and you are currently reviewing the working papers of the audit for the year ended 28 February 20X2. In the working papers dealing with payroll, the audit junior has commented as follows.

'Several new employees have been added to the company's payroll during the year, with combined payments of $125,000 being made to them. There does not appear to be any authorisation for these additions. When I questioned the payroll supervisor who made the amendments, she said that no authorisation was needed because the new employees are only working for the company on a temporary basis. However, when discussing staffing levels with management, it was stated that no new employees have been taken on this year. Other than the tests of controls planned, no other audit work has been performed.'

Required

In relation to the audit of Coot Co's payroll, explain the meaning of the term 'professional scepticism', and recommend any further actions that should be taken by the auditor.

(6 marks)

(c)   You are also the manager responsible for the audit of the Nassau Group, which comprises a parent company and six subsidiaries. The audit of all individual companies' financial statements is almost complete, and you are currently carrying out the audit of the consolidated financial statements. One of the subsidiaries, Exuma Co, is audited by another firm, Jalousie & Co. Your firm has fulfilled the necessary requirements of ISA 600 *Special*

Considerations – Audits of Group Financial Statements (Including the Work of Component Auditors) and is satisfied as to the competence and independence of Jalousie & Co.

You have received from Jalousie & Co the draft auditor's report on Exuma Co's financial statements, an extract from which is shown below:

'Qualified Opinion (extract)

'In our opinion, except for effects of the matter described in the Basis for Qualified Opinion paragraph, the financial statements give a true and fair view of the financial position of Exuma Co as at 31 March 20X2...'

An extract of Note 12 to Exuma Co's financial statements is shown below.

'Basis of Qualified Opinion (extract)

'The company is facing financial damages of $2 million in respect of an on-going court case, more fully explained in Note 12 to the financial statements. Management has not recognised a provision but has disclosed the situation as a contingent liability. Under International Financial Reporting Standards, a provision should be made if there is an obligation as a result of a past event, a probable outflow of economic benefit, and a reliable estimate can be made. Audit evidence concludes that these criteria have been met, and it is our opinion that a provision of $2 million should be recognised. Accordingly, net profit and shareholders' equity would have been reduced by $2 million if the provision had been recognised.

An extract of Note 12 to Exuma Co's financial statements is shown below.

Note 12 (extract)

The company is the subject of a court case concerning an alleged breach of planning regulations. The plaintiff is claiming compensation of $2 million. The management of Exuma Co, after seeking legal advice, believe that there is only a 20% chance of a successful claim being made against the company.

Figures extracted from the draft financial statements for the year ending 31 March 20X2 are as follows.

	Nassau Group $m	Exuma Co $m
Profit before tax	20	4
Total assets	85	20

Required

Identify and explain the matters that should be considered, and actions that should be taken by the group audit engagement team, in forming an opinion on the consolidated financial statements of the Nassau Group.

(10 marks)

(Total = 25 marks)

2 Plant (P7 12/12) (amended)   49 mins

(a)   You are an audit manager in Weller & Co, an audit firm which operates as part of an international network of firms. This morning you received a note from a partner regarding a potential new audit client:

'I have been approached by the audit committee of the Plant Group, which operates in the mobile telecommunications sector. Our firm has been invited to tender for the audit of the individual and group financial statements for the year ending 31 March 20X3, and I would like your help in preparing the tender document. This would be a major new client for our firm's telecoms audit department.

The Plant Group comprises a parent company and six subsidiaries, one of which is located overseas. The audit committee is looking for a cost effective audit, and hopes that the strength of the Plant Group's governance and internal control mean that the audit can be conducted quickly, with a proposed deadline of 31 May 20X3. The Plant Group has expanded rapidly in the last few years and significant finance was raised in July 20X2 through a stock exchange listing.'

Required

(i) Explain why a firm of auditors may decide **NOT** to seek re-election as auditor.

(6 marks)

(ii) Evaluate the specific matters to be included in the tender document for the audit of the Plant Group. **(9 marks)**

(b) Weller & Co is facing competition from other audit firms, and the partners have been considering how the firm's revenue could be increased. Two suggestions have been made:

1 Audit partners and managers can be encouraged to sell non-audit services to audit clients by including in their remuneration package a bonus for successful sales.

2 All audit managers should suggest to their audit clients that as well as providing the external audit service, Weller & Co can provide the internal audit service as part of an 'extended audit' service.

Required

Comment on the ethical and professional issues raised by the suggestions to increase the firm's revenue.

(10 marks)

(Total = 25 marks)

3 Becker (P7 12/08)   39 mins

You are a senior manager in Becker & Co, a firm of Chartered Certified Accountants offering audit and assurance services mainly to large, privately owned companies. The firm has suffered from increased competition, due to two new firms of accountants setting up in the same town. Several audit clients have moved to the new firms, leading to loss of revenue, and an over staffed audit department. Bob McEnroe, one of the partners of Becker & Co, has asked you to consider how the firm could react to this situation. Several possibilities have been raised for your consideration:

1 Murray Co, a manufacturer of electronic equipment, is one of Becker & Co's audit clients. You are aware that the company has recently designed a new product, which market research indicates is likely to be very successful. The development of the product has been a huge drain on cash resources. The managing director of Murray Co has written to the audit engagement partner to see if Becker & Co would be interested in making an investment in the new product. It has been suggested that Becker & Co could provide finance for the completion of the development and the marketing of the product. The finance would be in the form of convertible debentures. Alternatively, a joint venture company in which control is shared between Murray Co and Becker & Co could be established to manufacture, market and distribute the new product.

2 Becker & Co is considering expanding the provision of non-audit services. Ingrid Sharapova, a senior manager in Becker & Co, has suggested that the firm could offer a recruitment

advisory service to clients, specialising in the recruitment of finance professionals. Becker & Co would charge a fee for this service based on the salary of the employee recruited. Ingrid Sharapova worked as a recruitment consultant for a year before deciding to train as an accountant.

3   Several audit clients are experiencing staff shortages, and it has been suggested that temporary staff assignments could be offered. It is envisaged that a number of audit managers or seniors could be seconded to clients for periods not exceeding six months, after which time they would return to Becker & Co.

Required

Evaluate the ethical and practice management implications in respect of:

(a)   A business arrangement with Murray Co   **(7 marks)**
(b)   A recruitment service offered to clients   **(7 marks)**
(c)   Temporary staff assignments   **(6 marks)**

                                                                          (Total = 20 marks)

4 Peaches (P7 12/09) (amended)   49 mins

(a)   Recent surveys of the quality of audits being performed have noted that auditors too often treat the requirements of the IESBA *Code of Ethics* and of ISAs as though they were prescriptive (rules-based) requirements, when in fact they are intended to be principles-based.

Required

(i)   Contrast the prescriptive and the principles-based approaches to auditing; and
(ii)   Outline the arguments for and against a prescriptive (rules-based) approach to auditing.
                                                                              (6 marks)

(b)   You are a manager in the audit department of Peaches & Co, a firm of Chartered Certified Accountants. One of your responsibilities is to act as a mentor to new recruits into the department. A new junior auditor, Glen Rambaran, has asked you to answer some questions which relate to issues encountered in his first few weeks working at Peaches & Co. The questions are shown below.

(i)   When I was on my initial training course, there was a session on ethics in which the presenter talked about being intimidated by a client. I assume this does not mean physical intimidation, so what is an intimidation threat?

(ii)   I know that Peaches & Co is facing competition from a new audit firm, and that our firm is advertising its services in a national newspaper. What are the rules on advertising for new clients?

(iii)   I heard one of the audit managers say that our firm had lost an audit client to a competitor because of lowballing. What is lowballing and is it allowed?
                                                                              (9 marks)

Required

For each of the three questions raised, provide a response to the audit junior, in which you identify and explain the ethical or professional issue raised.   **(9 marks)**

(c)   You are also responsible for the audit of Adderley Co, which operates a chain of cinemas across the country. Currently its cinemas are out of date, and management is planning to invest in all of its cinemas. The company has sufficient cash to fund half of the necessary capital expenditure, but has approached its bank with a loan application of $8 million for the remainder of the funds required.

The audit strategy for this audit concludes that the company has a relatively high risk associated with money laundering, largely due to the cash-based nature of its activities. The

majority of customers purchase their cinema tickets and refreshments in cash, and the company transfers its cash to overseas bank accounts on a regular basis.

Required

(i) Explain the stages used in laundering money, commenting on why Adderley Co has been identified as high risk. **(4 marks)**

(ii) Recommend the elements of an anti-money laundering programme which audit firms such as Peaches & Co should have in place. **(6 marks)**

(Total = 25 marks)

5 Cobra (P7 Sep/Dec 17)   39 mins

You are a senior manager at Cobra & Co, a firm of Chartered Certified Accountants. You are responsible for reviewing quality control and ethical matters which arise with the firm's portfolio of clients. During recent investigations you identified the following matters:

Asp Co

Asp Co currently qualifies as a small company in the jurisdiction in which it operates, with turnover of $7.5 million (20X6 – $5.3 million), and as such is not required by law to have an audit. Until recently, your firm has provided a range of non-audit services to Asp Co including bookkeeping, payroll and tax computation and advice. The company recently obtained an offer for a significant amount of finance to help the company grow. The management of Asp Co has ambitious plans for growth which they believe will result in revenue doubling within one year and then continuing to grow at a similar rate for at least the next five years. In order to secure the funding, the directors have decided to have the financial statements audited and have asked if Cobra & Co will become the company's auditors, as well as continuing to provide the existing services. This will include auditing the financial statements for the year ended 31 July 20X7 at the request of the new financers.

Viper Co

You have been approached by Viper Co, a retail company, to provide audit and tax services. In response you have written to the outgoing auditor to ask if there are any matters which you should be made aware of which might prevent you from accepting the assignment. Despite a number of follow up phone calls, you have not been able to obtain a response from the outgoing audit firm. On discussing this with the management team of Viper Co, you are made aware that the company is suing the outgoing auditor for damages due to the detrimental effect on their reputation following the auditor issuing a modified opinion, which the directors of Viper Co felt was inappropriate. The reason for the modified opinion was the application of an accounting treatment which the outgoing auditor considered to be inappropriate and a material misstatement.

Adder Co

Adder Co is a listed audit client of your firm. The management team of Adder Co has asked you to perform a valuation of the shares of another audit client, Slowworm Co, with a view to buying the entire shareholding. Slowworm Co is a private company whose shares are owned entirely by the original founder, Mr Jim Slow.

Required

Comment on the ethical and other professional issues raised, and recommend any actions which should be taken in respect of:

(a) Asp Co **(7 marks)**
(b) Viper Co **(7 marks)**
(c) Adder Co **(6 marks)**

(Total = 20 marks)

6 Smith & Co (P7 6/08) (amended) 49 mins

You are an audit manager in Smith & Co, a firm of Chartered Certified Accountants. You have recently been made responsible for reviewing invoices raised to clients and for monitoring your firm's credit control procedures. Several matters came to light during your most recent review of client invoice files:

Norman Co, a large private company, has not paid an invoice from Smith & Co dated 5 June 20X7 for work in respect of the financial statement audit for the year ended 28 February 20X7. A file note dated 30 November 20X7 states that Norman Co is suffering poor cash flows and is unable to pay the balance. This is the only piece of information in the file you are reviewing relating to the invoice. You are aware that the final audit work for the year ended 28 February 20X8, which has not yet been invoiced, is nearly complete and the auditor's report is due to be issued imminently.

Wallace Co, a private company whose business is the manufacture of industrial machinery, has paid all invoices relating to the recently completed audit planning for the year ended 31 May 20X8. However, in the invoice file you notice an invoice received by your firm from Wallace Co. The invoice is addressed to Valerie Hobson, the manager responsible for the audit of Wallace Co. The invoice relates to the rental of an area in Wallace Co's empty warehouse, with the following comment handwritten on the invoice: 'rental space being used for storage of Ms Hobson's speedboat for six months – she is our auditor, so only charge a nominal sum of $100'. When asked about the invoice, Valerie Hobson said that the invoice should have been sent to her private address. You are aware that Wallace Co sometimes uses the empty warehouse for rental income, though this is not the main trading income of the company.

In the 'miscellaneous invoices raised' file, an invoice dated last week has been raised to Software Supply Co, not a client of your firm. The comment box on the invoice contains the note: 'referral fee for recommending Software Supply Co to several audit clients regarding the supply of bespoke accounting software'.

Required

Identify and discuss the ethical and other professional issues raised by the invoice file review, and recommend what action, if any, Smith & Co should now take in respect of:

(a) Norman Co **(8 marks)**
(b) Wallace Co **(5 marks)**
(c) Software Supply Co **(4 marks)**

Another client, Sci-Tech Co, is a pharmaceutical research company. Your firm is engaged to provide an assurance conclusion on some key performance indicators (KPIs) that it discloses in its operating and financial review. Sci-Tech Co receives funding from governmental health departments, as well as several large charitable donations, the amount of which depends whether three KPI targets are met annually. All three of the targets must be met in order to secure the government funding.

Extracts from Sci-Tech Co's operating and financial review are as follows.

KPI target	Draft KPI 20X7	Actual KPI 20X6
Pharmaceutical products donated free of charge to health care charities: 1% revenue	1% revenue	1.2% revenue
Donations to, and cost of involvement with, local community charities: 0.5% revenue	0.6% revenue	0.8% revenue
Accidents in the work place: Fewer than 5 serious accidents per year	4 serious accidents	2 serious accidents

Required

(d) (i) Discuss why it may not be possible to provide a high level of assurance over the stated key performance indicators.

(ii) Describe the procedures to verify the number of serious accidents in the year ended 30 November 20X7.

(8 marks)

(Total = 25 marks)

7 Ryder (P7 6/14)   39 mins

You are a manager in Ryder & Co, a firm of Chartered Certified Accountants, and you have taken on the responsibility for providing support and guidance to new members of the firm. Ryder & Co has recently recruited a new audit junior, Sam Tyler, who has come across several issues in his first few months at the firm which he would like your guidance on. Sam's comments and questions are shown below:

(a) I know that auditors are required to assess risks of material misstatement by developing an understanding of the business risks of an audit client, but I am not clear on the relationship between business risk and risk of material misstatement. Can you explain the two types of risk, and how identifying business risk relates to risk of material misstatement? **(4 marks)**

(b) I worked on the interim audit of Crow Co, a manufacturing company which outsources its payroll function. I know that for Crow Co payroll is material. How does the outsourcing of payroll affect our audit planning? **(4 marks)**

(c) Crow Co is tendering for an important contract to supply Hatfield Co. I know that Hatfield Co is also an audit client of our firm, and I have heard that Crow Co's management has requested our firm to provide advice on the tender it is preparing. What matters should our firm consider in deciding whether to provide advice to Crow Co on the tender? **(5 marks)**

(d) I also worked on the audit of Campbell Co, where I heard the managing director, Ting Campbell, discussing a potential new business opportunity with the audit engagement partner. Campbell Co is an events organiser, and is planning to run a programme of nationwide events for accountants, at which speakers will discuss technical updates to financial reporting, tax and audit regulations. Ting proposed that our firm could invest some cash in the business opportunity, supply the speakers, market the events to our audit clients, and that any profit made would be shared between Ryder & Co and Campbell Co. What would be the implications of our firm considering this business opportunity? **(7 marks)**

Required

For each of the issues raised, respond to the audit junior, explaining the ethical and professional matters arising from the audit junior's comments.

Note. The split of the mark allocation is shown against each of the issues above.

(Total = 20 marks)

8 Chennai (P7 Mar/Jun 16) (amended)   39 mins

You are a manager at Chennai & Co, a firm of Chartered Certified Accountants. One of the partners has asked you to investigate and respond to a number of issues which have arisen with two different companies.

(a) Delhi Co, a potential new client, is a privately owned and rapidly expanding company which currently operates below the audit threshold in the country in which it is based. The company's management is currently considering having either a full audit or a limited assurance review of their financial statements. The partner would like you to assist the management of Delhi Co by writing a response to them in which you:

(i) Explain the difference between an audit of historical financial statements and a limited assurance review; and

(ii) Discuss the relative advantages and disadvantages to Delhi Co of having an audit of their historical financial statements as opposed to a limited assurance review.

(12 marks)

Delhi Co was incorporated in 20X5, with founder and chief executive Mr Nimesh Dattani as the sole shareholder. After a period of rapid growth, Delhi Co took out a ten-year bank loan facility in June 20X7 to finance Mr Dattani's ambitious expansion plans. This was supported by a further injection of financial capital in 20X4 through a new issue of shares in the company. The shares were sold to Mr Robert Hyland, an ex-business partner of Mr Dattani. The sale gave Mr Hyland a 40% shareholding in Delhi Co. He has no involvement in the management of the company.

Until recently Delhi Co operated with a small accounting department, comprising one full-time member of staff and one part-time employee. Due to the expansion of the company and Mr Dattani's plans to expand the customer base internationally, it has been necessary to increase the size of the accounting function to include two new full-time members of staff. Both of the new recruits are part-qualified accountants and Mr Dattani has committed to sponsoring them through their remaining training and ACCA examinations.

Required

Prepare the response to the management of Delhi Co as requested by the partner.

(b) The audit committee of another client, Mumbai Co, has asked the partner to consider whether it would be possible for the audit team to perform a review of the company's internal control system. A number of recent incidents have raised concerns amongst the management team that controls have deteriorated and that this has increased the risk of fraud, as well as inefficient commercial practices. The auditor's report for the audit of the financial statements of Mumbai Co for the year ended 31 March 20X6 was signed a few weeks ago. Mumbai Co is a listed company.

Required

In respect of the request for Chennai & Co to review Mumbai Co's internal control systems:

Identify and discuss the relevant ethical and professional issues raised, and recommend any actions necessary. **(8 marks)**

(Total = 20 marks)

QUALITY CONTROL AND PRACTICE MANAGEMENT

Questions 9 to 15 cover Quality control and practice management, the subject of Part C of the BPP Workbook for AAA.

9 Bunk (P7 6/15)   39 mins

You are a senior manager in Bunk & Co, a global audit firm with offices in more than 30 countries. You are responsible for monitoring audit quality and ethical situations which arise in relation to audit clients. Wire Co is an audit client whose operations involve haulage and distribution. The auditor's report for the financial statements of Wire Co for the year ended 31 December 20X4 was issued last week. You are conducting a review of the quality of that audit, and of any ethical issues which arose in relation to it. Relevant information obtained from a discussion with Lester Freeman, the audit engagement partner, is given below.

(a)   Wire Co's audit committee refused to agree to an increase in audit fees despite the company's operations expanding into new locations. In response to this, the materiality level was increased during the audit, and some review procedures were not carried out. To reduce sample sizes used in tests of detail, the samples were selected based on judgement rather than statistical methods. In addition, only parts of the population being tested were sampled, for example, certain locations were not included in the sample of non-current assets selected for physical verification.   **(6 marks)**

(b)   Some of the audit work was performed by an overseas office of Bunk & Co in an 'off-shoring' arrangement. This practice is encouraged by Bunk & Co, whose managing partners see it as a way of improving audit efficiency. The overseas office performs the work at a lower cost, and it was largely low-risk, non-judgemental work included in this arrangement for the audit of Wire Co, for example, numerical checks on documentation. In addition, the overseas office read the minutes of board meetings to identify issues relevant to the audit.   **(5 marks)**

(c)   In July 20X4, Russell Bell, Wire Co's former finance director, joined Bunk & Co as an audit partner, working in the same office as Lester Freeman. Although Russell was not a member of the audit team, he did update Lester on some business developments which had taken place at the company during the period before he left. Russell held a number of equity shares in Wire Co, which he sold in January 20X5. Since joining Bunk & Co, Russell has been developing initiatives to increase the firm's income. One initiative is that audit team members should be encouraged to cross-sell non-audit services and references to targets for the cross-selling of non-audit services to audit clients is now included in partner and employee appraisal documentation.   **(9 marks)**

Required

Comment on the quality control, ethical and professional issues raised in respect of the audit of Wire Co and the firm-wide policies of Bunk & Co, and recommend any actions to be taken by the audit firm.

Notes

(1)   The split of the mark allocation is shown against each of the issues above.

(2)   Assume it is 6 June 20X5.   **(Total = 20 marks)**

10 Grape (P7 12/09)   70 mins

You are a manager in Grape & Co, a firm of Chartered Certified Accountants. You have been temporarily assigned as audit manager to the audit of Banana Co, because the engagement manager has been taken ill. The final audit of Banana Co for the year ended 30 September 20X9 is nearing completion, and you are now reviewing the audit files and discussing the audit with the junior members of the audit team. Banana Co designs and manufactures equipment such as cranes and scaffolding, which are used in the construction industry. The equipment usually follows a

BPP
LEARNING

standard design, but sometimes Banana Co designs specific items for customers according to contractually agreed specifications. The draft financial statements show revenue of $12.5 million, net profit of $400,000, and total assets of $78 million.

The following information has come to your attention during your review of the audit files.

During the year, a new range of manufacturing plant was introduced to the factories operated by Banana Co. All factory employees received training from an external training firm on how to safely operate the machinery, at a total cost of $500,000. The training costs have been capitalised into the cost of the new machinery, as the finance director argues that the training is necessary in order for the machinery to generate an economic benefit. After the year end, Cherry Co, a major customer with whom Banana Co has several significant contracts, announced its insolvency, and that procedures to shut down the company had commenced. The administrators of Cherry Co have suggested that the company may be able to pay approximately 25% of the amounts owed to its trade payables (creditors). A trade receivable of $300,000 is recognised on Banana Co's statement of financial position in respect of this customer.

In addition, one of the junior members of the audit team voiced concerns over how the audit had been managed. The junior said the following.

'I have only worked on two audits prior to being assigned the audit team of Banana Co. I was expecting to attend a meeting at the start of the audit, where the partner and other senior members of the audit team discussed the audit, but no meeting was held. In addition, the audit manager has been away on holiday for three weeks, and left a senior in charge. However, the senior was busy with other assignments, so was not always available.

'I was given the task of auditing the goodwill which arose on an acquisition made during the year. I also worked on the audit of inventory, and attended the inventory count, which was quite complicated, as Banana Co has a lot of work-in-progress. I tried to be as useful as possible during the count, and helped the client's staff count some of the raw materials. As I had been to the inventory count, I was asked by the audit senior to challenge the finance director regarding the adequacy of the provision against inventory, which the senior felt was significantly understated.

'Lastly, we found that we were running out of time to complete our audit procedures. The audit senior advised that we should reduce the sample sizes used in our tests as a way of saving time. He also suggested that if we picked an item as part of our sample for which it would be time consuming to find the relevant evidence, then we should pick a different item which would be quicker to audit.'

Required

In respect of the specific information provided:

(a) Comment on the matters to be considered, and explain the audit evidence you should expect to find during your file review in respect of:

(i) The training costs that have been capitalised into the cost of the new machinery; and

(ii) The trade receivable recognised in relation to Cherry Co. **(12 marks)**

(b) Evaluate the audit junior's concerns regarding the management of the audit of Banana Co.

(10 marks)

(c) There are specific regulatory obligations imposed on accountants and auditors in relation to detecting and reporting money laundering activities. You have been asked to provide a training session to the new audit juniors on auditors' responsibilities in relation to money laundering.

Required

Prepare briefing notes to be used at your training session in which you:

(i)   Explain the term 'money laundering'. Illustrate your explanation with examples of money laundering offences, including those which could be committed by the accountant

(ii)   Explain the policies and procedures that a firm of Chartered Certified Accountants should establish in order to meet its responsibilities in relation to money laundering

(10 marks)

Professional marks will be awarded in part (c) for the format of the answer, and the quality of the explanations provided. **(4 marks)**

Note. Assume it is 6 December 20X9. **(Total = 36 marks)**

11 Nate & Co (P7 12/07)   39 mins

You are an audit manager in Nate & Co, a firm of Chartered Certified Accountants. You are reviewing three situations, which were recently discussed at the monthly audit managers' meeting:

1   Nate & Co has recently been approached by a potential new audit client, Fisher Co. Your firm is keen to take the appointment and is currently carrying out client acceptance procedures. Fisher Co was recently incorporated by Marcellus Fisher, with its main trade being the retailing of wooden storage boxes.

2   Nate & Co provides the audit service to CF Co, a national financial services organisation. Due to a number of errors in the recording of cash deposits from new customers that have been discovered by CF Co's internal audit team, the directors of CF Co have requested that your firm carry out a review of the financial information technology systems. It has come to your attention that while working on the audit planning of CF Co, Jin Sayed, one of the juniors on the audit team and who is a recent information technology graduate, spent three hours providing advice to the internal audit team about how to improve the system. As far as you know, this advice has not been used by the internal audit team.

3   LA Shots Co is a manufacturer of bottled drinks, and has been an audit client of Nate & Co for five years. Two audit juniors attended the annual inventory count last Monday. They reported that Brenda Mangle, the new production manager of LA Shots Co, wanted the inventory count and audit procedures performed as quickly as possible. As an incentive she offered the two juniors ten free bottles of 'Super Juice' from the end of the production line. Brenda also invited them to join the LA Shots Co office party, which commenced at the end of the inventory count. The inventory count and audit procedures were completed within two hours (the previous year's procedures lasted a full day), and the juniors then spent four hours at the office party.

Required

(a)   Define 'money laundering' and state the procedures specific to money laundering that should be considered before, and on the acceptance of, the audit appointment of Fisher Co.

(5 marks)

(b)   With reference to CF Co, explain the ethical and other professional issues raised. **(9 marks)**

(c)   Evaluate the ethical and professional matters raised at the inventory count of LA Shots Co.
(6 marks)

(Total = 20 marks)

12 Sepia & Co

39 mins

(a) Explain what the term 'lowballing' means and discuss current guidance in this area.

(5 marks)

(b) You are an audit manager in Sepia & Co ('Sepia'), a firm of Chartered Certified Accountants. Your specific responsibilities include advising the senior audit partner on the acceptance of new assignments. The following matters have arisen in connection with three prospective client companies.

(i) Your firm has been nominated to act as external auditor to Squid, a private limited company. You have been waiting for a response to your letter of 'professional enquiry' to Squid's auditor, Krill & Co, for several weeks. Your recent attempts to call the current engagement partner, Anton Fargues, in Krill & Co have been met with the response from Anton's personal assistant that 'Mr Fargues is not available'.

(ii) Sepia has been approached by the management of Hatchet, a company listed on a recognised stock exchange, to advise on a take-over bid which they propose to make. The target company, Vitronella, is an audit client of your firm. However, Hatchet is not.

(iii) A former colleague at Sepia, Edwin Stenuit, is now employed by another firm, Keratin & Co. Sepia and Keratin & Co and three other firms have recently tendered for the audit of Benthos, a limited liability company. Benthos is expected to announce the successful firm next week. Yesterday, at a social gathering, Edwin confided to you that Keratin & Co 'lowballed' on their tender for the audit as they expect to be able to provide Benthos with lucrative other services.

(15 marks)

Required

Comment on the professional issues raised by each of the above matters and the steps, if any, that Sepia should now take.

(Total = 20 marks)

13 Groom (P7 6/13) (amended)

49 mins

(a) You are a manager in Groom & Co, a firm of Chartered Certified Accountants. You have just attended a monthly meeting of audit partners and managers at which the audit of Spaniel Co was discussed.

The auditor's report on the financial statements of Spaniel Co, a long-standing audit client, for the year ended 31 December 20X2 was issued in April 20X3, and was unmodified. In May 20X3, Spaniel Co's audit committee contacted the audit engagement partner to discuss a fraud that had been discovered. The company's internal auditors estimate that $4.5 million has been stolen in a payroll fraud, which has been operating since May 20X2.

The audit engagement partner commented that neither tests of controls nor substantive audit procedures were conducted on payroll in the audit of the latest financial statements as in previous years' audits there were no deficiencies found in controls over payroll. The total assets recognised in Spaniel Co's financial statements at 31 December 20X2 were $80 million. Spaniel Co is considering suing Groom & Co for the total amount of cash stolen from the company, claiming that the audit firm was negligent in conducting the audit.

Required

Explain the matters that should be considered in determining whether Groom & Co is liable to Spaniel Co in respect of the fraud.

(11 marks)

(b) You are also responsible for the audit of Clooney Co, the final audit of which is nearing completion. The following points have been noted for your attention by the audit senior:

Clooney Co is one of the world's leading leisure travel providers, operating under several brand names to sell package holidays. The company catered for more than 10 million customers in the last 12 months. Draft figures for the year ended 31 March 20X3 show revenue of $3,200 million, profit before tax of $150 million, and total assets of $4,100 million. Clooney Co's executives earn a bonus based on the profit before tax of the company.

In January 20X3, thousands of holiday-makers were left stranded abroad after the company operating the main airline chartered by Clooney Co went into liquidation. The holiday-makers were forced to wait an average of two weeks before they could be returned home using an alternative airline. They have formed a group which is claiming compensation for the time they were forced to spend abroad, with the total claim amounting to $20 million. The items which the group is claiming compensation for include accommodation and subsistence costs, lost income and distress caused by the situation. The claim has not been recognised or disclosed in the draft financial statements, as management argues that the full amount payable will be covered by Clooney Co's insurance.

One part of the company's activities, operating under the Shelly's Cruises brand, provides cruise holidays. Due to economic recession, the revenue of the Shelly's Cruises business segment has fallen by 25% this year, and profit before tax has fallen by 35%. Shelly's Cruises contributed $640 million to total revenue in the year to 31 March 20X3, and has identifiable assets of $235 million, including several large cruise liners. The Shelly's Cruises brand is not recognised as an intangible asset, as it has been internally generated.

Required

Comment on the matters that you should consider, and state the audit evidence you should expect to find in your review of the audit working papers for the year ended March 20X3 in respect of:

(b)   The compensation claim

(c)   Shelly's Cruises   **(14 marks)**

(Total = 25 marks)

14 Raven (P7 6/12) (amended)   49 mins

You are a senior manager in the audit department of Raven & Co. You are reviewing two situations which have arisen in respect of audit clients, which were recently discussed at the monthly audit managers' meeting:

1   Grouse Co is a significant audit client which develops software packages. Its managing director, Max Partridge, has contacted one of your firm's partners regarding a potential business opportunity. The proposal is that Grouse Co and Raven & Co could jointly develop accounting and tax calculation software, and that revenue from sales of the software would be equally split between the two firms. Max thinks that Raven & Co's audit clients would be a good customer base for the product.

2   Plover Co is a private hospital which provides elective medical services, such as laser eye surgery to improve eyesight. The audit of its financial statements for the year ended 30 September 20X2 is currently taking place. The audit senior overheard one of the surgeons who performs laser surgery saying to his colleague that he is hoping to finish his medical qualification soon, and that he was glad that Plover Co did not check his references before employing him. While completing the subsequent events audit procedures, the audit senior found a letter from a patient's solicitor claiming compensation from Plover Co in relation to alleged medical negligence resulting in injury to the patient.

Required

Evaluate the ethical, commercial and other professional issues raised, and recommend any actions that should be taken in respect of:

(a)   Grouse Co   **(8 marks)**

(b)   Plover Co   **(7 marks)**

You are also the manager responsible for the audit of another client, Dylan Co, which is a listed company. You are reviewing the working papers of the audit file for the year ended 30 September 20X2, and the audit senior has left a note for your attention:

'Dylan Co outsources its entire payroll, invoicing and credit control functions to Hendrix Co. In August 20X2, Hendrix Co suffered a computer virus attack on its operating system, resulting in the destruction of its accounting records, including those relating to Dylan Co. We have therefore been unable to perform the planned audit procedures on payroll, revenue and receivables, all of which are material to the financial statements. Hendrix Co has manually reconstructed the relevant figures as far as possible, and has supplied a written statement to confirm that they are as accurate as possible, given the loss of accounting records.'

Required

(c)   (i)   Comment on the actions that should be taken by the auditor, and the implications for the auditor's report.

        (ii)   Discuss the quality control procedures that should be carried out by the audit firm prior to the auditor's report being issued.

                                                                                                     (10 marks)

                                                                                          (Total = 25 marks)

15 Dragon Group (P7 6/09) (amended)   49 mins

The Dragon Group is a large group of companies operating in the furniture retail trade. The group has expanded rapidly in the last three years, by acquiring several subsidiaries each year. The management of the parent company, Dragon Co, a listed company, has decided to put the audit of the group and all subsidiaries out to tender, as the current audit firm is not seeking re-election. The financial year end of the Dragon Group is 30 September 20X9.

You are a senior manager in Unicorn & Co, a global firm of Chartered Certified Accountants, with offices in over 150 countries across the world. Unicorn & Co has been invited to tender for the Dragon Group audit (including the audit of all subsidiaries). You manage a department within the firm which specialises in the audit of retail companies, and you have been assigned the task of drafting the tender document. You recently held a meeting with Edmund Jalousie, the group finance director, in which you discussed the current group structure, recent acquisitions, and the group's plans for future expansion.

Meeting notes – Dragon Group

Group structure

The parent company owns 20 subsidiaries, all of which are wholly owned. Half of the subsidiaries are located in this country, and half overseas. Most of the foreign subsidiaries report under the same financial reporting framework as Dragon Co, but several prepare financial statements using local accounting rules.

Acquisitions during the year

Two companies were purchased in March 20X9, both located in this country:

- Mermaid Co, a company which operates 20 furniture retail outlets. The audit opinion expressed by the incumbent auditor on the financial statements for the year ended 30 September 20X8 was modified by a material misstatement over the non-disclosure of a contingent liability. The contingent liability relates to a court case which is still ongoing.

- Minotaur Co, a large company, whose operations are distribution and warehousing. This represents a diversification away from retail, and it is hoped that the Dragon Group will benefit from significant economies of scale as a result of the acquisition.

Other matters

The acquisitive strategy of the group over the last few years has led to significant growth. Group revenue has increased by 25% in the last three years, and is predicted to increase by a further 35% in the next four years as the acquisition of more subsidiaries is planned. The Dragon Group has raised finance for the acquisitions in the past by becoming listed on the stock exchanges of three different countries. A new listing on a foreign stock exchange is planned for January 20Y0. For this reason, management would like the group audit completed by 31 December 20X9.

Required

(a) Recommend and describe the principal matters to be included in your firm's tender document to provide the audit service to the Dragon Group;   **(10 marks)**

(b) Evaluate the matters that should be considered before accepting the audit engagement, in the event of your firm being successful in the tender; and   **(8 marks)**

(c) Define 'transnational audit', and discuss the features of a transnational audit that may contribute to a high level of audit risk in such an engagement. Explain the relevance of the term to the audit of the Dragon Group.   **(7 marks)**

(Total = 25 marks)

PLANNING AND CONDUCTING AN AUDIT OF HISTORICAL FINANCIAL INFORMATION

Questions 16 to 46 cover Planning and conducting an audit of historical financial information, the subject of Part D of the BPP Workbook for AAA.

16 Goldfinch (P7 Sep/Dec 17)   49 mins

You are a manager in the audit department of Pigeon & Co, a firm of Chartered Certified Accountants. You are responsible for the audit of Goldfinch Gas Co, a company which is the main supplier of gas to business and residential customers across the country.

The audit fieldwork for the year ended 30 June 20W7 is nearing completion. The draft financial statements recognise profit before tax of $130 million (20W6 – $110 million), and total assets of $1,900 million (20W6 – $1,878 million).

You are reviewing the audit files and the following matters have been noted for your attention by the audit senior:

(a)   **Decommissioning provision**

A provision of $430 million (20W6 – $488 million) is recognised as a long-term liability. The provision is in respect of decommissioning a number of gas production and storage facilities when they are at the end of their useful lives. The estimate of the decommissioning costs has been based on price levels and technology at the reporting date, and discounted to present value using an interest rate of 8% (20W6 – 6%). The timing of decommissioning payments is dependent on the estimated useful lives of the facilities but is expected to occur by 20Z6, with the majority of the provision being utilised between 20X5 and 20Z0.

The accounting policy note discusses the methodology used by management for determining the value of the decommissioning provision and states that this is an area of critical accounting judgements including key areas of estimation uncertainty. The estimate has been made by management. In previous years, a management expert was engaged to provide the estimate but as this was expensive, management decided to produce their own estimate for the year ended 30 June 20W7.   **(10 marks)**

(b)   **Depreciation**

The draft statement of financial position includes plant and equipment, unrelated to gas production and storage facilities, at a carrying amount of $65 million. There was a change in the estimation technique used to determine the depreciation in respect of these assets during the year. Depreciation was previously calculated on a straight line basis over a 10-year useful life, but from 1 July 20W6, the useful life has been amended to 15 years. The finance director explained to the audit team that the review of estimated useful life has been made on the basis that the assets are lasting longer than originally anticipated.

The change in depreciation policy has been accounted for as a prior year adjustment, resulting in an increase of $20 million to property, plant and equipment and to retained earnings. The depreciation expense recognised in draft profit for the year to 30 June 20W7 is $12 million (20W6 – $15 million).   **(8 marks)**

(c)   **Trade receivables**

The draft statement of financial position recognises total trade receivables of $450 million (20W6 – $390 million).

The audit team has performed substantive analytical procedures on trade receivables with the following results:

Receivables collection period:	20W7	20W6
Residential customers	65 days	58 days
Business customers	50 days	55 days

The notes to the financial statements contain the following information relating to trade receivables:

Trade receivables:	20W7 $ million	20W6 $ million
Residential customers	158	145
Business customers	356	289
Less: allowance for credit losses	(64)	(44)
Net trade receivables	450	390

Receivables from business customers are generally reviewed for impairment on an individual basis when a customer changes their gas supplier, discontinuing their relationship with the Group. Receivables from residential customers are reviewed for impairment where they are more than 90 days late in paying their bill, or where customers have a history of late payment. Since a new customer billing system was introduced in September 20W6, management has exercised additional judgement regarding the appropriate level of allowance for these trade receivables.
(7 marks)

Required

Comment on the matters to be considered, and explain the audit evidence you should expect to find during your file review in respect of each of the issues described above.

You are **NOT** required to explain the potential impact of the matters on the auditor's opinion or report.

Note. The split of the mark allocation is shown against each of the issues above.

(Total = 25 marks)

17 Ted (P7 6/15) (amended)   98 mins

You are an audit manager in Craggy & Co, which is an international firm of Chartered Certified Accountants with branches in many countries, and which offers a range of audit and assurance services to its clients. Your responsibilities include, in addition to audit work, reviewing ethical matters which arise with audit clients, and dealing with approaches from prospective audit clients.

You have been provided with the following exhibits:

1   An email which you have received from Jack Hackett, the audit engagement partner.
2   Information regarding a request received to submit an audit proposal.
3   Notes from a meeting between Jack Hackett and Len Brennan, Ted Co's finance director.
4   Extracts from the draft financial statements and results of preliminary analytical review.

Required

Respond to the instructions in the email from the audit engagement partner.   **(46 marks)**

Note. The split of the mark allocation is shown in the partner's email (Exhibit 1).

Professional marks will be awarded for the presentation and logical flow of the briefing notes and the clarity of the explanations provided.   **(4 marks)**

Note. Assume it is 6 June 20X5.   **(Total = 50 marks)**

Exhibit 1 – Email from audit engagement partner

To: Audit manager

From: Jack Hackett

Regarding: Ted Co tender and audit planning

Hello

Our firm has been invited to submit an audit proposal to the management of Ted Co. If we are successful in gaining the work I will need you to begin planning the audit of Ted Co.

I have already gathered some information about Ted Co and also had an initial meeting with the company's finance director, Len Brennan, and have provided you with that information. In addition, I have asked one of the audit seniors to begin to carry out preliminary analytical review procedures on Ted Co's draft financial statements, and the results of the review performed so far are also provided to you.

For the purpose of providing some practical training to some of our audit supervisors, please can you use the information in Exhibit 2 to:

(a)   (i)   Explain the specific matters to be included in the audit proposal (tender document), other than those relating to the audit fee; and   **(8 marks)**

        (ii)   Discuss the issues to be considered by the audit firm in determining a fee for the audit including any ethical matters raised assuming that Craggy & Co is appointed auditor of Ted Co.   **(6 marks)**

Then, using the remaining information, I need you to prepare briefing notes for my use in which you:

(b)   Discuss the matters specific to the planning of an initial audit engagement which should be considered in developing the audit strategy.   **(6 marks)**

(c)   Evaluate the audit risks to be considered in planning the audit of Ted Co.   **(18 marks)**

(d)   Recommend the principal audit procedures to be performed in the audit of:

        (i)   The portfolio of short-term investments; and
        (ii)   The earnings per share figure.   **(8 marks)**

Thank you.

Exhibit 2 – Information regarding proposed audit

The management of Ted Co has invited Craggy & Co to submit an audit proposal (tender document) for their consideration. Ted Co has grown rapidly in the last few years, and has recently achieved a stock exchange listing. The previous auditors of Ted Co, a small and unrelated firm called Crilly & Co, resigned in September 20X4. The audit opinion on the financial statements for the year ended 31 May 20X4 was unmodified.

The company designs, develops and publishes computer games, and some of its start-up funding was raised from a venture capital company. The software used in the computer games is developed in this country, but the manufacture of the physical product takes place overseas. Ted Co has two full-time accountants who use an off-the-shelf accounting package to record transactions and to prepare financial information. The company has a financial year ending 31 May 20X5.

The following comment was made by Dougal Doyle, the company's founder and managing director, in relation to the audit proposal and potential audit fee:

'I am looking for a firm of auditors who will give me a competitive audit fee. I am hoping that the fee will be quite low, as I am willing to pay more for services that I consider more beneficial to the business, such as strategic advice. I would like the audit fee to be linked to Ted Co's success in expanding overseas as a result of the audit firm's advice. Hopefully the audit will not be too disruptive and I would like it completed within four months of the year end.'

Exhibit 3 – Notes from meeting with Len Brennan

Ted Co was formed ten years ago by Dougal Doyle, a graduate in multimedia computing. The company has published many highly successful games which have won industry awards. In the last two years the company invested $100m in creating games designed to appeal to a broad, global audience and sales are now made in over 60 countries.

Computer games are largely sold through retail outlets, but approximately 25% of Ted Co's revenue is generated through sales made on the company's website. In some countries Ted Co's products are distributed under licences which give the licence holder the exclusive right to sell the products in that country. The cost of each licence to the distributor depends on the estimated sales in the country to which it relates, and licences last for an average of five years. The income which Ted Co receives from the sale of a licence is deferred over the period of the licence. At 31 May 20X5 the total amount of deferred income recognised in Ted Co's statement of financial position is $18 million.

As part of a five-year strategic plan, Ted Co obtained a stock market listing in December 20X4. The listing and related share issue raised a significant amount of finance, and many shares are held by institutional investors. Dougal Doyle retains a 20% equity shareholding, and a further 10% of the company's shares are held by his family members.

Despite being listed, the company does not have an internal audit department, and there is only one non-executive director on the board. These problems, which Ted Co's management is hoping to resolve in the next few months, are explained in the company's annual report, as required by the applicable corporate governance code.

Recently, a small treasury management function was established to manage the company's foreign currency transactions, which include forward exchange currency contracts. The treasury management function also deals with short-term investments. In January 20X5, cash of $8 million was invested in a portfolio of equity shares held in listed companies, which is to be held in the short term as a speculative investment. The shares are recognised as a financial asset at cost of $8 million in the draft statement of financial position. The fair value of the shares at 31 May 20X5 is $6 million.

As a listed company, Ted Co is required to disclose its earnings per share figure. Dougal Doyle would like this to be based on an adjusted earnings figure which does not include depreciation or amortisation expenses.

Exhibit 4 – Extract from draft financial statements and results of preliminary analytical review

STATEMENT OF PROFIT OR LOSS (EXTRACT)

	Year to 31 May 20X5 Draft $'000	Year to 31 May 20X4 Actual $'000	% change
Revenue	98,000	67,000	46.3% increase
Gross profit	65,000	40,000	62.5% increase
Operating profit	12,000	9,200	30.4% increase
Finance charge	4,000	3,800	5.3% increase
Profit before tax	8,000	5,400	48.1% increase
Earnings per share	89.6 cent per share	–	

Note. Earnings per share has been calculated as follows:

	$,000
Profit before tax	8,000
Add depreciation	1,100
Amortisation	6,000
Adjusted profit before tax	15,100
Adjusted profit before tax	15,100,000
Number of equity shares at 31 May 20X5	16,850,000 = 89.6 cents per share

STATEMENT OF FINANCIAL POSITION (EXTRACT)

	31 May 20X5 Draft $'000	31 May 20X4 Actual $'000	% change
Non-current assets			
Intangible assets – development costs	58,000	35,000	65.7% increase
Total assets	134,000	105,000	27.6% increase

18 Francis (P7 12/14)   49 mins

You are a manager in the audit department of Williams & Co and you are reviewing the audit working papers in relation to the Francis Group (the Group), whose financial year ended on 31 July 20X4. Your firm audits all components of the Group, which consists of a parent company and three subsidiaries – Marks Co, Roberts Co and Teapot Co.

The Group manufactures engines which are then supplied to the car industry. The draft consolidated financial statements recognise profit for the year to 31 July 20X4 of $23 million (20X3 – $33 million) and total assets of $450 million (20X3 – $455 million).

Information in respect of three issues has been highlighted for your attention during the file review.

(a)   An 80% equity shareholding in Teapot Co was acquired on 1 August 20X3. Goodwill on the acquisition of $27 million was calculated at that date and remains recognised as an intangible asset at that value at the year end. The goodwill calculation performed by the Group's management is shown below:

	$'000
Purchase consideration	75,000
Fair value of 20% non-controlling interest	13,000
	88,000
Less: Fair value of Teapot Co's identifiable net assets at acquisition	(61,000)
Goodwill	27,000

In determining the fair value of identifiable net assets at acquisition, an upwards fair value adjustment of $300,000 was made to the book value of a property recognised in Teapot Co's financial statements at a carrying value of $600,000.

A loan of $60 million was taken out on 1 August 20X3 to help finance the acquisition. The loan carries an annual interest rate of 6%, with interest payments made annually in arrears. The loan will be repaid in 20 years at a premium of $5 million.   **(12 marks)**

(b)   In September 20X4, a natural disaster caused severe damage to the property complex housing the Group's head office and main manufacturing site. For health and safety reasons, a decision was made to demolish the property complex. The demolition took place three weeks after the damage was caused. The property had a carrying value of $16 million at 31 July 20X4.

A contingent asset of $18 million has been recognised as a current asset and as deferred income in the Group statement of financial position at 31 July 20X4, representing the amount claimed under the Group's insurance policy in respect of the disaster. **(7 marks)**

(c)   Marks Co supplies some of the components used by Roberts Co in its manufacturing process. At the year end, an intercompany receivable of $20 million is recognised in Marks Co's financial statements. Roberts Co's financial statements include a corresponding intercompany payables balance of $20 million and inventory supplied from Marks Co valued at $50 million. **(6 marks)**

Required

Comment on the matters to be considered, and explain the audit evidence you should expect to find during your review of the audit working papers in respect of each of the issues described above.

Note. The split of the mark allocation is shown against each of the issues above. Assume it is 10 December 20X4.

(Total = 25 marks)

19 Thurman (P7 Sep/Dec 16)   49 mins

You are the manager responsible for the audit of Thurman Co, a manufacturing company which supplies stainless steel components to a wide range of industries. The company's financial year ended on 31 July 20X6 and you are reviewing the audit work which has been completed on a number of material balances and transactions: assets held for sale, capital expenditure and payroll expenses. A summary of the work which has been performed is given below and in each case the description of the audit work indicates the full extent of the audit procedures carried out by the audit team.

(a)   **Assets held for sale**

Due to the planned disposal of one of Thurman Co's factory sites, the property and associated assets have been classified as held for sale in the financial statements. A manual journal has been posted by the finance director to reclassify the assets as current assets and to adjust the value of the assets for impairment and reversal of depreciation charged from the date at which the assets met the criteria to be classified as held for sale. The finance director asked the audit senior to check the journal before it was posted on the basis of there being no one with the relevant knowledge to do this at Thurman Co.

The planned disposal was discussed with management. A brief note has been put into the audit working papers stating that in management's opinion the accounting treatment to classify the factory as held for sale is correct. The manual journal has been arithmetically checked by a different member of the audit team, and the amounts agreed back to the non-current asset register. **(9 marks)**

(b)   **Capital expenditure**

When auditing the company's capital expenditure, the audit team selected a material transaction to test and found that key internal controls over capital expenditure were not operating effectively. Authorisation had not been obtained for an order placed for several vehicles, and appropriate segregation of duties over initiating and processing the transaction was not maintained.

The audit team noted details of the internal control deficiencies and updated the systems notes on the permanent audit file to reflect the deficiencies. The audit work completed on this order was to agree the purchase of the vehicles to purchase invoices and to the cash book and bank statement. The rest of the audit work on capital expenditure was completed in accordance with the audit programme. **(7 marks)**

(c)   **Payroll expenses**

The payroll function is outsourced to Jackson Co, a service organisation which processes all of Thurman Co's salary expenses. The payroll expenses recognised in the financial statements have been traced back to year-end reports issued by Jackson Co. The audit team has had no direct contact with Jackson Co as the year-end reports were sent to Thurman Co's finance director who then passed them to the audit team.

Thurman Co employs a few casual workers who are paid in cash at the end of each month and are not entered into the payroll system. The audit team has agreed the cash payment made back to the petty cash records and the amounts involved are considered immaterial.

(9 marks)

Required

In respect of each of the three matters described above:

(i)   Comment on the sufficiency and appropriateness of the audit evidence obtained;

(ii)   Recommend further audit procedures to be performed by the audit team; and

(iii)   Explain the matters which should be included in a report in accordance with ISA 265 *Communicating Deficiencies in Internal Controls to Those Charged with Governance and Management*.

Note. The split of the mark allocation is shown against each of the matters above.

(Total = 25 marks)

20 Faster Jets (P7 12/14) (amended)   49 mins

Faster Jets Co is an airline company and is a new audit client of Brown & Co. You are responsible for the audit of the financial statements for the year ended 30 November 20X4. The draft financial statements recognise revenue of $150 million and total assets of $250 million.

(a)   The purpose of ISA 510 *Initial Audit Engagements – Opening Balances* is to establish standards and provide guidance regarding opening balances when the financial statements are audited for the first time or when the financial statements for the prior period were audited by another auditor.

Required

Explain the auditor's reporting responsibilities that are specific to initial engagements.

(5 marks)

(b)   During the year, Faster Jets Co purchased several large plots of land located near major airports at a cost of $12.5 million. The land is currently rented out and is classified as investment property, which is recognised in the draft financial statements at a fair value of $14.5 million. The audit partner has suggested the use of an auditor's expert to obtain evidence in respect of the fair value of the land.

Required

In respect of the land recognised as investment property:

(i)   Explain the additional information which you require to plan the audit of the land; and

(ii)   Explain the matters to be considered in assessing the reliance which can be placed on the work of an auditor's expert.

Note. The total marks will be split equally between each part. **(10 marks)**

(c)   Your firm has also been engaged to perform a separate assurance engagement on Faster Jets Co's corporate social responsibility (CSR) report. This engagement will be performed by Brown & Co's specialist social and environmental assurance department and there are no ethical threats created by the provision of this service in addition to the audit. An extract from the draft CSR report is shown below.

CSR objective	CSR target	Performance in 20X4
Continue to invest in local communities and contribute to charitable causes	Make direct charitable cash donations to local charities	Donations of $550,000 were made to local charities
	Build relationships with global charities and offer free flights to charitable organisations	800 free flights with a value of $560,000 were provided to charities
	Develop our Local Learning Initiative and offer free one-day education programmes to schools	$750,000 was spent on the Local Learning Initiative and 2,250 children attended education days
Reduce environmental impact of operations	Reduce the amount of vehicle fuel used on business travel by our employees	The number of miles travelled in vehicles reduced by 5%, and the amount spent on vehicle fuel reduced by 7%

Required

(i)   Discuss the difficulties in measuring and reporting on social and environmental performance; and **(4 marks)**

(ii)   Recommend the procedures to be used to gain assurance on the validity of the performance information in Faster Jets Co's CSR report. **(6 marks)**

(Total = 25 marks)

21 Magpie (P7 6/12) (amended)   98 mins

You are a manager in Magpie & Co, responsible for the audit of the CS Group.

You have been provided with the following exhibits:

1   An email which you have received from Jo Daw, the audit engagement partner.
2   Extracts from the permanent file on the audit of the CS Group.
3   Notes from a meeting between Jo Daw and Steve Eagle, the finance director of the CS Group

Required

Respond to the instructions in the email from the audit engagement partner. **(46 marks)**

Note. The split of the mark allocation is shown in the partner's email (Exhibit 1). Assume it is 30 August 20X2.

Professional marks will be awarded for the presentation and logical flow of the briefing notes and the clarity of the explanations provided. **(4 marks)**

(Total = 50 marks)

Exhibit 1 – Email from the audit engagement partner

To:	Audit manager
From:	Jo Daw
Regarding:	CS Group audit planning

Hello

I have just been to a meeting with Steve Eagle, the finance director of the CS Group. We were discussing recent events which will have a bearing on our forthcoming audit, and my notes from the meeting are attached to this email. One of the issues discussed is the change in group structure due to the acquisition of Canary Co earlier this year. Our firm has been appointed as auditor of Canary Co, which has a year ending 30 June 20X2, and the terms of the engagement have been agreed with the client. We need to start planning the audits of the three components of the Group, and of the consolidated financial statements.

Using the information provided, I require you to prepare briefing notes for my use, in which you:

(a)   Evaluate the implications of the acquisition of Canary Co for the audit planning of the individual and consolidated financial statements of the CS Group   **(8 marks)**

(b)   Evaluate the risks of material misstatement to be considered in the audit planning of the individual and consolidated financial statements of the CS Group, identifying any matters that are not relevant to the audit planning   **(22 marks)**

(c)   Recommend the principal audit procedures to be performed in respect of:

   (i)   The goodwill initially recognised on the acquisition of Canary Co   **(5 marks)**
   (ii)   The share options granted to employees of Crow Co   **(5 marks)**

During the discussion, Steve Eagle said that he would like me to attend the CS Group's board meetings on a monthly basis so that our firm can be made aware of any issues relating to the audit as soon as possible. Also, Steve asked if one of our audit managers could be seconded to Starling Co in temporary replacement of its finance director who recently left, and asked for our help in recruiting a permanent replacement.

Please provide me with a response to Steve in which you:

(d)   Evaluate the ethical implications of these three requests.   **(6 marks)**

Thank you.

Exhibit 2 – Permanent file (extract)

An extract from the permanent audit file describing the CS Group's history and operations is shown below.

Crow Co was incorporated 100 years ago. It was founded by Joseph Crow, who established a small pottery making tableware such as dishes, plates and cups. The products quickly grew popular, with one range of products becoming highly sought after when it was used at a royal wedding. The company's products have retained their popularity over the decades, and the Crow brand enjoys a strong identity and good market share.

Ten years ago, Crow Co made its first acquisition by purchasing 100% of the share capital of Starling Co. Both companies benefited from the newly formed CS Group, as Starling Co itself had a strong brand name in the pottery market. The CS Group has a history of steady profitability and stable management.

Crow Co and Starling Co have a financial year ending 31 July 20X2, and your firm has audited both companies for several years.

Exhibit 3 – Notes from meeting with Steve Eagle, finance director of the CS Group

Acquisition of Canary Co

The most significant event for the CS Group this year was the acquisition of Canary Co, which took place on 1 February 20X2. Crow Co purchased all of Canary Co's equity shares for cash consideration of $125 million, and further contingent consideration of $30 million will be paid on the third anniversary of the acquisition, if the Group's revenue grows by at least 8% per annum. Crow Co engaged an external provider to perform due diligence on Canary Co, whose report indicated that the fair value of Canary Co's net assets was estimated to be $110 million at the date of acquisition. Goodwill arising on the acquisition has been calculated as follows.

	$m
Fair value of consideration:	
Cash consideration	125
Contingent consideration	30
	155
Less fair value of identifiable net assets acquired	(110)
Goodwill	45

To help finance the acquisition, Crow Co issued loan stock at par on 31 January 20X2, raising cash of $100 million. The loan has a five-year term, and will be repaid at a premium of $20 million. 5% interest is payable annually in arrears. It is Group accounting policy to recognise financial liabilities at amortised cost.

Canary Co manufactures pottery figurines and ornaments. The company is considered a good strategic fit to the Group, as its products are luxury items like those of Crow Co and Starling Co, and its acquisition will enable the Group to diversify into a different market. Approximately 30% of its sales are made online, and it is hoped that online sales can soon be introduced for the rest of the Group's products. Canary Co has only ever operated as a single company, so this is the first year that it is part of a group of companies.

Financial performance and position

The Group has performed well this year, with forecast consolidated revenue for the year to 31 July 20X2 of $135 million (20X1 – $125 million), and profit before tax of $8.5 million (20X1 – $8.4 million). A breakdown of the Group's forecast revenue and profit is shown below.

	Crow Co $m	Starling Co $m	Canary Co $m	CS Group $m
Revenue	69	50	16	135
Profit before tax	3.5	3	2	8.5

Note. Canary Co's results have been included from 1 February 20X2 (date of acquisition), and forecast up to 31 July 20X2, the CS Group's financial year end.

The forecast consolidated statement of financial position at 31 July 20X2 recognises total assets of $550 million.

Other matters

Starling Co received a grant of $35 million on 1 March 20X2 in relation to redevelopment of its main manufacturing site. The government is providing grants to companies for capital expenditure on environmentally friendly assets. Starling Co has spent $25 million of the amount received on solar panels which generate electricity, and intends to spend the remaining $10 million on upgrading its production and packaging lines.

During the year to 31 July 20X2 it was discovered that an error had been made by a member of Crow Co's finance department which had resulted in the overstatement of deferred revenue by $10,000 in the prior period.

On 1 January 20X2, a new IT system was introduced to Crow Co and Starling Co, with the aim of improving financial reporting controls and to standardise processes across the two companies. Unfortunately, Starling Co's finance director left the company last week.

Share options

Crow Co granted 150 of its employees 600 share options each on 1 August 20X1. The options vest on 31 July 20X3. Only those employees working for Crow Co at the vesting date will actually vest.

The fair value of the options at various dates has been estimated as follows:

1 August 20X1	$6
31 July 20X2	$8
31 July 20X3	$9

During 20X2, five employees left the company, and Crow Co anticipates that a total of 10% of the current employees will leave in the course of the vesting period.

Crow Co has recognised $720,000 (150 × 600 × 8) as an expense, and a non-current liability of the same amount.

22 Adder (P7 6/15) (amended)   49 mins

The Adder Group (the Group) has been an audit client of your firm for several years. You have recently been assigned to act as audit manager, replacing a manager who has fallen ill, and the audit of the group financial statements for the year ended 31 March 20X5 is underway. The Group's activities include property management and the provision of large storage facilities in warehouses owned by the Group. The draft consolidated financial statements recognise total assets of $150 million, and profit before tax of $20 million.

(a)   The audit engagement partner, Edmund Black, has asked you to review the audit working papers in relation to two audit issues which have been highlighted by the audit senior. Information on each of these issues is given below:

(i)   In December 20X4, a leisure centre complex was sold for proceeds equivalent to its fair value of $35 million, the related assets have been derecognised from the Group statement of financial position, and a profit on disposal of $8 million is included in the Group statement of profit or loss for the year. The sale qualifies as a sale in line with IFRS 15 *Revenue from Contracts with Customers*.

At the date of the sale the fair value of the complex was $33 million. According to the Group's website, it continues to operate services from this leisure centre and a lease liability of $22 million has been created on the 20X5 draft financial statements in relation to the complex.

(ii)   In January 20X5, the Group acquired 52% of the equity shares of Baldrick Co. This company has not been consolidated into the Group as a subsidiary, and is instead accounted for as an associate. The Group finance director's reason for this accounting treatment is that Baldrick Co's operations have not yet been integrated with those of the rest of the Group. Baldrick Co's financial statements recognise total assets of $18 million and a loss for the year to 31 March 20X5 of $5 million.

Required

In respect of the issues described above:

Comment on the matters to be considered, and explain the audit evidence you should expect to find in your review of the audit working papers.

(16 marks)

(b)   The audit senior also left the following note for your attention:

'I have been working on the audit of properties, including the Group's storage facility warehouses. Customers rent individual self-contained storage areas of a warehouse, for which they are given keys allowing access by the customer at any time. The Group's employees rarely enter the customers' storage areas.

It seems the Group's policy for storage contracts which generate revenue of less than $10,000, is that very little documentation is required, and the nature of the items being stored is not always known. While visiting one of the Group's warehouses, the door to one of the customers' storage areas was open, so I looked in and saw what appeared to be potentially hazardous chemicals, stored in large metal drums marked with warning signs. I asked the warehouse manager about the items being stored, and he became very aggressive, refusing to allow me to ask other employees about the matter, and threatening me if I alerted management to the storage of these items. I did not mention the matter to anyone else at the client.'

Required

Discuss the implications of the audit senior's note for the completion of the audit, commenting on the auditor's responsibilities in relation to laws and regulations, and on any ethical matters arising.   **(9 marks)**

Note. Assume it is 6 June 20X5.   **(Total = 25 marks)**

23 Setter (P7 6/13) (amended)   39 mins

You are the manager responsible for the audit of Setter Stores Co, a company which operates supermarkets across the country. The final audit for the year ended 31 January 20X3 is nearing completion and you are reviewing the audit working papers. The draft financial statements recognise total assets of $300 million, revenue of $620 million and profit before tax of $47.5 million.

(a)   **Assets held for sale**

Setter Stores Co owns a number of properties which have been classified as assets held for sale in the statement of financial position. The notes to the financial statements state that the properties are all due to be sold within one year. On classification as held for sale, in October 20X2, the properties were re-measured from carrying value of $26 million to fair value less cost to sell of $24 million, which is the amount recognised in the statement of financial position at the year end.   **(8 marks)**

(b)   **Lease**

A 'sale and leaseback' arrangement involving a large property complex was entered into on 31 January 20X3. The property complex is a large warehousing facility, which was sold for $37 million, which is both its fair value at the date of the disposal and the present value of the lease payments. Setter Stores Co retains control of use of the asset. The lease term is 20 years, the same as the useful life of the property.

The facility was held under the cost model – together with other assets of its class – at its carrying amount at that date of $27 million.

BPP
LEARNING

Setter Stores Co has made accounting entries to recognise the cash received and a non-current liability classified as a 'Lease liability'. It has recognised a revaluation gain on the property asset of $10 million. **(7 marks)**

(c) **Distribution licence**

The statement of financial position includes an intangible asset of $15 million, which is the cost of a distribution licence acquired on 1 September 20X2. The licence gives Setter Stores Co the exclusive right to distribute a popular branded soft drink in its stores for a period of five years. **(5 marks)**

Required

Comment on the matters to be considered, and explain the audit evidence you should expect to find during your file review in respect of each of the issues described above.

Note. The split of the mark allocation is shown against each of the issues above.

(Total = 20 marks)

24 York (P7 Mar/Jun 16) (amended) 49 mins

(a) According to ISA 240 *The Auditor's Responsibilities Relating to Fraud in an Audit of Financial Statements*:

'When identifying and assessing the risks of material misstatement due to fraud, the auditor shall, based on a presumption that there are risks of fraud in revenue recognition, evaluate which types of revenue, revenue transactions or assertions give rise to such risks.'

Required

Discuss why the auditor should presume that there are risks of fraud in revenue recognition and why ISA 240 requires specific auditor responses in relation to the risks identified.

(7 marks)

(b) You are the manager responsible for the audit of York Co, a chain of health and leisure clubs owned and managed by entrepreneur Phil Smith. The audit for the year ended 30 November 20X5 is nearing completion and the draft financial statements recognise total assets of $27 million and profit before tax of $2.2 million. The audit senior has left the following file notes for your consideration during your review of the audit working papers:

(i) **Cash transfers**

During a review of the cash book, a receipt of $350,000 was identified which was accompanied by the description 'BD'. Bank statements showed that the following day a nearly identical amount was transferred into a bank account held in a foreign country. When I asked the financial controller about this, she requested that I speak to Mr Smith, as he has sole responsibility for cash management. According to Mr Smith, an old friend of his, Brian Davies, has loaned the money to the company to fund further expansion and the money has been invested until it is needed. Documentary evidence concerning the transaction has been requested from Mr Smith but has not yet been received.

(ii) **Legal dispute**

At the year end York Co reversed a provision relating to an ongoing legal dispute with an ex-employee who was claiming $150,000 for unfair dismissal. This amount was provided in full in the financial statements for the year ended 30 November 20X4 but has now been reversed because Mr Smith believes it is now likely that York Co will successfully defend the legal case. Mr Smith has not been available to discuss this matter and no additional documentary evidence has been made available since the end

of the previous year's audit. The auditor's report was unmodified in the previous year.

(13 marks)

Required

Evaluate the implications for the completion of the audit, recommending any further actions which should be taken by your audit firm.

(c)   You are also responsible for the audit of Squire Co, a listed company, and you are completing the review of its interim financial statements for the six months ended 31 October 20X5. Squire Co is a car manufacturer, and historically has offered a three-year warranty on cars sold. The financial statements for the year ended 30 April 20X5 included a warranty provision of $1.5 million and recognised total assets of $27.5 million. You are aware that on 1 July 20X5, due to cost cutting measures, Squire Co stopped offering warranties on cars sold. The interim financial statements for the six months ended 31 October 20X5 do not recognise any warranty provision. Total assets are $30 million at 31 October 20X5.

Required

Assess the matters that should be considered in forming a conclusion on Squire Co's interim financial statements, and the implications for the review report.   **(5 marks)**

(Total = 25 marks)

25 Mondrian (P7 Sep/Dec 15) (amended)   **98 mins**

You are a manager in the audit department of Mondrian & Co, a firm of Chartered Certified Accountants. You are responsible for the audit of Dali Co, a longstanding client of your firm and a listed company specialising in the design and manufacture of equipment and machinery used in the quarrying industry. You are planning the audit of the financial statements for the year ending 31 December 20X5. The projected financial statements for the 20X5 year end recognise revenue of $138 million (20X4 – $135 million), profit before tax of $9.8 million (20X4 – $9.2 million) and total assets of $90 million (20X4 – $85 million). Dali Co became listed in its home jurisdiction on 1 March 20X5, and is hoping to achieve a listing on a foreign stock exchange in June 20X6.

You have been provided with the following exhibits:

1   An email which you have received from Sam Hockney, the audit engagement partner.

2   Information about Dali plc's general background and activities.

3   Notes from a meeting held between Sam Hockney and Dali Co's audit committee.

4   Results of preliminary analytical review procedures performed on Dali Co's projected financial statements and other financial information.

Required

Respond to the instructions in the email from the audit engagement partner.   **(46 marks)**

Note. The split of the mark allocation is shown in the partner's email (Exhibit 1).

Professional marks will be awarded for the presentation and logical flow of the briefing notes and for the clarity of the explanations provided.   **(4 marks)**

(Total = 50 marks)

Exhibit 1 – Email from audit engagement partner

To: Audit manager

From: Audit engagement partner, Sam Hockney

Subject: Audit planning – Dali Co

Hello

I need you to start planning the audit of Dali Co. I know you are new to this audit client, so I have provided you with some background information, the results of some preliminary analytical review performed by one of the audit team members, and notes from a discussion I had with the company's audit committee yesterday. I require you to prepare briefing notes for use in the audit planning meeting which will be held next week. More junior members of the audit team will be present at the meeting, and I would like to give them an explanation of the term 'fraudulent financial reporting' so that they know what to look out for.

In these notes you are required to:

(a)   Explain the term 'fraudulent financial reporting', illustrating your explanation with examples.

(4 marks)

(b)   (i)   Evaluate the audit risks to be considered in planning the audit of Dali Co; and

(20 marks)

         (ii)   Recommend the additional information which would be relevant in the evaluation of audit risk.

(6 marks)

(c)   Explain the principal audit procedures to be performed in respect of:

         (i)   The valuation of work in progress and;   **(5 marks)**

         (ii)   The recognition and measurement of the government grant.   **(5 marks)**

(d)   Identify and discuss the ethical and other professional issues raised, and recommend any actions that should be taken in relation to the request to perform a valuation of the company's pension plan.   **(6 marks)**

Thank you.

Exhibit 2 – Company background

Dali Co was established 20 years ago and has become known as a leading supplier of machinery used in the quarrying industry, with its customers operating quarries which extract stone used mainly for construction. Its customer base is located solely in its country of incorporation but most of the components used in Dali Co's manufacturing process are imported from foreign suppliers.

The machines and equipment made by Dali Co are mostly made to order in the company's three manufacturing sites. Customers approach Dali Co to design and develop a machine or piece of equipment specific to their needs. Where management considers that the design work will be significant, the customer is required to pay a 30% payment in advance, which is used to fund the design work. The remaining 70% is paid on delivery of the machine to the customer. Typically, a machine takes three months to build, and a smaller piece of equipment takes on average six weeks. The design and manufacture of bespoke machinery involving payments in advance has increased during the year. Dali Co also manufactures a range of generic products which are offered for sale to all customers, including drills, conveyors and crushing equipment.

Exhibit 3 – Notes from meeting between Sam Hockney and Dali Co's audit committee

This year has been successful from a strategic point of view in that Dali Co achieved its stock exchange listing in March 20X5, and in doing so raised a significant amount of equity finance. The

company's corporate governance was reviewed as part of the flotation process, resulting in the recruitment of three new non-executive directors and a new finance director.

In March 20X5, a cash-settled share-based payment plan was introduced for senior executives, who will receive a bonus on 31 December 20X7. The amount of the bonus will be based on the increase in Dali Co's share price from that at the date of the flotation, when it was $2.90, to the share price at 31 December 20X7. On the advice of the newly appointed finance director, no accounting entries have been made in respect of the plan, but the details relating to the cash-settled share-based payment plan will be disclosed in the notes to the financial statements.

The finance director recommended that the company's manufacturing sites should be revalued. An external valuation was performed in June 20X5, resulting in a revaluation surplus of $3.5 million being recognised in equity. The finance director has informed the audit committee that no deferred tax needs to be provided in respect of the valuation because the property is part of continuing operations and there is no plan for disposal.

In July 20X5, a government grant of $10 million was received as part of a government scheme to subsidise companies which operate in deprived areas. Specifically $2 million of the grant compensates the company for wages and salaries incurred in the year to 31 December 20X5. The remaining grant relates to the continued operations in the deprived area, with a condition of the grant being that the manufacturing site in that area will remain operational until July 20Y0.

In December 20X5 Dali Co entered into a new contract for the lease of several portable cleaning machines. The present value of the lease payments is $850,000. The contract is for 5 years, and the supplier has a substantive right to substitute alternative machines.

All of the company's manufacturing sites will be closed at the year end to allow the inventory counts to take place. According to the most recent management accounts which are available, at 30 November 20X5 work in progress is valued at $12 million (20X4 – $9.5 million) and the majority of these orders will not be complete until after the year end. In recent weeks several customers have returned equipment due to faults, and Dali Co offers a warranty to guarantee that defective items will be replaced free of charge.

Dali Co's newly established audit committee has asked Mondrian & Co to perform an actuarial valuation on the company's defined benefit pension plan. One of the audit partners is a qualified actuary and has the necessary skills and expertise to perform the service. The pension liability in the 20X4 financial statements was $255,000.

Exhibit 4 – Preliminary analytical review (extract) and other financial information

	Based on projected figures to 31 December 20X5	Based on audited figures to 31 December 20X4
Operating margin	15%	13%
Inventory days	175 days	150 days
Receivables collection period	90 days	70 days
Trade payables payment period	60 days	55 days
Earnings per share	75 cents per share	–
Share price	$3.50	–

26 Bill (P7 6/11) (amended)   76 mins

(a)   You are a senior audit manager in Suki & Co, a firm of Chartered Certified Accountants. This morning you have been reassigned to the audit of Bill Co, a long-standing audit client of your firm, as the manager previously assigned to the client has been taken ill. Bill Co has a year ending 30 June 20X1, and the audit planning has been largely completed by the previously assigned audit manager, Tara Lafayette, who had been recruited by your firm four months ago.

Bill Co is a property development company, specialising in the regeneration and refurbishment of old industrial buildings, which are sold for commercial or residential use. All property developments are performed under specifically negotiated fixed-price contracts. The company was founded 35 years ago by two brothers, Alex and Ben Bradley, who own the majority of the company's share capital. Alex and Ben are nearing retirement age, and are planning to sell the company within the next two years. The forecast revenue for the year ending 30 June 20X1 is $10.8 million, and the forecast profit before tax is $2.5 million. The forecast statement of financial position recognises total assets of $95 million.

You have just received the following email from the audit engagement partner.

To:	Audit manager
From:	Audit partner
Re:	Bill Co – audit planning

Hello,

Thanks for taking on the role of audit manager for the forthcoming audit of Bill Co. I have just received some information on two significant issues that have arisen over the last week, from Sam Compton, the company's finance director. This information is provided in Attachment 1. Please prepare briefing notes which:

(i) Explain the matters that should be considered, and the risks of material misstatement, in relation to the treatment of these two issues in the financial statements. **(8 marks)**

(ii) Recommend the planned audit procedures that should be performed in order to address those risks. **(8 marks)**

(iii) Critically evaluate the planning that has been completed by the previously assigned audit manager. Relevant details are provided in Attachment 2, which contains notes made by her, and placed on the current year audit file. Make sure you include discussion of any ethical matters arising from the notes, and recommend any actions you think necessary. **(11 marks)**

Thanks.

Attachment 1: Information from Sam Compton, finance director of Bill Co

In the last week, two significant issues have arisen at Bill Co. The first issue concerns a major contract involving the development of an old riverside warehouse into a conference centre in Bridgetown. An architect working on the development has discovered that the property will need significant additional structural improvements, the unavoidable extra cost of which is estimated to be $350,000. The contract was originally forecast to make a profit of $200,000, and cannot be cancelled. The development is currently about one third complete, and will take a further 15 months to finish, including this additional construction work. The customer has been told that the completion of the contract will be delayed by around two months. However, the contract price is fixed, and so the additional costs must be covered by Bill Co.

The second issue concerns one of Bill Co's specialist divisions, which trades under the name 'Treasured Homes' and which deals exclusively in the redevelopment of non-industrial historic buildings such as castles and forts. These buildings are usually acquired as uninhabitable ruins, and are then developed into luxury residences for wealthy individuals. The management of Bill Co decided last week to sell this division, as although it is profitable, it generates a lower margin than other business divisions. 'Treasured Homes' operates separately from the rest of the business, and generates approximately 15% of the total revenue of the company. In a board minute dated 1 June 20X1, it was noted that 'interest has already been expressed in this division from a potential buyer, and it is hoped that sale negotiations will soon commence, leading to sale in August 20X1. There is a specific office building and some other tangible assets that will be sold as part of the deal. These assets are recorded at $7.6 million in the

financial statements. No redundancies will be necessary as employees' contracts will transfer to the new owners.'

Attachment 2: Planning Summary – Bill Co, year ending 30 June 20X1, prepared by Tara Lafayette, manager previously assigned to the audit

The planning for the forthcoming audit is almost complete. Time has been saved by not carrying out procedures considered unnecessary for this long-standing audit client. Forecast accounts have been obtained and placed on file, and discussions held with management concerning business developments during the year. Analytical procedures have been performed on the statement of profit or loss and other comprehensive income, but not on the statement of financial position, as there did not appear to be any significant movements in assets or liabilities since last year.

Management confirmed that there have been no changes to accounting systems and controls in the financial year. For this reason we do not need to carry out walk-through tests or review our documentation of the systems and controls.

Management also confirmed that there have been no changes to business operations, other than the potential sale of 'Treasured Homes'. All divisions are operating normally, generating sufficient profit and cash. For this reason, the business risk of Bill Co is assessed as low, and no further comments or discussions about business operations have been placed on file.

The matter that will demand the most audit work is the valuation of properties currently under development, especially the determination of the percentage completion of each development at the reporting date. Historically, we have engaged a property valuation expert to provide a report on this area. However, Bill Co has recently employed a newly qualified architect, who will be happy to provide us with evidence concerning the stage of completion of each property development contract at the year end. Using this person to produce a report on all properties being developed will save time and costs.

Bill Co has recently completed the development of a luxury new office building in Newtown. Several of the office units are empty, and the management of Bill Co has offered the office space to our firm for a nominal rent of $100 per year.

Required

Respond to the partner's email.   **(27 marks)**

Note. The split of the mark allocation is shown within the partner's email.

Professional marks will be awarded for the format and clarity of your response.   **(4 marks)**

(b)   Ben and Alex Bradley have a sister, Jo, who runs an interior design company, Lantern Co. During a review of board minutes, performed as part of the planning of Bill Co's audit, it was discovered that Bill Co has paid $225,000 to Lantern Co during the year, in respect of refurbishment of development properties. On further enquiry, it was also found that Lantern Co leases an office space from Bill Co, under an informal arrangement between the two companies.

Required

(i)   Explain the inherent limitations which mean that auditors may not identify related parties and related party transactions.

(ii)   Recommend the audit procedures to be performed in relation to Bill Co's transactions with Lantern Co.

                                                                              (8 marks)

Note. Assume it is 6 June 20X1.   **(Total = 39 marks)**

27 Parker (P7 6/13)

You are an audit manager in Hound & Co, responsible for the audit of Parker Co, a new audit client of your firm. You are planning the audit of Parker Co's financial statements for the year ending 30 June 20X3, and you have just attended a meeting with Ruth Collie, the finance director of Parker Co, where she gave you the projected results for the year. Parker Co designs and manufactures health and beauty products including cosmetics.

You have just received an email from Harry Shepherd, the audit engagement partner:

To:	Audit manager
From:	Harry Shepherd, Partner
Subject:	Parker Co

Hello,

I understand you met with Ruth Collie at Parker Co recently and that you are planning the forthcoming audit. To bring me up to date on this new client, I would like you to use the information obtained in your meeting to prepare briefing notes for my use in which you:

(a) Perform preliminary analytical procedures and evaluate the audit risks to be considered in planning the audit of the financial statements, and identify and explain any additional information that would be relevant to your evaluation; and **(24 marks)**

(b) Discuss any ethical issues raised and recommend the relevant actions to be taken by our firm. **(7 marks)**

Thank you.

PARKER CO – STATEMENT OF PROFIT OR LOSS AND OTHER COMPREHENSIVE INCOME

	Notes	30 June 20X3 Projected $'000	30 June 20X2 Actual $'000
Revenue		7,800	8,500
Cost of sales	1	(5,680)	(5,800)
Gross profit		2,120	2,700
Operating expenses		(1,230)	(1,378)
Operating profit		890	1,322
Finance costs		(155)	(125)
Profit before tax		735	1,197
Taxation		(70)	(300)
Profit for the year		665	897

Note 1. Cost of sales includes $250,000 relating to a provision for a potential fine payable. The advertising regulatory authority has issued a notice of a $450,000 fine payable by Parker Co due to alleged inappropriate claims made in an advertising campaign. The fine is being disputed and the matter should be resolved in August 20X3.

PARKER CO – STATEMENT OF FINANCIAL POSITION

	Notes	30 June 20X3 Projected $'000	30 June 20X2 Actual $'000
Non-current assets			
Property, plant and equipment		21,500	19,400
Intangible asset – development costs	2	2,250	–
		23,750	19,400
Current assets			
Inventory		2,600	2,165
Trade receivables		900	800
Cash		–	1,000
		3,500	3,965
Total assets		27,250	23,365
Equity			
Share capital		8,000	8,000
Revaluation reserve	3	2,500	2,000
Retained earnings		1,275	1,455
		11,775	11,455
Non-current liabilities			
2% preference shares		3,125	3,125
Bank loan		3,800	2,600
Lease liabilities		4,900	4,000
		11,825	9,725
Current liabilities			
Trade payables		1,340	1,000
Taxation		50	300
Lease liabilities		860	685
Provisions		500	200
Overdraft		900	–
		3,650	2,185
Total equity and liabilities		27,250	23,365

Notes

2   The development costs relate to a new range of organic cosmetics.

3   All of the company's properties were revalued on 1 January 20X3 by an independent, professionally qualified expert.

Notes from your meeting with Ruth Collie

Business review

Parker Co is facing difficult trading conditions. Consumer spending is depressed due to recession in the economy. The health and beauty market remains very competitive and a major competitor launched a very successful new cosmetics range during the year, which led to a significant decline in sales of one of Parker Co's most successful brands. It has been necessary to cut prices on some of the company's product ranges in an attempt to maintain market share. However, a new brand using organic ingredients is being developed and is due to launch in September 20X3.

Financial matters

Cash flow has been a problem this year, largely due to the cash spent on developing the new product range. Cash was also needed to pay dividends to both equity and preference shareholders. To help to reduce cash outflows, some new assets were acquired under leases and an extension to the company's bank loan was negotiated in December 20X2.

Human resources

In December 20X2 Parker Co's internal audit team performed a review of the operation of controls over the processing of overtime payments in the human resources department. The review found that the company's specified internal controls procedures in relation to the processing of overtime payments and associated tax payments were not always being followed. Until December 20X2 this processing was split between the human resources and finance departments. Since then, the processing has been entirely carried out by the finance department.

Expansion plans

Management is planning to expand Parker Co's operations into a new market relating to beauty salons. This is a growing market, and there is synergy because Parker Co's products can be sold and used in the salons. Expansion would be through the acquisition of an existing company which operates beauty salons. A potential target, Beauty Boost Co, has been identified and preliminary discussions have taken place between the management of the two companies. Parker Co's managing director has asked for our firm's advice about the potential acquisition, and specifically regarding the financing of the transaction. Beauty Boost Co is an audit client of our firm, so we have considerable knowledge of its business.

Required

Respond to the email from the audit partner. **(31 marks)**

Note. The split of the mark allocation is shown within the partner's email.

Professional marks will be awarded for the presentation, logical flow and clarity of explanation of the briefing notes. **(4 marks)**

(Total = 35 marks)

28 Stow (P7 12/13) (amended) 68 mins

You are an audit manager in Compton & Co, responsible for the audit of the Stow Group (the Group). You are planning the audit of the Group financial statements for the year ending 31 December 20X3. The Group's projected profit before tax for the year is $200 million and projected total assets at 31 December are $2,500 million.

The Group is a car manufacturer. Its operations are divided between a number of subsidiaries, some of which focus on manufacturing and distributing the cars, while others deal mainly with marketing and retail. All components of the Group have the same year end. The Group audit engagement partner, Chad Woodstock, has just sent you the following email.

To:	Audit manager
From:	Chad Woodstock, audit partner
Subject:	The Stow Group – audit planning

Hello,

We need to start planning the audit of The Stow Group. Yesterday, I met with the Group finance director, Marta Bidford, and we discussed some restructuring of the Group, which has taken place this year. A new wholly-owned subsidiary has been acquired – Zennor Co, which is located overseas in Farland. Another subsidiary, Broadway Co, was disposed of.

I have provided you with a summary of issues I discussed with Marta, and using this information I would like you to prepare briefing notes for my use in which you:

(a) (i)   Evaluate the risks of material misstatement to be considered in planning the Group audit, commenting on their materiality to the Group financial statements. **(12 marks)**

     (ii) Identify any further information that may be needed. **(4 marks)**

(b) Recommend the principal audit procedures to be performed in respect of the disposal of Broadway Co. **(8 marks)**

Marta has told me that Zennor Co has a well-established internal audit team. She has suggested that we use the internal audit team as much as possible when performing our audit of Zennor Co as this will reduce the audit fee. The Group audit committee appreciates that with the audit of the new subsidiary there will be some increase in our costs, but has requested that the audit fee for the Group as a whole is not increased from last year's fee. I have provided you with some information about the internal audit team and in your briefing notes I would like you to:

(c) Discuss how Marta's suggestion impacts on the planning of the audit of Zennor Co's and of the Group's financial statements, and comment on any ethical issue raised. **(7 marks)**

Thank you.

Acquisition of Zennor Co

In order to expand overseas, the Group acquired 100% of the share capital of Zennor Co on 1 February 20X3. Zennor Co is located in Farland, where it owns a chain of car dealerships. Zennor Co's financial statements are prepared using International Financial Reporting Standards and are measured and presented using the local currency of Farland, the Dingu. At the present time, the exchange rate is 4 Dingu = $1. Zennor Co has the same year end as the Group, and its projected profit for the year ending 31 December 20X3 is 90 million Dingu, with projected assets at the same date of 800 million Dingu.

Zennor Co is supplied with cars from the Group's manufacturing plant. The cars are sent on cargo ships and take approximately six weeks to reach the main port in Farland, where they are stored until delivered to the dealerships. At today's date there are cars in transit to Zennor Co with a selling price of $58 million.

A local firm of auditors was engaged by the Group to perform a due diligence review on Zennor Co prior to its acquisition. The Group's statement of financial position recognises goodwill at acquisition of $60 million.

Compton & Co was appointed as auditor of Zennor Co on 1 March 20X3.

Disposal of Broadway Co

On 1 September 20X3, the Group disposed of its wholly owned subsidiary, Broadway Co, for proceeds of $180 million. Broadway Co operated a distribution centre in this country. The Group's statement of profit or loss includes a profit of $25 million in respect of the disposal.

Broadway Co was acquired by a retail organisation, the Cornwall Group, which wished to bring its distribution operations in house in order to save costs. Compton & Co resigned as auditor to Broadway Co on 15 September 20X3 to be replaced by the group auditor of the Cornwall Group.

Zennor Co – Internal audit team

The internal audit team was established several years ago and is headed up by a qualified accountant, Jo Evesham, who has a lot of experience in designing systems and controls. Jo and her team monitor the effectiveness of operating and financial reporting controls, and report to the board of directors. Zennor Co does not have an audit committee as corporate governance rules in Farland do not require an internal audit function or an audit committee to be established.

During the year, the internal audit team performed several value for money exercises such as reviewing the terms negotiated with suppliers.

Required

Respond to the instructions in the partner's email. **(31 marks)**

Note. The mark allocation is shown against each of the instructions in the partner's email above.

Professional marks will be awarded for the structure and presentation of the briefing notes and for the clarity of explanations. **(4 marks)**

(Total = 35 marks)

29 Cooper (P7 6/14) (amended)   39 mins

(a) You are an audit manager in Rose & Co, responsible for the audit of Cooper Co. You are reviewing the audit working papers relating to the financial year ended 31 January 20X4. Cooper Co is a manufacturer of chemicals used in the agricultural industry. The draft financial statements recognise profit for the year to 31 January 20X4 of $15 million (20X3 – $20 million) and total assets of $240 million (20X3 – $230 million).

The audit senior, Max Turner, has brought several matters to your attention:

(i) Cooper Co's factories are recognised within property, plant and equipment at a carrying value of $60 million. Half of the factories produce a chemical which is used in farm animal feed. Recently the government has introduced a regulation stipulating that the chemical is phased out over the next three years. Sales of the chemical are still buoyant, however, and are projected to account for 45% of Cooper Co's revenue for the year ending 31 January 20X5. Cooper Co has started to research a replacement chemical which is allowed under the new regulation, and has spent $1 million on a feasibility study into the development of this chemical.

(ii) In October 20X3, Cooper Co's finance director, Hannah Osbourne, purchased a car from the company. The carrying value of the car at the date of its disposal to Hannah was $50,000, and its market value was $75,000. Cooper Co raised an invoice for $50,000 in respect of the disposal, which is still outstanding for payment.

(15 marks)

Required

Comment on the matters to be considered and explain the audit evidence you should expect to find during your review of the audit working papers in respect of each of the issues described above.

(b) Max noticed that a section of the audit file had not been completed on the previous year's audit. The incomplete section relates to expenditure incurred in the year to 31 January 20X3, which appears not to have been audited at all in the prior year. The expenditure of $1.2 million was incurred in the development of an internally generated brand name. The amount was capitalised as an intangible asset at 31 January 20X3, and that amount is still recognised at 31 January 20X4.

Required

Explain the implications of this matter for the completion of the audit, and any other professional issues raised, recommending any actions to be taken by the auditor. **(5 marks)**

(Total = 20 marks)

30 Grohl (P7 12/12) (amended)   98 mins

(a)   You are a manager in Foo & Co, responsible for the audit of Grohl Co, a company which produces circuit boards which are sold to manufacturers of electrical equipment such as computers and mobile phones. It is the first time that you have managed this audit client, taking over from the previous audit manager, Bob Halen, last month. The audit planning for the year ended 30 November 20X2 is about to commence.

You have been provided with the following exhibits:

1   An email which you have received from Mia Vai, the audit engagement partner.
2   Notes from your meeting with Mo Satriani, the finance director of Grohl Co.
3   Financial information provided by Mo Satriani.

Required

Respond to the instruction in the email from the audit engagement partner.   **(38 marks)**

Note. The split of the mark allocation is shown within the partner's email (Exhibit 1).

Professional marks will be awarded for the presentation and logical flow of the briefing notes and the and clarity of the explanations provided.   **(4 marks)**

Exhibit 1 – Email from the audit engagement partner

To:	Audit manager
From:	Mia Vai, Audit partner, Foo & Co
Subject:	Grohl Co – audit planning

Hello,

I am meeting with the other audit partners tomorrow to discuss forthcoming audits and related issues. I understand that you recently had a meeting with Mo Satriani, the finance director of Grohl Co. Using the information from your meeting together with the financial information that I understand Mo has sent you, I would like you to prepare briefing notes for my use in which you:

(i)   Evaluate the business risks faced by Grohl Co;   **(15 marks)**

(ii)   Evaluate the risks of material misstatement to be considered in planning the audit; and   **(15 marks)**

(iii)   Discuss any ethical issues raised, and recommend the relevant actions to be taken by our firm.   **(8 marks)**

Thank you.

Exhibit 2 – Notes from the meeting with Mo Satriani

Business overview

Grohl Co's principal business activity remains the production of circuit boards. One of the key materials used in production is copper wiring, all of which is imported. As a cost cutting measure, in April 20X2 a contract with a new overseas supplier was signed, and all of the company's copper wiring is now supplied under this contract. Purchases are denominated in a foreign currency, but the company does not use forward exchange contracts in relation to its imports of copper wiring.

Grohl Co has two production facilities, one of which produces goods for the export market, and the other produces goods for the domestic market. About half of its goods are exported, but the export market is suffering due to competition from cheaper producers overseas. Most domestic sales are made under contract with approximately 20 customers.

BPP
LEARNING

Recent developments

In early November 20X2, production was halted for a week at the production facility which supplies the domestic market. A number of customers had returned goods, claiming faults in the circuit boards supplied. On inspection, it was found that the copper used in the circuit boards was corroded and therefore unsuitable for use. The corrosion is difficult to spot as it cannot be identified by eye, and relies on electrical testing. All customers were contacted immediately and, where necessary, products recalled and replaced. The corroded copper remaining in inventory has been identified and separated from the rest of the copper.

Work has recently started on a new production line which will ensure that Grohl Co meets new regulatory requirements prohibiting the use of certain chemicals, which come into force in March 20X3. In July 20X2, a loan of $30 million with an interest rate of 4% was negotiated with Grohl Co's bank, the main purpose of the loan being to fund the capital expenditure necessary for the new production line. $2.5 million of the loan represents an overdraft which was converted into long-term finance.

Website sales

Grohl Co started to develop a website for sales on 1 December 20X1, which was completed and available for use by 31 May 20X2. The website has facilities for customers to design their own circuit boards, to choose the products they need and to make a payment. The total cost of website development in the year ended 30 November 20X2 was $200,000. This was capitalised and is to be written off over five years.

After initial development, the operation of the website, including collection of payments from customers, was outsourced to a specialist provider, Khalifa Co. Khalifa Co pays Grohl Co each month, after deducting its fee. Grohl Co's prices have been reduced by roughly 10% for online sales, which by the end of the year made up about a quarter of Grohl Co's total revenue.

The website initiates the fulfilment process automatically once payment has been made by the customer, working on the basis of the information entered by the customer. Grohl Co has also outsourced the final delivery of goods to a courier company.

Grohl Co has experienced some difficulties with the website, including relatively high rates of returns from customers. There have also been errors in goods delivered arising from customers' misunderstanding of the website.

Other matters

Several of Grohl Co's executive directors and the financial controller left in October 20X2, to set up a company specialising in the recycling of old electronic equipment. This new company is not considered to be in competition with Grohl Co's operations. The directors left on good terms, and replacements for the directors have been recruited. One of Foo & Co's audit managers, Bob Halen, is being interviewed for the role of financial controller at Grohl Co. Bob is a good candidate for the position, as he developed good knowledge of Grohl Co's business when he was managing the audit.

At Grohl Co's most recent board meeting, the audit fee was discussed. The board members expressed concern over the size of the audit fee, given the company's loss for the year. The board members would like to know whether the audit can be performed on a contingent fee basis.

Exhibit 3 – Financial information provided by Mo Satriani

EXTRACT OF DRAFT STATEMENT OF PROFIT OR LOSS FOR THE YEAR ENDED
30 NOVEMBER 20X2

	20X2 Draft $'000	20X1 Actual $'000
Revenue	12,500	13,800
Operating costs	(12,000)	(12,800)
Operating profit	500	1,000
Finance costs	(800)	(800)
Profit/(loss) before tax	(300)	200

The draft statement of financial position has not yet been prepared, but Mo states that the total assets of Grohl Co at 30 November 20X2 are $180 million, and cash at bank is $130,000. Based on draft figures, the company's current ratio is 1.1, and the quick ratio is 0.8.

(b) After having completed your briefing notes for Mia Vai, you received a phone call from Mo Satriani, Grohl Co's finance director, in which he made the following comments.

'There is something I forgot to mention in our meeting. Our business insurance covers us for specific occasions when business is interrupted. I put in a claim on 28 November 20X2 for $5 million which I have estimated to cover the period when our production was halted due to the problem with the corroded copper. This is not yet recognised in the financial statements, but I want to make an adjustment to recognise the $5 million as a receivable as at 30 November.'

Required

Comment on the matters that should be considered, and recommend the audit procedures to be performed, in respect of the insurance claim. **(8 marks)**

(Total = 50 marks)

31 Champers (P7 6/09) (amended)   70 mins

You are an audit senior in Carter & Co, working on the audit of Champers Co, and you have received the following email from Geoff Forest, the engagement partner responsible for the Champers audit.

To:	Audit Senior
From:	Geoff Forest
Date:	2 June 20X9
Subject:	Audit of Champers Co

Hi,

I need you to draft some briefing notes for me to use at the Champers audit planning meeting. The permanent file contains a report on Champers that was produced recently by an external business consultant. You may find this useful. The briefing notes should:

(a) (i) Identify and explain the aspects of a client's business which should be considered in order to gain an understanding of the company and its operating environment.
(6 marks)

(ii) Recommend the procedures an auditor should perform in order to gain business understanding. **(4 marks)**

The following is an extract from the permanent file.

Champers Co operates a large number of restaurants throughout the country, which are operated under four well-known brand names. The company's strategy is to offer a variety of different dining experiences in restaurants situated in city centres and residential areas, with the objective of maximising market share in a competitive business environment.

Key financial information

	31 May	
	20X9	20X8
	Draft	Final
	$m	$m
Company revenue	1,500	1,350
Revenue is derived from four restaurant chains, each having a distinctive brand name:		
Happy Monkeys family bistros	800	660
Quick-bite outlets	375	400
City Sizzler grills	300	290
Green George cafés	25	–
Company profit before tax	135	155
Company total assets	4,200	3,350
Company cash at bank	116	350

Business segments

The Happy Monkeys chain of restaurants provides family-friendly dining in an informal setting. Most of the restaurants are located in residential areas. Each restaurant has a large children's play area containing climbing frames and slides, and offers a crèche facility, where parents may leave their children for up to two hours. Recently there has been some media criticism of the quality of the child care offered in one crèche, because a child had fallen from a climbing frame and was slightly injured. One of the Happy Monkeys restaurants was closed in December 20X8 for three weeks following a health and safety inspection which revealed some significant breaches in hygiene standards in the kitchen.

The Quick-bite chain offers fast-food. The restaurants are located next to busy roads, in shopping centres, and at railway stations and airports. Champers Co has launched a significant marketing campaign to support the Quick-bite brand name. The draft statement of profit or loss and other comprehensive income for the year ended 31 May 20X9 includes an expense of $150 million in relation to the advertising and marketing of this brand. In January 20X9 the company started to provide nutritional information on its menus in the Quick-bite restaurants, following pressure from the government for all restaurants to disclose more about the ingredients of their food. 50% of the revenue for this business segment is derived from the sale of 'chuckle boxes' – self-contained children's meals which contain a small toy.

The City Sizzler grills offer a more sophisticated dining experience. The emphasis is on high quality food served in luxurious surroundings. There are currently 250 City Sizzler grills, and Champers Co is planning to expand this to 500 by May 20Y0. The grills are all situated in prime city centre locations and are completely refurbished every two years.

The Green George café chain is a recent addition to the range of restaurants. There are only 30 restaurants in the chain, mostly located in affluent residential areas. The restaurants offer eco-friendly food, guaranteed to be free from artificial flavourings and colourings, and to have been produced in an environmentally sustainable manner. All of the 30 restaurants have been newly constructed by Champers Co, and are capitalised at $210 million. This includes all directly attributable costs, and borrowing costs capitalised relating to loans taken out to finance the acquisition of the sites and construction of the restaurants. Champers Co is planning to double the number of Green George cafés operating within the next twelve months.

Laws and regulations

Two new regulations were issued by the government recently which will impact on Champers Co. The regulations come into effect from September 20X9:

(a) Minimum wage regulation has increased the minimum wage by 15%. One third of Champers Co's employees earn the minimum wage.

(b) Advertising regulations now forbid the advertising of food in a manner specifically aimed at children.

Three audit juniors are joining your team for the forthcoming audit of Champers Co, and you have asked them to read through the permanent file to familiarise themselves with the client. One of the juniors has told you that he appreciates that auditors need to have a thorough understanding of the business of their client, but he does not know what aspects of the client's business this relates to, or how the understanding is developed.

Required

Respond to the partner's email. **(32 marks)**

Note. Professional marks will be awarded in part (b) for the clarity, format and presentation of the briefing notes. **(4 marks)**

(Total = 36 marks)

32 Grissom (P7 6/10) (amended) 74 mins

You are a senior audit manager in Vegas & Co, responsible for the audit of the Grissom Group, which has been an audit client for several years. The group companies all have a financial year ending 30 June 20Y0, and you are currently planning the final audit of the consolidated financial statements. The group's operations focus on the manufacture and marketing of confectionery and savoury snacks. Information about several matters relevant to the group audit is given below. These matters are all potentially material to the consolidated financial statements. None of the companies in the group is listed.

Grissom Co

This is a non-trading parent company, which wholly owns three subsidiaries – Willows Co, Hodges Co and Brass Co, all of which are involved with the core manufacturing and marketing operations of the group. This year, the directors decided to diversify the group's activities in order to reduce risk exposure. Non-controlling interests representing long-term investments have been made in two companies – an internet-based travel agent, and a chain of pet shops. In the consolidated statement of financial position, these investments are accounted for as associates, as Grissom Co is able to exert significant influence over the companies.

As part of their remuneration, the directors of Grissom Co receive a bonus based on the profit before tax of the group. In April 20Y0, the group finance director resigned from office after a disagreement with the chief executive officer over changes to accounting estimates. A new group finance director is yet to be appointed.

 BPP LEARNING

45

Willows Co

This company manufactures and distributes chocolate bars and cakes. In July 20X9, production was relocated to a new, very large factory. One of the conditions of the planning permission for the new factory is that Willows Co must, at the end of the useful life of the factory, dismantle the premises and repair any environmental damage caused to the land on which it is situated.

Hodges Co

This company's operations involve the manufacture and distribution of packaged nuts and dried fruit. The government paid a grant in November 20X9 to Hodges Co, to assist with costs associated with installing new, environmentally friendly, packing lines in its factories. The packing lines must reduce energy use by 25% as part of the conditions of the grant, and they began operating in February 20Y0.

Brass Co

This company is a new and significant acquisition, purchased in January 20Y0. It is located overseas, in Chocland, a developing country, and has been purchased to supply cocoa beans, a major ingredient for the goods produced by Willows Co. It is now supplying approximately half of the ingredients used in Willow Co's manufacturing. Chocland has not adopted International Financial Reporting Standards, meaning that Brass Co's financial statements are prepared using local accounting rules. The company uses local currency to measure and present its financial statements.

Further information

Your firm audits all components of the group with the exception of Brass Co, which is audited by a small local firm, Sidle & Co, based in Chocland. Audit regulations in Chocland are not based on International Standards on Auditing.

You have just received the following email from Warwick Stokes, the audit engagement partner.

To: Audit manager

From: Warwick Stokes

Re: Grissom Group audit planning

Hello,

I need you to help me get started on planning for the audit of the consolidated financial statements of the Grissom Group. To this end, please prepare briefing notes for my attention in which you:

(a)   Evaluate the principal audit risks to be considered in planning the audit.   **(18 marks)**

Ignore those risks that relate to reliance on another auditor, as that will be dealt with separately.

(b)   Explain the factors that should be considered, and the procedures that should be performed, in deciding the extent of reliance to be placed on the work of Sidle & Co.   **(8 marks)**

(c)   Recommend the principal audit procedures that should be performed on:

    (i)   The classification of non-controlling investments made by Grissom Co

    (ii)   The condition attached to the grant received by Hodges Co

                                                     (8 marks)

Thanks.

Required

Respond to the email from the engagement partner.   **(34 marks)**

Professional marks will be awarded for the clarity, format and presentation of the briefing notes.

(4 marks)

(Total = 38 marks)

33 Sunshine (P7 Sep/Dec 17) (amended)   98 mins

You are a manager in the audit department of Dove & Co, responsible for the audit of the Sunshine Hotel Group (the Group), which has a financial year ending 31 December 20X7. The Group operates a chain of luxury hotels and it is planning to expand its operations over the next three years by opening hotels in countries with increasingly popular tourist destinations.

You have been provided with the following exhibits:

1   An email which you have received from John Starling, the audit engagement partner.

2   Information about the Group's general background and activities.

3   Notes from a meeting held between John Starling, the Group's finance director and a representative of the Group audit committee

4   Extract of an email from the Group finance director to John Starling, audit engagement partner

Required

Respond to the instructions in the email from the audit engagement partner.   **(46 marks)**

Note. The mark allocation is shown in the partner's email.

Professional marks to be awarded for the presentation and logical flow of the briefing notes and the clarity of the explanations provided.   **(4 marks)**

(Total = 50 marks)

Exhibit 1 – Email from audit engagement partner

To:	Audit manager
From:	John Starling, audit engagement partner
Subject:	Audit planning, the Sunshine Hotel Group

Hello,

I need you to begin planning the audit of the Sunshine Hotel Group for the year ended 31 December 20X7. I have provided you with several pieces of information in relation to this audit.

Using the information provided you are required to prepare briefing notes for my use in which you:

(a)   Evaluate the business risks facing the Group.   **(13 marks)**

(b)   Evaluate the significant risks of material misstatement which should be evaluated as part of our audit planning.   **(14 marks)**

(c)   In respect of the email received from the finance director:

(i)   Discuss the additional implications for planning the Group audit and explain any relevant actions to be taken by the firm, and   **(5 marks)**

(ii)   Recommend the planned audit procedures to be performed on the claim of $10 million, assuming that the audit team is given access to all relevant sources of audit evidence.

(6 marks)

BPP
LEARNING

(d)   Identify and discuss the ethical and other professional issues raised, and recommend any actions that should be taken, in relation to the request to tender for taxation services for the Group.   **(8 marks)**

Thank you.

Exhibit 2 – Background information

The Group owns 20 hotels, all located in popular beachside holiday resorts. The hotels operate on an 'all-inclusive' basis, whereby guests can consume unlimited food and drink, and take part in a variety of water sports including scuba diving as part of the price of their holiday. Each hotel has at least four restaurants and a number of bars. The 'Sunshine Hotel' brand is a market leader, with significant amounts spent each year on marketing to support the brand. The hotels are luxurious and maintained to a very high standard and are marketed as exclusive adult-only luxury holiday destinations.

When customers book to stay in the hotel, they are charged a deposit equivalent to 20% of the total cost of their stay, and a further 20% is payable eight weeks before arrival. The remaining 60% is settled on departure. If a booking is cancelled prior to a week before a guest's stay commences, then a full refund is given, but no refunds are given for cancellations within the week leading up to a guest's stay.

Exhibit 3 – Notes from meeting with finance director and representative of Group audit committee

The Group has seen continued growth, with revenue for the year to 31 December 20X7 projected to be $125 million (20X6 – $110 million), and profit before tax projected to be $10 million (20X6 – $9 million).

According to the latest management accounts, the Group's total assets are currently $350 million. The 'Sunshine Hotel' brand is not recognised as an asset in the financial statements because it has been internally generated. The Group has cash of $20 million at today's date. Most of this cash is held on short-term deposit in a number of different currencies. Based on the latest management accounts, the Group's gearing ratio is 25%.

In January 20X7, the Group entered into an agreement with an internationally acclaimed restaurant chain, Moulin Blanche, to open new restaurants in its five most popular hotels. The agreement cost $5 million, lasts for 10 years, and allows the Group to use the restaurant name, adopt the menus and decorate the restaurants in the style of Moulin Blanche. The cost of $5 million has been recognised within marketing expenses for the year. After a period of refurbishment, the new restaurants opened in all five hotels on 1 July 20X7. Unfortunately there were some problems with the quality of some of the seafood served in the restaurants' opening week, which led to several customers being taken ill, and a report in a small newspaper local to one of the hotels.

Part of the Group strategy is to expand into new countries, and in July 20X7 the Group purchased land in three new locations in Farland at a cost of $75 million. There are currently no specific plans for the development of these locations due to political instability in the country. In addition to the Farland acquisitions, an existing hotel complex was purchased from a competitor for $23 million. The hotel complex is located in a country where local legislation prohibits the private ownership and use of beaches, so the Group's hotel guests cannot enjoy the private and exclusive use of a beach which is one of the Group's key selling points. For this reason, the Group has not yet developed the hotel complex and it is currently being used as a location for staff training. All of these assets are recognised at cost as property, plant and equipment in the Group statement of financial position. Due to the problems with these recent acquisitions, the Group is planning to invest in alternative locations, with capital expenditure on sites in new locations of $45 million budgeted for 20X8. This will be funded entirely from an undrawn borrowing facility with the Group's bank which has a fixed interest rate of 3.5% per annum.

The Group's management is considering further overseas expansion in the coming year, and intends to obtain professional tax planning advice in relation to a planned acquisition. Dove & Co has been invited to submit a tender for these services, with the finance director commenting that it should be able to leverage its existing knowledge of the Group and thus be able to give a competitive price.

Improvements in technology have resulted in efficiency savings in the Group's central catering facilities, which supply the hotel restaurants. This has meant that the Group has been able to bring catering functions in its domestic country together into one building. One building thus became surplus to the Group's requirements, and on 30 September 20X7, the Group contracted to sell this building for $5.5 million. The building had last been revalued in September 20X4, and had a carrying amount of $4.2 million at the date of sale. The gain on disposal has been credited to revenue and the balance of the revaluation surplus relating to the building, $1.7 million, has been credited against other operating charges in the statement of profit or loss.

Two of the Group's hotels are located in an area prone to hurricanes, and unfortunately only last week, a hurricane caused severe damage to both of these hotels. Under the Group's 'hurricane guarantee scheme', customers who were staying at the hotels at the time of the hurricane were transferred to other Group hotels, at no cost to the customer. Customers with bookings to stay at the closed hotels have been offered a refund of their deposits, or to transfer their reservation to a different Group hotel, under the terms of the scheme. The hotels are closed while the necessary repair work, which will take two months, is carried out at an estimated cost of $25 million. The repair work will be covered by the Group's insurance policy, which typically pays half of the estimated cost of repair work in advance, with the balance paid when the repair work is completed. No accounting entries have been made as yet in relation to the hurricane.

Exhibit 4 – Extract from email from the Group finance director to John Starling, audit engagement partner

> **John**
>
> The Group's lawyer has received a letter from Ocean Protection, a multi-national pressure group which aims to safeguard marine environments. Ocean Protection is claiming that our hotel guests are causing environmental damage to delicate coral reefs when scuba diving under the supervision of the Group's scuba diving instructors.
>
> Ocean Protection is pressing charges against the Group, and alleges that our activities are in breach of international environmental protection legislation which is ratified by all of the countries in which the Group operates. Damages of $10 million are being sought, Ocean Protection suggesting that this amount would be used to protect the coral reefs from further damage.
>
> The Group is keen to avoid any media attention, so I am hoping to negotiate a lower level of payment and an agreement from Ocean Protection that they will not make the issue public knowledge.
>
> From an accounting point of view, we do not want to recognise a liability, as the disclosures will draw attention to the matter. We will account for any necessary payment when it is made, which is likely to be next year.
>
> I understand that your audit team will need to look at this issue, but I ask that you only speak to me about it, and do not speak to any other employees. Also, I do not want you to contact Ocean Protection as this could impact on our negotiation.

34 Laurel (P7 Mar/Jun 17) (amended)   98 mins

You are a manager in Holly & Co, a firm of Chartered Certified Accountants, and you are responsible for the audit of the Laurel Group (the Group), with a financial year ending 31 May 20X7. The Group produces cosmetics and beauty products sold under various brand names which are globally recognised and which are sold in more than 100 countries.

BPP
LEARNING

You have been provided with the following exhibits:

1   An email which you have received from Brigitte Sanders, the audit engagement partner.

2   Extracts of the permanent file for the audit of the Group

3   Extracts of the Group's projected and actual financial statements, together with associated notes from meeting with Group finance director

4   Notes on the planned acquisition of Azalea Co by the Group

5   Notes on the audit of Bulldog Co

Required

Respond to the instructions in the email from the audit engagement partner.   **(46 marks)**

Note. The split of the mark allocation is shown in the partner's email (Exhibit 1).

Professional marks will be awarded for the presentation and logical flow of the briefing notes and the clarity of the explanations provided in parts (a)–(c).   **(4 marks)**

(Total = 50 marks)

Exhibit 1 – Email from audit engagement partner

To:	Audit manager
From:	Brigitte Sanders, Audit Engagement Partner
Subject:	Audit planning – the Laurel Group, and Bulldog Co

Hello

It is time for you to begin planning the audit of the Laurel Group. I have provided you with some information – a summary of relevant points from the permanent audit file, notes from a meeting with the Group finance director and some extracts from the latest forecast financial statements with comparative figures.

Using this information, I require you to prepare briefing notes for my use, in which you:

(a)   Evaluate the risks of material misstatement to be considered in planning the Group audit. Your evaluation should utilise analytical procedures as a method for identifying relevant risks.
(19 marks)

(b)   Recommend any additional information which should be requested from the Group which would allow a more detailed preliminary analytical review to be performed.   **(6 marks)**

(c)   Recommend the principal audit procedures to be performed on:

(i)   The impairment of the Chico brand; and   **(5 marks)**
(ii)   The planned acquisition of Azalea Co.   **(5 marks)**

In addition to these briefing notes, there is one further matter I require your assistance with. I have provided you with some information that relates to the audit of another, separate audit client, Bulldog Co (Exhibit 5), whose audit is about to commence. Using this information, please can you:

(d)   Explain the matters Holly & Co should have considered before continuing with the engagement to audit Bulldog Co.   **(3 marks)**

(e)   Discuss why the audit of financial instruments is particularly challenging, and explain the matters to be considered in planning the audit of Bulldog Co's forward exchange contracts.
(8 marks)

Your response to these final two requirements need not be in the form of briefing notes.

Thank you.

Exhibit 2 – Points from the permanent audit file

Holly & Co was appointed as Group auditor three years ago, and the firm audits all components of the Group, which is a listed entity.

The Group sells its products under well-known brand names, most of which have been acquired with subsidiary companies. The Group is highly acquisitive, and there are more than 40 subsidiaries and 15 associates within the Group.

Products include cosmetics, hair care products and perfumes for men and women. Research into new products is a significant activity, and the Group aims to bring new products to market on a regular basis.

Exhibit 3 – Extract from projected and actual financial statements and associated notes from meeting with Group finance director

CONSOLIDATED STATEMENT OF FINANCIAL POSITION

	Notes	Projected 31 May 20X7 $m	Actual 31 May 20X6 $m
Assets			
Non-current assets			
Property, plant and equipment	1	92	78
Intangible assets – goodwill		18	18
Intangible assets – acquired brand names	2	80	115
Intangible assets – development costs		25	10
Total non-current assets		215	221
Current assets		143	107
Total assets		358	328
Equity and liabilities			
Equity			
Equity share capital		100	100
Retained earnings		106	98
Non-controlling interest		23	23
Total equity		229	221
Non-current liabilities			
Debenture loans	3	100	80
Deferred tax	4	10	2
Total non-current liabilities		110	82
Current liabilities		19	25
Total liabilities		129	107
Total equity and liabilities		358	328

CONSOLIDATED STATEMENT OF PROFIT OR LOSS FOR THE YEAR TO 31 MAY

	Notes	Projected 20X7 $m	Actual 20X6 $m
Revenue		220	195
Operating expenses	5	(185)	(158)
Operating profit		35	37
Finance costs		(7)	(7)
Profit before tax		28	30
Tax expense		(3)	(3)
Profit for the year		25	27

BPP
LEARNING

Notes

1 Capital expenditure of $20 million has been recorded so far during the year. The Group's accounting policy is to recognise assets at cost less depreciation. During the year, a review of assets' estimated useful lives concluded that many were too short, and as a result, the projected depreciation charge for the year is $5 million less than the comparative figure.

2 Acquired brand names are held at cost and not amortised on the grounds that the assets have an indefinite life. Annual impairment reviews are conducted on all brand names. In December 20X6, the Chico brand name was determined to be impaired by $30 million due to allegations made in the press and by customers that some ingredients used in the Chico perfume range can cause skin irritations and more serious health problems. The Chico products have been withdrawn from sale.

3 A $20 million loan was taken out in January 20X7, the cash being used to finance a specific new product development project.

4 The deferred tax liability relates to timing differences in respect of accelerated tax depreciation (capital allowances) on the Group's property, plant and equipment. The liability has increased following changes to the estimated useful lives of assets discussed in note 1.

5 Contracts were signed in February 20X7 for the hire of 5 new machines for use in production. Contract payments of $1m have been charged to operating expenses as they were made, on the basis that the machines are of low value.

Exhibit 4 – Details of planned acquisition of Azalea Co

Group management is currently negotiating the acquisition of Azalea Co, a large company which develops and sells a range of fine fragrances. It is planned that the acquisition will take place in early June 20X7, and the Group is hopeful that Azalea Co's products will replace the revenue stream lost from the withdrawal of its Chico perfume range. Due diligence is taking place currently, and Group management is hopeful that this will support the consideration of $130 million offered for 100% of Azalea Co's share capital. The Group's bank has agreed to provide a loan for this amount.

Exhibit 5 – Bulldog Co audit

You are also responsible for the audit of another audit client, Bulldog Co, a clothing manufacturer that has been a client of Holly & Co for many years, but which has recently expanded its operations overseas. To manage exposure to cash flows denominated in foreign currencies, the company has set up a treasury management function, which is responsible for entering into hedge transactions such as forward exchange contracts. These transactions are likely to be material to the financial statements.

35 Dasset (P7 12/13) (amended)   39 mins

Dasset Co operates in the coal mining industry. The company owns ten mines across the country from which coal is extracted before being sold onto customers who are energy providers. Coal mining companies operate under licence from the National Coal Mining Authority, an organisation that monitors the environmental impact of coal mining operations, and requires coal mines to be operated in compliance with strict health and safety regulations.

You are an audit manager in Burton & Co, responsible for the audit of Dasset Co and you are reviewing the audit working papers for the year ended 31 August 20X3. The draft financial statements recognise profit before tax of $18 million and total assets of $175 million. The audit senior has left a note for your attention:

Accident at the Ledge Hill Mine

On 15 August 20X3, there was an accident at the Ledge Hill Mine, where several of the tunnels in the mine collapsed, causing other tunnels to become flooded. This has resulted in one-third of the mine becoming inaccessible and for safety reasons, the tunnels will be permanently closed. However,

Dasset Co's management thinks that the rest of the mine can remain operational, as long as improvements are made to ensure that the mine meets health and safety regulations.

Luckily no one was injured in the accident. However, the collapse caused subsidence which has damaged several residential properties in a village located above the mine. A surveyor has been commissioned to report on whether the properties need to be demolished or whether they can be safely repaired. A group of 20 residents has been relocated to rental properties in the local area and Dasset Co is meeting all expenses in relation to this. The Ledge Hill Mine was acquired several years ago and is recognised in the draft statement of financial position at $10 million. As no employees were injured in the accident, Dasset Co's management has decided not to report the accident to the National Coal Mining Authority.

Required

In respect of the accident at the Ledge Hill Mine:

(a) (i) Comment on the matters which you should consider; and

(ii) Describe the audit evidence which you should expect to find

in undertaking your review of the audit working papers and financial statements of Dasset Co.

(14 marks)

(b) In relation to management's decision not to report the accident to the National Coal Mining Authority, discuss Burton & Co's responsibilities and recommend the actions which should be taken by the firm. **(6 marks)**

(Total = 20 marks)

36 Soprano (P7 6/15)   39 mins

You are an audit manager in Soprano & Co, working on the audit of the Tony Group (the Group), whose financial year ended on 31 March 20X5. This is the first time you have worked on the Group audit. The draft consolidated financial statements recognise profit before tax of $6 million (20X4 – $9 million) and total assets of $90 million (20X4 – $82 million). The Group manufactures equipment used in the oil extraction industry.

Goodwill of $10 million is recognised in the Group statement of financial position, having arisen on several business combinations over the last few years. An impairment review was conducted in March 20X5 by Silvio Dante, the Group finance director, and this year an impairment of $50,000 is to be recognised in respect of the goodwill.

Silvio has prepared a file of documentation to support the results of the impairment review, including notes on the assumptions used, his calculations, and conclusions. When he gave you this file, Silvio made the following comment:

'I don't think you should need any evidence other than that contained in my file. The assumptions used are straightforward, so you shouldn't need to look into them in detail. The assumptions are consistent with how we conducted impairment reviews in previous years and your firm has always agreed with the assumptions used, so you can check that back to last year's audit file. All of the calculations have been checked by the head of the Group's internal audit department.'

Silvio has also informed you that two members of the sales team are suspected of paying bribes in order to secure lucrative customer contracts. The internal audit team were alerted to this when they were auditing cash payments, and found significant payments to several new customers being made prior to contracts being signed. Silvio has asked if Soprano & Co would perform a forensic investigation into the alleged bribery payments.

Required

(a)   Explain the importance of professional scepticism in planning and performing an audit, and discuss how professional scepticism should be applied to the statement made by Silvio.

(11 marks)

(b)   Explain the principal audit procedures to be performed on the impairment of goodwill.

(5 marks)

(c)   Recommend the procedures to be used in performing a forensic investigation on the alleged bribery payments.

(4 marks)

Note. Assume it is 6 June 20X5.   **(Total = 20 marks)**

37 Willow (P7 12/11) (amended)   49 mins

Willow Co is a print supplier to businesses, printing catalogues, leaflets, training manuals and stationery to order. It specialises in using 100% recycled paper in its printing, a fact which is promoted heavily in its advertising.

You are a senior audit manager in Bark & Co, and you have just been placed in charge of the audit of Willow Co after the manager previously assigned to the audit was moved to another urgent assignment. The audit for the year ended 31 August 20X1 is nearing completion, and the auditor's report is due to be issued in two weeks' time. You are currently reviewing a summary of matters for your considering, prepared by the audit senior.

Summary of issues for manager's attention

Materiality has been determined as follows.

* $800,000 for assets and liabilities
* $250,000 for income and expenses

Issues related to audit work performed:

(i)   **Audit work on inventory**

Audit procedures performed at the inventory count indicated that printed inventory items with a value of $130,000 were potentially obsolete. These items were mainly out of date training manuals. The finance director, Cherry Laurel, has not written off this inventory as she argues that the paper on which the items are printed can be recycled and used again in future printing orders. However, the items appear not to be recyclable as they are coated in plastic. The junior who performed the audit work on inventory has requested a written representation from management to confirm that the items can be recycled and no further procedures relevant to these items have been performed.

(ii) **Audit work on provisions**

Willow Co is involved in a court case with a competitor, Aspen Co, which alleges that a design used in Willow Co's printed material copies one of Aspen Co's designs which are protected under copyright. Our evidence obtained is a verbal confirmation from Willow Co's lawyers that a claim of $125,000 has been made against Willow Co, which is probable to be paid. Cherry Laurel has not made a provision, arguing that it is immaterial. Cherry refused our request to ask the lawyers to confirm their opinion on the matter in writing, saying it is not worth bothering the lawyers again on such a trivial matter.

(iii) **Audit work on current assets**

Willow Co made a loan of $6,000 to Cherry Laurel, the finance director, on 30 June 20X1. The amount is recognised as a current asset. The loan carries an interest rate of 4% which we have confirmed to be the market rate for short-term loans and we have concluded that the loan is an arm's length transaction. Cherry has provided written confirmation that she intends to repay the loan by 31 March 20X2. The only other audit work performed was to agree the

cash payment to the cash book. Details of the loan made to Cherry have not been separately disclosed in the financial statements.

Other issues for your attention:

Property revaluations

Willow Co currently adopts an accounting policy of recognising properties at cost. During the audit of non-current assets Willow Co's property manager said that the company is considering a change of accounting policy so that properties would be recognised at fair value from 1 January 20X2.

Non-current asset register

The audit of non-current assets was delayed by a week. We had asked for the non-current asset register reconciliation to be completed by the client prior to commencement of our audit procedures on non-current assets, but it seems that the person responsible for the reconciliation went on holiday having forgotten to prepare the reconciliation. This happened on last year's audit as well, and the issue was discussed with the audit committee at that time.

Procurement procedures

We found during our testing of trade payables that an approved supplier list is not maintained, and invoices received are not always matched back to goods received notes. This was mentioned to the procurement manager, who said that suppliers are switched fairly often, depending on which supplier is the cheapest, so it would be difficult to maintain an up-to-date approved supplier list.

Financial controller

Mia Fern, Willow Co's financial controller, owns a holiday home overseas. It appears that she offered the audit team free use of the holiday home for three weeks after the audit, as a reward for the team's hard work. She also bought lunch for the audit team on most days.

Required

(a) Assess the audit implications of the issues related to audit work performed, that have been raised by the audit senior. Your assessment should consider the sufficiency of evidence obtained, explain any adjustments that may be necessary to the financial statements, and describe the impact on the auditor's report if these adjustments are not made. You should also recommend any further audit procedures necessary. **(17 marks)**

(b) Explain the matters, arising from the 'Other issues for your attention', which should be brought to the attention of the audit committee of Willow Co. **(8 marks)**

(Total = 25 marks)

38 Jovi (P7 12/12)   55 mins

(a) You are a manager in Sambora & Co, responsible for the audit of the Jovi Group (the Group), which is listed. The Group's main activity is steel manufacturing and it comprises a parent company and five subsidiaries. Sambora & Co currently audits all components of the Group.

You are working on the audit of the Group's financial statements for the year ended 30 June 20X2. This morning the audit engagement partner left a note for you:

Hello,

The audit senior has provided you with the draft consolidated financial statements and accompanying notes which summarise the key audit findings and some background information.

At the planning stage, materiality was initially determined to be $900,000, and was calculated based on the assumption that the Jovi Group is a high risk client due to its listed status. During the audit, a number of issues arose which meant that we needed to revise the materiality level for the financial statements as a whole. The revised level of materiality is now determined to be $700,000. One of the audit juniors was unsure as to why the materiality level had been revised. There are two matters you need to deal with:

(i)   Explain why auditors may need to reassess materiality as the audit progresses.

(4 marks)

(ii)   Assess the implications of the key audit findings for the completion of the audit. Your assessment must consider whether the key audit findings indicate a risk of material misstatement. Where the key audit findings refer to audit evidence, you must also consider the adequacy of the audit evidence obtained, but you do not need to recommend further specific procedures. **(18 marks)**

Thank you

The Group's draft consolidated financial statements, with notes referenced to key audit findings, are shown below:

DRAFT CONSOLIDATED STATEMENT OF PROFIT OR LOSS AND OTHER COMPREHENSIVE INCOME

	Notes	30 June 20X2 Draft $'000	30 June 20X1 Actual $'000
Revenue	1	98,795	103,100
Cost of sales		(75,250)	(74,560)
Gross profit		23,545	28,540
Operating expenses	2	(14,900)	(17,500)
Operating profit		8,645	11,040
Share of profit of associate		1,010	900
Finance costs		(380)	(340)
Profit before tax		9,275	11,600
Taxation		(3,200)	(3,500)
Profit for the year		6,075	8,100
Other comprehensive income/expense for the year, net of tax:			
Gains on property revaluation	3	800	–
Actuarial losses on defined benefit plan	4	(1,100)	(200)
Other comprehensive income/expense		(300)	(200)
Total comprehensive income for the year		5,775	7,900

Notes. Key audit findings – statement of profit or loss and other comprehensive income

1   Revenue has been stable for all components of the Group with the exception of one subsidiary, Copeland Co, which has recognised a 25% decrease in revenue.

2   Operating expenses for the year to June 20X2 is shown net of a profit on a property disposal of $2 million. Our evidence includes agreeing the cash receipts to bank statement and sale documentation, and we have confirmed that the property has been removed from the non-current asset register. The audit junior noted, when reviewing the sale document, that there is an option to repurchase the property in five years' time, but did not discuss the matter with management.

3   The property revaluation relates to the Group's head office. The audit team have not obtained evidence on the revaluation, as the gain was immaterial based on the initial calculation of materiality.

4   The actuarial loss is attributed to an unexpected stock market crash. The Group's pension plan is managed by Axle Co – a firm of independent fund managers who maintain the necessary accounting records relating to the plan. Axle Co has supplied written representation as to the value of the defined benefit plan's assets and liabilities at 30 June 20X2. No other audit work has been performed other than to agree the figure from the financial statements to supporting documentation supplied by Axle Co.

DRAFT CONSOLIDATED STATEMENT OF FINANCIAL POSITION

	Notes	30 June 20X2 Draft $'000	30 June 20X1 Actual $'000
Assets			
Non-current assets			
Property, plant and equipment		81,800	76,300
Goodwill	5	5,350	5,350
Investment in associate	6	4,230	4,230
Assets classified as held for sale	7	7,800	–
		99,180	85,880
Current assets			
Inventory		8,600	8,000
Receivables		8,540	7,800
Cash and cash equivalents		2,100	2,420
		19,240	18,220
Total assets		118,420	104,100
Equity and Liabilities			
Equity			
Share capital		12,500	12,500
Revaluation reserve		3,300	2,500
Retained earnings		33,600	29,400
Non-controlling interest	8	4,350	4,000
Total equity		53,750	48,400
Non-current liabilities			
Defined benefit pension plan		10,820	9,250
Long-term borrowings	9	43,000	35,000
Deferred tax		1,950	1,350
Total non-current liabilities		55,770	45,600
Current liabilities			
Trade and other payables		6,200	7,300
Provisions		2,700	2,800
Total current liabilities		8,900	10,100
Total liabilities		64,670	55,700
Total equity and liabilities		118,420	104,100

Notes. Key audit findings – statement of financial position

5   The goodwill relates to each of the subsidiaries in the Group. Management has confirmed in writing that goodwill is stated correctly, and our other audit procedure was to arithmetically check the impairment review conducted by management.

6   The associate is a 30% holding in James Co, purchased to provide investment income. The audit team have not obtained evidence regarding the associate as there is no movement in the amount recognised in the statement of financial position.

7   The assets held for sale relate to a trading division of one of the subsidiaries, which represents one third of that subsidiary's net assets. The sale of the division was announced in May 20X2, and is expected to be complete by 31 December 20X2. Audit evidence obtained includes a review of the sales agreement and confirmation from the buyer, obtained in July 20X2, that the sale will take place.

8   Two of the Group's subsidiaries are partly owned by shareholders external to the Group.

9   A loan of $8 million was taken out in October 20X1, carrying an interest rate of 2%, payable annually in arrears. The terms of the loan have been confirmed to documentation provided by the bank.

Required

Respond to the note from the audit engagement partner.   **(22 marks)**

Note. The split of the mark allocation is shown within the partner's note.

(b)   The audit engagement partner now sends a further note regarding the Jovi Group:

'The Group finance director has just informed me that last week the Group purchased 100% of the share capital of May Co, a company located overseas in Farland. The Group audit committee has suggested that due to the distant location of May Co, a joint audit could be performed, starting with the next financial statements for the year ending 30 June 20X3. May Co's current auditors are a small local firm called Moore & Co who operate only in Farland.'

Required

Discuss the advantages and disadvantages of a joint audit being performed on the financial statements of May Co.   **(6 marks)**

(Total = 28 marks)

39 Jolie (P7 12/10) (amended)   98 mins

You are a manager in Jen & Co, a firm with three offices and 12 partners. About one third of the firm's clients are audit clients, the remainder are clients for whom Jen & Co performs tax, accounting and business advisory services.

You are responsible for the audit of Jolie Co, a large company operating in the retail industry, which has a year ended 30 November 20Y0. As this is the first year that your firm will be acting as auditor for Jolie Co, you need to gain an understanding of the business risks facing the new client.

You have been provided with the following exhibits:

1   An email which you have received from the audit engagement partner.

2   Notes from a meeting held between the audit engagement partner and Mo Pitt the finance director of Jolie Co.

3   Extract from financial and non-financial information of Jolie Co.

4   Revenue-raising suggestions for Jen & Co.

Required

Respond to the instructions in the email from the audit engagement partner   **(46 marks)**

Professional marks will be awarded for the presentation and logical flow of the briefing notes and the clarity of the explanations provided in part (a).   **(4 marks)**

(Total = 50 marks)

Exhibit 1 – Email from audit engagement partner

To:	Audit Manager
From:	Audit Partner
Re:	Jolie Co audit planning

Hello

I need you to begin planning the audit of Jolie Co for the year ended 30 November 20Y0. I have just attended a planning meeting with Mo Pitt, the finance director of the company, and have provided you with notes.

Using this information, you are required to:

(a) Prepare briefing notes to be used at a planning meeting with your audit team, in which you evaluate the business risks facing Jolie Co to be considered when planning the final audit for the year ended 30 November 20Y0. **(16 marks)**

(b) Using the information provided, evaluate the principal risks of material misstatement. **(14 marks)**

(c) Recommend the principal audit procedures to be performed in respect of the valuation of the JLC brand name. **(5 marks)**

Our firm has been considering how, in general terms, it might improve its revenue figures going forward. Our firm's business development manager has made some suggestions of how we might do this, and I have provided you with a summary of these.

Using this information, please:

(d) Evaluate each of the revenue-raising suggestions made, commenting on the ethical and professional issues raised. **(11 marks)**

Thank you.

Note that briefing notes are only required for part (a).

Exhibit 2 – Notes from meeting with Mo Pitt

Jolie Co sells clothing, with a strategy of selling high fashion items under the JLC brand name. New ranges of clothes are introduced to stores every eight weeks. The company relies on a team of highly skilled designers to develop new fashion ranges. The designers must be able to anticipate and quickly respond to changes in consumer preferences. There is a high staff turnover in the design team.

Most sales are made in-store, but there is also a very popular catalogue, from which customers can place an order online, or over the phone. The company has recently upgraded the computer system and improved the website, at significant cost, in order to integrate the website sales directly into the general ledger, and to provide an easier interface for customers to use when ordering and entering their credit card details. The new on-line sales system has allowed overseas sales for the first time.

The system for phone ordering has recently been outsourced. The contract for outsourcing went out to tender and Jolie Co awarded the contract to the company offering the least cost. The company providing the service uses an overseas call centre where staff costs are very low.

A new inventory system was introduced in June 20Y0, with the aim of keeping better track of the movement of inventory within and across Jolie's sites, including factories, stores and online distribution centres. The system keeps track of all cost inputs as inventory is produced, allowing management to keep close control over these processes.

Jolie Co has recently joined the Ethical Trading Initiative. This is a 'fair-trade' initiative, which means that any products bearing the JLC brand name must have been produced in a manner which is clean and safe for employees, and minimises the environmental impact of the manufacturing process. A significant advertising campaign promoting Jolie Co's involvement with this initiative has recently taken place. The JLC brand name was purchased a number of years ago and is recognised at cost as an intangible asset, which is not amortised. The brand represents 12% of the total assets recognised on the statement of financial position.

The company owns numerous distribution centres, some of which operate close to residential areas. A licence to operate the distribution centres is issued by each local government authority in which a centre is located. One of the conditions of the licence is that deliveries must only take place between 8 am and 6 pm. The authority also monitors the noise level of each centre, and can revoke the operating licence if a certain noise limit is breached. Two licences were revoked for a period of three months during the year.

Jolie Co owns a manufacturing division which is located in Nearland, and comprises a small factory and office, together with various items of plant and equipment. This division processes raw materials such as fabrics and dyes, which are then transported to Jolie Co's own jurisdiction, where they are worked into finished products. Jolie Co decided to sell some of this division's assets during the year, on the grounds that it is now possible to purchase processed materials, which are of equivalent or better quality, more cheaply from elsewhere. The factory and office belonging to the division were advertised for sale in November 20Y0; offers have been received and the sale is expected to be completed within six months. The factory and office were therefore classified as 'held for sale' in the financial statements, and are carried at revalued amounts of $14m and $8m respectively.

Exhibit 3 – Extract of financial and non-financial information

Year ending 30 November	20Y0 Draft $m	20X9 Actual $m
Revenue:		
Retail outlets	1,030	1,140
Phone and online sales	425	395
Total revenue	1,455	1,535
Operating profit	245	275
Finance costs	(25)	(22)
Profit before tax	220	253

Additional information:

Total assets	$1,675m	$1,625m
Number of stores	210	208
Average revenue per store	$4.905m	$5.48m
Number of phone orders	680,000	790,000
Number of online orders	1,020,000	526,667
Average spend per order	$250	$300

Exhibit 4 – Revenue-raising suggestions for Jen & Co

Jen & Co is considering how to generate more revenue, and the following suggestions have been made by the firm's business development manager

(i)   An advertisement could be placed in national newspapers to attract new clients. The draft advertisement has been given to you for review:

> Jen & Co is the largest and most professional accountancy and audit provider in the country. We offer a range of services in addition to audit, which are guaranteed to improve your business efficiency and save you tax.
>
> If you are unhappy with your auditors, we can offer a second opinion on the report that has been given.
>
> Introductory offer: for all new clients we offer a 25% discount when both audit and tax services are provided. Our rates are approved by ACCA.

(ii)   A new partner with experience in the banking sector has joined Jen & Co. It has been suggested that the partner could specialise in offering a corporate finance service to clients. In particular, the partner could advise clients on raising debt finance, and would negotiate with the client's bank or other provider of finance on behalf of the client. The fee charged for this service would be contingent on the client obtaining the finance with a borrowing cost below market rate.

40 Vancouver (P7 Mar/Jun 16) (amended)   98 mins

You are an audit manager in Montreal & Co, a firm of Chartered Certified Accountants, and you are responsible for the audit of the Vancouver Group (the Group). The Group operates in the supply chain management sector, offering distribution, warehousing and container handling services.

The Group comprises a parent company, Vancouver Co, and two subsidiaries, Toronto Co and Calgary Co. Both of the subsidiaries were acquired as wholly owned subsidiaries many years ago. Montreal & Co audits all of the individual company financial statements as well as the Group consolidated financial statements.

You have been provided with the following exhibits:

1   An email which you have received from Albert Franks, the audit engagement partner.

2   Notes from a meeting between Albert Franks, the Group finance director and a representative of the audit committee

3   Financial information on the Group, provided by the Group finance director

Required

Respond to the instructions in the email from the audit engagement partner.   **(46 marks)**

Note. The split of the mark allocation is shown within the partner's email (Exhibit 1).

Professional marks will be awarded for the presentation and logical flow of the briefing notes and the clarity of the explanations provided.   **(4 marks)**

(Total = 50 marks)

Exhibit 1 – Email from audit engagement partner

To: Audit manager

From: Albert Franks, audit engagement partner

Subject: The Vancouver Group – audit planning, year ending 31 July 20X6

Hello

I would like you to begin to plan the Group audit for the financial year ending 31 July 20X6.

I held a meeting yesterday with Hannah Peters, the Group finance director. A representative of the Group audit committee was also at the meeting to discuss two issues raised for our attention by the committee. Hannah gave me some projected financial information for the Group's forthcoming year end, along with comparatives and explanatory notes, and we discussed some matters relevant to the Group this year. I am preparing for the audit team briefing next week at which there will be a number of recent recruits into the audit department whose first assignment will be the Vancouver Group.

I have attached some notes from my meeting as well as the financial information provided by Hannah. Using this information you are required to prepare briefing notes for use in the audit team briefing in which you:

(a)   Explain why analytical procedures are performed as a fundamental part of our risk assessment at the planning stage of the audit.   **(5 marks)**

(b)   Evaluate the audit risks which should be considered in planning the Group audit. You should ensure that you consider all of the information provided as well as utilising analytical procedures, where relevant, to identify the audit risks.   **(25 marks)**

(c)   Recommend the principal audit procedures that should be performed on the consolidation process.   **(8 marks)**

(d)   Discuss the ethical issues relevant to Montreal & Co, and recommend any actions which should be taken by our firm.   **(8 marks)**

Thank you.

Exhibit 2 – Notes from meeting with the Group finance director and audit committee representative

The Group has not changed its operations significantly this year. However, it has completed a modernisation programme of its warehousing facilities at a cost of $25 million. The programme was financed with cash raised from two sources: $5 million was raised from a debenture issue, and $20 million from the sale of 5% of the share capital of Calgary Co, with the shares being purchased by an institutional investor.

The Group fell victim during the year to a significant cyber attack, which fortunately did not adversely affect its operations. It did, however, result in the loss of files containing the contact details of many of the Group's employees.

An investigation into the Group's tax affairs started in January 20X6. The tax authorities are investigating the possible underpayment of taxes by each of the companies in the Group, claiming that tax laws have been breached. The Group's tax planning was performed by another firm of accountants, Victoria & Co, but the Group's audit committee has asked if our firm will support the Group by looking into its tax position and liaising with the tax authorities in respect of the tax investigation on its behalf. Victoria & Co has resigned from their engagement to provide tax advice to the Group. The matter is to be resolved by a tribunal which is scheduled to take place in September 20X6.

The Group audit committee has also asked whether one of Montreal & Co's audit partners can be appointed as a non-executive director and serve on the audit committee. The audit committee lacks a financial reporting expert, and the appointment of an audit partner would bring much needed knowledge and experience.

Exhibit 3 – Financial information provided by the Group finance director

CONSOLIDATED STATEMENT OF FINANCIAL POSITION

	Notes	Projected 31 July 20X6 $m	Actual 31 July 20X5 $m
Assets			
Non-current assets			
Property, plant and equipment	1	230	187
Intangible assets – goodwill		30	30
Deferred tax asset	2	10	15
Total non-current assets		270	232
Current assets			
Inventories		35	28
Trade and other receivables		62	45
Cash and cash equivalents		–	10
Total current assets		97	83
Total assets		367	315
Equity and liabilities			
Equity			
Equity share capital		50	50
Retained earnings		126	103
Non-controlling interest	3	5	–
Total equity		181	153
Non-current liabilities			
Debenture		60	55
Provisions	4	6	12
Total non-current liabilities		66	67
Current liabilities			
Trade and other payables		105	95
Overdraft		15	–
Total current liabilities		120	95
Total liabilities		186	162
Total equity and liabilities		367	315

CONSOLIDATED STATEMENT OF PROFIT OR LOSS FOR THE YEAR TO 31 JULY

	Notes	Projected 20X6 $m	Actual 20X5 $m
Revenue	5	375	315
Operating expenses		(348)	(277)
Operating profit		27	38
Profit on disposal of shares in Calgary Co		10	–
Finance costs		(4)	(3)
Profit before tax		33	35
Tax expense		(10)	(15)
Profit for the year		23	20

Notes

1   Several old warehouses were modernised during the year. The modernisation involved the redesign of the layout of each warehouse, the installation of new computer systems, and the replacement of electrical systems.

2   The deferred tax asset is in respect of unused tax losses (tax credits) which accumulated when Toronto Co was loss making for a period of three years from 20W9 to 20X2.

3   The non-controlling interest has arisen on the disposal of shares in Calgary Co. On 1 January 20X6, a 5% equity shareholding in Calgary Co was sold, raising cash of $20 million. The profit made on the disposal is separately recognised in the Group statement of profit or loss.

4   The provisions relate to onerous leases in respect of vacant properties which are surplus to the Group's requirements.

5   The Group has always recognised distribution revenue when a shipment leaves its distribution centre.

41 Bluebell (P7 12/08) (amended)   70 mins

Bluebell Co operates a chain of 95 luxury hotels. This year's results show a return to profitability for the company, following several years of losses. Hotel trade journals show that on average, revenue in the industry has increased by around 10% this year. Despite improved profitability, Bluebell Co has poor liquidity, and is currently trying to secure further long-term finance.

You have been the manager responsible for the audit of Bluebell Co for the last four years. Extracts from the draft financial statements for the year ended 30 November 20X8 are shown below.

EXTRACTS FROM THE STATEMENT OF PROFIT OR LOSS

	Notes	20X8 $m	20X7 $m
Revenue	1	890	713
Operating expenses	2	(835)	(690)
Other operating income	3	135	10
Operating profit		190	33
Finance charges		(45)	(43)
Profit/(loss) before tax		145	(10)

Notes

1   **Revenue recognition**

Revenue comprises sales of hotel rooms, plus conference and meeting rooms. Revenue is recognised when a room is occupied. A 20% deposit is taken when the room is booked.

2   **Significant items included in operating expenses**

	20X8 $m	20X7 $m
Share-based payment expense (i)	138	–
Damaged property repair expenses (ii)	100	–

3   **Other operating income includes**

	20X8 $m	20X7 $m
Profit on property disposal (iii)	125	10

(i)   In June 20X8 Bluebell Co granted 50 million share options to executives and employees of the company. The cost of the share option scheme is being recognised over the three-year vesting period of the scheme. It is currently assumed that all of the options will vest and the expense is calculated on that basis. Bluebell Co operates in a tax jurisdiction in which no deferred tax consequences arise from share-based payment schemes.

(ii)   In September 20X8, three hotels situated near a major river were severely damaged by a flood. All of the hotels, which were constructed by Bluebell Co only two years ago, need extensive repairs and refurbishment at an estimated cost of $100 million, which has been provided in full. All of the buildings are insured for damage caused by flooding.

(iii)   Eight properties were sold in March 20X8 to Daffodil Fund Enterprises (DFE). Bluebell Co entered into a management contract with DFE and is continuing to operate the eight hotels under a 15-year agreement. Under the terms of the management contract, Bluebell Co receives an annual financial return based on the profit made by the eight hotels. At the end of the contract, Bluebell Co has the option to repurchase the hotels, and it is likely that the option will be exercised.

EXTRACTS FROM THE STATEMENT OF FINANCIAL POSITION	20X8	20X7
	$m	$m
Property, plant and equipment (Note 4)	1,265	1,135
Deferred tax asset (Note 5)	285	335
Deferred tax liability (Note 6)	(735)	(638)
Total assets	2,870	2,230

4   **Property, Plant and Equipment (extract)**

On 31 October 20X8 all of Bluebell Co's owned hotels were revalued. A revaluation gain of $250 million has been recognised in other comprehensive income and in the statement of financial position.

5   **Deferred Tax Asset (extract)**

The deferred tax asset represents unutilised tax losses which accumulated in the loss making periods 20X4–20X7 inclusive. Bluebell Co is confident that future taxable trading profits will be generated in order for the tax losses to be utilised.

6   **Deferred Tax Liability (extract)**

	Temporary differences relating to Property, plant and equipment
	$m
1 December 20X7	638
Charged to equity	88
Charged to tax expense	9
30 November 20X8	735

Required

(a) Using the specific information provided, identify and explain the risks of material misstatement to be addressed when planning the final audit of Bluebell Co for the year ended 30 November 20X8.   **(14 marks)**

(b) Describe the principal audit procedures to be carried out in respect of the following.

(i)   The measurement of the share-based payment expense   **(6 marks)**
(ii)   The recoverability of the deferred tax asset   **(4 marks)**

(c)   A new internal auditor, Daisy Rosepetal, has recently joined Bluebell Co. She has been asked by management to establish and to monitor a variety of social and environmental Key Performance Indicators (KPIs). Daisy has no experience in this area, and has asked you for some advice. It has been agreed with Bluebell Co's audit committee that you are to provide guidance to Daisy to help her in this part of her role, and that this does not impair the objectivity of the audit.

You have just received the following email from the audit engagement partner on the Bluebell audit.

To: Audit manager

From: Audit partner

Re: Bluebell Co

Hello,

I have a meeting with Daisy Rospetal tomorrow for which I need you to prepare some briefing notes. Please prepare notes in which you:

(Recommend EIGHT KPIs which could be used to monitor Bluebell Co's social and environmental performance, and outline the nature of evidence that should be available to provide assurance on the accuracy of the KPIs recommended.

Thanks.

Required

Respond to the partner's email above.   **(8 marks)**

Professional marks will be awarded for the presentation, logical flow and clarity of explanation of the briefing notes.   **(4 marks)**

(Total = 36 marks)

42 Robster (06/09) (amended)   **49 mins**

Robster Co is a company which designs and creates high-value items of jewellery. You are the manager responsible for the audit of Robster Co, and you are reviewing the audit working papers for the year ended 28 February 20X9. The draft financial statements show profit before tax of $3.2 million, and total assets of $45 million.

The audit senior has left you the following note on the audit file, relating to assets recognised in the statement of financial position for the first time this year, and a consignment inventory arrangement.

Leases

In July 20X8, Robster Co entered into five new rental contracts for land and buildings. The contracts have been recognised as leases, and the statement of financial position includes right-of-use assets presented as tangible non-current assets at a value of $3.6 million, and a total lease liability of $3.2 million.

Financial assets

Non-current assets include financial assets recognised at $1.26 million. A note to the financial statements describes these financial assets as investments classified as at 'fair value', and the investments are described in the note as 'held for trading'. The investments are all shares in listed companies. A gain of $350,000 has been recognised in net profit in respect of the revaluation of these investments.

Consignment inventory

Approximately half of Robster's jewellery sold is from its own retail outlets. The other half is sold by external vendors under a consignment inventory arrangement, the terms of which specify that Robster Co retains the ability to change the selling price of the jewellery, and that the vendor is required to return any unsold jewellery after a period of nine months. When the vendor sells an item of jewellery to a customer, legal title passes from Robster Co to the customer.

On delivery of the jewellery to the external vendors, Robster Co recognises revenue and derecognises inventory. At 28 February 20X9, jewellery at cost price of $1 million is held at external vendors. Revenue of $1.25 million has been recognised in respect of this jewellery.

Required

(a) In your review of the audit working papers, comment on the matters you should consider, and state the audit evidence you should expect to find in respect of:

   (i) The lease
   (ii) The financial assets
   (iii) The consignment inventory

   (21 marks)

(b) ISA 260 *Communication with Those Charged with Governance* requires the auditor to communicate with those charged with governance about the significant findings from the audit.

   Required

   Explain the matters that would be communicated with those charged with the governance of Robster Co in relation to the issues above. **(4 marks)**

   (Total = 25 marks)

43 Connolly (P7 12/14) 68 mins

You are an audit manager in Davies & Co, responsible for the audit of Connolly Co, a listed company operating in the pharmaceutical industry. You are planning the audit of the financial statements for the year ending 31 December 20X4, and the audit partner, Ali Stone, has sent you this email:

To:	Audit manager
From:	Ali Stone, Audit partner
Subject:	Audit planning – Connolly Co

Hello

I would like you to start planning the audit of Connolly Co. The company's finance director, Maggie Ram, has sent to me this morning some key financial information discussed at the latest board meeting. I have also provided you with minutes of a meeting I had with Maggie last week and some background information about the company. Using this information I would like you to prepare briefing notes for my use in which you:

(a) Evaluate the business risks faced by Connolly Co; **(11 marks)**

(b) Evaluate the principal risks of material misstatement to be considered in planning the audit; **(8 marks)**

(c) Recommend the principal audit procedures to be performed in respect of the acquired 'Cold Comforts' brand name; and **(5 marks)**

BPP LEARNING

(d) Discuss the ethical issues relevant to the audit firm, and recommend appropriate actions to be taken. **(7 marks)**

Thank you.

Background information

Connolly Co is a pharmaceutical company, developing drugs to be licensed for use around the world. Products include medicines such as tablets and medical gels and creams. Some drugs are sold over the counter at pharmacy stores, while others can only be prescribed for use by a doctor. Products are heavily advertised to support the company's brand names. In some countries television advertising is not allowed for prescription drugs.

The market is very competitive, encouraging rapid product innovation. New products are continually in development and improvements are made to existing formulations. Four new drugs are in the research and development phase. Drugs have to meet very stringent regulatory requirements prior to being licensed for production and sale. Research and development involves human clinical trials, the results of which are scrutinised by the licensing authorities.

It is common in the industry for patents to be acquired for new drugs and patent rights are rigorously defended, sometimes resulting in legal action against potential infringement.

Minutes from Ali Stone's meeting with Maggie Ram

Connolly Co has approached its bank to extend its borrowing facilities. An extension of $10 million is being sought to its existing loan to support the on-going development of new drugs. Our firm has been asked by the bank to provide a guarantee in respect of this loan extension.

In addition, the company has asked the bank to make cash of $3 million available in the event that an existing court case against the company is successful. The court case is being brought by an individual who suffered severe and debilitating side effects when participating in a clinical trial in 20X3.

In January 20X4, Connolly Co began to sell into a new market – that of animal health. This has been very successful, and the sales of veterinary pharmaceuticals and grooming products for livestock and pets amount to approximately 15% of total revenue for 20X4.

Another success in 20X4 was the acquisition of the 'Cold Comforts' brand from a rival company. Products to alleviate the symptoms of coughs and colds are sold under this brand. The brand cost $5 million and is being amortised over an estimated useful life of 15 years.

Connolly Co's accounting and management information systems are out of date. This is not considered to create any significant control deficiencies, but the company would like to develop and implement new systems next year. Management has asked our firm to give advice on the new systems as they have little specialist in-house knowledge in this area.

Key financial information

	20X4 – Projected unaudited $'000	20X3 – Actual audited $'000
Revenue	40,000	38,000
Operating profit	8,100	9,085
Operating margin	20%	24%
Earnings per share	25c	29c
Net cash flow	(1,200)	6,000
Research and development cash outflow in the year	(3,000)	(2,800)
Total development intangible asset recognised at the year end	50,000	48,000
Total assets	200,000	195,000
Gearing ratio (debt/equity)	0.8	0.9

Required

Respond to the email from the audit partner. **(31 marks)**

Note. The split of marks is shown within the partner's email. Assume it is 10 December 20X4.

Professional marks will be awarded for the presentation, clarity of explanations and logical flow of the answer. **(4 marks)**

(Total = 35 marks)

44 Osier (P7 Mar/Jun 17) (amended)   49 mins

(a)   You are the manager responsible for the audit of Osier Co, a jewellery manufacturer and retailer. The final audit for the year ended 31 March 20X7 is nearing completion and you are reviewing the audit working papers. The draft financial statements recognise total assets of $1,919m (20X6 – $1,889 million), revenue of $1,052 million (20X6 – $997 million) and profit before tax of $107 million (20X6 – $110 million). Two issues from the audit working papers are summarised below:

(i)   **Cost of inventory**

Inventory costs include all purchase costs and the costs of conversion of raw materials into finished goods. Conversion costs include direct labour costs and an allocation of production overheads. Direct labour costs are calculated based on the average production time per unit of inventory, which is estimated by the production manager, multiplied by the estimated labour cost per hour, which is calculated using the forecast annual wages of production staff divided by the annual scheduled hours of production. Production overheads are all fixed and are allocated based upon the forecast annual units of production. At the year end, inventory was valued at $21 million (20X6 – $20 million). **(7 marks)**

(ii)   **Impairment**

At the year end, management performed an impairment review on its retail outlets, which are a cash generating unit for the purpose of conducting an impairment review. While internet sales grew rapidly during the year, sales from retail outlets declined, prompting the review. At 31 March 20X7 the carrying amount of the assets directly attributable to the retail outlets totalled $137 million, this includes both tangible assets and goodwill.

During the year management received a number of offers from parties interested in purchasing the retail outlets for an average of $125 million. They also estimated the disposal costs to be $1.5 million, based upon their experience of corporate acquisitions and disposals. Management estimated the value in use to be $128 million. This was based upon the historic cash flows attributable to retail outlets inflated at a general rate of 1% per annum. This, they argued, reflects the poor performance of the retail outlets.

Consequently the retail outlets were impaired by $9 million to restate them to their estimated recoverable amount of $128 million. The impairment was allocated against the tangible assets of the outlets on a pro rata basis, based upon the original carrying amount of each asset in the unit. **(7 marks)**

Required

Comment on the matters to be considered, and explain the audit evidence you should expect to find during your file review in respect of each of the issues described above.

Note. The split of the mark allocation is shown against each of the issues above. You are not required to discuss any potential implications for the auditor's report.

Your firm is required to conduct an audit of the performance information of another client, Moosewood Hospital. You are required to provide assurance with regard to both the accuracy and completeness of three key performance measures which are used to monitor the hospital's efficiency and effectiveness. The performance measures, all of which the Hospital claims to have met, are:

(1)   To maintain an average patient to nurse ratio of no more than 6:1.

(2)   To achieve a minimum 75% annual usage of surgical rooms.

(3)   To ensure that the rate of admissions within 28 days for previously treated conditions does not exceed 3%.

Required

(b)   Explain the difference between a 'performance audit' and an 'audit of performance information.'   **(3 marks)**

(c)   Recommend the examination procedures which should be used in auditing the performance information of Moosewood Hospital.   **(8 marks)**

(Total = 25 marks)

45 Macau (P7 Mar/Jun 16)   49 mins

You are a senior manager in Macau & Co, a firm of Chartered Certified Accountants. In your capacity as engagement quality control reviewer, you have been asked to review the audit files of Stanley Co and Kowloon Co, both of which have a financial year ended 31 December 20X5, and the audits of both companies are nearing completion.

(a)   Stanley Co is a frozen food processor, selling its products to wholesalers and supermarkets. From your review of the audit working papers, you have noted that the level of materiality was determined to be $1.5 million at the planning stage, and this materiality threshold has been used throughout the audit. There is no evidence on the audit file that this threshold has been reviewed during the course of the audit.

From your review of the audit planning, you know that a new packing machine with a cost of $1.6 million was acquired by Stanley Co in March 20X5, and is recognised in the draft statement of financial position at a carrying amount of $1.4 million at 31 December 20X5. The packing machine is located at the premises of Aberdeen Co, a distribution company which is used to pack and distribute a significant proportion of Stanley Co's products. The machine has not been physically verified by a member of the audit team. The audit working papers conclude that 'we have obtained the purchase invoice and order in relation to the machine, and therefore can conclude that the asset is appropriately valued and that it exists. In addition, the managing director of Aberdeen Co has confirmed in writing that the machine is located at their premises and is in working order. No further work is needed in respect of this item.'

Inventory is recognised at $2 million in the draft statement of financial position. You have reviewed the results of audit procedures performed at the inventory count, where the test counts performed by the audit team indicated that the count of some items performed by the company's staff was not correct. The working papers state that 'the inventory count was not well organised' and conclude that 'however, the discrepancies were immaterial, so no further action is required'.

The audit senior spoke to you yesterday, voicing some concerns about the performance of the audit. A summary of his comments is shown below:

'The audit manager and audit engagement partner came to review the audit working papers on the same day towards the completion of the audit fieldwork. The audit partner asked me if there had been any issues on the sections of the audit which I had worked on, and when I said there had been no problems, he signed off the working papers after a quick look through them.

When reading the company's board minutes, I found several references to the audit engagement partner, Joe Lantau. It appears that Joe recommended that the company use the services of his brother, Mick Lantau, for advice on business development, as Mick is a management consultant. Based on that recommendation, Mick has provided a consultancy service to Stanley Co since September 20X5. I mentioned this to Joe, and he told me not to record it in the audit working papers or to discuss it with anyone.'

Required

Comment on the quality of the audit performed discussing the quality control, ethical and other professional issues raised. **(13 marks)**

(b) Kowloon Co works on contracts to design and manufacture large items of medical equipment such as radiotherapy and X-ray machines. The company specialises in the design, production and installation of bespoke machines under contract with individual customers, which are usually private medical companies. The draft financial statements recognise profit before tax of $950,000 and total assets of $7.5 million.

The audit senior has left the following note for your attention:

'One of Kowloon Co's major customers is the Bay Medical Centre (BMC), a private hospital. In June 20X5 a contract was entered into, under the terms of which Kowloon Co would design a new radiotherapy machine for BMC. The machine is based on a new innovation, and is being developed for the specific requirements of BMC. It was estimated that the design and production of the machine would take 18 months with estimated installation in December 20X6. As at 31 December 20X5, Kowloon Co had invested heavily in the contract, and design costs totalling $350,000 have been recognised as work in progress in the draft statement of financial position. Deferred income of $200,000 is also recognised as a current liability, representing a payment made by BMC to finance part of the design costs. No other accounting entries have been made in respect of the contract with BMC.

As part of our subsequent events review, inspection of correspondence between Kowloon Co and BMC indicates that the contract has been cancelled by BMC as it is unable to pay for its completion. It appears that BMC lost a significant amount of funding towards the end of 20X5, impacting significantly on the financial position of the company. The manager responsible for the BMC contract confirms that BMC contacted him about the company's financial difficulties in December 20X5.

The matter has been discussed with Kowloon Co's finance director, who has stated that he is satisfied with the current accounting treatment and is not proposing to make any adjustments in light of the cancellation of the contract by BMC. The finance director has also advised that the loss of BMC as a customer will not be mentioned in the company's integrated report, as the finance director does not consider it significant enough to warrant discussion.

Kowloon Co is currently working on six contracts for customers other than BMC. Our audit evidence concludes that Kowloon Co does not face a threat to its going concern status due to the loss of BMC as a customer.'

Your review of the audit work performed on going concern supports this conclusion.

Required

(i)   Comment on the matters to be considered, and recommend the actions to be taken by the auditor; and   **(7 marks)**

(ii)   Explain the audit evidence you would expect to find in your review of the audit working papers.   **(5 marks)**

(Total = 25 marks)

46 Northwest (P7 Sep/Dec 16) (amended)   49 mins

You are an audit manager at Thornhill & Co responsible for the audit of Northwest Co, a subsidiary of Valerian Co. A different audit firm is responsible for the audit of Valerian Co and the Valerian Group financial statements.

The audit of the financial statements of Northwest Co for the year ended 31 July 20X6 is nearing completion, but the following issues require your attention before the auditor's report is signed and your final communication is made to the group auditor in response to their request for information. The draft financial statements of Northwest Co recognise a loss before tax of $50,000.

Northwest Co has been loss making for several years and it generates insufficient cash to meet its significant debt obligations. The company relies on support from Valerian Co in order to continue trading. The management of Valerian Co has confirmed verbally that it will continue to support Northwest Co, but has not provided a formal letter of support despite a number of requests.

You are aware that Valerian Co is the subject of a major lawsuit following an industrial accident which resulted in significant pollution of local agricultural land and, most seriously, loss of life. You attempted to discuss the matter with the directors of Valerian Co but they refused, saying that it had already been investigated by the group auditor. The group auditor informed you that the case is ongoing and that they have obtained satisfactory representations from both management and legal advisers stating that they were confident of successfully defending the claim. When you asked for copies of the representations, the group auditor refused saying it was a matter relevant to the parent company and that it was not relevant to the audit of Northwest Co.

Shortly after making your enquiries, you received a phone call from the group engagement partner who said that the board of Valerian Co was concerned that you might modify the auditor's report of Northwest Co. He also said that, as the only person with full oversight of audit matters relating to the Valerian Group, he did not think that it would be necessary to modify the auditor's report of Northwest Co and that he would oppose any attempt to do so. He suggested that if the debt in the financial statements of Northwest Co was the reason for seeking parental support that he would transfer it to the Group and the letter of support would no longer be necessary.

Required

(a)   Discuss the considerations the Group auditor should have made prior to requesting Thornhill & Co to perform work on the financial statements of a component.   **(6 marks)**

(b)   Discuss how professional scepticism should be applied to the statements made by the management and auditors of Valerian Co regarding the outstanding legal case.   **(5 marks)**

(c)   Comment on the ethical and professional issues raised, considering any implications for completion of the audit, in respect of:

       (i)   The evidence obtained in relation to the support offered by Valerian Co
       (ii)   The request not to modify the auditor's report of Northwest Co

       Note. The total marks will be split equally between each part.   **(14 marks)**

(Total = 25 marks)

COMPLETION, REVIEW AND REPORTING

Questions 47 to 63 cover Completion, review and reporting, the subject of Part E of the BPP Workbook for AAA.

47 Rope (P7 Sep/Dec 16) (amended)   49 mins

You are the manager responsible for the audit of Rope Co, a new audit client, for the year ended 30 September 20X6. During a visit to the team performing the fieldwork, the audit senior shows you a cash flow forecast covering six-month periods to 30 September 20X8 as prepared by management as part of their assessment of the going concern status of the company. The audit senior asks whether any of the forecast cash flows disclosed require any further investigation during the audit fieldwork.

The actual and forecast six-monthly cash flows for Rope Co for the periods ended:

	Actual				Forecast	
	31 March 20X6 $'000	30 Sept 20X6 $'000	31 March 20X7 $'000	30 Sept 20X7 $'000	31 March 20X8 $'000	30 Sept 20X8 $'000
Operating cash flows						
Receipts from customers	13,935	14,050	14,300	14,700	14,950	15,400
Payments to suppliers	(10,725)	(10,850)	(11,050)	(11,400)	(11,600)	(12,000)
Salaries	(1,250)	(1,300)	(1,275)	(1,326)	(1,301)	(1,353)
Other operating cash payments	(1,875)	(1,850)	(1,913)	(1,887)	(1,951)	(1,925)
Other cash flows						
Sale of investments	–	–	–	–	–	500
Repayment of J Stewart loan	–	–	–	–	–	(500)
Repayment of bank loan	–	–	–	–	(1,500)	–
Receipt of bank loan	–	–	–	–	1,500	–
Cash flow for the period	85	50	62	87	98	122
Opening cash	(275)	(190)	(140)	(78)	9	107
Closing cash	(190)	(140)	(78)	9	107	229

The following additional information has been provided in support of the forecasts:

- Receipts from customers and payments to suppliers have been estimated based on detailed sales forecasts prepared by the sales director.

- Salaries and overheads have been estimated as the prior year cost plus general inflation of 2%.

- The bank loan expires on 5 January 20X8. The finance director expects to take out a matching facility with the current lender to pay off the existing debt.

- On 1 October 20X5, the chief executive, Mr J Stewart, gave the company a three-year, interest-free loan secured by a fixed charge over the operational assets of Rope Co. The audit team was unaware of this loan prior to obtaining the cash flow forecast.

- The directors plan to sell some investments in listed shares to fund the repayment of the chief executive's loan. At 30 September 20X6, the investments were carried in the statement of financial position at their fair value of $350,000.

Required

(a) Evaluate the appropriateness of the cash flow forecast prepared by Rope Co and recommend the further audit procedures which should be performed. **(14 marks)**

(b) Comment on the matters to be considered in respect of the loan from Mr J Stewart. **(3 marks)**

The finance director of Rope Co, Uma Thorton, has requested that your firm present the draft financial statements into a format appropriate for publication at the forthcoming company general meeting. Uma has also commented that the previous auditors did not use a liability disclaimer in their auditor's report, and would like more information about the use of liability disclaimer paragraphs.

Required

(c) Discuss the ethical issues raised by the request for your firm to prepare the financial statements of Rope Co. **(3 marks)**

(d) In the context of a standard unmodified auditor's report, describe the content of a liability disclaimer paragraph, and discuss whether its use should be considered appropriate. **(5 marks)**

(Total = 25 marks)

48 Kandinsky (P7 Sep/Dec 15)   49 mins

Malevich & Co is a firm of Chartered Certified Accountants offering audit and assurance services to a large portfolio of clients. You are a manager in the audit department responsible for the audit of two clients, Kandinsky Co and the Rothko University, both of which have a financial year ended 31 July 20X5. The audits of both clients are being completed and you are reviewing issues which have been raised by the audit seniors.

(a) Kandinsky Co is a manufacturer of luxury food items including chocolate and other confectionery which are often sold as gift items individually or in hampers containing a selection of expensive items from the range of products. Due to an economic recession sales of products have fallen sharply this year, and measures have been implemented to support the company's cash flow. You are aware that the company only has $150,000 in cash at the year end.

Extracts from the draft financial statements and other relevant information are given below.

	Note	July 20X5 (Draft) $'000	July 20X4 (Actual) $'000
Revenue		2,440	3,950
Operating expenses		(2,100)	(2,800)
Finance charge		(520)	(500)
(Loss)/profit before tax		(180)	650
Total assets		10,400	13,500
Long-term liabilities – bank loan	1	3,500	3,000
Short-term liabilities – trade payables	2	900	650
Disclosed in notes to financial statements:			
Undrawn borrowing facilities	3	500	1,000
Contingent liability	4	120	–

Notes

1   The bank loan was extended in March 20X5 by drawing on the borrowing facilities offered by the bank. The loan carries a fixed interest rate and is secured on the company's property including the head office and manufacturing site. The first repayment of loan capital is due on 30 June 20X6 when $350,000 is due to be paid.

2   Kandinsky Co renegotiated its terms of trade with its main supplier of cocoa beans, and extended payment terms from 50 days to 80 days in order to improve working capital.

3   The borrowing facilities are due to be reviewed by the bank in April 20X6 and contain covenants including that interest cover is maintained at 2, and the ratio of bank loan to operating profit does not exceed 4:1.

4   The contingent liability relates to a letter of support which Kandinsky Co has provided to its main supplier of cane sugar which is facing difficult trading conditions.

Required

In respect of the audit of Kandinsky Co:

(i)   Evaluate the matters which may cast significant doubt on the company's ability to continue as a going concern; and   **(9 marks)**

(ii)   Recommend the audit procedures to be performed in relation to the going concern matters   identified.
(6 marks)

(b)   The Rothko University, a public sector entity, is a small university with approximately 2,000 students, which was established 10 years ago and specialises in vocational study programmes leading to the award of degrees in business, accountancy, finance, law and marketing. The highest performing students achieve a distinction on completing their degree programme, indicating excellence in the knowledge and understanding of their subject. Students pay tuition fees of $10,000 per year, and the degree programme is typically three years long.

The audit work in respect of the year ended 31 July 20X5 is almost complete, but the audit senior has not yet completed the audit work in respect of performance information which is being published with the annual financial statements for the first time this year. It is a requirement in the jurisdiction in which the Rothko University is located that the performance information is audited as part of the external audit.

Details of the performance information are given below.

Performance area	Performance measure	20X5 result
Graduation rate	% of students who complete their degree programme	85%
Academic performance	% of students achieving a distinction	20%
Employability	% of students who on graduation obtain graduate level employment	65%
Course satisfaction	% of students who rate their university experience as excellent or very good	70%

Required

(i)   Discuss the relevance and measurability of the reported performance information; and

(ii)   Recommend the examination procedures to be used in auditing the performance information.

Note. The total marks will be split equally between each part.   **(10 marks)**

(Total = 25 marks)

49 Butler (P7 6/11) (amended)   49 mins

(a)   Butler Co is a new audit client of your firm. You are the manager responsible for the audit of the financial statements for the year ended 31 May 20X1. Butler Co designs and manufactures aircraft engines and spare parts, and is a subsidiary of a multi-national group. There are concerns about the future of the company: against a background of economic recession, sales have been declining, several significant customer contracts have been cancelled unexpectedly, and competition from overseas has damaged the market share previously enjoyed by Butler Co.

Extracts from the draft financial statements are shown below, together with a cash flow forecast for the three months after the year end, which was prepared by Butler Co.

STATEMENT OF FINANCIAL POSITION

	Notes	31 May 20X1 Draft $m	31 May 20X0 Actual $m
Assets			
Non-current assets			
Intangible assets	1	200	180
Property, plant and equipment	2	1,300	1,200
Deferred tax asset	3	235	20
Financial assets		25	35
		1,760	1,435
Current assets			
Inventory		1,300	800
Trade receivables		2,100	1,860
		3,400	2,660
Total assets		5,160	4,095
Equity and liabilities			
Equity			
Share capital		300	300
Retained earnings		(525)	95
		(225)	395
Non-current liabilities			
Long-term borrowings	4	1,900	1,350
Provisions	5	185	150
		2,085	1,500
Current liabilities			
Short-term borrowings	6	800	400
Trade payables		2,500	1,800
		3,300	2,200
Total equity and liabilities		5,160	4,095

Notes

1   Intangible assets comprise goodwill on the acquisition of subsidiaries ($80 million), and development costs capitalised on engine development projects ($120 million).

2   Property, plant and equipment includes land and buildings valued at $25 million, over which a fixed charge exists.

3   The deferred tax asset has arisen following several loss-making years suffered by the company. The asset represents the tax benefit of unutilised tax losses carried forward.

4   Long-term borrowings include a debenture due for repayment in July 20X2, and a loan from Butler Co's parent company due for repayment in December 20X2.

5   Provisions relate to warranties provided to customers.

6   Short-term borrowings comprise an overdraft ($25 million), a short term loan ($60 million) due for repayment in August 20X1, and a bank loan ($715 million) repayable in September 20X1.

ATTACHMENT: CASH FLOW FORECAST FOR THE THREE MONTHS TO 31 AUGUST 20X1

	30 June 20X1 $m	31 July 20X1 $m	31 August 20X1 $m
Cash inflows			
Cash receipts from customers (Note 1)	175	195	220
Loan receipt (Note 2)		150	
Government subsidy (Note 3)			50
Sales of financial assets	50		
Total cash inflows	225	345	270
Cash outflows			
Operating cash outflows	200	200	290
Interest payments	40	40	40
Loan repayment			60
Total cash outflows	240	240	390
Net cash flow for the month	(15)	105	(120)
Opening cash	(25)	(40)	65
Closing cash	(40)	65	(55)

Notes

This cash flow forecast has been prepared by the management of Butler Co, and is based on the following assumptions.

1   Cash receipts from customers should accelerate given the anticipated improvement in economic conditions. In addition, the company has committed extra resources to the credit control function, in order to speed up collection of overdue debts.

2   The loan expected to be received in July 20X1 is currently being negotiated with our parent company, Rubery Co.

3   The government subsidy will be received once our application has been approved. The subsidy is awarded to companies which operate in areas of high unemployment and it subsidises the wages and salaries paid to staff.

Required

(i)   Review the draft statement of financial position and cash flow forecast, and identify and explain any matters which may cast significant doubt on the company's ability to continue as a going concern   **(9 marks)**

(ii) Recommend the principal audit procedures to be carried out on the cash flow forecast, and identify any additional information that would be needed in order to carry out these procedures   **(10 marks)**

Note. The split of the mark allocation is shown above.

(b)   Given the information provided relating to Butler Co, it is likely that the auditor may conclude on completion of all necessary audit procedures, that the use of the going concern assumption in the financial statements is appropriate, but that a material uncertainty, or several uncertainties, exist regarding the company's ability to continue as a going concern.

Required

If audit procedures indicate that one or more material uncertainties exist regarding Butler Co's ability to continue as a going concern, explain the matters that should be considered in forming the audit opinion and the potential impacts on the auditor's report.   **(6 marks)**

Note. Assume it is 7 June 20X1.   **(Total = 25 marks)**

50 Yew (P7 12/11) (amended)   49 mins

(a)   Auditors should accept some of the blame when a company on which they have expressed an unmodified audit opinion subsequently fails, and they should also do more to highlight going concern problems being faced by a company.

Required

Discuss this statement.   **(7 marks)**

(b)   You are the manager responsible for the audit of Yew Co, a company which designs and develops aircraft engines. The audit for the year ended 31 July 20X1 is nearing completion and the audit senior has left the following file note for your attention.

'I have just returned from a meeting with the management of Yew Co, and there is a matter I want to bring to your attention. Yew Co's statement of financial position recognises an intangible asset of $12.5 million in respect of capitalised research and development costs relating to new aircraft engine designs. However, market research conducted by Yew Co in relation to these new designs indicated that there would be little demand in the near future for such designs. Management has provided written representation that they agree with the results of the market research.

'Currently, Yew Co has a cash balance of only $125,000 and members of the management team have expressed concerns that the company is finding it difficult to raise additional finance.

'The new aircraft designs have been discussed in the chairman's statement which is to be published with the financial statements. The discussion states that 'developments of new engine designs are underway, and we believe that these new designs will become a significant source of income for Yew Co in the next 12 months.

'Yew Co's draft financial statements include profit before tax of $23 million, and total assets of $210 million.

'Yew Co is due to publish its annual report next week, so we need to consider the impact of this matter urgently.'

Required

Discuss the implications of the audit senior's file note on the completion of the audit and on the auditor's report, recommending any further actions that should be taken by the auditor.
     (12 marks)

(c)   You are responsible for answering technical queries from other managers and partners of your firm. An audit partner left the following note on your desk this morning.

(i)   'I am about to draft the auditor's report for my client, Sycamore Co. I am going on holiday tomorrow and want to have the auditor's report signed and dated before I leave. The only thing outstanding is the written representation from management – I have verbally confirmed the contents with the finance director who agreed to send the

representations to the audit manager within the next few days. I presume this is acceptable?'

(ii)   'We are auditing Sycamore Co for the first time. The prior period financial statements were audited by another firm. We are aware that the auditor's opinion on the prior period was qualified due to a material misstatement of trade receivables. We have obtained sufficient appropriate evidence that the matter giving rise to the misstatement has been resolved and I am happy to issue an unmodified opinion. But should I refer to the prior year modification in this year's auditor's report?'

Required

Respond to the audit partner's comments.   **(6 marks)**

Note. The split of the mark allocation is shown within the question.   **(Total = 25 marks)**

51 Fern (P7 Mar/Jun 17) (amended)   49 mins

(a)   You are a manager working in the public sector audit department of Fern & Co. You are responsible for the audit of Moosewood Hospital, for the year ended 31 March 20X7. You have recently visited the audit team, who are currently on site performing the fieldwork, to review the work performed to date and to discuss their progress. During your visit the audit senior informed you of the following matter:

During a review of the valuation of medical inventories, including medicines used in a variety of treatments at the hospital, it was noted that a number of items had passed their recommended use by dates. These were recorded on an inventory spreadsheet maintained by the financial controller and were easy to spot because they were highlighted in red. One of the audit team inspected a sample of the inventories in question and confirmed that their use by dates had expired. When asked about this, the financial controller stated that the audit team must be mistaken. The audit team requested to look at the spreadsheet again but he refused. The next day the finance director confronted the audit team accusing them of extending their investigations 'beyond their remit'. He also threatened to remove them from the premises if they continued to ask questions which were not relevant to the audit of the hospital's financial statements. Since then the audit team have been unable to complete their audit of medical inventories. They have also noted that the room where the inventories were previously kept has been emptied.

Required

Identify and explain the ethical and professional issues raised and recommend any actions which should be taken in respect of the matter described by the audit senior.   **(9 marks)**

(b)   You are the manager responsible for the audit of Lear Co, a jewellery manufacturer and retailer. The final audit for the year ended 31 March 20X7 is nearing completion and you are reviewing the audit working papers. The draft financial statements recognise total assets of $1,919 million (20X6 – $1,889 million), revenue of $1,052 million (20X6 – $997 million) and profit before tax of $107 million (20X6 – $110 million).

Each year management makes a provision for jewellery returned under warranty. It is based upon an estimate of returns levels for each product type (rings, bracelets, necklaces, watches, earrings, etc) and is calculated on an annual basis by the sales director. The breakdown for the current provision, as extracted from the notes to the financial statements, is as follows:

	$m
At 1 April 20X6	11.5
Provisions charged during the year	0.5
Provisions utilised during the year	(1.9)
Unutilised provisions reversed	(3.1)
At 31 March 20X7	7.0

Required

Comment on the matters to be considered, and explain the audit evidence you should expect to find during your file review in respect the issue described above. **(5 marks)**

(c) You are also currently involved in the completion stage of the audit of Rocket Co, which is a listed client operating in the engineering industry. The company manufactures machinery for use in the aircraft, defence and marine sectors. The audit for the year ended 30 April 20X7 is almost complete. The revenue and profit before tax figures recognised in the draft financial statements are $1,437 million and $139 million, respectively (20X6 – $1,489 million and $175 million respectively).

Audit procedures identified two sales transactions in the final quarter of the year that related to two different customers but where the goods were delivered to the same location. Further investigations revealed that the goods were delivered to a third party, who agreed to store them until the customers were ready to receive delivery. The goods have yet to be delivered to the customers because they are both building new facilities and neither is sufficiently progressed to receive the new machinery. The contract terms explicitly state that Rocket Co is obliged to deliver the goods to the customers for final inspection and acceptance and the client has not agreed to any consequent amendments to these terms. The sales invoices were raised and the revenue recognised upon despatch of the goods to the storage facility. During discussions with the audit team, the finance director stated that the company had fulfilled its contractual obligations to provide the goods by a specified date. The revenue attributable to the two transactions totalled $17 million.

Required

(i) Comment upon the matter described above and explain the further actions necessary before the auditor's report can be signed. **(6 marks)**

(ii) Discuss the implications for the auditor's report if no adjustments are made to the financial statements. **(5 marks)**

(Total = 25 marks)

52 Boston (P7 Mar/Jun 16) (amended)   49 mins

You are the manager responsible for the audit of Boston Co, a producer of chocolate and confectionery. The audit of the financial statements for the year ended 31 December 20X5 is nearly complete and you are reviewing the audit working papers. The financial statements recognise revenue of $76 million, profit before tax for the year of $6.4 million and total assets of $104 million.

The summary of uncorrected misstatements included in Boston Co's audit working papers, including notes, is shown below. The audit engagement partner is holding a meeting with the management team of Boston Co next week, at which the uncorrected misstatements will be discussed.

Summary of uncorrected misstatements:	Statement of profit or loss		Statement of financial position	
	Debit $	Credit $	Debit $	Credit $
(i) Impairment	400,000			400,000
(ii) Borrowing costs		75,000	75,000	
(iii) Irrecoverable debt	65,000			65,000
(iv) Investment		43,500	43,500	
Totals	465,000	118,500	118,500	465,000

(i)   During the year Boston Co impaired one of its factories. The carrying value of the assets attributable to the factory as a single, cash-generating unit totalled $3.6 million at the year end. The fair value less costs of disposal and the value in use were estimated to be $3 million and $3.5 million respectively and accordingly the asset was written down by $100,000 to reflect the impairment. Audit procedures revealed that management used growth rates attributable to the company as a whole to estimate value in use. Using growth rates attributable to the factory specifically, the audit team estimated the value in use to be $3.1 million.

(ii)   Interest charges of $75,000 relating to a loan taken out during the year to finance the construction of a new manufacturing plant were included in finance charges recognised in profit for the year. The manufacturing plant is due for completion in November 20X6.

(iii)   One of Boston Co's largest customers, Cleveland Co, is experiencing financial difficulties. At the year end, Cleveland Co owed Boston Co $100,000, against which Boston Co made a 5% specific allowance. Shortly after the year end Cleveland Co paid $30,000 of the outstanding amount due but has since experienced further problems, leading to their primary lender presenting a formal request that Cleveland Co be liquidated. If successful, only secured creditors are likely to receive any reimbursement.

(iv)   During the year Boston Co purchased 150,000 shares in Nebraska Co for $4.00 per share. Boston Co classified the investment as a financial asset held at fair value through profit or loss. On 31 December 20X5, the shares of Nebraska Co were trading for $4.29. At the year end the carrying value of the investment in Boston Co's financial statements was $600,000.

Required

(a)   Explain the matters which should be discussed with management in relation to each of the uncorrected misstatements, including an assessment of their individual impact on the financial statements; and   **(14 marks)**

(b)   Assuming that management does not adjust any of the misstatements, discuss the effect on the audit opinion and auditor's report.   **(6 marks)**

As a result of the audit engagement partner's meeting with management, all uncorrected misstatements were corrected and an auditor's report was issued with an unmodified opinion.

Three days after the auditor's report was issued, management informed the audit engagement partner that it had discovered that significant errors had been made in the processing of the company's payroll. The overall effect of these errors is not yet clear, but they appear to have been ongoing for several months and are likely to be significant.

Required

(c)   Explain the auditor's responsibilities in relation to this matter, and the actions that should be taken by the auditor.   **(5 marks)**

                                                                                        (Total = 25 marks)

53 Coram (Sep 18)   49 mins

(a)   You are an audit manager in Coram & Co, a firm of Chartered Certified Accountants. The audit of one of your clients, Clark Co, for the year ended 31 May 20X8 is nearly complete and the auditor's report is due to be issued next week. Clark Co is an unlisted, family owned business which specialises in the service and repair of both commercial and privately owned motor vehicles. The company operates from seven geographically distinct sites, each of which is considered a separate cash generating unit for impairment review purposes. The draft financial statements recognise profit before taxation for the year of $2.3 million and total assets of $22 million.

The schedule of uncorrected misstatements included in Clark Co's audit working papers and prepared by the audit supervisor is shown below. You are due to attend a meeting with the

BPP
LEARNING

finance director of Clark Co tomorrow, at which the uncorrected misstatements will be discussed.

		Statement of profit or loss		Statement of financial position	
Schedule of uncorrected misstatements		Debit $	Credit $	Debit $	Credit $
(i)	**Lease of testing equipment**				
	• lease assets			475,000	
	• lease liabilities				475,000
(ii)	**Legal claim**				
	• contingent assets			1,200,000	
	• provision for liabilities				1,200,000
(iii)	**Asset impairment**				
	• assets				85,000
	• expenses	85,000			
Total		85,000	–	1,675,000	1,760,000

(i) Lease of testing equipment

In the jurisdiction in which Clark Co operates, all motor vehicles over three years old are required to undergo an annual test of vehicle safety and roadworthiness. The annual test requires specialist testing equipment which is inspected by government officials on a regular basis. Following inspection visits in May 20X8, the government inspection report required Clark Co to replace the testing equipment at three of its sites. In order to comply with this requirement, Clark Co has agreed to lease new testing equipment from a leasing company on six-month leases. Under the terms of the leases, the company has no option to purchase the equipment. The testing equipment was made available for use by Clark Co at each of the three sites on 31 May 20X8. The client has capitalised leases with a total carrying amount of $625,000 at two of the sites but has elected to take advantage of the IFRS 16 *Leases* exemption not to capitalise short-term leases at the largest of the three sites. As a result, the present value of the lease payments of $475,000 relating to this site has not been recognised on the company's statement of financial position. **(7 marks)**

(ii) Legal claim

A customer of Clark Co successfully sued the company for negligence in April 20X8 after suffering a personal injury at one of its sites. The court awarded the customer $1.2 million in damages and this had not yet been paid as at 31 May 20X8. The audit working papers include a copy of a verified letter dated 25 May 20X8 from an insurance company confirming that the claim is fully covered under Clark Co's public liability insurance policy. On the basis that the company has no net liability as a result of the claim, the finance director has not recognised any amounts in the financial statements and has not made any disclosures in relation to the matter. **(5 marks)**

(iii) Asset impairment

During the year, a significant new competitor entered the market place at one of Clark Co's seven sites. As a result, the site has experienced a decline in market share and revenue. The company has therefore conducted an impairment test on the site's assets. The company's working papers for the impairment test have been audited and the following figures have been agreed by the audit team:

	Site assets
	$
Carrying amount on statement of financial position as at 31 May 20X8	3.6 million
Value in use	2.9 million
Fair value	3.9 million

Related costs of selling the assets:

– legal costs	126,000
– transaction taxes	174,000
– costs of removing the assets	85,000
– costs of reorganising the business following the asset disposals	96,000

On the basis of the results of these figures, the client has calculated the recoverable amount of the assets as $3.6 million and concluded that the site has not suffered an impairment. No adjustments have therefore been made to the financial statements in this regard. **(5 marks)**

Required

Recommend and explain the matters which should be discussed with management in relation to each of the proposed adjustments, including an assessment of their individual impact on the financial statements and on the auditor's opinion if management does not make the proposed adjustments.

Note. The split of the mark allocation is shown against each of the issues above.

(b)   Your client portfolio as an audit manager at Coram & Co also includes Turner Co which is a listed financial institution offering loans and credit facilities to both commercial and retail customers. You have received an email from the audit supervisor who is currently supervising interim testing on systems and controls in relation to the audit for the year ending 31 October 20X8. The email gives the following details for your consideration:

One of the audit team members, Janette Stott, has provisionally agreed to take out a loan with Turner Co to finance the purchase of a domestic residence. The loan will be secured on the property and the client's business manager has promised Janette that he will ensure that she gets 'the very best deal which the bank can offer.'

The payroll manager at Turner Co has asked the audit supervisor if it would be possible for Coram & Co to provide a member of staff on secondment to work in the payroll department. The payroll manager has struggled to recruit a new supervisor for the organisation's main payroll system and wants to assign a qualified member of the audit firm's staff for an initial period of six months.

Required

Comment on the ethical and professional issues raised in respect of the audit of Turner Co and recommend any actions to be taken by the audit firm. **(8 marks)**

(Total = 25 marks)

54 Dexter (P7 12/08)   39 mins

You are the manager responsible for performing hot reviews on audit files where there is a potential disagreement between your firm and the client regarding a material issue. You are reviewing the going concern section of the audit file of Dexter Co, whose financial statements are prepared on the going concern basis of accounting. Dexter Co's financial statements show an increase in profit before tax from the previous year, but the company has experienced a number of difficulties, such as

BPP
LEARNING

the resignations of key senior management personnel, and a shortage of some of the principal raw materials that are needed for production. Dexter Co has a positive cash balance.

Dexter Co has made a number of new appointments to its senior management team since the end of the reporting period, who have undertaken a reassessment of the company's immediate objectives. With a renewed focus on generating cash from operations, the company has sought to extend its payables payment period from 30 to 45 days, and its receivables collection period from 20 to 60 days.

Dexter Co has applied for a new loan that would provide it with a significant cash boost, which it hopes to use to fund investment in a new production facility. The outcome of this application is not yet known.

Required

(a) (i)   Compare and contrast the responsibilities of management with those of auditors, in relation to the assessment of going concern.

     (ii) Explain the matters to consider, and the audit evidence you should expect to find, in your file review in relation to Dexter Co's assessment of the going concern assumption.

(7 marks)

The audit working papers indicate that since Dexter Co is currently trying to raise finance to fund operating cash flows, if the finance is not received then this will give rise to a significant doubt over the going concern status of the company. The working papers conclude that the going concern assumption is appropriate, but it is recommended that the financial statements should contain a note explaining the cash flow problems faced by the company, along with a description of the finance being sought, and an evaluation of the going concern status of the company. The directors do not wish to include the note in the financial statements.

Required

(b) Consider and comment on the possible reasons why the directors of Dexter Co are reluctant to provide the note to the financial statements. **(5 marks)**

(c) Identify and discuss the implications for the auditor's report if:

     (i)   The directors refuse to include the disclosure note   **(4 marks)**
     (ii) The directors agree to include the disclosure note   **(4 marks)**

(Total = 20 marks)

55 Willis (P7 12/10) (amended)   49 mins

(a) You are the manager responsible for the audit of Willis Co, a large client of your audit firm (Neeson & Co) which operates in the pharmaceutical industry. The audit work for the year ended 31 August 20X0 is nearly complete, and you are reviewing the draft auditor's report which has been prepared by the audit senior. You are aware that Willis Co is developing a new drug and has incurred significant research and development costs during the year, most of which have been capitalised as an intangible asset. The asset is recognised at a value of $4.4 million, the total assets recognised on the draft statement of financial position are $55 million, and Willis Co has a draft profit before tax of $3.1 million.

Having reviewed the audit working papers, you are also aware that management has not allowed the audit team access to the results of scientific tests and trials performed on the new drug being developed.

An extract from the draft auditor's report is shown below.

> **Basis of opinion (extract)**
>
> Evidence available to us in respect of the intangible asset capitalised was limited, because of restrictions imposed on our work by management. As a result of this we have been unable to verify the appropriateness of the amount capitalised, and we are worried that the asset may be overvalued. Because of the significance of the item, and the lack of integrity shown by management, we have been unable to form a view on the financial statements as a whole.
>
> **Opinion (extract): Disclaimer on view given by financial statements**
>
> Because of the lack of evidence that we could gain over the intangible asset, we are unable to form an opinion as to whether the financial statements are properly prepared in accordance with the relevant financial reporting framework.

Required

(i) Critically appraise the draft auditor's report of Willis Co for the year ended 31 August 20X0, prepared by the audit senior.

Note. You are **NOT** required to redraft the extracts from the auditor's report.

(9 marks)

(ii) Identify and explain any other matters to be considered, and the actions to be taken by the auditor, in respect of the management-imposed limitation on scope. **(5 marks)**

(b) You are also responsible for the audit of Moore Co, with a year ended 30 September 20X0. The following notes have been left for your attention by the audit senior.

'Our audit testing performed so far on trade payables revealed some internal control deficiencies. Supplier statement reconciliations have not always been performed by the client, and invoices were often not approved before payment. We have found a few errors in the payables ledger and the individual accounts of suppliers making up the trade payables balance, the total of which is material to the statement of financial position.'

Required

Recommend the further actions that should be taken by the auditor, and outline any reporting requirements in respect of the internal control deficiencies identified. **(5 marks)**

(c) You have set up an internal discussion board, on which current issues are debated by employees and partners of Neeson & Co. One posting to the board concerned the compulsory rotation of audit firms, whereby it has been suggested in the press that after a pre-determined period, an audit firm must resign from office, to be replaced by a new audit provider.

Required

(i) Explain the ethical threats created by a long association with an audit client.
(ii) Evaluate the advantages and disadvantages of compulsory audit firm rotation.

(6 marks)

(Total = 25 marks)

56 Newman (P7 12/10) (amended)   49 mins

You are a manager in Newman & Co, a global firm of Chartered Certified Accountants. You are responsible for evaluating proposed engagements and for recommending to a team of partners whether or not an engagement should be accepted by your firm.

Eastwood Co is an existing audit client and is an international mail services operator, with a global network including 220 countries and 300,000 employees. The company offers mail and freight services to individual and corporate customers, as well as storage and logistical services.

BPP
LEARNING

Eastwood Co takes its corporate social responsibility seriously, and publishes social and environmental key performance indicators (KPIs) in a Sustainability Report, which is published with the financial statements in the annual report. Partly in response to requests from shareholders and pressure groups, Eastwood Co's management has decided that in the forthcoming annual report, the KPIs should be accompanied by an independent assurance report. An approach has been made to your firm to provide this report in addition to the audit.

To help in your evaluation of this potential engagement, you have been given an extract from the draft Sustainability Report, containing some of the KPIs published by Eastwood Co. In total, 25 environmental KPIs, and 50 social KPIs are disclosed.

Extract from Sustainability Report	Year ended 31 October 20Y0 Draft	Year ended 31 October 20X9 Actual
CO2 emissions (million tonnes)	26.8	28.3
Energy use (million kilowatt hours)	4,895	5,250
Charitable donations ($ million)	10.5	8.2
Number of serious accidents in the workplace	60	68
Average annual spend on training per employee	$180	$175

You have also had a meeting with Ali Monroe, the manager responsible for the audit of Eastwood Co, and notes of the meeting are given below.

Notes from meeting with audit manager, Ali Monroe

Newman & Co has audited Eastwood Co for three years, and it is a major audit client of our firm, due to its global presence and recent listing on two major stock exchanges. The audit is managed from our office in Oldtown, which is also the location of the global headquarters of Eastwood Co.

We have not done any work on the KPIs, other than review them for consistency, as we would with any 'other information' issued with the financial statements. The KPIs are produced by Eastwood Co's Sustainability Department, located in Fartown. We have not visited Eastwood Co's offices in Fartown as it is in a remote location overseas, and the departments based there are not relevant to the audit.

We have performed audit procedures on the charitable donations, as this is disclosed in a note to the financial statements, and our evidence indicates that there have been donations of $9 million this year, which is the amount disclosed in the note. However, the draft KPI is a different figure – $10.5 million, and this is the figure highlighted in the draft Chairman's Statement as well as the draft Sustainability Report. $9 million is material to the financial statements.

The audit work is nearly complete, and the annual report is to be published in about four weeks, in time for the company meeting, scheduled for 31 January 20Y1.

Your firm has recently established a sustainability reporting assurance team based in Oldtown, and if the engagement to report on the Sustainability Report is accepted, it would be performed by members of that team, who would not be involved with the audit.

Required

(a) Identify and explain the matters that should be considered in evaluating the invitation to perform an assurance engagement on the Sustainability Report of Eastwood Co. **(11 marks)**

(b) Recommend procedures that could be used to verify the following draft KPIs.

   (i) The number of serious accidents in the workplace
   (ii) The average annual spend on training per employee. **(6 marks)**

(c) You have a trainee accountant assigned to you, who has read the notes taken at your meeting with Ali Monroe. She is unsure of the implications of the charitable donations being disclosed

as a different figure in the financial statements compared with the other information published in the annual report.

Required

Prepare briefing notes to be used in a discussion with the trainee accountant, in which you:

(i)   Explain the responsibility of the auditor in relation to other information published with the financial statements.

(ii)   Recommend the action to be taken by Newman & Co if the figure relating to charitable donations in the other information is not amended.   **(8 marks)**

(Total = 25 marks)

57 Marr (P7 6/14) (amended)   **49 mins**

(a)   Your firm is responsible for the audit of Marr Co, a listed company with a year ended 28 February 20X4. The draft financial statements recognise profit for the year of $11 million. The audit for the year end is nearing completion, and several matters have been highlighted for your attention by another audit senior, Xi Smith. The matters have been discussed with management and will not be adjusted in the financial statements:

1   In January 20X4 a major customer went into administration. There was a balance of $2.5 million owing to Marr Co from this customer at 28 February 20X4, which is still included in trade receivables.

2   A court case began in December 20X3 involving an ex-employee who is suing Marr Co for unfair dismissal. Lawyers estimate that damages of $50,000 are probable to be paid. The financial statements include a note describing the court case and quantifying the potential damages but no adjustment has been made to include it in the statement of financial position or the statement of profit or loss.

Xi Smith has produced a draft auditor's report for your review, an extract of which is shown below:

Basis for opinion and disclaimer of opinion

We have performed our audit based on a materiality level of $1.5 million. Our audit procedures have proven conclusively that trade receivables are materially misstated. The finance director of Marr Co, Rita Gilmour, has refused to make an adjustment to write off a significant trade receivables balance. Therefore, in our opinion the financial statements of Marr Co are materially misstated and we therefore express a disclaimer of opinion because we do not think they are fairly presented.

Key audit matters

The audit team spent considerable time working on Marr Co's revenue recognition policies, which are highly complicated. We were concerned that Marr Co might recognise revenue too early, but in our opinion revenue is presented fairly in accordance with IFRSs.

Emphasis of Matter paragraph

Marr Co is facing a legal claim for an amount of $50,000 from an ex-employee. In our opinion this amount should be recognised as a provision but it is not included in the statement of financial position. We draw your attention to this breach of the relevant IFRS.

Required

Critically appraise the proposed auditor's report of Marr Co for the year ended 28 February 20X4.

Note. You are **NOT** required to redraft the extracts from the auditor's report.   **(15 marks)**

(b) After this year's audit, Bobby Wellington will have acted as audit engagement partner for Marr Co for seven years. He understands that a new audit partner needs to be appointed to take his place.

Bobby is hoping to stay in contact with the client by acting as the engagement quality control reviewer in forthcoming audits of Marr Co.

Required

Explain the ethical threats raised by the long association of senior audit personnel with an audit client and the relevant safeguards to be applied, and discuss whether Bobby Wellington can act as engagement quality control reviewer in the future audits of Marr Co. **(5 marks)**

(c) Having been appointed as the new audit engagement partner to Marr Co, Afzal Siddiqui has stated that he would like to use 'data analytics' on the next audit engagement. He has heard that many large audit firms now make use of these techniques, but he does not know what the term means.

Required

Explain what the term 'data analytics' means, and discuss current thinking about their anticipated impact on the auditing profession. **(5 marks)**

(Total = 25 marks)

58 Pluto (P7 6/09) (amended) 49 mins

(a) You are a partner at Neptune Co, and are currently conducting several engagement quality control reviews. You are currently reviewing the engagement partner's proposed auditor's report on the financial statements of Pluto Co, a listed company, for the year ended 31 March 20X8. During the year the company has undergone significant reorganisation, involving the discontinuance of two major business segments. Extracts of the proposed auditor's report are shown below.

Basis for adverse opinion arising from material misstatement in respect of IAS 37

The directors have not recognised a provision in relation to redundancy costs associated with the reorganisation during the year. The reason is that they do not feel that a reliable estimate of the amount can be made, and so the recognition criteria of IAS 37 have not been met. We disagree with the directors as we feel that an estimate can be made. This matter is more fully explained in a note to the financial statements. We feel that this is a material misstatement as the profit for the year is overstated.

In our opinion, the financial statements do not give a true and fair view of the financial position of the company as of 31 March 20X8, and of its financial performance and its cash flows for the year then ended in accordance with International Financial Reporting Standards.

Emphasis of Matter

The directors have decided not to disclose the earnings per share for 20X8, as they feel that the figure is materially distorted by significant discontinued operations in the year. Our opinion is not qualified in respect of this matter.

Required

Critically appraise the proposed auditor's report of Pluto Co for the year ended 31 March 20X8.

Note. You are **NOT** required to redraft the extracts from the auditor's report. **(9 marks)**

(b) You are also the engagement quality control reviewer for the audit of the Retriever Group (Retriever), a manufacturer of mobile phones and laptop computers. Retriever obtained a stock exchange listing in July 20X7. The audit of the consolidated financial statements for the year ended 28 February 20X8 is nearing completion.

You have discussed the Retriever audit with some of the junior members of the audit team, one of whom made the following comments about how it was planned and carried out:

'The audit has been quite time-pressured. The audit manager told the juniors not to perform some of the planned audit procedures on items such as directors' emoluments and share capital as they are considered to be low risk. He also instructed us not to use the firm's statistical sampling methods in selecting trade receivables balances for testing, as it would be quicker to pick the sample based on our own judgement.

'Two of the juniors were given the tasks of auditing trade payables and going concern. The audit manager asked us to review each other's work as it would be good training for us, and he didn't have time to review everything.

'I was discussing Retriever's tax position with the financial controller, when she said that she was struggling to calculate the deferred tax asset that should be recognised. The deferred tax asset has arisen because several of Retriever's subsidiaries have been loss-making this year, creating unutilised tax losses. As I had just studied deferred tax at college I did the calculation of Retriever's deferred tax position for her. The audit manager said this saved time as we now would not have to audit the deferred tax figure.

'The financial controller also asked for my advice as to how the tax losses could be utilised by the Retriever Group in the future. I provided her with some tax planning recommendations, for which she was very grateful.'

Required

In relation to the audit of the Retriever Group, evaluate the quality control, ethical and other professional matters arising in respect of the planning and performance of the audit.

(12 marks)

(c) Explain the matters to be considered in deciding who is eligible to perform an engagement quality control review for a listed client. **(4 marks)**

(Total = 25 marks)

59 Burford (P7 12/13) 39 mins

(a) You are the manager responsible for the audit of Burford Co, a company which designs and manufactures engine parts. The audit of the financial statements for the year ended 31 July 20X3 is nearing completion and you are reviewing the working papers of the going concern section of the audit file. The draft financial statements recognise a loss of $500,000 (20X2 – profit of $760,000), and total assets of $13.8 million (20X2 – $14.4 million).

The audit senior has left the following note for your attention.

'I have performed analytical review on Burford Co's year-end financial statements. The current ratio is 0.8 (20X2 – 1.2), the quick ratio is 0.5 (20X2 – 1.6). The latest management accounts show that ratios have deteriorated further since the year end, and the company now has a cash balance of only $25,000. Burford Co has a long-term loan outstanding of $80,000 with a covenant attached, which states that if the current ratio falls below 0.75, the loan can be immediately recalled by the lender.'

You are also aware that one of Burford Co's best-selling products, the QuickFire, has become technically obsolete during 20X3 as customers now prefer more environmentally friendly engine parts. Historically, the QuickFire has generated 45% of the company's revenue. In response to customers' preference, $1.3 million has been spent on designing a new product, the GreenFire, due for launch in February 20X4, which will be marketed as an environmentally friendly product.

A cash flow forecast has been prepared for the year to 31 July 20X4, indicating that based on certain assumptions, the company's cash balance is predicted to increase to $220,000 by the end of the forecast period. Assumptions include:

1   The successful launch of the GreenFire product

2   The sale of plant and machinery which was used to manufacture the QuickFire, generating cash proceeds of $50,000, forecast to take place in January 20X4

3   A reduction in payroll costs of 15%, caused by redundancies in the QuickFire manufacturing plant

4   The receipt of a grant of $30,000 from a government department which encourages innovation in environmentally friendly products, scheduled to be received in February 20X4

Required

(i)   Evaluate the matters that cast doubt on the going concern status of Burford Co.

(6 marks)

(ii)   Explain the audit evidence you should expect to find in your file review in respect of the cash flow forecast.   **(8 marks)**

(b)   Having completed the file review, you have concluded that the use of the going concern assumption is appropriate, but that there is significant doubt over Burford Co's ability to continue as a going concern. You have advised the company's audit committee that a note is required in the financial statements to describe the significant doubt over going concern. The audit committee is reluctant to include a detailed note to the financial statements due to fears that the note will highlight the company's problems and cause further financial difficulties, but have agreed that a brief note will be included.

Required

In respect of the note on going concern to be included in Burford Co's financial statements, discuss the implications for the auditor's report and outline any further actions to be taken by the auditor.   **(6 marks)**

(Total = 20 marks)

60 Basking (P7 Sep/Dec 17)   39 mins

(a)   Discuss the three types of misstatement identified in ISA 450 *Evaluation of Misstatements Identified During the Audit* and comment on why it is important for the auditor to consider the type of misstatement when evaluating their effect on the financial statements and determining the further actions to be taken.   **(5 marks)**

(b)   You are responsible for the audit of Basking Co, a large, listed package delivery company. The audit of the financial statements for the year ended 31 July 20X7 is nearly complete and you are reviewing the audit working papers. The financial statements recognise revenue of $56,360 million (20X6 – $56,245 million), profit for the year of $2,550 million (20X6 – $2,630 million) and total assets of $37,546 million (20X6 – $38,765 million).

The uncorrected misstatements identified during the audit of Basking Co are described below. The audit engagement partner is holding a meeting with the management team of Basking Co next week, at which the uncorrected misstatements will be discussed.

1   The accuracy of the depreciation charge was investigated for a sample of motor vehicles with a carrying value of $4.5 million. The investigation revealed that the accounting system had failed to correctly depreciate vehicles acquired during the year.

Consequently, depreciation in the sample had been understated, and the carrying value of the vehicles overstated, by $350,000. The total value of all motor vehicles at the year end was $125 million (20X6 – $131 million).

2   In January 20X7, the board of Basking Co approved a loan to Mrs C Angel, who is a key member of the senior management team of the company. The total amount of the loan was $75,000. Following a review of the board minutes, it was discovered that the directors agreed that the amount was clearly trivial and have, therefore, not disclosed the loan in the notes to the financial statements.

3   During the year Basking Co reduced the value of their provision for customer refunds which is recognised in the financial statements. For the past five years the value of the provision has been calculated based on 7% of one month's sales, using an average monthly sales value. Management argued that due to improved internal processing systems, such a high rate of provision was no longer necessary and reduced it to 4%.

Audit procedures found that refund levels were similar to previous years and there was insufficient evidence at this early stage to confirm whether the new system was more effective or not.

Required

For each of the matters described above:

(i)   Explain the matters which should be discussed with management in relation to each of the uncorrected misstatements; and

(ii)   Assuming that management does not adjust the misstatements identified, evaluate the effect of each on the audit opinion.

Note. The total marks will be split equally between each matter.   **(15 marks)**

(Total = 20 marks)

61 Hopper (P7 Sep/Dec 15) (amended)   49 mins

You are an audit manager at Rockwell & Co, a firm of Chartered Certified Accountants. You are responsible for the audit of the Hopper Group, a listed audit client which supplies ingredients to the food and beverage industry worldwide.

The audit work for the year ended 30 June 20X5 is nearly complete, and you are reviewing the draft auditor's report which has been prepared by the audit senior. During the year the Hopper Group purchased a new subsidiary company, Seurat Sweeteners Co, which has expertise in the research and design of sugar alternatives. The draft financial statements of the Hopper Group for the year ended 30 June 20X5 recognise profit before tax of $495 million (20X4 – $462 million) and total assets of $4,617 million (20X4 – $4,751 million).

An extract from the draft auditor's report is shown below:

Basis for modified opinion (extract)

In their calculation of goodwill on the acquisition of the new subsidiary, the directors have failed to recognise consideration which is contingent upon meeting certain development targets. The directors believe that it is unlikely that these targets will be met by the subsidiary company and, therefore, have not recorded the contingent consideration in the cost of the acquisition. They have disclosed this contingent liability fully in the notes to the financial statements. We do not feel that the directors' treatment of the contingent consideration is correct and, therefore, do not believe that the criteria of the relevant standard have been met. If this is the case, it would be appropriate to adjust the goodwill balance in the statement of financial position.

We believe that any required adjustment may materially affect the goodwill balance in the statement of financial position. Therefore, in our opinion, the financial statements do not give a true and fair view of the financial position of the Hopper Group and of the Hopper Group's financial performance and cash flows for the year then ended in accordance with International Financial Reporting Standards.

Emphasis of Matter Paragraph

We draw attention to the note to the financial statements which describes the uncertainty relating to the contingent consideration described above. The note provides further information necessary to understand the potential implications of the contingency.

Required

(a)   Critically appraise the draft auditor's report of the Hopper Group for the year ended 30 June 20X5, prepared by the audit senior.

   Note. You are **NOT** required to redraft the extracts from the auditor's report.   **(10 marks)**

(b)   The audit of the new subsidiary, Seurat Sweeteners Co, was performed by a different firm of auditors, Fish Associates. During your review of the communication from Fish Associates, you note that they were unable to obtain sufficient appropriate evidence with regard to the breakdown of research expenses. The total of research costs expensed by Seurat Sweeteners Co during the year was $1.2 million. Fish Associates has issued a qualified audit opinion on the financial statements of Seurat Sweeteners Co due to this inability to obtain sufficient appropriate evidence.

   Required

   Comment on the actions which Rockwell & Co should take as the auditor of the Hopper Group, and the implications for the auditor's report on the Hopper Group financial statements.
   (6 marks)

(c)   Discuss the quality control procedures which should be carried out by Rockwell & Co prior to the auditor's report on the Hopper Group being issued.   **(4 marks)**

(d)   During the course of the audit, the Hopper Group's finance director commented on growing competition in the Group's sector. One rapidly expanding competitor, Pissarro Co, was referred to specifically. You are aware that your firm recently acquired another accountancy firm, and that Pissarro Co is one of its clients. It is hoped that the audit of Pissarro Co will be transferred to your department to take advantage of your experience in media and publishing.

   Required

   Evaluate the ethical and professional issues raised by this situation, and recommend any actions necessary for the auditor.   **(5 marks)**

   (Total = 25 marks)

62 Darren (P7 6/15)   39 mins

You are a manager in the audit department of Nidge & Co, a firm of Chartered Certified Accountants, responsible for the audit of Darren Co, a new audit client operating in the construction industry. Darren Co's financial year ended on 31 January 20X5, and the draft financial statements recognise profit before tax of $22.5 million (20X4 – $20 million) and total assets of $370 million, including cash of $3 million. The company typically works on three construction contracts at a time.

The audit is nearly complete and you are reviewing the audit working papers. The audit senior has brought several matters to your attention:

(a)   Darren Co is working on a major contract relating to the construction of a bridge for Flyover Co. Work started in July 20X4, and it is estimated that the contract will be completed in September 20X5. The contract price is $20 million, and it is estimated that a profit of $5 million will be made on completion of the contract. The full amount of this profit has been included in the statement of profit or loss for the year ended 31 January 20X5. Darren Co's management believes that this accounting treatment is appropriate given that the contract was signed during the financial year, and no problems have arisen in the work carried out so far.

(8 marks)

(b) A significant contract was completed in September 20X4 for Newbuild Co. This contract related to the construction of a 20-mile highway in a remote area. In November 20X4, several large cracks appeared in the road surface after a period of unusually heavy rain, and the road had to be shut for ten weeks while repair work was carried out. Newbuild Co paid for these repairs, but has taken legal action against Darren Co to recover the costs incurred of $40 million. Disclosure on this matter been made in the notes to the financial statements. Audit evidence, including a written statement from Darren Co's lawyers, concludes that there is a possibility, but not a probability, of Darren Co having to settle the amount claimed.

(6 marks)

(c) For the first time this year, the financial statements are presented as part of an integrated report. Included in the integrated report are several key performance indicators, one of which states that Darren Co's profit before tax has increased by 20% from the previous year.

(6 marks)

Required

Discuss the implications of the matters described above on the completion of the audit and on the auditor's report, recommending any further actions which should be taken by the auditor.

Notes

1   The mark allocation is shown next to each of the matters above.
2   Assume it is 6 June 20X5.   **(Total = 20 marks)**

63 Chester & Co (P7 12/13) (amended)   49 mins

You are an audit manager in Chester & Co, a firm of Chartered Certified Accountants, and you are reviewing two situations which have arisen recently with respect to potential and existing audit clients of your firm.

Tetbury Co's managing director, Juan Stanton, has approached Chester & Co to invite the firm to tender for its audit. Tetbury Co is a small, owner-managed company providing financial services such as arranging mortgages and advising on pension plans. The company's previous auditors recently resigned. Juan Stanton states that this was due to 'a disagreement on the accounting treatment of commission earned, and because they thought our controls were not very good'. You are aware that Tetbury Co has been investigated by the financial services authority for alleged non-compliance with its regulations. As well as performing the audit, Juan would like Chester & Co to give business development advice.

The audit of Stratford Co's financial statements for the year ended 30 November 20X3 will commence shortly. You are aware that the company is in financial difficulties. Stratford Co's managing director, Colin Charlecote, has requested that the audit engagement partner accompanies him to a meeting with the bank, where a new loan will be discussed and the draft financial statements reviewed. Colin has hinted that if the partner does not accompany him to the meeting, he will put the audit out to tender. In addition, an invoice relating to interim audit work performed in August 20X3 has not yet been paid.

Required

Identify and discuss the ethical and other professional issues raised, and recommend any actions that should be taken in respect of:

(a)   Tetbury Co   **(7 marks)**

(b)   Stratford Co   **(6 marks)**

(c) You are also responsible for the audit of Crow Co, a designer and manufacturer of mobile information technologies. The audit for the year ended 30 June 20X6 is nearly complete and the auditor's report is to be signed imminently. The following outstanding matters still require your consideration. The draft reported profit before tax and total assets for the year are $65 million (20X5 – $111 million) and $650 million (20X5 – $910 million) respectively. Crow Co is not a listed company.

Military research project

During the year $7 million of expenses relating to a new military research project were recorded in the statement of profit or loss. The audit team was given brief summaries of the costs incurred but when asked for further corroborating evidence, management stated that it had signed a confidentiality agreement with the military and was unable to provide any further details. The only additional information provided was that they anticipated the project to last for three years and that it may lead to a highly lucrative contract.

Fire

During the year a major catastrophe took place when a fire caused significant damage to the operations of the company, leading to production ceasing for several months. While operations have resumed, repairs are ongoing and it is anticipated that full production will not resume for at least another six months. Audit procedures revealed that the matter has been fully and satisfactorily reflected and disclosed in the financial statements and that it does not pose a significant risk to the going concern status of Crow Co.

Required

In respect of each of the matters described above, discuss the implications for the auditor's report and recommend any further actions necessary.

Note. The total marks will be split equally between each matter. **(12 marks)**

(Total = 25 marks)

OTHER ASSIGNMENTS

Questions 64 to 70 cover Other assignments, the subject of Part F of the BPP Workbook for AAA.

64 Leopard (P7 Sep/Dec 17)   **39 mins**

(a)   You are a manager in one of the assurance departments of Leopard & Co, a large firm of Chartered Certified Accountants. You are currently assigned to a due diligence engagement for one of your firm's audit clients, Cheetah Co, a manufacturer of bespoke furniture. The audit of Cheetah Co is conducted by a team from a different department; you have never been involved in the audit of this client.

The engagement is to conduct a financial and operational due diligence review of Zebra Co, a company which has been identified as a potential acquisition target by Cheetah Co, due to the synergies offered and the potential to expand the existing production facilities. As part of the due diligence review, you have been asked to provide a valuation of Zebra Co's assets and liabilities and an analysis of the company's operating profit forecasts. This will assist Cheetah Co in determining an appropriate purchase price for Zebra Co.

During the engagement fieldwork your team identified two matters, which require your further consideration, as follows:

1   While reviewing correspondence with customers in relation to outstanding receivables, one of the team found a letter from a large retailer, for which Zebra Co produces a number of unique products, providing advanced notice that they are not renewing their purchasing agreement when the current one expires. The customer advised that they are switching to a new entrant to the market who is substantially cheaper than Zebra Co. A brief analysis identified that the customer provides, on average, almost 5% of Zebra Co's annual revenues.

2   Zebra Co owns a piece of land which was given to it as a gift by the local authorities ten years ago. The land surrounds the entrance to the main production premises and is designated as a nature reserve. Restrictions were imposed on the usage of the land which also limit who the owner is able to sell the land to in the future. The land has zero carrying value in the financial statements.

No additional matters have arisen for your consideration. You are also aware that the financial statements for the last ten years have been audited and no modifications have been made to the auditor's opinion during this period.

Required

In respect of the two matters identified above:

(i)   Explain why each matter requires further investigation as part of the due diligence review; and   **(6 marks)**

(ii)   Recommend the investigation procedures to be performed.   **(6 marks)**

(b)   The management team of Cheetah Co has also approached Leopard & Co to ask whether representatives of the firm would be available to attend a meeting with the company's bankers, who they are hoping will finance the acquisition of Zebra Co, to support the management team in conveying the suitability of the acquisition of Zebra Co. For the meeting the bank requires the most up-to-date interim accounts of Cheetah Co with the accompanying auditor's independent interim review report. Your firm is due to complete the interim review shortly and the management team of Cheetah Co has requested that the interim review is completed quickly so that it does not hold up negotiations with the bank, stating that if it does, it may affect the outcome of the next audit tender, which is due to take place after the completion of this year's audit.

Required

Comment on the ethical and professional issues raised, and recommend any actions which should be taken in respect of the request from the management team of Cheetah Co.

(8 marks)

(Total = 20 marks)

65 Apricot and Lychee (P7 12/09) (amended)　　　49 mins

Your audit client, Apricot Co, is intending to purchase a new warehouse at a cost of $500,000. One of the directors of the company, Pik Choi, has agreed to make the necessary finance available through a director's loan to the company. This arrangement has been approved by the other directors, and the cash will be provided on 30 March 20X0, one day before the purchase is due to be completed. Pik's financial advisor has asked to see a cash flow projection of Apricot Co for the next three months. Your firm has been asked to provide an assurance report to Pik's financial advisor on this prospective financial information.

The cash flow forecast is shown below.

	January 20X0 $'000	February 20X0 $'000	March 20X0 $'000
Operating cash receipts			
Cash sales	125	135	140
Receipts from credit sales	580	600	625
Operating cash payments			
Purchases of inventory	(410)	(425)	(425)
Salaries	(100)	(100)	(100)
Overheads	(175)	(175)	(175)
Other cash flows			
Dividend payment		(80)	
Purchase of new licence	(35)		
Fixtures for new warehouse			(60)
Loan receipt			500
Payment for warehouse			(500)
Cash flow for the month	(15)	(45)	5
Opening cash	100	85	40
Closing cash	85	40	45

The following information is relevant:

1　Apricot Co is a wholesaler of catering equipment and frozen food. Its customers are mostly restaurant chains and fast food outlets.

2　Customers who pay in cash receive a 10% discount. Analysis has been provided showing that for sales made on credit, 20% of customers pay in the month of the sale, 60% pay after 45 days, 10% after 65 days, 5% after 90 days, and the remainder are bad debts.

3　Apricot Co pays for all purchases within 30 days in order to take advantage of a 12% discount from suppliers.

4　Overheads are mainly property rentals, utility bills, insurance premiums and general office expenses.

5　Apricot Co needs to have a health and safety licence as it sells food. Each licence is valid for one year and is issued once an inspection has taken place.

6　A profit forecast has also been prepared for the year ending 31 December 20X0 to help with internal planning and budgeting.

This is the first time that Apricot Co has requested an assurance report, and the directors are unsure about the contents of the report that your firm will issue. They understand that it is similar in format to an auditor's report, but that the specific contents are not the same.

Required

(a)   Recommend the procedures that should be performed on the cash flow forecast for the three months ending 31 March 20X0 in order to provide an assurance report as requested by Apricot Co.   **(11 marks)**

(b)   Explain the main contents of the report that will be issued on the prospective financial information.   **(5 marks)**

Another audit client of yours, Lychee Co, is a manufacturing company with a year ended 30 September 20W9. The audit work has been completed and reviewed and you are due to issue the auditor's report in three days. The draft audit opinion is unmodified. The financial statements show revenue for the year ended 30 September 20W9 of $15 million, net profit of $3 million, and total assets at the year end are $80 million.

The finance director of Lychee Co telephoned you this morning to tell you about the announcement yesterday, of a significant restructuring of Lychee Co, which will take place over the next six months. The restructuring will involve the closure of a factory, and its relocation to another part of the country. There will be some redundancies and the estimated cost of closure is $250,000. The financial statements have not been amended in respect of this matter.

Required

(c)   In respect of the announcement of the restructuring:

(i)   Comment on the financial reporting implications, and advise the further audit procedures to be performed   **(5 marks)**

(ii)   Recommend the actions to be taken by the auditor if the financial statements are not amended   **(4 marks)**

                                                                                                        (Total = 25 marks)

66 Mizzen (P7 12/13)   **49 mins**

You are a manager in the business advisory department of Goleen & Co. Your firm has been approached to provide assurance to Baltimore Co, a company which is not an audit client of your firm, on a potential acquisition. You have just had a conversation with Mark Clear, Baltimore Co's managing director, who made the following comments.

'Baltimore Co is a book publisher specialising in publishing textbooks and academic journals. In the last few years the market has changed significantly, with the majority of customers purchasing books from online sellers. This has led to a reduction in profits, and we recognise that we need to diversify our product range in order to survive. As a result of this, we decided to offer a subscription-based website to customers, which would provide the customer with access to our full range of textbooks and journals online.

'On investigating how to set up this website, we found that we lack sufficient knowledge and resources to develop it ourselves and began to look for another company which has the necessary skills, with a view to acquiring the company. We have identified Mizzen Co as a potential acquisition, and we have approached the bank for a loan which will be used to finance the acquisition if it goes ahead.

BPP
LEARNING

'Baltimore Co has not previously acquired another company. We would like to engage your firm to provide guidance regarding the acquisition. I understand that a due diligence review would be advisable prior to deciding on whether to go ahead with the acquisition, but the other directors are not sure that this is required, and they don't understand what the review would involve. They are also unsure about the type of conclusion that would be issued and whether it would be similar to the opinion in an auditor's report.

'To help me brief the other directors and using the information I have provided, I would like you to:

(a)   Discuss the principal benefits to Baltimore Co of a due diligence review being performed on Mizzen Co. **(6 marks)**

(b)   Identify and explain the matters you would focus on in your due diligence review and recommend the additional information you will need to perform your work. **(16 marks)**

(c)   Describe the type of conclusion which would be issued for a due diligence report and compare this to an auditor's report.' **(3 marks)**

Mark Clear has sent you the following information about Mizzen Co.

Company background

Mizzen Co was established four years ago by two university graduates, Vic Sandhu and Lou Lien, who secured funds from a venture capitalist company, BizGrow, to set up the company. Vic and Lou created a new type of website interface which has proven extremely popular, and which led to the company growing rapidly and building a good reputation. They continue to innovate and have won awards for website design. Vic and Lou have a minority shareholding in Mizzen Co.

Mizzen Co employs 50 people and operates from premises owned by BizGrow, for which a nominal rent of $1,000 is paid annually. The company uses few assets other than computer equipment and fixtures and fittings. The biggest expense is wages and salaries and due to increased demand for website development, freelance specialists have been used in the last six months. According to the most recent audited financial statements, Mizzen Co has a bank balance of $500,000.

The company has three revenue streams:

1   Developing and maintaining websites for corporate customers. Mizzen Co charges a one-off fee to its customers for the initial development of a website and for maintaining the website for two years. The amount of this fee depends on the size and complexity of the website and averages at $10,000 per website. The customer can then choose to pay another one-off fee, averaging $2,000, for Mizzen Co to provide maintenance for a further five years.

2   Mizzen Co has also developed a subscription-based website on which it provides access to technical material for computer specialists. Customers pay an annual fee of $250 which gives them unlimited access to the website. This accounts for approximately 30% of Mizzen Co's total revenue.

3   The company has built up several customer databases which are made available, for a fee, to other companies for marketing purposes. This is the smallest revenue stream, accounting for approximately 20% of Mizzen Co's total revenue.

Extracts from audited financial statements

STATEMENT OF PROFIT OR LOSS AND OTHER COMPREHENSIVE INCOME

	Year ended 30 September 20X3 $'000	Year ended 30 September 20X2 $'000	Year ended 30 September 20X1 $'000	Year ended 30 September 20X0 $'000
Revenue	4,268	3,450	2,150	500
Operating expenses	(2,118)	(2,010)	(1,290)	(1,000)
Operating profit/(loss)	2,150	1,440	860	(500)
Finance costs	(250)	(250)	(250)	–
Profit/(loss) before tax	1,900	1,190	610	(500)
Tax expense	(475)	(300)	(140)	–
Profit/(loss) for the year	1,425	890	470	(500)

There were no items of other comprehensive income recognised in any year.

Required

Respond to the request from Mark Clear.

Note. The mark allocation is shown against each of the instructions from Mark Clear above.

(Total = 25 marks)

67 Titian (P7 Sep/Dec 15) (amended)   49 mins

You are a manager at Raphael & Co, a firm of Chartered Certified Accountants. Sanzio Co is an audit client of your firm, and has requested it to perform a due diligence review of a potential acquisition target, Titian Tyres Co. The acquisition is planned to be structured as a joint venture with another company, Calloway Co, with each party taking joint control of Titian Tyres Co. Sanzio Co's finance director, Steven Cropper, has stated that he wants to share the completed report with Calloway Co.

As part of the due diligence review and to allow for consideration of an appropriate offer price, Sanzio Co has requested that you identify and value all the assets and liabilities of Titian Tyres Co, including items which may not currently be reported in the statement of financial position.

Sanzio Co is a large, privately owned company operating only in this country, which sells spare parts and accessories for cars, vans and bicycles. Titian Tyres Co is a national chain of vehicle service centres, specialising in the repair and replacement of tyres, although the company also offers a complete range of engine and bodywork services as well. If the acquisition is successful, the management of Sanzio Co intends to open a Titian Tyres service centre in each of its stores.

One of the reasons for Titian Tyres Co's success is their internally generated customer database, which records all customer service details. Using the information contained on the database software, the company's operating system automatically informs previous customers when their vehicle is due for its next service via email, mobile phone text or automated letter. It also informs a customer service team to telephone the customer if they fail to book a service within two weeks of receiving the notification. According to the management of Titian Tyres Co, repeat business makes up over 60% of annual sales and management believes that this is a distinct competitive advantage over other service centres.

Titian Tyres Co also recently purchased a licence to distribute a new, innovative tyre which was designed and patented in the United States. The tyre is made of 100% recycled materials and, due to a new manufacturing process, is more hardwearing and therefore needs replacing less often. Titian Tyres Co paid $5 million for the licence in January 20X5 and the company is currently the sole, licenced distributor in this country.

BPP LEARNING

During a brief review of Titian Tyres Co's financial statements for the year ended 30 June 20X5, you notice a contingent liability disclosure in the notes relating to compensation claims made after the fitting of faulty engine parts during 20X4. The management of Titian Tyres Co has stated that the fault lies with the manufacturer of the part and that they have made a claim against the manufacturer for the total amount sought by the affected customers.

Required

(a) Describe the purpose of a due diligence assignment and compare the scope of a due diligence assignment with that of an audit of historical financial statements. **(6 marks)**

(b) Identify and discuss the relevant ethical and professional issues raised if the due diligence engagement is accepted, and recommend any actions necessary. **(5 marks)**

(c) (i) Recommend, with reasons, the principal additional information which should be made available to assist with your valuation of Titian Tyres Co's intangible assets.

   (ii) Explain the specific enquiries you should make of Titian Tyres Co's management relevant to the contingent liability disclosed in the financial statements.

   Note. The total marks will be split equally between each part. **(14 marks)**

   (Total = 25 marks)

68 Jacob (P7 6/11) (amended)   49 mins

You are a manager at Thyme & Co, a firm of Chartered Certified Accountants. Jacob Co, an audit client of your firm, is a large privately owned company whose operations involve a repair and maintenance service for domestic customers. The company offers a range of services, such as plumbing and electrical repairs and maintenance, and the repair of domestic appliances such as washing machines and cookers, as well as dealing with emergencies such as damage caused by flooding. All work is covered by a two-year warranty.

The directors of Jacob Co have been seeking to acquire expertise in the repair and maintenance of swimming pools and hot-tubs as this is a service increasingly requested, but not offered by the company. They have recently identified Locke Co as a potential acquisition. Preliminary discussions have been held between the directors of the two companies with a view to the acquisition of Locke Co by Jacob Co. This will be the first acquisition performed by the current management team of Jacob Co. Your firm has been asked to perform a due diligence review on Locke Co prior to further discussions taking place. You have been provided with the following information regarding Locke Co.

1   Locke Co is owner-managed, with three of the five board members being the original founders of the company, which was incorporated 30 years ago. The head office is located in a prestigious building, which is owned by the founders' family estate. The company recently acquired a separate piece of land on which a new head office is to be built.

2   The company has grown rapidly in the last three years as more affluent customers can afford the cost of installing and maintaining swimming pools and hot-tubs. The expansion was funded by a significant bank loan. The company relies on an overdraft facility in the winter months when smaller operating cash inflows arise from maintenance work.

3   Locke Co enjoys a good reputation, though this was tarnished last year by a complaint by a famous actor who claimed that, following maintenance of his swimming pool by Locke Co's employees, the water contained a chemical which damaged his skin. A court case is on-going and is attracting media attention.

4   The company's financial year end is 31 August. Its accounting function is outsourced to Austin Co, a local provider of accounting and tax services.

Required

(a) Explain the principal potential benefits of an externally provided due diligence review to Jacob Co. **(6 marks)**

(b) Recommend additional information which should be made available for your firm's due diligence review, and explain the need for the information. **(11 marks)**

Note. Assume it is 7 June 20X1.

Tulip Co is another client of your firm, for which you are currently reviewing the draft assurance report in relation to the examination of a forecast. The forecast is included in a proposal due to be sent to Tulip Co's lenders as part of an effort to secure a new loan. Audit procedures concluded that there is no reason to believe that the forecast is unrealistic or that it has not been properly prepared. You are currently reviewing the draft assurance report, which is provided below.

Independent auditor's report on the forecast of Tulip Co to the shareholders of Tulip Co:

We have examined the forecast information of Tulip Co contained in the loan proposal in accordance with the relevant standards on assurance engagements applicable to the examination of prospective financial information. Thyme & Co is not responsible for the forecast, including the assumptions on which it is based.

Based on our examination of the evidence supporting the assumptions, we believe that these assumptions provide a reasonable basis for the forecast. Further, in our opinion the forecast is properly prepared on the basis of the assumptions and is presented in accordance with IFRS.

Actual results are likely to be different from the forecast since the assumptions on which the forecast is based are unlikely to be accurate.

Signed by assurance engagement partner, Thyme & Co

Required

(c) Critically appraise the proposed assurance report extract of Tulip Co.

Note. You are **NOT** required to redraft the assurance report. **(8 marks)**

(Total = 25 marks)

69 Crocus   49 mins

You are a manager in the forensic investigation department of your audit firm. The directors of a local manufacturing company, Crocus Co, have contacted your department regarding a suspected fraud, which has recently been discovered operating in the company, and you have been asked to look into the matter further. You have held a preliminary discussion with Gita Thrales, the finance director of Crocus Co, the notes of this conversation are shown below.

Notes of discussion with Gita Thrales

Four months ago Crocus Co shut down one of its five factories, in response to deteriorating market conditions, with all staff employed at the factory made redundant on the date of closure.

While monitoring the monthly management accounts, Gita performs analytical procedures on salary expenses. She found that the monthly total payroll expense had reduced by 3% in the months following the factory closure – not as much as expected, given that 20% of the total staff of the company had been made redundant. Initial investigations performed last week by Gita revealed that many of the employees who had been made redundant had actually remained on the payroll records, and salary payments in respect of these individuals were still being made every month, with all payments going into the same bank account. As soon as she realised that there may be a fraud being conducted within the company, Gita stopped any further payments in respect of the redundant

BPP
LEARNING

employees. She contacted our firm as she is unsure how to proceed, and would like our firm's specialist department to conduct an investigation.

Gita says that the senior accountant, Miles Rutland, has been absent from work since she conducted her initial investigation last week, and it has been impossible to contact him. Gita believes that he may have been involved with the suspected fraud.

Gita has asked whether your department would be able to provide a forensic investigation, but is unsure what this would involve. Crocus Co is not an audit client of your firm.

Required

(a) Identify and explain the matters that should be considered before accepting the engagement to perform a forensic investigation at Crocus Co. **(4 marks)**

(b) (i) Describe the objectives of a forensic investigation

  (ii) Explain the steps involved in a forensic investigation into the payroll fraud, including examples of procedures that could be used to gather evidence **(14 marks)**

(c) Assess how the fundamental ethical principles of the IESBA's *Code of Ethics for Professional Accountants* should be applied to the provision of a forensic investigation service. **(7 marks)**

(Total = 25 marks)

70 Jansen (Sep 18)   49 mins

You are an audit manager in Jansen & Co which offers a range of audit and other assurance services to its clients. One of your audit clients is Narley Co which operates a commercial haulage company. Narley Co has been an audit client for the last five years and is currently planning a significant expansion of its operations into a new geographical area and jurisdiction. In order to finance the planned expansion, Narley Co needs funds to purchase additional heavy goods vehicles, expand its warehousing facilities and recruit more drivers. The company is also planning a major advertising and marketing campaign targeted at potential customers in the new jurisdiction.

Narley Co's finance director, Suzanne Seddon, has approached you to ask if your firm will provide a report on the prospective financial information which has been prepared in support of a loan application. The application is for a new long-term loan of $22 million from the company's current lender which it intends to use exclusively to finance the planned expansion. The company currently has an existing long-term loan of $31 million from the same bank which is redeemable in five years' time.

Suzanne Seddon has provided you with the following extract from the prospective financial information which will form part of the company's loan application:

Forecast statements of profit or loss

	Notes	Year ended 31 August 20X8 Unaudited $'000	Year ending 31 August 20X9 Forecast $'000	Year ending 31 August 20Y0 Forecast $'000
Revenue	1	138,861	174,965	225,705
Cost of sales	2	(104,862)	(124,786)	(157,230)
Administrative expenses	3	(22,936)	(21,984)	(20,743)
Operating profit		11,063	28,195	47,732
Finance costs	4	(1,450)	(1,638)	(1,597)
Profit before tax		9,613	26,557	46,135

Notes

1 Revenue represents the amounts derived from the provision of haulage services to commercial customers operating principally in the retail sector. Narley Co's board of directors believes that trade in both its existing and new markets will experience significant growth over the next two years.

2 Cost of sales comprises the costs of warehousing and distribution including relevant staff costs, maintenance and repair of vehicles and depreciation of property, equipment and vehicles.

3 Administrative expenses are mainly the costs of running Narley Co's central head office facility.

4 Finance costs represent the cost of servicing long-term finance from Narley Co's bankers.

(a) **Required**

(i) Explain the matters which should be considered by Jansen & Co before accepting the engagement to review and report on Narley Co's prospective financial information.
(6 marks)

(ii) Assuming Jansen & Co accepts the engagement, recommend the examination procedures to be performed in respect of Narley Co's forecast statements of profit or loss. **(9 marks)**

(b) One of your colleagues at Jansen & Co, Rodney Evans, has been taken ill at short notice and you have been temporarily assigned as audit manager on Watson Co, an IT consultancy company which is listed on a second tier investment market. The final audit of Watson Co for the year ended 30 June 20X8 is approaching completion and you are in the process of reviewing the audit working papers. The draft financial statements for the year recognise profit before taxation for the year of $54.2 million and total assets of $23.1 million.

The audit supervisor, who is a part-qualified chartered certified accountant, has sent you an email from which the following extract is taken:

'It's great to have you on board as I was beginning to worry that there would be no manager review of our working papers prior to the final audit clearance meeting next week. The audit assistant and myself have done our best to complete all of the audit work but we only saw Rodney on the first day of the audit about a month ago when I think he was already feeling unwell. We had a short briefing meeting with him at which he told us 'if in doubt, follow last year's working papers.'

One issue which I wanted to check with you is that Watson Co has introduced a cash-settled share-based payment scheme by granting its directors share appreciation rights (SARs) for the first time this year. This was not identified at planning as a high risk area. The SARs were granted on 1 July 20X7 at which date the client obtained a valuation of the rights which was performed by an external firm of valuers. I have filed a copy of the valuation report and I have looked up the valuers online and have found a very professional looking website which confirms that they know what they are doing. The cost of the SARs scheme based on this valuation is being appropriately recognised over the three-year vesting period and a straight line expense of $195,000 has been recognised in the statement of profit or loss on this basis. A corresponding equity reserve has also been correctly recognised on the statement of financial position. The amount also seems immaterial and I can't see any need to propose any amendments to the financial statements in relation to either the amounts recognised or the disclosures made in the notes to the financial statements.'

Required

Comment on the quality of the planning and performance of the audit of Watson Co discussing the quality control and other professional issues raised. **(10 marks)**

(Total = 25 marks)

Answer Bank

1 Lark

Workbook references. Chapters 1, 2 and 11.

Top tips. This question examined two connected issues: money laundering and professional scepticism. In part (a), you needed to spot that money laundering was taking place. If you weren't sure, then requirement (ii) contains a little hint by referring to 'any reporting that should take place' – this confirms that there is money laundering going on in the scenario.

Part (a)(i) was mainly a matter of explaining what is going on in the scenario. You should be aware of the three stages of a money laundering regime (placement, layering and integration), and could have scored well by simply applying them to the scenario. But even if you had forgotten what the stages were, you could still have done well by just explaining how each bit of the scenario might be evidence of a money laundering regime.

Part (a)(ii) was more of a test of knowledge, but you should have been able to remember that the senior should report his suspicions to the MLRO, and that the MLRO then decides what to do about the matter. If you explained this well then you could have got two marks out of three here without too much effort.

Part (b) should have been straightforward, as this was a topical area that you should have been aware of – given that there was an IAASB Q&A paper on this area.

Part (c) of this question was deceptively difficult. At first sight it may appear to be a standard question on group audits, but delve into it more deeply and you will find that it is actually relatively tricky. The key issue is making sense of what has already happened: the component auditor has sent you a draft report.

This report contains a qualified opinion which appears to be drafted correctly – you need to draw on your knowledge of ISA 705 *Modifications to the Opinion in the Independent Auditor's Report* to make this assessment. If you didn't know ISA 705 well enough to do this correctly, then you might have struggled with this question.

The auditor says in the report that a provision should have been made, but in Note 12 to the financial statements, management says that the probability of an outflow is only 20%, so no provision is necessary. The question for the group auditor (which is you!) is: who is right? In order to decide this, the auditor must review the audit evidence that the component auditor based its conclusion on. If the evidence is sufficient and appropriate, then the draft auditor's report is OK; if the evidence is not sufficient and appropriate, then either further evidence must be obtained, or the draft auditor's report is wrong.

You then have to think about the matter practically: what would happen from here? If Exuma is right, then the draft auditor's report is wrong. If the auditor is right, then Exuma may change the financial statements.

If this does not happen, then the group accounts may or may not need changing, all of which will have an impact on the group auditor's report.

This is quite a lot of work for the ten marks on offer, and you should make sure that you do not go over time on this part of the question. The important thing is to be scoring marks with each point you make.

Easy marks. The point about 'tipping off' is always an easy mark in a question on money laundering. It's one of the more important things to be aware of in the real world, so markers tend to like it when you mention it.

Also calculating materiality in part (c) was easy – but don't just do the figures, make sure you say what you are doing and conclude on whether or not the matter is material to the group, and whether the component is significant or not.

BPP LEARNING

Marking scheme

Marks

(a) (i) **Implications of the audit senior's note**
Generally 1 mark for each matter discussed relevant to money laundering:
- Definition of money laundering
- Placement – cash-based business
- Owner posting transactions
- Layering – electronic transfer to overseas
- Secrecy and aggressive attitude
- Audit to be considered very high risk
- Senior may have tipped off the client
- Firm may consider withdrawal from audit
- But this may have tipping off consequences

Maximum 6

(ii) **Reporting that should take place**
Generally 1 mark for each comment:
- Report suspicions immediately to MLRO
- Failure to report is itself an offence
- Examples of matters to be reported (identity of suspect, etc)
- Audit senior may discuss matters with audit manager but senior responsible for the report

Maximum 3

Marks

(b) **Professional scepticism**

Generally 1 mark for each comment:

– Definition of professional scepticism
– Explain – alert to contradictory evidence/unusual events/fraud indicator
  (up to 2 marks)
– Part of ethical codes
– Coot Co – evidence is unreliable and contradictory
– Absence of authorisation is fraud indicator
– Additional substantive procedures needed
– Management's comments should be corroborated
– Control deficiency to be reported to management/those charged with governance
– Audit junior needs better supervision/training on how to deal with deficiencies identified

Maximum   6

(c) **Matters/actions**

Up to 2 marks for each matter/action identified and explained
(max 3 marks for identification):

– Exuma Co is a significant component
– Matter is material to individual and group financial statements
– Accounting treatment/qualification for Exuma Co's financial statements
– Review of audit work performed
– Consideration of further audit work
– Discuss with group management and those charged with governance
– Request that Exuma Co's management adjust financial statements
– Adjustment could be made on consolidation
– Impact on group opinion if no adjustment made

Maximum   10

Total   **25**

(a) (i) The implication of the circumstances described is that there may be money laundering going on at Heron Co, involving its owner-manager Jack Heron.

Money laundering is a process by which criminals may attempt to conceal the origins of the proceeds of criminal activity. The aim is to transform 'dirty' money, which can be tied to its criminal origin, into 'clean' money which can be spent.

The fact that Heron Co's revenue is almost entirely cash makes it an ideal 'front' business for a money laundering regime. The aim here would be to transform the 'dirty' money into revenue from the legitimate business. What appears to be happening here is that the legitimate cash receipts of $3.5m are being topped up with $2m 'dirty' money. This is the placement stage of the money laundering regime. The idea is that the $5.5m revenue will eventually appear legitimate if it can be said to all come from a legitimate business (Heron Co).

The $2m electronic transfer is then part of the layering process, which aims to maximise the distance between the placement of the 'dirty' money and its eventual 'integration' into the financial system as 'clean' money. The fact that this is an overseas transfer only

BPP
LEARNING

109

heightens its suspiciousness, as money launderers often move money across national boundaries to make it harder to trace.

The fact that Jack Heron has sole responsibility for cash receipts and postings gives him the opportunity to launder money in this way. The fact that no documentation was available to support the transfer means it is possible that it was done to launder money. The fact that Jack did not answer the senior's questions and became aggressive seems to confirm his desire for secrecy here.

There is a risk that the senior has 'tipped off' Jack Heron by questioning him about the transfer. This is itself an offence, although it may be argued here that the senior was not aware that the disclosure could prejudice any future money laundering investigation.

From the point of view of the audit, the amount is clearly highly material. It is possible that Lark & Co may seek to withdraw from the engagement; however, there is a risk that this could be construed as 'tipping off' if Jack Heron thinks it is because the audit firm has suspicions over money laundering. The firm should obtain advice from its legal counsel.

(ii)   The audit senior should report the situation to Lark & Co's Money Laundering Reporting Officer (MLRO). The MLRO is the internal person responsible for receiving and evaluating reports of suspected money laundering, and for making any reports to external bodies.

The report would typically include the name of the suspect, the amounts involved, the reasons for suspicion and the whereabouts of any laundered cash.

The report must be made as soon as possible, as it is an offence to not report suspicions as soon as practicable.

The senior would be allowed to discuss his suspicions with the audit manager – in order to assure himself that his suspicions were reasonable – but should alert the MLRO himself.

(b)   **Professional scepticism**

Professional scepticism is an attitude that includes a questioning mind, being alert to conditions which may indicate possible misstatement due to error or fraud, and a critical assessment of audit evidence (ISA 200: para. 13).

This means being alert to the actual circumstances of the engagement and the work being done, and to the possibility that things may not be as they appear to be on first sight, eg that evidence obtained is unreliable, or may point to fraud. If an auditor is not sceptical in this way then they may not realise that something is unusual; they may not tailor audit procedures to the actual risk at hand; or they may jump to hasty conclusions.

Professional scepticism lies at the heart of auditing, both in the sense that it is part of being a competent auditor, and that it is an important part of being ethically independent.

Further actions

The evidence obtained already may not be reliable.

The payroll supervisor's assertion that no authorisation is needed for temporary workers must be corroborated. Evidence should also be gathered about the claim that the employees are temporary.

If the supervisor is correct that no authorisation is required for new employees, then this is a major deficiency of internal controls that should have been identified as part of controls testing. It may be a point to include in the report to management.

There is a contradiction between the supervisor's claim that there were new temporary staff, and management's claim that there are no new staff. It should be clarified that when management said there were no new employees, this included temporary staff.

It is possible that there is a fraud taking place here, possibly by the payroll supervisor. The new employees could be 'ghost employees' to whom money is paid via payroll but who do not exist. The money is then taken criminally, eg by the payroll supervisor or an associate of hers.

The audit junior should be made aware that when he comes across issues like this, he must raise them with his supervisor.

(c) **Materiality to group**

ISA 600 *Special Considerations – Audits of Group Financial Statements (Including the Work of Component Auditors* suggests that a component is significant (material to a group) where a chosen benchmark is more than 15% of the same figure for the group as a whole.

Exuma Co's profit before tax is 20% of group profit before tax (PBT), and total assets is 23.5%. Exuma is therefore a significant component.

Materiality of issue

The $2m legal claim represents 50% of Exuma's PBT, and 10% of total assets.

The claim is also material to the group, at 10% of PBT and 2.4% of total assets.

Qualified opinion – Exuma

Jalousie & Co have expressed a qualified opinion on Exuma in relation to IAS 37 *Provisions, Contingent Liabilities and Contingent Assets*. Audit evidence was obtained that led the auditor to conclude that the Note 12 to the financial statements of Exuma materially misstates the probability of the claim against the company being successful. Presumably Jalousie & Co must have obtained audit evidence that the claim's chance of success was not 20% as stated, but was 50% or more. This would mean that a liability should have been recognised in accordance with IAS 37.

This misstatement is material but is unlikely to be deemed pervasive, so the qualified opinion is correct provided that the audit evidence obtained is sufficient and appropriate.

Audit evidence

Exuma Co is material to the group, as is this specific issue. The group auditor should therefore review Jalousie & Co's audit evidence in relation to it.

The key question is the assessment of the probability of the court-case being lost, and the consequent future outflow of $2m. The group auditor should discuss the matter with Jalousie & Co's audit engagement partner. Audit evidence should include copies of all legal correspondence, as well as written representations from Exuma's management regarding their accounting treatment of the matter.

Depending on the strength of this evidence, it may have been appropriate for Jalousie & Co to have used an auditor's expert to provide a separate legal opinion on the matter.

Further evidence

The group auditor may determine that further audit evidence needs to be obtained, such as the opinion of an auditor's expert if this has not been sought. This can be done either by collaboration with the component auditor, or by the group auditor alone.

It is possible that there is not sufficient appropriate evidence to qualify the opinion on this matter, and that Exuma Co's management is correct. In this case, Jalousie & Co would have to redraft its auditor's report to show an unmodified opinion.

BPP LEARNING

Impact on group – discussion with group management

The matter should be discussed with group management in order to ascertain what the impact will be on the group financial statements and auditor's report. There are a number of possible outcomes, examined below.

Exuma's financial statements changed

The group auditor should request that Nassau Group's management ask Exuma to adjust its financial statements and recognise a provision. This would mean that Jalousie & Co's auditor's report, which has not yet been issued, could potentially be issued with an unmodified opinion if the adjusted financial statements are not materially misstated.

Only group accounts changed

If Exuma's financial statements are not adjusted, then the group financial statements themselves could still be adjusted to rectify the material misstatement. The auditor's opinion on Exuma would still be qualified, but the group auditor's opinion would not be modified in relation to this matter.

No adjustment made at all

If no adjustment is made to Exuma's or the Nassau Group's financial statements, then the group audit opinion is qualified ('except for') due to a material misstatement. The work of the component auditor would not be referred to in the group auditor's report.

2 Plant

Workbook references. Chapters 2 and 5.

Top tips. Part (a)(i) is a relatively straightforward standalone requirement, which you should have been able to pass, perhaps identifying and explaining three reasons, and simply identifying a fourth within the time available. Note that the model answer below contains five reasons, whereas only four are necessary to gain full marks (the extra reason is provided to illustrate the style of answer required).

Part (a)(ii) should not have posed you many difficulties. The contents of the audit tender document are basic knowledge at this level, but here you really need to apply your knowledge to the situation of the Plant Group. You can use the basic contents of the tender as a starting point, and then bring in points from the scenario where they are relevant. For example, the tender must assess 'the needs of the prospective client': here, the tender must clarify that all of the subsidiaries will require audits.

There are also points that come out of the scenario itself. These are likely to be practical points: here, the proposed deadline was very close to the year end, and should be discussed in the tender document as a practical issue.

In part (b), the first suggestion might have been trickier than the second, which was clear-cut. With the first suggestion (on the bonus for cross-selling to audit clients), you should have been able to work out that there is a self-interest threat here. You then needed to know that the crucial issue was whether the person was a key audit partner or not.

With suggestion 2, you should be well aware of the ethical issues surrounding the provision of internal audit services, and this part of the question was pretty much just knowledge recall. You should have scored well on this part of the question, and if you didn't then you need to make sure that you are happy with this area in the future.

Easy marks. There were easy marks in part (a)(ii) for noting that the tight deadline would cause problems – this came straight from the scenario and should stand out prominently. Part (b) contains easy marks.

ACCA examining team's comments. In part (a)(i), too few candidates actually provided an explanation of the reasons they gave.

Requirement (a)(ii) was generally well-attempted, with a significant minority of answers achieving close to full marks. The best answers went through each of the typical contents of a tender document and related them specifically to the Group in the question, resulting in focused and well-explained answer points. Interestingly, these answers were often relatively brief, but still managed to attract a high mark through application of knowledge to the question scenario.

Some answers tended to either be much too brief – sometimes little more than a list of bullet points – or did not answer the question requirement, and instead of explaining matters to be included in a tender document, discussed the matters that may impact client acceptance, such as whether the audit firm has sufficient resources, and whether a fee dependency would be created. Candidates are advised to read question requirements carefully and not to make assumptions about what is being asked for.

Answers to requirement (b) tended to discuss one of the suggestions reasonably well, but then repeat almost identical points in relation to the second suggestion. There was some overlap given that both involved the provision of a non-audit service to an audit client, but there were enough separate points that could be made to avoid repetition. In relation to the financial incentives for partners and manager selling services to audit clients, hardly any candidates discussed the issue of the significance of the ethical threat depending on seniority and that partners couldn't have the arrangement. Many also discussed the self-interest threat in relation to the audit firm rather than its personnel.

In relation to the extended audit, most answers explained the self-review threat and suggested appropriate safeguards, usually that of separate teams. Fewer discussed the need for extended review procedures or for separate engagement letters and billing arrangements were the internal audit service provided to an audit client. Fewer still knew the position of the ethical codes in relation to this matter, and there was very little in the way of discussion of the topic as a current issue.

Marking scheme

Marks

(a) (i) **Identify and explain using examples why an audit firm may not seek re-election**
Generally ½ mark for identification and 1 mark for explanation/example:
- Disagreement
- Lack of integrity
- Fee level
- Late payment of fees
- Resources
- Overseas expansion
- Competence
- Independence
- Conflict of interest

Maximum 6

(ii) **Matters to be included in tender document**
Up to 1½ marks for each matter identified and explained with relevance to the Plant Group (up to a maximum of 2 marks in total for matters identified only):
- Outline of the audit firm including international network
- Audit firm specialism in telecoms

- Client audit requirements
- Outline of audit firm's audit methodology
- Deadlines
- Discuss provision of audit-related services
- Quality control and ethics
- Fees
- Discuss provision of non-audit services

Maximum   9

(b) **Ethical matters**

Up to 1 mark for each relevant comment:

- Explain self-interest threat arising on bonus suggestion
- Significance depends on seniority of person, materiality of compensation
- Partners may not have this arrangement
- Safeguard could be put in place for other audit team members
- Explain self-review threat arising on internal audit service
- Identify impact on professional scepticism
- Explain management threat arising in internal audit service
- Safeguards (1 mark each), eg separate team
- Not allowed for public interest clients
- Separate engagement letter/billing arrangements
- Approval of those charged with governance

Maximum   10

Total   **25**

(a) (i) **Reasons for not seeking re-election**

Disagreement with client

The auditor may have disagreed with the client in past, for instance over accounting treatments. There is a possibility that the relationship between auditor and client could break down, which would make it very difficult to carry out the audit effectively.

Resources

An auditor may find that it lacks the resources to carry out an audit, perhaps because the client has grown rapidly so that the firm lacks the staff to provide a big enough audit team.

Competence

An auditor might believe itself not to be competent enough to carry out the audit, perhaps because the client operates in an industry with highly specialised accounting requirements, in respect of which the firm lacks the necessary expertise.

Ethics – management's integrity

The auditor might feel that it has reason to doubt the integrity of management, for instance because of a breakdown in relationship, or an unproven suspected fraud. This would lead to a breakdown in the relationship between auditor and management.

Ethics – fee level

The fees necessary to make a profit may have reached an inappropriate level, for instance 15% of total practice income in line with ACCA guidance (ACCA *Code of Ethics*). If the fees are too high, there is considered to be an independence problem because the audit opinion might be influenced by a fear of losing the client.

(ii) **Matters to include in tender**

Overview of Weller & Co

A brief overview of the firm's structure. This should state that the firm is part of an international network of firms, and that it therefore has access to a considerable depth of audit expertise.

This could be particularly relevant to the audit of the Plant Group's overseas subsidiary.

Areas of expertise and key staff

The firm has a telecoms audit department, and therefore already has staff with expertise in the Plant Group's specific industry. This may make it particularly well placed to audit the Plant Group. Details should also be provided of the approximate size and makeup of the audit team, as well as of the expected audit engagement partner together with details of his or her relevant experience.

It is possible that the addition of a significant new telecoms audit client could create conflicts with existing clients in this industry. It should be possible to manage these, however, by applying safeguards to reduce the risk of independence being threated.

Assessment of Plant Group's needs

The Plant Group is composed of a parent and six subsidiaries, and it should be clarified that the tender includes the audit of each of the subsidiaries as single companies, together with the parent company and the group as a whole.

Audit approach

A brief description of Weller & Co's audit approach. In the case of the Plant Group, this is likely to include reliance on the internal controls, which are described as strong. The tender document should point out that controls would be tested before they were relied upon, but that if they did prove reliable then the audit should indeed be cost-effective.

Deadline

The proposed deadline is just two months after the year end. It would be very difficult to meet such a deadline while still maintaining audit quality. It might make it difficult to obtain evidence in specific areas, such as receivables recoverability or going concern. There is also a risk of putting significant pressure on the audit team to do work quickly rather than thoroughly, which could result in things being missed.

The tender should therefore propose a later deadline for audit completion.

Fees

The tender should state the proposed audit fee, together with a breakdown of the fee. The fee proposed should be sufficient to ensure that a high-quality audit could be conducted.

Non-audit services

The firm may wish to outline any relevant non-audit services that it could provide to the Plant Group. These will be curtailed by the fact that the Plant Group is now listed and thus a public interest entity, but there may still be some areas in which Weller & Co could provide help.

Quality control & ethics

Weller & Co should state its adherence to the IESBA's *Code of Ethics for Professional Accountants*, and to International Standards on Quality Control. This will give the Plant Group confidence in the auditor's report that would be issued.

(b) **Selling bonus**

The first suggestion would be a 'compensation and evaluation policy', in the terms of the IESBA *Code of Ethics*. This creates a self-interest threat. If the partner or manager receives a bonus from selling services to the client, then they might be less willing to disagree with the client during the audit.

The significance of this threat depends upon several factors:

- The proportion of the individual's compensation or performance evaluation that is based on the sale of such services

- The role of the individual on the audit team

- Whether promotion decisions are influenced by the sale of such services (IESBA *Code of Ethics*)

The *Code* specifically states that a key audit partner shall not be given a bonus based on selling non-audit services to audit clients. Therefore this bonus should not be offered to key audit partners.

The suggestion is to offer the bonus to audit managers too. This may be ethically acceptable if adequate safeguards were put in place: the manager's work should be reviewed by another professional accountant. If this is not done, then the bonus cannot be offered.

It may also be that if the manager is a particularly senior manager, then their role will be so significant in the audit team that no safeguard would be sufficient. They should not receive the bonus.

Internal audit

There are two potential issues here: a self-review threat, and the threat from taking on a management responsibility.

Self-review threat

If Weller & Co seeks to rely on work performed by internal audit as part of its external audit, then there will be a self-review threat if it has itself performed the internal audit. The risk is that the internal audit work relied upon is not treated with enough professional scepticism. It may be possible to surmount this problem by using a team or department that is separate from the external audit team, to perform the internal audit.

Management responsibility

If firm personnel assume a management responsibility as part of the internal audit, then this threat would be so significant that either the internal audit service must not be provided, or the firm must withdraw from the external audit.

A management responsibility would be assumed where, for example, the auditor performs internal control procedures, or takes responsibility for designing, implementing and maintaining internal controls.

Public interest entities

If the audit client is a public interest entity (eg a listed company), then internal audit services relating to the following areas cannot be provided:

- A significant part of controls over financial reporting

- Accounting systems that generate information significant to the client's accounting records or financial statements

- Amounts or disclosures that are material to the financial statements (IESBA *Code of Ethics*)

3 Becker

Workbook reference. Chapters 2 and 5.

Top tips. Ethical questions where you are asked to consider a number of scenarios come up frequently in this exam. The best way to be prepared is to practise as many of this type of question as you can. Always try to explain the risks fully rather than just stating what they are and try to come up with relevant safeguards.

Easy marks. All three areas were roughly similar in difficulty. If you are well prepared, this type of question should not be difficult.

ACCA examining team's comments. This question focused on ethics and practice management. Answers tended to be inadequate overall. This is disappointing, given that ethics is regularly tested, and that many candidates seem to think that the ethics question is the 'easy question'. The scenario relevant to requirement (a) described a business opportunity for which an audit client required funding. Most candidates spotted the obvious ethical problems of making loans to clients, and of having a mutual financial interest. However, few candidates really explained why this is a problem. Many candidates would simply state a type of threat – 'self-interest' and 'intimidation' being the most common, with little attempt to explain how the threat arose and if anything could be done to mitigate the threat. Stronger candidates responded well to the practice management issues, discussing whether the audit firm has the relevant skills for such a business venture and whether attention would be better focused on attracting new audit and assurance clients.

Requirement (b)'s scenario discussed the audit firm potentially setting up a recruitment advisory service. Similar problems appeared here, with many candidates stating threats but not explaining them. Some candidates devoted much of their answer to the fee based on salary, maintaining that it was a contingent fee, banned under ethical guidelines.

Requirement (c) tended to be unsatisfactorily answered. Many candidates simply repeated the same comments they had made for requirement (b), seeming not to realise that the two were entirely different proposals. This shows the importance of explaining the threats, as similar threats may indeed arise from the possibilities described in (b) and in (c), but why they arise and the implication for the audit firm is completely different.

Marking scheme

Marks

(a) **Joint business arrangement**

Generally 1–1½ marks per comment:
- Self-interest independence threats:
  - Loans to clients generally prohibited
  - Convertible loan stock would lead to equity stake in client – prohibited
  - Joint venture arrangement is significant business interest
  - Audit firm would share control of JV with audit client
  - Finance involved likely to be significant
- Can only proceed with business venture if resign as auditors
- Potentially lucrative business opportunity **but**
- Auditors lack commercial experience in this type of venture
- Should spend time on client retention and attraction

Maximum   7

BPP
LEARNING

(b) **Recruitment service**

Generally 1–1½ marks per comment:
- Explanation of self-interest threat
- Explanation of familiarity threat
- Explanation of management involvement threat
- Threats increase with seniority of recruitee
- Can look at CVs and draw up shortlist but management to take final decision
- Ingrid lacks specific, recent experience
- May not be much demand for the service
- Need to train second person – cost implication
- Consider setting up as separate business

Maximum   7

(c) **Temporary staff assignment**

Generally 1–1½ marks per comment:
- Explanation of self-review threat
- Explanation of management involvement threat
- Explanation of familiarity threat
- Description of safeguards
- Problem when secondee returns to audit firm – reassign to other client
- Individual benefits from different work experience
- But may be offered permanent employment by the client
- Issues with competence of people seconded
- Eases audit forms over-staffing problem

Maximum   6

Total   **20**

(a) **Murray Co**

Threat to independence and objectivity

If the investment in Murray Co were to go ahead, Becker & Co would create self-interest and intimidation threats to their objectivity and independence. The IESBA's *Code of Ethics for Professional Accountants* states that the audit firm must be seen to be independent of the client. If Becker & Co and Murray Co are working together on the new product, the audit firm will not be seen to be independent.

Loan to audit client

Under the first option, Becker & Co would provide finance in the form of convertible debentures. This is a loan between the audit firm and its client and creates a self-interest threat to independence. The *Code* specifically states that audit firms should not enter into any loan arrangement with a client that is not a bank or similar institution and no safeguard would reduce the self-interest threat to an acceptable level. Becker & Co should therefore not provide finance to Murray Co unless they resign as auditors.

Equity shares in audit client

The convertible debentures will eventually be converted to equity resulting in Becker & Co holding shares in Murray. This presents a self-interest threat to independence as Becker & Co will hold a financial interest in an audit client. The *Code* states that an audit firm is not allowed to own a direct financial interest in a client. Disposing of the equity or resigning from the audit will be the only applicable safeguards in this instance.

Joint venture

Under the second option, Becker & Co would form a joint venture with Murray Co. This would create a self-interest threat to independence as the audit firm and audit client would have an inappropriately close business relationship. Under the *Code*, an assurance provider should not participate in such a venture with an assurance client unless the interest is clearly insignificant. In this case the interest would be significant. Becker & Co should therefore not enter into the joint venture unless they resign as auditors of Murray Co.

Diversification

Entering into a business arrangement with Murray Co would be a new area of business for Becker & Co. The firm should consider whether it wants to diversify into an area in which it has little expertise or knowledge. It would be necessary to carry out a full commercial evaluation and business risk analysis before deciding if this is a growth strategy the firm would like to pursue.

Additionally, the firm needs to consider whether it has the time and resources to devote to this new area without the audit business suffering. Time may be better spent attracting and retaining audit clients, rather than pursuing new areas of business.

Business opportunity

If the firm does decide (after research and careful consideration) that this is a business opportunity it would be lucrative to pursue, then they should immediately resign as auditors of Murray Co.

(b) ### Recruitment service

Providing a recruitment service to a client is not specifically prohibited by the IESBA *Code of Ethics*. However, the *Code* does say certain threats to independence could be created.

Self-interest threat

Becker & Co are considering the provision of recruitment services to audit clients, earning fees based on a percentage of the salary of the person recruited. This creates a financial self-interest threat to independence. The firm may be tempted to recommend an individual to a client in order to earn a fee, and not consider whether that individual is suited to the role.

Familiarity threat

The provision of recruitment services will create a familiarity threat. During audits, Becker & Co will have to assess the work of individuals they helped recruit. The firm may be or may be perceived to be less likely to criticise or challenge such individuals because this could discredit their recruitment services.

Self-review threat

A self-review threat occurs where an audit firm makes management decisions for an audit client. Becker & Co could be seen to be making such decisions by providing recruitment services to audit clients. The firm could review candidates' CVs and recommend individuals to interview but the final decision of who to recruit should always rest with the client.

This threat is increased with the seniority of the individual being recruited, for example if Becker & Co were to advise on a new finance director. The threat could be reduced by only providing services for the recruitment of junior staff members.

Demand for services

Becker & Co would need to carry out market research to ensure that there is a demand for recruitment services before embarking on any new business venture.

Training costs

The firm should also consider whether it has the time and resources to enter into a new area of business. Ingrid Sharapova only worked in recruitment for a year and seems to be the only employee with any experience. She may require further training in order to recruit finance professionals and update her skills.

An additional member of staff at Becker & Co will also require some training so the recruitment business can be kept running whilst Ingrid is away or on sick leave.

If successful, the recruitment business may prove too much for Ingrid to handle alone and the firm will have to either train or hire additional staff to assist her.

Damage to reputation

Becker & Co's reputation could be damaged if the quality of recruitment services is low. This risk can be reduced by setting up the recruitment services as a separate company.

(c) ### Temporary staff assignments

Self-review threat

Becker & Co are proposing audit managers and seniors to be seconded to audit clients. This creates a self-review threat as there is the risk that the manager or senior will be auditing their own work on return to the audit firm. Even if the seconded individual is not on the audit team, there is a risk that the audit firm over relies on work carried out by their own employee.

Safeguards would need to be in place to ensure that staff are not assigned to audit teams for clients where they have completed a secondment. This safeguard could cause some internal difficulties at Becker & Co as clients are likely to request staff who are familiar with their business and have been part of the audit team. Becker & Co may find that they can no longer allocate the staff with the most experience to clients where there has been a secondment. This difficulty could be overcome somewhat if staff are seconded to areas outside of the finance department.

Management involvement

By seconding an audit manager or senior, Becker & Co could be or could be perceived to be making management decisions for audit clients. This poses a problem as it creates a self-review threat to independence. The threat is greater when a more senior staff member is seconded as there is an increased likelihood the individual will be making important decisions.

The firm would need to apply safeguards to ensure that Becker & Co employees are not involved in any management decisions, responsible for approving or signing agreements or given the authority to enter into commitments whilst on secondment at the client.

Familiarity threat

An individual from Becker & Co could be seconded to a client for a time period covering the audit. A familiarity threat to independence arises as the audit team may be over familiar with the seconded individual and not apply professional scepticism.

Reputation risk

Becker & Co's reputation could be adversely affected if seconded staff do not have the correct level of expertise for the role in question. The firm should make sure that any seconded employees are suitably competent and qualified for the seconded role.

Loss of staff

There is a risk that key staff may leave Becker & Co if clients offer them a permanent position. The situation could be exacerbated by staff being concerned about redundancy as the audit department is over-staffed.   Signed agreements where clients agree not to offer seconded staff permanent roles would reduce this risk.

Benefits

The main benefit of this suggestion is that it will ease the problems with over-staffing in the audit department in the short term. In the long term, Becker & Co will still need to find new business or consider where they could reassign excess staff.

Individuals seconded to clients may learn and gain new perspectives from working in a finance department rather than in an accountancy firm. These new skills will benefit Becker & Co on their return.

4 Peaches

Workbook references. Chapters 1, 2 and 5.

Top tips. Part (a) tested around the edge of the syllabus, but you should have been able to score very well, as you should already be familiar with the arguments in favour of principles- and rules-based approaches from your earlier studies. In addition to this, the examining team did discuss this issue in an article in *Student Accountant* shortly before the exam. This underlines again the advantage that you can gain just by carefully reading the examining team's articles there!

There is a possibility that students might have been put off by the question text on recent surveys of the audit market, but if you read the requirement you'll see that all you need to do is talk about the different approaches to auditing in general. Take care in part (ii), though, only to talk about the pros and cons of a prescriptive approach – the question is not asking you to talk about a principles-based approach at all (although the advantages of one and pretty much the same as the disadvantages of the other).

Part (b) was a standard question on ethics. You should have scored well here, as was mainly a test of factual knowledge but in the guise of a scenario.

Part (c) on money laundering was quite a nice requirement in this area. Part (i), on the stages of money laundering, was partly pre-learned knowledge in an area that is quite interesting by AAA standards, and partly application to Adderley Co. If you explained each stage well, then you only needed to say two further things in relation to Adderley Co to get maximum marks – and there were two strong hints in the scenario (tickets purchased in cash, and the regular overseas bank transfers). Part (ii) was knowledge-based and in a key area of the syllabus, so it's important that you get a good number of these marks.

Easy marks. Part (a)(i) should have been very easy. There was an easy mark available for defining lowballing in part (b)(iii) – an example of the kind of mark you might miss out on if you mess up your timing and don't answer all the parts of the question.

ACCA examining team's comments. This question focused on ethical and professional issues. The topic should not have been a surprise to candidates given the importance of this current issue, and the examining team's recent article covering the subject.

Requirement (a) tested candidates' knowledge and understanding of prescriptive and principles-based approaches to auditing. Generally, this requirement was answered well.

Requirement (b) contained three sub-requirements, testing candidates understanding of the terms 'intimidation threat', 'lowballing', and also including a section on the advertising rules which auditors should abide by. Most candidates could demonstrate that they knew the basic facts about each, but generally did not explain their points in sufficient detail to score a high mark on requirement (b) as a whole. For example, with regard to lowballing, most candidates could state that this involves charging a low fee for the performance of an audit engagement, but not all candidates then developed the point into issues relating to the quality of the audit performed. It was pleasing that the requirement on advertising rules was well answered, given that this is a relatively peripheral area of the syllabus. Unusually for the ethics question, at this sitting it tended to be the optional question in which candidates scored the highest mark.

Part (c) of the question focused on money laundering, and in contrast to previous sittings where this subject has been examined, the answers were generally of a reasonable standard. Most answers were reasonably well attempted, and most candidates demonstrated knowledge of both the stages of money laundering, and the elements of an anti-money laundering programme. The weaker answers tended to simply be too short, limiting the marks that could be awarded. Some answers failed to comment on why Adderley Co had been assessed as having a high risk of money laundering, even though the reasons were fairly obvious from the information provided.

Marking scheme

Marks

(a) (i) **Prescriptive and principles-based approach to auditing**
   – 1 mark per point up to a maximum of 2

(ii) **Arguments for and against prescriptive approach**
   – 1 mark for each advantage – clarity, increase in quality, uniformity, easy to monitor
   – 1 mark for each disadvantage – lack of tailoring, over-auditing, no use of skill/judgement, process becomes mundane/routine

   Maximum 6

(b) (i) **Intimidation threat**
   1 mark per comment explained:
   – Independence/objectivity threat
   – Example – aggressive individual
   – Link to familiarity (or other) threat
   – Safeguards needed

(ii) **Advertising**
   1 mark per comment explained:
   – Must abide by professional principles
   – Must not make false/exaggerated claims
   – Must not make disparaging remarks about other firms
   – Must abide by local rules on advertising generally

(iii) **Lowballing**
   1 mark per comment explained:
   – Definition
   – Why is problem – low quality audit, not acting with due care/competence
   – Not prohibited but not encouraged

   Maximum 9

(b) (i) **Stages of money laundering**
   Up to 2 marks for each stage explained with relevance to Adderley Co:
   – Placement – cash based business and mixing of illegal and legitimate sources of cash

Marks

- Layering – complex transactions to hamper tracing the cash such as transfer overseas
- Integration – investing or spending cash to place it into the legitimate economy

Maximum 4

(ii) **Elements of an anti-money laundering programme**
Up to 1½ marks for each element recommended:
- MLRO – senior person, responsibilities
- Firm-wide training programme
- Know your client procedures
- Record keeping

Maximum 6

Total **25**

(a) (i) Rules-based (prescriptive) auditing is where the auditor follows prescribed rules on how to audit a particular area, but does not use any judgement about how to apply the rules.

Principles-based auditing is where no detailed rules are prescribed, but where the auditor must apply more general, guiding principles to the particular area being audited.

(ii) **Arguments for**

Improved clarity and understandability. Prescriptive auditing standards leave the auditor in no doubt as to what he needs to do to audit a particular area. He just needs to follow the rules precisely and to the letter. As long as he has done this, he will be able to say that he has audited in accordance with the standards.

It can be argued that prescriptive standards lead to an improvement in the quality of audits because they leave less scope for the auditor to choose how to audit each area, which reduces the risk that the auditor might make the wrong choice or might make a poor judgement. This also makes it much easier for the regulatory authorities to monitor audit quality, as it is much clearer what the auditor needs to do in accordance with the standards.

Arguments against

The key disadvantage is that it reduces the auditor's ability to take into account the individual circumstances of the entity that is actually being audited. There is a danger of just applying the rules irrespective of whether the audit procedures are appropriate in this particular case. Worse than this, there may not even be a rule for the particular situation being audited, leaving the auditor in a very difficult position. This would lead to audit procedures being done that may not be adequate to gather sufficient appropriate audit evidence.

Prescriptive approaches diminish the extent to which auditors need to use their own judgement. This may not be too much of a problem in the case of a simple entity that is straightforward to audit, but it can be problematic in the case of a complex entity that is difficult to audit.

There is therefore a danger that a prescriptive approach might actually reduce the quality of audits.

(b) (i) An intimidation threat is a threat to compliance with the fundamental principle of an auditor's objectivity, which is a crucial part of his independence.

An example of an intimidation threat would be a client threatening to replace the auditor if the auditor intends to qualify the audit opinion (IESBA *Code of Ethics*).

When an auditor identifies that there is a threat to his independence, he should apply safeguards to reduce the threat to an acceptably low level. There may, for instance, be a specific mode of recourse available through the individual regulatory framework that the auditor is operating in.

(ii) The ACCA's general rule on advertising is that the medium used should not reflect adversely on the member, ACCA or the accountancy profession (ACCA *Rulebook*).

In particular, adverts should not discredit the services offered by others, whether by claiming superiority for the member's or firm's own services or otherwise. They should also not be misleading, either directly or by implication – they must not make false claims.

It is important that short adverts do not include information about fees. It is possible to mention fees in longer adverts, but these must include information about the basis on which fees would be calculated, such as hourly rates, etc.

(iii) Lowballing is tendering for an audit for a very low fee, with the hope of under-cutting competitors and winning the audit tender. It is associated with audit firms recovering any losses they incur from the low fee, by just raising the fees significantly in future years.

The short answer is that lowballing is allowed, but the fact that a firm is charging a low fee does not mean that it can cut costs by doing less audit work. It must do the same amount of work as on any other audit, ie the amount required to provide reasonable assurance that the financial statements are not materially misstated. The danger is that the firm tries to cut back on the audit work done in order to lessen any loss it is making on the audit – which is a serious risk to its independence.

The ACCA's *Code of Ethics and Conduct* emphasises that where a firm obtains an appointment with a significantly lower fee than competitors, it must be able to demonstrate that the audit has been conducted in accordance with auditing standards.

(c) (i) There are three stages in money laundering: placement, layering and integration.

Placement

This is the initial placing of ill-gotten cash into the financial system. Cash-based business provide good cover for this, as it is easier for criminals to disguise dirty money as clean, eg by mixing it in with cash receipts.

For Adderley, it might be possible to place dirty money into the system in the guise of till receipts, after which it could be mixed with the clean money and subsequently treated as such.

Layering

This is the creation of 'layers' of transactions which seek to disguise the original origin of the placed cash. In practice this can be so complex that the cash is almost impossible to trace.

For Adderley, the regular transfer of cash into overseas bank accounts could be a way of introducing complexity to the layering process.

Integration

This is the integration of the money back into the legitimate economy, so that the criminals can use it to make purchases or investments.

For Adderley, the use of $8m of its own cash could be a way of integrating laundered money back into a legitimate activity for the purpose of investment.

(ii) **Money Laundering Reporting Officer**

Peaches & Co should appoint a Money Laundering Reporting Officer (MLRO) who should occupy a senior position in the firm. Suspicions of money laundering are reported to the MLRO, who then considers whether to pass them on to the National Crime Agency.

Firm-wide

Firm-wide elements include a training programme for staff, so that they are aware of relevant legislation and what they must do if they suspect or encounter money laundering. Training should include money laundering risk factors, so that individuals are better able to spot money laundering and respond appropriately.

Customer due diligence

Customer due diligence (know your client) procedures involve an audit firm establishing the identity of clients, eg through passports, and understanding the sources of clients' income and the rationale for business transactions.

Records

Peaches & Co must maintain records of client identification procedures and of any transactions, eg the receipt of payment of the audit fee. This helps ensure that the auditor does not inadvertently become involved in laundering money for its clients.

5 Cobra

Workbook reference. Chapters 2 and 5.

Top tips. This was a typical ethics question and was a fair test. The requirement asks for comments on the issues raised, but also actions which should be taken. These are sometimes slightly easier marks to get, although to get them you must say both **what** the auditor should do, and **why** they should do it.

Part (a) was about a small but growing company that was choosing to have an audit. Most candidates would have realised that providing these non-audit services would threaten Cobra & Co's independence as auditor, however the question tested candidates' knowledge of the *Code of Ethics*: it is permissible to provide these services to a non-listed audit client, provided that any threats are reduced to an acceptable level.

When answering part (b), don't overlook the first point, which is about an auditor providing tax services to an audit client. This is not the core of this question part but nevertheless, there are marks available. The central issue in part (b) is the conflict between the client and the outgoing auditor. The issue is relatively clear-cut and should have provided you with ample opportunity to score marks.

Part (c) contained plenty of possible marks too, as it is clear that there is a conflict of interest between the two clients, irrespective of their ownership.

Easy marks. There were marks available for simply stating the types of threats that were present, as well as for explaining why these are threats. Note, however, that the examining team does not like it when candidates simply list out all of the categories of threat – this is not likely to score any marks.

BPP
LEARNING

Marks

Generally up to 1½ marks for each well explained matter and 1 mark for each well explained and relevant response to the matters identified.

Note. Only ½ mark will be awarded for brief identification of a matter. Further marks will be awarded for explaining why the threat/matter is relevant in this specific context. Likewise only ½ mark will be awarded for a brief response. Only well explained responses should score a full mark.

(a) **Asp Co**
   - Self-review threat due to financial statements impact of other services
   - Not prohibited because Asp Co is not listed
   - Use different teams and make sure that this is possible and acceptable to client (max 1 mark)
   - Potential management threat
   - No safeguards available for management threat relating to an audit client
   - Communicate management threat issues with management and potentially obtain new engagement letter (max 1 mark)
   - Second partner review of audit for 31 July 20X7 (max 1 mark)

	Maximum	7

(b) **Viper Co**
   - Self-review threat to objectivity
   - Inadequate acceptance procedures
   - Preconditions for accepting audit
   - Question over integrity of management
   - Possible that previous auditor is at fault, not management
   - Obtain further information relating to financial reporting dispute (max 1 mark)
   - Investigate matter independently (max 1 mark)
   - Decision based on outcome of further investigations (max 1 mark)

	Maximum	7

(c) **Adder Co**
   - Conflict of interest with competing audit clients
   - Potentially private information held by Cobra & Co in relation to Slowworm Co
   - Self-review threat caused by valuation service
   - Possible use of separate teams (max 1 mark)
   - Not permitted to conduct valuation for audit client (max 1 mark)

	Maximum	6

Total	**20**

(a) **Asp Co**

Self-review threat

If Cobra & Co accepts the audit of Asp Co and continues to provide the other services, this would create a self-review threat to objectivity. This would arise because all of the other services would have an impact on the financial statements which Cobra & Co would then be responsible for forming an opinion on. Given the nature of the services, the impact on the financial statements would most likely be material.

The IESBA *Code of Ethics for Professional Accountants* (the *Code*) does not prohibit firms from providing bookkeeping and tax services to non-listed audit clients but requires that sufficient safeguards are implemented to reduce any threat to an acceptable level. The response should, however, be considered in light of the complexity of the other services and amount of judgement required in providing the other services, particularly in relation to the application of relevant tax regulations.

Management responsibility

Undertaking bookkeeping and taxation services on behalf of a client may require the service provider to make decisions on behalf of the client or may create the perception that the service provider is acting in a managerial capacity. If Cobra & Co were to assume such responsibility for an audit client, this would create a threat to their objectivity.

This is particularly relevant for a small company such as Asp Co where management is more likely to rely on Cobra & Co for advice. To avoid the risk of assuming a management responsibility, the firm should ensure that Asp Co has procedures in place to ensure that the management team makes all judgements and decisions including:

–   designating an individual who possesses suitable skill, knowledge and experience to be responsible for the client's decisions and to oversee the services being provided;

–   provision of oversight of the services and evaluation of the results of services performed for the client's purposes; and

–   accepting responsibility for the actions to be taken as a result of the services.

If all the services currently provided to Asp Co are administrative and routine, then the threat will be minimal. If, however, Cobra & Co assumes any responsibilities normally carried out by management, then the *Code* states that this threat is so significant that no safeguards can reduce this to an acceptable level.

Audit of financial statements for 31 July 20X7

Cobra & Co has already had significant involvement in the preparation of amounts which have been included in the financial statements for this year end and they may have already applied significant judgement in determining those figures, particularly in relation to any tax amounts or liabilities. Given this heightened risk, as well as using a separate team to do the audit, it would be prudent to ensure that an engagement quality control review is carried out prior to signing the auditor's report.

Actions

If Cobra & Co accepts the audit engagement, they will need to use different staff to undertake the audit to those involved in the other services. Cobra & Co must ensure that they have sufficient staff with the necessary competence within the firm to enact such segregation of duties and they must ensure that the client understands that different teams will be used for the various services provided.

If Cobra & Co has been responsible for any managerial decisions, they must cease this if they accept the audit engagement. However, it is likely that the firm would have to wait a period of time before they would be able to audit the financial statements, as even if they cease to assume management responsibility in the current year, the firm will have influenced the financial statements for the year ended 31 July 20X7. They should communicate this to the management of Asp Co and obtain written confirmations from the client that they understand and accept this. If this requires any change in the nature of the engagements provided, new engagement letters must be issued and signed before the services can be continued.

(b)   **Viper Co**

Self-review threat

Once again, providing both audit and tax services creates a self-review threat to objectivity, but as Viper Co is a non-listed client, Cobra & Co may accept the assignment provided sufficient safeguards are implemented. However, the issue identified in relation to the outgoing auditor does raise concern as to whether these engagements should be accepted.

Acceptance procedures

ISA 220 *Quality Control for an Audit of Financial Statements* requires that Cobra & Co obtains sufficient information to consider a range of matters before accepting an audit engagement. One of the matters is considering the integrity of the owners and management of the client. One such procedure to obtain this information is to communicate with the outgoing auditor. If the engagement partner is not satisfied that they have obtained sufficient information and that they have not concluded sufficiently rigorous procedures to investigate this matter, they should not accept the engagement.

Previously modified opinion

It appears that the management of Viper Co has had a significant disagreement with their outgoing auditor over a certain accounting treatment. This raises a number of separate issues:

–   If management is applying an incorrect accounting treatment and the effect on the financial statements is material, it will lead to a modification in future periods. If management does not accept their responsibility to apply appropriate accounting treatment, then the preconditions for accepting the audit, as prescribed in ISA 210 *Agreeing the Terms of Audit Engagements,* will not have been met. In these circumstances Cobra & Co must not accept the engagement.

–   There is a doubt over the integrity of management as they appear to have disagreed with the auditor, an expert in the application of financial reporting standards, over an accounting treatment. This may indicate an unwillingness to accept financial reporting requirements or a conscious effort to distort the financial statements. Either way, if Cobra & Co is not satisfied as to the integrity of management, they should not accept the engagement.

–   The lawsuit indicates that Viper Co believes that they are correct and that the auditor is incorrect in the matter disputed. This may indicate that, contrary to the previous point, management is not at fault. If this is the case and the auditor is indeed negligent, then there is no reason for Cobra & Co to refuse the engagement.

Actions

Cobra & Co should try to obtain further information from management relating to the lawsuit. It is likely that in these circumstances additional expertise has been sought to determine if the auditor has acted negligently or not. If this is the case, Cobra & Co should request to see any communications with the experts, if permitted.

If not, Cobra & Co should request to review information relating to the matter under dispute. Cobra & Co should be able to use their own expertise to determine an appropriate accounting treatment.

If, following these procedures, Cobra & Co decides that they can proceed with the engagement they should first of all consult with their own legal team, or at least with senior

partners responsible for executive decisions, before accepting given the potentially litigious nature of Viper Co.

If Cobra & Co determines that Viper Co is incorrect or that there is insufficient information to enable a satisfactory conclusion, then it would be prudent in the circumstances to politely decline the engagement.

(c) **Adder Co**

The *Code* defines a conflict of interest as arising when a firm provides a service in relation to two or more clients whose interests in respect of the matter are in conflict.

In this case, the interests of Adder Co and Slowworm Co will be conflicting; Adder Co will want to purchase the shares for the lowest possible amount and the owner of Slowworm Co will want to sell them for the highest possible amount. This creates, therefore, a significant threat to the objectivity of Cobra & Co, who may be seen to be acting in the interest of one party at the expense of the other.

The problem is exacerbated by the nature of the engagement; Adder Co will use information about the company, including operational information, to bargain over the price. Cobra & Co may be privy to private information gained during their time as auditor of Slowworm Co which Adder Co might not have become aware of during normal due diligence procedures. If Cobra & Co were to divulge this to Adder Co, it would give them a potentially unfair advantage over the other client and would be a breach of confidentiality.

Self-review threat

Performing the valuation service for Adder Co would also create a self-review threat because Cobra & Co would have a significant influence over the valuation of Slowworm Co, which would consequently be used to consolidate their accounts into the new, enlarged group which Cobra & Co would be responsible for auditing in the future.

Actions

It is possible to reduce both the conflict of interest and self-review threats by using different teams to conduct the various services provided.

The *Code* stipulates, however, that a firm should not provide valuation services for a listed client if the valuation has a material effect on the financial statements which are consequently audited.

Therefore, before accepting the assignment, Cobra & Co should consider the potential impact of the transaction and, if they believe it will be material, they should politely decline the engagement.

6 Smith & Co

Workbook reference. Chapters 2 and 15.

Top tips. In this type of question it is important to pay attention to the mark allocation and make sure you allocate your time accordingly. Norman Co is worth eight marks so you need to spend more time on this than the other two.

Part (d) would appear difficult as there is no specific technical material on which to base an answer. What was needed here was a common-sense approach, thinking about factors that affect the levels of assurance, and the natures of information that would be likely to exist about the particular performance indicators given in the question.

Easy marks. By suggesting some sensible action points – such as reviewing credit control procedures – you should be able to score some easy marks in this question.

BPP
LEARNING

Marking scheme

Marks

(a) **Norman Co**

Generally 1 mark each per comment and action point:

–   Poor credit control
–   Independence threat – free audit/loan
–   Independence threat – self-interest in 20X8 report
–   Financial distress leads to going concern threat for the company
–   Non-payment due to financial distress does not necessitate resignation
–   Discuss with client – ethical problem/payment arrangements
–   Ethics partner notification
–   Assess significance of amount outstanding
–   Policy to check prior invoices paid
–   Continue to improve credit control
–   Second partner review
–   Review of audit work performed on going concern

Maximum   8

(b) **Wallace Co**

Generally 1 mark each per comment and action point:

–   Non arm's length commercial transaction
–   Material to audit manager
–   Self-interest/intimidation threat
–   Question audit manager's integrity
–   Potential disciplinary action
–   Remove Valerie from audit team
–   Review all work performed on Wallace Co

Marks

- Consider Valerie's relationship with and likelihood of bias towards her other clients
- Disclosure of ethical threat to those charged with governance
- Provide clear communication to all staff regarding transactions with clients

Maximum   5

(c)   **Software Supply Co**

Generally 1 mark each per comment and action point:

- Self review threat
- Self-interest threat
- Independence check
- Client disclosure and acknowledgement
- QC monitoring

Maximum   4

(d)   (i)   **KPI assurance difficulties**
- Discussion of problems in defining KPI terms (max 2 marks)
- Discussion of difficulty in gathering evidence (max 2 marks)

(ii)   **Procedures on number of accidents**
Generally 1 mark per procedure:
Ideas list:
- Review log book
- Discuss and clarify criteria
- HR/payroll records
- Employee correspondence
- Board minute review
- Legal letter review
- Discuss with employees

Maximum   8

Total   25

(a)   **Norman Co**

Credit control

The fees for the 20X7 audit have been outstanding for over 12 months and it seems that little has been done to collect them. Since the file note states that Norman Co is suffering poor cash flows, the balance may no longer be recoverable. Credit control has been poorly managed at Smith & Co regarding this client and the debt should not have remained outstanding for so long.

Action

Credit control procedures at the firm need to be reviewed to prevent this situation reoccurring. It appears that some improvements have already been made with the audit manager now being responsible for reviewing client invoices raised and monitoring credit control procedures.

Independence

The overdue fees for the 20X7 audit may make it appear the audit has been performed for free or could effectively be seen as a loan from Smith & Co to Norman Co. The IESBA *Code of Ethics for Professional Accountants* specifically states that an audit firm should not enter into a loan arrangement with a client that is not a bank or similar institution. It highlights overdue fees as an area where a self-interest threat could arise and independence is threatened. Smith & Co should not have allowed outstanding fees to build up as their independence is now compromised.

Action

Smith and Co should discuss the recoverability of the 20X7 audit fee with the audit committee (if one exists) or those charged with governance. A payment plan should be put into place.

If the overdue fees are not paid, the firm should consider resigning as auditors. In this case a valid commercial reason appears to exist as to why the fees remain unpaid. Smith & Co can remain as auditors provided that adequate safeguards are in place and the amount outstanding is not significant. If the overdue fees are significant, it may be that no safeguards could eliminate the threats to objectivity and independence or reduce them to an acceptable level.

The ethics partner at Smith & Co should be informed of the situation. The ethics partner should evaluate the ethical threat and document the conclusions including the significance of the overdue fees.

20X8 audit

The 20X7 audit fee and arrangements for payment should have been agreed before Smith & Co formally accepted appointment as auditor for the 20X8 audit. Since the 20X8 audit has now almost been completed, it appears this could not have happened.

Action

The ethics partner at Smith & Co should take steps to ensure that there are no outstanding audit fees before commencing new client work. This could involve a new firm-wide policy that audit managers check payment of previous invoices.

Self-interest in 20X8 report

The 20X8 auditor's report has not yet been signed. This creates a self-interest threat to Smith & Co's objectivity and independence because the issue of an unmodified auditor's report may enhance their prospects of securing payment of the overdue 20X7 audit fees.

Action

The working papers for the 20X8 audit of Norman Co should undergo an independent review by the engagement quality control reviewer.

Going concern

Norman Co is known to be having cash flow problems and so there is an issue of whether the company is a going concern for the 20X8 auditor's report.

Action

Smith & Co should carry out a review of the 20X8 audit working papers on going concern. It may be necessary to carry out further audit procedures to ensure that sufficient evidence has been gathered to support the audit opinion.

(b) **Wallace Co**

Business relationship

Under the IESBA's *Code of Ethics,* persons in a position to influence the conduct and outcome of the audit should not enter into business relationships with a client, except where they involve the purchase of goods and services from the client in the ordinary course of business, are on an arm's length basis and are clearly inconsequential to each party.

As audit manager of Wallace Co, Valerie Hobson has influence over the outcome of the audit and should only rent the warehouse space if the conditions prescribed by the *Code* are met. Since the warehouse space is already known to be used for rental income, this transaction is in the ordinary course of business. However, the note on the invoice about only charging a nominal sum indicates that the transaction is not on an arm's length basis. The criteria in the *Code* have therefore been breached. It is also worth noting that the transaction may represent a material discount for Valerie Hobson.

Action

Valerie Hobson should not retain the position of audit manager at Wallace Co and a new manager should be assigned. All planning work for the 20X8 audit should be independently reviewed as planning decisions may have been influenced by the transaction. The situation should be disclosed to those charged with governance at Wallace Co and the audit committee, if one exists.

Self-interest threat

Valerie Hobson has created a self-interest threat, by renting the warehouse space at a reduced rate. Valerie's objectivity could be biased by her desire to please Wallace Co so that she can benefit financially.

Action

Valerie Hobson may need to be disciplined for her actions by Smith & Co who could also send her for ethics training. Smith & Co should investigate for evidence of bias in other audits where Valerie Hobson has had influence.

(c) **Software Supply Co**

Self-interest threat

Smith & Co may have entered into an inappropriate close business relationship by accepting a fee for recommending Software Supply Co to audit clients. This could be seen as a self-interest threat and compromise the independence and objectivity of Smith & Co. The business relationship can be allowed to continue provided that Smith & Co put safeguards in place.

Action

Smith & Co should ensure that where Software Supply Co has been used by a client the following safeguards exist.

- Audit staff have no financial or personal interest in Software Supply Co.

- The arrangement between Smith & Co and Software Supply Co has been fully disclosed.

- Smith & Co should obtain written confirmation that the client is aware of the referral fee.

Additionally, Smith & Co should monitor the quality of the products supplied to ensure they are not associated with inferior goods.

Key performance indicators

(i) **Level of assurance over meeting KPIs**

There are two main reasons why the level of assurance given in relation to the KPIs cannot be a high level of assurance:

- Lack of precision in the description of the KPIs
- Likely lack of appropriate audit evidence

Lack of precision

The KPIs are defined imprecisely and involve a high degree of subjectivity. For example:

- Donated product should be 1% of revenue, but what price will be free product be valued at – cost or retail price?

- Similarly, how will 'donations' to local charities be valued if these donations are more than just financial donations, such as the use of Sci-Tech's expert employees or products?

- 'Serious' accidents should be fewer than five, but what constitutes 'serious'?

Audit evidence

Some of these matters may be well documented, such as cash donations or accidents, because of health and safety procedures, but others, such as time spent by employees at local charities, may not be so well documented.

(ii) **Evidence in relation to serious accidents**

- Obtain and review health and safety accident log-books for all Sci-Tech's premises and review the number of accidents.

- Discuss the definition of 'serious' with the directors and obtain written verification of this definition.

- Select a number of accidents designated serious and not-serious and review associated correspondence, payroll records and compensation payments to determine whether the accidents have been properly designated serious or not.

- Review correspondence with legal advisors to ascertain if any action has been taken in relation to accidents not designated serious by the directors.

- Review board minutes to obtain directors' opinions on the increase in serious accidents in 20X7.

- Review correspondence and reports from regulatory bodies to ensure that controls over health and safety reporting are considered to be strong.

- Discuss health and safety controls with health and safety officer to ensure that all accidents are reported.

7 Ryder

Workbook reference. Chapters 2, 5, 6 and 7.

Top tips. The requirement here was to respond to the junior's question, and to explain the ethical and professional matters arising. There might have been a little bit of confusion here, because the requirement could be read as saying that ethical and professional matters arose from each mini-scenario, which was not the case.

Part (a) was a discussion-type requirement on business risk and the risk of material misstatement. The junior's question suggests a format for your answer – explain the two types of risk (1 mark each),

then identify the relation between them (2 marks for a good discussion). The first two marks here were not difficult, so all you then needed to do was muster a reasonable discussion to pass this part of the question.

Part (b) was quite a theoretical discussion of the use of 'service organisations' (outsourcing). Questions like this are a reminder that AAA students need to be familiar with ISAs, specifically ISA 402, as there were plenty of marks available for knowledge that comes straight from the ISA, eg of Type 1 and Type 2 reports.

Part (c) contained a fairly clear conflict of interests between two clients, and was a standard ethics-type question at AAA. Your approach should therefore be to identify and explain the issue; explain which ethical principles are threatened and why; suggest safeguards (where relevant), or suggest that the engagement be declined.

Part (d) was another ethics requirement, and was fairly clear-cut although there were a lot of marks available here.

Easy marks. The first part of part (a) was fairly easy, even if it did not look it at first sight.

ACCA examining team's comments. In issue (a), most candidates could attempt the definitions, but some went into far too much detail for the marks available. The relationship between the two types of risk was usually explained by way of example, which was acceptable, and many of the examples were appropriate. The most common mistake seen in answers here was to explain audit risk rather than risk of material misstatement.

Issue (b) saw some good attempts, with most answers identifying issues in relation to access to information, assessment of the internal controls at the service organisation, and the competence of the service organisation. Disappointingly, few answers mentioned type 1 and type 2 reports that are typically obtained in this situation, and many tried to focus on ethical matters such as independence, and therefore didn't specifically address the requirement.

On issue (c), many candidates did correctly determine that a conflict of interest would arise and could recommend appropriate safeguards. However, many answers failed to identify the potential issues surrounding the confidentiality of client information. Some candidates tried to include a comment on every one of the ethical principles – many of which were irrelevant. It is a better exam technique to focus on the most relevant of the ethical threats, and not to try to cover all of them, especially when there are only 5 marks available.

On issue (d), most answers picked up on the potential for a close business relationship to be created with an audit client, and many could discuss that the severity of the ethical threats resulting from such an investment are unlikely to be acceptable. Some answers also considered the commercial angle, and many also reached an appropriate conclusion. Weaker answers listed out all of the possible threats to objectivity without any real application to the scenario.

Marking scheme

Marks

In general up to 1½ marks for each comment/explanation/definition:

(a) **Risk assessment**

- Definition of business risk (1 mark)
- Definition of risk of material misstatement (1 mark)
- Business risks impact on the financial statements and therefore risk of material misstatement
- Business risk impacts inherent risk
- Business risk impacts control risk

Maximum   4

BPP
LEARNING

(b) **Outsourcing**

- Need to assess significance of outsourced function on financial statements
- Need to understand relationship and interaction between audited entity and service organisation
- Obtain understanding of the service organisation including internal controls
- Means of obtaining understanding – type 1 and type 2 reports
- Other means of obtaining understanding – requesting information, performing tests on controls at the service organisation

Maximum   4

(c) **Conflict of interest**

- Identify/explain the conflict of interest
- Threats to objectivity and confidentiality created
- Safeguard of disclosure to both parties
- Other safeguards (½ mark each), eg separate teams, confidentiality agreements, review of situation by independent partner
- If threats too significant the advice should not be given

Maximum   5

(d) **Business opportunity**

- Identify the opportunity as a close business relationship/financial interest in a client
- Threat created – self-interest
- Can only be accepted if the interest is insignificant
- Unlikely to be insignificant due to nationwide programme
- Consider commercial angle – return on investment/cash availability
- Skills and competence to provide speakers
- Resource availability

Maximum   7

Total   **20**

(a) **Explanation of risks**

Business risk is the risk inherent to the company in its operations, and can be considered in three aspects: operational risk, financial risk and compliance risk. Business risk considers the company in its operational aspect only.

The risk of material misstatement (RoMM) can be thought of as part of audit risk, comprising inherent risk and control risk but excluding detection risk. Like audit risk, RoMM is concerned with whether or not the financial statements are materially misstated; the difference is that RoMM excludes the work done by the auditor to detect those misstatements.

Relation between risks

In general terms, business risk can affect RoMM because almost everything that the business does has a financial effect which must be reported. For instance, a company might launch a new revenue stream. This business activity results in revenue which must be reported in line with IFRS 15 *Revenue from Contracts with Customers*. There is a risk of this being done incorrectly, which is a RoMM.

A business risk might affect inherent risk (part of RoMM). For example, a company might have high levels of debt with covenants attached. There is a business risk of these covenants being breached; there is also an inherent risk of the financial statements being manipulated in order prevent this from happening.

A business risk could affect control risk (also part of RoMM). For example, a company may be subject to a business risk as a result of losing key members of staff from the accounting department. This could also increase control risk because it could mean that fewer staff are available to operate controls.

(b) Outsourcing is covered in ISA 402 *Audit Considerations Relating to an Entity Using a Service Organisation*. The effect at the planning stage is that the auditor must consider what risks might arise from the outsourcing (ie from using a service organisation) and plan how to respond to them. ISA 402 requires consideration of:

- The nature and significance of the services provided to the audited entity (eg the effect on internal control)

- The nature and materiality of the transactions processed by the service organisation

- The degree of interaction between the activities of the service organisation and the audited entity

- The nature of the relationship, including contractual terms   (ISA 402)

Crow Co should also have its own internal controls over the outsourced payroll. The auditor should evaluate them and obtain an understanding of the control risk in this area. If the outsourced payroll is not subject to checks by Crow Co then control risk is higher.

The starting point is information available from Crow Co about the service organisation, but it may be necessary to obtain a report on the controls at the service organisation. A Type 1 report here focuses on the description and design of controls; a Type 2 report also considers whether they are effective (ISA 402).

The auditor may also contact the service organisation, and may plan to visit them to perform tests of controls. This requires client permission and can be time-consuming (and therefore costly).

Once an understanding of Crow Co's use of the service organisation has been obtained, control risk can be properly assessed and thus the procedures the auditor plans to perform.

(c) This is a potential conflict of interests, with the auditor being asked to provide advice to Crow Co in its tender to another audit client.

The key threat here is confidentiality, as either party could benefit from information obtained from the audit firm about the other party.

The IESBA *Code of Ethics* requires the significance of any threats to be evaluated, and safeguards to be applied when necessary to eliminate the threats or reduce them to an acceptable level.

The chief safeguard here is disclosure of the situation to both of the audit clients. Ryder & Co should not accept the engagement until both clients have given their consent.

Other possible safeguards could include:

- Using separate engagement teams

- Information barriers between the teams (eg, strict physical separation of the teams, confidential and secure data filing)

- Clear guidelines for members of the engagement team on security and confidentiality

- Confidentiality agreements signed by employees and partners of the firm

- Regular review of the application of safeguards by a senior individual not involved with relevant client engagements (IESBA *Code of Ethics*)

It is possible that the threat cannot be reduced to an acceptable level, in which case Ryder & Co should decline to give advice in relation to the tender.

(d) This arrangement could be considered a close business relationship, in the terms of the IESBA *Code of Ethics*, resulting from a commercial relationship or common financial interest. Ryder & Co would be investing money in the relationship and therefore stands to gain or lose financially from it; its fate is in this respect tied up with that of Campbell Co.

There is a self-interest threat here, because Ryder & Co may be inclined to treat Campbell Co more favourably in order to protect its own interest in this joint business arrangement.

Ryder & Co must evaluate the significance of these threats, and whether there are safeguards available to reduce them to an acceptable level. If the financial interest is material or the business relationship significant, then no safeguards would be able to reduce the threat to an acceptable level, and Ryder & Co should not take part in the arrangement. The fact that the events are nationwide implies that it is a reasonably large operation and could therefore be assessed as significant.

Further, Ryder & Co must be independent not only in substance but in appearance too. Even if the interest were immaterial and the business relationship insignificant, the appearance of closeness that might be suggested would be enough to compromise Ryder & Co. For this reason the invitation should be declined.

There may be practical and commercial problems here too. Ryder & Co may not have staff with the requisite technical expertise to deliver the technical updates, in which case to deliver them would violate the principle of professional competence and due care. There could also be resourcing issues if staff need to be diverted away from audit engagements in order to deliver lectures.

Even if these ethical problems did not exist, a commercial judgement would need to be made. Ryder & Co may not have sufficient cash to invest, and needs to consider what return it might expect to receive for its investment.

8 Chennai

Workbook reference. Chapters 2 and 12.

Top tips. Part (a)(i) was a real bread-and-butter question for AAA – this material should be very familiar to you indeed. The main issue here should have been avoiding writing too much. If you did find this requirement tricky then you will need to make sure you know this material well for your exam.

Part (a)(ii) followed on from (i). The key was that the requirement asked for 'advantages and disadvantages **to Delhi**', ie you had to apply yourself to the scenario. In many respects this makes the question easier, as all you need to do is to read the scenario and think about how an audit might help in this situation. As usual, each part of the scenario is there to tell you something, so try to think about what bearing it might have on whether an audit is needed.

Don't forget that it's about disadvantages as well; some are implied by the scenario, eg the part about staff studying for their ACCA exams hints at staff being less experienced at dealing with auditors, and also perhaps having less time available.

Part (b) should have been a reasonable ethics question. The self-review threat is fairly clear. You should have been able to spot that designing internal controls is management's responsibility – not the auditor's – and therefore should not be undertaken.

In a way the question was a little tricky, because the existence of internal control problems hints at the audit process – how can the auditor rely on these controls? – but the requirement asks only for the ethical and professional issues. If your answer focuses on the audit process then presumably there will be no marks for this, but there are marks available for the effect on governance (communication with the audit committee), and for whether the audit was conducted properly. In any case, you only need four to five marks to pass this part of the question.

It should be noted that the solutions given for this question in particular are significantly longer than anything a student could produce in an exam, so you should not be aiming to write this much in your answer.

Easy marks. Part (a)(i) was easy, and was probably why many people chose this question in their real exam.

ACCA examining team's comments. This question required candidates to provide advice to two clients around the difference between an audit and a limited assurance review and providing non-audit services.

In relation to the differences between audit and limited review, most candidates demonstrated a sound understanding of both and were able to succinctly explain the differences between them including the different audiences for each.

Strong answers were tailored based on the specifics of the scenario and therefore provided relevant advice to the client in question. For example strong answers highlighted that a full audit would be beneficial to the fast-growing client as it would give more credibility to the company, especially as it may be seeking bank finance. Candidates are reminded that at this level answers need to be responsive to the question requirements and should not simply be an exercise in reproducing everything that they know about a topic.

Candidates were also asked to advise a listed audit client, asking for a review of their control systems due to concerns about weaknesses in controls shortly after your firm had signed off the most recent auditor's report.

Few candidates recognised the potential implications on the accuracy of the auditor's report which had been recently issued and that these potential weaknesses could undermine that opinion. Clearly further details were needed to establish if the deficiencies in control would have had any significant impact on those financial statements.

Many candidates simply provided a discussion of the advantages to the client of having a review of the internal control system but failed to appreciate that undertaking such a review for a listed client would be prohibited by the *Code*, and this again demonstrated that many candidates did not have a good enough understanding of the requirement of the ethical guidelines. In such circumstances opting for a separate team is not an effective safeguard and the review should not be done.

Marking scheme

Marks

(a)   Generally 1 mark available for each well explained point:

    (i)   **Audit v limited review**

        –   Regulatory requirements
        –   Determination of scope
        –   Nature of procedures
        –   Reasonable v moderate levels of assurance
        –   Audit **opinion**
            'The financial statements are true and fair.......'
        –   Review engagement **conclusion**

BPP
LEARNING

'Based on our review nothing has coming to our attention.......'
- Negative v positive wording

(ii) **Advantages and disadvantages of audit**
- Accountability to external shareholder
- Renegotiation of loan facility
- Reliability of information for internal decisions
- Potential mandatory audit if company grows
- Overseas trading relationships
- Review of internal controls
- Risk of misstatement due to changes in accounting staff
- Cost of full audit
- Potentially no need for high level of assurance
- More invasive nature of audit

Maximum   12

(b) **Mumbai Co**
Generally 1 mark for each well explained ethical and professional threat; ½ mark available for each recommended safeguard:

- Self-review threat
- Management responsibility: self-interest and familiarity threat
- No safeguards which can reduce management threat
- Possible safeguards to avoid management threat
- Restriction on internal audit services for listed clients
- Competence if review is not related to financial controls
- Responsibilities of auditor in relation to internal controls
- Possible deficiency in external audit procedures
- Nature/severity of deficiencies not clear

Maximum   8

Total   20

(a) (i) **Difference between an audit and a limited assurance review**

An audit is a mandatory requirement in most countries, although some small companies below a certain threshold may be exempted. Limited assurance reviews are not usually required by law.

The scope of and procedures performed during an audit are determined by the audit firm in accordance with the auditing standards adopted by the professional regulatory body. The scope of a limited review is agreed by the firm providing the services and the client, although this must be in accordance with any relevant standards on assurance and related services adopted by professional regulators.

In particular, an audit involves a wide range of procedures used to obtain evidence, including both tests of controls and substantive procedures. The latter include inspection of documents, recalculation, observation, enquiry and analytical procedures, amongst others. Limited reviews use a narrower range of procedures, focusing primarily on enquiry and analytical procedures.

Overall, the level of assurance provided by an audit is much higher than that provided by a limited review. In an audit the practitioner gives a reasonable level of assurance, whereas in a review engagement the practitioner gives a moderate level of assurance.

This has a significant impact on the wording of the respective reports. In an auditor's report the practitioner expresses an opinion as to the fair presentation of the financial statements. An example of this would be:

'In our opinion the financial statements present fairly, in all material respects, the financial position of the company, its financial performance and its cash flows for the year ended in accordance with International Financial Reporting Standards (IFRSs).'

(ISA 700)

A review engagement report does not express any opinion on the fair presentation of the financial statements reviewed, instead the report expresses a conclusion based only upon the work performed. For example:

'Based on the review performed, nothing has come to our attention which causes us to believe that the financial statements do not present fairly, in all material respects, ... in accordance with International Financial Reporting Standards.'   (ISRE 2400)

The review engagement report is often referred to as a negative form of opinion, whereas the auditor's report is referred to as a positive statement regarding the fair presentation of the financial statements.

(ii) **Advantages and disadvantages to Delhi Co of having an audit**

Advantages

One of the key differences between an audit and a review engagement is that an audit provides a reasonable level of assurance, whereas a review only provides limited assurance. This means that an audit provides stronger assurances to users of the financial statements regarding their accuracy and credibility.

This would be significant for Delhi Co for a number of reasons. The first is that the company now has an external shareholder, Robert Hyland, who is not part of the executive management team. With this separation of ownership and control comes an increased need to hold the management of the company accountable to the external shareholders and having a full audit will provide a much stronger form of accountability.

Second, Delhi Co has a bank loan facility which is due to expire in 20X7. Given the ambitious expansion plans of Delhi Co, it is likely that the company will want to renew this facility and they may even seek to obtain more loan finance.

If this is the case, it is very likely that the bank will seek a reasonable level of assurance over the financial statements. By electing to have an annual audit now, it may avoid delays in 20X7 when the company comes to renegotiate terms with the bank.

Finally, the internal management team needs good quality information on which to base their operational and strategic decisions. As the business grows and the significance of those decisions increases, it becomes more important that the management team has information that they can rely on. Having fully audited financial statements, as opposed to a limited review, will increase the confidence of management in the accuracy of the information used.

Another benefit of having a full audit now is that, whilst the business is currently under the audit exemption threshold, it is rapidly expanding and may soon exceed the threshold and be subject to mandatory audit. One of the key problems of auditing a business for the first time is that there is no existing assurance over the opening balances and comparative figures. In this case the first audit is much more time consuming, and therefore expensive, as the audit team has to invest more time investigating prior year figures. The requirement to review the prior year would be much less onerous if the company began to have their financial statements audited now while they were still relatively small and this would lead to a more efficient audit in the future.

Delhi Co also plans to expand its customer base. Trading internationally usually adds extra complications due to the added complexity in the supply chain, foreign exchange and simple lack of familiarity with the company. Customers may want assurances that any company they sign a trading agreement with has the resources to satisfy their contractual obligations. For this reason, having fully audited accounts, as opposed to accounts which have had a limited review, may give potential customers increased confidence in the financial position of Delhi Co and may improve their chances of forming new trade partnerships.

There has also been a recent change in the accounting department of Delhi Co. This is normal in a rapidly expanding business but it creates new challenges. Often the accounting systems of small companies are unsophisticated but as the company grows the systems soon become outdated and less effective. An audit incorporates a review of effectiveness of the internal control systems relevant to the production of the financial statements and any deficiencies identified by the auditor would be reported to management. Given the changes Delhi Co has experienced, a full audit may help them assess the effectiveness of their internal systems and make changes where necessary. The systems would not be assessed with a limited review.

The change in staff in the accounts department also increases the risk of misstatement of the financial statements due to their lack of familiarity with the company and the accounting systems. The fact that the new recruits are both part qualified further increases the risk of misstatement of the financial statements because the trainees may not be fully able to process all of the transactions and events relevant to the business. An audit is a more thorough investigation of the financial statements than a review and would be much more likely to identify misstatements, providing management with more reliable figures upon which to base their decisions.

Disadvantages

While an audit is a more thorough investigation, it is also more expensive than a review. For a small company an audit may be prohibitively expensive, whereas a review may be more affordable.

If the company is exempt, an audit may also be an unnecessary cost. Delhi Co already managed to raise a loan without the need for audited accounts. The external shareholder is also an ex-business partner of Mr Dattani and it is likely that they have a good working relationship. If Mr Hyland needs assurances, it is possible that Mr Dattani could satisfy this on an informal basis without the need to incur the costs of an audit. Mr Hyland also decided to invest knowing that the company was not subject to audit, so it may not be a concern of his.

An audit is also more invasive than a limited review and would require the staff of Delhi Co to provide more information to the auditor and give up more of their time than would be the case with a limited review. Given the relative inexperience of the accounts team, Mr Dattani may prefer to choose the less invasive limited review now and perform a full audit in the future when the team is more knowledgeable of the business.

(b)   **Mumbai Co**

Review of internal controls

Reviewing the internal controls of an audit client which are relevant to the financial reporting system would create a self-review threat as the auditor would consequently assess the effectiveness of the control system during the external audit.

The design, implementation and maintenance of internal controls are also management responsibilities. If the auditor were to assist in this process, it may be considered that they were assuming these management responsibilities. The IESBA *Code of Ethics for Professional Accountants* identifies this as a potential self-review, self-interest and familiarity threat.

The latter arises because the audit firm could be considered to be aligning their views and interests to those of management.

The *Code* states that the threats caused by adopting management responsibilities are so significant that there are no safeguards which could reduce the threats to an acceptable level.

The only effective measures which could be adopted would be those which ensured the audit firm did not adopt a management responsibility, such as ensuring that the client has assigned competent personnel to be responsible at all times for reviewing internal control review reports and for determining which of the recommendations from the report are to be implemented.

Furthermore, the *Code* stipulates that if the client is listed and also an audit client, then the audit firm shall not provide internal audit services which relate to a significant part of the internal controls relevant to financial reporting. Given that this is the main expertise of the audit firm, it is likely that they will be required to perform some work in this area and this service would therefore not be appropriate.

If Mumbai Co would like the firm to perform a review of internal controls not related to the financial reporting system, Chennai Co would need to consider whether they have the professional competencies to complete the engagement to the necessary standard of quality.

Concerns regarding deterioration in controls

One of the responsibilities of the auditor is to evaluate the design and implementation of the client's controls relevant to the audit in order to assist with the identification of risks of material misstatement. This includes the specific requirement to consider the risk of material misstatement due to fraud.

If deficiencies in internal controls are identified, the auditor has to assess the potential impact on the financial statements and design a suitable response in order to reduce audit risk to an acceptable level. The auditor is also responsible for communicating significant deficiencies in internal control to those charged with governance on a timely basis.

The audit committee has suggested that a number of internal control deficiencies have recently been identified which they were not previously aware of. This suggests that these were not issues identified or reported to those charged with governance by the auditor.

If these internal control deficiencies relate to systems relevant to the audit, it may suggest that the audit firm's consideration of the internal control system failed to detect these potential problems, which may indicate ineffective audit planning. If so, this increases the risk that the audit procedures designed were inappropriate and that there is a heightened risk that the audit team failed to detect material misstatements during the audit. In the worst case scenario this could mean that Chennai & Co issued an inappropriate audit opinion.

The circumstances are not clear though; the audit committee of Mumbai Co has not specified which controls appear to have deteriorated and whether these are related to the audit or not. There is also no indication of the potential scale of any fraud or inefficient commercial practice. It is possible that the risks resulting from the deficiencies are so small that they did not lead to a risk of material misstatement. In these circumstances, the audit team may have identified the deficiencies as not being significant and reported them to an appropriate level of operating management.

In order to assess this further, the manager should examine the audit file and review the documentation in relation to the evaluation of the internal controls of Mumbai Co and assess any subsequent communications to management and those charged with governance. The concerns raised by the audit committee should be noted as points to take forward into next year's audit, when they should be reviewed and evaluated as part of planning the audit for the 20X7 year end.

Additionally, Chennai & Co should contact the audit committee of Mumbai Co to seek further clarification on the nature and extent of the deficiencies identified and whether this has resulted in any actual or suspected acts of fraud.

9 Bunk

Workbook references. Chapters 2 and 4.

Top tips. The requirement for this question contained several different elements, so you had a lot to bear in mind when reading the scenarios and constructing your answer. There are at least four elements that you had to think of: ethics, quality control, firm-wide policies, and actions for the firm to take. The marking scheme contains quite a few marks for actions, and it would have been difficult to score well if you had not included any.

Part (a) was a nice mini-scenario on fee pressure and a related drop in audit quality. You needed to respond to the issues in the scenario and connect them up with your book-knowledge. For example, the scenario contains the issue of the audit committee refusing to increase the fee – you needed to note this, and state that it is an intimidation threat. Likewise, you should note that materiality was increased in order to reduce the amount of audit work done, and then connect this to your book-knowledge of quality control.

Part (b) should not have been difficult, provided that you read the scenario carefully. This may have been more difficult, however, if you do not have experience of working in an audit firm (and thus of off-shoring). In some ways there was not that much to say for the 5 marks available. Essentially, it is OK to off-shore non-judgmental work, but it is not OK to off-shore work that requires judgement and, in particular, work which requires knowledge of the client (which those working off-shore are unlikely to have). It's fairly clear in the scenario that the numerical checks on documentation are OK, but that reviewing board minutes is not OK. This then raises quality control issues, which connect to the 'firm-wide policies' asked for by the requirement because the scenario states that Bunk & Co encourages this practice, ie this is a firm-wide policy that may have implications for quality control.

Part (c) featured a slightly tricky situation in that the finance director was not the audit engagement partner, but merely another audit partner in the firm. This means that the issue is not quite cut-and-dried, but it is clear that this partner had an influence on the audit of the company he had just left, and that ethical threats arose from this. This was a good place to suggest actions for the auditor, such as discussing the issue with the ethics partner and the audit committee.

Easy marks. Part (a) contained some easy marks for identifying the intimidation threat, and the quality control issues there were fairly clear-cut.

ACCA examining team's comments. Part (a) described how the audit committee of Wire Co had refused to agree to an increase in audit fees despite an increase in the company's operations. Consequently the audit firm increased the materiality level used during the audit, reduced sample sizes used when obtaining audit evidence and cut out some review procedures. Many candidates attempted this part of the question well. **Effective answers** explained the intimidation threat to objectivity caused by fee pressure and went on to discuss the impact of each of the issues raised in the scenario on the quality of the audit that had been performed. It was pleasing to see many candidates discuss matters such as sampling risk and the need for review procedures to assure the quality of audit work and to reduce the audit firm's detection risk. **Weaker answers** tended to be repetitive, and for each of the issues simply say that 'not enough evidence could be obtained' resulting in material misstatements and an inappropriate audit opinion.

Part (b) focused on the issue of off-shoring audit work, which had been discussed in an article before this exam. Answers ranged in quality, with some good attempts which identified that while off-shoring can bring efficiencies to an audit, care must be taken in deciding the type of work that is performed by the overseas office. From this scenario it should have been identified that off-shoring procedures such as the reading of board minutes to identify audit issues was not appropriate, but relatively few answers mentioned this point. Weaker answers tended to suggest that overseas offices would be incompetent and unable to perform even the simplest of audit procedures. Some candidates misinterpreted the information provided and assumed that the scenario was about using component auditors in a group situation, which was not the case.

BPP Note. The article referred to is entitled 'Audit quality', and is available here:

http://www.accaglobal.com/uk/en/student/exam-support-resources/professional-exams-study-resources/p7/technical-articles/audit-quailty.html

In part (c) most candidates realised that the former finance director could have influenced the partner and had motivation to do so given that he held shares in Wire Co for a period of time after joining the audit firm. **Stronger candidates** were able to clearly explain the specific ethical threats that arose from the scenario, provided sensible recommendations, and also commented on the audit firm needing stronger firm-wide policies in the event of recruiting new audit partners from audit clients.

The scenario also stated that audit team members were being encouraged to cross-sell non-audit services to audit clients and that they would be appraised on this. The answers here tended not to focus on the problems caused by appraising staff on their success in selling services to audit clients but instead discussed generally the ethical problems of providing non-audit services to audit clients. While not irrelevant, these discussions tended to be very general and not applied to the information in the scenario, resulting in answers that lacked focus.

It was also clear that **many candidates were not guided by the mark allocation for the various parts of the question**, and a significant number of answers to part (c) were the same length as the answer to part (a). As mentioned earlier, candidates should bear the mark allocation in mind, and use it to determine how long to spend in answering each part of the question.

Marking scheme

Marks

Generally up to 1½ marks for each relevant point explained, to include 1 mark for each action recommended and ½ mark for identification of ethical threats.

(a) **Fee pressure and sampling risk**
   – Intimidation threat identified and explained
   – Fee should not remain the same when the scope of audit is increased
   – Discuss with audit committee and communicate with those charged with governance
   – Increased materiality level reduces audit work and increases detection risk
   – Audit work to be reviewed for completeness and sufficiency (1 mark)
   – Use of judgement increases sampling risk
   – Some items excluded from sample, so sample cannot be representative of population

Maximum   6

(b) **Off-shoring audit work**
   – No regulation to prohibit off-shoring arrangements
   – Increasingly common way to improve audit efficiency
   – Problem is those performing audit work lack knowledge and experience of the client
   – Off-shoring should focus on low-risk and low-judgement areas of the audit
   – Strong controls and monitoring should be in place

Maximum   5

BPP
LEARNING

(c) **Recent service with audit client, financial self-interest and cross-selling services**

- Recent service with client creates self-interest, self-review and familiarity threats
- Persons joining audit firm from a client should not be part of that client's audit team
- Russell seems to have acted as if he were a member of the audit team
- A quality control review should be performed
- Russell's shareholding creates a self-interest threat
- The shareholding should have been disposed of immediately
- Consider why this did not happen – firm's policies should be reviewed
- Cross-selling creates a self-interest threat
- Key audit partners should not be evaluated based on cross-selling
- Other audit team members can cross-sell if appropriate safeguards are in place

Maximum   9

Total   **20**

(a) **Intimidation threat**

When the audit client imposes fee pressure on the audit firm, an intimidation threat to objectivity arises. IESBA's *Code of Ethics* defines the intimidation threat as the threat that a professional accountant will be deterred from acting objectively because of actual or perceived pressures, and gives an example of an intimidation threat where the audit firm is being pressured to reduce inappropriately the extent of work performed in order to match the fee they can obtain to the work performed.

Action

The matter should have been discussed with Wire Co's audit committee, with the audit firm stressing that the new locations would lead to an increased scope of the audit, and therefore the fee should increase rather than remain the same. It should also be brought to the attention of Bunk & Co's partner responsible for ethics.

Materiality – quality control

The fee pressure has resulted in the materiality level being increased, presumably in order to reduce the level of audit procedures performed and thus the cost of the audit. This leads to a risk that insufficient audit evidence may have been obtained to support the audit opinion, with the risk heightened by the fact that some review procedures were not carried out. This in itself indicates that appropriate quality control procedures have not been applied to the audit.

ISA 220 *Quality Control for an Audit of Financial Statements* requires the audit engagement partner to review the audit documentation to be satisfied that audit work is complete and that sufficient appropriate audit evidence has been obtained to support the conclusions reached and for the auditor's report to be issued.

Sample sizes

There are also quality control issues with the selection of samples to be used in tests of detail. First, the use of judgmental sampling may result in sample sizes which are smaller than would have been selected using statistical sampling methods, or in the selection of items which are not representative of the whole population. ISA 530 *Audit Sampling* requires the auditor to determine a sample size sufficient to reduce sampling risk to an acceptably low level, and to select items for the sample in such a way that each sampling unit in the population has an equal chance of selection. The risk is that the use of judgement has led to inappropriate audit conclusions being made.

Second, it seems that some items in the populations were completely excluded from the sample. There is a high risk that these items have not been subject to sufficient audit procedures and that the relevant assertions have not been covered by audit testing. For example, if the non-current assets have not been physically verified, and no other procedures relevant to their existence have been performed, then assets recognised in the financial statements may be overstated.

Conclusion

Given the pressure on fees which seems to be affecting the quality of audit work performed, Bunk & Co may wish to consider whether it is appropriate to continue with the audit engagement. The audit firm's concerns should be communicated to those charged with governance of Wire Co, and the audit committee should be made aware of the implications of the fee pressure on the audit.

(b) **Off-shoring of audit work**

The off-shoring of audit work has become increasingly common in the audit profession in the last few years, with global audit firms using low-cost overseas audit offices or service centres to perform some audit procedures. There is no regulation to prohibit this practice, but quality control implications have been brought into question.

If the overseas office is performing only low-risk and non-judgmental work, the risk to audit quality is relatively low. However, it seems in the case of Wire Co's audit other more subjective tasks were included in the off-shoring arrangement, such as the review of board minutes. In order to properly assess the contents of the board minutes for audit implications, the work should be performed by an auditor with sufficient knowledge and understanding of the audit client to be able to identify matters which are significant in the context of that audit. It is unlikely that an auditor in an overseas office with no direct understanding or experience of Wire Co would be able to identify relevant matters for the attention of the rest of the audit team.

If Bunk & Co wishes to continue the off-shoring of audit procedures, then controls must be put in place to ensure that only appropriate tasks are included in the arrangement, and that monitoring and review procedures are performed to give comfort on the quality of the work performed. The audit firm must ensure that its firm-wide policies adhere to the requirements of ISQC 1 *Quality control for firms that perform audits and reviews of financial statements, and other assurance and related services engagements*, and that commercial considerations do not take priority over the performance of high quality audits.

> **Tutorial note.** Credit will be awarded for other relevant comments on the issue of off-shoring audit work.

(c) **Finance director becoming audit partner**

Russell Bell moving from Wire Co to Bunk & Co to take up the position of audit partner creates potential threats to objectivity.

The IESBA *Code* states that self-interest, self-review or familiarity threats may be created if a member of the audit team has recently served as a director, officer, or employee of the audit client. Though the threats may be mitigated somewhat by him not being a formal member of the audit team of Wire Co, the fact that Russell helped the audit team (by providing information about the audited entity) means that the threats described above apply in this situation. There is a perception that the audit team is not independent.

BPP
LEARNING

The IESBA *Code* requires that if, during the period covered by the auditor's report, a member of the audit team served as a director or officer of the audit client (or was an employee in a position to exert significant influence over the preparation of the client's accounting records or the financial statements on which the firm will express an opinion), that person may not be included in the audit team. Clearly Russell's former position as finance director of Wire Co means that this requirement should have been applied to him.

Action

The matter should be discussed with Bunk & Co's partner responsible for ethics, and it should also be discussed with Wire Co's audit committee, who are responsible for oversight of auditor independence.

Shareholding in client

The second issue is that Russell retained a shareholding in Wire Co for six months after his appointment as an audit partner in Bunk & Co. This gives rise to a self-interest threat to objectivity, as it would have been in Russell's interests to act in such a way as to maximise his financial interest in Wire Co until the point when he sold his shares. There is a general prohibition on auditors holding a financial interest in an audit client. The IESBA *Code* states that when a financial interest arises, it should be disposed of immediately in the case of an audit team member, or as soon as possible in the case of an individual who is not a member of the audit team. Given Russell's seniority, and the fact that he seems to have closely advised the audit team on matters relating to Wire Co, he should have made the disposal immediately.

Concerns may arise over Bunk & Co's procedures in relation to staff and partner disclosure of financial interests in audited entities. Six months is a long period for the shares to have been held, and the firm should have procedures in place to ensure that such matters are monitored and quickly resolved.

Action

A review of the firm's procedures should take place, and Russell should be asked why he did not dispose of the shares more quickly.

Cross-selling

Finally, the audit firm's policy on cross-selling non-audit services raises ethical issues. The IESBA *Code* states that a self-interest threat is created when a member of the audit team is evaluated on or compensated for selling non-assurance services to that audit client. This is because the audit team member clearly has a financial interest in successful cross-selling, which may result in the selling of services which are inappropriate to the client, or which give rise to other independence threats which exist when non-audit services are provided to audited entities, or when fees from non-audit services are dependent on the audit service.

The significance of the self-interest threat depends on:

- The proportion of the individual's compensation or performance evaluation which is based on the sale of such services;

- The role of the individual on the audit team; and

- Whether promotion decisions are influenced by the sale of such services.   (IESBA *Code*)

The IESBA *Code* states that a key audit partner shall not be evaluated on or compensated based on that partner's success in selling non-assurance services to the partner's audit client. Therefore if Bunk & Co is to continue with this policy, care must be taken that partners' performance is not evaluated based on their success in cross-selling to their audit clients.

It is not prohibited for other audit team members to cross-sell, but safeguards must be in place to reduce the potential threat to an acceptable level, such as a review of audit work performed.

It may be prudent, however, for the audit firm to consider other ways to increase revenue and to evaluate staff performance which do not raise threats to objectivity.

10 Grape

Workbook reference. Chapters 1, 4 and 9.

Top tips. The scenario gives you the figures to calculate materiality in a fairly obvious way (by stating that the 'draft financial statements show revenue of $12.5m, net profit of $400,000, and total assets of $78m'). This is almost always a hint that you're going to have to calculate materiality at some point in your answer, and the opportunity to do so comes up straight away in part (a)(i)'s requirement for 'matters to consider' in relation to audit evidence.

These are easy marks, so to make sure you get them, calculate materiality, and then apply it to the scenario by stating whether or not the matter in question is actually material.

Part (a)(i) was a tricky requirement. If you read the question carefully, you could have noticed that it is asking for the 'audit evidence you should expect to find **DURING your file review**' in relation to the 'training costs **that have been capitalised**'. In other words, you're being asked for the evidence that you would find for the training costs as non-current asset additions in the year, **given that the audit team have not yet realised that the accounting treatment is wrong**. This is tricky, but these questions do come up. When they do, it's important not to panic. Read the requirement very carefully – as long as you answer the requirement, you should get marks for every (correct) thing that you say. Once you've understood the requirement correctly, it's actually a very straightforward question on audit evidence.

Part (b) should have been straightforward, as there were plenty of points in the scenario that you should have picked up on. You should have been looking to pass this part of question well – but without exceeding the time allocation for it!

Part (c) did require you to go into quite a lot of detail about money laundering. If you have trouble remembering the policies and procedures (part (ii)), then you could try just thinking of the sorts of procedures that firms could implement in order not to get caught money laundering, as many of them are fairly common-sense.

Easy marks. There is one mark for just writing a conclusion to your answer to part (b), indicated by the word 'evaluate' in the requirement. As a general point, this examining team does like candidates to write introductions and conclusions to their answers, so get into the habit of writing something, no matter how short.

As usual, make sure you get at least two of the four professional marks available in part (c) (eg by using headings within your answer, writing an introduction and a conclusion).

ACCA examining team's comments. This question was the best answered on the exam. It was pleasing to see that many candidates appeared to have read and understood the examining team's article on audit evidence and matters to be considered, as the quality of answers was undoubtedly better than previous sittings. Most candidates could discuss the relevant accounting treatments with a degree of confidence, most determined materiality, and most could come up with several specific pieces of audit evidence.

Approximately 10% of answers agreed with the accounting treatment for the capitalised training costs, which is not allowed. A further disappointment was how few candidates considered any inventory held by Banana Co in relation to its insolvent customer, which would need to be considered in terms of obsolescence.

BPP
LEARNING

For requirement (b), the vast majority of answers were sound, with almost all candidates able to identify some, if not all, of the quality control issues in the scenario. The lack of a planning meeting, inappropriate delegation of work, poor direction and supervision were identified by most. Some candidates considered not only the most obvious issues from the scenario, but also the overall impact on the audit, and went beyond simply repeating points from the scenario. However, some candidates failed to really evaluate the quality control issues, and did little more than copy out sentences from the question, providing little explanation and development of the issue identified.

Requirement (c) was on money laundering. This topic seemed to polarise candidates. Well-prepared candidates performed very well here, and while most candidates could at least define money laundering, a significant minority of candidates attempted this requirement inadequately, if at all. Candidates are reminded that money laundering is a crucial issue that auditors must consider with every client engagement, and the anti-money laundering rules are an important part of the syllabus.

Marking scheme

Marks

(a)   (i)   **Training costs**

Generally 1 mark per matter/evidence point:

Matters

- Correct calculation and assessment of materiality
- Cannot capitalise training costs
- Expenditure does not create an asset which the entity controls
- Potential qualification re material misstatement

Evidence

- Schedule of costs (½ only)
- Agree costs to supporting documentation
- Agree costs to cash book/bank statement (½ mark only)
- Cut-off procedure
- Compare to budgeted cost

Maximum   6

(ii)   **Trade receivable**

Generally 1 mark per matter/evidence point:

Matters

- Correct calculation and assessment of materiality (max 1½ marks)
- Receivable impaired
- Consider any inventory in relation to Cherry Co
- Potential qualification re material misstatement
- Impact of the two issues together on the audit opinion

Evidence

- Initial correspondence with administrators of Cherry Co
- Confirmation with the administrators
- Agreement to receivables ledger
- Recalculations of impairment losses
- Review of inventory schedules

Maximum   6

Marks

(b) **Quality control matters**

Up to 1½ marks for each point evaluated from ideas list, plus 1 mark
for overall conclusion:
- No audit planning meeting – lack of direction
- Absence of manager and senior – lack of supervision
- Junior assigned difficult audit work (goodwill and WIP)
- Junior helped out with inventory count – lack of
  understanding/supervision
- Junior asked to challenge FD – inappropriate delegation
- Audit running out of time – poor planning?
- Changed sample size – inappropriate response to time pressure
- Changed item selected in sample – inappropriate response to
  time pressure

Maximum   10

(c) **Money laundering briefing notes**

Professional marks to be awarded for format (heading, introduction,
conclusion) – 1 mark, and clarity of explanation – 1 mark
Generally up to 1½ marks for each explanation from list below:
- Definition of money laundering (1 mark)
- Examples of money laundering activities (½ mark each up to
  3 marks)
- Procedures – appoint MLRO
- Procedures – enhanced record keeping systems
- Procedures – know your client
- Procedures – staff training
- Procedures – internal controls, monitoring and management of
  compliance

Maximum   10

Professional marks   4

Total   **36**

(a) (i) **Matters to consider**

Materiality

Materiality on revenue: $\dfrac{\$500,000}{\$12.5m} = 4\%$

Materiality on net profit: $\dfrac{\$500,000}{\$400,000} = 125\%$

Materiality on total assets: $\dfrac{\$500,000}{\$78m} = <1\%$

The training costs are not material to the statement of financial position. They would,
however, be material to revenue and profit if they were reclassified as expenses, turning
a profit into a loss.

Accounting treatment

The training costs are currently recognised as non-current assets. This is not in
accordance with IAS 16 *Property, Plant and Equipment*, which states that the costs of
training staff should always be treated as an expense, as they do not meet the definition

BPP
LEARNING

of an asset, which requires that the entity has control of the asset (IAS 16: para. 19). This is very unlikely to be the case with training costs, as the staff will probably have the right to leave the company, meaning that Banana Co would not receive any subsequent economic benefit from having trained them.

The training costs should be treated as an expense in the statement of profit or loss.

Audit opinion

If Banana Co does not amend its financial statements, the audit opinion will be modified due to a material misstatement. This would probably be an 'except for' qualification as the misstatement is material but not pervasive.

Evidence

The file should contain:

- A review of the nature of the expenses themselves to verify that they are classified correctly and that they are in fact training costs

- Testing of entries selected according to sampling procedures detailed in the audit plan to supporting documentation, such as purchase invoices, and agreement of payment of related payables to the cashbook and to bank statements

- Evidence that a sample (selected according to audit plan) of entries are included in the accounts in the correct period

Testing for completeness and that all invoices that should have been accrued for were in fact accrued for.

(ii) **Matters to consider**

Materiality for whole receivable

Materiality on revenue: $\dfrac{\$300,000}{\$12.5m} = 2.4\%$

Materiality on net profit: $\dfrac{\$300,000}{\$400,000} = 75\%$

Materiality on total assets: $\dfrac{\$300,000}{\$78m} = <1\%$

The receivable is not material to the statement of financial position. It would, however, be material to the statement of profit or loss if an impairment loss were recognised in relation to it.

Accounting treatment

IFRS 9 *Financial Instruments* requires receivables to be recognised at fair value. The fair value of the Cherry Co receivable is the 25% that the administrators suggest it may be able to pay, ie $75,000. $225,000 should therefore be recognised as an impairment loss in the statement of profit or loss.

Calculating materiality for the impairment loss:

Materiality on revenue: $\dfrac{\$225,000}{\$12.5m} = 1.8\%$

Materiality on net profit: $\dfrac{\$225,000}{\$400,000} = 56\%$

This is clearly material to profit for the year.

Inventory

As Cherry Co is a customer, it is possible that Banana Co is holding inventory or work in progress that was ordered by Cherry Co. Grape & Co needs to ascertain whether this is the case, and if so whether the inventory can in fact be sold. If it cannot be, then it may be impaired and should be written down, recognising the loss in profit for the year.

Audit opinion

If Banana Co does not amend its financial statements, the auditor's opinion will be modified due to a material misstatement. This would probably be an 'except for' qualification as the misstatement is material but not pervasive.

If the misstatement in respect of the receivable is taken together with the misstatement in respect of the training costs, the overall result may be that Grape & Co judges the statement of profit or loss to be rendered meaningless (pervasive effect). In this case it would issue an adverse audit opinion.

Audit evidence

- External documentation confirming the insolvency of Cherry Co and the possible repayment of only 25% of the receivable

- Confirmation from the administrator of the 25% to be paid, including an indication of when this is likely to happen

- Agreement of the amount owed from the receivables listing to the ledger

- Review of inventory documentation, and evidence of enquiries made of management, regarding the value and the potential recoverability of any inventory relating to contracts with Cherry Co

- Calculations regarding the amount to be recognised as an impairment loss

(b) **Selection of engagement staff**

The fact that the junior had only worked on two audits before this is not a problem. However, it is important that they be given work appropriate to their level of skill and experience. This does not appear to have happened here, as detailed below.

No audit planning meeting

The audit planning meeting, led by the partner, is a crucial part of the audit. It is the best way of giving the team an understanding of the client, and should discuss both the overall strategy and the detailed audit plan, perhaps going into difficulties that have been experienced in previous years and which could come up again. The discussion should focus on what individual members of the team need to do. This is particularly important for less experienced and junior members of the team.

Audit manager away

The manager should not have given the senior responsibility for the audit while they were away on holiday for three weeks. It is important that an audit is properly supervised, and it may have been more appropriate for another manager to take responsibility for the audit.

Senior busy

Not only is there a question mark over whether they have the experience to manage the audit, but the senior is also busy with other assignments and thus unable to devote sufficient time to this one. It is very important that someone is available to supervise junior members of the audit team. This is not happening here.

It is also possible that the lack of attention paid by both the manager and the senior has led to the misstatements in respect of the training costs and trade receivables not being picked up by the audit team.

Junior auditing goodwill and inventory

Goodwill is a complex accounting area to audit, and should not be given to a junior to do. The same can be said of inventory and in particular work-in-progress. A junior is very unlikely to have developed the judgement needed to audit these areas. This seems to be the case here, as shown by the junior's error at the inventory count (see below).

Inventory count

The junior helped the client's staff to count raw materials at the inventory count, when they should instead have been observing that the client's staff were counting them correctly and in accordance with the count procedures. This would seem to imply that the junior had not been properly briefed on their responsibilities at the inventory count, as this is a relatively basic error.

It is likely that more audit evidence will be needed to be collected on inventory as a result of this error.

Junior asked to challenge FD

It is not appropriate for a junior to be asked to challenge a client's finance director regarding an accounting issue that they are unlikely to understand fully. This should have been done by either the audit manager or the partner, as they would be in a position to understand the technical issues involved, and would carry sufficient authority with the client to make the challenge effective.

Running out of time to complete procedures

Pressure of time is an important contributor to audit risk. Audit time budgets should allow staff enough time to complete the audit to the required quality. It is also possible that the lack of supervision of the audit team's work has led to the audit being conducted inefficiently, with inadequate monitoring of progress and discussion of issues as they arise.

Reduction of sample sizes

It is clearly unacceptable to reduce sample sizes as a way of saving time. The sample sizes detailed in the audit plan should have been designed to gather sufficient appropriate audit evidence. Reducing the sample size beneath this point increases detection risk, and the risk of the auditor giving the wrong opinion.

Basis of sample selection

Selecting a sample on the basis of the ease of finding evidence for an item, is not an appropriate basis. Indeed, this might actively increase detection risk as it means by definition that those items for which evidence is not readily available, or might not even exist, are not tested.

Conclusion

The litany of failures above suggests that this engagement has not been adequately supervised, and that the audit work performed is inadequate in some areas. A detailed review should be performed so that any other shortcomings can be addressed.

Doubt is also cast over the sufficiency of the firm's quality control procedures. This matter should be referred to the relevant partner for consideration.

(c) (i) **Briefing notes for training session**

By: Audit manager

Subject: Money laundering

Introduction

These notes explain what money laundering is, using examples of offences including those that could be committed by an accountant. They also explain the policies and procedures that a firm of Chartered Certified Accounts should establish in order to meet its responsibilities in relation to money laundering.

Definition

Money laundering is the process by which criminals attempt to conceal the true origin and ownership of the proceeds of their criminal activity, allowing them to maintain control over the proceeds and, ultimately, providing a legitimate cover for their sources of income.

Explanation

The money laundering process has three stages:

1   Placement: getting money (usually cash) into the system in the first place. This could be by making bank deposits, making investments (eg in a unit trust), or through a 'front' business, which is a legitimate business that is used to launder money (eg a betting shop, which legitimately receives high levels of cash, could be used to deposit stolen cash).

2   Layering: using lots of different transactions to create so many 'layers' of transactions between the initial placement of 'dirty' money and the money that is taken out at the end, that it is difficult to trace.

3   Integration: extracting funds from the laundering system, and 'integrating' them back into the world of legitimate and use-able money.

Examples of offences

•   Handling the proceeds of criminal activities.

•   Arranging the acquisition or use of criminal property. This may include becoming involved with tax evasion.

•   Tipping off – when the MLRO (see below) or any individual discloses something that might prejudice any investigations

(ii) **Appoint a Money Laundering Reporting Officer (MLRO) and implement internal reporting procedures**

The MLRO should have a suitable level of seniority and experience. Individuals should make internal reports of money laundering to the MLRO. The MLRO must then consider whether to report to the relevant authority (in the UK, this would be the National Crime Agency), and document this process.

Train individuals

Train individuals to ensure that they are aware of the relevant legislation, know how to recognise and deal with potential money laundering, how to report suspicions to the MLRO, and how to identify clients.

Internal procedures

Establish internal procedures appropriate to forestall and prevent money laundering, and make relevant individuals aware of the procedures. Procedures should cover:

BPP
LEARNING

- Client acceptance
- Gathering 'know your client' (KYC) information
- Controls over client money and transactions through the client account
- Advice and services to clients that could be of use to a money launderer

Verify client identities

The firm must be able to establish that new clients are who they claim to be. They should verify the identity of new and existing clients, and keep the evidence of this on file – typically, copies of evidence such as passports, driving licences and utility bills. For a company this will include identities of directors and certificates of incorporation.

Record keeping

Maintain records of client identification, and any transactions undertaken for or with the client. Special care needs to be taken when handling clients' money to avoid participating in a transaction involving money laundering.

Conclusion

There are a number of ways that the accountant could become involved in money laundering. It is important that a firm has adequate procedures in place to ensure that it does not fall foul of anti-money laundering legislation, and that it ensures that these procedures are adhered to.

11 Nate & Co

Workbook references. Chapters 1, 2 and 4.

Top tips. In part (a) it is important to make your answer specific to the scenario, it is not just a straight 'textbook knowledge' requirement. In parts (b) and (c) you need to focus on **explaining** and **discussing** the issues, it is not enough to state facts from the question or to quote from the *Code of Ethics and conduct*. You need to apply your knowledge to the facts given and show that you understand **why** they may be seen as problematic.

Easy marks. There are not many easy marks to be found in this question – each requirement demands professional judgement and application of knowledge. The basic definition in part (a) and the broad issues relating to the acceptance of the appointment are probably the easiest elements.

ACCA examining team's comments. Requirement (a) asked candidates to define money laundering and to state procedures relevant to money laundering that should take place on the acceptance of a new audit client. Candidates appeared to have prepared for the topic of money laundering, as the definitions were usually sound. Unfortunately, few candidates could provide many, if any, specific procedures. A significant minority of answers suggested that Fisher Co should appoint an MLRO, totally misunderstanding the facts of the scenario, ie that Fisher Co is a potential audit client, not a firm of auditors. Only the best answers discussed 'know your client' procedures, and the need for clarification in the engagement letter of matters to do with money laundering.

Candidates should remember to allocate their time carefully between question requirements. Most scripts contained answers to requirements (a), (b) and (c) of a similar length, when it is clear that the mark allocation differs significantly for requirement (b).

Marking scheme

Marks

(a) **Money laundering**

Definition – 1 mark

Procedures – generally 1 mark each

Ideas list:

- Client identity
- Client business activity
- Client address
- Client principal shareholders and directors
- Engagement letter clarification

Maximum 5

(b) **Ethical and professional issues**

Generally 1–1½ marks per issue explained:

- Extra work on control deficiencies
- Review work of internal audit
- Expand audit testing
- Cost/budget implication
- Two-partner review
- Lack of supervision and direction
- Lack of understanding of extent of responsibilities
- Inappropriate advice
- Provision of non-audit service
- Safeguards

Maximum 9

(c) **Ethical and professional issues**

Generally 1–1½ marks per issue explained:

- Perception of bribe
- Modesty of gift
- Interference with count procedures
- Review of work performed
- Possible reperformance/alternative procedures
- Lack of professional behaviour
- QC issues

Maximum 6

Total **20**

(a) **Money laundering**

Money laundering is the process by which criminals attempt to conceal the true origin and ownership of the proceeds of their criminal activity, allowing them to maintain control over the proceeds and, ultimately, providing a legitimate cover for their sources of income.

Money laundering procedures – before acceptance

The firm should carry out client identification procedures, such as:

- Obtaining evidence that the client exists, such as looking at the certificate of incorporation and establishing the identities of all directors (Mr Fisher and any others) by taking copies of passports or driving licences

- Conducting a search on Fisher Co, eg using Companies House in the UK

- Confirming the registered address (by obtaining headed paper)

- Obtaining a list of shareholders and directors

Money laundering procedures – after acceptance

The firm should obtain 'know your client' information, such as:

- The expected patterns of Fisher Co's business, are there peak seasons for selling wooden storage boxes, are there any major clients or suppliers?

- The business model of the client (in this instance Marcellus Fisher appears to be acting individually through a company – does he own any other companies and what activities do they have?)

- The source of the client's funds (is Mr Fisher the only investor, or are there others, does the company also have debt finance and, if so, from whom?)

The firm should include a paragraph about money laundering responsibilities in the engagement letter.

(b) **CF Co**

Ethical and professional considerations in connection with audit

There seems to have been a failure in quality control over the planning of the audit if an audit junior found time to spend three hours offering informal advice on the systems rather than carrying out planning work. As an audit junior, he should have been supervised, and the senior member of staff should have prevented him giving this informal advice.

It would have been appropriate for the audit team to make formal advice on systems in a report to management (management letter) that was therefore reviewed by the audit partner and documented between the parties. The informal advice given was inappropriate and does create the possibility that the firm will be liable if the advice was found to be inappropriate.

The audit junior appears to misunderstand his role on the audit team and therefore should be given additional training in what is expected of an audit junior. The firm's initial training procedures should be reviewed to see if this is a general failing of that training.

The errors in the system will also have an impact on the audit which the firm should consider and take steps about. The increased control risk over cash deposits from customers should lead to extended testing in this area, which is likely to be significant to CF Co. Due to the problems in controls, additional substantive testing should be carried out.

The extent of the problems in controls should be determined, to discover if the problem is more widespread than cash deposits and whether it continued throughout the year. The auditors should review internal audit's work to assess this, and the materiality of the errors should be documented. Then the approach to any other areas affected should be documented.

The industry is highly regulated and such breaches might eventually result in the need for the firm to report them to the relevant authorities (eg the Financial Conduct Authority in the UK). First, however, Nate & Co should consider whether its understanding of the issue is sufficient, and whether it needs to obtain more information about relevant laws and regulations, and whether the entity is required to report breaches to the authorities (IESBA *Code of Ethics*: para. 360.25 A1). If it is determined that there has been a breach, then this should be discussed with management or those charged with governance at CF Co. Only if management's response is not satisfactory – eg they fail to disclose any breaches – might Nate & Co consider disclosing any breaches to the relevant authorities.

The failure to record client monies correctly is also an indication that money laundering might have occurred, and this suspicion should be raised in a report to the firm's money laundering reporting officer, who must review the evidence and determine whether to make a report to the relevant authorities.

Ethical and professional considerations in connection with proposed review

When considering whether to accept an additional service at an audit client, the firm must consider whether it will adversely affect the independence of the audit. Two key things to consider are:

(i)   The nature of the work
(ii)   The fee level

In this instance, the firm have been asked to carry out a review of the financial information technology system as a result of errors found in it by the internal audit department, with a view to improving it. The firm must make sure that it follows the guidance of the IESBA *Code of Ethics and Conduct* in relation to non-audit services provided to audit clients.

The auditors are likely to review the IT systems and possibly rely on them as part of their audit, so carrying out an engagement to improve the systems represents a self-review threat. The firm should assess whether the risk is too great for the firm to take on the engagement, or whether appropriate safeguards might be applied.

In this instance, appropriate safeguards might include using staff not involved with the audit to carry out this engagement. The firm would have to ensure that the staff members used are suitably qualified. The audit junior, who is a recent IT graduate, appears to be qualified to be involved in such an engagement. If he were, he should not be involved with the audit again.

If the firm decides it can reduce the self-review threat to a reasonable level to accept the engagement, then it must consider whether a self-interest threat is raised by taking on additional work for the same client (IESBA *Code of Ethics*).

As the review would be a one-off exercise, the fees would also be a one-off amount and would not affect the recurring fee income from the client. As a result, it is unlikely to threaten the independence of the audit sufficiently to decline the engagement.

(c)   **LA Shots Co**

Control problems

It is a problem in the control over the inventory count that the office party was scheduled to start 'at the end of the inventory count', because it meant that the staff involved in the count were motivated to complete the count quickly rather than well. It would have been better if the party did not start until a specified later time.

The control environment for the count appears to have been poor, as the person in charge of the count seems keen to get it finished fast, with the implication being that this was rather than well. She may also have been unaware that it is inappropriate to offer gifts and hospitality to auditors, but this should be communicated to her.

Giving inventory away during the inventory count is also a sign of poor controls, as ideally there would be no unnecessary movements of inventory during the count.

Due to these problems with controls, it might have been appropriate for the auditors to have extended samples and taken longer over their procedures due to the higher control risk, but in the event, they did the opposite.

Ethical problems

The IESBA *Code of Ethics* states that a gift or hospitality from a client affects independence unless it is clearly inconsequential. In this case, while bottles of juice and attendance at an office party may seem insignificant, whether they were or not should have been determined by a more senior member of the audit team than the juniors, probably their manager. Given that the juniors accepted the incentives and then appeared to be motivated by them, their independence does appear to have been compromised.

These matters should be discussed with the juniors and disciplinary action taken, particularly if they attended the party in work hours without permission from their manager.

BPP
LEARNING

159

Quality control

The fact that two audit juniors with so little understanding of what they should have done on being offered incentives, were sent out on this inventory count may be a sign that it was not planned or reviewed properly.

Possible action to take

As the inventory count was carried out so recently, it is probable that the firm could carry out other procedures now in order to ensure that they can rely on the figure for inventory in the financial statements if the manager determines that it is not possible to rely on the work carried out by the juniors. The work should be reviewed and concluded on as a point of priority to determine this.

12 Sepia & Co

Workbook references. Chapters 2 and 5.

Top tips. When trying to identify professional and ethical issues, think about general themes such as independence, integrity, objectivity and confidentiality. Try to relate relevant ethical and professional guidance that you are aware of to each situation, and explain why it is relevant.

Easy marks. There are easy marks available in this question for knowledge brought forward from your earlier auditing studies, such as being able to give a definition of lowballing and knowing the etiquette with regard to professional clearance letters. Easy marks can also be obtained for coming up with simple steps to take in respect of each issue – for example, if no answer has been received in part (i), it seems logical to repeat the request.

ACCA examining team's comments. The technical content of this question was not difficult.

In part (b)(i), many candidates made a big issue of the preliminary procedures of the professional etiquette already gone through and ended their answers with Sepia & Co no closer to a resolution to the problem than when they started.

In part (b)(ii), nearly everyone identified a 'conflict of interest' but few stated that they would refuse the assignment. Many referred to information barriers but did not consider how unacceptable to Vitronella the assignment would be. Those that proposed resigning the audit (of Vitronella) showed a lack of professionalism.

Part (b)(iii) was probably the worst answered part. Many candidates referred the matter to the partner for his/her decision. Weaker candidates proposed unsuitable 'solutions' (eg that Sepia withdraw their tender). Few candidates acknowledged that little could be done. Candidates who referred to 'insider dealing' clearly had no understanding of the term.

Marking scheme

		Marks
(a)	Lowballing	
	Generally 1 mark for each well-explained point	5
(b)	Generally 1 mark each comment	
	Maximum 5 marks each of the three matters	
	Ideas	
	Professional issues raised	
	– Integrity (management and/or audit firm)	
	– Objectivity/independence	
	– Confidentiality	

Marks

- Relevant ethical guidance – ie
    (i)   Changes in professional appointment
    (ii)   Corporate finance advice including take-overs
    (iii) Fees
- Meaning of 'lowballing'
Steps (ie **actions**)
- Obtain ... what? ... why?
- Ask/advise ... who?   When?   15

Total   **20**

(a)   **Lowballing** is the practice of a firm quoting a significantly lower fee level for an assurance service than would have been charged by the predecessor firm. This creates a significant self-interest threat. If the firm's tender is successful, the firm must apply safeguards such as maintaining records such that the firm is able to demonstrate that appropriate staff and time are spent on the engagement and complying with all applicable assurance standards, guidelines and quality control procedures

Current guidance in the form of IESBA's *Code of Ethics* states that members can quote whatever fee is deemed appropriate.

It is not considered unethical for one firm to offer a lower fee than another – however doing so may create threats to compliance with the fundamental principles. For example, a **self-interest threat** to professional competence and due care would arise if the fee quoted was so low that it would be difficult to perform the engagement in accordance with applicable technical and professional standards.

Safeguards to mitigate such threats could include making the client aware of the terms of the engagement and the basis on which fees are charged and what services are covered by the quoted fees, and also assigning appropriate time and staff to the engagements.

The IESBA has recently made changes to enhance the independence and objectivity of accountants performing assurance engagements with a view to strengthening the independence requirements of the IESBA's *Code of Ethics for Professional Accountants*.

(b)   (i)   **Squid**

Professional issues

Sepia & Co ('Sepia') has requested a professional clearance letter from Krill & Co in respect of the audit of Squid. Krill & Co has not responded. Krill & Co has a professional duty of confidence to Squid, and therefore should have sought permission from Squid to respond to Sepia's request.

The fact that Krill & Co has not responded could indicate that Squid has refused permission for Krill & Co to respond to Sepia. However, this seems unlikely for two reasons: firstly, that Squid nominated Sepia to act as auditors and therefore should have no objection to Krill & Co responding to them and allowing them to take up that nomination, and secondly, that if Krill & Co had simply been refused permission to give that clearance, then as a professional courtesy they should have responded to Sepia informing them that they could not give them the information they requested and why.

Therefore it is possible that Anton Fargues, on behalf of Krill & Co, is not replying because he has a concern as to the integrity of the directors of Squid that he does not wish to share with Sepia due to concerns over confidentiality issues. However, if Squid has given them permission to respond, this should not be a problem. Therefore, it appears that Anton Fargues is acting unprofessionally in not responding to Sepia's request.

 BPP
LEARNING

Steps

The manager at Sepia should ask Squid whether the company has given Krill & Co permission to respond to Sepia, and if they confirm that permission has been given, Sepia should get this confirmed in writing.

He should send a duplicate request for professional clearance by recorded delivery so that receipt has to be acknowledged by Krill & Co and gives legal evidence that it was received.

This should include a letter stating that lack of response to his letter will be taken to mean that there are no professional issues preventing Sepia accepting appointment and that if Krill & Co fails to respond, Sepia will report Anton Fargues to his professional body for unprofessional conduct.

If a reply is received, Sepia's actions will then be directed by the contents of the reply.

If there is still no reply within reasonable time, Sepia should accept the appointment and report Anton Fargues to his professional body so that his behaviour can be investigated.

(ii) **Hatchet**

Professional issues

Sepia has been approached by Hatchet to offer a non-audit service. Sepia does not provide audit services to Hatchet, so in relation to Hatchet itself, there is no independence bar to accepting appointment.

However, the service is advice in relation to a proposed takeover of Vitronella, an audit client of Sepia. This is likely to raise a conflict of interest such that it is necessary to refuse the appointment. This depends on several factors:

1   Whether Hatchet or Vitronella object to Sepia offering the services

2   What the services are in detail

3   Whether Sepia would be Vitronella's primary advisor in the event of a takeover

1   The fact that Sepia are Vitronella's auditors is public information reported in the financial statements. As such, it is likely that Hatchet are aware that Sepia are Vitronella's auditors and therefore do not mind. Vitronella, the target company, will be unaware at this point that their auditors have been asked to advise a company about a proposed takeover of themselves and might mind very much. Professional advice in respect of such conflicts of interest states that the firm (Sepia) should make both parties aware of the conflict so that they can decide whether they want Sepia to be advisors.

2/3   The professional guidance states that one firm should not be principal advisor to both parties involved in a takeover. Therefore, if Hatchet wants Sepia to be its principal advisor, and Sepia anticipates that as auditor, it is likely to be Vitronella's principal advisor, the partners of Sepia will have to decide which side they want to advise. Being auditor does not automatically mean they would be Vitronella's principal advisors, but there is often an advantage to a company in having its auditor advise in such situations and, providing that the combined fees do not cause a problem, there should be no bar to independence in doing so. It is possible that Vitronella would expect Sepia to act as their principal advisors.

It would not be possible for Sepia to resign from the Vitronella audit in order to be able to be Hatchet's principal advisors as this would still pose a conflict of interest as far as Vitronella was concerned.

If Sepia was not principal advisor to both parties, and both parties agreed, it could advise Hatchet and do Vitronella's audit. The best way to ensure confidentiality was maintained in this instance would be to have entirely separate engagement teams and set up strict procedures for ensuring information was kept secret – for example, having teams in different areas of the office or from different offices of a national firm.

Steps

Sepia should determine whether Hatchet requires Sepia to be their principal advisors in relation to this takeover. The partners should inform Hatchet that before they accepted any engagement of this nature they would require permission from Vitronella.

Sepia should notify Vitronella that Hatchet has asked them to be principal advisor and gauge the reaction.

Ultimately it is likely that Sepia would refuse to advise Hatchet due to the conflict of interest being so great.

(iii) **Keratin**

Professional issues

Lowballing is the practice of tendering for audits at a lower price than the audit can actually be carried out for, often with the intention of obtaining other, more profitable, work from the audit client.

Lowballing is not forbidden by professional rules, because it is seen as a reasonable marketing tactic. However, it is important that the client is aware of the scope of the work that is going to be carried out and is aware that prices might rise in the future.

Professional guidance indicates also that auditors must ensure that they do not provide a service lower than is required by quality standards regardless of the price that it is being done for. Keratin must ensure that they do not fall into the trap of providing a poor audit service because they have tendered at an unreasonable price. They would be putting themselves at risk of being found to be negligent by a professional body or even in a court of law should problems arise.

Keratin would be within their rights to provide other services to an audit client as long as this did not affect the independence of the audit. However, given that the provision of other services to audit clients is increasingly frowned upon, for example, in the US, where audit firms are prohibited from providing other services to audit clients, Keratin should be careful of taking such an approach.

Edwin Stenuit may be in breach of a duty of confidentiality to his employer, discussing the firm's affairs in such a way at a social gathering.

Steps

Sepia can take no steps against Keratin in the matter of this tender as Benthos is entitled to choose whichever audit firm they like to do their audit.

If Keratin is successful, Sepia may have to review its own pricing policy if it is likely to be tendering against Keratin in the future.

Sepia could report Edwin Stenuit to ACCA for misconduct as a result of his breach of confidentiality to his employer, but it is unlikely that they would do so.

13 Groom

Workbook references. Chapters 3, 4 and 8.

Top tips. Part (a) represented a little bit of a twist on this issue. Usually one might expect questions on auditors and fraud to require candidates to state that the auditor is not responsible for preventing and detecting fraud. While you should have done this here, there was also the twist that the auditor appears to have been negligent in performing the audit.

As you are reading through the information for part (b), jot down the accounting standards you believe are relevant and note down the matters to consider that arise from them. Think if any ISAs are relevant as well (this is particularly important as your examining team has recently commented that candidates tend to show too little knowledge of the requirements of ISAs). Always comment on the materiality of matters.

Easy marks. Calculating materiality in parts (a) and (b) was easy, as was listing out the three things to prove in order to prove negligence (a duty of care existed; this duty was breached; financial loss resulted from this breach).

ACCA examining team's comments. There were some excellent answers to requirement (a). The best ones clearly outlined the factors that have to be proven to determine negligence, and applied them methodically to the scenario. Some answers tended to only provide a rote-learnt description of responsibilities in relation to fraud, and usually failed to reach an appropriate conclusion. With little application to the scenario there is limited scope for marks to be awarded.

For requirement (b)(i), almost all candidates were able to generate marks by calculating the materiality of the amount, and describing the basic accounting treatment for provisions. Fewer went on to discuss the potential impact of the insurance cover, and some answers drifted into a discussion of going concern and other business risks. Audit procedures were often inadequately focused, with no regard to the scale of the issue. Although most suggested looking at legal documents, candidates rarely mentioned looking at the group claim document. Some candidates proposed lots of very detailed tests on the validity of individual claims, such as checking hotel bills and airline tickets.

Requirement (b)(ii) was not dealt with well. Very few candidates recognised that the business segment represented a cash generating unit that required an impairment test. Even those candidates that did pick up on the impairment issue could rarely provide evidence points other than 'check the value of the assets' (too vague) or 'inspect the assets' (irrelevant).

Marking scheme

Marks

(a) **Fraud and auditor's liability**

Generally up to 2 marks for each point explained:

- Not auditor's primary responsibility to detect fraud unless it is material in impact on financial statements
- Determine that the payroll fraud would have been material (include calculation)
- Reasons why fraud is hard to detect
- Audit firm may not have been sufficiently sceptical
- Non-adherence to ISAs on controls assessment and evidence obtained
- Discuss whether duty of care owed to client
- Discuss breach of duty of care
- Identify financial loss suffered and firm likely to have been negligent

Maximum   11

Marks

(b)   (i)   **Compensation claim**

1 mark per matter, 1 mark per specific procedure

Matters

- Materiality
- Provision/contingent liability
- Recoverability under insurance
- Management reluctant to provide

Evidence

- Copy of legal claim
- Legal correspondence
- Press releases/news stories to establish constructive obligation
- Booking conditions to verify legal obligation
- Advice given by the company at the time of the incident
- Copy of insurance contract
- Copy of claim made on insurance
- Written representation on outcome

(ii)   **Shelley's Cruises**

1 mark per matter, 1 mark per specific procedure

Matters

- Materiality
- Impairment of assets (**not** brand)
- Cash-generating unit
- Subjective elements in impairment calculations

Evidence

- Review management impairment test (max 2 marks if detailed)
- Discuss future strategy re Shelly's Cruises
- Review post year end performance/bookings in advance   Maximum   <u>14</u>

Total   <u>**25**</u>

(a)   **Responsibilities**

Detecting fraud is the primary responsibility of management, not the auditor. However, the matter is complicated because the auditor is required to give reasonable assurance that the financial statements are not materially misstated as a result of fraud (or error). Moreover, auditors are required by ISA 240 *The Auditor's Responsibilities Relating to Fraud in an Audit of Financial Statements* to identify and assess the risks of material misstatement due to fraud. This means that an audit conducted in line with ISAs should obtain evidence specifically in relation to fraud.

The audit process is, however, subject to inherent limitations which are particularly pertinent to the problem of fraud. Fraud may involve sophisticated attempts at concealment, which can make it difficult to detect. Furthermore, there may be collusion by management which makes the auditor's task even more difficult. It is therefore quite possible for the auditor to have conducted an audit in accordance with ISAs, but still have failed to detect a material misstatement resulting from fraud.

BPP
LEARNING

Materiality

The total amount stolen is 5.6% of total assets. Not all of this took place within the year, so the amount could be pro-rated as follows: if the theft was at a constant rate, then 8/12 months fall within the year in question, which is $3m or 3.8% of total assets. This is material, and appears to have result in an incorrect auditor's opinion having been expressed.

Conduct of audit

Professional scepticism is a key weapon in the auditor's attempt to detect misstatements resulting from fraud. The audit of Spaniel does not appear to have been conducted with an attitude of professional scepticism, possibly as a result of it being a long-standing audit client.

However, irrespective of the auditor's specific duties in relation to fraud, sufficient appropriate evidence does not in any case seem to have been obtained in relation to payroll. ISAs require the auditor to design and perform tests of controls in each period under audit. Substantive evidence should have been obtained in relation to payroll. This is particularly important given that payroll is likely to be a material area.

On this basis it is apparent that the audit was not conducted in accordance with ISAs. The audit partner may therefore find it very difficult to defend the conduct of the audit.

Negligence?

Three things must be proved for the auditor to be found to have been negligent:

- A duty of care existed
- The duty of care was breached
- A financial loss resulted from the negligence

As there is a contract between Groom & Co and Spaniel, a duty of care can be shown to have existed (in this case, to the shareholders as a body).

The financial loss here would be the value of the theft, although it is not clear whether the auditor could be held responsible for the full amount of the theft.

It is likely that Groom & Co were negligent, and that Spaniel would be able to prove this in court.

(b)　(i)　**Matters to consider**

The claim is material to profit at 13.3% of profit before tax (20 / 150 × 100%). It is not material to the statement of financial position at only 0.49% of total assets (20 / 4,100 × 100%).

Management have an incentive to manipulate the financial statements through fraudulent financial reporting, as their bonus is based on profit before tax. There is a risk that profit may be overstated. They may not want to provide for the claim because this would reduce profit.

IAS 37 *Provisions, Contingent Liabilities and Contingent Assets* requires a provision to be recognised where, as a result of a past event, an outflow of economic benefits is probable, the amount of which can be estimated reliably (IAS 37: para. 14). If such an outflow is only possible but not probable then it is a contingent liability, and should be disclosed in a note to the financial statements. Further evidence is required to determine whether the compensation claim should be provided for or not.

If Clooney can make a claim on its insurance policy in respect of the legal case, then per IAS 37 this is treated as a separate event, in accordance with IAS 37's requirements on contingent assets. For an asset to be recognised, IAS 37 states that it should be certain to be received (IAS 37: paras. 31–35). As in this case receipt of an insurance payment is only probable, no asset should be recognised. The insurance claim should be disclosed by way of a note.

In addition to the provision that must be created, it may be necessary for Clooney to provide for any legal costs associated with defending the claim, which would further reduce its profit for the year.

Evidence

- Copy of claim made by the group of holiday makers, detailing the $20 million claimed and the basis of the claim

- Review of correspondence between 'claim group' and the company

- Correspondence from Clooney's legal counsel, showing their opinion on the likely outcome

- Copy of any press releases made by Clooney, which could help establish there is a constructive obligation

- Review of press coverage of the situation, to assess any comments made in public by company representatives regarding the claim

- Review of the standard terms and conditions that holiday-makers agree to on booking a holiday – this could help to establish any legal obligation, eg to cover the cost of accommodation before being returned home

- Details of any helpline or other means by which the stranded holiday-makers were given advice at the time of the incident (eg if the company advised them to book alternative accommodation this may imply that the company is liable for the cost)

- Copy of insurance contract detailing level of cover, if any, provided for this situation, and any amount that will not be covered (eg an excess on the policy)

- Correspondence between insurance company and Clooney to establish whether an insurance claim has been made

- Written representation stating management's opinion on the outcome of the court case, and the likelihood of reimbursement from the insurance cover

- Review of invoices received pre and post year end in respect of legal costs, to ensure adequately included in expenses and accrued for if necessary

(ii) **Matters to consider**

The Shelly's Cruises (SC) operation is material to the financial statements, contributing 20% to revenue ($640/3,200 \times 100\%$). The identifiable assets of the business segment represent 5.7% of total assets ($235 / 4,100 \times 100\%$), and are thus material to the statement of financial position.

The brand is (correctly) not recognised as an intangible asset in accordance with IAS 38 *Intangible Assets*, so there is no intangible asset that may be impaired. However, in accordance with IAS 36 *Impairment of Assets*, SC's assets represent a cash generating unit as they are independent of the assets of the rest of the entity. The question is whether these are impaired.

The drops in revenue and profit are indicators of impairment per IAS 36. Management must have conducted an impairment test, calculating the value-in-use of the cash-generating unit, and also the fair value less cost to sell, to determine the recoverable amount of the SC assets collectively. Any impairment loss should be expensed. Management will want to avoid recognising an impairment loss as it will reduce their bonus payment.

The impairment test will involve a number of subjective elements, eg the discount rate used to determine the present value of cash flows. Management's assumptions here should be approached with professional scepticism.

Evidence

- Review management's impairment test, including:

    - Assessment that an appropriate discount rate has been used

    - Agreement that the assumptions to determine future cash flows are reasonable

    - Agreement that correct carrying value of assets has been used for comparison of recoverable amount

    - Agreement that all identifiable assets have been included in the cash generating unit

    - Recalculation of all figures

- Discussion with management of the expected future performance of SC

- Review of post year end management accounts for the performance of Shelly's Cruises

- Review of the level of bookings made in advance for cruises to be taken in the future

14 Raven

Workbook references. Chapters 1, 2, 4 and 11.

Top tips. The main difficulty that many students will have faced with part (a) is that eight marks are available for what seems like quite a clear-cut issue. However, if you read the requirement carefully you will have seen that it is not only about ethics, but the 'commercial and other professional issues' raised by the scenario. This question is typical of the current examining team's approach to AAA in that it mixes together different areas – here, ethics and commercial matters. To answer this part well, you needed to know the main categories of ethical threat and then think whether any circumstances in the scenario fell into any of these categories.

Part (b) may have been a bit easier, with seven marks for an issue that is clear-cut and that there is quite a lot to write about. The main thing here is to be sceptical and question the information in the scenario – eg whether there really is a connection between the surgeon's comments and the solicitor's letter. The best approach here is often to break the scenario down into parts and take each one in turn.

Part (c)(i) on auditor's reports was a fairly difficult question in this area. You should have known that either a qualified opinion or a disclaimer of opinion would be issued, but the difficulty comes from the fact that you cannot be entirely sure from the information given in the question.

Notice that there are marks available here for actions such as communicating with those charged with governance before issuing a report with a modified opinion. The examining team likes this kind of point because it shows that you are thinking practically about what would happen, rather than simply reciting your knowledge about the different kinds of audit opinions. There are also usually marks available for the format of any modified report, eg stating that there should be a 'basis for modification paragraph', what the paragraph should say, and that it should be immediately after the opinion paragraph.

Part (c)(ii) required you to have noticed that the company was listed, and that an engagement quality control reviewer was necessary. However, even if you had missed this, you still could have thought to yourself, 'What quality controls would be relevant to this engagement?' A review of the audit file before the auditor's report is issued should have been at the top of your list!

Easy marks. Part (b) contains easy marks for just recognising that there may be a breach of law and regulations in respect of the possibly unqualified surgeon.

ACCA examining team's comments. Sound answers to part (a) used a logical approach, being prompted by the question requirement to discuss in turn the ethical issues, then commercial issues, then professional issues and leading to a set of recommended actions. Weaker answers tended to just list in bullet point format all of the possible threats to objectivity without any real discussion or development of the threats specific to the scenario. Candidates are reminded that the IESBA's *Code of Ethics for Professional Accountants* provides a framework for the evaluation of threats to objectivity, including the identification of threats, the evaluation of the significance of threats identified, and the use of professional judgement in deciding whether the application of safeguards can reduce threats identified to an acceptable level.

In part (b), most candidates identified that the main issues for the audit firm to consider related to a potential breach of law and regulations by the hospital, and that the audit firm should consider disclosure in the public interest. Most answers identified that confidentiality was in issue, and that the matter should be firstly discussed with those charged with governance.

Some candidates focused on disciplinary action to be taken against the employee of the hospital, and on the possibility that the hospital's management were somehow colluding with the employee to deliberately breach law and regulations and commit some type of fraud, which missed the point. Weaker answers also failed to consider the financial statement and therefore audit implications of a letter claiming negligence, which could lead to the recognition of a provision or disclosure of a contingent liability, and could potentially have going concern implications. These matters were relevant as the audit was ongoing.

In requirement (c)(i), most candidates correctly discussed that fact that the auditor was unable to obtain sufficient, appropriate audit evidence based on the reconstructed records, leading them to explain that the audit opinion should be disclaimed. Fewer candidates suggested that alternative procedures could be used to obtain evidence, and fewer still recognised that as the accounting records were available for eleven months of the year, the auditor's report may not necessarily be subject to a disclaimer of opinion, or even qualified at all if alternative procedures could take place.

On requirement (c)(ii), sound answers appreciated that because the client in the scenario was listed, an Engagement Quality Control review would be required, and the answers that described what such a review would entail achieved the maximum marks. Most answers were too general however, simply describing the quality control procedures that would be relevant to any audit. Many answers were extremely brief, with little more than a sentence or two provided.

Marking scheme

Marks

(a) **Grouse Co**
Generally 1 mark for each matter discussed:
- Situation is a close business arrangement giving rise to threat to objectivity
- Explain self-interest threat
- Explain intimidation threat
- Only acceptable if financial interest immaterial and relationship insignificant

- Sale of software to audit clients would require full disclosure of financial benefit
- Sale of software to audit clients creates self-review threat
- Sale of software perceived as providing non-audit service
- Risks heightened for listed/public interest entities
- If enter business arrangement must withdraw from audit of Grouse Co
- Commercial consideration – demand for product
- Commercial consideration – experience of partners

Maximum   8

(b) **Plover Co**

Generally 1 mark for each matter discussed:

- Potential breach of law and regulations
- Further understanding to be obtained
- Consider potential impact on financial statements
- Discuss with those charged with governance
- Management should disclose to relevant regulatory body
- Auditor could disclose in public interest
- Issues with confidentiality
- Take legal advice
- Extend audit work in relation to the legal claim
- Risk of material misstatement
- Consider integrity of audit client

Maximum   7

(c) (i) **Actions and implications in respect of the auditor's report on Dylan Co**

Up to 1½ marks for each action/implication:

- Insufficient appropriate audit evidence so far obtained
- Possible to extend audit procedures on reconstructed figures/other procedures
- Majority of transactions during the year likely to have sufficient evidence
- If no further evidence available, consider modification to opinion
- Discuss whether material or pervasive
- Description of auditor's report contents if opinion modified
- Communicate with those charged with governance

(ii) **Quality control procedures**

Up to 1 mark for each comment:

- EQCR required as Dylan Co is listed
- EQCR to review sufficiency and appropriateness of evidence obtained
- EQCR to consider judgement used in forming audit opinion
- EQCR to ensure matters communicated to those charged with governance

Maximum   10

Total   **25**

(a) **Close business relationship**

Grouse Co's proposal would create very significant threats to Raven's independence.

This would be a 'close business relationship' per the IESBA *Code of Ethics*, and may give rise to a self- threat. The *Code* states that unless the financial interest is immaterial, and the business relationship insignificant, then no safeguards can reduce the threat to an acceptable level. Therefore Raven should not enter into this relationship if it still wants to be Grouse's auditor.

It should be remembered that independence includes independence in appearance (IESBA *Code of Ethics*). A joint venture with an audit client would probably have a severe effect on how Raven appeared, so even if it had been acceptable on ethical grounds, the fact that it looks so bad may well have ruled it out anyway.

Selling to clients

In addition to the close business relationship, Grouse is also proposing that the software be sold to Raven's audit clients. There are several issues here.

Firstly, there is a self-interest threat to Raven's independence if its joint venture is selling to its clients. It may be possible to reduce this to an acceptable level by using the safeguard of disclosing the relationship to clients, along with the benefit that Raven would receive from any sales.

Secondly, there would be a self-review threat if any of the audit clients used the accounting and tax software to prepare its financial statements. It may be possible to use an auditor's expert here; however, accounting software is usually pervasive to the internal controls over financial reporting, so it may be that the expert would have to be used to conduct most of the audit. This would be extremely expensive and impracticable.

Thirdly, the use of the firm's accounting and tax software could be seen as a non-audit service. This could create a perception of taking on management's responsibilities. The risk would be greater still for clients that are public interest entities, and the firm should not be involved in any tax calculations for these clients.

Taking into account these factors, Raven must choose between selling the software to its clients, and continuing to act as their auditor. It would not be possible to sell this software to clients and continue to audit them. Raven must therefore make a business decision to choose between the potential income from the software, and the loss of audit fees from every client to whom the software is sold. Raven should also take into account the loss of the audit fee from Grouse itself.

The software joint venture therefore represents a major diversification from audit to the preparation of accounting and tax software. This is a major decision that must be considered very carefully, taking into account the firm's long-term interests, where its expertise really lies, and the potential risks from diversifying into such an unknown area.

(b) **Unqualified surgeon?**

The audit senior has heard that one of the surgeons has not finished his medical qualification. This may be connected to the solicitor's letter that was later found which alleged medical negligence. As an auditor, we need to deal with each issue separately.

ISA 250 *Consideration of Laws and Regulations in an Audit of Financial Statements* states that compliance with laws and regulations is management's responsibility, and that it is not the auditor's responsibility to either prevent or detect it. However, if – as here – we become aware of possible NOCLAR (Non-Compliance with Laws and Regulations) then we must consider its effect on the financial statements. This breach could have an indirect but material effect on the financial statements.

As auditors we have no expert knowledge of medicine, and it is possible that we may be jumping to conclusions about whether the surgeon is qualified to do his work. It may be, for example, that he is a qualified doctor, and the 'medical qualification' he is hoping to finish is merely a further qualification that is not a requirement for his work as a surgeon. Although he was glad that Plover did not check his references, this could be a separate issue from whether or not he is qualified.

We must therefore obtain further evidence about this surgeon's qualifications, and whether they meet the requirements for his job. This could entail simply reviewing the personnel file, which may contain evidence about his qualifications.

Effect of unqualified surgeon

If we find that the surgeon is not qualified to do his job, then we must consider the effect on the financial statements. There are two main risks:

(i)   Risk of litigation resulting from errors made by the surgeon
(ii)   Risk of action by regulatory bodies

In relation to (i), this is potentially a very serious problem. If the surgeon has made many errors then this could result in multiple patients suing the company. The potential cost of these actions is not known, but could be very considerable indeed. It is even possible that Plover's ability to continue as a going concern could be affected. Further evidence must be obtained about the extent of further errors and possible legal actions. It may be necessary to obtain advice from our legal counsel.

In relation to (ii), the medical profession is highly regulated and it is possible that Plover will be fined by any relevant regulatory authorities. There is a legal question about whether Plover's management could be found guilty of possible negligence as a result of breaking its duty of care to patients. It may be necessary to obtain legal advice here.

It is even possible that any licences which Plover requires to operate will be removed, and that its ability to continue as a going concern will be in doubt. It may be necessary to use an auditor's expert here to provide advice about the possible regulatory consequences, and/or to obtain legal advice.

Control failure?

The surgeon's comment that his references were not checked raises questions about the effectiveness of Plover's internal controls over recruitment. It will be necessary to obtain evidence about whether or not there are other employees in this position – the main issue being that there could be other employees (eg surgeons) who are not qualified to do their work. Uncovering these could lead to the discovery of further liabilities.

Public interest?

If the surgeon is not qualified, then it is possible that management will not disclose this to the relevant authorities. They should be encouraged to do so by the auditor, but if they do not then it may be necessary to make this disclosure in the public interest. This is a difficult issue to decide, as the auditor must balance the duty of confidentiality that is owed to Plover, with the duty to the public. Matters to consider here include the gravity of the situation, whether members of the public may be affected, and the likelihood of further non-compliance. This will all depend on whether the surgeon was in fact unqualified, and on what impact this may have had on patients.

Disclosure in the public interest would require careful consideration, and it may be necessary to obtain legal advice before doing so.

Legal claim

The letter that was found in the subsequent events review may be evidence of a liability under IAS 37 *Provisions, Contingent Liabilities and Contingent Assets*. The key question is whether the event in question took place before or after the year end. The crucial date here is likely to be the date on which the medical service was provided.

If the surgery was after the year end, then this is a non-adjusting event and no provision is necessary. If the surgery was before the year end, then a provision may be required. This will depend on how probable it is that Plover will have to pay to settle the claim, with a provision being necessary if it is probable that a payment will be made. If the matter is material and Plover's management refuse to make any necessary provisions or disclosures, then it may be necessary to express a qualified auditor's opinion.

(c) (i) **Actions**

We have not performed audit procedures on payroll, revenue and receivables, and have not obtained sufficient appropriate audit evidence as yet.

Hendrix Co has reconstructed the figures 'as far as possible', which means that they could still be materially and pervasively misstated. In any event, their representation is not sufficient audit evidence.

It may be possible to perform additional procedures on the information that Hendrix Co has reconstructed. This could obtain evidence about revenue and payroll. Receivables could still be tested by a circularisation.

It is not clear, however, what records may still be in existence: Hendrix Co may have sent information to Dylan Co during the year. As the virus attack only happened in August, Dylan Co could have 10 or 11 months' information on which it might be possible to perform audit procedures.

As a listed company, Dylan Co may have issued interim financial statements, which could provide accounting information for part of the year that could be audited.

Practically, it may be necessary to request an extension to any deadlines for completion of the audit.

Auditor's report

It is possible that additional procedures may obtain sufficient appropriate evidence, in which case an unmodified report could be issued.

If this evidence is not obtained, then either a qualified opinion will be expressed, or the auditor will disclaim an opinion.

A qualified opinion would be expressed if the auditor judges that the inability to obtain sufficient appropriate audit evidence is material but not pervasive. The auditor would then state that the financial statements give a true and fair view 'except for' the areas where there is insufficient evidence – payroll, revenue and/or receivables.

A disclaimer of opinion would be made if the problem is both material and pervasive.

Further actions

The details of any potential modification should be communicated in advance to those charged with governance, who should be given a chance to provide further explanations.

(ii) Dylan Co is a listed company, so in line with ISA 220 *Quality Control for an Audit of Financial Statements* an engagement quality control reviewer must be appointed. The review must be completed before the auditor's report is issued.

BPP
LEARNING

The reviewer should review the financial statements and the proposed auditor's report, together with relevant audit documentation.

The issue of whether sufficient audit evidence has been obtained in relation to payroll, revenue and receivables should be paid very close attention, considering in particular whether it might be possible to obtain evidence about these balances by any other means. This is important, because if it is in fact possible to obtain this evidence, then the auditor must not express an opinion saying otherwise.

The review should ensure that there is adequate documentation supporting any judgements made in forming the opinion, and that adequate communications have been made where necessary to those charged with governance.

15 Dragon Group

Workbook references. Chapter 5 and 9.

Top tips. Part (a) was probably the hardest part of this question. You should try to strike a balance between making general remarks about what a tender document should include, and sticking to the specific information given in the scenario.

Part (b) offered a lot of marks in this area, and was a good test of your knowledge.

Part (c) should have been straightforward provided that you knew what a transnational audit was.

Easy marks. Part (c) contained a number of marks for pure knowledge, and thus the opportunity to score easy marks.

ACCA examining team's comments. In part (a), sound answers appreciated that the point of the tender document is to sell your audit firm's services to the client. Those candidates who tailored their answer to the question scenario tended to do well. However, candidates who provided a list of points to be included in **any** tender scored inadequately. Weak answers simply stated vague comments: 'we should discuss fees', 'we should set a deadline', etc. Answers to part (b), which asked for matters to consider re: acceptance were weak, despite this being a regularly examined syllabus area. Most answers were not tailored to the question, and just provided a list of questions or actions. Requirement (c) was the worst answered on the exam. Clearly, very few candidates had studied the issue of transnational audits, and answers displayed a lack of knowledge.

Marks

(a)   **Contents of tender document**

Up to 1½ marks per matter described:
- Outline of firm
- Specialisms
- Audit requirement of Dragon Group
- Outline audit approach (max 3 marks if detailed description)
- QC
- Communication with management
- Timing
- Key staff/resources
- Fees
- Extra services

Maximum   10

Marks

(b) **Matters to consider re acceptance**

Generally ½ mark for identification – cap at max 3, 1 further mark for explanation, from ideas list:
– Large and expanding group – availability of staff now and in the future
– Use of overseas offices
– Visits to overseas audit teams
– Skills/experience in retail/foreign subsidiaries consolidation
– Timing – tight deadline
– Mermaid Co – implication of prior year qualification
– Minotaur Co – implication of different business activity
– Highly regulated – risk/additional reporting requirements
– Reason for previous auditors leaving office

Maximum   8

(c) **Define transnational audit and relevance to Dragon Group**

1 mark for definition
2 marks for relevance to Dragon Group

Audit risk factors in a transnational audit

2 marks per difference explained:
– Auditing standards
– Regulation of auditors
– Financial reporting standards
– Corporate governance/control risk

Maximum   <u>7</u>

Total   **<u>25</u>**

(a) **Fees**

The proposed fee should be included, along with an explanation of how it is calculated. This would include details of the charge-out rates of the staff likely to be used on the audit, along with estimates of the amount of time the audit would be likely to take.

Dragon Group's needs and how Unicorn & Co could meet them

(i) An explanation of the need for each subsidiary (as well as Dragon Co) to have its own individual audit, and for the consolidated financial statements then to be audited too.

That Unicorn & Co is a large firm and would be capable of auditing a large group such as this.

(ii) The Dragon Group may also need some non-audit services (see below).

That Unicorn & Co can provide a variety of non-audit services, should they be required.

(iii) Several subsidiaries prepare accounts under local accounting rules, so the auditor of these would need to audit under different financial reporting frameworks.

That Unicorn & Co is a global firm with offices in over 150 countries. It would be well-placed to conduct an audit under local accounting rules, and to audit their consolidation into the group accounts.

BPP
LEARNING

(iv)   The Dragon Group operates in the furniture retail trade.

That Unicorn & Co has a specialist retail department and therefore has the experience to audit the group efficiently.

Proposed audit approach

This section should include a description of the methodology to be used in the audit. For instance:

(i)   How the firm would acquire knowledge of the business
(ii)   Methods used in planning and risk assessment
(iii) Procedures used to gather audit evidence

Brief outline of Unicorn & Co

A short history of the firm, including a description of its organisational structure, the services it can offer and the locations in which it operates.

Other services

A description of any other services Unicorn & Co can offer, such as offering advice in relation to the proposed stock exchange listing. Careful consideration should be given to ethical requirements relating to independence when offering other services to a potential audit client.

Key staff

Details of the proposed engagement partner and of his experience that is relevant to this audit. Details should also be given of the approximate size and composition of the audit team, together with a description of the relevant experience of key members of that team.

Communication with management

An outline of the various communications that will be made to management over the course of the audit. This may include information on the way in which these reports could add value to the Dragon Group's business, for instance the production of a written report on the effectiveness of internal control procedures.

Timing

Details should be provided of the timeframe envisaged for the various aspects of the audit. This might include details of when the subsidiaries would be audited, when the consolidation process would be audited, and an estimate of by when the group audit opinion could be completed.

Conclusion

This is a large, transnational group, carrying a high level of risk. Unicorn & Co should take on the audit only once it is sure that it is able to do so, and is assured of a fee that adequately compensates it for the level of risk involved in undertaking the audit.

(b)   **Matters to consider before accepting engagement**

Size of Dragon Group

The Dragon Group is large and expanding group of companies, and would therefore require a high level of resources to audit. Unicorn & Co must consider whether it has sufficient staff available to audit a growing group of this size.

Overseas subsidiaries

Half of the subsidiaries are located overseas. Unicorn & Co has a large number of overseas offices which could perform some or all of the overseas audits. However, these offices may not all have specialist retail audit departments, so consideration needs to be given to whether there is enough experienced staff to carry out the audit.

If some of the overseas audit work needs to be done by auditors outside of Unicorn & Co, then this work would need to be evaluated in order to express an opinion on the group financial statements.

Relevant expertise

As Unicorn & Co has a department specialising in retail audits, it is likely that it will have sufficient expertise in this country.

As a large auditing firm, it is also likely that Unicorn & Co will have staff sufficiently experienced in auditing the consolidation process to audit the consolidation of the Dragon Group's results.

Time pressure

The group's year end is 30 September 20X9, and management wants the audit completed by 31 December 20X9. This represents a tight deadline, given that the audit involves a large number of subsidiaries located in several different countries and reporting under a number of different accounting rules. The fact that this would be the first year that Unicorn & Co would have audited the group also makes the deadline tight. There is also a possibility that management does not fully understand what is required for an audit.

Planned listing

Management are planning a new listing on a foreign stock exchange. This will increase the risk of management manipulation of the accounts, as management may be under pressure to report favourable results. Audit risk is also increased by the fact that as a result of the listing, the financial statements will be subject to heavy scrutiny by regulators.

Previous auditor

Unicorn & Co should consider the reason for the group seeking to change its auditor, as this might affect the decision to accept the engagement. On the face of it, it appears likely that the quickly growing group has outgrown its previous auditors, but Unicorn & Co should still seek to obtain the reason for the change from the previous auditors.

Mermaid Co

Mermaid Co's previous auditors expressed a qualified audit opinion. Unicorn & Co should gather information about the related contingent liability, part of which would involve contacting the previous auditors. Management's refusal to disclose the contingent liability may indicate a lack of integrity on their part, which would increase audit risk. Consideration then needs to be given to whether any future non-disclosure would be material to the group financial statements.

Minotaur Co

Minotaur Co operates in a different business area from the rest of the group, so Unicorn & Co must consider whether it has staff available with the appropriate level of expertise. This difficulty should be straightforward for a firm of Unicorn & Co's size to overcome.

(c) A transnational audit means an audit of financial statements which are or may be relied upon outside the audited entity's home jurisdiction for purposes of significant lending, investment or regulatory decisions (TAC, 2010).

This will include the Dragon Group because it is listed on the stock exchange, and also because it is listed on the stock exchanges of several different countries, and is therefore bound by regulations emanating from more than one national jurisdiction.

The fact that the group contains many overseas subsidiaries means that their accounts are likely to be relied upon both at home and abroad, and so are transnational in nature.

Regulation and oversight of auditors differs from country to country

In some countries audits are self-regulated, whereas in others a legislative approach is used. There is a risk that auditors of transnational groups may not be sufficiently aware of the requirements in all of the relevant countries.

Differences in auditing standards from country to country

Although ISAs are now in operation in many countries, these standards are frequently modified by individual countries. Moreover, not all countries have adopted the standards.

There is a risk that auditors may not have the required understanding of the relevant auditing standards in each country.

Variability in audit quality in different countries

It may be the case that the quality of auditing required may differ between relevant countries. There is a risk either that the auditor does not perform an audit that is up to the required standard in some countries, or that the audits performed on some overseas subsidiaries are not up to the standard required to express an opinion on the group financial statements.

16 Goldfinch

Workbook references. Chapters 7 and 8.

Top tips. This was a reasonable question in a format that should be familiar to AAA students.

Part (a) featured a decommissioning provision. In a way this was an easy question part, because the only hard pieces of information you are given tell the story of the provision going down. If you had thought about it, you could have worked out that the provision should be going up; however, even if you didn't get this point you could have spotted the change in the discount rate used, which signals what is going on. The audit points themselves should be straightforward.

Part (b) gave us another suspicious-looking adjustment by management, this time a change in how depreciation is estimated. This should not have posed you significant problems, as the scenario was clear and the points coming out of it were not too complex – the main things being the change in the useful lives themselves, and then accounting for it retrospectively instead of prospectively.

One thing to bear in mind with questions like this is that the examining team tends not to like it when students go too far in criticising management, or do not use professional language when doing so. Notice that the answer here is quite restrained in its language, and that the key response is to apply professional scepticism.

Part (c) may have seemed more difficult as it is full of inconsistencies. You might have been thrown off by the existence of two different types of trade receivable; by the unexplained differences in collection periods between the types of receivable; or by the unexplained change in the allowance for credit losses. The question does not actually give you a great deal to go on here, so it is reasonable to feel unsure of how to answer it. The model answer keeps things simple – more information is needed. Two of the evidence points are for 'notes of a discussion with management' – this is a type of evidence that is very useful in questions like this one.

Easy marks. The marks for calculating materiality are the easiest on the question.

Marking scheme

Marks

Generally up to 1 mark for each relevant matter considered, and 1 mark for each well explained point on audit evidence.

(a) **Decommissioning provision**

Matters
- Materiality of the provision
- Requirements of ISA 540 regarding obtaining appropriate evidence
- Unusual that a decommissioning provision has reduced in value but there could be valid reasons
- Provision should be measured at best estimate and discounted to present value
- The reason for the change in interest rate needs to be fully understood
- Consideration of accounting entries and whether they indicate an attempt to boost profit for the year
- Whether it is appropriate that management has not used an expert to determine the estimate

Evidence
- A copy of management's calculation of the $430 million provision, with all components agreed to underlying documentation, and arithmetically checked
- Notes of a meeting with management, at which the reasons for the reduction in the provision were discussed
- Copies of the source data used to produce management's estimate
- A comparison of the calculation for this year's provision with previous years, confirming consistency in the overall approach used by management
- Copies of the underlying information relating to the expected costs of the decommissioning
- An evaluation of all key assumptions, considering consistency with the auditor's knowledge of the business, and a conclusion on their validity
- An independent estimate prepared by the audit team, compared to management's estimate, and with significant variances discussed with management
- Alternatively, an estimate prepared by an auditor's expert, with all workings and assumptions evaluated by the audit team
- A schedule of the movement in the provision, checked for arithmetical accuracy, opening and closing figures agreed to the draft financial statements and general ledger
- Evaluation, and a conclusion on the appropriateness of the accounting entries used, especially in relation to the profit impact of the entries
- A copy of the notes to the financial statements which describe the decommissioning provision, reviewed for completeness and accuracy

Maximum   10

BPP
LEARNING

(b)   **Depreciation**

Matters
- Materiality
- Annual review of estimated useful life is required
- Amendment has a significant impact on profit and could be an attempt to inflate profit
- Professional scepticism should be applied
- Incorrectly accounted for as a prior year adjustment, should be a prospective adjustment
- Retained earnings and PPE are overstated

Evidence

- Notes of a meeting with management on incorrect accounting treatment
- Confirmation from management that a correction will be made to account for it prospectively rather than retrospectively
- Agreement of the carrying value of the plant and equipment to the non-current asset register
- Documentation supporting the extension of the useful lives of the assets
- A written representation from management explaining the justification for the amendment to the estimated life of the assets
- A copy of management's calculation of the amended depreciation charge, checked for arithmetical accuracy, and each element of the calculation agreed to supporting documentation

Maximum   8

(c)   **Trade receivables**

Matters

- Materiality
- Trend in receivables collection periods is inconsistent
- New billing system could explain the change in trends
- Management using more judgement in determining allowance, the increase is significant and not adequately explained by management

Evidence

- Notes of a discussion with management on the results of the analytical procedures
- A copy of the aged receivables analysis, reviewed for significant changes in year
- Documentation on the new billing system, to confirm our understanding of the system and relevant controls
- Further analytical procedures performed on the allowance for credit losses
- Notes of a discussion with management which include the assumptions used by management in determining the amount of the allowance, and the method by which it was calculated

Maximum   7

Total   **25**

(a) **Decommissioning provision**

Matters

The provision is material as it amounts to 22.6% of total assets. The provision has changed in value over the year, declining by $58 million, which is a significant reduction of 11.9%.

According to ISA 540 *Auditing Accounting Estimates Including Fair Value Accounting Estimates and Related Disclosures*, the audit team should have tested how management made the accounting estimate, and the data on which it is based. The audit team should also have tested the operating effectiveness of any relevant controls, and developed their own point estimate or range in order to evaluate management's estimate.

The value of a decommissioning provision would normally be expected to increase, as the date of the anticipated settlement of the liability draws closer, so the audit team must fully understand the reasons for the reduction in the provision. There could be valid reasons – for example, the estimated costs of dismantling the assets have reduced, or the estimated date of decommissioning is later – but the change in value should have been fully investigated by the audit team.

IAS 37 *Provisions, Contingent Liabilities and Contingent Assets* requires that the amount recognised as a provision should be the best estimate of the expenditure required to settle the present obligation at the reporting date, and that provisions are measured at present value. For the decommissioning provision recognised by Goldfinch Gas Co, where the obligation will not be settled for many years, the method used to discount the liability to present value will have a significant impact on the measurement of the provision. For example, the use of 8% to determine the discount factor, rather than 6%, will have reduced the value of the provision and the reasons for the change in interest rate should have been an important consideration for the audit team.

Consideration should be given to the accounting entries which have been made to effect the change in the value of the provision. When a decommissioning provision is first recognised, there is no profit impact, because the cost is capitalised as part of the relevant non-current asset. Subsequent adjustments to the value of the provision could be charged or credited to profit, or recognised as an adjustment to the asset value, depending on the reason for the adjustment. The audit work should conclude on the appropriateness of how the change to the provision of $58 million has been recognised in the current year financial statements. In particular, the validity of any credit entries made to profit should be scrutinised, as this could indicate creative accounting, specifically earnings management.

In previous years management has engaged an expert to provide the estimate, but this year the estimate has been prepared by management. There are therefore increased risks of both error and management bias in the estimation techniques and methodology which have been used. The audit team should approach this issue with professional scepticism and consider whether the expense of engaging an expert is the real reason as to why a management estimate has been used this year.

Evidence

- A copy of management's calculation of the $430 million provision, with all components agreed to underlying documentation, and arithmetically checked.

- Notes of a meeting with management, at which the reasons for the reduction in the provision were discussed, including the key assumptions used by management. In particular, management should provide justification of the change in interest rate used in their estimation from 6% to 8%.

- Copies of the source data used to produce management's estimate, including information on the relevant assets' estimated useful lives and expected date of their

BPP
LEARNING

decommissioning, which may be part of a licence agreement to operate gas production and storage facilities.

- A comparison of the calculation of this year's provision with previous years, confirming consistency in the overall approach and methodology applied in creating the estimate.

- Copies of the underlying information relating to the expected costs of the decommissioning, evaluated for reasonableness by the audit team, for example, by comparison to the cost of any current decommissioning which is taking place.

- An evaluation of all key assumptions, considering consistency with the auditor's knowledge of the business, and a conclusion on their validity.

- An independent estimate prepared by the audit team, compared to management's estimate, and with significant variances discussed with management.

- As an alternative to the above, if the audit team does not have the necessary skill to prepare the estimate, an estimate prepared by an auditor's expert should be included in the audit file, with all workings and assumptions evaluated by the audit team.

- A schedule obtained from management showing the movement in the decommissioning provision in the accounting period, checked for arithmetic accuracy, and with opening and closing figures agreed to the draft financial statements and general ledger.

- Evaluation by the audit team, and a conclusion on the appropriateness of the accounting entries used, especially in relation to the profit impact of the entries.

- A copy of the notes to the financial statements which describe the decommissioning provision, reviewed for completeness and accuracy.

(b) **Depreciation**

The plant and equipment is recognised at $65 million; this is material to the financial statements as it represents 3.4% of total assets. The depreciation which has been recognised in profit for the year represents 9.2% of profit before tax, and is also material.

There are two main issues to be considered regarding the accounting treatment of the depreciation. First, the reason for the change in the estimated useful life needs to be properly justified. There is nothing wrong in amending the estimated useful life of non-current assets – indeed it is a requirement of IAS 16 *Property, Plant and Equipment* that the useful life of an asset should be reviewed at least at each financial year end.

However, the adjustment to the estimated useful life appears to be fairly significant, resulting in a $3 million reduction in the annual depreciation charge, equivalent to a reduction of 20% of the expense recognised in the previous year, and increasing profit before tax in 20W7 by 2.3%. Management could have changed the estimated useful life with the intention of boosting profit, and the audit team should be sceptical of the reasons used to justify the change in estimated useful life. The need to be sceptical is augmented by the boost to profit which may have been achieved through the reduction in the decommissioning provision.

Second, the change in estimate has been accounted for incorrectly. According to IAS 16, when a change in estimated useful life is recognised, this is accounted for prospectively as a change in estimate under IAS 8 *Accounting Policies, Changes in Accounting Estimates and Errors*. In this case, it has been incorrectly accounted for as a prior year adjustment, effectively being treated as an error rather than a change in estimation technique.

Based on the information provided, both non-current assets and retained earnings are overstated by $20 million. This represents 1.1% of total assets, and is borderline in terms of its materiality to the financial statements, though given the possibility of earnings management techniques being used to boost profit, the audit team should consider revising its risk assessment for the audit as a whole and reducing the level of materiality applied when

evaluating the risk of material misstatement. Further, this is effectively the misapplication of an accounting policy and is therefore likely to be considered material by nature.

Evidence

- Notes of a meeting with management where the incorrect accounting treatment of the change in estimate has been discussed, along with confirmation from management that a correction will be made to account for it prospectively rather than retrospectively.

- Confirmation that the carrying value of the plant and equipment and the retained earnings have been adjusted to remove the $20 million incorrectly recognised as a prior year adjustment.

- Agreement of the carrying value of the plant and equipment to the non-current asset register and physical verification of a sample of assets where the asset life has been extended to confirm condition and operation of the asset.

- Documentation supporting the extension of the useful lives of the assets concerned, for example, maintenance reports indicating continued efficiency of the assets, and engineer's reports showing that there are no major operational problems with the assets.

- A written representation from management explaining the justification for the amendment to the estimated life of the assets.

- A copy of management's calculation of the amended depreciation charge, checked for arithmetical accuracy by the audit team, and each element of the calculation agreed to supporting documentation.

(c) **Trade receivables**

The total trade receivables is material to the financial statements, representing 23.7% of total assets.

The analytical procedures performed by the audit team reveal an unusual trend in that the trade receivables collection period for residential customers has increased from 58 to 65 days, whereas the collection period for business customers has reduced from 55 to 50 days. The reasons for this inconsistent trend should be fully explored with management. Net trade receivables in total have increased by 15.4%. The use of additional judgement could increase the risk of material misstatement, particularly in relation to the residential customers who are deemed to be historically late in paying their bills.

The changes in collection period could be related to the new customer billing system which has been introduced during the year, and management should confirm whether this relates to both residential and business customers, or to just one of them.

The allowance for credit losses has increased significantly, by 45.5%. The allowance is material to the financial statements as it represents 3.4% of total assets and the movement in the allowance in the year represents 15.3% of profit. The note to the financial statements indicates that the introduction of the new billing system has impacted on how management estimates the allowance for credit losses, and the reasons for this should be discussed with management. It would seem unusual that the introduction of a new billing system would have such a significant effect on the level of bad or doubtful debts, so possibly there is another reason to explain why the allowance has increased by such a large amount.

The audit team should have documented and evaluated the new system, using walk through tests to confirm understanding of how the system works, and controls should also have been evaluated for effectiveness in their design and operation. This is particularly important given that there are significant changes in the collection periods for both residential and business customers since last year end, which could indicate that customers are not being billed in the same way or that there is some misallocation between residential and business customers' accounts.

Evidence

- Notes of a discussion with management on the change in the trade receivables collection period, including management's reasons for the increase in the residential customers' collection period, and reduction in the business customers' collection period.

- A copy of the aged receivables analysis, reviewed for significant changes in the year, for example, an increase in the age profile of the receivables could justify the increase in allowance against old receivables balances.

- Documentation on the new billing system, to confirm understanding of the system and the results of the evaluation of the controls which operate over the system.

- Further analytical procedures performed on the allowance for credit losses, for example, procedures which show a breakdown of the allocation of the allowance against residential and business customers.

- Notes of a discussion with management which include the assumptions used by management in determining the amount of the allowance, and the method by which it was calculated, for example as a % of receivables balances or specific allocation to individual customers' balances, and how the introduction of the new billing system has impacted on the determination of the allowance.

Tutorial note. Credit will be awarded for audit evidence on the collectability and existence of trade receivables including after date cash tests, relevant enquiries with credit controllers and receivables confirmations and reconciliations.

---

17 Ted

Workbook references. Chapters 2, 5, 6, and 8.

Top tips. As ever you needed to stick closely to the scenario to do well – including reading it carefully.

Part (a) was a good question on audit tendering and ethics, which provided you with a fair test. Audit tendering is a slightly peripheral but still important part of the syllabus. You can approach questions like part (a)(i) by using a standard set of issues to include in the tender (eg taken from the Workbook), which you must then adapt to the scenario. The easy marks here come from the scenario, and you do not need to know very much about tendering to get those marks.

One obvious point to bear in mind when answering part (a)(i) is that there are no marks for mentioning fees in this part of your answer! Also it was possible to mention ethics in both part (i) and part (ii), but your answer needed to be focused on the requirement in each part, so do not discuss detailed ethical issues in part (i), but only the coverage of ethical matters in the tender.

Part (a)(ii) was again fair, and most candidates would have been able to muster up enough comments about how fees are determined and the necessity of maintaining quality. This part of the requirement breaks down into two elements – the issues to consider in determining a fee, and the ethical matters – so you need to cover both of these.

Part (b) was almost standalone, and although it is better if you can bring bits of the scenario into your answer you do not strictly have to do so to answer the requirement. It is important to stick to your allotted time here – it may have been a temptation to go over the 12 minutes available (6 marks × 1.95 minutes).

The wording of the requirement itself was quite complicated, containing several subordinate clauses – to discuss planning matters, specific to an initial audit engagement, which should be considered in developing the audit strategy. Yet in the end most planning matters would affect the audit strategy, so your focus should have been mainly on planning matters for initial audit engagements, provided that the points you come up with are not so detailed as to be irrelevant to the strategy.

Note that the audit has now been accepted, so matters related to obtaining professional clearance from the predecessor auditor were not relevant to this part of the question. (This is one way in which you needed to bear the scenario in mind in order to answer this question part.)

Although the client is a new client, it has previously been audited so the matters to consider here do not include matters where the prior year financial statements are unaudited.

Part (c) was a typical AAA question on audit risk. Your approach here should be to work through the scenario, noting and thinking about audit risks as you spot them.

There were marks available for calculating an item's materiality, and for saying whether or not it was material. These are easy marks and you should make sure you get them, although there is likely to be a cap on the number of marks you can get here.

Although a preliminary analytical review has already been performed, there are still marks available for calculating a few extra figures – for example, profit margins. These are easy marks, but to get them you need to calculate the comparative as well (ie both this year's margin and last year's margin). Again, these marks are likely to be capped so don't spend all of your time doing calculations!

The requirement is on audit risk – rather than the risk of material misstatement – so this includes detection risk, as well as any more practical issues that could affect the audit planning.

Part (d) may have looked harder than it was. You can get quite a few marks for saying simple things like: the need to vouch the payment for purchasing the investments to the cashbook and bank statement; to review board minutes for evidence of authorisation; and to review the disclosure note to ensure that disclosure is accurate and complete. Once you have these points you only need to think of a few more in order to pass this question part. It should go without saying that you need to make your procedures as specific as possible, eg do not just say 'vouch to documentation', but rather state which piece of documentation you would use.

Easy marks. The marks for calculating and assessing materiality in part (c) are simple. Not to mention the professional marks: notice that the professional marks are for presentation (among other things), something which will also help to get your marker on your side.

ACCA examining team's comments. The first part of the question focused on practice management and client acceptance issues. The scenario described a potential new audit client, Ted Co, a small but rapidly growing company. The audit firm had been approached to tender for the audit of Ted Co, and this would be the first year that the company required an audit.

Requirement (a)(i) for eight marks asked candidates to explain the specific matters to be included in the audit proposal document, other than those relating to the audit fee. This was **quite well attempted by many**, with almost all candidates understanding the main components of an audit proposal document such as a background of the audit firm, discussion of audit methodology, an outline of the firm's resources and timings and deadlines. Where **candidates did not score well** on this requirement was where the answer provided was very generic and was not made specific to the requirements of Ted Co.

Requirement (a)(ii) for six marks went on to ask candidates to discuss the issues relating to determining the audit fee to be considered by the audit firm, assuming its appointment as auditor of Ted Co. Unfortunately many answers to this requirement did not identify the relevant matters in the question scenario, including the issue of contingent fees, intimidation on fees and lowballing that were implied by the comments made by the owner-manager of Ted Co. **Better candidates** were able to make the very valid point that the potential client needed a better understanding of the purpose of an audit and why it needs to be seen to be independent and tied this back to the content of the proposal document.

BPP
LEARNING

Where these matters were not discussed, answers tended to be generic, and simply focused on the fact that audit fees should be determined by time, resources and charge-out rates. Many of the weaker answers did not focus on the specific nature of the question requirement, and instead discussed matters that had little to do with the audit fee, such as self-review threats and other irrelevant acceptance procedures such as customer due diligence.

Answers to part (b) were very mixed in quality, with the best answers concentrating on practical matters such as reviewing the previous audit firm's working papers, planning procedures to obtain evidence on opening balances, and ensuring that the audit team developed a thorough understanding of the business.

Unfortunately the majority of candidates provided generic answers discussing whether or not the firm could take on the audit, engagement letters, fees, customer due diligence and checking to see if the previous auditors had been correctly removed from office. It was not relevant to discuss whether the audit firm should take on the client and associated acceptance issues as it was clearly expressed in the scenario that this decision had already been taken and consequently answers of this nature scored limited credit.

Other weaker answers discussed general audit planning matters such as the need to determine a materiality level. This was not tailored to the specifics of this scenario as this would be relevant for any audit. **Candidates are reminded to answer the specific question that has been set**, which in this case should have meant answers focusing on matters relevant to planning an initial audit engagement after the engagement has been accepted.

Some candidates wrote a lot for what was only a six-mark requirement. Candidates are reminded that the marks for each requirement are a guide as to how long should be spent on answering the question. In some cases the answers to this question part ran to several pages, leading to time pressure on subsequent answers.

There were some excellent answers to requirement (c), with many responses covering a range of audit risks, all well explained, and all relevant to the scenario. The best answers demonstrated that a methodical approach had been applied to the information in the scenario, and the better candidates had clearly worked through the information logically, identifying the risk factors, then going on to explain them fully and specifically.

The audit risks that were generally dealt with well included those relating to the foreign currency transactions and to the portfolio of short term investments. The risk relating to whether research and development costs could be capitalised was also identified by the majority of candidates, but the issue of amortisation was not often discussed.

To achieve a good mark for this type of requirement, candidates should look for a range of audit risks, some of which are risks of material misstatement and some are detection risks. **Candidates** however **do not need to categorise the risks they are discussing** or to spend time explaining the components of the audit risk model.

When discussing audit risks relating to a specific accounting treatment, well explained answers will include an evaluation of the potential impact of the risk factor on the financial statements, for example, in this scenario there was a risk that the short-term investments were overstated in value and that profit also was overstated. Materiality should be calculated when possible, as this allows prioritisation of the risks identified. **Strong candidates**, as well as providing detailed analysis and explanation of the risks, also **attempted to prioritise the various risks identified**, thus demonstrating appropriate judgment and an understanding that the audit partner would want to know about the most significant risks first. Candidates are reminded that it is those risks that could result in a material misstatement in the financial statements, which need to be identified and addressed.

Weak answers included answer points that were too vague to be awarded credit. Comments such as 'there is a risk this has not been accounted for properly', 'there is risk that this is not properly disclosed' and 'there is a risk that the accounting standard has not been followed' are unfortunately too common and will not earn marks due to the lack of specificity. It would be beneficial for candidates to review their answers and to consider whether what they have written would provide the audit engagement partner with the necessary knowledge to understand the risk profile of the client in question.

Regarding requirement (d), some candidates proved able to provide a good list of recommendations, but this was the minority. Answers tended to be better in relation to the investment portfolio, with many candidates appreciating that determining the short-term nature of the investments was an important issue and that the fair value of the shares at the year end could be agreed to stock market listings. However, most candidates could only provide vague suggestions such as 'discuss with the board' or 'agree to supporting documentation', and in relation to the fair value of the share many candidates could only suggest to 'rely on an expert' which was not necessary given that the investment relates to the shares of listed companies. Some candidates tried to make the recommended procedures much too complicated, not fully appreciating that traded equity shares can be easily valued and documented.

The procedures in relation to EPS were often very vague, with many candidates only able to suggest a recalculation of components of the calculation provided, or check the board had approved the calculation, neither of which were relevant given that the calculation was incorrect. Very few candidates picked up on the fact that the weighted average number of shares would need to be verified given that the company had a share issue during the year.

Marking scheme

Marks

(a) (i) **Matters to be included in the audit proposal**
Generally up to 1½ marks for each matter explained:
- Outline of the audit firm
- Audit requirement of Ted Co
- Audit approach (allow up to 3 marks for well-explained points made relevant to scenario)
- Deadlines
- Quality control and ethics
- Additional non-audit and assurance services

Maximum   8

(ii) **Matters to be considered in determining audit fee**
Generally up to 2 marks for each point discussed:
- Fee to be based on staffing levels and chargeable hours
- Low fees can result in poor-quality audit work and increase audit risk
- Lowballing and client expectation issues
- Contingent fees not allowed for audit services

Maximum   6

(b) **Initial audit engagement**
Generally up to 1½ marks for each point discussed, including:
- Communicate with the previous auditor, review their working papers
- Consider whether any previous auditor reports were modified
- Consider any matters which were raised when professional clearance was obtained

    –   Consider matters discussed with management during our firm's appointment

    –   Need to develop thorough business understanding

    –   Risk of misstatement in opening balances/previously applied accounting policies

Other points included:

    –   Firm's quality control procedures for new audit clients

    –   Need to use experienced audit team to reduce detection risk

Maximum   6

(c)   **Evaluation of audit risk**

Generally up to 1½ marks for each point discussed, and 1 mark for each calculation of materiality:

    –   Management bias due to recent stock market listing – pressure on results

    –   Management bias due to owner's shareholding – incentive to overstate profit

    –   Management lacks knowledge and experience of the reporting requirements for listed entities

    –   Weak corporate governance, potential for Dougal to dominate the board

    –   Revenue recognition – should the revenue be deferred

    –   Revenue recognition – whether deferred income recognised over an appropriate period

    –   E-commerce (allow up to 3 marks for discussion of several risks factors)

    –   Foreign exchange transactions – risk of using incorrect exchange rate

    –   Forward currency contracts – risk derivatives not recognised or measured incorrectly

    –   Portfolio of investments – risk fair value accounting not applied

    –   New team dealing with complex issues of treasury management

    –   EPS – incorrectly calculated (allow 3 marks for detailed discussion)

    –   EPS – risk of incomplete disclosure

    –   Rapid growth – control risk due to volume of transactions

    –   Profit margins – risk expenses misclassified (also allow 1 mark for each margin correctly calculated with comparative)

    –   Development costs – risk of over-capitalisation of development costs

    –   Inventory – year-end counts already taken place, difficulties in attending inventory counts

    –   Opening balances (give mark here if not given in (a) above)

Maximum   18

(d) (i)   **Procedures on portfolio of investments**

Generally 1 mark for each procedure explained:

    –   Agree the fair value of the shares held as investments to stock market share price listings

    –   Confirm the original cost of the investment to cash book and bank statements

    –   Discuss the accounting treatment with management and confirm that an adjustment will be made to recognise the shares at fair value

Marks

- Review the notes to the financial statements to ensure that disclosure is sufficient to comply with the requirements of IFRS 9
- Enquire with the treasury management function regarding disposals and reinvestment
- Review board minutes to confirm the authorisation and approval of the amount invested
- Confirm the number of shares held to supporting documentation such as dividend received vouchers
- Review documentation relating to the scope and procedures of the new treasury management function

(ii) **Procedures on EPS**

Generally 1 mark for each procedure explained:

- Review documentation relating to the scope and procedures of the new treasury management function
- Review board minutes to confirm the authorisation of the issue of share capital, the number of shares and the price at which they were issued
- Confirm the share issue complies with the company's legal documentation such as the memorandum and articles of association
- Inspect any other supporting documentation for the share issue, such as a share issue prospectus
- Recalculate the weighted average number of shares for the year to 31 May 20X5
- Recalculate EPS using the profit as disclosed in the statement of profit or loss and the weighted average number of shares
- Discuss with management the existence of any factors which may impact on the calculation and disclosure of a diluted EPS figure, for example, convertible bonds
- Read the notes to the financial statements in respect of EPS to confirm that disclosure is complete and accurate and complies with IAS 33

| | Maximum | 8 |

Professional marks for the overall presentation, structure and logical flow of the briefing notes, and for the clarity of the evaluation and discussion provided.

| | Maximum | 4 |
| **Total** | | **50** |

(a) (i) **Outline of audit firm**

An outline of Craggy & Co (Craggy) should be provided, perhaps including a brief history and a summary of key information about the firm (eg the number of partners and offices).

Any specialisms of Craggy should be mentioned, particularly if it has expertise in auditing software development companies. It should also be stated that Craggy has branches in many countries, as this may prove useful if any audit work needs to be performed overseas.

BPP
LEARNING

Client requirements

The statutory audit requirements in Ted Co (Ted)'s jurisdiction should be stated, to confirm that an audit is needed. It should be stated that the audit must conform to ISAs. Any additional reporting requirements that result from Ted's listing should be stated.

Audit approach

The tender should outline the stages of an audit. This should include the possibility that Craggy will need to test Ted's opening balances, which were audited by a predecessor auditor. It should be stated that this will depend on whether Craggy is able to review the predecessor auditor's working papers and is satisfied with the evidence obtained.

Craggy should describe the proposed audit approach, including the firm's audit methodology, and should explain that audit is risk-based, involving an assessment of the company's accounting systems and internal controls. It is possible that Ted's controls may not be reliable, given the accounting function's limited resources (there are only two full-time accountants), which would affect the audit approach.

Client expectations

Dougal Doyle hopes that the audit will not be disruptive. Craggy may attempt to manage his expectations here, as a certain degree of disruption is unavoidable. It will be necessary, for example, to receive explanations from employees, including the accountant, which will take time.

Communications

The tender should outline the various communications which will be made to management and those charged with governance, including the value which Ted may derive from them, particularly in relation to any control deficiencies identified.

Deadlines

The tender should seek to clarify the timeframe for the audit. The proposed deadline of four months may be reasonable, although Ted is a recently listed company so the audit is likely to be a large one (and potentially time-consuming). If there are problems with the audit, eg Ted's internal controls are less reliable than expected, then the audit may take longer. Ted needs to be prepared for this possibility.

Quality control and ethics

Craggy should state its adherence to the IESBA's *Code of Ethics for Professional Accountants*, and to International Standards on Quality Control. This will give Ted and its venture capitalist investor confidence in the auditor's report that would be issued.

Predecessor auditor

Crilly & Co, the predecessor auditor, resigned and it is crucial that professional clearance is obtained before proceeding with the audit.

Additional services

The tender should make mention of any other non-audit services which Craggy is in a position to provide. These are particularly relevant to Ted in light of Dougal Doyle's comments. It should be stated that these services can only be provided subject to meeting the ethical requirements by which Craggy is bound.

(ii) **Commercial factors**

The audit firm has a commercial desire to make a profit, which it does by offering a fee which is high enough to be profitable but low enough to attract business. It must do this without compromising its professional independence or its standards of quality.

Costs

The fee should be linked to costs incurred. The main cost is the time spent by the audit team, so this component of the fee is calculated using a charge-out rate which is multiplied by the time spent. Basing the fee on the costs incurred is both commercially sound (it ensures that costs and normal profits are covered), and ethically relevant because it ensures that the fee is sufficient to pay for the work that needs to be done.

Additional costs included in the audit fee are the fees of any auditor's experts, and the costs of any travel that is needed for the audit team. The cost of auditing Ted may be increased by its stock exchange listing, which will impose more extensive reporting requirements on it and thus more audit work.

Low fees

There is a suggestion that the fee for the Ted audit may be set below market rate in order to win the audit. This is known as lowballing, and while this is not prohibited as such, it does carry the ethical risk that the fees may not be sufficient to pay for the work required. Craggy must not, therefore, reduce the amount of audit work done because the fee is insufficient, but must do whatever work is necessary to reduce audit risk to an acceptable level.

Contingent fee

To link the audit fee to the success of the company is to charge a contingent fee. This creates a self-interest threat.

The threat is so significant that no safeguards could reduce it to an acceptable level, so such an arrangement should not be entered into.

Intimidation

Taken together, Dougal Doyle's two suggestions in relation to fees (low and contingent fees) and his hope for a fixed deadline may amount to an intimidation threat. If this is the case then Craggy must consider not continuing with the tender.

Briefing notes

To: Jack Hackett

From: Manager

Subject: Audit of Ted Co, y/e 31 May 20X5

Introduction

These briefing notes will discuss planning matters to consider in relation to the audit strategy of an initial audit engagement, evaluate the audit risks relevant to planning the Ted audit, and recommend the principal audit procedures for the portfolio of investments and the earnings per share (EPS) figure.

(b)   Although professional clearance should already have been obtained, we should consider the effect on our strategy of any matters that the predecessor auditor may have brought to our attention. The reason for the predecessor auditor's resignation should be established, as this may have a bearing on our assessment of risk and our planning of resources for the audit.

ISA 300 *Planning an Audit of Financial Statements* suggests contacting the predecessor auditor in order to review their working papers (as long as this is not prohibited by laws or regulation). This would help Craggy to plan its audit if there are any matters which would still be relevant to the current year, such as accounting policies. It is possible, however, that the predecessor auditor may refuse access to their working papers.

Although last year's auditor's opinion was unmodified, if any previous years' auditors' reports were modified then the reason for the modification(s) should be sought, as the matter(s) may continue to be relevant in the current year.

It is possible that, during the appointment process, matters were discussed which might have a bearing on the audit, eg there might have been a discussion of accounting policies. This may affect the audit strategy.

Craggy must obtain evidence on opening balances. Procedures should be performed on whether they have been brought forward correctly, and whether accounting policies are consistent.

Understanding the entity is crucial with an initial audit engagement, and this understanding would clearly have an impact on the audit strategy. It would help Craggy to decide on the areas of audit risk, would facilitate analytical review, and would help to plan practical matters such as the use of auditor's experts.

(c) **Development costs**

Development costs capitalised are 43% of total assets. This is material.

The 65.7% increase over last year is significant, so there is a risk of misstatement. Given that $100m was invested, however, capitalising 58% may be reasonable; this can only be known once audit evidence has been obtained in this area. Professional scepticism will be important, given the highly material nature of the asset but also the risk of management bias (see below).

Development costs are capitalised only when they meet the IAS 38 *Intangible Assets* criteria, such as whether it is probable that future economic benefits will flow to the entity, whether the cost can be measured reliably, whether the asset is technically and commercially feasible, or whether Ted has the resources to complete the development (IAS 38: para. 57). Costs not meeting these criteria are expensed in profit or loss.

Overseas manufacturing

Overseas manufacture of physical product brings a detection risk in relation to inventory. For example, it may be difficult for the firm to attend inventory counts overseas at the year end if inventory is held overseas, in which case alternative sources of evidence should be consulted.

Website sales

25% of revenue is generated through the website. This is material.

There is a control risk here, and this is particularly acute given the company's rapid expansion – there is a danger that the website cannot cope with a large increase in sales, which could affect the figures reported in the financial statements.

There is a detection risk, because the website may not leave a significant audit trail.

There is a cut-off risk, because it may be difficult to determine the exact time when performance obligations are satisfied in line with IFRS 15 *Revenue from Contracts with Customers*, ie when control is passed from Ted to the customer.

Licence income

Deferred income from licences is 13.4% of total assets. This is material.

This income should be accounted for in line with IFRS 15, and again it may be difficult to determine exactly when performance obligations are satisfied. This depends on whether the promise to grant a licence includes any other promised goods or services, for example whether the software will be updated during the period of the licence. If no such goods or services are included, then it may be that performance obligations are satisfied at that point in time, ie when the licence is sold. In this case no licence income should be deferred at all and there is a material misstatement, understating revenue and overstating assets. The audit plan should ensure that sufficient resources are devoted to this technical area.

Listing

Ted obtained a listing during the year, which brings a risk of manipulation. This is an inherent risk at the financial statement level. Management will want to present good results for the new (and potential) shareholders, so there is an incentive to overstate profit and assets. Profit before tax is up 48.1%, and there is a risk that this is overstated.

The listing may bring further reporting responsibilities (eg in relation to earnings per share), so there is a risk of misstatement here which is heightened given that it is probably the first time this has been reported.

Many shares are held by institutional investors, bringing an increased level of scrutiny to the financial statements and the audit process. This increases the risk of litigation to the auditor.

Corporate governance

Corporate governance structures do not appear to be strong: there are too few non-executive directors, and there is no internal audit department. There is a risk of Dougal Doyle dominating the board and influencing the preparation of the financial statements. This is amplified by the incentive for management bias in relation to the listing.

Foreign exchange

Ted must have significant foreign currency transactions, as it sells in over 60 countries and manufactures products overseas. The risk is that IAS 21 *The effects of changes in foreign exchange rates* is not followed. IAS 21 requires all items to be translated into Ted's functional currency ($) when the transactions occur (historical rate) (IAS 21: paras. 21–22). All monetary balances at the year end must then be retranslated at the closing rate (IAS 21: para. 23). Misstatements may occur in either of these processes, leading to over- or under-statement of assets, liabilities, income, expenses, and exchange gains or losses.

The establishment of a treasury management function may help reduce this risk by improving controls. However, the fact that the team is new may mean it takes time to become effective, and there is a risk of mistakes being made while it gains experience.

The use of forward contracts to try to manage business risk represents an audit risk. First, unless they are managed properly, these contracts may not have the desired effect (the team is new), which could result in an audit risk if problems occur. Second, they are derivative financial instruments and are accounted for in line with IFRS 9 *Financial Instruments*. This is complex, and there is a risk that not all contracts may be identified. Further, the contracts should be measured at fair value, which may be difficult and judgemental to determine. Hedge accounting rules must be followed, which are complex in nature. Taken together, there is a significant control risk in, this area.

Investment portfolio

The cost of the shares of $8m is 6% of total assets. This is material.

The fall in value of $2m is 25% of profit before tax. This is material.

In line with IFRS 9, shares held in the short term as a speculative investment should be held at fair value through profit or loss (they are not being held to collect contractual cash flows). They are currently held at cost, which is therefore incorrect. They should be remeasured to fair value; if this is not done, then both profit and total assets are overstated by $2 million.

The fact that such a large sum of money was lost on speculative investments raises a number of questions. This seems an ill-advised venture, and it is not clear why Ted has established a new treasury function which has spent (and lost) such sums speculating in shares, outside the company's principal activity. This may be further evidence of poor governance, and a lack of internal control which could affect the assessment of audit risk.

Rapid growth

Ted has grown rapidly in recent years, which often results in control risk as systems and people struggle to keep up with both greater volumes and new types of transactions. This may be the case here, as a lack of proper governance and control structures appears evident in several places.

Earnings per share (EPS)

IAS 33 *Earnings per Share* requires Ted to present both EPS and diluted EPS on the face of the statement of profit or loss.

The EPS calculation must be based on profit (or loss) attributable to ordinary shareholders, from the statement of profit or loss (IAS 33: para. 66). To calculate it otherwise is a material misstatement. It is possible to present an alternative figure in the notes to the financial statements, however.

There are two further errors in the EPS calculation. Profit before tax should not be used, and the number of shares used should be a weighted average for the year – not just the number at the year end, as here.

This is significant given the new listing during the year which will expose Ted to significant scrutiny in this area.

Profit margins

	20X5	20X4
Gross margin	65,000 / 98,000 = 66.3%	40,000 / 67,000 = 59.7%
Operating margin	12,000 / 98,000 = 12.2%	9,200 / 67,000 = 13.7%

There is a risk that the coincidence of a rising gross margin with a falling operating margin is a result of the misclassification of expenses between cost of sales and operating expenses. This could also indicate an understatement of cost of sales. Alternatively, it could be that Ted has simply incurred more operating expenses as it has grown – for example backroom and administrative functions (such as treasury management). In any case, explanations need to be obtained of the reasons for this discrepancy.

(d) (i) **Procedures on investment portfolio**

- Agree fair value of shares to stock market listings at 31 May 20X5.

- Confirm original cost of investment to cash book and bank statements.

- Discuss accounting treatment with management and confirm that an adjustment will be made to recognise the shares at fair value.

- Review notes to the financial statements to ensure that disclosure is sufficient.

- Enquire with treasury management function whether there have been any disposals of the original shares and reinvestment of proceeds into the portfolio.

- Review board minutes to confirm authorisation and approval of the investment.

- Review documentation relating to the scope and procedures of the new treasury management function, for example, to understand how the performance of investments is monitored.

- For investments from which dividends have been received, confirm the number of shares held to supporting documentation, eg dividend certificates.

(ii) **Procedures on EPS**

- Discuss IAS 33 with management and request it to recalculate EPS in line with IAS 33.

- Review board minutes to confirm authorisation and details of issue of share capital.

- Inspect supporting documentation for the share issue, eg share issue prospectus.

- Confirm that share issue complies with company's legal documentation, eg memorandum and articles of association.

- Recalculate weighted average number of shares for the year to 31 May 20X5.

- Recalculate EPS using the correct figures for profit and number of shares.

- Discuss with management whether there is anything that may affect the calculation of diluted EPS, eg convertible bonds.

- Read the notes to the financial statements in respect of EPS to confirm that disclosure complies with IAS 33.

Conclusion

These briefing notes depict a high level of audit risk for this engagement, which is due to the possibility of management bias and a number of indicators of poor internal controls.

18 Francis

Workbook references. Chapters 8, 9 and 10.

Top tips. This question may have been deceptively simple; it really was a question about goodwill, a non-adjusting event and intercompany transactions. It was therefore quite possible to score well.

Throughout the question, your evidence points need to be as specific as possible, stating the evidence that you would want to see (eg the particular document – purchase documentation, say), and then why you want to see it. A simple list of pieces of evidence is unlikely to score well if it does not also say why the evidence is needed.

In part (a), you need to go through the various pieces of information thinking of what might go wrong in relation to each of them. Some housekeeping points in relation to FR: goodwill is not amortised; assets are revalued to fair value on acquisition, which does not involve a revaluation reserve; loans are held at amortised cost using an effective interest rate.

In part (b), it should be clear that this event is non-adjusting. Always try to think of when the obligating event happened – in this case it was after the year end, so it is never going to require adjustment to the financial statements. Mentioning IAS 37 in relation to the contingent asset is OK, but not strictly relevant because it's a non-adjusting event, so the fact that it may not be virtually certain to be received does not really matter. With this part of the question, there were so many marks available for calculating materiality that if you got them, you could still pass this part of the question even if you were wrong about the non-adjusting event.

In part (c), there may have been some confusion about what was being asked for. The ACCA answer focuses on the issues that would arise in the Group financial statements, which is valid on the grounds that the question strongly implies that your firm is the Group auditor. However, the question also states that your firm audits all components of the Group. The requirement does not specify whether the working papers being reviewed relate to the Group audit only or the audit of components as well. Therefore in BPP's view it would be legitimate to discuss issues arising in the audit of the individual components, although it would not have been possible to calculate component materiality with the information provided.

Note that throughout this question, the evidence points in particular are far more comprehensive in our answer than any candidate would be able to include in their exam answer.

Easy marks. There are plentiful marks just for calculating materiality in each section, and for saying whether or not an item is material.

 BPP LEARNING

ACCA examining team's comments. This type of requirement is common in AAA, and it was encouraging to see that many candidates had obviously practised past exam questions containing similar requirements. Most candidates approached each of the issues in a sensible manner by firstly determining the materiality of the matters involved, considering the appropriate financial reporting treatment and risk of misstatement, and then providing some examples of appropriate audit evidence relevant to the matters discussed. However, the question was not well attempted by all, and it was usually a lack of knowledge of financial reporting requirements, and / or an inability to explain the relevant audit evidence that let some candidates down.

Requirement (a) related to an acquisition of a subsidiary that had taken place during the year. A goodwill calculation had been provided, along with information regarding a fair value adjustment relevant to the net assets of the subsidiary at acquisition. In addition, a loan had been taken out to finance the acquisition and information relating to the interest rate and loan premium was given in the scenario.

Candidates were able to achieve a good mark here if they tackled each component of the information provided in turn and used that approach to deliver a structured answer. In relation to the goodwill calculation, many candidates identified that no impairment had been recognised, and therefore that the goodwill balance may be overvalued. Only the strongest candidates mentioned that a significant drop in the Group's profit for the year meant that it would be very likely that an impairment loss should be recognised. It was worrying to see how many candidates referred to the need for goodwill to be amortised over a useful life – a practice that has not been allowed under IFRS 3 *Business Combinations* for many years. Fewer candidates touched on the measurement issues in relation to the non-controlling interest component of goodwill, which was usually ignored in answers. Looking at the fair value adjustment to net assets, most candidates recognised that this would be a subjective issue and that ideally an independent valuer's report or due diligence report would be required as audit evidence to justify the adjustment. Weaker candidates thought that the accounting treatment of goodwill was incorrect and set about correcting the perceived errors.

The loan element tended to be well dealt with – most candidates seemed to be aware of the principles of IFRS 9 *Financial Instruments* in discussing the financial reporting implications of the loan taken out to finance the acquisition, and the need to measure the loan at amortised cost including the premium was frequently identified. It was encouraging to see many candidates also refer to the extensive disclosure requirements that would be necessary in relation to the acquisition itself, as well as the loan, and that a significant risk would be insufficient disclosure in the notes to the financial statements.

Some incorrect accounting treatments frequently discussed included:

- Goodwill should be amortised over an estimated useful life (discussed above)
- Goodwill only needs to be tested for impairment when indicators of impairment exist
- Non-controlling interest should not be part of the goodwill calculation
- Borrowing costs should be capitalised into the cost of investment / goodwill figures
- Fair value adjustments are not required and are an indication of fraudulent financial reporting

The evidence points provided by candidates for this requirement tended to revolve around recalculations of the various balances, and confirming figures to supporting documentation such as the loan agreement, purchase documentation and due diligence reports. These were all valid evidence points but it would benefit candidates to consider a wider range of evidence that may be available especially in relation to the more subjective and therefore higher risk elements, for example a discussion with management regarding the need for an impairment review of goodwill or a review and assessment of the methods used to determine the fair value of the non-controlling interest.

Requirement (b) related to a natural disaster that had taken place two months after the year end, resulting in the demolition of the Group's head office and main manufacturing site. The Group had claimed under its insurance an amount in excess of the value of the demolished property, and the whole amount of the claim was recognised in the statement of financial position as a current asset and deferred income. **This requirement was generally well answered**, with almost all candidates correctly determining the materiality of the property complex and the contingent asset.

Most candidates also appreciated that the auditor should consider the event to be a non-adjusting event after the reporting date, requiring disclosure in the notes to the financial statements, in line with the requirements of IAS 10 *Events after the Reporting Period*. The audit evidence suggested was usually relevant and sensible, tending to focus on the insurance claim, discussing the need for demolition with management, and evidence from documents such as health and safety reports on the necessity for the demolition. Many answers identified that a key part of the audit evidence would be in the form of a review of the sufficiency of the required notes to the financial statements describing and quantifying the financial implications of the non-adjusting event. In a minority of scripts candidates suggested that the event was actually an adjusting event and that impairment of the property complex should be recognised in this financial year.

Weaker answers to this requirement suggested that the event should be recognised by impairing the property complex and recognising the contingent asset. However, encouragingly even where candidates had discussed the incorrect accounting treatment, the evidence points provided were generally appropriate to the scenario.

Requirement (c) for 6 marks briefly described the details of intercompany trading that had taken place between components of the Group resulting in intercompany receivables and payables in the individual financial statements of the components, and inventory within the recipient company including a profit element. Most candidates correctly determined that at Group level the intercompany transactions should be eliminated and that a provision for unrealised profit would be necessary to remove the profit element of the transaction. Most candidates also correctly calculated the relevant materiality figures and could provide a couple of evidence points. **The main concern with responses** to this requirement was that they were often brief, with the audit evidence described usually amounting to little more than recalculations and 'check the elimination has happened'.

In summary, part (b) was well attempted by many candidates, with the matters to consider element of the requirements usually better attempted than the audit evidence points. As in part (a), it was clear that many candidates had practised past questions of this type and were well prepared for the style of question requirement.

Marking scheme

Marks

(a) **Teapot Co**
   Matters
   - Materiality of the goodwill
   - Purchase price/consideration to be at fair value
   - Risk of understatement if components of consideration not included
   - Non-controlling interest at fair value – determination of fair value if Teapot Co is listed
   - Non-controlling interest at fair value – determination of fair value if Teapot Co is not listed
   - Use of fair value hierarchy to determine fair value
   - Risk that not all acquired assets and liabilities have been separately identified
   - Risk in the measurement of acquired assets and liabilities – judgemental
   - Additional depreciation to be charged on fair value uplift
   - Group accounting policies to be applied to net assets acquired on consolidation
   - Impairment indicator exists – fall in revenue
   - Impairment review required regardless for goodwill

BPP
LEARNING

197

- Risk goodwill and Group profit overstated if necessary impairment not recognised
- Loan – initial measurement at fair value
- Loan – subsequent measurement at amortised cost
- Risk effective interest not properly applied – understated finance cost and liability
- Risk of inadequate disclosure in relation to financial liability

Evidence

- Agreement of the purchase consideration to the legal documentation, and a review of the documents
- Agreement of the $75 million to the bank statement and cash book
- Review of board minutes for discussions relating to the acquisition, and for board approval
- A review of the purchase documentation and a register of significant shareholders of Teapot Co to confirm the 20% non-controlling interest
- If Teapot Co's shares are not listed, a discussion with management as to how the fair value of the non-controlling interest has been determined and evaluation of the appropriateness of the method used
- If Teapot Co's shares are listed, confirmation that the fair value of the non-controlling interest has been calculated based on an externally available share price at the date of acquisition
- A copy of any due diligence report relevant to the acquisition, reviewed for confirmation of acquired assets and liabilities and their fair values
- An evaluation of the methods used to determine the fair value of acquired assets, including the property, and liabilities to confirm compliance with IFRS 3 and IFRS 13
- Review of depreciation calculations, and recalculation, to confirm that additional depreciation is being charged on the fair value uplift
- A review of the calculation of net assets acquired to confirm that Group accounting policies have been applied
- Discussion with management regarding the potential impairment of Group assets and confirmation as to whether an impairment review has been performed
- A copy of any impairment review performed by management, with scrutiny of the assumptions used, and reperformance of calculations
- Reperformance of management's calculation of the finance charge in relation to the loan, to ensure that effective interest has been correctly applied
- Agreement of the loan receipt and interest payment to bank statement and cash book
- Review of board minutes for approval of the loan to be taken out
- A copy of the loan agreement, reviewed to confirm terms including the maturity date, premium to be paid on maturity and annual interest payments

Marks

    –   A copy of the note to the financial statements which discusses the loan to ensure all requirements of IFRSs 7 and 13 have been met

Maximum   12

(b) **Subsequent event**

Matters

- Materiality of the asset (calculation) and significance to profit
- Identify event as non-adjusting
- Describe content of note to financial statements
- Consider other costs, eg inventories to be written off
- Contingent asset/deferred income should not be recognised

Evidence

- A copy of any press release/media reports
- Photographic evidence of the site after the natural disaster and of the demolished site
- A copy of the note to the financial statements describing the event
- A schedule of the costs of the demolition, with a sample agreed to supporting documentation
- A schedule showing the value of inventories and items such as fixtures and fittings
- A copy of the insurance claim
- Confirmation of the removal of the contingent asset from the financial statements

Maximum   7

(c) **Intercompany trading**

Matters

- Materiality of the intercompany balance and the inventory
- At Group level the intercompany balances must be eliminated
- If they are not eliminated, Group current assets and liabilities will be overstated
- A provision for unrealised profit may need to be recognised in respect of the inventory

Evidence

- Review of consolidation working papers to confirm that the intercompany balances have been eliminated
- A copy of the terms of sale scrutinised to find out if a profit margin or mark-up is part of the sales price
- A reconciliation of the intercompany balances between Roberts Co and Marks Co to confirm that there are no other reconciling items to be adjusted, eg cash in transit or goods in transit
- Copies of inventory movement reports for the goods sold from Marks Co to Roberts Co to determine the quantity of goods transferred
- Details of the inventory count held at Roberts Co at the year end, reviewed to confirm that no other intercompany goods are held at the year end

Maximum   6

Total   **25**

(a) **Goodwill**

Goodwill is 6% of total assets, and is therefore material.

Impairment

Management should review goodwill for impairment at the end of the year. No impairment loss has been recognised, and there is a risk that this is because no impairment review was conducted.

Group profit has declined by 30.3% ($10m / $33m) and assets have declined by 1.1% ($5m / $455m). These are both impairment indicators, although it is possible that the downward trends do not relate to Teapot Co's ('Teapot') activities. In any case, there is a risk that assets and profit are both overstated.

Consideration

Consideration should be measured at its fair value. There is a risk that the calculation is incomplete, eg if there is any deferred or contingent consideration not included.

Non-controlling interest (NCI)

IFRS 3 *Business Combinations* permits NCI to be measured at fair value, so this is acceptable. However there is a risk in relation to the estimation of fair value. If Teapot is listed then this is just the market price of the shares and is reliable; however, if it is not listed then the estimation must be done in line with IFRS 13 *Fair Value Measurement*. This involves an element of judgement, the basis of which must be clearly understood by the auditor.

Net assets

There is a risk that not all net assets will be identified, or that the estimation of their fair values is not reliable. Some form of due diligence should have been performed as part of the acquisition, which may have valued the business and identified its assets and liabilities.

Fair value adjustment

The adjustment of $300,000 is not material, at less than 1% of total assets. However, additional depreciation should be charged at group level on these assets (also not material).

Loan

The loan is 13.3% of total assets, and is material.

Under IFRS 9 *Financial instruments* it is measured at its fair value when initially recognised, and then subsequently at amortised cost as it is not held for trading (although there is a fair value option).

An effective interest rate should thus be used to allocate the premium over the 20-year life of the loan. There is a risk that the finance charge is not calculated using the effective rate, or that the premium is recognised incorrectly (for example, it may be recognised as a liability at its present value, which is incorrect).

IFRS 7 *Financial Instruments: Disclosure* contains extensive disclosure requirements, and there is a risk of misstatement in respect of inadequate disclosures in relation to the loan (eg of its significance for Teapot Co's financial position and performance).

Evidence

- Agreement of consideration to legal documentation, reviewing to ensure that the figures included in the goodwill calculation are complete

- Agreement of $75 million to bank statement

- Review of board minutes for discussions of acquisition, and for approval of the acquisition

- Review of purchase documentation, and a register of significant shareholders of Teapot Co, to confirm 20% NCI

- If Teapot Co's shares are not listed, discuss with management how the fair value of the NCI was determined and evaluation of the appropriateness of the method used

- If Teapot Co's shares are listed, confirmation that the fair value of NCI was calculated based on an externally available share price at the date of acquisition

- Copy of due diligence report, reviewed for details of assets and liabilities and their fair values

- Evaluation of methods used to determine fair value of assets and liabilities to confirm compliance with IFRS 3 and IFRS 13

- Review of depreciation calculations, and recalculation, to confirm that additional depreciation is being charged on fair value uplift

- Review of the calculation of net assets acquired to confirm that Group accounting policies have been applied

- Discussion with management regarding the potential impairment of Group assets and confirmation of whether an impairment review has been performed

- Copy of any impairment review performed by management, with scrutiny of the assumptions used, and reperformance of calculations

- Reperformance of management's calculation of the finance charge on the loan, to ensure that the loan premium has been correctly accrued

- Agreement of the loan receipt and interest payment to bank statement

- Review of board minutes for approval of the loan to be taken out

- Copy of the loan agreement, reviewed to confirm terms including the maturity date, premium to be paid on maturity and annual interest payments

- Copy of the note to the financial statements which discusses the loan to ensure all requirements of IFRSs 7, 9 and 13 have been met

(b) **Property**

The carrying value is material, at 3.6% of total assets ($16m/$450m).

Under IAS 10 *Events after the Reporting Period*, the natural disaster is a non-adjusting event because it relates to conditions which did not exist until two months after the year end (IAS 10: para. 3). Therefore, the value of the property complex should not be written off in the 20X4 financial statements.

The event should be disclosed in a note describing its impact, and quantifying its anticipated effect on next year's financial statements. Consideration should be given to any other effects, eg other damage sustained in the disaster, and the costs of the demolition itself.

Contingent asset

The contingent asset is material, at 4.0% of total assets (= $18m/$450m).

This should not have been recognised, as it also relates to a non-adjusting event deriving from conditions which did not exist at the end of the reporting period. This fact is saliently admitted by the recognition as 'deferred income', which is itself incorrect because the amount has not yet been received.

Evidence

- Copy of any press release made by the Group after the natural disaster, and relevant media reports of the natural disaster, in particular focusing on its impact on the property complex

- Photographic evidence of the site after the natural disaster, and of the demolished site

- Copy of the note to the financial statements describing the event, reviewed for completeness and accuracy

- Schedule of the costs of the demolition, with a sample agreed to supporting documentation, eg invoices for work performed

- Schedule showing the value of inventories and items such as fixtures and fittings at the time of the disaster, and confirmation that this is included in the costs described in the note to the financial statements

- Copy of the insurance claim and correspondence with the Group's insurers to confirm that the property is insured

- Confirmation that an adjustment has been made to reverse out the contingent asset and deferred income which has been recognised

(c) **Intercompany trading**

Intercompany receivables and payables are 4.4% of Group assets, and are material. The inventory is 11% of Group assets, and is also material.

Intercompany balances should be eliminated on consolidation. There is a risk that this has not been done correctly, overstating Group assets and liabilities.

If these transactions included a profit element then Group inventory needs to be reduced in value by an adjustment for unrealised profit. If this is not made then Group assets and profits will be overstated.

Individual companies

It is not clear why Roberts Co has recognised inventory at $50m but a payable at $20m, or where the remaining $30m (credit) has been recorded. If it is because the goods were sold at a mark-up of $30m, then the inventory can continue to be recognised at the cost of $50m, but the payable must also be $50m. These amounts need to be recognised, and more information is needed on why there is a mismatch within Roberts Co's own records.

The transaction should be disclosed in the financial statements of each individual company in line with IAS 24 *Related Party Disclosures*.

Evidence

- Review of consolidation working papers to confirm that intercompany balances were eliminated

- Copy of terms of sale between Marks Co and Roberts Co, showing whether a profit margin is part of the sales price

- Reconciliation of intercompany balances between Roberts Co and Marks Co to confirm that there are no other items to be adjusted, eg cash in transit or goods in transit

- Copies of inventory movement reports for the goods sold from Marks Co to Roberts Co, to determine the quantity of goods transferred

- Details of the inventory count held at Roberts Co at the year end, reviewed to confirm that no other intercompany goods are held at the year end

19 Thurman

Workbook references. Chapters 8 and 11.

Top tips. This was quite a practical auditing question that you should have been able to pass well, particularly if you have experience of working in audit.

The format of the question and the requirement almost suggests a tabular format for your answer, but this is unlikely to be appropriate at this level (it would lead you away from writing full sentences, which you need to do in AAA). Instead, you should lay your answer out in the same way as the model answer, ie part (a) has (i), (ii) and (iii), and so on.

Regarding **timings**, one of the difficulties with this question was knowing how much to write for each sub-part (i, ii, iii). There are different amounts that can be said in relation to each sub-part, so if you had divided your time equally between them then you might have struggled. The best method here would be to work out your time for each part (a, b, c), and then make sure you answer each sub-part within it.

Part (a) was typical of the things that can happen to an auditor in the real world. Much of the audit work that has been done is OK, but it is not enough. You should be able to pick some holes in it by asking yourself questions about how much more could have been done, eg not just checking that the journal is arithmetically correct, but that all the figures in it are included in line with IFRS 5 – and that there are no other adjustments that should have been made. Try to think about what other requirements the standard might have.

There were a few little distractors in this scenario that it's worth noting – the phrase 'manual journal' might have made you think of some kind of manual override of controls, suggesting that there was something amiss when in fact there was not (how else would this adjustment be made?). There is a hint that the audit senior is taking on a management role, but remember, the requirement does not ask for ethical issues so you should not write about them.

It is important to note that the requirement really focuses on the auditor's response to these issues, so that in eg part (a) the problem is not necessarily the accounting treatment per se, but rather whether the auditor has sufficient evidence for its reasonableness.

Make sure you spend enough time writing further audit procedures – they're worth a mark if explained properly, and these are relatively easy marks. State **what** should be done, and then say **why**.

Almost every statement in the scenario for part (a) that related to audit evidence contained an issue. Your task was simply to draw this out of the question, state some procedures that should now be performed, and consider what should be included in the management letter (report to management/those charged with governance). Parts (b) and (c) were similar in this respect.

Easy marks. The marks for audit procedures are easy. It is key to passing this question that you address each part of the requirement (i, ii, iii) so that you picked up the easiest marks available in each.

ACCA examining team's comments. This question was set in the completion stage of the audit and as is generally the case with completion questions, it was focused on the accounting treatment and audit evidence obtained on three issues. In this case, candidates were also required to discuss the impact of the issues found on the report to those charged with governance. Candidates generally demonstrated a good knowledge of the financial reporting implications of the areas and were often able to identify that the evidence obtained was insufficient and suggest further procedures. For many candidates the control weaknesses in the company and the implication of a deficiency in controls on further audit strategy and testing was not always identified. Candidates' responses to the matters to include in the report were variable with some candidates discussing auditor's report qualifications (despite no errors being flagged) or giving general answers to the contents of the report with no reference to the scenario in the exam.

Marks

Generally 1 mark for each relevant point of discussion and well explained audit procedure:

(a)   **Asset held for sale**

    (i)   **Audit evidence**

        –   Discussion is relevant but management's assertions must be corroborated

        –   Discussion alone is not sufficient to reach an audit conclusion

        –   Evidence not obtained on whether IFRS 5 classification criteria have been met

        –   Evidence not obtained on whether disclosure of discontinued operations is necessary

    (ii)   **Further procedures**

        –   Review board minutes to confirm the sale approval and date

        –   Correspondence with estate agents to confirm that the factory is being actively marketed

        –   Confirmation, for example, by a review of production schedules, inventory movement records and payroll records that production at the factory has stopped

        –   Auditor's expert to confirm the fair value of the property and agree that this figure has been used in the impairment calculation

        –   Using management accounts, determine whether the factory is a separate major line of business in which case its results should be disclosed as a discontinued operation

    (iii)   **Report to those charged with governance**

        –   Should be controls in place over year-end journals (2 marks for detailed discussion)

        –   Finance director should not have to ask the audit team to check his work

                                    Maximum   9

(b)   **Capital expenditure**

    (i)   **Audit evidence**

        –   Testing should have been extended after the control deficiency was identified

        –   Reason for the controls not operating effectively should be investigated

        –   Increases the fraud risk in relation to capital expenditure

        –   Not all assertions have been covered by audit testing in respect of the vehicles purchased

Marks

(ii) **Further audit procedures**

– Obtain the insurance documents to confirm that Thurman Co is paying the relevant insurance for the vehicles

– Physically verify the vehicles and confirm that they are being used by employees on company business

– Obtain the log book and other relevant ownership documents such as those issued by the vehicle licensing body, to confirm the right of Thurman Co to recognise the vehicles

– Trace the vehicles to the company's fixed asset register

– Recompute the depreciation which should have been charged on the vehicles and agree to the statement of profit or loss for the year.

(iii) **Report to those charged with governance**

– Explain the deficiencies and the implications, ie increased fraud risk

– Recommend improvements to specific controls and to the general control environment

Maximum   7

(c) **Payroll**

(i) **Audit work**

– Agreeing payroll to the service organisation's report does not provide sufficient evidence on completeness, accuracy or validity of the amounts

– The controls at the service organisation must be assessed for their adequacy

– No further work needed on the petty cash payments to casual workers as the amount is not material

(ii) **Further audit procedures**

– Review the service agreement between Thurman Co and Jackson Co to understand the exact work which is conducted by Jackson Co as a service organisation

– Read all reports made by Jackson Co during the year to identify any risks of misstatement in the payroll figure

– Discuss and document relevant controls in place at Thurman Co over the information received from Jackson Co and the management of casual employees, and perform tests of controls on a sample basis

– Recalculate the amount of any unpaid tax which may be due to the tax authorities

– Read any user manuals or systems overviews to assess the efficacy of controls in place over the processing of payroll

– If necessary, obtain a type 1 or type 2 report from Jackson Co to obtain further assurance on the controls which the service organisation has in place

Marks

- Perform a substantive analytical review on payroll, preparing an auditor's expectation of the payroll figures and comparing it to that recognised in the financial statements and discussing any variance with management
- Perform test of detail by selecting a sample from the payroll records and agreeing the amounts to payslips and HR records

(iii) **Report to those charged with governance**

- There is not a significant control deficiency as the amounts involved are immaterial
- Potential non-compliance with regulations, eg tax regulation should be reported
- Recommend that all workers are put through payroll to ensure compliance

	Maximum	9
Total		**25**

(a) **Assets held for sale**

(i) **Audit evidence obtained**

The evidence does not appear to be sufficient to draw a conclusion on the appropriateness of classifying the property and any other related assets and liabilities as held for sale. A discussion with management regarding the accounting treatment is relevant, as the audit team will need to understand management's rationale. However, management's explanation should not be accepted at face value and should be corroborated through further audit procedures. It is not sufficient to simply put management's justification for the accounting treatment on the audit file and conclude that it is correct. For example, the factory can only be classified as held for sale if it is available for immediate sale in its current condition, which may not be the case.

In terms of the manual journal, checking that it is arithmetically correct, while relevant, is not sufficient evidence. Further evidence should be obtained in order to conclude that the basis of the calculation is in accordance with IFRS 5 *Non-current Assets held for sale and discontinued operations* and there should be consideration as to whether other requirements of the standard other than those related to the reclassification and measurement of the asset have been complied with. For example, the results specific to the factory may need to be disclosed as a discontinued operation in the statement of profit or loss and the statement of cash flows. No audit evidence appears to have been obtained in respect of these issues.

(ii) **Further audit procedures**

- Review board minutes to confirm that the sale of the factory has been approved and to agree the date of the approval to the board minutes and relevant staff announcements.
- Obtain correspondence with estate agents to confirm that the factory is being actively marketed.

- Obtain confirmation, for example, by a review of production schedules, inventory movement records and payroll records, that production at the factory has stopped and thus it is available for immediate sale.

- Use an auditor's expert to confirm the fair value of the property and agree that this figure has been used in the impairment calculation.

- Using management accounts, determine whether the factory is a separate major line of business in which case its results should be disclosed as a discontinued operation.

(iii) **Report to those charged with governance**

ISA 265 *Communicating Deficiencies in Internal Controls to Those Charged with Governance and Management* requires the auditor to communicate significant deficiencies in internal control to those charged with governance and management. In deciding whether a control deficiency is significant, one of the matters which should be considered is the importance of the control to the financial reporting process. Controls over the period-end financial reporting process such as controls over non-recurring journal entries can be important as they often deal with one-off material matters which are being accounted for outside the normal accounting system.

Therefore the journal posted by the finance director should be subject to some form of internal control, for example, approval by the board or the audit committee. The report to those charged with governance should recommend that controls are established over period-end journals posted to ensure their accuracy and validity.

In addition, the finance director should not be asking the audit team to check his figures; this could be perceived as a self-review threat to independence. This should potentially be flagged to the audit committee.

The fact that there is, according to the finance director, no one else at the company with relevant knowledge is concerning. The audit committee should be made aware of this and appropriate steps taken to ensure that sufficiently knowledgeable personnel are hired or appropriate training is provided to existing staff.

(b) **Capital expenditure**

(i) **Audit work performed**

The audit work has revealed that internal controls have not been operating and this should have led to more extensive testing of capital expenditure, rather than the audit programme being completed as planned. Generally, the audit team should extend audit testing on capital expenditure, for example, by extending sample testing and reducing the level of materiality applied in audit tests.

The audit team should also investigate why the controls are not operating, considering whether they are being deliberately ignored or overridden, whether time pressure or lack of resources is making the controls difficult to operate, or if there is a suspicion of collusion and possible fraud.

The procedures on the purchase of the vehicles do not appear to cover all relevant assertions, for example, there is nothing to confirm that Thurman Co has correctly depreciated the vehicles or that they are actually owned and being used by the company, or even that they exist.

(ii) **Further audit procedures**

- Obtain the insurance documents to confirm that Thurman Co is paying the relevant insurance for the vehicles.

- Physically verify the vehicles and confirm that they are being used by employees on company business.

BPP
LEARNING

- Obtain the log book/vehicle registration document and other relevant ownership documents such as those issued by the vehicle licensing body, to confirm the right of Thurman Co to recognise the vehicles.

- Trace the vehicles to the company's non-current asset register.

- Recalculate the depreciation which should have been charged on the vehicles and agree to the statement of profit or loss for the year.

(iii) **Report to those charged with governance**

The auditor should report to those charged with governance that there appears to be a deficiency in internal controls. While the audit team's findings do not indicate that a fraud is taking place, the lack of segregation of duties and the failure to obtain appropriate authorisation makes it easy for assets to be misappropriated and creates a significant fraud risk.

The audit firm should explain the implications of the control deficiencies to management and recommend improvements. For example, authorisation should be a pre-requisite for any order over a certain monetary amount. Thurman Co should also be encouraged to improve the control environment, for example, by training staff on the importance of controls and setting an appropriate tone at the top so that there is no tolerance of controls being ignored or deliberately circumvented.

(c) **Payroll**

(i) **Audit work**

The audit work in respect of the payroll needs to be much more thorough; simply agreeing the amounts to the reports issued by Jackson Co provides no evidence on the completeness, accuracy or validity of the payroll figures recognised in the financial statements. The audit team seems to have relied on Jackson Co's year-end reports as being accurate and the requirements of ISA 402 *Audit Considerations Relating to an Entity using a service organisation* do not appear to have been followed.

The audit team needs to obtain assurance on the controls which Jackson Co has implemented in order to assess the risk of material misstatement in the payroll figures and to respond to the risk with appropriate audit procedures. The controls which Thurman Co uses to verify the information received from Jackson Co also need to be understood. With the permission of Thurman Co, the audit team should contact Jackson Co with the objective of obtaining more information which can be used to assess how the payroll has been processed, and the controls which are in place. The controls in place at Thurman Co should be documented and tested.

It is recommended that further substantive procedures should be carried out to provide a wider range of evidence on the payroll expense recognised in the financial statements.

In relation to the casual employees, the fact that the amount involved is immaterial means that the audit team does not need to perform any further detailed audit procedures as there is no risk of material misstatement. However, as there is a risk over the completeness of these costs, the controls in place to ensure this process is effectively managed should be discussed with management and documented.

(ii) **Further audit procedures**

- Review the service agreement between Thurman Co and Jackson Co to understand the exact work which is conducted by Jackson Co as a service organisation.

- Read all reports made by Jackson Co during the year to identify any risks of misstatement in the payroll figure.

- Discuss and document relevant controls in place at Thurman Co over the information received from Jackson Co and the management of casual employees, and perform tests of controls on a sample basis.

- The amount of unpaid taxes in respect of the casual workers should be quantified by recalculations of the amounts due.

- Read any user manuals or systems overviews to assess the efficacy of controls in place over the processing of payroll.

- If necessary, obtain a type 1 or type 2 report from Jackson Co to obtain further assurance on the controls which the service organisation has in place.

- Perform a substantive analytical review on payroll, preparing an auditor's expectation of the payroll figures and comparing it to that recognised in the financial statements and discussing any variance with management.

- Perform test of detail by selecting a sample from the payroll records and agreeing the amounts to payslips and HR records.

(iii) **Report to those charged with governance**

The fact that casual employees are being paid from petty cash without being put onto the company's payroll indicates that Thurman Co may not be complying with relevant regulations, for example, that appropriate payroll taxes are not being paid. Despite the amounts involved being immaterial, the potential non-compliance should be reported to those charged with governance, along with a recommendation that all employees, whether casual or not, should be processed through the company's payroll system. There may be implications for the financial statements if fines or penalties are imposed by the tax authorities in respect of the non-compliance.

20 Faster Jets

Workbook references. Chapters 6, 7 and 15.

Top tips. Part (a) was a relatively straightforward discussion of ISA 510 – provided you knew the material well.

In part (b)(i), it is important that you stick to stating additional information that is needed rather than audit procedures that should be performed. Also the ACCA examining team's answer uses questions in places (presumably addressed to the client), however you are on safer ground if you phrase your answer as factual pieces of information that are needed. Writing questions could be construed as informal language. For each piece of information needed, try to state why you need it.

Part (c) was perhaps more difficult. In part (c)(i), you only needed to make a few simple points (but in sufficient detail) to pass the question – for example, the difficulty of attaching quantities to KPIs, of making comparisons between companies, and the lack of information systems relevant to social and environmental performance.

In part (c)(ii), many of the procedures were just like other audit procedures – for example, agreeing payments to the cashbook. There are four performance measures given in Faster Jets Co's report in the scenario, so if you tried to think of one or two procedures for each measure then you could have scored well.

Easy marks. Calculating materiality is simple in part (b).

ACCA examining team's comments. In part (a) the requirement was to explain the auditor's reporting responsibilities specific to initial engagements. However many candidates did not read the question and produced an answer that related to new engagements and pre-acceptance procedures. Where answers were answered by considering ISA 510, marks were not awarded for detailing audit work to verify the balances.

BPP
LEARNING

The next part of the question, which was for ten marks spilt evenly over two requirements, focused on planning the audit work relating to several large plots of land that had been purchased by the company during the year and were being accounted for as investment property in the company's financial statements. The first requirement asked candidates to explain the additional information that would be required to plan the audit of the land. This type of requirement is often seen in audit planning questions and again, as in previous sittings, disappointingly candidates tended to provide specific audit procedures rather than considering information that would be helpful in determining the type of procedures that would be relevant. Candidates for future examinations should bear in mind that answer points for this type of requirement can be phrased as questions, eg 'what is management's future plans for the land?', as this helps to determine its classification as investment property. Many candidates may find this type of requirement difficult if they have limited practical audit experience, in which case it is especially important to use past questions to practise how to answer these questions.

The next requirement asked candidates to explain the matters to be considered in assessing the reliance to be placed on the work of an auditor's expert being used in the audit of the land. This was much better answered than the first requirement, with almost all answers identifying that the auditor's expert must be independent and competent. However most answers went little further than explaining those two matters, indicating little knowledge of the requirements of ISA 620 *Using the Work of an Auditor's Expert* in relation to agreeing the scope of the expert's work, and evaluating the relevance of their conclusions. The answers to this requirement were also often very brief, amounting to little more than a few sentences or bullet points. Candidates are reminded that the number of marks available should be used as a guide for the number of points and depth required. A couple of bullet points or brief sentences are unlikely to be sufficient to score the five marks that were available here.

The next part of the question focused on measuring and reporting on social and environmental information. The audit firm in the scenario had been asked to perform an assurance engagement on Faster Jets Co's corporate social responsibility (CSR) report, and a number of CSR objectives and targets were provided along with the performance indicators for 20X4 to be included in the CSR report. The first requirement asked for a discussion of the difficulties in measuring and reporting on social and environmental performance for which there was four marks available. This short requirement was well attempted by many candidates, with most identifying that it can be difficult to define and quantify CSR measures, that systems are often not in place to capture the relevant information and that comparisons are difficult due to the lack of a regulatory framework. This again indicates that many candidates had practised past exam questions, as this type of requirement has featured in an AAA exam on several previous occasions.

Candidates found the final requirement of this question more difficult, as they were asked for recommendations of procedures that could be used to gain assurance on the validity of the performance information included in the CSR report for six marks.

The main weakness in responses was that candidates simply repeated the same procedures for each of the performance measures given, even if they weren't appropriate. For example, one of the performance measures related to free flights that had been donated to charities, and many candidates recommended that this should be agreed to bank statements or cash book even though it is not a cash transaction. Candidates are encouraged to think about whether the procedures they are recommending are sensible in the context of the scenario. As is often the case when presented with a requirement to detail procedures, many candidates provided procedures that were not well explained, and in many cases weren't procedures at all, eg 'review the free flights', 'inspect the education days', 'confirm the vehicle fuel'. This type of comment cannot be given credit as it is too vague and does not answer the question requirement.

Marking scheme

Marks

(a) **Auditor's reporting responsibilities for initial engagements**
Generally 1 mark each point of explanation
Ideas (ISA 510)
Sufficient appropriate evidence
– Opening balances
– Prior period's closing balances
– Appropriate accounting policies
If insufficient ⇒ inability to obtain sufficient appropriate audit evidence
– Modified opinion ('except for')
– Disclaimer
– If permitted, qualified/disclaimed on results
  (unqualified on financial position)
Material misstatement ⇒ modified opinion/adverse
– Misstatement not properly accounted for
– Inconsistent accounting policies
Prior period modification
– Modify again if still relevant

Maximum   5

(b) (i) **Further information requirements**
1 mark for each further information point explained:
–   The reason for the purchase, to understand the business rationale
–   Any specific plans for how Faster Jets Co may make use of the land in the future
–   The date of purchase
–   Whether the land was purchased for cash or if finance was taken out
–   Who is leasing the land? This could establish whether the arrangement is with a related party
–   Whether the rental arrangement is a lease
–   What is the land being used for?
–   The location of the purchased land – this is necessary to plan the logistics of the audit
–   Does the company hold any other investment property, and if so is that also held at fair value?
–   What is management's rationale for the accounting policy choice to measure the land at fair value?

(ii) **Matters to consider regarding the use of the auditor's expert**
Up to 1½ marks for each of the following explained:
–   Objectivity
–   Competence
–   Scope of work
–   Relevance and reasonableness of conclusions

Maximum   10

(c) (i) **Difficulties in measuring and reporting on social and environmental performance**

Up to 1½ marks for each point discussed:
 – Measures are difficult to define
 – Measures are difficult to quantify
 – Systems not set up to capture data
 – Hard to make comparisons

Maximum 4

(ii) **Procedures on Faster Jets Co's performance measures**

Generally 1 mark for a well explained procedure:
 – Obtain a summary of all amounts donated to charitable causes and agree to cash book
 – For large donation confirm that authorisation for the payment has been made
 – Review correspondence with charities for confirmation of the amounts paid
 – Review relevant press releases and publicity campaigns
 – For the $750,000 spent on the local education scheme, obtain a breakdown of the amounts spent and scrutinise to ensure all relate to the scheme, eg payments to educators
 – Obtain a sample of registers to confirm attendance of children on certain days
 – For the free flights donated to charity, perform analytical review to confirm that the average value of a flight seems reasonable – the average being $700
 – For a sample of the 800 free flights, obtain confirmation that the passenger was a guest of Faster Jets Co
 – Agree a sample of business miles travelled in vehicles and fuel costs to employee expenses claims forms

Maximum 6

Total **25**

(a) **Auditor's responsibilities for initial engagements**

The auditor must obtain sufficient, appropriate audit evidence that the opening balances do not contain misstatements that materially affect the current period's financial statements. The auditor must obtain evidence that the prior period's closing balances have been brought forward correctly to the current period or have been restated, if appropriate. The auditor should also obtain sufficient, appropriate audit evidence that appropriate accounting policies are consistently applied or changes in accounting policies have been properly accounted for and adequately disclosed.

If this evidence cannot be obtained, the auditor's report should include a qualified opinion (inability to obtain sufficient appropriate audit evidence) or a disclaimer of opinion or, in those jurisdictions where it is permitted, a qualified opinion or disclaimer of opinion regarding the results of operations, and an unmodified opinion on the financial position.

If the opening balances contain misstatements that could materially affect the current period's financial statements, the auditor should inform the client's management and the predecessor auditor. If the effect of the misstatement is not properly accounted for and disclosed, a qualified or adverse opinion will be expressed.

If the current period's accounting policies have not been consistently applied to the opening balances and the change not accounted for properly and disclosed, a qualified or adverse opinion will be expressed.

If the prior period's auditor's report was modified, the auditor should consider the effect of this on the current period's financial statements. If the modification remains relevant and material to the current period's accounts then the current period's auditor's report should also be modified.

An Other Matter paragraph should be included in the auditor's report in the case of the prior period financial statements not having been audited at all, or having been audited by another auditor. This is irrespective of whether or not they are materially misstated, and does not relieve the auditor of the need to obtain sufficient appropriate audit evidence on opening balances.

(b) (i) Additional information includes:

- Details of the reason for the purchase, to understand the business purpose, eg whether the land is held for capital appreciation. This will help determine whether it is classified correctly as investment property.

- Whether management has any specific plans for how Faster Jets Co may make use of the land in the future, eg to construct buildings and if so, what their purpose will be.

- The date of purchase, to ascertain how long it has taken for the land to increase in value by $2 million and whether this is in line with the auditor's understanding of the entity and its environment.

- Whether the land was purchased for cash, or if finance was taken out to raise the $12.5 million paid.

- Details of who is renting the land, in order to establish whether the arrangement is with a related party.

- The type of rental arrangement, to determine whether it represents a lease.

- What the land is being used for. As the legal owner, Faster Jets Co should be aware of its use and any associated risks, eg activities close to airports may convey security risks, eg terrorism.

- The location of the purchased land, in order to plan the logistics of the audit.

- Whether the company holds any other investment property, and if so, whether it is also held at fair value. This will help determine whether the accounting treatment is consistent for all investment property.

- Information on management's reasoning behind the accounting policy choice to measure the land at fair value.

- Details of who holds the title deeds to the land as this may need to be inspected.

(ii) **Relying on an auditor's expert**

Independence

The auditor must evaluate whether the expert is independent of the client, and so should enquire into whether they have any interests or relationships which may threaten their independence.

For example, the expert must not be connected to Faster Jets Co, and must not be a related party of anyone having influence over its financial statements. Less reliance will be placed on their work if they are not independent.

Competence

The expert's competence must be evaluated, eg by considering whether they are members of any relevant professional bodies. The expert's relevant experience should also be considered. An expert with extensive experience of valuing land and investment properties will be more reliable than a newly-qualified one with relatively little experience.

In this case, an expert valuer may be a Chartered Surveyor, which would give the auditor confidence in the reliability of their work.

Scope of work

The auditor should agree the scope of the work with the expert, include its objectives, how it will be used (in relation to the audit), the methodology and any key assumptions to be used. These assumptions should agree with the auditor's understanding of the entity and its environment.

The scope should be agreed at the start of the engagement. If the expert deviates from it, then their work will be less useful to the auditor.

Conclusions

The auditor considers the source data used by the expert, focusing whether it is reliable and consistent with the auditor's understanding. The auditor then evaluates the conclusions drawn by expert, and whether they are warranted by the evidence obtained. Any inconsistencies should be investigated.

(c)   (i)   **Definition**

A company's social and environmental (S&E) performance is a very wide subject area, as a company is likely to have multiple effects on a number of complex systems, so that any one measure is likely to present only a partial picture. In defining S&E performance in simple terms, there is a risk of distorting a complex reality. This diminishes the usefulness of any information produced.

Setting KPIs

Performance is defined by setting KPIs, but this process is not straightforward. If it is decided that S&E performance is to be considered in terms of the stakeholders affected by the company's operations, then there is the problem of deciding firstly which stakeholders are most important, and secondly which aspects of the company's operations are of interest to them.

Quantification

It can be difficult to quantify KPIs in monetary terms. As a result of the complexity of the underlying social and natural environments, a qualitative approach may be more faithful to the reality, but this foregoes the possibility of measurement. Assigning quantitative KPIs buys precision but at the risk of arbitrariness and distortion.

There are also difficulties deciding how to quantify performance. For example Faster Jets Co's provision of free flights can be quantified in monetary terms, but it is not clear what price should be used – cost price or market value?

Systems and controls

Companies are used to reporting on their financial performance, and are required by law to have systems of internal control over financial reporting. This is not the case with S&E performance, so there may not be reliable systems and controls over the processing of relevant information.

Lack of standards

There is no single set of guidelines on reporting S&E performance that all companies have to apply, but rather a multiplicity of reporting practices based on the different situations of the different entities. This makes it very difficult to compare performance between different companies. Year on year comparisons for the same company may also be difficult if its targets change during the period.

(ii) **Procedures**

- Obtain a summary of all amounts donated to charitable causes and agree a sample to the cash book.

- For large donations above a certain limit (say $10,000) confirm that authorisation for the payment has been made, eg by agreeing to minutes of management meetings.

- Review correspondence with charities for confirmation of the amounts paid.

- Review relevant press releases and publicity campaigns, eg the free flight scheme and the local education schemes are likely to have been publicised.

- For the $750,000 spent on the local education scheme, obtain a breakdown of the amounts spent and scrutinise to ensure all relate to the scheme, eg payments to educators.

- Obtain a sample of classroom registers to confirm attendance of children on certain days.

- For the free flights donated to charity, perform analytical review to confirm that the average value of a flight seems reasonable – the average being $700 ($560,000/800).

- For a sample of the 800 free flights, obtain confirmation that the passenger was a guest of Faster Jets Co, eg through correspondence with the passenger and relevant charity.

- Agree a sample of business miles travelled in vehicles to a mileage log, and fuel costs to employee expenses claims forms and the general ledger.

21 Magpie

Workbook references. Chapters 2, 4, 6, 8 and 9.

Top tips. Part (a) was a fair requirement, but one that may have left you struggling for ideas to make up eight marks. The requirement divides itself naturally into two parts, with four marks each for the individual company and the consolidated financial statements. Make sure you noticed what point we were at in the audit process: it is audit planning, after the engagement has been accepted but before the audit work as such has begun. Comments relating to specific procedures will get no marks here, and neither will comments relating to eg audit acceptance procedures.

Part (b) was the longest part of the question, and was a fairly typical test of applying your knowledge to the scenario. The question did require perhaps a bit more financial reporting knowledge than in some previous sittings of AAA – IFRS 3, IFRS 9, IAS 20 and IFRS 2 came up – but you should not have struggled with any of it. Passing this part of the question is a matter of working steadily through the issues contained in the scenario. You can flag to your marker that you are answering the question by specifically stating for each issue something like 'the risk here is', and then using auditing terminology to pick out where there may be eg an understatement or an overstatement.

It should be possible to pass part (c) fairly easily, as there is one mark available per specific procedure. As with many questions asking for audit procedures in a specific area of financial reporting, a good approach is to think of each of the specific figures involved, and then think of what could go wrong with each of them and how you would test them. The question makes it easy for you here, as you have a goodwill calculation laid out for you. All you need to do is think of one or two good procedures for each figure in the calculation, and hey presto, you have passed the requirement!

Part (d) contained three tricky ethical issues. Even if you were not sure of the final answer in a given situation, you can try approaching questions like this by (1) working out what the issue is, perhaps using the general types of threats as a guide (self-interest, self-review, advocacy, familiarity and intimidation); then (2) trying to think of safeguards that might remove the issue; and then (3) if no safeguards would make the threat go away, recommending that the auditor doesn't do it.

As ever it is important that you stick to the scenario and do not offer too much theory. Your knowledge of ISAs should be applied rather than simply stated. Overall this was a requirement on which you should have looked to score well.

Easy marks. There were plenty of easy marks in part (c) for thinking of procedures – provided you had not gone over time on the part (b) that preceded them.

ACCA examining team's comments. With respect to requirement (a), most answers identified the main planning implications, such as the determination of component and group materiality levels, the audit firm's need to obtain business understanding and assess the control environment in relation to the new subsidiary, and practical aspects such as the timings and resources needed for the group audit. Weaker answers tended to just list out financial reporting matters, eg that in the group financial statements related party transactions would have to be disclosed, and inter-company balances eliminated, but failed to link these points sufficiently well to audit planning implications.

Answers to (b) tended to cover a wide range of points but very often did not discuss the points in much depth. For example, almost all candidates identified that accounting for goodwill can be complex, leading to risk of misstatement, but few candidates explained the specific issues that give rise to risk. Many answers also went into a lot of detail about how particular balances and transactions should be audited, recommending procedures to be performed by the auditor, which was not asked for. Weaker answers simply stated an issue, for example, that a grant had been received, and said the risk was that it would not be accounted for properly. Clearly this is not really an evaluation, as required, and will lead to minimal marks being awarded.

It was pleasing to see many candidates determining the materiality of the transactions and balances to the individual company concerned and to the group. However, candidates are reminded that materiality should be calculated appropriately, eg the materiality of an asset or liability should be based on total assets and not revenue.

Generally candidates did well on requirement (c)(i), with many providing well described, relevant procedures.

Most answers to part (d) of the question went through the issues in order and identified the ethical threats that arose. However, a lot of answers took a scattergun approach, and said that all of the issues would give rise to the same threats of familiarity, management, self-review and self-interest, but then did not go on to explain how, or why, the threats arose and whether it would be possible for safeguards to reduce the threats to an acceptable level.

Marking scheme

Marks

(a) **Audit implications of Canary Co acquisition**

Up to 1½ marks for each implication explained (3 marks maximum for identification):

- Develop understanding of Canary Co business environment
- Document Canary Co accounting systems and controls
- Perform detailed analytical procedures on Canary Co
- Communicate with previous auditor
- Review prior year audit opinion for relevant matters
- Plan additional work on opening balances
- Determine that Canary Co is a significant component of the Group
- Plan for audit of intra-company transactions
- Issues on auditing the one month difference in financial year ends
- Impact of acquisition on analytical procedures at Group level
- Additional experienced staff may be needed, eg to audit complex goodwill

Maximum   8

(b) **Risk of material misstatement**

Up to 1½ marks for each risk (unless a different maximum is indicated below):

- General risks – diversification, change to group structure
- Goodwill – contingent consideration – estimation uncertainty (probability of payment)
- Goodwill – contingent consideration – measurement uncertainty (discounting)
- Goodwill – fair value of net assets acquired
- Goodwill – impairment
- Identify that the issues in relation to cost of investment apply also in
  Crow Co's individual financial statements (1 mark)
- Loan stock – premium on redemption
- Loan stock – accrued interest
- Loan stock – inadequate disclosure
- Identify that the issues in relation to loan stock apply to cost of investment in Crow Co's individual financial statements (1 mark)
- Online sales and risk relating to revenue recognition (additional 1 mark if calculation provided of online sales materiality to the Group)
- No group accounting policy for online sales
- Canary Co management have no experience regarding consolidation
- Financial performance of Crow Co and Starling Co deteriorating (up to 3 marks with calculations)
- Possible misstatement of Canary Co revenue and profit
- Grant received – capital expenditure
- Grant received – amount not yet spent
- Prior period error – clearly trivial

- New IT system
- Starling Co – no finance director in place at year end
- Share options – wrong FV used
- Share options – cost not spread over vesting period
- Share options – no adjustment for employees leaving
- Share options – recognised as liability instead of equity

Maximum   22

(c)   (i) **Goodwill**

Generally 1 mark per specific procedure (examples shown below):

- Confirm acquisition date to legal documentation
- Confirm consideration details to legal documentation
- Agree 100% ownership, eg using Companies House search/register of significant shareholdings
- Vouch consideration paid to bank statements/cash book
- Review board minutes for discussion/approval of acquisition
- Obtain due diligence report and agree net assets valuation
- Discuss probability of paying contingent consideration
- Obtain written representation regarding contingency
- Recalculate goodwill including contingency on a discounted basis

Maximum   5

(ii) **Share options**

Generally 1 mark per specific procedure (examples shown below):

- Agree number of employees to details set out in contracts
- Confirm fair value at the grant date to documentation
- Obtain information regarding the model used to estimate fair value.
- Consider using an auditor's expert for the valuation
- Obtain written representations
- Agree other contractual terms to legal documentation
- Obtain supporting documentation for management's estimate of the 10% leaving rate for employees
- Compare staffing numbers to forecasts and numbers of leavers to prior years

Maximum   5

(d) **Ethical matters**

Generally 1 mark per comment:
- Reasonable for partner to attend board meetings
- But must avoid perception of management involvement
- Partner must not be appointed to the board
- Seconded manager would cause management and self-review threat
- Safeguards could not reduce these threats to an acceptable level

Marks

- Some recruitment services may be provided – interviewing/CV selection
- But avoid making management decision and put safeguards in place

	Maximum	6
Professional Marks		4
Total		**50**

Briefing notes

For: Jo Daw

From: Audit manager

Subject: CS Group audit

Introduction

These notes identify and explain the implication of the Canary Co acquisition for planning the CS Group and individual companies' audits. The notes evaluate the risks of material misstatement for this audit. Finally, they recommend the principal audit procedures in respect of goodwill recognised on the acquisition of Canary Co, and the share options granted to Crow Co employees.

(a) **Planning implications of Canary Co acquisition**

Individual financial statements

ISA 315 *Identifying and Assessing the Risks of Material Misstatement through Understanding the Entity and its Environment* requires us to understand the entity and its environment, and internal control.

To understand Canary Co ('Canary') and its environment, we must consider any relevant regulatory factors, eg whether it uses the same financial reporting ('FR') framework as the group; the nature of the entity's operations, ownership and governance, and the kinds of transactions and balances that should be expected in the financial statements; and its selection and application of accounting policies, and whether they are in line with its business and the FR framework.

To understand Canary's internal controls, we must consider its accounting systems as well as any other controls relevant to the audit. Our understanding of these controls must be documented. This is particularly important with a new audit client because we have not had time to build up knowledge of the entity, and so need to place special emphasis on this area now.

IT is likely to form a significant part of Canary's systems (since 30% of sales are online), and these will be different from the rest of the group. We should consider if we need to use an auditor's expert in this area.

It will be necessary to perform detailed analytical procedures on Canary at the planning stage. This will be necessary to determine planning materiality, and to help identify any significant events or transactions in the period.

ISA 300 *Planning an Audit of Financial Statements* requires us to communicate with Canary's predecessor auditor, asking if there is anything we should be aware of that may influence our plan. We should also review the prior period audit opinion and auditor's report.

Finally, we will need to perform additional procedures on Canary's opening balances, as these were audited by a predecessor auditor.

BPP
LEARNING

Consolidated financial statements

The first thing to consider is whether Canary is a significant component according to ISA 600 *Special Considerations – Audits of Group Financial Statements (Including the Work of Component Auditors)*. Canary's forecast revenue is 11.9% (16/135) of group revenue, and profit is 23.5% (2/8.5), so it is definitely a significant component.

Although we are both the group auditors and Canary's individual auditors, we still need to (i) consider whether audit evidence obtained for the individual company is sufficient and appropriate for the group, and (ii) perform procedures on matters relevant to the consolidated accounts. This includes procedures to determine whether intra-group balances have been eliminated, and whether IFRS 3 *Business Combinations* has been applied correctly in relation to the acquisition itself.

A particular issue is that Canary's 30 June year end is different from the rest of the group. In practice this will usually be changed soon after the company is acquired, so we need to obtain evidence to determine whether or not this has happened. This matter is absolutely crucial to the audit. If the year end has not been changed, then additional procedures must be performed on Canary's financial information so that its financial statements as at 31 July 20X2 can be consolidated.

Care must be taken when performing analytical review at a group level, as Canary's figures are only included since the acquisition date and will not be comparable with the whole-year figures of the rest of the group.

Finally, the new acquisition introduces new complexities into the audit, so we must ensure that these aspects of the audit are done by staff with appropriate levels of experience, eg the goodwill asset and the contingent consideration.

(b) ### General

There are several factors which together mean that this is a high risk audit: there has been a significant acquisition, a move into a new line of business, and the introduction of new IT systems relating to financial reporting.

Goodwill

Goodwill is material to the financial statements, at 8.2% of total assets (45/550).

The contingent consideration is a significant audit risk. It is currently recognised in full as an asset, which is in line with the IFRS 3 *Business Combinations* requirement to recognise it at its fair value at the acquisition date. However, this amount should be discounted to its present value, because the consideration is not payable until 1 February 20X5. As this has not been done, goodwill appears to be overstated.

A further risk relates to the valuation of identifiable net assets. This has been done by a management's expert in the context of a due diligence review. ISA 500 *Audit Evidence* requires the auditor to evaluate the expert's competence, capability and objectivity; to obtain an understanding of their work; and to evaluate the work's appropriateness as audit evidence. The auditor's evaluation of each of these issues should be documented.

IAS 36 *Impairment of Assets* requires goodwill to be tested for impairment annually (IAS 36: para. 36), and there is no mention of this having been done at the year end. There is therefore a risk that goodwill may be overstated.

Loan stock

The loan stock issued is material, at 18.2% of total assets (100/550).

The premium of $20m should be recognised as a finance cost over the period of the loan using the amortised cost method, in line with IFRS 9 *Financial Instruments*. The risk is that this has not been done, and that finance costs are understated.

An interest cost of 5% is also payable in arrears, and there is a risk of further understatement of finance costs if this has not been accrued for.

These issues apply to both the group accounts and Crow Co's individual company financial statements.

Online sales

Canary's online sales represent 30% of its revenue, with approximately $4.8m (0.3 × 16) included in the group accounts, which is material at 3.6% of group revenue. This figure should be even higher in future, when a full year's revenue will be included in the group accounts.

There is a risk that the strictures of IFRS 15 *Revenue from Contracts with Customers* on when revenue should be recognised are not met. This will be heavily dependent on the reliability of the IT system involved, its appropriateness for financial reporting, and its integration with the accounting system.

E-commerce can also represent a business risk as it may expose Canary to eg lost sales or reputational damage if its website does not operate effectively. With online sales at 30% of revenue, any significant problems in this area could affect Canary's status as a going concern.

Canary's management

Canary's management have no prior experience of the consolidation process at the CS Group, so it is possible that the process will operate inefficiently and that errors will be made. It is likely that more audit work will need to be done on the consolidation of Canary's results than on the rest of the group.

Financial performance

At first sight, the group's results are encouraging – revenue is up 8% and profit before tax is up 1.2%. However, this is not comparing like with like: the prior year figures do not include any of Canary's results, whereas the current year figures include Canary for six months.

If we include only Crow Co and Starling Co's results and compare them with the prior year, then a different picture emerges:

	20X2 Crow + Starling forecast	20X1 Group actual	% change
Revenue	119	125	(4.8%)
Profit before tax	6.5	8.4	(22.6%)

Instead of profit and revenue both growing, the picture these figures paint is of profit and revenue shrinking. This may be for operational reasons, but it is also possible that there has been a misstatement, with either costs being overstated or revenue understated.

Government grant

The grant is material, at 6.4% of total assets (35/550).

There are two issues in relation to the grant. The first is that in line with IAS 20 *Accounting for Government Grants and Disclosure of Government Assistance*, this is a grant related to assets. This may either be deducted from the cost of the related assets (in this case, solar panels), or recognised as deferred income that is released systematically into profit or loss (IAS 20: para. 24). At the year end only $25m of the $35m grant had been spent, so some of the grant should be deferred until the next year. There is a risk that this has not been done, and eg the $35m has simply been recognised in income during the year.

The second issue is that the grant is for capital expenditure on environmentally friendly assets, but Starling Co intends to spend the remaining $10m on upgrading its production and packing lines. This seems unlikely to meet the conditions of the grant, and it is possible that some of it will need to be repaid if it is spent in this way. The matter is likely to be material to the group, at 1.8% of total assets (10/550).

Prior period error not relevant

Deferred revenue in the prior period was overstated by $10,000. This is 0.014% of Crow Co's forecast revenue (= 10,000 / 69,000,000), and 0.29% of profit. It is clearly immaterial, and is not relevant to the audit planning.

New IT system

The new IT system, which is relevant to financial reporting, represents a risk of material misstatement per ISA 315. There are two main issues: firstly, errors may have been made in transferring the data from the old to the new system; and secondly, the new system is likely to take time to bed in, and it is possible for teething problems to lead to a loss of data.

New FD

The fact that Starling Co's FD has recently left increases the risk of errors as it deprives the company of accounting skills it may need when producing its financial statements, and for the consolidation process. It may also make the audit more difficult to conduct, as it may not be possible to obtain explanations that are needed if there is no FD.

Finally, the reasons for the FD leaving should be ascertained, as it is possible that there has been a disagreement over accounting policies, or even a fraud.

Share options

An expense has been recognised of $720,000. This is 20.6% of profit before tax (= $720,000/$3.5m), and is a material area of the statement of profit or loss. The options may also be material by nature if they have been granted to related parties, such as company directors.

In accordance with IFRS 2 *Share-based Payment*, Crow Co should recognise the remuneration expense as the employees' services are received, based on the fair value of the share options granted. The principal risk is that the accounting treatment will be inappropriate; there appear to be several misstatements in this regard.

The fair value at the grant date was $6. The calculation performed by the entity currently uses the fair value at the end of the reporting period of $8, which is incorrect.

Crow Co has recognised the full expense in profit or loss in the year of issue. This is incorrect; IFRS 2 requires the cost to be spread over the vesting period of 2 years.

Crow Co's calculation has not adjusted for the number of options expected to vest. IFRS 2 requires Crow Co to take into account estimates of the number of employees expected to leave.

Finally, a long-term liability has been recognised instead of equity.

Taking all of these points together, the expense should have been recognised as $243,000 (150 × 600 × 90% × $6 × ½ years), rather than $720,000. Profit is therefore understated by $477,000, This constitutes 13.6% of profit before tax (= 477 / 3,500), which is material.

(c)   (i)   **Audit procedures on goodwill**

- Obtain the legal purchase agreement and confirm the acquisition date
- Confirm (from the legal agreement) the consideration, and details of the contingent consideration
- Confirm that Canary is wholly owned by Crow Co through a review of its register of shareholders
- Agree cash payment of $125 million to cash book and bank statements

- Review board minutes for discussion regarding, and approval of, the purchase of Canary
- Obtain due diligence report on Canary and confirm estimated fair value of net assets

(ii) **Audit procedures on share options**

- Agree the number of employees in the scheme to details set out in employment contracts
- Confirm that the fair value at the grant date to supporting documentation
- Obtain information from management regarding the model used to estimate fair value. Consider whether this is in accordance with IFRS is appropriate in the circumstances.
- Consider whether it will be necessary to make use of an auditor's expert for the valuation
- Obtain written representations from management that the assumptions used in the calculation are reasonable.
- Agree other contractual terms to legal documentation, eg agree number of shares awarded to each employee, vesting terms and length of vesting period
- Obtain supporting documentation for management's estimate of the 10% leaving rate for employees
- Compare staffing numbers to forecasts and numbers of leavers to prior years

(d) **Partner at board meetings**

It is acceptable for the audit engagement partner to attend board meetings. There are even some times when the partner should attend, eg to raise issues with management and/or those charged with governance.

The important thing is that the partner does not take on a management role, and that they are not involved in any discussions that are not relevant to the audit. If the partner served as a director of an audit client, then the self-review and self-interest threats created would be insurmountable.

Audit manager secondment

This is a temporary staff assignment, and is acceptable as long as it is for a short period of time, and no management responsibilities are taken on. In this case, the member of staff would probably be involved in making management decisions as they would be the finance director. They would not be under the control of the audit client.

It is therefore unlikely that any safeguards could reduce this threat to an acceptable level, so no member of staff should be seconded into this role.

Recruitment help

It is possible for help to be provided with recruitment, but only if the auditor does not make any management decisions. It would be possible to eg review a shortlist of candidates' CVs, but only against criteria set out by the CS Group itself.

If help is provided then the final decision about recruitment must be left to the client. Safeguards should also be put in place, such as obtaining written acknowledgement from the client that they are responsible for the recruitment decision.

Conclusion

These briefing notes have address the issues around the Canary acquisition and the goodwill recognised thereon, around the share options scheme, and have highlighted a number of key risks of material misstatement which must now form the focus of audit procedures.

BPP
LEARNING

22 Adder

Top tips. In part (a), you must calculate materiality for each issue – the hint is that the question includes the figures for profit and total assets. This should be the first thing you write for each part of your answer. (Also note that marks are likely to be capped here, so don't go overboard and calculate it for every single number in the question if this is not needed.)

The question is on matters and evidence, which suggests the form for your answer to take.

Part (a)(i) was a sale and leaseback arrangement which should be accounted for under IFRS 16 *Leases*. This is a relatively new standard which features some complex calculations. This question was a good test of your mettle in this area.

The key to answering part (a)(ii) well was being confident in your knowledge of subsidiaries and associates. Specifically, you needed to be sure that a 52% shareholding would normally mean it's a subsidiary, but that the issue is really whether this stake gives control **or** significant influence. The client in the question doesn't even claim that it doesn't have control, but instead makes a spurious argument about integration into group operations. You needed to stick to your guns about control.

Part (b), on laws and regulations, is an area that is examined quite frequently. As ever, the auditor is in the tricky situation of discovering something and then finding themselves stuck in a dilemma about reporting vs confidentiality. The usual track is first to report to management, and then if management does not report it to the authorities, consider reporting it if there is a legal duty to do so, or if it's in the public interest. If in doubt, saying to 'obtain legal advice' allows you to sit on the fence in your exam!

Easy marks. The marks for calculating and assessing materiality in part (a) are simple.

ACCA examining team's comments. Answers to part (a)(i) on the whole were good. Most candidates proved able to confidently discuss whether the lease had been appropriately classified and accounted for. In addition almost all candidates correctly determined the materiality of the balances and could provide some specific and well explained points on audit evidence.

In answers to part (a)(ii), candidates were able to identify that the accounting treatment seemed incorrect, and could explain their reasoning. Fewer candidates appreciated that the loss-making status of Baldrick Co was the possible explanation for the Group's reluctance to consolidate it as a subsidiary and therefore that the Group's profits were overstated. Most candidates could provide some evidence points, with the most commonly cited being the board approval of the acquisition and agreeing the cash paid to bank statements.

Fewer candidates could suggest how the audit firm should obtain evidence on the exercise of control by the parent company or on the mechanics of the consolidation that should have taken place.

In answers to part (b), most candidates identified the obvious issues, namely that this was likely to be a breach of laws and regulations, internal controls were poor, and that an intimidation threat existed. Beyond this, the quality of answers varied dramatically. The **best answers** used a methodical approach to explain the auditor's responsibilities in relation to a suspected breach of laws and regulations; including the need to obtain more evidence, the auditor's reporting responsibilities, and the need to consider client confidentiality as well as possibly reporting the matter in the public interest. It was pleasing to see many candidates deal well with these issues, as well as the ethical threat raised by the employee's behaviour.

BPP
LEARNING

Weaker answers focused solely on the potential money laundering implications, which while not irrelevant should not have been the only matter discussed. In addition, weaker answers simply stated facts without much attempt to apply the requirements of ISA 250 *Consideration of Laws and Regulations in an Audit of Financial Statements*, to the scenario. Some candidates suggested that the audit firm was responsible for ensuring that the Group was complying with relevant laws and regulations, saying that the audit firm should 'ensure compliance', and there were occasionally suggestions that the audit senior should be 'disciplined' for not taking further action when threatened by the employee of the Group. These comments, especially the latter, demonstrate a lack of judgment or real understanding of the role of the auditor in this regard.

This question was for many candidates the best attempted question on the exam.

Marking scheme

Marks

Generally up to 1½ marks for each matter discussed, and 1 mark for each well-explained procedure:

(a)   (i)   **Sale and leaseback**

Matters

- Correct determination of materiality
- Substance of transaction is a lease with a right-of-use asset
- Assets and liabilities understated, profit overstated
- Adjustment recommended
- Implications for auditor's report if not adjusted

Evidence

- A copy of the lease, signed by the lessor, and a review of its major clauses to confirm that control has been transferred, and that the arrangement is a lease
- Review of forecasts and budgets to confirm that economic benefit is expected to be generated through the continued use of the property complex
- Physical inspection of the property complex to confirm it is being used by the Group
- Confirmation of the fair value of the property complex, possibly using an auditor's expert
- Evaluation of the expert's work including the appropriateness of assumptions and use of the correct financial reporting framework
- Agreement of the $35 million cash proceeds to bank statement and cash book
- Minutes of a discussion with management regarding the accounting treatment and including an auditor's request to amend the financial statements
- A copy of insurance documents stating that the Group is responsible for insuring the property complex

(ii)   **Baldrick Co**

Matters

- Correct determination of materiality of Baldrick Co
- If Group exercises control, Baldrick Co is a subsidiary not an associate
- Need to determine nature of the Group's interest in Baldrick Co

BPP
LEARNING

- Impact on audit opinion is at least qualification due to material misstatement
- Discussion of impact on Group profit if Baldrick Co is treated as a subsidiary
- Presentation issues
- Impact could be pervasive in combination with the sale and leaseback

Evidence

- Agreement of the cash paid to acquire Baldrick Co to cash book and bank statements
- Review of board minutes for discussion of the change in Group structure and for authorisation of the acquisition and disposal
- Review of legal documentation pertaining to the acquisition of Baldrick Co, to confirm the number of equity shares acquired, and the rights attached to the shareholding, eg the ability to appoint board members
- Inspection of other supporting documentation relating to the acquisition such as due diligence reports
- Notes of discussion with management regarding the exercise of control over Baldrick Co, eg the planned level of participation in its operating and financial decisions
- Review of forecasts and budgets to assess the plans for integrating Baldrick Co into the Group
- Ensure that losses from the date of acquisition only are consolidated
- Evaluation and recalculation of amounts recognised in Group equity in respect of Baldrick Co, in particular the determination of pre- and post-acquisition results

Maximum   16

(b) **Completion issues and laws and regulations**
Generally up to 1½ marks for each point discussed:
- Storage of hazardous chemicals likely to be a breach of laws and regulations
- Auditor needs to understand laws and regulations applicable to the Group
- Further evidence should be obtained about the storage of chemicals
- Implications for the financial statements to be considered, eg provisions for fines and penalties
- Matter to be reported as soon as possible to those charged with governance
- Auditor may have a legal duty to disclose, or consider disclosing in the public interest
- Intimidation and threatening behaviour should be reported to those charged with governance
- Control deficiency and recommendation to be communicated to those charged with governance
- The audit firm may wish to seek legal advice regarding the situation

Maximum   9

Total   **25**

(a)   (i)   The sale and leaseback transaction is material to the group statement of financial position. The proceeds received on the sale of the property, equivalent to the fair value of the assets, represents 23.3% of Group assets, and the carrying amount of the assets disposed of were $27 million ($35m – $8m), representing 18% of group assets. In addition, the profit recognised on the disposal represents 40% of the Group's profit for the year, so it is highly material to the statement of profit or loss.

The transaction is a sale and leaseback because part of the asset has been leased back after the sale. The accounting treatment is not in line with IFRS 16 *Leases*. IFRS 16 would see this effectively as a part-disposal. Part of the right-of-use asset is retained, and a gain is recognised only in relation to the part that is sold/transferred.

First we must work out the size of the gain. This is the difference between the selling price and the fair value on the date of the sale: $35m – $33m = $2m. Since the selling price is higher than the fair value, this is recognised as additional financing provided to the Group.

Next we must work out the proportion of the asset that has been retained for use. We do this by comparing the present value (PV) of the lease liability (which is the value of the right-of-use asset retained), with the fair value. We must, however, adjust the PV of the liability for the additional financing, since this does not relate to the asset retained for use. In this case, the PV of the liability is $22m, from which we deduct the $2m gain ('additional financing') to give $20m.

The proportion of the asset that is retained for use is therefore $20m / $33m = 0.606.

IFRS 16 requires us to continue recognising the leased asset in terms of cost/carrying amount, so the asset is recognised at carrying amount × 0.606 = $27m × 0.606 = $16.4m. This asset must be recognised on the statement of financial position. The amount is material, at 11% of total assets.

There is a gain on the sale of the building, which is the difference between the fair value and the carrying amount, ie $35m – $27m = $8m. The Group can only recognise the part of the gain that relates to the part of the asset that was sold/transferred. Using the same proportion as before, we get $8m × 0.606 = $4.85m retained. This amount is material at 24% of profit. The rest relates to the part that was sold/transferred, ie the balancing amount of $8m – $4.85m = $3.15m.

Therefore, the Group's profit is materially overstated, and the total assets and liabilities are materially understated. An adjustment should be recommended to management, whereby the right-of-use asset would be reinstated, with a lease liability established.

If the adjustment is not made, the group financial statements will contain a material misstatement. The auditor's opinion would be modified due to a material misstatement following the misapplication of IFRS 16 to the sale and leaseback transaction.

Evidence:

- A copy of the lease, signed by the lessor, and a review of its major clauses to confirm that control has been transferred, and that the arrangement should be recognised as a lease in line with IFRS 16

- Review of forecasts and budgets to confirm that economic benefit is expected to be generated through the continued use of the portion of the property complex now being leased

- Physical inspection of the property complex to confirm that it is being used by the Group

- Confirmation of the fair value of the property complex, possibly using an auditor's expert, in which case the expert's report should be included in the audit working papers

- Where fair value has been established using an auditor's or management expert, evaluation of the expert's work including confirmation that the fair value is determined according to the applicable financial reporting framework, and that all assumptions are reasonable

- Agreement of the $35 million cash proceeds to bank statement and cash book

- Minutes of a discussion with management regarding the accounting treatment and including an auditor's request to amend the financial statements

- A copy of insurance documents stating that the Group is responsible for insuring the property complex

- Recalculation of finance charge and depreciation expense in relation to the leased asset

- Review of the financial statements to confirm that appropriate adjustments have been made, and recalculation of right-of-use asset, lease liability and the gain on part-disposal

(ii) The Group's interest in Baldrick Co is material, as the company's assets are equivalent to 12% of total Group assets, and its loss is equivalent to 25% of the Group's profit.

It is questionable whether Baldrick Co should have been accounted for as an associate. An associate arises where there is significant influence over an investee, according to IAS 28 *Investments in Associates and Joint Ventures*. Significant influence is typified by an equity shareholding of 20–50%, so the Group's shareholding of 52% would seem to indicate that the Group exercises control, rather than significant influence.

However, it may be that even with a 52% shareholding, the Group cannot exercise control, for example, if it is prevented from doing so due to agreements between other shareholders, or because it cannot appoint members to the board of Baldrick Co. This would be unusual though, so audit evidence must be sought on the nature of the shareholding in Baldrick Co and whether the Group actually exercises control or significant influence over the company. Baldrick Co not having been integrated into the Group's activities is not a valid reason for its non-consolidation as a subsidiary.

If the Group does have a controlling interest, and Baldrick Co remains recognised as an associate, the Group financial statements will be materially misstated, with implications for the auditor's opinion, which would be modified due to the application of an inappropriate accounting treatment.

If Baldrick Co should be treated as a subsidiary rather than an associate, then the company's loss for the year should be consolidated from the date of acquisition which was 1 January 20X5. Therefore, a loss of $1.25 million ($5 million $\times$ $^3/_{12}$) should be consolidated into Group profit. The loss which has already been recognised, assuming that equity accounting has been correctly applied, would be $650,000 ($5 million $\times$ $^3/_{12} \times 52\%$), therefore an additional loss of $600,000 needs to be recognised.

In addition, there are presentation issues to consider. Equity accounting requires the investment in the associate to be recognised on one line in the statement of financial position, and the income from the associate to be disclosed on one line of the statement of profit or loss. Treating Baldrick Co as a subsidiary will require a line-by-line consolidation in the statement of financial position as well as the statement of profit or loss. This will have a significant impact on numerous balances and transactions within the financial statements.

The combination of adjustments in relation to the sale and leaseback transaction and the consolidation of Baldrick Co as a subsidiary may be considered pervasive to the Group financial statements, and if so, and the necessary adjustments are not made, then the audit opinion could be adverse.

Evidence:

- Agreement of the cash paid to acquire Baldrick Co to cash book and bank statements

- Review of board minutes for discussion of the change in Group structure and for evidence that the acquisition was authorised by the board

- Review of legal documentation pertaining to the acquisition of Baldrick Co, to confirm the number of equity shares acquired, and the rights attached to the shareholding, eg the ability to appoint board members

- Review of notes of discussion with management regarding the exercise of control over Baldrick Co, eg the planned level of participation in its operating and financial decisions, for evidence of control

- Inspection of other supporting documentation relating to the acquisition, such as due diligence reports, for evidence that Baldrick's assets have been measured at fair value

- Review of forecasts and budgets to assess the plans for integrating Baldrick Co into the Group

- Review of supporting workings for Baldrick's loss for the year in the consolidated financial statements, to ensure that correct time apportionment has been applied in calculating the amount of losses recognised in the consolidation of Baldrick Co

- Evaluation and recalculation of amounts recognised in Group equity in respect of Baldrick Co, in particular the determination of pre- and post-acquisition results

(b)   The storage of the potentially hazardous chemicals raises concerns that the Group may not be complying with regulations such as health and safety legislation. The auditor needs to consider the requirements of ISA 250 *Consideration of Laws and Regulations in an Audit of Financial Statements* and the IESBA *Code of Ethics*. It is management's responsibility to ensure that the entity's operations are conducted in accordance with the provisions of laws and regulation (IESBA *Code*: para. 360.8 A1). However, the auditor does have some responsibility, especially where Non-Compliance with Laws and Regulations ('NOCLAR') has an effect on the financial statements.

The auditor is required by ISA 315 *Identifying and Assessing the Risks of Material Misstatement through Understanding the Entity and its Environment* to obtain an understanding of the legal and regulatory framework in which the audited entity operates. This will help the auditor to identify NOCLAR and to assess its implications. Therefore, the auditor should obtain a full knowledge and understanding of the laws and regulations relevant to the storage of items in the Group's warehouses, focusing on health and safety issues and the implications of NOCLAR.

ISA 250 requires that when NOCLAR is identified or suspected, the auditor shall obtain an understanding of the nature of the act and of the circumstances in which it has occurred, and further information to evaluate the possible effect on the financial statements. Therefore, procedures should be performed to obtain evidence about the suspected non-compliance, and to identify any further instances of NOCLAR in the Group's other warehouses.

Management may not be aware that the warehouse manager is allowing the storage of these potentially hazardous items. ISA 250 requires the matter to be discussed with management, and, where appropriate, with those charged with governance. The IESBA *Code of Ethics* requires the NOCLAR to be communicated with the most appropriate level of management, ie at least one level above the person involved (IESBA *Code*: para. R360.11). The auditor must therefore ignore the warehouse manager's threats and communicate the suspected NOCLAR. Given the potential severity of the situation, and that the chemicals may not be safe, there is

BPP
LEARNING

the risk of injury to the Group's employees or the general public, so the matter should be communicated as soon as possible.

The auditor needs to consider the potential implications for the financial statements. The NOCLAR could lead to regulatory authorities imposing fines or penalties on the Group, which may need to be provided for directly in the financial statements. Audit procedures should be performed to determine the amount, materiality and probability of payment of any such fine or penalty imposed.

In terms of reporting NOCLAR to the relevant regulatory authorities, ISA 250 requires the auditor to determine whether they have a responsibility to report the identified or suspected NOCLAR to parties outside the entity. In the event that management or those charged with governance of the Group fail to make the necessary disclosures to the regulatory authorities, the auditor should consider whether they should make the disclosure. This will depend on matters including whether there is a legal duty to disclose or whether it is considered to be in the public interest to do so. Confidentiality is also an issue, and if disclosure were to be made by the auditor, it would be advisable to seek legal advice on the matter. This is very much a worst case scenario, however, as the Group's management is likely to make the necessary disclosures, and should be encouraged by the auditor to do so.

There is also an ethical issue arising from the warehouse manager's aggressive attitude and threatening behaviour. It would seem that the manager has something to hide, and that he was the only person who knew about the storage of the chemicals. He may have been bribed to allow the storage of the dangerous chemicals. His behaviour amounts to intimidation of the auditor, which is not acceptable behaviour, and those charged with governance should be alerted to the situation which arose. ISA 260 *Communication with Those Charged with Governance* requires the auditor to communicate significant difficulties encountered during the audit, which may include examples of lack of co-operation with the auditor, and imposed limitations on auditors performing their work.

The final issue is that the Group should review its policy of requiring limited documentation for contracts less than $10,000. This would seem to be inappropriate because it may lead to other instances of unknown items being stored in the Group's warehouses. This would seem to be a significant control deficiency, and should be reported to those charged with governance in accordance with both ISA 260 and ISA 265 *Communicating Deficiencies in Internal Control with Those Charged with Governance and Management*. The auditor could recommend improvements to the controls over the storage of items which should prevent any further non-compliance with laws and regulations from occurring.

23 Setter

Workbook reference. Chapter 8.

Top tips. Don't forget to calculate materiality, as these are easy marks.

Your general approach to questions of this sort should be to state the correct accounting treatment of the issue at hand, and then compare this with what has actually happened in the question. Even if you're not absolutely certain of what the correct treatment is (part (b) was tricky here), you can still score marks by setting out the requirements of the standard. (But note that marks will be limited for 'identification' only, so you should not spend too long doing this.)

Part (a) should have been OK, as the question contained quite a lot of information that should have helped to remind you of the requirements of IFRS 5 *Non-current Assets held for sale and discontinued operations*. Note that there are no marks available for naming the standard, so do not waste time in the exam doing so – especially when its name is as long as this one!

Part (b) was hard, as the correct accounting treatment was not entirely obvious. However, you could still have scored well by picking up the easier points and by talking about the criteria from the standard.

Part (c) was probably the easiest part of this question, so it was important here that you had not run out of time and could therefore pick up plenty of the marks that were available. Note in particular that there are many more marks available if you adjust your amortisation calculation for the mid-year acquisition, compared with simply dividing the cost by the useful life.

Easy marks. If you calculated materiality correctly for each part of the question, then you would have scored an easy 1.5–2 marks (½ mark for each calculation).

ACCA examining team's comments. Candidates were well prepared for this type of question, and as one of the optional questions, it was attempted by the majority of candidates. On requirement (a), most answers were satisfactory, largely because candidates were confident in explaining the relevant financial reporting requirements and applying them to the brief scenario.

On requirement (b), some answers were excellent, covering all of the financial reporting issues and correctly concluding that the treatment was wrong and if not corrected could have implications for the auditor's opinion. Inadequate answers discussed the points in a vague manner, seeming uncertain as to whether the accounting treatment was correct or not, resulting in the suggestion of a few unclear audit evidence points.

On requirement (c), candidates seemed more comfortable with this requirement than the preceding one, and many discussed all of the relevant financial reporting concerns, particularly in relation to amortisation and/or impairment of the asset.

Overall this was a well attempted question by many. I would however point out that candidates need to think carefully when calculating and commenting on materiality. Most candidates calculated the materiality of every figure given in the question in relation to each of revenue, profit before tax and assets. By this stage in their studies candidates should appreciate that often this is not necessary, for example there is little relevance in calculating an item of expense in relation to assets. Performing all of these calculations must take some time, and the irrelevant calculations will not generate marks.

Marking scheme

Marks

(a)   **Assets held for sale**
Generally 1 mark for each matter considered/evidence point explained:

Matters

-   Assets held for sale are material (calculation)
-   Amount written off is not material (calculation)
-   Conditions required to classify assets as held for sale (up to 2 marks)
-   Re-measurement at classification appears correct
-   Further impairment review may be needed at year end
-   Depreciation should not be charged after reclassification
-   Disclosure in notes to financial statements

Evidence

-   Board minutes at which the disposal of the properties was agreed by management
-   Details of the active programme in place to locate a buyer
-   A copy of any minutes of meetings held with prospective purchasers of any of the properties
-   Written representation from management that the assets will be sold before October 20X3
-   Subsequent events review
-   Confirm depreciation ceased on reclassification
-   Details of any impairment review conducted by management

Maximum   8

BPP
LEARNING

(b) **Sale and leaseback**

Generally 1 mark for each matter considered/evidence point explained:

Matters

– Asset is material (calculation)
– Accounting treatment currently not correct re. asset revaluation
– Discuss materiality of adjustments needed
– Treatment of liability appears correct

Evidence

– A copy of the contract to confirm that the arrangement is a lease
– Confirmation of the fair value of the property complex, possibly using an auditor's expert
– Agreement of the $37 million cash proceeds to bank statement and cash book
– A schedule showing the adjustment required in the financial statements
– Minutes of a discussion with management regarding the accounting treatment and including an auditor's request to amend the financial statements

Maximum 7

(c) **Distribution licence**

Generally 1 mark for each matter considered/evidence point explained:

Matters

– Materiality of the asset (calculation)
– Identify event as intangible asset that should be capitalised
– Identify that no amortisation has been charged
– The non-amortisation is not material

Evidence

– A copy of the licence
– Agreement of cost to bank statement and cash book
– Discussion with management regarding the non-amortisation
– Sales records of the soft drink since 1 September 20X2

Maximum 5

Total 20

(a) **Matters**

The assets held for sale are material to the financial statements at 8% of total assets (= $24m ÷ $300m).

The amount written off is not material, at less than 1% of revenue (= $2m ÷ $620m) and 4.2% of profit before tax (= $2m ÷ $47.5m).

Assets are classified as held for sale if they meet the following criteria (among others):

• Management is committed to a plan to sell

• The assets are available for immediate sale in their present condition

• An active programme exists to locate a buyer

• The sale is highly probable, within 12 months of reclassification (IFRS 5)

The accounting treatment appears to be correct, measuring the assets at the lower of carrying amount and fair value less costs to sell.

The classification took place mid-year, so an impairment review should be conducted as it is possible that the assets have become impaired by the year end.

Depreciation should have ceased from when the reclassification took place in October.

Evidence

- Copy of board minutes to show management's intention to sell assets
- Physical inspection of assets to confirm that they are saleable in present condition
- Evidence of programme to locate buyer, eg copies of advertisements, correspondence with estate agent
- Written representation for management's commitment to sell within 12 months
- Copy of management's impairment review
- Confirmation that $2m written off is recognised in profit or loss
- Confirmation that depreciation ceased on reclassification

(b) **Matters**

The proceeds are material at 12% of total assets (= $37m ÷ $300m).

The asset has not been transferred in line with IFRS 15 *Revenue from Contracts with Customers*, because Setter Stores still has control. The cash received is therefore effectively a secured loan, to be accounted for as a financial liability in line with IFRS 9 *Financial Instruments*. This is not a lease under IFRS 16 *Leases*.

The full amount of the cash received is recognised as a financial liability. The property is held under the cost model of IAS 16 *Property, Plant and Equipment* (IAS 16: para. 30), and continues to be held at its carrying amount of $27m – it is not revalued. Setter Stores has therefore wrongly recognised a revaluation gain of $10m. This is a material overstatement of total assets at 3.3% (= $10m ÷ $300m). The gain should be reversed so that the asset is held under the cost model.

The financial liability is initially recognised at the fair value of the consideration received, which is $37m. This appears to have been done correctly. The liability should then be held at amortised cost, being amortised over 20 years. This would result in other income recognised in the statement of profit or loss – this would be $1.85m each year (= $37m ÷ 20 years). However, the amount recognised in the current year is $nil because the transaction took place at the year end.

Depreciation should also be charged over 20 years. The amount recognised in this period will be based on the carrying amount of $27m.

As the lease is for 20 years, the effect of discounting is likely to be material. The liability should be recognised at its present value, with the effect of discounting being recognised as a finance cost in future periods.

Evidence

- A copy of the signed lease should be on file, with confirmation of its major clauses affecting its classification as a lease
- Copy of insurance documents showing that Setter Stores is responsible for insurance
- Copy of board minutes of discussion of lease for indication of any conditions relating to the cash received
- Agreement of $37m cash received to bank statement
- Confirmation of fair value of $37m, possibly using an auditor's expert

(c)   **Matters**

The licence is material at 5% of total assets (= $15m ÷ $300m).

The asset can be recognised if:

- It is probable that future economic benefits will flow to the entity

- The cost can be measured reliably   (IAS 38: para. 8)

As the licence has been acquired separately, it should be treated as an intangible non-current asset.

Amortisation should be recognised based on the useful life of five years, but this does not appear to have been done. This gives an additional expense of $1.25m (= ($15m ÷ 5 years) × 5 months). This amount is not material at less than 1% of revenue ($1.25m ÷ $620m) and 2.6% of profit before tax ($1.25m ÷ $47.5m).

Evidence

- A copy of the licence, confirming five-year term and cost of $15m

- Agreement of $15m cash paid to bank statement

- Minutes of discussion with management of non-amortisation of the licence

- Sales information in relation to the soft drink to confirm the probability of receiving economic benefits

24 York

Workbook references. Chapters 1, 3, 8 and 12

Top tips. Although it's discussion-based, part (a) is not horribly difficult. It's really important here that you answer the requirement set, which asks why there is a risk of fraud in revenue recognition. Although it mentions fraud, the requirement is absolutely not about the responsibilities of management vs auditors in relation to fraud. There are no marks available for this, so even if you're panicking, you're still better off using your time to do something else.

The matter is slightly confused by the fact that there is a second part of the requirement, about 'why ISA 240 requires specific auditor responses in relation to the risks identified' – but this is not really addressed by the examining team's answer. Anything you wrote in relation to this should, however, get credit from the marker as long as it is relevant and true.

You could probably have thought of the following points, and developed them just a bit, in order to pass the question:

- Performance targets for management lead to risk of manipulation

- Cut-off can be relatively easy to manipulate, particularly where judgment is needed to determine

- IFRS 15 is complex in some areas, eg how to account for warranties provided with products

- Cash sales can be manipulated relatively easily.

If you developed these then you should have been able to get one mark each, and thus pass.

Part (b)(i) was a bit nicer, so you could have made up for any shortfall in your marks from part (a). The first part was a sly little question on money laundering. The tell-tale signs here were:

- It's a cash deposit
- It's then transferred abroad
- It isn't part of the company's business activities
- No evidence is provided

Although it's possible that there's a reasonable explanation for all this – more information is needed – it's also quite possibly money laundering. You should have been able to spot this, so it's then a question of having the confidence to base your answer on this rather than anything else. From then on it's fairly straightforward!

An approach to writing your answer would be to state the reasons why it might be money laundering, and then use a bit of terminology to describe it: this is 'layering'. The rest follows on from this – both anti-money laundering implications, but also audit implications (eg the need for increased scepticism).

Note that there are easy marks for calculating materiality in (b), so make sure you do this (and say if the issue is material).

By the time you'd arrived at part (b)(ii) you might have expected to encounter another dodgy situation, and you wouldn't have been wrong. Mr Smith has shown himself to be an unreliable character (in part (b)(i)), and continues to be so here. His lack of availability to discuss the issue with auditors should raise the alarm.

The issue here is whether there should be a provision at the year end, in line with IAS 37. You should therefore state the IAS 37 requirements and apply them. Given that the provision was included in last year's accounts, it should only be removed: if it is no longer needed as a result of something happening, or if last year's accounts (and auditor's report) were wrong. Last year's audit file should therefore be examined to see why the provision was included (ie what evidence there was).

Nothing has actually changed in the situation, so if there was nothing wrong with last year's audit file/report, it seems that Mr Smith has simply decided by himself to remove the provision. This is unlikely to be acceptable to the auditor!

Note that there are **no marks for auditor's report** implications here, even if it was something that seemed to follow on logically from the question. If you did write about this then you need to be careful to only include it if it's asked for.

Part (c) was straightforward, as long as you were familiar with the reporting requirements for review engagements of this sort.

Easy marks. Calculating materiality gets you easy marks. You should also be aiming to score well in part (b)(ii) here (say 4.5 marks at least), as it was quite a nice question. Stick to your time limit though – 6 marks = 12 minutes.

ACCA examining team's comments. Part (a) required candidates to discuss why auditors should presume that there is a risk of fraud in revenue recognition and this requirement was poorly answered with most candidates setting out lengthy explanations of the respective duties of the auditor and management for the identification and prevention of fraud and thereby not answering the question. Strong answers considered management bias and targets, judgments in complex business and cut-off errors.

Part (b) explored two unusual issues which had occurred in an entrepreneurial audit client. Many candidates were able to identify the potential money laundering transaction and identified the placement and layering stages which were involved. Most candidates answered this part of the question well and were able to identify; the need for proper evidence, the poor controls over payments, notification to the MLRO and avoiding tipping-off the client.

Candidates were also asked to consider the release of a provision relating to a legal claim for which evidential documentation was not available. Most candidates discussed the implications of the reversal quite well but failed to identify the creative accounting and profit smoothing which was the purpose behind the provision reversal.

In both parts numerous candidates demonstrated poor exam technique and diverted into highlighting what would be included in the auditor's report which was not required.

Most answers to requirement (c) were good at discussing the accounting treatment for the warranty provision, that the non-recognition was not appropriate, and the majority correctly assessed the

materiality of the issue. Answers were inadequate in discussing the impact of this on the review report, being mostly unable to say much more than the auditor would need to mention it in the review report. There seemed to be a lack of knowledge on anything other than the standard wording for a review report, with many answers stating that the wording should be 'nothing has come to our attention' followed by a discussion that there actually was something to bring to shareholders' attention but with no recommendation as to how this should be done.

Marking scheme

Marks

(a) **Fraud and revenue recognition**

Generally 1 mark for each point of discussion:

- Management targets/incentives
- High volume of transactions
- Use of judgement
- Complexity of accounting
- Cash sales
- Common in recent accounting frauds
- Not always complex/rebuttable permitted

Maximum   7

(b) **Implications for completion of audit**

Generally 1 mark for each well explained implication for the audit or recommendation for further action:

(i) **Cash transfers**

- Indication of money laundering
- Layering
- Weakness in controls over cash
- Need to understand the accounting entries
- Failure to provide evidence
- Increased risk/need for scepticism
- Need for independent review
- Report to MLRO
- Care in avoiding 'tipping off'

(ii) **Legal dispute**

- Potential creative accounting
- Material impact on profit for the year
- Review evidence on previous file
- Criteria for recognition (½ each to max of 1)
- Insufficiency of current evidence
- Request for further evidence (1 mark for each well described procedure to obtain further evidence)
- Possible need to reinstate provision to be discussed with management

Maximum   13

(c) **Interim financial statement review**

Up to 1½ marks for each matter to be considered in forming conclusion/implication for report:

- Interim financial information should use applicable financial reporting framework
- Identify and explain unrecognised provision

Marks

- Correct calculation of materiality (1 mark)
- Communicate necessary adjustment to management/those charged with governance
- If amount unadjusted, the conclusion will be qualified
- Reason for qualified conclusion to be explained in the report
- Consider withdrawing from engagement/resign from audit appointment   Maximum   5

Total   **25**

(a) There are a number of reasons why there should be a presumption of risks of fraud in revenue recognition. One is that managers of companies are often under pressure, particularly in listed companies, to achieve certain performance targets. The achievement of those targets often affects their job security and their compensation. These performance targets often include measures of revenue growth, providing an incentive for management to use earnings management techniques.

In other companies there may be incentives to understate revenues, for example, to reduce reported profits and, therefore, company taxation charges. This may be more relevant to private limited companies where management may not be under such pressure to achieve revenue-based targets.

There is also usually a high volume of revenue transactions during a financial period. As the volume of transactions increases, the risk of failing to detect fraud and error using traditional, sample-based auditing techniques also increases. This means that it is potentially easier for management to successfully manipulate these balances than other balances which are subject to a lower volume of transactions. Material misstatement through the manipulation of revenue recognition can be readily achieved by recording revenue in an earlier or later accounting period than is proper or by creating fictitious revenues.

Revenue recognition can also be a judgemental area. Examples include the recognition of revenues on long-term contracts, such as the construction of buildings, and from the provision of services. These require the estimation of the percentage of completion at the period end, increasing the scope for management to manipulate reported results.

As well as requiring judgement, revenue recognition can also be a complex issue. For example, some sales have multiple elements, such as the sale of goods and the separate sale of related maintenance contracts and warranties. This added complexity increases the risk of manipulation.

In some companies, for example, those in the retail industry, a high proportion of revenue may be earned through cash sales. This increases the risk of the theft of cash and the consequent manipulation of recorded revenues to conceal this crime.

Methods of revenue manipulation have also featured prominently in cases of accounting fraud, such as Enron and WorldCom.

The prevalence of these methods in modern accounting frauds and the failure of auditors to detect this in these cases suggests that it is one of the more common methods of earnings management and one which auditors should rightly consider as high risk.

While revenue recognition in general may be considered a high-risk area, it is not always the case; companies with simple revenue streams or a low volume of transactions may be considered at low risk of fraud through revenue manipulations. Accordingly ISA 240 *The Auditor's Responsibility Relating to Fraud in an Audit of Financial Statements* permits the rebuttal of the fraud risk presumption for revenue recognition. One example of simple revenue streams would be where a company leases properties for fixed annual amounts over a fixed period of time. If this is the case, the reasons for not treating revenue as a high fraud risk area must be fully documented by the auditor.

(b) (i) **Cash transfers**

This unusual, unexplained cash transfer into a foreign bank account may indicate that Phil Smith is using York Co to carry out money laundering. Money laundering is defined as the process by which criminals attempt to conceal the origin and ownership of the proceeds of their criminal activity, allowing them to maintain control over the proceeds and, ultimately, providing a legitimate cover for the sources of their income.

It is possible that the proceeds of criminal activity have been placed into York Co's bank account to enable them to transfer the funds into a foreign account, thus providing them with the appearance of legitimacy and creating a trail which is difficult to trace to the original source. This process is known as 'layering'. According to ACCA's Technical Factsheet 145 *Anti-money laundering guidance for the accountancy sector*, money laundering can result from a single transaction such as the cash placed into York Co's bank account.

The fact that Mr Smith retains sole control over cash management and that the financial controller has no oversight or involvement in this indicates weak controls over cash, for example, there appears to be no segregation of duty which may be the intention of Mr Smith to facilitate illegal activity. That he has failed to provide any documentary evidence, despite the request to do so by the audit team, only arouses suspicion further. It is also possible that the company is being used as a vehicle for money laundering without Mr Smith's knowledge. It is possible that the money has been accepted in good faith without the source of the funding being adequately verified.

The amount which has been transferred represents 1.3% of total assets, which is material to the financial statements. The engagement, and particularly matters relating to cash transactions, should now be considered as high risk and approached with a high degree of professional scepticism. The audit files should now be subject to an independent second partner review. The firm may also wish to seek legal advice given the potential legal implications of dealing with a client involved in money laundering.

To properly assess the impact of the transaction on the financial statements, the audit firm needs to understand the accounting entries which have been made. The debit side of the entry would be to cash, and the audit team should enquire as to where the credit side of the entry has been recognised. Possibly the credit has been recognised as revenue or possibly it has been contra-d against the cash payment which was made the next day.

The situation should be reported as soon as possible to the firm's Money Laundering Reporting Officer (MLRO). The MLRO is responsible for receiving and evaluating reports of suspected money laundering from colleagues within the firm. They will make a decision as to whether further enquiries are required and, if necessary, will make reports to the appropriate authorities.

Finally, care must now be taken during the remaining audit that no-one 'tips off' the client that their activity is being treated as suspicious and that a report will be made to the MLRO. 'Tipping off' the client could prejudice any consequent investigation and may itself be considered a criminal offence, depending on relevant legislation. According to Technical Factsheet 145, a tipping-off disclosure may be made in writing or verbally, and either directly or indirectly so the audit team must ensure that when discussing the matter with Mr Smith, he is not alerted to the suspicions of money laundering.

(ii) **Legal dispute**

The creation of provisions and their reversal in consequent years is a commonly used creative accounting technique. As such, this is a potentially high-risk area of the audit. The reversal of the provision in the current year increases the reported profit before tax by $150,000, which represents 6.8% of profit. This is therefore material and should be treated with appropriate professional scepticism.

In accordance with IAS 37 *Provisions, Contingent Liabilities and Contingent Assets*, the provision should only have been recorded originally if: York Co had an obligation as a result of a past event; if it was considered probable that an outflow of cash would occur; and if a reliable estimate of the amount was available (IAS 37: para. 14). Given that this is a material amount, there should be audit evidence on the prior year file concerning the appropriateness of the original amount recorded.

It would be prudent to review the evidence held on the prior year audit file to assess the quality of evidence which was obtained relating to the assumptions made regarding the probability of payment. With legal disputes one would expect to see some documentary evidence from legal experts, such as the company's lawyers. It is unlikely that management assumptions and a written representation would have been considered appropriate as evidence in a matter where legal expertise is required.

For the same reason it is unlikely that the opinions of Mr Smith are likely to be considered as sufficient justification for reversing the provision in the current year. The lack of additional documentary evidence and Mr Smith's lack of availability to discuss the matter with the audit team further arouses suspicions of the validity of the decision to reverse the provision.

The audit manager should contact the client and request confirmation of Mr Smith's opinions from the company lawyers, along with any relevant documentation of legal proceedings or agreements reached with the ex-employee.

If the client is unable (or unwilling) to provide any further documentation, then the provision should be reinstated in full. This should be noted on the summary of proposed adjustments to the financial statements and sent to the client along with a request that they amend all the adjustments identified.

(c) The review should be conducted in line with ISRE 2410 *Review of Interim Financial Information Performed by the Independent Auditor of the Entity*. The key elements of the review are enquiry and analytical procedures, which do not lead to reasonable assurance.

The applicable financial reporting framework should be the same as for the annual financial statements, so IFRSs apply.

In line with IAS 37 *Provisions, Contingent Liabilities and Contingent Assets*, a provision should be recognised for the warranty on the cars. Thus the treatment in the 20X5 annual financial statements appears correct.

Squire Co has stopped offering warranties on cars sold from 1 July 20X5 onwards. However, it still has an obligation to honour warranties on cars already sold. Hence it should still provide for the cost of honouring those warranties. The interim financial statements therefore appear to understate liabilities and overstate profit.

If the same warranty provision needed to be recognised in the interim financial statements as at the year end, this would be $1.5m. This is 5% of total assets (= $1.5m / $30m), and is material.

The auditor should communicate this misstatement to management. If management does not respond appropriately, then the auditor must inform those charged with governance.

If appropriate adjustments are not made, then the report should contain a qualified or adverse conclusion. The report must include a 'Basis for qualified conclusion' paragraph immediately before the 'Qualified conclusion' paragraph.

25 Mondrian

Workbook references. Chapters 2, 6, 8 and 10.

Top tips. Part (a) was straightforward, and you should have been looking to score close to maximum marks here. Note that you don't need to write as much as this model answer contains. Write your best points first, and make sure that you don't go over your time allocation – which is very easy to do on a requirement that you know well.

Part (b) is a typical question on audit risk that should not have carried too many surprises. There are marks available for calculating materiality, so you really should get these. With materiality, it is best not to calculate the general thresholds at the start of your answer because the marks are available in relation to each item. The best approach is that taken by the model answer, ie select the relevant figure (revenue, PBT or total assets), calculate the percentage and then state whether it is material.

Any extra trend calculations that you can do can be a source of easy marks, eg calculating that revenue has increased by 2.2%, which is not included in the analytical review given in the question. These will usually earn ½ a mark.

It should not need saying, but the question does not ask for business risks so you should not be mentioning these in your answer, no matter how tempting it is to do so!

It is also a bad idea to include any theoretical discussions of the nature of audit risk (ie inherent risk vs detection risk vs control risk). Further, it is not really necessary to classify risks as eg inherent risks or control risks; the best answers might do this and the ability to do so easily is certainly a sign of a strong answer, but there are no marks available for this, so it is unlikely to be a good use of your time to rack your brains over it.

The requirement in part (b)(ii) to recommend additional information is a common one, and the 6 marks available are relatively easy ones (each well-explained piece of information should get a full mark, which is quite a good return given how little needs to be written). It's really important that you devote enough time to this part of the question, and it is probably a good idea to answer this separately from part (b)(i), to make sure that you give it enough attention. You could do this by making a sheet of paper just for additional information and adding things to it as you write your answer to part (i), and then spending time at the end thinking of anything else that might get marks.

Part (c) asked for audit procedures on work in progress and the government grant. The relevant parts are towards the end of the scenario, just before the preliminary analytical review. The paragraph on the government grant contains a bit of a steer by stating that the grant comes with conditions – the audit procedures must surely test whether these conditions will be met. You should thus be able to get two relatively easy marks in this area just by thinking of procedures to verify that $2m has been spent on wages, and that the manufacturing site is likely to operate until 20Y0.

With part (c)(i) on work in progress, notice that the mark for materiality is in part (b) in relation to audit risk, so do not put your materiality calculation in your answer to part (c). This was quite an unusual requirement for AAA – the model answer is quite detailed here, and is perhaps more like something one would expect in AA. This could be good news for candidates, though, because all you needed to do was think of some generic procedures and hey presto, two marks (or more).

Part (d) was a typical ethics requirement. Be very wary about writing about the risk of % fee thresholds being breached, as your examining team may consider these to be general points that betoken a lack of application to the scenario at hand.

Easy marks. The knowledge marks available in part (a) for explaining 'fraudulent financial reporting' were easy.

The marks for additional information in part (b)(ii), and for calculating materiality in (b)(i). The professional marks are absolutely basic and there is no reason not to get at least 3 of them.

ACCA examining team's comments. This question was set at the planning stage of the audit/assurance cycle and covered risks, audit procedures and other information required.

Requirement (a) asked for an explanation of the term 'fraudulent financial reporting', with some examples to illustrate the explanation. Answers on the whole were reasonable, and in terms of illustration, a range of examples were usually provided.

Candidates were required to provide an analysis of audit risks for a manufacturer of bespoke and generic machines. Performance on this requirement was good with the majority of candidates correctly describing audit risks rather than business risks. This is an area that most candidates are well prepared on. However, stronger answers were able to develop and apply the relevant accounting treatment. Those able to identify specific areas of the financial statements which would be affected and to correctly identify whether the risk was over or understatement tended to score the strongest marks. A significant minority of candidates thought that the client was new to the firm as opposed to simply having a change in manager and spent time addressing opening balances and new client procedures which were not relevant to the question. Candidates are again reminded to read the question carefully and consider the context of the scenario both in terms of client history and timeframe before answering the question.

Candidates were further required to provide additional information needed to effectively plan the audit, and candidates showed a marked improvement over previous sittings where this requirement has been examined. This type of question requires candidates to identify information that would be available in advance of the audit that would assist in the planning of the audit. Such information would generally help in the identification or evaluation of risks rather than the information available at the year end for performing audit procedures. This is particularly relevant as the question was set almost a month prior to the year end so financial statements and year-end balances would not yet be available.

Candidates were further required to provide audit procedures for the valuation of work in progress (WIP) and a government grant. With respect to the former, candidates often cited the need for an expert to value WIP rather than focusing on the components of cost and NRV in the machines. Similarly, there were a number of candidates who requested written representations from management on WIP despite the figure not being an issue where the knowledge was confined to management or one of management's intentions. Candidates are once again reminded that a written representation is not a suitable substitute for sufficient appropriate evidence. The audit procedures relevant to the grant were generally well described.

There were four professional marks available, and most candidates secured most of these marks by providing an introduction and using headings to create an appropriate structure for their answer. However, presentation was not always good and candidates are reminded to pay attention to determining an appropriate layout for their answer.

Marking scheme

Marks

(a)   **Fraudulent financial reporting**

Generally 1 mark per comment/example:
- Material misstatement in financial statements
- Deliberate/intentional
- Manipulation of underlying accounting records
- Misrepresentation/omission in financial statements

- Misapplication of IFRS
- Earnings management

Maximum   4

(b)   (i)   **Evaluation of audit risks**

Up to 2 marks for each audit risk evaluated, and 1 mark for relevant calculations (eg materiality, trends) up to a maximum of 6 marks for calculations:

- Stock exchange listing and pressure on results
- Disclosure for listed companies
- Foreign exchange transactions and potential derivatives (up to 3 marks)
- Payment in advance and revenue recognition
- Potential for cancelled contracts and implication for valuation of work in progress
- New directors
- Cash-settled share-based payment scheme
- Revaluation of property
- Deferred tax recognition
- Government grant recognition and potential for repayment if terms are breached
- Lease contract
- Inventory valuation
- Provision in respect of returned goods
- Working capital

Maximum   20

(ii)   **Additional information**

1 mark for each relevant piece of relevant information recommended. The list below is indicative, and credit should be given for other relevant recommendations:

- Details of the stock exchange listing during the year
- Information on the specific listing rules relevant to the stock exchange
- Details on the planned foreign stock exchange listing
- Information on the background and experience of the new non-executive directors and the new finance director
- A full set of draft financial statements including a statement of cash flows
- Details on the valuation of properties such as date of valuation and name of the valuer
- Documentation on the cash-settled share-based payment scheme

Maximum   6

(c)   (i)   **Audit procedures on the valuation of work in progress**

1 mark for each well explained audit procedure:

- Obtain a schedule itemising the jobs included in work in progress at the year end, cast it and agree the total to the general ledger and draft financial statements

- Agree a sample of items from the schedule to the inventory count records

242

- For a sample of jobs included on the schedule:
    - Agree costs to supporting documentation such as supplier's invoice and payroll records
    - For any overheads absorbed into the work in progress valuation, review the basis of the absorption and assess its reasonableness
    - Assess how the degree of completion of the job has been determined at the year end and agree the stage of completion of the job to records taken at the inventory count
    - Agree the details of the job specification to customer order
    - Confirm that net realisable value is greater than cost by agreeing the contract price and cash received from the customer post year end

- To assess the completeness of work in progress, select a sample of customer orders and trace through to the list of jobs included in work in progress

Maximum   5

(ii) **Audit procedures in respect of the government grant**

1 mark for each well explained audit procedure:

- Obtain the documentation relating to the grant to confirm the amount, the date the cash was received, and the terms on which the grant was awarded

- Review the documentation for any conditions attached to the grant, for example, is there a requirement that a certain number of people are employed at the manufacturing plant?

- Discuss with management the method of recognition of the amount received, in particular how much of the grant has been recognised in profit and the treatment of the amount deferred in the statement of financial position

- For the part of the grant relating to continued operation of the manufacturing plant, determine the basis on which this is being released into profit, assess its reasonableness and recalculate to confirm accuracy of management's calculations

- Review forecasts and budgets in relation to the manufacturing plant to assess the likelihood of its continued operations until 20Y0

- Using the draft financial statements, confirm the accounting treatment outlined by discussion with management has been applied and recalculate the amounts recognised

- Confirm the cash received to bank statement and cash book

Maximum   5

BPP
LEARNING

(d)   **Ethical issue**

–   Provision of valuation service creates self-review and self-interest threats to objectivity

–   Service cannot be provided if the pension deficit is material

–   Calculate and comment on materiality in 20X3 financial statements

–   Other matters to consider including level of subjectivity, lack of informed management (1 mark each)

–   Safeguards may be used to reduce threat to acceptable level (1 mark each)

Maximum   6

Professional marks for headings, introduction, conclusion and quality of explanations provided   <u>4</u>

Total   **<u>50</u>**

Briefing notes

To: Audit partner

From: Audit manager

Subject: Audit planning in respect of Dali Co

Introduction

These briefing notes are prepared to assist in the audit planning meeting for Dali Co, our manufacturing client supplying machinery and equipment to the quarrying industry. The notes explain, and give examples of, fraudulent financial reporting. The notes contain an evaluation of audit risk along with recommendations of the additional information which is relevant to audit risk evaluation. The notes explain the principal audit procedures to be performed in respect of the valuation of work in progress, and the government grant received during the year. The notes also identify and discuss the ethical and other professional issues raised in respect of the client's request for a valuation service.

(a)   There are two aspects to fraudulent financial reporting. Firstly, it involves misstatements in the financial statements, either by misstating the information they contain or by omitting information from them. Secondly, like all fraud it is not a result of error but of a fraudulent **intention**. It is the intentional creation of misstatements in the financial statements.

This falls into three general categories:

•   Manipulation, falsification or alteration of accounting records/supporting documents. An example of this would be changing the date on a sales invoice so as to manipulate the year-end cut-off for revenue.

•   Misrepresentation (or omission) of events, transactions or other significant information in the financial statements. An example of this might be failing to include a provision for a future liability.

•   Intentional misapplication of accounting principles. An example of this could be misapplying IAS 23 *Borrowing Costs* so as to include interest payments as an expense when they should be capitalised.

Such fraud may be carried out by overriding controls that would otherwise appear to be operating effectively, for example by recording fictitious journal entries or improperly adjusting assumptions or estimates used in financial reporting.

Aggressive earnings management is a topical issue and, at its most aggressive, may constitute fraudulent financial reporting.

(b) (i) **Audit risk evaluation**

Stock exchange listing and pressure on results

The listing obtained during the year can create inherent risk at the financial statement level because management may feel under pressure to achieve good results in this financial year. The flotation raised equity capital, so there will be new shareholders who will want to see strong performance in the expectation of a dividend pay-out. In addition, the introduction of the cash-settled share-based payment plan motivates management to produce financial statements which show a favourable performance and position which is likely to lead to an increase in the company's share price. There is a risk that revenue and profits may be overstated. Revenue has increased by 2.2% and profit before tax by 6.5%, which may indicate overstatement.

Disclosure for listed companies

This is the first set of financial statements produced since Dali Co became listed. There is a risk that the new finance director will not be familiar with the requirements specific to listed companies, for example, the company now falls within the scope of IAS 33 *Earnings per Share* and IFRS 8 *Operating Segments* for the first time. There is a risk of incomplete or inaccurate disclosures in respect of these standards and also in respect of any listing rules in the jurisdiction in which the company is listed.

Foreign exchange transactions

Dali Co purchases many components from foreign suppliers and is therefore likely to be transacting and making payments in foreign currencies. According to IAS 21 *The Effects of Changes in Foreign Exchange Rates*, transactions should be initially recorded using the spot rate (IAS 21: para. 21), and monetary items such as trade payables should be retranslated at the year end using the closing rate (IAS 21: para. 23). Exchange gains and losses should be recognised within profit for the year (IAS 21: para. 28).

The risk is that the incorrect exchange rate is used for the translation and retranslation, or that the retranslation does not happen at the year end, in which case trade payables and profit could be over- or understated, depending on the movement in the exchange rate. The company may have entered into hedging arrangements as a way to reduce exposure to foreign exchange fluctuations. There is a risk that hedging arrangements are not identified and accounted for as derivatives according to IFRS 9 *Financial Instruments*, which could mean incomplete recognition of derivative financial assets or liabilities and associated gains or losses.

Payment in advance and revenue recognition under contract with customers

For items where significant design work is needed, Dali Co receives a payment in advance. This gives rise to risk in terms of when that part of the revenue generated from a sale of goods is recognised. There is a risk that revenue is recognised too early, especially given the risk of management bias and the incentive to overstate revenue and profit as discussed above. According to IFRS 15 *Revenue from Contracts with Customers*, revenue should only be recognised as control is passed, either over time or at a point in time. The timing of revenue recognition will depend on the contractual terms with the customer, with factors which may indicate the point in time at which control passes including the transference of the physical asset, transference of legal title, and the customer accepting the significant risks and rewards related to the ownership of the asset. It is likely that the payments in advance should be treated as deferred revenue at the point when the payment is received as the conditions for recognition of revenue are unlikely to have been met at this point in time. There is additional audit risk created if a customer were to cancel a contract part way through its completion, the bespoke work in progress may be worthless and would need to be written off according to IAS 2 *Inventories*. There is therefore a risk of overstated work in progress.

New directors

During the year several new non-executive directors were appointed, as well as a new finance director. While this may serve to strengthen the corporate governance structure including the control environment, equally the introduction of new personnel could mean inexperience and a control risk, particularly if the finance director is lacking in experience. Some of the suggestions and accounting treatments made by the finance director indicate that their knowledge of the applicable financial reporting framework is weak, signalling that errors may occur in the preparation of the financial statements.

Cash-settled share-based payment scheme

This falls under the scope of IFRS 2 *Share-based Payment* which states that the liability in respect of the plan should be measured at fair value at the year end. The increase in the share price from $2.90 at flotation to $3.50 (projected) at the year end indicates that a liability should be recognised at 31 December 20X5 based on the fair value of the liability which has accrued up to that date, with the expense recognised in the statement of profit or loss. This accounting treatment has not been followed, leading to understated liabilities and overstated profit, and the disclosure in respect of the plan may not be sufficient to meet the requirements of IFRS 2 which requires extensive disclosures including the effect of share-based payment transactions on the entity's profit or loss for the period and on its financial position.

Revaluation of property

The decision to revalue the company's manufacturing sites creates several risks. First, revaluation involves establishing a current market price or fair value for each property included in the revaluation, which can be a subjective exercise, leading to inherent risk that the valuations may not be appropriate. A risk also arises in that IAS 16 *Property, Plant and Equipment* requires all assets in the same class to be revalued (IAS 16: para. 36), so if any properties which are manufacturing sites have not been included in the revaluation exercise, the amounts recognised will not be correct. There is also a risk that depreciation has not been recalculated on the new, higher value of the properties, leading to overstatement of non-current assets and understatement of operating expenses. IAS 16 also requires a significant level of disclosure in relation to a policy of revaluation (IAS 16: para. 77), so there is a risk that the necessary disclosures are incomplete. The revaluation gain recognised in equity represents 3.9% of total assets and is therefore material to the financial statements.

Deferred tax recognition

IAS 12 *Income Taxes* requires deferred tax to be recognised in respect of taxable temporary differences which arise between the carrying amount and tax base of assets and liabilities, including the differences which arise on the revaluation of non-current assets, regardless of whether the assets are likely to be disposed of in the foreseeable future (IAS 12: paras. 5, 15 and 20). The finance director's suggestion that deferred tax should not be provided for is therefore incorrect, and at present liabilities are understated, representing an error in the statement of financial position. There is no profit impact, however, as the deferred tax would be recognised in equity. Depending on the rate of tax which would be used to determine the necessary provision, it may not be material to the financial statements.

Government grant recognition

The government grant represents 11.1% of total assets and is material to the financial statements. A risk arises in relation to the recognition of the grant. IAS 20 *Accounting*

for Government Grants and Disclosure of Government Assistance requires that a grant is recognised as income over the period necessary to match the grant received with the related costs for which they are intended to compensate (IAS 20: para. 12). Therefore, the $2 million relating to costs incurred this year should be recognised as income, but the remainder should be released to profit on a systematic basis; in this case it would seem appropriate to release on a straight line basis until July 20Y0. The risk is that the grant has been recognised on an inappropriate basis leading to over or understated profit for the year. The part of the grant not recognised in profit should be recognised in the statement of financial position. IAS 20 allows classification as deferred income, or alternatively the amount can be netted against the assets to which the grant relates (IAS 20: para. 24). There is therefore also a risk that the amount is recognised elsewhere in the statement of financial position, leading to incorrect presentation and disclosure.

If the terms of the grant have been breached, the grant or an element of it may need to be repaid. There is therefore a risk that if there is any breach, the associated provision for repayment is not recognised, understating liabilities.

Lease recognition

The present value of the contract represents 0.9% of total assets (= $850,000 / $90m), and is on the borderline of being material. Misstatements here could become material when aggregated with any other uncorrected misstatements.

IFRS 16 *Leases* states that a lease is a contract that gives control of the use of an identified asset for a period of time in exchange for consideration. Although Dali Co may have the right to control the use of the cleaning machines, the supplier has substantive substitution rights, ie it could feasibly substitute other machines for the ones Dali Co is using. There is therefore no identified asset, so the lease should not be recognised. The risk is that Dali Co may have recognised a non-current asset and a lease liability, which would overstate both assets and liabilities. Dali Co should have recognised the lease payments in profit or loss as they occur.

Inventory valuation

Work in progress is material at 13.3% of total assets and has increased by 26.3% in the current year. The valuation of work in progress is likely to be complex as many different jobs for different customers are ongoing at the year end, and each will have a different stage of completion and cost base at the year end. There are also issues more generally with the valuation of inventory, due to the customer returns of items which have recently occurred showing that there are problems with the quality of the goods supplied. For items which have been returned, the net realisable value is likely to be less than the cost of the item indicating that a write-off may be necessary to reduce the value of the inventory according to IAS 2. The increase in the inventory holding period, as demonstrated by the increase in inventory days, shows that inventory has become more slow-moving during the year also indicating that inventory may be overstated.

Provision in respect of returned goods

A provision should be recognised where a reliable estimate can be made in relation to a probable outflow of economic resources and an obligating event has taken place. The fact that Dali Co replaces faulty products free of charge indicates that a provision should be recognised based on the best estimate of the future economic outflow. The risk is that no provision or an insufficient provision in relation to the warranty has been recognised, leading to understated liabilities and operating expenses.

Working capital

The preliminary analytical review reveals that Dali Co is struggling to manage its working capital. The liquidity ratios provided show that the operating cycle has increased from 165 days in 20X4 (150 + 70 – 55) to 205 days in 20X5 (175 + 90 –

60). The company may be finding it difficult to collect cash from customers, as the receivables period has increased by 20 days, and in turn the payment period to suppliers has increased by five days. If there is doubt over the collectability of receivables, then certain balances may need to be written off, and there is a risk of overstatement of receivables and understatement of operating expenses if bad debts are not recognised.

> **Tutorial note.** Credit will be awarded for other relevant audit risks.

(ii) **Recommended additional information**

- Details of the stock exchange listing during the year including the terms of the flotation, number of equity shares issued and amount of equity capital raised.

- Any information available in relation to the flotation – for example, investor prospectus, pre- and post-flotation press releases, communications with the stock exchange registrar.

- Information on the specific listing rules relevant to the stock exchange – for example, the corporate governance code and disclosures necessary in company annual reports and financial statements.

- Details on the planned foreign stock exchange listing in 20X6 including the jurisdiction, the strategic rationale for seeking the listing and proposed timescales.

- Information on the background and experience of the new non-executive directors and the new finance director – for example, their professional qualifications and previous employment or directorships held.

- A full set of forecast financial statements including a statement of cash flows to assess the working capital issues faced by the company.

- Details on the valuation of properties including the date of the revaluation and information on the valuer such as their professional qualification and relationship with the company and a copy of the valuation report.

- Documentation on the cash-settled share-based payment scheme to gauge the number of members of the scheme and its potential materiality to the financial statements.

> **Tutorial note.** Credit will be awarded for other relevant information which would be available at this stage of the audit to help in the evaluation of audit risk.

(c) (i) **Audit procedures in respect of the valuation of work in progress**

- Obtain a schedule itemising the jobs included in work in progress at the year end, cast it and agree the total to the general ledger and draft financial statements.

- Agree a sample of items from the schedule to the inventory count records.

- For a sample of jobs included on the schedule:

  - Agree costs to supporting documentation such as supplier's invoice and payroll records

  - For any overheads absorbed into the work in progress valuation, review the basis of the absorption and assess its reasonableness

- Assess how the degree of completion of the job has been determined at the year end and agree the stage of completion of the job to records taken at the inventory count;

- Agree the details of the job specification to customer order and

- Confirm that net realisable value is greater than cost by agreeing the contract price and cash received from the customer post year end

- To assess the completeness of work in progress, select a sample of customer orders and trace through to the list of jobs included in work in progress.

(ii) **Audit procedures in respect of the recognition and measurement of the government grant**

- Obtain the documentation relating to the grant to confirm the amount, the date the cash was received, and the terms on which the grant was awarded.

- Review the documentation for any conditions attached to the grant, for example, is there a requirement that a certain number of people are employed at the manufacturing plant?

- Discuss with management the method of recognition of the amount received, in particular how much of the grant has been recognised in profit and the treatment of the amount deferred in the statement of financial position.

- For the part of the grant relating to wages and salaries, confirm that the grant criteria have been complied with by examining payroll records and timesheets to verify that $2m has been spent on wages in the deprived area.

- For the part of the grant relating to continued operation of the manufacturing site, determine the basis on which this is being released into profit and recalculate to confirm accuracy of management's calculations.

- Review forecasts and budgets in relation to the manufacturing site to assess the likelihood of its continued operations until 20Y0.

- Using the draft financial statements, confirm the accounting treatment outlined by discussion with management has been applied and recalculate the amounts recognised.

- Confirm the cash received to bank statement and cash book.

(d) **Ethical issues**

Threats

There is a self-interest threat here in respect of the fee for the non-assurance service.

A self-review threat is present because the partner's actuarial valuation may need to be audited, in which case Mondrian & Co would be reviewing its own work. It is not clear whether the audit partner in question is an audit engagement partner for the Dali Co audit. If this is the case then the service cannot be performed unless the engagement partner is changed.

Assuming that the partner involved is not the engagement partner, and subject to the further considerations below, relevant safeguards here could include:

- Using separate teams to work on the actuarial valuation and on the audit, separated by information barriers

- Independent review of the audit and/or the valuation by an independent professional

Valuation

In assessing the significance of the self-review threat, a number of factors must be considered. Chief among these are:

- The materiality of the valuation to the audited financial statements

- The degree of subjectivity involved in the valuation

- The extent to which the client is involved in making any judgements necessary to the valuation

(IESBA *Code of Ethics*: para. 603.3 A23)

If, for instance, the valuation involves a high degree of subjectivity, and cannot be performed according to an established methodology then the self-review threat might be considered severe.

Materiality

Dali is a listed – and therefore public interest – entity, so its auditor must not provide valuation services which materially affect the financial statements.

The pension liability was 0.3% of total assets last year (= $255,000 / $85m) and was thus immaterial. If the figures this year are similar, then materiality would not be a barrier to providing the service.

Conclusion

These briefing notes indicate that there are many areas of potential audit risk to be considered when developing the audit strategy for Dali Co, and that additional information should be requested from the client to be obtained as soon as possible to facilitate a more in-depth evaluation of certain audit risks identified. The audit procedures recommended in respect of work in progress and the government grant received will provide assurance on these significant issues.

26 Bill

Workbook references. Chapters 2, 6, 7 and 8.

Top tips. As this was a large question, it was vital that you worked methodically and kept to your timings throughout its sections.

You should have noticed when reading the question that the second paragraph of the information gives figures for calculating materiality. Remember, whenever a question includes these figures, it is very likely that you will have to calculate materiality at some point in your answer. These are easy marks, so be sure to get them.

Parts (a)(i) and (ii) should have been relatively straightforward, provided that your financial reporting knowledge is up to scratch. This is relatively in-depth financial reporting for AAA, and is a good example of the kind of knowledge you need to be able to demonstrate. Assuming that you are comfortable with the accounting, the question itself should have been within your grasp if you are systematic and address all parts of the requirement for each of the two accounting issues.

Part (a)(iii) tested your knowledge of ISAs and your ability to apply them. Your examining team has stated that knowledge of ISAs is a common weakness amongst candidates. You should have scored well on this part of the question, and may have found yourself going over your allocated time of 21 minutes (11 marks × 1.95). Make sure you stick to your timings, or you will struggle later in the exam.

Part (b) was relatively difficult. Part (b)(i) required you to think on your feet, as it did not ask you to explain how something should be audited, but rather to reflect on the difficulties involved in doing so. You should be looking to score at least 2–3 marks here. It's important not to panic, and to make sure you don't go over your time trying to think of things to write – especially given that the next part of

the question was a bit easier. Part (b)(ii) should have been simpler, and required you to recommend audit procedures. A good bullet pointed list should have been able to score 3–4 marks (one mark per good, specific point).

Easy marks. Calculating materiality in part (a). There is one mark just for drawing an overall conclusion to the notes in part (a), which you should get (make sure you include a subheading, 'conclusion', signal to the marker that you want this mark!).

ACCA examining team's comments. In answers to requirement (a)(i), most candidates recognised the loss-making nature of the contract described in the scenario, and correctly calculated the loss, and the majority then went on to discuss the risk of material misstatement that profit would be overstated if the loss were not recognised in full. However, having gone this far, many candidates then went on to consider other potential accounting issues and different financial reporting standards, leading to confused answers and often contradictory advice. No conclusion was provided and the contradictory comments clearly detract from the overall quality of an answer. Some candidates simply could not decide which financial reporting standard was most relevant. **It was common to see answers of this type stretching over many pages, when all that was needed was a succinct discussion of the loss-making contract, which could be done in a few short paragraphs. This wasted time and meant answers were overly long and largely irrelevant.**

On the whole answers to requirement (b)(i) were satisfactory. However, answers to (b)(ii) were often unsatisfactory, as many candidates ignored the question requirement and just provided a rote-learnt list of procedures to identify related party transactions in general, not focusing on the transactions in the scenario. Even those that did think about the scenario provided inadequate procedures – eg 'check the lease is market rate' – but not explaining how the auditor should do this.

Marking scheme

Marks

(a) (i) **Loss-making contract**
Generally 1 mark per comment on matter/risk of material misstatement:
- Identify loss-making status of contract (only ½ mark if no calculation of loss)
- Per IFRS 15 and IAS 37 the irrecoverable costs are recognised as a liability
- Risk of MM is overstated profit if loss not recognised
- Penalties for late completion may exist
- Risk of MM is overstated profit/understated liabilities if not recognised
- Incentive for loss not to be recognised due to planned sale of company
- Consideration of materiality

Held for sale disposal group
Generally 1 mark per comment on matter/risk of material misstatement:
- Identify 'Treasured Homes' as a disposal group per IFRS 5
- Explain why meets criteria for treatment as a disposal group
- Assets should be presented separately and tested for impairment
- Risk of material misstatement is overvalued assets and incorrect presentation
- Identify 'Treasured Homes' as a discontinued operation per IFRS 5

- Risk of material misstatement is incorrect presentation of its results in SoPLOCI and SoCF
- Consideration of materiality

Maximum   8

(ii) **Audit procedures to be performed**
Generally 1 mark per evidence point:
Loss-making contract
- Obtain budget and recompute anticipated loss
- Agree fixed price to contract
- Review contract for late-completion penalty clauses
- Review internal architect's report
- Inspect quote or other supporting document for amount of additional costs
- Consider use of an expert regarding amount of additional costs
- Discuss estimate of additional costs and timeframe with contractors
- Review cash flow forecasts

Held for sale disposal group
- Review board minutes to confirm management's commitment to the sale
- Inspect any documents relevant to the negotiation
- Inspect 20X2 budgets to confirm 'Treasured Homes' not included
- Confirm disclosures made according to IFRS 5 in draft financial statements

Maximum   8

(iii) **Critical evaluation of planning**
Up to 2 marks for each point evaluated from ideas list, plus 1 mark for overall conclusion:
- Insufficient analytical review performed
- No systems work or controls evaluation carried out
- Inadequate assessment and documentation of business risk
- Inappropriate to plan to use client employee as auditor's expert
- Ethical threats raised by offer to use office space
- Conclusion (1 mark)

Maximum   11

(b) (i) **Limitation on identification of related party relationships and transaction**
1 mark each point explained:
- Management not aware of relationship or transaction
- Subjectivity/complexity in deciding on who or what is a related party
- Deliberate concealment of relationship or transaction
- Accounting systems do not specifically identify related party transactions
- Transactions at nil value especially hard to detect

Marks

(ii) **Audit procedures**

1 mark each specific procedure:
- Review invoices/inspect cash book to confirm amount of cash paid
- Review payables ledger to confirm any amount outstanding
- Consider if transaction is arm's length by comparing value to non-related party transaction
- Discuss/obtain written representation on details of informal lease
- Review any written documentation that may exist regarding the lease
- Review disclosures on draft financial statements

| | Maximum | 8 |

Professional marks for the overall presentation of the briefing notes, and the clarity of the explanation and assessment provided   4

Total   **39**

(a) **Briefing notes**

To: Audit partner

From: Audit manager

Re: Bill Co audit plan

Introduction

The following notes explain the risks of material misstatement (MM) and matters to consider, in relation to Bill Co, and then recommend audit procedures to address these risks.

The notes then evaluate the planning done so far, including ethical matters, before recommending actions to perform.

(i) **First issue (Bridgetown)**

Matters to consider

Contract loss

This contract has become onerous, as it contains unavoidable costs which exceed the economic benefits expected to be received under it.

In accordance with IFRS 15 *Revenue from Contracts with Customers*, costs should only be recognised as an asset if they are expected to be recovered. In this case, of the additional expected costs of $350,000, $200,000 will be recovered based on contract revenue, but $150,000 will not be.

The recoverable portion of the costs ($200,000) will continue to be recognised as an asset.

However, the irrecoverable portion of the costs must be provided for in line with IAS 37 *Provisions, Contingent Liabilities and Contingent Assets*. This will reduce profit before tax and total assets by $150,000.

At 6% of profit before tax, the irrecoverable costs are material to forecast profit before tax.

BPP
LEARNING

Possible penalties

The contract will be completed two months late. This may result in penalties being incurred by Bill Co for late completion. These should be provided for in accordance with IAS 37.

Possible management bias

Alex and Ben plan to sell the company in the next two years, and therefore may seek to increase its value.

Risks of MM

Provision

There is a risk that profit is overstated by up to $200,000 if the onerous costs are not recognised in profit or loss. There is also a risk that the expected costs of $350,000 have not been recognised in the financial statements at all.

Possible penalties

The risk is that if there are indeed penalties and no provision has been made, then liabilities are understated and profits are overstated by the amount of those penalties.

Possible bias

The risk is that a provision, or a loss on a contract, are not recognised in an effort to increase Bill Co's valuation.

Second issue (Treasured Homes)

Matters to consider

Discontinued operations

The sale of the division appears to be a discontinued operation in accordance with IFRS 5 *Non-current Assets Held for Sale and Discontinued Operations*. It meets IFRS 5's requirements as it is an independent business division which can be distinguished operationally and for financial reporting purposes.

The division's results for the year should be presented separately as a discontinued operation on the face of the statement of profit or loss. Comparatives will also need to be restated.

Disposal group

The assets of the division are a disposal group per IFRS 5.

At 8% of total assets, the amount is material to the forecast statement of financial position.

IFRS 5 requires that a disposal group is recognised as held for sale where the assets are available for sale in their present condition, the sale is highly probable, and these conditions are met before the year end.

This is the case here, as a buyer is interested in the division and a sale is expected in August 20X1, two months after the year end.

In accordance with IFRS 5, the assets in the disposal group should be measured at the lower of their carrying amount and their fair value less costs to sell, and should no longer be depreciated. They should be presented separately in the statement of financial position.

Risks of MM

Discontinued operation

The risk is that the division's results are not presented separately in the statement of profit or loss, in line with IFRS 5, or that comparatives are not restated.

Disposal group

The risk is of non-compliance with IFRS 5 if the disposal group is not presented separately in the FS, and is not measured in accordance with IFRS 5. Measurement would be incorrect if depreciation is charged, for instance.

(ii) **First issue – audit procedures**

Inspect basis of estimate for the $350,000 extra costs, eg architect's report.

- Discuss $350,000 estimate with employees to assess if it is reasonable.

- Discuss two-month additional timeframe with employees to assess if it is reasonable.

- Recalculate extent to which costs are expected to be recoverable ($150,000 are onerous).

- Inspect the signed contract to verify the price and to check if there are any penalties for late completion.

- Review financial statements for provisions in relation to penalties.

- Consider using an auditor's expert to estimate the contract costs to completion.

Second issue – audit procedures

- Review board minutes for evidence that the sale is imminent.

- Obtain calculations of the disposal group's fair value less costs to sell, and of its carrying amount.

- Obtain evidence of the estimated fair value, possibly by engaging an auditor's expert valuer.

- Confirm that results of the discontinued operation are presented separately in the statement of profit or loss.

- Confirm that the disposal group is presented as assets held for sale in the statement of financial position.

(iii) **Critical evaluation of audit plan**

The notes provided indicate that the audit has not been planned in line with the requirements of ISAs.

Ethics – long association

The IESBA *Code of Ethics* states that a familiarity threat to independence may arise with long-standing audit clients. This appears to be the case here, as some analytical procedures have not been performed because of past experience with the client. It may be necessary to implement further safeguards to reduce this threat to an acceptable level.

Analytical procedures

The need for analytical procedures must be reviewed each year in line with the requirements of ISAs, including the need for procedures not done in previous years.

No procedures have been performed on the statement of financial position, on the basis that there did not appear to be any significant movements. This is not an adequate reason for not performing more detailed procedures, but is in fact just an inadequate procedure itself. It may be the case that, given other changes in the accounts, movement would be expected in assets and liabilities, so 'no movement' is not in itself a sign that nothing is wrong.

Forecast accounts

Forecast accounts have been placed on file, but it is not clear if any procedures have been performed using them, for example to assess the adequacy of the going concern basis. Discussions have been held with management, but it is not clear whether the forecasts have been assessed in the light of these discussions.

Controls testing

Management said there were no changes to internal controls in the year, but no walkthrough tests were performed to verify whether this is in fact the case. Walkthrough tests should have been performed to ascertain whether controls are operating as described.

The auditor is effectively relying on previous years' audit work which showed that the long-standing controls were adequate in the past. However, they may no longer be suitable. ISA 315 *Identifying and Assessing the Risks of Material Misstatement through Understanding the Entity and its Environment* requires that the auditor obtain an understanding of the entity's internal controls. This has not been done here.

Business risk

Business risk has been assessed as low on the basis that all divisions are 'operating normally'. However, ISA 315 requires that the auditor obtain evidence of the specific objectives and strategies of the entity, and of its performance in relation to these objectives. This does not appear to have been done.

ISA 315 states that business risks need to be identified in relation to financial reporting. Without assessing specific business risks, this cannot be done.

Moreover, past performance is not necessarily a guide to the future. No assessment appears to have been done of the business environment and of the risks it may pose to the entity.

Risk assessment (material misstatement)

ISA 315 requires that the risks of material misstatement be assessed both at the financial statement level and at the assertion level. No risk assessment appears to have been carried out at the assertion level.

Property valuation/stage of completion

It is right that an expert be engaged to provide evidence regarding property valuations. In previous years this was an auditor's expert, this year it is a management's expert.

ISA 500 *Audit Evidence* requires that the competence, capabilities and objectivity of the management's be assessed. This has not been done here.

The architect is newly qualified, which may cast doubt over whether she has sufficient experience and competence to do this work.

The architect is employed by the entity, which according to ISA 500 is an indication that she may be less objective than if she were engaged for a specific task. Furthermore, there is a risk that the business owners, who intend to sell the business, may seek to inflate the valuations in order to achieve a better price on the sale.

Therefore the architect's work cannot be relied upon for the purposes of the audit. An auditor's expert should be engaged to provide independent valuations.

Office space rent

The IESBA *Code of Ethics* states that gifts and hospitality may create a self-interest threat to independence. Suki & Co must assess the nature, value and intent of the offer.

The fact that the rent is of a nominal amount means that the effective value of the gift is likely to be substantial.

The intent is not clear, but it could be considered a bribe, given in the hope of obtaining an unmodified audit opinion before the sale of the company.

The offer should therefore be declined.

Conclusion

The audit has been inadequately planned, and fails to meet the requirements of ISAs. There are also a number of ethical threats to Suki & Co's independence.

Actions include possible further training for Tara Lafayette, and a reconsideration of the firm's ethical safeguards in place regarding long association with audit clients.

(b)   (i)   Related party transactions (RPTs) are difficult to identify because management may not themselves be fully aware of what constitutes a RPT, and may not therefore disclose all RPTs to the auditor.

IAS 24 *Related Party Disclosures* requires a degree of subjective judgement in deciding who is a related party. This makes it less likely that management will be able to prepare adequate disclosures in line with IAS 24.

Management may deliberately attempt to conceal RPTs, for example because they are being used to manipulate the financial statements. This is particularly difficult for the auditor to address, as knowledge of related parties must come largely from representations made by management.

Finally, accounting systems are not set up to identify RPTs separately from transactions in the normal course of business.

(ii)   Audit procedures include:

- Review invoices from Lantern Co to verify the amount of the expense. Confirm cash payments to the cash book
- Inspect Lantern Co's trade payables account to confirm any amount outstanding at the year end
- Compare the cost of refurbishment carried out by Lantern Co to the cost of refurbishment carried out by other suppliers, to determine if the transaction is at arm's length
- Discuss the informal lease with management, and obtain a written representation regarding the nature of the arrangement, and whether any amount is payable to Bill Co
- Confirm through enquiry with management the date the lease arrangement commenced, and the expected period of the lease
- Enquire if any written documentation exists regarding the lease arrangement – if so, review and place on file
- Review disclosures made (if any) regarding these transactions in the draft financial statements

27 Parker

Top tips. In part (a) you needed to stick to the material in the question. There are no marks available for pre-learned knowledge, so do not be tempted to recite information, eg on obtaining an understanding of the entity and its environment, or on the theory of audit risk.

Try to strike a balance between words and numbers. Marks for calculations tend to be capped, so if you spend almost all your time performing calculations then you are unlikely to pass the question. The BPP answer given here, for example, contains more calculations than would be needed to reach the cap.

Equally, it is important that you do not go to the other extreme and perform too few calculations, as these are some of the easiest marks on the whole exam. Note that marks are available for:

- Trends, eg that revenue has decreased by 8.2%. This would normally get a half mark.

- Ratios, eg that gross profit has fallen from 31.8% to 27.2%. You must calculate the ratio for both years (so that a comparison can be made), which normally gets a mark.

Any adjustments or additional calculations you can make will tend to look good to the marker and will score well, eg adjusting cost of sales for the effect of reclassifying the provision.

In terms of organising your answer, little advantage is to be gained from dividing your answer into the different components of audit risk. You are advised to stick to picking risks out of the information in the question and then evaluating them.

You should note that the audit engagement has already been accepted, so there are no marks available for matters in relation to client acceptance (eg contacting the previous auditors). Again, you are advised to stick to evaluating the audit risks that are present in the scenario.

Finally, there are plenty of marks available for explaining additional information that is needed. You can gain an easy mark on most of the audit risks by simply thinking of some relevant information that would be helpful. However, you must take care not to start recommending audit procedures here, as that is not what is asked for.

In part (b), the main pitfall would be discussing ethical issues from throughout the scenario. What is being asked for here are issues of professional ethics for the auditor, ie relating to auditor independence. No marks are available for discussing whether Parker's management is ethical, or whether the human resources arrangements might give rise to the possibility of ethical failings or fraud.

Easy marks. Some of the four professional marks were easy to come by. To get them you must include a header, an introduction and a conclusion, and make sure that your answer is written clearly and concisely, without waffling!

Calculations in part (a) are easy marks, as long as you perform them quickly and accurately.

ACCA examining team's comments. This question scenario was based on Parker Co, a new audit client, and information was provided in the form of extracts from financial statements, and notes from a meeting with the company's finance director. The notes covered matters including a brief business review, financing arrangements, internal control issues, and future plans for expansion.

As this style of question appears regularly it was no surprise that most candidates seemed well prepared for a question on audit planning, and there were some detailed and well-focused answers. However, there were some common problems seen in candidates' answers, which will be discussed below.

Requirement (a) was for 24 marks and asked candidates to perform analytical procedures and evaluate audit risks to be considered in planning the audit of Parker Co, and also to identify and explain additional information relevant to the evaluation. Looking first at the audit risk evaluation, this was generally reasonably well attempted, with most answers working through the information given in the scenario to identify and then discuss the audit risks. Almost all answers spotted the going concern risk facing Parker Co, and could evaluate it appropriately. The majority of answers also included commentary on the internal control weakness in payroll, and a discussion of several risks of material misstatement including classification and measurement of a provision, a revaluation of properties, and the classification of leases. Each of these had been clearly signposted in the scenario as issues related to audit planning.

Fewer candidates picked up on the less obvious audit risks. This was often because analytical review had not been conducted, or it had been done but then not used to help identify audit risks. One of the purposes of performing analytical review is to help the auditor to identify potential risks of material misstatement, and there were many audit risks that could have been identified in this scenario from properly prepared analytical review. For example the increase in inventory days indicates potentially obsolete inventory which may be overvalued and the deterioration in margins and interest cover add weight to the company's going concern problems. It is therefore important that when asked to perform analytical review that candidates do not just calculate trends and ratios but go on to assess them as part of the evaluation of audit risk. Calculating trends and ratios and then leaving them unused in the written part of the answer is poor exam technique and to some extent a waste of time.

Some candidates did no analytical review at all, which meant that as well as not picking up marks for relevant calculations, they also failed to achieve marks on identifying some audit risks. There were also many scripts that focused exclusively on calculating trends rather than ratios, which often resulted in less detailed answers. A significant number of answers included incorrect calculations, with gearing ratios and return on capital employed being the most commonly miscalculated.

Some of the problems noted above arise from lack of knowledge, others from poor exam technique. It is vital with this type of question to spend enough time reading the information provided, including the extracts from the financial statements, and to think about how the information gives rise to risk factors. It is obvious that when faced with an audit risk scenario, many candidates see a heading or word, for example 'brand' and write an answer point that is totally irrelevant to the scenario.

As well as asking for analytical review and audit risk evaluation, this requirement also asked candidates for additional information that would help in the evaluation. Most answers contained at least a few requests for additional information, often those relating to the evaluation of going concern risk, such as cash flow forecasts and market research findings. It was pleasing to see in many scripts a wide range of information requests, and candidates are encouraged to read the model answer to this requirement in preparing for AAA, to see examples of the kind of information requests included. Some answers however overlooked this part of the requirement, missing out on marks.

Other problems often seen in answers that scored less well on this requirement included the following:

- Long sections at the start of the answer describing the audit risk model in enormous depth

- Discussions of client acceptance matters such as the need for know your client procedures

- Detailed description of analytical procedure and its use in the audit (including at completion stage) with no application at all to the scenario

- Concentration on going concern risk and very little discussion of any other risk

- Repeating long sections of wording from the question requirement

The ethical issues in respect of confidentiality and conflicts of interest were particularly well discussed, as was the self-review threat associated with providing a non-audit service to Parker Co.

However, there were still many answers, which failed to recommend actions to be taken by the audit firm. Also, some answers tended to identify almost every possible threat without really explaining their relevance to the scenario. There also is an increasing trend for answers to consider ethical matters that have little, if anything, to do with the audit, and sometimes make little sense, for example whether it is 'ethical' for Parker Co's management to develop a new organic product range, or whether the company's management 'lacks integrity' for the company's going concern problems. Candidates are strongly advised to focus their answer on ethical threats directly related to the planning and performance of the audit.

Finally there were four professional marks available for this question, which were awarded for the structure of the answer, and for the clarity of explanations given and evaluation performed. Almost all candidates used a reasonable structure, with appropriate use of headings, and having an introduction. Fewer candidates provided a conclusion to their briefing notes. Though not essential, it is recommended that the calculations provided as part of analytical review are given in a separate section of the briefing notes, and then referred to in the main text, as this creates a well-structured answer. Again, not essential, but as part of exam technique candidates may want to consider having their requests for additional information as a separate part of the answer, presented in a clear list. Generally the presentation of answers was satisfactory, though as mentioned earlier in this report, a significant number of candidates have such illegible handwriting that it is very difficult to award many marks to the answer they have provided.

Marking scheme

Marks

(a) **Audit risk**

Audit risk evaluation, preliminary analytical review and additional information requests

In relation to the matters listed below:

Up to 2 marks for each audit risk/area from preliminary analytical review evaluated

1 mark for each ratio and comparative calculated (½ mark for a trend) to a maximum of 6 marks

1 mark for each additional information request to a maximum of 5 marks

- – Profitability
- – Liquidity
- – Solvency
- – Going concern
- – Provisions
- – Finance costs
- – Tax expense
- – Development costs
- – Property revaluation
- – Overtime payments control risk
- – New client detection risk
- – Opening balances

Maximum   24

Marks

(b) **Ethical matters**

Generally 1 mark per comment:
- Conflict of interest threat to objectivity
- Evaluate significance of threat and potential safeguards
- Contact both parties to request consent to act
- If consent not obtained cannot act for both parties
- Explain why corporate finance service creates advocacy threat
- Explain why corporate finance service creates self-review threat
- Identify safeguards (1 mark each)

Maximum   7

Professional marks for the overall presentation, structure and logical flow of the briefing notes, and for the clarity of the evaluation and explanations provided.

Maximum   4

Total   **35**

Briefing notes

To: Harry Shepherd

From: A Manager

Date: 3 June 20X3

Subject: Parker Co (Parker)

Introduction

The following briefing notes contain: the results of preliminary analytical procedures in relation to the Parker Co audit; an evaluation of the audit risks to be considered in planning the audit; and a discussion of ethical issues raised along with a recommendation of relevant actions for our firm.

Analytical procedures are contained in an Appendix at the end of these notes. All figures quoted are in $000.

(a) **Trading**

Revenue declined by 8.2%, but cost of sales only declined by 2.1%. The two are not in line, as would be expected. This points to a possible overstatement of cost of sales.

Indeed, cost of sales does appear to have been overstated by the misclassification of a provision there, which should have been classified within operating expenses. Removing the provision from cost of sales gives a decline of 6.4% (= (5,680 – 250)/5,800), which is closer to the 8.2% fall in revenue. This degree of discrepancy might be explained by eg not all costs of sales being fully variable.

This misclassification casts doubt over the efficacy of Parker's internal controls. This increase in control risk may mean that more substantive testing will be required.

The decline in revenue is dramatic, but if anything a steeper decline might be expected given Parker's price cutting and the economic conditions. Revenue may therefore be overstated.

It is possible that the price cuts may not have been properly reflected in reported revenue. Further information is needed here, such as a detailed breakdown of revenue by product line, including information about prices and volumes.

Profitability

Parker's profitability has dropped during the year, with the projected operating margin of 11.4% (20X2: 15.6%). This is worrying, but the projections do still show a profit. However, as

 BPP
LEARNING

indicated later in these notes, some adjustments may be required to the financial statements which would worsen the picture further. This gives rise to significant uncertainties over Parker's future profitability, and so also its going concern.

Fine provision

IAS 37 *Provisions, Contingent Liabilities and Contingent Assets* requires a provision to be recognised where:

- There is a present obligation as a result of a past event. The past event here was the inappropriate advertising

- An outflow of resources embodying economic benefits is at least probable

(IAS 37: para. 14)

The fact that Parker has recognised a provision at all implies that it thinks an outflow of resources is probable. Therefore it is likely that an obligation exists.

Further information is required here on why management has only recognised 250. We would need to examine the notice from the regulatory authority.

As this is a one-off event, IAS 37 requires measurement at the most likely amount, which in this case is likely to be the full 450. The required adjustment of 200 is material to net profit.

Finance costs

Finance costs have risen by 24%, presumably as a result of the increase in debt finance during the year.

Some initial calculations suggest that this may be understated. Interest-bearing debt at the year end is 13,585 (= 11,825 + 860 + 900), against which there is a finance cost of 155. This implies an interest rate of 1.1%, which is very low.

Further information needed would include:

- Bank loan agreement, with details of interest rates and any restrictive covenants imposed

- Bank overdraft agreement, with details of interest rate applicable to interest bearing balances

- Lease agreements, with details of interest rate implied in the lease

Taxation

The tax charge has fallen by 76.7%, and looks low. Indeed, the implied tax rate in 20X3 is 9.5% (= 70/735), which is significantly lower than the 25% (= 300/1,197) in 20X2.

The charge in the statement of profit or loss (70) does not agree with the liability (50), so there must be some misstatement. It seems likely that the tax computation has not yet been performed for the projected figures, and that adjustments will need to be made once this is done. The amount is material to profit for the year, at 10.5%.

Taken together with the misclassification of the provision to cost of sales, this is further evidence of poor internal controls over financial reporting at Parker.

Further information needed would be the ledger accounts for both tax figures, along with tax computations for the expense.

Revaluation

The revaluation of PPE has given rise to a revaluation reserve, but the statement of profit or loss and other comprehensive income does not include a revaluation gain, or indeed any other comprehensive income at all. This appears to be a material misstatement, which could be argued to be pervasive.

We will be able to place some reliance on the management's expert's valuation, in line with ISA 500 *Audit Evidence*. Further information is needed on the expert's qualifications and independence, as well as a copy of the report itself.

Given Parker's imperfect internal controls, it is possible that the depreciation may not have been remeasured at the point of the revaluation, leading to an understatement of expenses. Parker may have revalued assets selectively, whereas it is required to revalue all assets within a class. Finally, extensive disclosures are required in the notes to the financial statements, and there is a risk that these have not been made.

The main risk with the revaluation is that assets are overstated. Given Parker's poor profitability and liquidity position (see below), management has an incentive to overstate assets. There is therefore a risk of management bias in the revaluation.

Development costs

Further information is required regarding the costs capitalised, as there is a risk that Parker is capitalising internally generated brands, which is prohibited by IAS 38 *Intangible Assets*. This would be in line with the possible management bias discussed above.

IAS 38 requires only development costs to be capitalised, with research costs being expensed (IAS 38: para. 68). Given that operating expenses fell by 10.7% during year – more than the fall in revenue – it appears unlikely that significant research costs have been treated as expenses. Therefore it is very likely that assets are overstated.

Costs can only be capitalised if they meet specific criteria, such as the probability of future economic benefits flowing to Parker, and that costs can be measured reliably. The first criterion here is problematic, since it depends on the claim that there is a market for the product, and that Parker has the financial resources to complete the development.

It is possible that Parker's new range will arrive on the market too late to compete effectively with the competitor's new range. Further information is required, such as details of market research conducted.

Parker is also currently in dire straits when it comes to liquidity (see below), which raises doubts over its ability to complete the development.

At 2,250, the amounts involved here are highly material. If only half of these were expensed, it would completely wipe out profit for the year, from a profit of 625 to a loss of 500.

Leases

New assets were acquired under leases. There is a risk that these have been wrongly classified, or that any right-of-use assets have not been recognised at cost.

Liquidity

The bank balance of 900 at the end of 20X2 is projected to have become an overdraft of 1,000 by the end of 20X3. The current ratio has nearly halved, from 1.8 to 0.96, meaning that current assets do not cover current liabilities.

Receivables days have risen from 34 to 42. This could be down to poor credit control; we already know that Parker's internal controls may not be entirely reliable. Alternatively, it could indicate the presence of irrecoverable receivables not provided for, which would further reduce assets and profit were provision to be made for them.

Inventory days have risen from 136 to 167. This could be a sign of inventory obsolescence; this is particularly likely given the competition that Parker is facing. If net realisable value is lower than inventory cost then write-downs may be required, which would affect both assets and profit.

Payables days have risen from 63 to 86. This is a sign of cash flow difficulties, with Parker struggling to pay its suppliers (a feat made difficult by its slow debt collection from its customers). This could damage supplier relationships, leading to interest charges or lost discounts, or to the breakdown of relationships. This could make trading very difficult for Parker.

Parker is currently dependent on its overdraft for trading. If the overdraft were withdrawn, then it would be virtually impossible for it to continue as a going concern. Further information is needed here regarding the overdraft limit and the date of any reviews.

Solvency

Interest cover has fallen from 10.6 to 5.7. The fall is worrying, although 5.7 is not a terrible figure. That being said, given that finance costs may be understated, the figure could become worse once appropriate adjustments are made.

Gearing has risen from 0.8 to 1. This is high, and may make it harder to raise finance in future. Given Parker's liquidity problems, it appears unlikely that the bank would want to renew the bank loan again, which would again affect going concern. Further information is needed regarding the terms of the loan, and in particular the repayment date.

Further information is needed on Parker's preference shares, as these may be redeemable. If they were to be redeemed then Parker may not be able to make the required payment or issue new shares, which could hit going concern.

Going concern

Parker's plan to get itself out of its current difficulties appears to be twofold: increased sales from the new product in development, and synergies from the acquisition of Beauty Boost Co.

More information is needed regarding the projected sales from the new product. Cash flow forecasts in particular are crucial, as at present it appears that Parker is haemorrhaging cash and needs to start receiving substantial inflows very soon.

The proposed acquisition of Beauty Boost Co may indeed provide some synergies, but it appears unlikely that any savings would be significant enough to restore profitability. More likely, it would leave Parker with still more debt, which it would then have to find more cash to service.

In any event, in view of its solvency position it appears unlikely that Parker will be able to raise sufficient funds to make the acquisition.

There is a risk that Parker will not make sufficient disclosure of the doubts that exist over going concern. It is also possible that the financial statements will have to be prepared under an alternative assumption to going concern – eg the liquidation basis – but this would only become clear once audit evidence has been obtained in this area.

Control risk

As discussed, several factors point to high control risk on this engagement. In addition, Parker's internal auditors found deficiencies in the controls over payroll, which may mean that more substantive testing will need to be performed. The change during the year from HR to the finance department represents a risk, as procedures may not have been followed properly during the handover. Moreover, there is a risk of a lack of segregation of duties now that payments are handled by the finance department alone.

New client

As Parker is a new client, detection risk is increased as we will lack cumulative understanding of the business and its environment. We must therefore focus particularly on developing this understanding at the planning stage.

Appendix

	20X3		20X2
Revenue decrease		8.2%	
Cost of sales decrease		2.1%	
Finance costs increase		24%	
Taxation decrease		76.7%	
Operating expenses decrease		10.7%	
Operating profit margin	11.4%		15.6%
Current ratio	0.96		1.8
Interest cover (finance costs / operating profit)	5.7		10.6
Gearing (non-current liabilities / equity)	1		0.8
Receivables days	42		34
Inventory days	167		136
Payables days	86		63

(b) **Ethical issues**

Potential acquisition – conflict of interest

There is a potential conflict of interest here, as Hound & Co may effectively be advising both sides of a potential acquisition negotiation. The IESBA *Code of Ethics* requires safeguards to be applied here. Crucially, both parties should be informed of the potential conflict, and should be asked for their consent to the arrangement. If either party declines, then the engagement should not be accepted.

If both say yes, then safeguards could include:

* Separate engagement teams, separated by information barriers
* Confidentiality agreements signed by employees and partners of Hound & Co

Potential acquisition – self-review

There is also a self-review threat in relation to the due diligence, as we will be performing procedures on financial statements which we have already audited. Safeguards here would include:

* Separate engagement teams

* Pre-issuance review of the non-audit service report by an independent professional accountant

Financing – advocacy

Providing advice on financing raises an advocacy threat if Hound & Co is asked to represent Parker's interests, for example to any potential lenders. Such a role should therefore be avoided.

Financing – management role

There is a risk that we could be seen as playing (or could actually play) a management role. This would be the case if eg we recommended a particular form of finance to Parker. The threat can be mitigated by making it clear that any decisions rest with Parker's management, and that we are providing them with advice only.

Financing – self-review

There may be a self-review threat here if the financial statements come to include amounts in relation to any financing obtained using our advice. Possible safeguards include:

- Using a separate corporate finance team from the audit team

- Pre-issuance review of the corporate finance service, and of the relevant area of the financial statements, by an independent professional accountant

If safeguards would not reduce the threat to an acceptable level, the engagement should not be accepted.

Conclusion

From the above it can be concluded that the audit of Parker Co is of relatively high risk overall, with particular risks in relation to overstatement of assets, understatement of expenses, and the company's ongoing solvency and liquidity problems.

Several important ethical issues are raised by Parker's request, and these must be considered carefully before any engagements are accepted.

28 Stow

> **Workbook references.** Chapters 6, 7 and 9.
>
> **Top tips.** Be sure to get the **professional marks** here, for which you needed to: write out the heading for 'briefing notes'; write an introduction; set out your answer clearly using sub-headings; and write a conclusion. Your introduction and conclusion do not need to be too long – make sure you write the heading, and try to write a brief paragraph of about three or four lines. Make sure you get the marks, but don't spend too much time on it!
>
> Part (a) was on the risks of material misstatement, and therefore **excludes detection risks** – there are no marks available for risks that arise from difficulties in auditing the group, such as the need to obtain an understanding of the newly-acquired subsidiary.
>
> As ever you are advised not to spend time making **general points** about group audits, as many candidates in the real exam will have done. Almost everything you say needs to be based on the scenario, and if it isn't then you're in danger of spending time writing something which will get no marks.
>
> It is often the case in AAA that it's relatively easy to score marks for specifying **further information** – requirement (a)(ii) here. Be specific – state what information you need, and why you need it (you can think of it as a ½ mark for each). It is also important to bear in mind here that the requirement is **not** asking for audit **procedures**, so there are no marks for information that would be needed to perform procedures. What you need to think of are pieces of information that would be useful at the **planning** stage of the audit – things like last year's audited financial statements for Zennor, which we wouldn't have because we didn't audit them. Information on, for example, exchange rate fluctuations would only be useful for conducting procedures on the foreign subsidiary, and would not be useful at the planning stage.
>
> It is important that you calculate **materiality**, as you are asked to do so by requirement (a)(i). It is best to do this separately with each item (eg 'goodwill is 2.4% of total assets and is therefore material'), rather than calculating the general materiality thresholds at the start of the question. There are no marks for just saying that something is material without performing a calculation (so if you put thresholds at the start of the question, you would still have to calculate the materiality of each item in order to get the marks). It's also important that you use the **appropriate benchmark** – total assets for statement of financial position items, and profit for items affecting the statement of profit or loss. Materiality for inventory should be calculated using total assets, with the materiality of any impairment being calculated using profit before tax. Likewise goodwill.

Take care in your answer to part (a) not to spend time writing about business risks, eg the risk to the group of exposure to foreign exchange rate fluctuations. Unless you develop this into an audit risk (and this may be difficult to do) you won't get any marks for it at all.

A general point of exam technique that is relevant to this question is to read the question carefully. A careful reading shows that 'we' (ie Compton & Co) are auditing both the group and its components. This means that you can recite pre-learned knowledge about group and component auditors from ISA 600.

Part (b) on procedures for the Broadway disposal should not have been too problematic. This is another area where you can score well (like 'further information'), as long as you state the **procedure**, and then state **why** you are performing it.

In part (c), some candidates may have been tempted to write a lot about internal audit and the steps to take before deciding whether to rely on internal audit work. While this is valid and relevant, it is important not to go over your time allocation on this part. Finally, note that whenever an 'ethical issue' is raised in AAA, this is almost always referring to the auditor's ethics – whether Marta or the internal auditors are acting ethically is not really the issue.

Easy marks. The marks for further information are simple marks, as are those for audit procedures on the disposal of the subsidiary. Not to mention the professional marks.

Marking scheme

Marks

(a) (i) **Risks of material misstatement, materiality and further information requests**
Generally up to 1½ marks for each risk identified and explained (to a maximum of 4 marks for identification only):

Zennor Co
- High fashion items/high staff turnover in design team
- Treatment of exchange gains and losses arising on retranslation
- Goodwill not measured correctly at initial recognition
- Goodwill not tested for impairment before the year end
- Time apportionment of Zennor Co's income and expenses not correct
- Incomplete or inadequate disclosure
- Cancellation of intercompany balances
- Disclosure of related party transactions
- Completeness of inventory

Broadway Co
- Derecognition of assets, liabilities and goodwill
- Time apportionment of profit up to date of disposal
- Calculation of profit on disposal
- Classification and presentation regarding the disposal
- Treatment in parent company financial statements
- Accrual for tax payable

Generally 1 mark for each of the following calculations/comments on materiality:
- Appropriate retranslation of Zennor Co figures into $
- Calculate materiality of Zennor Co to the Group
- Determine if Zennor Co is a significant component of the Group

| | – Calculate materiality of goodwill arising on acquisition |
| | – Calculate materiality of inventory in transit to the Group |

Maximum   12

(ii) **1 mark for each piece of additional information identified:**
- Prior years' financial statements and auditor's reports
- Minutes of meetings where the acquisition was discussed
- Business background, eg from the company's website or trade journals
- Copies of systems documentation from the internal audit team
- Confirmation from Zennor Co's previous auditor of any matters that should be brought to our attention
- Projected financial statements for the year to 31 December 20X3
- A copy of the due diligence report
- Copies of prior year tax computations

Maximum   4

(b) **Audit procedures**

Generally 1 mark for each well described audit procedure:

- Confirm the value of assets and liabilities which have been derecognised from the Group

- Confirm goodwill that exists is derecognised from the Group

- Confirm that the Stow Group is no longer listed as a shareholder of the company

- Obtain legal documentation in relation to the disposal to confirm the date of the disposal and confirm that Broadway Co's profit has been consolidated up to this date only

- Agree or reconcile the profit recognised in the Group financial statements to Broadway Co's individual accounts as at 1 September 20X3

- Analytical procedures to gain assurance that the amount of profit consolidated from 1 January to 1 September 20X3 appears reasonable

- Reperform management's calculation of profit on disposal in the Group financial statements

- Agree proceeds received to legal documentation/cash book/bank statements

- Confirm that no deferred or contingent consideration is receivable in the future

- Confirm that the profit on disposal is correctly disclosed as part of profit for the year

- Confirm that all necessary notes are given in the Group financial statements

- Obtain the parent company's statement of financial position to confirm that the cost of investment is derecognised

- Reperform the calculation of profit on disposal in the individual financial statements

Marks

- Reconcile the profit on disposal recognised in the parent company's financial statements to the profit recognised in the Group financial statements

- Obtain management's estimate of the tax due on disposal, reperform the calculation and confirm the amount is properly accrued at parent company and at Group level

- Review any correspondence with tax authorities regarding the tax due

- If the tax is paid in the subsequent events period, agree to cash book and bank statement

Maximum   8

(c) **Reliance on internal audit**

Generally 1 mark for each discussion point:
- Impact on audit strategy, eg reliance on controls
- Impact on audit planning, eg systems documentation/business understanding
- Specific work can be performed, eg inventory counts
- Could lead to significant reduction in audit costs, eg travel costs can be avoided
- Need to evaluate how much reliance can be placed (objectivity, competence, quality control, etc) – up to 3 marks
- Reliance will impact on Group audit as well as on individual audit
- Pressure on fee is an intimidation threat
- Fee unlikely to be maintained given the change in Group structure

Maximum   7

Professional marks to be awarded for:
- Use of headings
- Introduction
- Logical flow/presentation
- Conclusion

Maximum   <u>4</u>

Total   <u>**35**</u>

Briefing notes

To: Audit Partner

From: Audit Manager

Subject: Stow Group planning, year end 31/12/X3

Introduction

Please find below an assessment of the risks of material misstatement in the Stow Group ('Stow') audit, indicating any further information needed, the principal audit procedures for the disposal of Broadway Co ('Broadway') and a discussion of Martha's suggestion and its effect on our audit.

(a) **Risks of material misstatement – Zennor**

Zennor's profit translates to $22.5m, which is 11.3% of Group profit and is thus material. Zennor's total assets translate to $200m, which is 8% of Group total assets and is also material. Zennor may therefore be adjudged a significant component of the Stow audit as it is financially significant to it.

BPP
LEARNING

As these are projected figures, materiality will be recalculated at the year end on the basis of Zennor's actual figures and the closing exchange rate at that date.

Foreign exchange

IAS 21 *The Effects of Changes in Foreign Exchange Rates* requires Zennor's assets and liabilities to be translated at the closing rate on 31/12/20X3, and income and expenses to be translated at the actual rates on the dates of the transactions. There is a risk that the wrong rates are used, which could over- or understate total assets and profit.

IAS 21 also requires any exchange gain or loss to be recognised within profit or loss (P/L). Calculations here can be complex, so there is a risk of profit being misstated if this is not done correctly. Exchange gains or losses on translating a subsidiary's balances are recognised in other comprehensive income (OCI), so there is a risk of this not being done and thus of misclassification of these sums between P/L and OCI.

Goodwill on acquisition must also be retranslated at the year end, and there is a risk of this not being done.

Inventory

Inventory in transit is likely to be in the region of $58m at the year end. This is 2.3% of total assets and is material.

The group's controls need to be robust here in order to mitigate the risk of inventory being recorded incorrectly. Given that Zennor is newly acquired, there is a risk that this may not be the case. The risk may, however, be lessened by the presence of an internal audit department in Zennor.

Revenue and inventory

It is important that the group is clear about who owns the inventory at each point. There are many possible types of error here, which could lead to misstatements in both the group financial statements and those of the individual companies. For instance, Stow might consider the inventory as sold and thus recognise revenue that would need to be eliminated on consolidation. In its individual accounts, this would be considered consignment inventory and should not be recognised in revenue. If Zennor did not yet recognise the inventory, then it would be entirely missing from the group accounts, understating inventory and overstating revenue.

Alternatively, both Stow and Zennor could recognise the cars in inventory, leading to an overstatement of group inventory if this double-counting were not eliminated on consolidation.

Unrealised profit

If the inventory was recognised as sold to Zennor at a mark-up, then a provision for unrealised profit must be included. The risk is that it is omitted, which would overstate both inventory and profit.

Related parties

The intra-group transactions fall within the scope of IAS 24 *Related Party Disclosures*, and must be disclosed in the individual financial statements of the group companies. There is a risk that if disclosure is inadequate, this will be a material misstatement.

Goodwill

Goodwill of $60m is 2.4% of total assets and is material.

There are several risks here. First, calculating goodwill requires estimating the fair values of Zennor's assets and liabilities. This may involve judgement and can be complex, particularly when dealing with assets that are hard to value.

Second, it is possible that some assets and liabilities may have been missed, leading to overstatement of goodwill.

Third, the fair value of the consideration transferred could include contingent consideration, which may be complex to calculate. Improper measurement here could under- or overstate goodwill.

Fourth, goodwill must be reviewed annually for impairment whether or not there are indicators of impairment. If this has not been done then goodwill could be impaired, overstating assets and profit.

It is possible that Stow's management has valued Zennor's net assets on the basis of the due diligence review. There is a risk that the work of this management's expert is not suitable for this purpose, leading to misstatements in both net assets and goodwill.

Mid-year acquisition

Zennor was acquired on 1 February 20X3, one month into the year. There is a risk that Zennor's 20X2 year-end reserves are mistaken for its pre-acquisition reserves in the group accounts, which would misstate group reserves.

There is also a risk of the full year of Zennor's statement of profit or loss being consolidated, rather than 11 months. Assuming profits accrue evenly, this would result in a misstatement of $22.5m \times {}^1/_{12} = \$1.875m$ in the group accounts. At 0.9% of group profit, this would be immaterial.

Disclosure

IFRS 3 *Business Combinations* requires extensive disclosures, eg in relation to goodwill. There is a risk that these are not included in the group financial statements.

Opening balances

Zennor's prior year financial statements may not have been audited, or were audited by another auditor. There may therefore be misstatements in this year's opening balances which could materially misstate both this year's financial statements (eg the statement of financial position) and the corresponding figures.

Risks of material misstatement – Broadway

Profit on disposal

The profit on disposal of $25m is 12.5% of group profit and is material.

There is a risk that this has not been calculated correctly. For example, if a contingent consideration is involved then its miscalculation could affect the figure for profit on disposal.

Net assets

Broadway's net assets were $155m ($180m proceeds less $25m profit), which is material at 6.2% of assets.

There is a risk that not all of these balances were derecognised from the group accounts. This could misstate profit on disposal, or just the group financial statements.

Mid-year disposal

Broadway was disposed of on 1 September 20X3, meaning that for the first eight months of the year it was in the Stow group. Its results should therefore be consolidated for this period. The risk is that this has not been done correctly, overstating group profit.

Presentation of financial statements

There is a risk that the profit on disposal of $25m is not presented separately on face of the statement of profit or loss, as is required by IAS 1 *Presentation of Financial Statements* (IAS 1: para. 98).

BPP
LEARNING

It is possible that Broadway is a disposal group of assets and a discontinued operation in line with IFRS 5 *Non-Current Assets Held for Sale and Discontinued Operations*. In this case its net assets and liabilities should have be measured at fair value before disposal. If this was not done, then profit on disposal may be misstated.

Further, IFRS 5 requires Broadway's profit or loss after tax to be disclosed on the face of the statement of profit or loss as a discontinued operation, together with detailed disclosures in the notes. There is a risk of material misstatement if this is not done.

Further information

- Zennor's prior year financial statements and the auditor's report thereon, to determine approach to opening balances

- A copy of the local auditor's due diligence report on Zennor

- Confirmation from Zennor's previous auditor of any matters which should be brought to our attention

- Background on Zennor's business, eg from trade journals or company's website, to gain understanding of the entity

(b) **Procedures on Broadway disposal**

- Recalculate profit on disposal.

- Obtain legal documentation of sale and confirm proceeds of $180m.

- Agree proceeds of $180m to bank statement.

- Inspect legal documentation for evidence of contingent or deferred consideration.

- Review register of shareholders to confirm that Stow is no longer a shareholder of the company.

- Review group statement of profit or loss and confirm separate disclosure of profit on disposal.

- Review group statement of profit or loss and confirm disclosure of discontinued operation is in line with IFRS 5.

- Review group asset register to confirm that Broadway's assets are not included.

- Confirm that Broadway's results for first eight months of the year are consolidated by reconciling consolidated profits to Broadway's individual financial records.

- Perform substantive analytical procedures to confirm that profit consolidated for Broadway is in line with expectations based on prior periods.

(c) **Internal audit**

The immediate impact on planning is that we may be able to rely on the work of the internal auditors. This may improve the efficiency of our audit, allowing us to rely on Zennor's controls and so reduce the level of our substantive procedures. This would indeed work to reduce our audit fee by comparison with the situation in which Zennor did not have an internal audit function.

The prospective reduction in audit costs is increased still further by the fact that Zennor is located overseas. By using the work of internal audit, we would avoid the substantial travel costs which would otherwise be incurred.

It may be possible to rely directly on the work of internal audit, eg on tests of control they have performed. Moreover, we may be able to deepen our knowledge of Zennor's systems and controls, as well as its business in general, through contact with the internal audit team.

The decision about relying on internal audit should be based upon our assessment of its objectivity, competence and the systematic nature of its approach.

Internal audit would appear to be competent on the grounds of it being led by a qualified accountant. We do not have information about the team as a whole, however, and this would be required before reliance could be placed on their work. Further information would also be needed on the level of supervision, review and documentation of the work performed.

Internal audit's standing within the organisation appears to be enhanced by the fact that it reports to the board of directors. However, this is in reality something which may count against its objectivity, since it may thereby be subject to management's potentially damaging influence. The presence of an audit committee would have helped improve internal audit's independence from management, and might have given its work weight with those charged with governance.

Ethical issue

Marta's statement that we should rely on the work of internal audit is inappropriate, as this is rightfully the decision of the external auditor alone.

The group audit committee's request that the audit fee remain unchanged is inappropriate. Although its argument is not entirely false, it overlooks the additional work that is required to audit a new subsidiary, for instance obtaining an understanding of it at the planning stage. Work would also still be required on the disposed subsidiary's statement of profit or loss, the majority of which will be consolidated this year.

It is instructive to observe that the audit fee must be charged based on the work done, rather than on the grounds of a purely commercial bargain between the client and the audit firm. There is a risk that charging too low a fee may induce the auditor to reduce inappropriately the extent of work performed. The request therefore amounts to an intimidation threat to the principle of professional competence and due care.

Conclusion

The audit of the Stow Group contains a high overall risk of material misstatements as a result of the substantial group restructuring that took place during the year. Audit procedures must now be designed to detect any misstatements arising. These may involve relying on the work of Zennor's internal auditors, but it is important that the audit fee is substantial enough to allow sufficient audit procedures to be performed.

29 Cooper

Workbook references. Chapters 4, 7, 8 and 10.

Top tips. In part (a), one of the first things to notice when you read the scenario is that you are given figures from the draft accounts (profit and total assets). This means that you are likely to need to do something with these figures: calculate materiality. An easy way to start off your consideration of audit evidence is to decide whether the issue is material or not. However, you need to keep your wits about you and not just apply this method mechanically: this approach works well with part (a)(i), but with part (ii) we have a transaction with a director which is material by nature.

This question tests your knowledge of several accounting standards to a level that you should be comfortable with. Terminology is important with these questions, but what matters most is that your discussion of the accounting issues is concise and accurate.

Part (b) was not a difficult question, but it did require you to think a little bit if you were to get the marks relating to the prior period error and quality control.

Easy marks. Easy marks are available for calculating materiality, but this is an area that requires care to select the right figure.

Marking scheme

Marks

(a) (i) **Factories**

Generally up to 1½ marks for each matter and up to 1 mark for each evidence point explained:

Matters

- Materiality of factories to statement of financial position
- Government regulation is an indicator of impairment
- Management need to conduct an impairment review
- Implication for financial statements if factories are overstated

- Impairment review may reveal that factories are not overstated
- Research costs may not be capitalised
- No going concern issues this year but could be a longer term problem

Evidence

- A copy of the government regulation
- Agreement of the carrying value of the factories making this product to the non-current asset register and general ledger
- A review of forecast financial statements and management accounts to confirm the amount of revenue still being generated by the factories
- A copy of and assessment of management's impairment test
- A discussion with management regarding the potential future use of the factories, and whether the potential new product can be produced by them
- Confirmation that the research costs are included in operating expenses, and have not been capitalised

(ii)　**Related party transaction**

Generally up to 1½ marks for each matter and up to 1 mark for each evidence point explained:

Matters
- Hannah is a member of key management personnel and therefore a related party
- Auditor required to review documents and to consider whether transaction authorised
- Materiality should not be based solely on monetary calculations – it is material by nature
- The amount is outstanding and may need to be written off
- Disclosure needed in notes to financial statements
- Implications for auditor's report if appropriate disclosure not made

Evidence
- A review of the notes to the financial statements to confirm that sufficient disclosure has been made
- A copy of the invoice raised, and agreement to the receivables ledger
- A copy of any contract or other document pertaining to the sale of the car to Hannah, and a review of its terms and conditions
- A post year end review of the bank statement and cash books to confirm if the amount has been received subsequent to the year end
- Confirmation that the carrying value of $50,000 has been removed from the non-current asset register and general ledger
- Confirmation that profit or loss on disposal has been included in profit or loss

    – A review of board minutes to confirm the transaction was appropriately authorised

    – A written representation from management

Maximum   15

(b) **Prior year material misstatement**

Generally 1 mark per point explained:

– The prior year error is material at 6% of profit for 20X3
– A prior year adjustment is required
– If no adjustment is made the audit opinion for 20X4 will be modified
– The client must be informed of the error
– Potential for legal action against the audit firm
– Audit of 20X4 financial statements to include procedures on the prior year adjustment
– Quality control on prior year audit was lacking and should be investigated
– May be implications for firm-wide quality control procedures

Maximum   <u>5</u>

Total **<u>20</u>**

(a) (i) At 25% (= \$60m / \$240m) of total assets, the factories are material to the financial statements. At 12.5% (= (half of \$60m) / \$240m) of total assets, the factories manufacturing the chemical being phased out are also material.

The new regulation which will lead to the chemicals being phased out is a significant adverse change in the regulatory environment. In line with IAS 36 *Impairment of Assets*, this is an indicator that these factories may be impaired (IAS 36: para. 12).

Since there is an indicator of impairment, IAS 36 requires management to have conducted an impairment review of the assets. The factories should be measured at their recoverable amount, which is the higher of fair value less cost to sell and the assets' value in use.

The new regulation will lead to falling revenues and value in use. This could be less than the carrying amount of \$30m, in which case an impairment loss may need to be recognised. If this is the case then profit and assets are overstated.

It is stated that sales are still buoyant, though, so an impairment test may find that the assets are not impaired. If an alternative use can be found for the factories then they may not be impaired – however, the development of the new chemical may still be at too early a stage for this to be relied upon as a value in use.

It is also possible that even if value in use is less than \$30m (carrying amount), the fair value less costs to sell could be higher. This would mean that no impairment loss would be due.

The \$1m spent on a feasibility study would be research costs, and under IAS 38 *Intangible Assets* they should be treated as an expense in profit or loss.

Evidence includes:

• Copy of government regulation stating that the product made by the factories is to be phased out in 20X7

• Agreement of carrying value of factories making this product to non-current asset register and general ledger, at an amount of \$30 million

- Review of forecast financial statements and management accounts to confirm amount of revenue still being generated by the factories

- Copy of management's impairment test, including an assessment of the validity of any assumptions used and confirmation that they are in line with auditor's understanding of the business

- Discussion with management regarding the potential future use of the factories, and whether the potential new product can be produced by them

- Confirmation that the research costs are included in operating expenses, and have not been capitalised

(ii)   In line with IAS 24 *Related Party Disclosures*, this is a related party transaction because Hannah Osbourne is key management personnel.

ISA 550 *Related Parties* requires the auditor to evaluate whether these transactions have been accounted for and disclosed correctly. This is a significant transaction outside the normal course of business, so the auditor must inspect the underlying contracts to evaluate whether:

- There has been fraudulent financial reporting or misappropriation of assets; and
- The terms of the transaction are consistent with management's explanations.

Evidence should be obtained regarding the proper authorisation and approval of the transactions.

Judging materiality in relation to the financial statements, the value of the car is less than 1% of total assets and thus immaterial. However since this is a transaction with key management personnel – a director – this is material by nature and must therefore be disclosed. If disclosure is not made, or is not adequate, then this may result in a qualified auditor's opinion.

IAS 24 requires disclosure of the nature of the relationship and details of the transaction, including the amount, any terms and conditions, and that the balance is currently outstanding.

The invoice for $50,000 is still outstanding, and may not be recoverable. Management should be encouraged to make any required adjustments even though they are not material. The auditor should keep a schedule of any uncorrected misstatements as they may become material in aggregate with other misstatements.

Evidence:

- Review of the notes to the financial statements, to confirm that sufficient disclosure has been made to comply with IAS 24

- Copy of invoice raised, and agreement to the receivables ledger to confirm amount of $50,000 outstanding

- Copy of any contract or other document pertaining to the sale of the car, and a review of its terms and conditions, eg specification of when the amount is due for payment

- Post year end review of the bank statement and cash books to confirm whether the amount has been received after the reporting period

- Confirmation that the carrying value of $50,000 has been removed from the non-current asset register and general ledger

- Confirmation that any profit or loss recognised on the disposal has been recognised in profit

- Review of board minutes to confirm the transaction was appropriately authorised
- Written representation from management stating that management has disclosed to the auditor the identity of the entity's related parties and all the related party relationships and transactions of which they are aware, and that management has appropriately accounted for and disclosed such relationships and transactions in line with IAS 24

(b) $1.2m expenditure is 0.5% of 20X3 total assets (= $1.2m / $230m), and 6% of 20X3 profits (= $1.2m / $20m). It is therefore material to profit in the prior year.

IAS 38 specifically prohibits the capitalisation of expenditure on internally-generated brands. This is therefore a material misstatement, because the expenditure should have been treated as an expense in profit or loss, reducing profit by a material amount (6%) to $18.8m.

Not only should the asset be derecognised from the 20X4 financial statements, but it is also a prior year error in line with IAS 8 *Accounting Policies, Changes in Accounting Estimates and Errors*. It should be accounted for retrospectively, adjusting comparatives and retained earnings in the 20X4 financial statements.

Ross & Co should inform Cooper Co of the situation and ask them to amend the financial statements. This is a difficult thing to do, but should be done in the interests of professionalism and integrity.

Procedures should be performed to ensure that appropriate amendments are made and that disclosures are appropriate. If the adjustment is not made, then this may result in a modified auditor's opinion being expressed.

The failure to audit a material area raises questions about quality control at Ross & Co. It is possible that Ross & Co has been negligent in performing last year's audit, as a result of which legal action could be taken against it.

Ross & Co should review last year's audit file in order to understand how such a mistake took place. It may be, for example, that the $1.2m was an adjustment made by the client after the audit file had been reviewed, but which was noticed in the final financial statements. In any case, it appears likely that Ross & Co's firm-wide quality control procedures were inadequate, so these should be reviewed and amended as necessary to ensure compliance with ISQC 1 *Quality Controls for Firms that Perform Audits and Reviews of Financial Statements, and Other Assurance and Related Services Engagements*.

30 Grohl

Workbook references. Chapters 2, 6 and 8.

Top tips. This was a fairly standard AAA question on audit planning, and should have been within your capabilities. Part (a)(i) required you to evaluate business risks. Your approach here should be to read the scenario closely, noting the risks as they occur. There were plenty of risks there for your 15 marks.

Part (a)(ii) was on the risks of material misstatement. One possible pitfall here might have been talking about risks to do with the auditors themselves (eg that the Board members leaving might make it difficult to obtain explanations), when these are **not** part of the 'risk of material misstatement'.

Part (a)(iii) covered ethics in the scenario. The parts of the scenario that were relevant here should have stood out, although you might have struggled to write eight marks' worth of material here. It is important, then, that you do not try to 'pad' your answer with irrelevant information, as this will not earn you marks. With a focused and systematic discussion, you should have been able to pass this part of the question.

Part (b) should not have been difficult. The issue was fairly clear-cut, and there were plenty of marks available for some fairly straightforward points. Most of the procedures are really common sense, and come straight from the scenario itself.

Easy marks. There were easy marks in part (b) for the matters to consider – the insurance claim was obviously implausible. Also in part (a), it is basic knowledge for ethics questions that a contingent fee is not appropriate for an audit engagement. Make sure you get some of the professional marks as well.

ACCA examining team's comments. It was clear that the majority of candidates were familiar with audit planning questions and seemed comfortable with the style of the question and with the amount of information that had been given in the scenario. There was little evidence of time pressure despite the length of the question.

Requirement (a)(i) was by far the best-answered requirement of the exam, with most candidates identifying and explaining a range of relevant business risks, which on the whole were developed in enough detail.

For candidates who achieved lower marks on this requirement, the problem was that they did not develop their discussion enough to achieve the maximum marks per point. Some of the answers just repeated the business issue as stated in the question without discussing any of the impact on the business at all. Most candidates discussed going concern, which was relevant, but instead of relating going concern to specific matters such as liquidity problems and the large loan, it was simply mentioned as a conclusion in relation to every business risk discussed, and therefore was not specific enough to earn credit. Many answers could have been improved in relation to business risk evaluation by including some simple analysis of the financial information made available, for example through the calculation of profit margins and trends. This would have been an easy way to develop the point that financial performance was suffering, as well as liquidity being poor.

Answers were very mixed for requirement (a)(ii). Some candidates clearly understood the meaning of a risk of material misstatement, and could apply their knowledge to the question requirement, resulting in sound explanations. However, despite this being a regularly examined topic and the cornerstone of audit planning, the majority of answers were unsatisfactory.

First, many candidates included a discussion about this being a first-year audit which would result in a risk of material misstatement, but this was both incorrect and showed that the question had not been read carefully enough. Then, when attempting to explain a risk of material misstatement, many candidates could do little more than state a financial reporting rule, and then say the risk was that 'this would be incorrectly accounted for'. It was not clear if this type of vague statement was down to candidates being reluctant to come to a decision about whether a balance would be over or understated, or if they thought that their answer was specific enough. Very few answers were specific enough on the actual risk of misstatement to earn credit.

Answers to requirement (a)(iii) were mixed, and generally the answers in relation to the contingent fee were better than those in relation to employment at a client company. On the contingent fee most candidates seemed confident in their knowledge, and correctly identified that a contingent fee is not allowed for an audit engagement, and recommended sensible actions such as ensuring a discussion of the matter with those charged with governance. The majority of candidates had the correct knowledge here, and could apply appropriately to the question. As usual, candidates appear reasonably comfortable with the ethics part of the syllabus, but are reminded that to score well on ethical requirements in AAA, they must do more than just identify a threat.

With respect to requirement (b), the audit procedures that were recommended were mixed in quality. Most candidates suggested a review of the terms and conditions of the insurance policy to see if the situation was covered, and most also recommended reviewing the actual claim and contacting the insurance provider. All of these are valid and appropriate procedures and generally were well described. Some answers tended to state that the matter should be 'discussed with management' with no further explanation, or that 'an expert should be consulted' but with no description of what evidence the expert should be asked to provide, or even who the expert should be. Too many candidates seemed to want to rely on representations and discussions about the possible outcome of the insurance claim when there were other stronger sources of audit evidence available.

BPP
LEARNING

Marks

(a)　(i)　**Business risks**

Up to 2 marks for each business risk evaluated (up to a maximum of 5 marks in total if risks identified but not evaluated):

- Exchange rate risk
- Imports – transportation costs and potential for disrupted supply
- Reliance on one supplier
- Quality control issues
- High-tech/competitive industry
- Reliance on key customer contracts
- Regulatory issues
- Website sales
- Outsourcing
- Liquidity/solvency issues
- Poor profitability
- Change in key management

Maximum　　15

(ii)　**Risk of material misstatement**

Up to 2 marks for each risk of material misstatement identified and explained (up to a maximum of 2 marks in total for identification only):

- Initial translation of foreign exchange transactions
- Retranslation and exchange gains and losses
- Obsolete inventory
- Refunds to customers
- Capitalisation of borrowing cost to new production line
- Impairment of old production line
- Loan classification, measurement and disclosure
- Inventory obsolescence
- Going concern
- Website development costs
- Website sales

Maximum　　15

(iii)　**Ethical issues**

Generally 1 mark per comment:

- Explain why familiarity threat arises
- Explain why intimidation threat arises
- Significant connections should be evaluated
- If significant connections remain, firm should resign
- If continue with audit, consider modifying audit approach and change audit team
- Review any work recently performed on Grohl Co audit by Bob Halen
- Consider firm's policies and procedures
- Contingent fee not acceptable
- The basis for calculation of the audit fee must be agreed with client

Maximum　　8

Marks

Professional marks

Generally 1 mark for heading, 1 mark for introduction, 1 mark for
use of headings within the briefing notes,
1 mark for clarity of comments made

	Maximum	4

(b) **Insurance claim**

Generally 1 mark per matter/procedure:

Matters

– Accounting treatment for contingent asset
– Claim may not be covered by insurance
– Amount of the claim seems unreasonable
– Materiality
– Potential risk of material misstatement and impact on report

Procedures

– Inspect claim and supporting documentation
– Inspect insurance terms and conditions
– Review correspondence
– Communicate with insurance provider
– Enquiry with lawyers

	Maximum	8
Total		**50**

(a) **Briefing notes**

For: Mia Vai

By: Audit manager

Date: Dec 20X2

Subject: Grohl Co audit planning

Introduction

These notes will evaluate the business risks faced by Grohl Co; identify and explain four risks of material misstatement to be considered in audit planning; and discuss relevant ethical issues and recommend actions to be taken by our firm.

(i) **Evaluation of business risks**

Overseas supplier

Copper wiring is a key production material, and is imported from overseas. There is therefore a risk of unstable supply as a result of it being transported over a long distance, across borders. Any of the following could pose problems.

• A rise in fuel prices could affect the cost of materials

• Political instability could lead to difficulties transporting across borders

• Goods may not be subject to the same regulatory standards as those in Grohl's own jurisdiction, and could be of poor quality

• Environmental disruption could affect eg shipping or aviation, and lead to disruption of the supply of materials

BPP
LEARNING

If there were a stock out of this key material then this would severely affect Grohl Co's production, and its ability to supply its customers. This could lead to a loss of revenue and of customer goodwill.

Exchange rate risk

Purchases are made in a foreign currency, and fluctuations are not hedged against. This leaves Grohl Co exposed to the risk of price rises, which could affect both its cash position and its short-run profitability. It may be advisable for the company to use forward contracts to help mitigate this risk.

Key supplier

Grohl Co is reliant on just one supplier for all its copper wiring. It is thus exposed to any risks resulting from problems with this supplier, eg price rises, problems with supply, quality control.

Grohl Co also moved all of its copper purchases to just one new supplier, before having used the supplier for a trial period. It was therefore highly exposed to any problems with the new supplier.

Competitive pressure

Grohl Co operates in a competitive industry and is subject to price competition from overseas. There is a risk that Grohl will be unable to keep its prices low enough to compete on this basis. It may need to consider alternative strategies.

The industry is dynamic and subject to rapid change, so in order to remain competitive Grohl Co must adapt quickly to any changes. It may not have sufficient resources to do this.

Quality control

Quality problems with the new copper supply have led to goods being returned by customers. This seems likely to be related to the use of a new, cheaper supplier. There is a risk of losing customers as a result of poor quality products, which may be particularly dangerous in this competitive market.

It may be necessary in future for Grohl Co to test the quality of copper purchased. This would incur costs, which would in turn put further pressure on Grohl Co's already tight operating margins.

New regulations

New regulations come into force after the year end. There is a risk that these may not be complied with, which could lead to significant penalties. These could be fines, or could result in suspending production.

New loan

The new $30m loan is significant at 1/6 (16.7%) of total assets. It is not known what proportion of net assets this constitutes. Annual interest on the loan is 4% × $30m = $1.2m, which is a significant amount in the context of a loss of $300,000 before tax and a cash balance of only $130,000.

The fact that Grohl Co has a $2.5m overdraft may be indicative of a cash shortage, a view that is borne out by low current and quick ratios. There is a risk that Grohl Co may not be a going concern for the next year.

Management change

The loss of several executive directors means that key business expertise has been lost, which might have been especially important given Grohl Co's current financial position.

Website sales

The introduction of website sales brings with it several risks. These include the risk of non-compliance with taxation, legal and other regulatory issues. There is a risk of technological failure (crashes) resulting in business interruption and possible brand damage.

There is a significant security risk from virus attacks, which could result in loss of company or customer data. This may in turn have legal ramifications.

The high rate of returns from the website is a concern, as this may indicate a flaw in the design of the website.

On balance the website is likely to help improve Grohl Co's sales, but it is notable that prices have been reduced by 10%. There is a risk of lost revenue if this reduction has not been given adequate consideration.

Outsourcing

Grohl Co has outsourced both its new website and the delivery service from it, which brings a risk that the services provided may not be of sufficient quality. Grohl Co is now reliant on two external entities for key elements of its business, over which it has now relinquished control.

There is also a cost risk with outsourced services, as they may be more expensive than performing the service in-house.

Profitability

Draft revenue is down by $1.3m from 20X1, or 9.4%. Operating profit has fallen by $500,000, or 50%, and the operating margin has fallen from 7.2% to 4%, a fall of 44%.

Grohl Co has made a pre-tax loss of $300,000, although this does not appear to include the finance costs from the new loan (finance costs for 20X2 are the same as 20X1). If these were included, then the loss would be about $0.5m higher, at $0.8m. This is a large loss, and may again indicate going concern problems.

(ii) ## Risks of material misstatement

Foreign exchange

There is a risk of non-compliance with IAS 21 *The Effects of Changes in Foreign Exchange Rates*. IAS 21 requires that non-monetary items are recognised at the historical rate, which is the rate at the date of the transaction (IAS 21: paras. 21–22). This would include income and expenses in the statement of profit or loss. There is a risk that non-monetary items are not recognised at the correct historical rate, leading to under- or over-statement of these items.

IAS 21 requires monetary items to be measured at the closing rate (IAS 21: para. 23). Thus any foreign currency payables and receivables must be retranslated at the year end, with any exchange gain or loss being recognised in the statement of profit or loss. There is a risk that the wrong rate is used, or that items are translated using the wrong rate. There is also a risk that no exchange gain or loss is recognised in relation to payables and receivables settled during the year.

Product recall

Grohl Co may be liable to customers in relation to faulty goods supplied. Although the issue appears to be resolved, it is possible that there may be further liabilities which should be recognised in line with IAS 37 *Provisions, Contingent Liabilities and Contingent Assets*. There is thus a risk that provisions are understated.

There is a risk that the accounting treatment of the product recall was incorrect. Any revenue recognised on recalled items should be cancelled against the corresponding receivables balance. The risk is therefore that revenue and receivables may be overstated.

New production line

The construction of the new production line is likely to result in new non-current assets which should be recognised in line with IAS 16 *Property, Plant and Equipment.* There is a risk that this has not been done correctly, leading to either under- or overstatement of assets.

The production line is likely to be a qualifying asset in line with IAS 23 *Borrowing Costs*, so all directly attributable borrowing costs should be capitalised. It is not clear how much of the $0.5m finance cost from the new loan would be capitalised, as the loan appears to have been used only 'mainly' for the new production line.

Old production line – impairment

The new regulations coming into force after the year end indicate that the existing production may be impaired. IAS 36 *Impairment of Assets* requires management to conduct an impairment review. If this is not done adequately, then non-current assets and profit may be overstated.

Inventory obsolescence

There is a risk that some inventory may have been rendered un-useable by the use of corroded copper. The matter is complicated by the fact that testing is required to determine whether an item has been affected.

IAS 2 *Inventories* requires inventory to be carried at the lower of cost and net realisable value. There is a danger that obsolete inventory has been included in the financial statements without being reviewed for impairment, resulting in an overstatement of inventory.

Website development costs

Website development costs may be treated as an internally generated intangible asset according to IAS 38 *Intangible Assets*, provided that the appropriate conditions are satisfied.

IAS 38 requires the website to be feasible, which seems to be the case since it is operational. Similarly, the costs appear to be able to be measured reliably at $200,000.There is a risk, however, that subsequent costs have been included within this figure, which could result in assets being overstated and expenses understated.

Website sales

A key risk is the use of an outsourced service provider. ISA 402 *Audit Considerations Relating to an Entity Using a Service Organisation* provides guidance on how auditors should obtain sufficient appropriate audit evidence when the audit client, which is a 'user entity', relies on such services.

The website sales are likely to be material to Grohl Co as they make up around a quarter of revenue, even though they have only been launched for half a year. The outsourced service therefore constitutes a key element of Grohl Co's internal control systems, so it will need to be assessed carefully.

Going concern

As indicated in the evaluation of business risks, there may be going concern problems at Grohl Co. The risk is either that the financial statements are prepared on the going

concern basis when they should not be, or that appropriate disclosures are not made regarding any significant doubts over going concern.

(iii) **Ethical issues**

Audit manager joining client

An audit manager from Foo & Co may leave to become a financial controller at Grohl Co. According to the IESBA *Code of Ethics*, this could create familiarity and intimidation threats.

The audit team may be so familiar with Bob Halen that they lose independence, for example they may not challenge him if this is necessary. They may fail to exercise enough professional scepticism. Bob is also likely to be familiar with Foo & Co's audit methodology, so would be well placed to think of ways of hiding things from the audit team.

The IESBA *Code* states that if a 'significant connection' remains between the firm and the individual who joined the client, then no safeguard could mitigate the threat and the firm should withdraw from the engagement. This would be the case if:

*   Bob is entitled to benefits or payments from Foo & Co, unless in line with fixed pre-determined arrangements

*   Bob is owed an amount by the firm that is material to the firm

*   Bob continues to participate in the firm's business or professional activities

Alternatively, if there is no significant connection then safeguards may be acceptable. The threat here is significant, as Bob was in charge of the Grohl Co audit only very recently, and would have maintained contact with Grohl Co's management.

Safeguards might include reviewing any work that Bob has done on the audit, although there is not likely to be much of this as planning is only just starting.

Contingent fee audit

The IESBA *Code* clearly states that an audit firm may not enter into a contingent fee arrangement, as the self-interest threat would be too great for safeguards to reduce to an acceptable level.

Conclusion

Grohl Co is facing some significant business risks, which may affect the going concern assertion. There are a number of significant risks of material misstatement in relation to which the audit plan should design procedures to obtain sufficient appropriate audit evidence. The ethical issue with Bob Halen requires that safeguards be put in place, and it should be communicated to Grohl Co's Board that the audit cannot be performed on a contingent fee basis.

(b) **Matters to consider**

At $5m, the claim represents 40% of draft revenue, and would turn a loss of $0.3m into a profit of $4.7. It is therefore highly material.

This is a contingent asset. IAS 37 requires that contingent assets are not recognised, unless it is virtually certain that the inflow of economic benefits will take place (IAS 37: paras. 31–35).

At the moment, it is not certain that the claim will even be paid, even if is more likely to be paid than not. Whether or not it is paid will depend on the specific terms of the insurance policy, which would need to be considered in detail and light of any communications with the insurer and/or Grohl Co's legal counsel.

BPP
LEARNING

Regarding the value of the claim, production was halted for just one week so 40% of annual revenue is far too high. It is very unlikely that this amount will be received.

Procedures

- Obtain a copy of the insurance claim made and confirm that $5 million is claimed.

- Enquire into the basis of the $5 million claimed, and review any supporting documentation such as extracts of management accounts showing lost revenue for the period of halted production.

- Inspect the terms of the insurance policy, to determine whether production halted in these specific circumstances would be covered.

- Seek Grohl Co's permission to contact the insurer to ask about the status of the claim, and request written confirmation of any payment that may be made.

- Review correspondence between Grohl Co and the insurance provider, looking for confirmation of any amounts to be paid.

31 Champers

Workbook references. Chapters 6 and 8.

Top tips. In part (a)(i), there is a ½ mark available for just mentioning ('identifying') each aspect that needs to be considered, so try to get lots of these (you only need to recall information from the Workbook) – but don't go overboard here, as the marks available for identification will be capped. Then try to explain as many of them as you can within the time allocated to this part of the question. In part (a)(ii), try to explain at least three procedures within the time available.

Part (b) is a standard question on business risks, and you should be scoring well on this part. Remember that you need to say enough about each risk (without waffling) to get the marks – don't just produce a list. There are 13 marks available here, so you should be looking to get around 8–10 of them on a requirement like this. Finally, be careful not to exceed the time allotted to this part of the question if you find you have lots to write. Part (c)(i) is for five marks, so you should seek to describe at least three **principal** audit procedures to pass the question. Part (c)(ii) is more difficult, so you should seek to get at least 2–3 marks on this part, making sure that your answer is properly focused on the requirement.

BPP note. This question focuses on business risk in part (b), but in the real exam an AAA question would be likely to also include a corresponding requirement dealing with audit risk or RoMM.

Easy marks. Make sure you get the four professional marks for: use of format and using appropriate language for an audit junior.

ACCA examining team's comments. Some candidates performed well overall, especially those who spent an appropriate amount of time on each of the question requirements. In part (a), few candidates recognised the need to understand the internal control environment, and fewer still mentioned the importance of understanding the relevant financial reporting framework and performance measures of the client. Candidates tended not to gain the professional mark available for the clarity of their answer, because explanations were often confused, repetitive, or non-existent. Candidates also need to bear in mind that professional marks are awarded partly for the quality of language used.

Common weaknesses is part (b) included: failure to use the financial information provided to identify risks; focusing on risk of material misstatement, which was **not** a requirement of the question; trying to link every risk identified to a going concern risk.

For part (c)(i), few candidates could suggest anything other than 'check the relevant invoices' or 'check the amount was approved'. Most candidates in part (c)(ii) failed to read the requirement, and the scenario, both of which stated that the advertising costs had been expensed. Most discussed the merits of recognising the amount as an intangible asset, which as well as being completely irrelevant is also technically incorrect.

Marking scheme

Marks

(a) (i) **Identify and explain aspects of understanding business and environment**
Generally ½ mark for identification and 1 mark for explanation:
–   External factors
–   Entity and accounting policies
–   Objectives, strategies and business risks
–   Performance measures
–   Internal control

Maximum   6

(ii) **Recommend procedures to gain understanding**
Generally 1 mark per procedure described:
–   Inquiry
–   Analytical procedure
–   Observation
–   Inspection

Maximum   4

(b) **Business risk**
Generally ½ mark for identification, 1 further mark for explanation, from ideas list
1 mark to be given for each appropriate calculation eg trends, materiality:
–   Risk of damage to brand name/bad publicity re injury to child and closed restaurant
–   Investment needed in play areas to prevent health and safety problems
–   Damage to the Happy Monkeys brand name may cross to other brand names
–   Compliance risk re health and safety regulations – food preparation
–   Fall in revenue from Quick-bite business segment
–   The above linked to reduced demand for fast food/more emphasis on healthy eating
–   Advertising ban could reduce revenue
–   Rapid expansion plans for City Sizzler chain – danger of overtrading
–   Potential lack of cash for the capital expenditure and on-going refurbishment costs
–   Potential lack of cash for continued advertising
–   Green George chain – need to monitor supply chain
–   PBT fallen 13% – poor cost control?
–   Minimum wage legislation will increase operating costs significantly next year
–   Cash position worsened during year
–   Cash based business – risk of fraud
–   Internal structure may need addressing

Maximum   13

(c) (i) **Audit procedures on amounts capitalised**
Generally 1 mark per specific audit procedure:
Ideas list:
- Agree sample of costs to invoice/tender documents
- Review capex budget and discuss variances actual v budget
- Agree interest rate of finance cost to terms of finance
- Agree period of capitalisation correct by reference to date of completion of restaurants
- Review list of items capitalised to ensure all capital in nature

Maximum   5

(ii) **Audit work for advertising expense**
Generally 1 mark per specific audit procedure:
Ideas list:
- Agree sample of costs to invoices/reports from consultants
- Analytical review
- Discuss with relevant personnel/review of business plan
- Inspect budgets
- Physically inspect the advertising
- After-date invoice review
- Assess date advertising conducted

Maximum   4

Professional marks to be awarded for format, use of introduction and conclusion, use of language that an audit junior could understand.   4
Total   **36**

Briefing notes

To: Champers audit team

From: Geoff Forest

Subject: Champers Co business risks

Introduction

These notes explain the aspects of a client's business to be considered when obtaining an understanding of the entity and its environment, recommending appropriate procedures. An evaluation is made of the business risks currently faced by Champers Co. Finally, a description is given of the principal audit procedures to be performed in relation to two areas of the financial statements.

(a) (i) **Aspects to be considered**

- **Industry, regulatory and other external factors**. For instance, some industries require businesses to carry specific levels of capital (such as 'bonded' travel agents). An auditor would need to gain knowledge of these regulations to assess their impact on the audit. This could also affect audit planning. If a client operates in an industry with unusual accounting treatments (construction or insurance, for example), it would be wise to choose an audit team with experience of that industry.

- **Nature of the entity**. An auditor must understand the legal structure of the entity (company or group). Complex ownership structures might increase the risk of misstatement – for instance if subsidiaries' results are not consolidated correctly.

- **Selection, application and reasons for changes of accounting policies**. An auditor must understand the entity's accounting policies together with the reasons for them being selected. This would include consideration of whether or not they are in line with the applicable financial reporting framework.

- **Objectives, strategies and related business risks**. Business risks are the risks that the company may not achieve its objectives. The main way this affects audit risk is that if there is a high risk of the company failing to meet its objectives (or if it adopts a risky strategy to try to meet them), there is a risk that the company may not be a going concern. Any financial statements prepared on the going concern basis would then be likely to be misstated.

- **Measurement and review of the entity's financial performance**. The auditor should understand how the entity's performance is assessed, because management could seek to manipulate the results so that it looks like the company is doing better than it is. This might trigger bonus payments, for example.

- **Internal control**. This is an absolutely crucial area in assessing audit risk, as the auditor may seek to place reliance on the entity's internal controls. The assessment of control risk would have a direct effect on audit strategy. This would include assessing the entity's control environment.

(ii) **Procedures recommended**

- **Inquiries of management**. This would usually be the first place to start – management should be the best people to give the auditor information on the aspects of the company and its environment referred to in ISA 315. The auditor could also consult others, such as an internal audit department.

- **Analytical procedures**. It is crucial to perform analytical procedures to gain an understanding of the major areas of the financial statements, as well as the dominant trends and anomalies (in financial information, and between financial and non-financial information). This will allow the auditor to assess the areas where there is a higher risk of material misstatement.

- **Observation**. Observing internal control activities, for instance, could help to cement the auditor's understanding of how they operate.

- **Inspection**. Documents such as business plans or internal control manuals may contain valuable information on how the entity operates. Inspecting these would supplement the inquiries already made of management.

(b) **Happy Monkeys children's crèches**

A child was slightly injured during the year in an incident at one of the crèches. The media criticism that was received could lead to significant damage of the Happy Monkeys brand, particularly given that the family-friendly orientation of the restaurants appears to be an important selling point. Although revenues from this segment rose 21% compared with 20X8 ((800 – 660) / 660 = 21%), this negative publicity probably did result in some lost revenue.

It is possible that regulatory bodies could take action as a result of this incident, with the potentially disastrous consequence of the crèches or even the whole restaurants being shut down.

If it wants to protect the Happy Monkeys brand, Champers will probably need to spend money to improve the standard of child care offered in the crèches. It would be difficult for it to do this given its falling cash balance ($116m in 20X9; $350, in 20X8). It would therefore have to divert funds away from other projects, such as the expansion of the City Sizzler grills.

Revenue derived from Happy Monkeys restaurants makes up 53% of total revenue (= 800 / 1500), so any damage to this revenue stream could have a significant effect on Champers as a whole.

Happy Monkeys – health and safety

One restaurant was actually closed during the year as a result of significant breaches in kitchen hygiene standards. Health and safety authorities often have significant powers, and it is crucial that Champers' restaurants comply with them. Moreover, this could cause significant damage to the Happy Monkeys brand, and even to the other brands that Champers owns by way of association with it. If this was to happen revenues could drop sharply, which would clearly affect Champers' ability to meet its objective of maximising market share.

The effect of damage to the Happy Monkeys brand on Champers as a whole could be very significant indeed, owing to the fact that it makes up 53% of Champers' total revenue in 20X9.

Quick-bite chain

- ### Marketing campaign

    A significant marketing campaign was launched to support the Quick-bite brand, costing $150m in 20X9. This represents 10% of Champers' total revenue for the year, and is a significant expense. Indeed, this outlay may have been partly responsible for the decrease in cash during the year, and because of Champers' poor cash position this level of spending is unlikely to be sustainable in the future.

- ### Falling revenue

    Revenue from this segment fell by 6% in 20X9. The fact that this happened even though $150m was spent on advertising during the year is a worrying sign, and may be indicative of a significant reduction in demand. This is borne out by the pressure exerted by government for the restaurants to provide nutritional information in its menus, which the company rightly responded to. It is possible that this highly competitive industry is experiencing falling demand as a result of increased public awareness of the importance of eating healthily. This would appear to cast significant doubt over the wisdom of the company having spent such a large amount on advertising during the year.

- ### New advertising regulations

    50% of Quick-bite's revenue derives from 'chuckle boxes' sold to children. These sales are likely to be affected by the new advertising regulations coming into force from September 20X9. Champers will have to consider how it is going to tackle this problem going forward.

City Sizzler grills

- ### Expansion plans

    Champers is planning to double the number of City Sizzler grills from 250 to 500 by the end of the current financial year. Given that the restaurants operate in the higher quality end of the market, this is likely to require significant expenditure to acquire new prime locations and to refurbish the locations acquired.

    It is possible that Champers may not be able to afford this level of investment in the next year, owing to its already declining cash balance. There is a risk that it will begin to expand the chain, but then run out of cash once it has started.

There is a possibility that Champers will have to raise new funds in order to finance the expansion. Given the scale of its plans, it may struggle to raise the necessary funds. If it takes on new debt, this would expose the company to increased liquidity risk if it cannot make the required repayments.

- **Refurbishment costs**

    Champers plans to refurbish each City Sizzler grill every two years. This is likely to represent a significant and ongoing drain on Champers' cash resources, and there is a risk that Champers will not be able to afford it. Champers should therefore consider whether it can reduce the outlay in some way, perhaps by extending the amount of time between refurbishments from two to three years.

Green George cafés

Champers plans to double the number of cafés within the next 12 months. This would probably be costly, and again there is a question mark over its affordability to Champers. The combination of the plans to expand the Green George cafés and the City Sizzler grills, as well as a potential fall in revenue from the Quick-bite outlets as a result of increased regulatory pressure, represents a significant risk to the future success of Champers as a whole.

This risk is exacerbated by the fact that Champers financed the expansion in the Green George cafés by taking on debt, which may pose a threat to the company's liquidity if Champers fails to keep up with the necessary repayments.

Falling cash balance

Champers' cash balance fell by $234m from $350m at 31 May 20X8 to $116m at 31 May 20X9, a fall of 67%. At this rate it will run out of money approximately 180 days into the year (116 / 234 × 365). It is vital to Champers' ongoing survival that this trend is stemmed.

Falling profits

Champers' profit after tax fell by 13% from $155m in 20X8 to $135m in 20X9. This may be a result of some one-off expenses, such as the $150m advertising expenses in respect of the Quick-bite chain, or any expenses related to the investment in the City Sizzler grills and the Green George cafés. However, it is crucial that Champers' management considers its cost-control procedures in the future. This is particularly pertinent in view of the impending 15% increase in the minimum wage, which will significantly increase Champers' costs, as it will affect a third of employees in the labour-intensive restaurant industry.

(c)　(i)　**Agree costs to invoice**

The audit team should agree a sample of costs capitalised to supporting documents. Labour costs should be agreed to payroll records and timesheets. Materials costs should be agreed to supplier purchase invoices. Costs relating to site acquisitions should be agreed to legal papers, such as completion statements.

Agree finance costs to contracts

Interest rates should be agreed to original finance agreements, and the interest charge for the period should be recalculated. If the rates are derived from an underlying figure (such as a central bank base rate), the rates applied should be agreed.

Agree cut-off for finance costs

Per IAS 23 *Borrowing Costs*, capitalisation must cease when the related asset is available for use (IAS 23: para. 22), so the date on which this was the case should be agreed to underlying operational documentation, eg surveyor's reports.

Agree classification between revenue and capital expenditure

A sample of costs capitalised should be agreed to underlying documentation (such as purchase invoices) and the classification agreed. There is a risk that eg staff training costs could have been capitalised.

Compare actual vs budget

Compare actual with budgeted capital expenditure, and discuss any significant variances with the appropriate employee (eg the manager for that budget area). If necessary carry out substantive testing in order to verify the actual amounts where there are significant variances.

(ii) **Analytical procedures**

Compare the current year expense with the prior year, discussing any significant variances with an appropriate employee (eg a marketing manager) and performing substantive procedures if necessary.

Compare actual expenditure with budgeted expenditure, discussing with an employee and performing further procedures if required.

Agree sample of costs to underlying documentation

Costs should be agreed to purchase invoices or other supporting documentation, and then to the actual advert itself, which may exist in archive form for eg newspaper adverts. If judged necessary, costs could be traced to purchase orders and then to budgets, making enquiries of management in relation to any costs not budgeted for.

Cut-off testing

Review after-date advertising invoices and ensure that those relating to the 20X9 financial year are accrued for.

Review the dates on which advertising actually took place and verify that adverts taking place after the year end are accounted for correctly as prepayments.

Understanding of the business

Discuss the nature of the advertising expenditure with an appropriate employee, in order to form an expectation of the expense likely to be incurred and to design specific testing procedures.

Conclusion

First, these notes have described the aspects of an entity that an auditor needs to understand, and the procedures needed to obtain this understanding. Second, these notes have found that the business risks currently faced by Champers are not insignificant, and there is even a risk that it may not survive the next financial year if its inability to generate sufficient cash inflows is not countered. Finally, audit procedures are recommended in relation to two areas of the financial statements.

32 Grissom

Workbook references. Chapters 6 and 9.

Top tips. To answer this question well, some time spent planning would be very advisable prior to launching into your answer. In part (a), remember to consider practical aspects and keep in mind the mark allocation – you need to make 10 well-explained points to achieve the maximum potential marks available, and you should be able to generate these from the clues in the question scenario. In part (b), you need to make sure you apply your knowledge of group audits to the scenario – there are lots of clues in the question, and it is important that you pick up on them.

Easy marks. You should be able to score reasonably well in part (a) if you use the information provided to you in the question scenario and explain the matters fully. Similarly, part (b) should be fairly straightforward on ISA 600. The professional marks are easy!

ACCA examining team's comments. Overall performance on this question varied considerably. Candidates who answered the specific question requirements scored well. However, despite the requirements of (a) and (c) covering familiar issues seen in many previous exams, a significant proportion of candidates did not answer the specific question requirements, leading to largely irrelevant answers scoring very few marks

Many scripts contained the following errors.

- Discussion of business risk without linking the business risk to audit risk (eg 'there is a risk of failing to comply with relevant laws and regulations', or 'there is a risk that inventories are obsolete')

- Including audit procedures (which were not asked for in part (a))

- Long description of the components of audit risk (inherent, control and detection risks) with no application to the scenario

- Explanations too vague to earn marks (eg 'the risk is it is not accounted for properly' or 'the risk is that the accounting standard is not followed')

- Discussing reliance on the component auditor (which the requirement explicitly said should not be considered)

Many candidates included the inevitable references to going concern problems, even though there was no hint in the scenario that the group faced operational or financial difficulties. Also, some candidates misread the scenario, leading to inappropriate comments.

A significant minority of candidates did not attempt to earn the four professional marks available for this requirement. Candidates are reminded that resources are available on ACCA's website providing guidance on the importance of professional marks.

Overall performance on this requirement was unsatisfactory. Candidates are reminded that group audit engagements are an important part of the AAA syllabus, and the requirements and practical implications of ISA 600 should be studied in detail.

Marks

(a) **Evaluation of audit risks and other matters to be considered**
½ mark for identification (to a maximum of 5 marks) and up to 1½ further marks for evaluation:
- Classification of non-controlling interests
- Auditors lack knowledge of activities of non-controlling interests
- Bonus and potential earnings management
- Change of accounting estimates (IAS 8)
- Lack of group finance director
- Capitalisation of dismantling costs (IAS 16)
- Provision – discounting and finance charge (IAS 37)
- Deferral of grant income (IAS 20)
- Potential provision or contingent liability (IAS 37)
- Mid-year acquisition
- Goodwill on acquisition – subjective (IFRS 3)
- Retranslation of Brass Co financial statements (IAS 21)
- Retranslation of goodwill

BPP
LEARNING

        –   Adjustments necessary to bring in line with group accounting policies

        –   Intra-group transactions

                                                              Maximum   18

Professional marks for presentation of answer, clarity of explanations   4

(b) **Evaluation of audit risks and other matters to be considered**

    1 mark per comment on matters/procedure:

    –   Ethics

    –   Competence/qualifications

    –   Skills/resources

    –   Quality control

    –   Monitoring activities

                                                             Maximum   8

(c) (i)   **Principal audit procedures for non-controlling interests**

          Generally 1 mark per procedure:

          –   Confirm % shareholding acquired

          –   Confirm if Grissom Co appointed any board members

          –   Consider relationship with other shareholders

          –   Discussion of involvement

          –   Written representation re involvement

                                           Maximum   4

    (ii)   **Principal audit procedures for condition attached to grant**

          Generally 1 mark per procedure:

          –   Confirm 25% to terms of grant

          –   Ascertain from grant document:

               •   The period required to demonstrate reduction

               •   The amount that would be repaid if condition breached

          –   Review results of monitoring performed

                                           Maximum   <u>4</u>

Total   **<u>38</u>**

Briefing notes

To: Audit team

Re: Grissom Co audit risks June 20Y0

Introduction

These notes consider the principal audit risks to be considered in planning the audit of the Grissom Group financial statements for June 20Y0. The notes explain the factors to consider, and procedures to perform, in deciding whether to rely on Sidle & Co's work. Finally, they recommend audit procedures in relation to two important areas of the financial statements.

(a) Grissom Co

Non-controlling interests

There is an inherent risk that these investments have been classified incorrectly as associates. IAS 28 *Investments in Associates and Joint Ventures* requires Grissom to have significant influence over the investee. If this is not the case, the investments should be treated as trade investments. Alternatively they may be joint arrangements if control is shared jointly with one or more other entities.

These two investments are in areas quite different from the group's core activity. There is thus a risk that the group's finance team may not have applied appropriate accounting policies – eg deferring revenue for the travel agent – resulting in misstatement of the group accounts.

Bonuses and accounting estimates

The existence of profit-based bonuses for directors represents an inherent risk of manipulation, with income and profit being overstated, and expenses being understated.

The fact that the group finance director left after a disagreement over accounting estimates may indicate that senior management have indeed attempted to manipulate the financial statements. It is crucial that professional scepticism is exercised in this area. There is a risk that IAS 8 *Accounting Policies, Changes in Accounting Estimates and Errors* has not been adhered to, for instance if a change in accounting policy has been mistaken for a change in accounting estimate.

Group finance director resigned

There is a risk that the financial statements, and in particular the consolidation, have not been properly prepared in the absence of a finance director overseeing the preparation process.

Moreover, the audit team may find it difficult to obtain appropriate explanations from management if there is no finance director, or if a new one is appointed who is not responsible for the accounts being audited.

Willow Co

New factory

The relocation to a new, very large factory may represent an increase in Willow's operational gearing, which may create a business risk to going concern if cash flow problems result. These could be exacerbated by any teething problems resulting from the new factory.

Dismantling costs

IAS 16 *Property, Plant and Equipment* requires the dismantling costs to be capitalised as non-current assets, and a provision created against them (IAS 16: paras. 16–17). Account should be taken of the effect of discounting if this is material, and a finance charge included in the statement of profit or loss to represent the unwinding of the discount. The risk is that the provision has not been created, and that assets and liabilities are therefore understated, and that the depreciation expense is understated, which would result in profit being overstated. There is also a risk that the provision has not been measured correctly in accordance with IAS 37 *Provisions, Contingent Liabilities and Contingent Assets*, eg in respect of the effect of discounting.

Hodges Co

Government grant

IAS 20 *Accounting for Government Grants and Disclosure of Government Assistance* requires that the grant income is matched to the costs it is intended to compensate for (IAS 20: para. 12). This will result in deferred revenue being held on the statement of financial position. There is a risk that this has not done, leading to liabilities being understated and profit being overstated.

BPP
LEARNING

IAS 20 also requires that a grant is recognised only when there is reasonable assurance that Hodges will meet the condition specified by the government. Where there is doubt over this, a provision should be recognised in line with IAS 37. The risk is that this has not been done, and that liabilities are understated and profits overstated.

Brass Co

Consolidation

The subsidiary was acquired mid-year, and there is a risk that its results have not been consolidated from the correct date. If they are included from too early a date and the company is profitable, then group profits may be overstated.

The acquisition should be accounted for in line with IFRS 3 *Business Combinations*. There is a risk that goodwill has not been calculated correctly, and that the fair values of Brass Co's assets and liabilities have not been estimated reliably.

Accounting standards

Brass Co's accounts must be restated so that they are in line with the group's accounting policies, which should conform to IFRS. This is a risky process, particularly in the absence of a group finance director, and there is a risk that Brass Co's accounts may not be in line with IFRS.

Intra-group trading

Brass Co supplies about half of Willow Co's ingredients. There are therefore a significant number of intra-group transactions which need to be eliminated from the group accounts. There may also be inventories containing unrealised profit, which needs to be provided for. The risk is that this has not been done, potentially overstating revenues, expenses, assets and liabilities.

(b) **Factors to consider**

Guidance is provided in ISA 600 *Special Considerations – Audits of Group Financial Statements (Including the Work of Component Auditors)*. Brass Co is a significant component of the group, and Sidle & Co are component auditors. As group auditors we should obtain an understanding of the component auditor, focusing on:

- Whether Sidle & Co complies with ethical requirements

- Sidle & Co's professional competence

- Whether the group audit team will be able to be sufficiently involved in the component auditor's work

- Whether Sidle & Co works in a regulated environment

Ethics

Sidle & Co should, per ISA 600, be subject to the same ethical requirements as the group auditor, irrespective of regulations applicable in Chocland. These are contained in the IESBA's *Code of Ethics for Professional Accountants* and the ACCA's *Code of Ethics and Conduct*.

Professional competence

As group auditor, Vegas & Co should check that Sidle & Co:

- Understand ISAs. Chocland audit regulations are not based on ISAs, so Vegas & Co must ensure that the work performed by Sidle & Co conforms to the requirements of ISAs.

- Have sufficient resources and skills to perform the necessary work. Various complex accounting issues will be involved in preparing the group accounts, such as the measurement of fair values on consolidation. The group auditor must assess whether Sidle & Co has the resources and skills to do this.

- Understand IFRSs. Chocland has not adopted IFRSs, and there is a risk that Sidle & Co is not competent to audit Brass Co's accounts after they have been adjusted to comply with IFRSs.

Procedures to perform

- Obtaining and reviewing the ethical code adhered to by Sidle & Co, and comparing it to those followed by Vegas & Co

- Obtaining a statement from Sidle & Co that it has adhered to this code

- Establishing through discussion or questionnaire whether Sidle & Co is a member of an auditing regulatory body, and the professional qualifications issued by that body

- Obtaining confirmations from the professional body Sidle & Co belong to, or the authorities licensing it

- Determining through discussion whether Sidle & Co is a member of a network of audit firms

- Discussion of the audit methodology used by Sidle & Co in the audit of Brass Co, and compare it with those used under ISAs (eg how the risk of material misstatement is assessed)

- A questionnaire or checklist could be used to provide a summary of audit procedures used

- Ascertaining the quality control policies and procedures used by Sidle & Co, both firm-wide and those applied to individual audit engagements

- Requesting any results of monitoring or inspection visits conducted by the regulatory authority under which Sidle & Co operates

- Communicating to Sidle & Co an understanding of the assurances that our firm will expect to receive, to avoid any subsequent misunderstandings

(c) (i)
- Determine the percentage shareholding acquired, using purchase documentation.

- Confirm that the percentage shareholding is between 20 and 50% of equity shares.

- Obtain a list of directors (eg using published financial statements) for the companies to confirm whether Grissom Co has appointed director(s) to the boards.

- Discuss with the directors of Grissom Co their level of involvement in policy decisions made at the companies.

- Obtain a written representation detailing the nature of involvement and influence exerted over the companies (eg a letter from the investee's board of directors confirming the voting power of Grissom Co).

- Consider the identity of the other shareholders and the relationship between them and Grissom Co. This may reveal that the situation is in substance a joint venture and would need to be accounted for as such.

(ii)
- Obtain the grant document and review the terms to verify that 25% reduction is specified.

- Determine over what period the 25% reduction must be demonstrated.

- Review the terms to establish the financial repercussions of breaching the condition – would the grant be repayable in full or in part, and when would repayment be made.

- Obtain documentation from management showing the monitoring procedures that have been put in place regarding energy use.

- Review the results and adequacy of any monitoring that has taken place before the year end to see if the condition has been breached (eg compare electricity meter readings pre- and post- installation of the packing line, to confirm reduced levels of electricity are being used).

- Discuss energy efficiency of the packing lines with an appropriate employee to obtain their views on how well the assets are performing.

Conclusion

These notes have discussed a number of audit risks which must be addressed during the planning of the audit of the Grissom Group financial statements for June 20Y0. There are several issues to consider in relation to relying on the work of Sidle & Co. Finally, the notes have recommended the principal audit procedures that should be performed in relation to two important areas of the financial statements.

33 Sunshine

Workbook references. Chapters 2, 6, 7 and 8.

Top tips. This question tested both business risks and risks of material misstatement (RoMM), which made it slightly unusual as AAA questions tend not to focus on business risk. It is clearly important that you keep the two separate. One approach might have been to mark each risk you notice as either a business risk or a RoMM, so that you can then return to them when writing your answers for parts (a) and (b) respectively.

Part (a), on evaluating business risks, required you to think a bit differently from usual, and to be critical of the company's actions. As ever, almost everything in the scenario can be seen as either a business risk or an audit risk, even if it doesn't appear to be at first sight. For instance, the significant expenditure on marketing the Group's brand gives rise to a business risk of the brand being damaged – for example by the pressure group's charge that the Group is damaging the environment.

Part (b) was more familiar territory. A number of key risks should have stood out, eg revenue recognition, the effect of the hurricane, and the potential provision. Your discussion of each risk should focus on the three elements for which marks are awarded: the accounting treatment, the RoMM itself, and materiality. Calculating and judging materiality is probably the easiest part of this, but the marks for the RoMM can be easy too – once you have the correct accounting treatment, you need to say whether there is a risk of under-/over-statement of a particular figure.

Part (c) focused on the potential provision. Part (c)(i) depicted an attempt to limit the scope of the audit, which you should be able to perceive and denounce (politely). Part (c)(ii) asked for procedures, and as with all requirements of this type it was important to be specific and to state **why** each procedure should be performed.

Easy marks. Make sure you get at least two or three of the four professional marks. The marks for calculating materiality – and stating whether the issue is material – are easy.

Marking scheme

Marks

(a) **Business risk evaluation**

Generally up to 1½ marks for each business risk evaluated, in addition allow ½ mark for each relevant calculation, eg profit margin:

- Luxury product – sensitive to changes in consumer's disposable income
- Rapid expansion and inappropriate business strategy
- Financial implications of business expansion including impact on gearing, interest cover and cash flows
- Profit margins and cash flows
- International operations
- Catering operations
- Hurricanes
- Claim relating to environmental damage - reputational issue, loss of customers

Maximum   13

(b) **Significant risks of material misstatement**

Generally up to 1 mark for discussion of the accounting treatment, 1 mark for identifying the associated risk of misstatement, and 1 mark for materiality (to a maximum of 2½ marks per issue):

- Revenue recognition
- Cash/foreign exchange
- Licence agreement
- Impairment of property, plant and equipment – political instability and regulatory issues
- Gain on disposal of property
- Impairment of assets – effect of hurricane
- Provision/contingent liability regarding legal claim
- Repairs to properties damaged by hurricane

Maximum   14

(c) (i) **Implications for audit planning**

Up to 1½ marks for each point of discussion/appropriate action:

- Limitation in scope imposed by finance director, not in accordance with agreeing the terms of an audit engagement
- Discuss with audit committee, who should intervene to remove the limitation
- Finance director lacks integrity, increase application of professional scepticism and increased audit risk
- Consider required response when an instance of non-compliance is suspected and the reporting responsibilities of the auditor

Maximum   5

(ii) **Audit procedures**

Up to 1 mark for each well described audit procedure:

- Obtain the letter received from Ocean Protection, review to understand the basis of the claim

- Discuss the issue with the Group's legal adviser, to understand whether in their opinion, the Group could be liable for the damages

- Discuss with legal advisers to obtain understanding of the remit and scope of the legislation in relation to environmental protection

- Discuss with management the procedures which the Group utilises to ensure that it is identifying and ensuring compliance with relevant legislation

- Obtain an understanding, through enquiry with relevant employees, such as those responsible for scuba diving and other water sports, as to the nature of activities which take place

- Obtain and read all correspondence between the Group and Ocean Protection up to the date that the auditor's report is issued

- Obtain a written representation from management

- Discuss the issue with those charged with governance

- Review the disclosures, if any, provided in the notes to the financial statements

- Read the other information published with the financial statements for consistency with the financial statements

Maximum   6

(d) **Ethics of tax engagement**

Generally up to 1½ marks for each well explained matter and 1 mark for each well explained and relevant action:

- Issue may only relate to next year's audit
- Self-review threat
- Factors affecting severity of threat
- Clarification of type of advice needed
- Audit firm's competence
- Safeguards
- Cannot use existing knowledge

Maximum   8

Professional marks

Generally 1 mark for heading, 1 mark for introduction, 1 mark for use of headings within the briefing notes, 1 mark for clarity of comments made.

Maximum   <u>4</u>

Total   <u>**50**</u>

Briefing notes

To: John Starling, audit engagement partner

From: Audit manager

Subject: Sunshine Hotel Group – audit planning

Introduction

These briefing notes relate to the initial audit planning for the Sunshine Hotel Group (the Group), for the year ending 31 December 20X7. As requested, the notes contain an evaluation of the business risks facing our client, and the significant risks of material misstatement to be considered in our audit planning. Finally, the notes contain a discussion of the impact which an email received from the Group finance director relating to a claim for damages will have on our audit planning, as well as the recommended actions to be taken by Dove & Co and principal procedures which should be carried out in relation to this claim.

(a)   **Evaluation of business risks**

Luxury product

The Group offers a luxury product aimed at an exclusive market. This in itself creates a business risk, as the Group's activities are not diversified, and any decline in demand will immediately impact on profitability and cash flows. The demand for luxury holidays will be sensitive to economic problems such as recession and travel to international destinations will be affected by events in the transportation industry, for example, if oil prices increase, there will be a knock-on effect on air fares, meaning less demand for the Group's hotels.

Business expansion – inappropriate strategy

It is questionable whether the Group has a sound policy on expansion, given the problems encountered with recent acquisitions which have involved expanding into locations with political instability and local regulations which seem incompatible with the Group's operations and strategic goals. The Group would appear to have invested $98 million, accounting for 28% of the Group's total assets, in these unsuitable locations, and it is doubtful whether an appropriate return on these investments will be possible. There is a risk that further unsuitable investments will be made as a result of poor strategic decisions on where to locate new hotels. The Group appears to have a strategy of fairly rapid expansion, acquiring new sites and a hotel complex without properly investigating their appropriateness and fit with the Group's business model. The intention to obtain tax planning advice in relation to the next planned investment may be a step in the right direction, but the existence of further plans for expansion may be too much too soon for the Group.

Business expansion – finance

The Group is planning further expansion with capital expenditure of $45 million planned for new sites in 20X8. This equates to 12.9% of the Group's total assets, which is a significant amount and will be financed by a bank loan. While the Group's gearing is currently low at 25%, the additional finance being taken out from the Group's lending facility will increase gearing and incur additional interest charges of $1.6 million per annum, which is 16% of the projected profit before tax for the year. The increased debt and finance charges could impact on existing loan covenants and the additional interest payments will have cash flow as well as profit implications.

In addition, $5 million has been spent on the Moulin Blanche agreement. A further $25 million is needed for renovating the hotels which were damaged following a hurricane. Despite the fact that the repair work following the hurricane will ultimately be covered by insurance, the Group's capital expenditure at this time appears very high, and needs to be underpinned by sound financial planning in order to maintain solvency, especially given that only half of the

BPP
LEARNING

insurance claim in relation to repair work will be paid in advance and it may take some time to recover the full amount given the significant sums involved.

Customer illness

Customers being taken ill as a result of eating poor quality food in some hotel restaurants has exposed the Group to some bad publicity. However, this does appear to have been limited to a small local newspaper report, so this is unlikely to have a significant effect on the performance of the new Moulin Blanche brand.

There is a risk that legal claims could be made against the Group, and that more significant bad publicity could arise from these. Such claim may be difficult to prove, however, and are unlikely to be financially significant to the Group.

Profit margins and cash management

The nature of the business means that overheads will be high and profit margins likely to be low. Based on the projected profit before tax, the projected margin for 20X7 is 8%, and for 20X6 was 8.2%. Annual expenses on marketing and advertising are high, and given the focus on luxury, a lot will need to be spent on maintenance of the hotels, purchasing quality food and drink, and training staff to provide high levels of customer service. Offering all-inclusive holidays will also have implications for profit margins and for managing working capital as services, as well as food and drink, will have to be available whether guests use or consume them or not. The Group will need to maintain a high rate of room occupancy in order to maintain cash flows and profit margins. Cash management might be particularly problematic given that the majority of cash is received on departure, rather than when the guests book their stay. Refunds to customers following the recent hurricane will also impact on cash flows, as will the repairs needed to the damaged hotels.

International operations

The Group's international operations expose it to a number of risks. One which has already been mentioned relates to local regulations; with any international operation there is risk of non-compliance with local laws and regulations which could affect business operations. Additionally, political and economic instability introduces possible unpredictability into operations, making it difficult to plan and budget for the Group's activities, as seen with the recent investment in a politically unstable area which is not yet generating a return for the Group. There are also foreign exchange issues, which unless properly managed, for example, by using currency derivatives, can introduce volatility to profit and cash flows.

Catering operations

The Group has introduced improved technologies into its in-house catering operations. This appears to have brought efficiency savings, but there may be risks associated with such a change, eg it is possible that the quality of the catering will not be maintained, or that there could be difficulties around managing the associated organisational changes.

Hurricanes

The hurricane guarantee scheme exposes the Group to unforeseeable costs in the event of a hurricane disrupting operations. The costs of moving guests to another hotel could be high, as could be the costs of refunding customer deposits if they choose to cancel their booking rather than transfer to a different hotel. The cost of renovation in the case of hotels being damaged by hurricane is also high, and while this is covered by insurance, the Group will still need to fund the repair work before the full amount claimed on insurance is received which as discussed above will put significant pressure on the Group's cash flow. In addition, having two hotels which have been damaged by hurricanes closed for several months while repair work is carried out will result in lost revenue and cash inflows.

Claim relating to environmental damage

This is potentially a very serious matter, should it become public knowledge. The reputational damage could be significant, especially given that the Group markets itself as a luxury brand. Consumers are likely to react unfavourably to the allegations that the Group's activities are harming the environment; this could result in cancellation of existing bookings and lower demand in the future, impacting on revenue and cash flows. The email relating to the claim from Ocean Protection refers to international legislation and therefore this issue could impact in all of the countries in which the Group operates. The Group is hoping to negotiate with Ocean Protection to reduce the amount which is potentially payable and minimise media attention, but this may not be successful, Ocean Protection may not be willing to keep the issue out of the public eye or to settle for a smaller monetary amount.

(b) **Significant risks of material misstatement**

Revenue recognition

The Group's revenue could be over- or understated due to timing issues relating to the recognition of revenue. Customers pay 40% of the cost of their holiday in advance, and the Group has to refund any bookings which are cancelled a week or more before a guest is due to stay at a hotel. There is a risk that revenue is recognised when deposits are received, which would be against the requirements of IFRS 15 *Revenue from Contracts with Customers*, which states that revenue should be recognised when, or as, an entity satisfies a performance obligation. Therefore, the deposits should be recognised within current liabilities as deferred revenue until a week prior to a guest's stay, when they become non-refundable. There is the risk that revenue is overstated and deferred revenue and therefore current liabilities are understated if revenue is recognised in advance of the date the amount becomes non-refundable.

> **Tutorial note.** Credit will be awarded for discussion of further risk of misstatement relating to revenue recognition – for example, when the Group satisfies its performance obligations and whether the goods and services provided to hotel guests are separate revenue streams.

Foreign exchange

The Group holds $20 million in cash at the year end, most of which is held in foreign currencies. This represents 5.7% of Group assets, thus cash is material to the financial statements.

According to IAS 21 *The Effects of Changes in Foreign Exchange Rates*, at the reporting date foreign currency monetary amounts should be reported using the closing exchange rate, and the exchange difference should be reported as part of profit or loss. There is a risk that the cash holdings are not retranslated using an appropriate year-end exchange rate, causing assets and profit to be over- or understated.

Licence agreement

The cost of the agreement with Moulin Blanche is 1.4% of Group assets, and 50% of profit for the year. It is highly material to profit and is borderline in terms of materiality to the statement of financial position.

The agreement appears to be a licensing arrangement, and as such it should be recognised in accordance with IAS 38 *Intangible Assets*, which requires initial recognition at cost and subsequent amortisation over the life of the asset, if the life is finite. The current accounting treatment appears to be incorrect, because the cost has been treated as a marketing expense, leading to understatement of non-current assets and understatement of profit for the year by a significant amount. If the financial statements are not adjusted, they will contain a material misstatement, with implications for the auditor's report. As the restaurants were opened on 1 July 20X7, six months after the licence was agreed, it would seem appropriate to amortise the asset over the remaining term of the agreement of 9.5 years as this is the timeframe over which the licence will generate economic benefit. The annual amortisation expense would be $526,316, so if six months is recognised in this financial year, $263,158 should be charged to operating expenses, resulting in profit being closer to $14.74 million for the year.

It is possible that the incident in which a newspaper reported that some customers were taken sick as a result of eating in Moulin Blanche restaurants could have an effect on the brand's performance. The brand should be tested for impairment in line with IAS 36 *Impairment of Assets*.

Impairment of non-current assets due to political instability and regulatory issues

The sites acquired at a cost of $75 million represent 21.4% of total assets, and the hotel complex acquired at a cost of $23 million represents 6.6% of total assets; these assets are material to the Group financial statements.

There are risks associated with the measurement of the assets, which are recognised as property, plant and equipment, as the assets could be impaired. None of these assets is currently being used by the Group in line with their principal activities, and there are indications that their recoverable value may be less than their cost. Due to the political instability and the regulatory issues, it seems that the assets may never generate the value in use which was anticipated, and their fair value may also have fallen below cost. Therefore, in accordance with IAS 36 *Impairment of Assets*, management should conduct an impairment review, to determine the recoverable amount of the assets and whether any impairment loss should be recognised. The risk is that assets are overstated, and profit overstated, if any necessary impairment of assets is not recognised at the end of the reporting period.

Property sale

The gain on disposal is $1.3m (= $5.5m – $4.2m), which is 13% of profit before tax (= $1.3m / $10m). This is material to the statement of profit or loss.

The gain should not be included in revenue, but should be disclosed separately in the statement of profit or loss. There is a risk that revenue will be overstated if the financial statements include this gain within revenue. This classification misstatement is material, as the gain on disposal is just over 1% of the revenue figure in which it has been included (= $1.3m / $125m).

The revaluation gain is also material at 17% of profit before tax (= $1.7m / $10m). This gain should not be credited against operating charges in the statement of profit or loss. This amount should originally have been recognised in other comprehensive income and then held within other components of equity; it should now be transferred to retained earnings.

The sale should only be recognised in the year if the contract to sell is binding. There is a risk of the sale being recognised incorrectly if this is not the case.

If the contract is not binding before the year end but is completed before the auditor's report is eventually signed, then it will be a non-adjusting event after the end of the reporting period requiring disclosure in the financial statements.

If the contract is binding but not completed at the year end, there will be a material receivable of $5.5m (1.5% of total assets).

As the asset that has been sold is a revalued asset, all the assets in the same class will also be revalued as required by IAS 16: para. 36.

IAS 16 requires that revalued assets are revalued with sufficient regularity that the carrying amount does not differ materially from that which would be determined using fair value at the date of the statement of financial position (IAS 16: para. 31). The valuation on the sold building appeared to be out of date, as it sold at 31% above the valuation, which is material.

It will therefore be necessary to ensure that the valuations on the other buildings are correct, particularly if the increase in capacity has increased their value.

Effect of the hurricane

Two of the Group's hotels are closed due to extensive damage caused by a recent hurricane. It is anticipated that the Group's insurance policy will cover the damage of $25 million and the terms of the policy are that half will be paid in advance and the remainder on completion of the repairs, although this will need confirming during our audit testing. The accounting for these events will need to be carefully considered as there is a risk that assets and profit are overstated if the damage and subsequent claim have not been accounted for correctly.

The damage caused to the hotels and resultant loss of revenue are likely to represent an indicator of impairment which should be recorded in line with IAS 36. IAS 16 *Property, Plant and Equipment* requires the impairment and derecognition of PPE and any subsequent compensation claims to be treated as separate economic events and accounted for separately in the period they occur. The standard specifically states that it is not appropriate to net the events off and not record an impairment loss because there is an insurance claim in relation to the same assets. As such, this may mean that the Group has to account for the impairment loss in the current year but cannot recognise the compensation claim until the next financial reporting period as this can only be recognised when the compensation becomes receivable. If it is indeed the case that the insurance company will pay half of the claim in advance, then it is likely that $12.5m could be included in profit or loss in the current year.

Provision/contingent liability

The letter received from Ocean Protection indicates that it may be necessary to recognise a provision or disclose a contingent liability, in respect of the $10 million damages which have been claimed. The amount is material at 2.9% of total assets, and 67.9% of profit before tax (adjusted for the incorrect accounting treatment of the licence agreement).

According to IAS 37 *Provisions, Contingent Liabilities and Contingent Assets*, a provision should be recognised if there is a present obligation as a result of a past event, and that there is a probable outflow of future economic benefits for which a reliable estimate can be made. It remains to be seen as to whether the Group can be held liable for the damage to the coral reefs. However, the finance director seems to be implying that the Group would like to reach a settlement, in which case a provision should be recognised.

A provision could therefore be necessary, but this depends on the negotiations between the Group and Ocean Protection, the outcome of which can only be confirmed following further investigation by the audit team during the final audit.

A contingent liability arises where there is either a possible obligation depending on whether some uncertain future event occurs, or a present obligation but payment is not probable or the amount cannot be measured reliably. There is a risk that adequate disclosure is not provided in the notes to the financial statements, especially given the finance director's reluctance to draw attention to the matter.

> **Tutorial note.** Credit would also be awarded for discussion of other relevant risks of material misstatements.

(c) (i) **Implications for audit planning**

The finance director's requests which restrict the audit team's ability to obtain audit evidence in relation to the environmental damage claim are inappropriate. In particular, the finance director should not dictate to the audit engagement partner that the audit team may not speak to Group employees. According to ISA 210 *Agreeing the Terms of Audit Engagements*, the management of a client should acknowledge their responsibility to provide the auditor with access to all information which is relevant to the preparation

BPP
LEARNING

of the financial statements which includes unrestricted access to persons within the entity from whom the auditor determines it necessary to obtain audit evidence.

This would appear to be an imposed limitation on scope, and the audit engagement partner should raise this issue with the Group's audit committee. The audit committee should be involved at the planning stage to obtain comfort that a quality audit will be performed, in accordance with corporate governance best practice, and therefore the audit committee should be able to intervene with the finance director's demands and allow the audit team full access to the relevant information, including the ability to contact Ocean Protection and the Group's lawyers.

The finance director would appear to lack integrity as he is trying to keep the issue a secret, possibly from others within the Group as well as the public. The audit engagement partner should consider whether other representations made by the finance director should be treated with an added emphasis on professional scepticism, and the risk of management bias leading to a risk of material misstatement could be high. This should be discussed during the audit team briefing meeting.

There is also an issue arising in relation to ISA 250 *Consideration of Laws and Regulations in an Audit of Financial Statements*, which requires that if the auditor becomes aware of information concerning an instance of non-compliance or suspected non-compliance with laws and regulations (NOCLAR), the auditor shall obtain an understanding of the act and the circumstances in which it has occurred, and further information to evaluate the possible effect on the financial statements. Therefore, the audit plan should contain planned audit procedures which are sufficient for the audit team to conclude on the accounting treatment and on whether the auditor has any reporting responsibilities outside the Group, for example, to communicate a breach of international environmental protection legislation to the appropriate authorities.

(ii)   **Planned audit procedures**

- Obtain the letter received from Ocean Protection and review to understand the basis of the claim, for example, to confirm if it refers to a specific incident when damage was caused to the coral reefs.

- Discuss the issue with the Group's legal adviser, to understand whether in their opinion, the Group could be liable for the damages, for example, to ascertain if there is any evidence that the damage to the coral reef was caused by activities of the Group or its customers.

- Discuss with the Group's legal adviser the remit and scope of the legislation in relation to environmental protection to ensure an appropriate level of understanding in relation to the regulatory framework within which the Group operates.

- Discuss with management and those charged with governance the procedures which the Group utilises to ensure that it is identifying and ensuring compliance with relevant legislation.

- Obtain an understanding, through enquiry with relevant employees, such as those responsible for scuba diving and other water sports, as to the nature of activities which take place, the locations and frequency of scuba diving trips, and the level of supervision which the Group provides to its guests involved in these activities.

- Obtain and read all correspondence between the Group and Ocean Protection, to track the progress of the legal claim up to the date that the auditor's report is issued, and to form an opinion on its treatment in the financial statements.

- Obtain a written representation from management, as required by ISA 250, that all known instances of non-compliance, whether suspected or otherwise, have been made known to the auditor.

- Discuss the issue with those charged with governance, including discussion of whether the Group has taken any necessary steps to inform the relevant external authorities, if the Group has not complied with the international environmental protection legislation.

- Review the disclosures, if any, provided in the notes to the financial statements, to conclude as to whether the disclosure is sufficient for compliance with IAS 37.

- Read the other information published with the financial statements, including chairman's statement and directors' report, to assess whether any disclosure relating to the issue has been made, and if so, whether it is consistent with the financial statements.

(d) **Tax planning engagement**

The invitation to tender for a tax planning engagement raises several issues. It is not stated when the engagement would take place, but if it is after the current year's auditor's report has been signed then it should not pose a problem for this year. If this is not the case, however, or if we continue to serve as the Group's auditor next year, then the following considerations are relevant.

Tax planning services encompass a range of different services, from advising a client how to structure its affairs in a tax-efficient manner, to advising on the application of a new tax law (IESBA *Code of Ethics*: para. 604.7 A2). There is a self-review threat if the planning advice affects matters to be reflected in the financial statements.

The significance of the threat depends on factors such as:

- The degree of subjectivity involved, and whether advice is supported by existing law
- The materiality of the effect of any advice on the financial statements
- Whether the tax planning advice given will depend on any accounting treatment

(IESBA *Code of Ethics*: para. 604.7 A3)

Given that this appears to be the first time the Group has obtained tax planning advice, the advice it wants may be relatively basic in nature. Dove & Co should ask the Group for further information about the advice it needs; more complex advice may pose a greater threat than simpler advice.

The Group is planning to make another acquisition but it is not known whether this would be material to the financial statements, or whether the effect of any advice would be material. This is, however, possible. For example, tax planning advice could determine whether an acquisition takes the form of acquiring an entity's assets and liabilities, or whether a new subsidiary is acquired. The latter would be more likely to be material.

Providing tax planning advice on an overseas acquisition may require knowledge of overseas tax legislation, which may fall outside of Dove & Co's competence. Before submitting any tender Dove & Co must find out where the acquisition is planned to take place so that it can determine whether it would be in a position to do the work.

Depending on these considerations, it is likely that an engagement could only be accepted on the basis that safeguards could be applied to reduce the self-review threat to an acceptable level. Safeguards could include:

- Using separate teams to perform the tax service and the audit
- Having an independent tax professional advise the audit team on the service

(IESBA *Code of Ethics*: para. 604.7 A4)

BPP
LEARNING

It has been suggested that Dove & Co would be able to make use of its existing knowledge of the Group. This is unlikely to be possible, as the tax engagement would be separate from the audit engagement.

Conclusion

These briefing notes highlight that the Group faces significant and varied business risk, in particular in relation to its expansion strategy which is possibly unsound. There are a number of significant risks of material misstatement which will need to be carefully considered during the planning of the Group audit, to ensure that an appropriate audit strategy is devised. Several issues are raised by the claim from Ocean Protection, and our audit programme should contain detailed and specific procedures to enable the audit team to form a conclusion on an appropriate accounting treatment. Finally, several matters should be clarified with the Group before tendering for a possible tax planning engagement.

34 Laurel

Workbook references. Chapters 4, 6 and 8.

Top tips. This was a relatively straightforward Section A case study-style question, albeit one with a fairly numerical focus. When attempting long questions such as this, it is crucial that you stick to your timings for each question part – if you multiply the number of marks by 2 then you'll come close to the number of minutes available.

Part (a) asked for risks of material misstatement AND analytical procedures. It is essential that you do calculate enough ratios if you are going to pass this question. There are 5 marks available for this, and they are easy marks that you should be banking on getting.

Although the model answer does not do this, it is a good idea to put your ratios in an appendix to your answer. This makes them easier to mark, and allows you to run through your calculations before you identify risks. You should also ensure that you're calculating relevant ratios, such as those shown here.

The requirement asks you to use analytical procedures as a way of identifying risks. If you work in this way then the question will actually be easier as this is the easiest way to discover some of the risks.

As you should be aware, a question asking for 'risks of material misstatement' does not want detection risks, so these will get no marks. In addition, weaker candidates often spend time writing long theoretical discussions of how audit risk is made up. This is a nice early signal to the marker that they are likely to fail – so take heed and do not do this!

Part (b) was closely connected to (a). One way of approaching this would be to write down additional information needed on a separate sheet of paper as you are answering part (a).

Part (c) was a straightforward question part featuring issues that have come up on past exam sittings and which should therefore have been familiar to you.

Part (d) was not difficult, and you could have made headway here using common sense alone.

Part (e) was difficult, but it was possible to pass this part of the question with some fairly generic remarks on the audit of financial instruments, mentioning things like the complexity of the accounting standards in this area and the difficulty in determining the correct treatment.

Easy marks. The marks for calculating ratios, and those for additional information, were among the easiest in the exam. The professional marks should also not be missed.

ACCA examining team's comments. This question presented the scenario of a large cosmetics group and candidates were presented with five requirements.

Part (a) required risks of material misstatement in the audit to be considered, including using analytical procedures, and a full statement of financial position and statement of profit or loss were provided. This was generally well answered as there were lots of potential risks to discuss. Candidates that did not score well often concentrated on explaining audit procedures rather than evaluating risks. Disappointingly, many candidates only calculated one or two ratios or trends even though the question asked for analytical procedures and contained a full page of numerical data to analyse. Candidates' inability to utilise all the information provided when evaluating risks continues to be an area of concern and continues to demonstrate that candidates must improve their exam technique in this regard.

Part (b) required candidates to highlight additional information to enable more detailed analytical review to be performed. Answers to this part were collectively disappointing with most candidates giving generic lists of additional items that may be required, such as board minutes or impairment reviews. These would be required as part of a wider audit plan but that was not what the question asked for. Very few candidates actually answered the question and highlighted what information was required for analytical review purposes, such as a breakdown of sales by product or market.

Part (c) was split into two sections, firstly the audit procedures related to the impairment of a brand. This was reasonably answered with some good procedures highlighted but many candidates erroneously digressed into seeking the original cost of the brand and discussing whether any claims were being made against the company which would have been better-included in part (a).

In part (c)(ii) the audit procedures related to a planned acquisition and were generally well answered with sensible procedures such as reviewing the due diligence report, board minutes and discussions with management about the likelihood of success. Theorising about whether the acquisition would be a subsidiary or associate or suggesting audit procedures for the enlarged group did not answer the requirement.

There were four **professional marks** available for presentation, logic and clarity. Candidates who presented their answers in a logical and reasoned manner with sub-headings and references scored well. Again candidates are advised to consider their exam technique in this area, for example only one concise paragraph is necessary as an introduction, not a whole page. **Candidates are advised to space out their work and start a new page for each sub-section**.

On requirement (e), answers here were extremely mixed in quality. Satisfactory answers focused on why financial instruments generally are difficult to audit, discussing their complex nature, the changing landscape of financial reporting requirements, the potential for both client and auditor to lack appropriate knowledge and skills, and the frequent need to rely on an expert.

Inadequate answers did not include much reference to audit at all, and simply listed out financial reporting rules, with no consideration of audit implications other than saying that financial instruments are complex and subjective. There were very few references to relevant ISA requirements, and little evidence that the audit of complex matters such as financial instruments had been studied at all, even though it is a topical current issue.

Marking scheme

Marks

(a) **Evaluation of risk of material misstatement**
Generally 1 mark for each ratio (including comparative) calculated, and ½ mark for relevant trends calculated, up to a maximum of 5 marks. In addition, up to 2 marks for discussion of risks in relation to the ratios calculated. Risks in relation to ratio analysis could include:
– Understatement of operating expenses excluding the impairment loss
– Understatement of finance costs

BPP
LEARNING

- Tax expense not in line with movement in deferred tax liability
- Overstatement of current assets/understatement of current liabilities
- Significant new loan liability to be taken on around the reporting date – recognition, measurement and disclosure risks
- Unexplained/ inconsistent movement in intangible assets/loan raised to finance development
- Unreconciled movement in retained earnings

Other risks of material misstatement – up to 2 marks for each risk identified and explained:
- Allow 1 mark for each correct calculation and comment on materiality up to a maximum of 2 marks
- New loan may breach existing loan covenants – risk that IFRS 7 disclosures not made
- Change to PPE useful lives may not be appropriate – overstated assets and profit
- Management bias risk due to new loan being taken out
- Impairment to Chico brand may be understated if full carrying value of brand not written off
- Impairment may need separate disclosure due to materiality – risk of inadequate disclosure
- Chico inventories will need to be written off – risk of overstated assets
- Risk that goodwill has not been tested for impairment
- A provision may be needed for customer claims – risk of understated liabilities
- Hire contracts appear to result in lease that has not been recognised
- Deferred tax liability appears incorrect and likely to be overstated

Maximum 19

(b) **Additional information to assist with preliminary analytical review**
Generally up to 1 mark for each piece of information recommended:
- Disaggregation of revenue into major brands to identify significant trends by brand
- Monthly breakdown of revenue to assess date at which Chico products were withdrawn
- Disaggregation of operating expenses to determine main categories and inclusion of impairment expense
- Disaggregation of current assets to assess movements in inventories, receivables and cash
- Disaggregation of current liabilities to assess significant decrease
- Details of the $20m loan taken out to evaluate appropriateness of finance charge
- Details of the new $130m loan to build into projected gearing and other ratios
- Details of machine hire contracts to determine size of any assets not recognised
- Reconciliation of brought forward and carried forward intangible assets
- Statement of changes in equity

Maximum 6

Marks

(c) **Audit procedures**
Up to 1 mark for each well described procedure:

(i) **Impairment of brand name**
- Obtain management's calculations relevant to the impairment and review to understand methodology
- Evaluate the assumptions used by management in their impairment review and consider their reasonableness
- Confirm the carrying value of the Chico brand pre-impairment to prior year financial statements or management accounts
- From management accounts, obtain a breakdown of total revenue by brand, to evaluate the significance of the Chico brand
- If the brand is not fully written off, discuss with management the reasons for this treatment given that the brand is now discontinued
- Obtain a breakdown of operating expenses to confirm that the impairment is included
- Review the presentation of the income statement, considering whether separate disclosure of the impairment is necessary given its materiality

Maximum   5

(ii) **Acquisition of Azalea Co**
- Read board minutes to understand the rationale for the acquisition, and to see that the acquisition is approved
- Discuss with Group management the way that control will be exercised over Azalea Co, enquiring as to whether the Group can determine the board members of Azalea Co
- Review the minutes of relevant meetings held between management of the Group and Azalea Co to confirm matters such as:
  - That the deal is likely to go ahead
  - The likely timescale
  - The amount and nature of consideration to be paid
  - The shareholding to be acquired and whether equity or non-equity shares
  - The planned operational integration (if any) of Azalea Co into the Group
- Obtain any due diligence reports which have been obtained by the Group and review for matters which may need to be disclosed in accordance with IAS 10 or IFRS 3
- After the reporting date, agree the cash consideration paid to bank records

Maximum   5

Professional marks
Generally 1 mark for heading, 1 mark for introduction, 1 mark for use of headings within the briefing notes, 1 mark for clarity of comments made.

Maximum   4

(d) **Matters re recurring audit**

Generally up to 1 mark for each point explained:
- Consider changes in circumstances
- Examples of changes in circumstances
- Bulldog's circumstances have not changed significantly
- No need to remind entity of terms

Maximum   3

(e) **Audit of financial instruments**

Generally up to 1½ marks for each point explained:

Why is audit of financial instruments challenging?
- Financial reporting requirements complex
- Transactions themselves difficult to understand
- Lack of evidence and need to rely on management judgement
- Auditor may need to rely on expert
- May be hard to maintain attitude of scepticism
- Internal controls may be deficient

Planning implications
- Obtain understanding of accounting and disclosure requirements
- Obtain understanding of client's financial instruments
- Determine resources, ie skills needed and need for an auditor's expert
- Consider internal controls including internal audit
- Determine materiality of financial instruments
- Understand management's method for valuing financial instruments

Maximum   8

Total   **50**

Briefing notes

To: Brigitte Sanders, audit engagement partner

From: Audit manager

Subject: Laurel Group audit planning Introduction

These briefing notes are intended for use in planning the audit of the Laurel Group (the Group). The notes contain an evaluation of risks of material misstatement, which have been identified using information provided by the client following a meeting with the Group finance director and performing selected analytical procedures. The notes also identify the additional information which should be requested from the Laurel Group to allow for a more detailed preliminary analytical review to be performed.

The notes also recommend the principal audit procedures to be performed in respect of an impaired brand and a planned acquisition which will take place after the reporting period.

(a) Evaluation of risk of material misstatement
(b) Additional information to help in performing analytical review

Selected analytical procedures and associated evaluation of risk of material misstatement

	20X7	20X6
Operating margin	$35/220 \times 100 = 15.9\%$	$37/195 \times 100 = 19\%$
Return on capital employed	$(35/229 + 110) \times 100 = 10.3\%$	$(37/221 + 82) \times 100 = 12.2\%$
Interest cover	$^{35}/_7 = 5$	$^{37}/_7 = 5.3$
Effective tax rate	$^3/_{28} \times 100 = 10.7\%$	$^3/_{30} \times 100 = 10\%$
Current ratio	$143/19 = 7.5$	$107/25 = 4.3$
Gearing ratio	$(100/100 + 229) \times 100 = 30.4\%$	$(80/80 + 221) \times 100 = 26.6\%$

Revenue is projected to increase by 12.8% in the year, whereas operating expenses increase by 17.1%, explaining the reduction in operating margin from 19% in 20X6 to 15.9% in 20X7. The trend in return on capital employed is consistent, with the return falling from 12.2% to 10.3%.

The notes from the meeting with the finance director state that an impairment loss of $30m has been recognised during the year. Assuming that this cost has been included in operating expenses, it would be expected that operating expenses should increase by at least $30m. However, operating expenses have increased by only $27m during the year. If the $30m impairment loss is excluded, it would seem that operating expenses have actually decreased by $3m, which is not in line with expectations given the substantial increase in revenue. There is therefore a risk that operating expenses are understated and consequently profit is overstated. Detailed audit procedures will need to be performed to investigate the possible omission of expenses from the statement of profit or loss.

Conversely, there is also the risk that revenue is overstated given the withdrawal of the Chico branded products, implying that revenue should decrease due to lost sales from this revenue stream.

To assist with the analytical review on operating profit, the following additional information should be obtained:

- A disaggregation of revenue to show the revenue associated with the key brands of the Group, in particular the level of sales and contribution from the withdrawn Chico brand.

- A breakdown of revenue month by month, to establish when sales of the Chico brand cease.

- A disaggregation of the main categories of expenses included in operating expenses, which would confirm that the impairment loss has been included.

The interest cover is stable and indeed the finance cost recognised is constant at $7m each year. Given that the Group took out a $20m loan in January 20X7, it would be expected that finance charges should increase to take account of interest accruing on the new element of the loan. There is therefore a risk that finance charges and the associated loan liability are understated.

Additional information to help the analytical review here would include:

- Details of the loan taken out, including a copy of the new loan agreement to establish the interest rate payable, repayment terms and whether any borrowing costs other than interest were incurred.

The Group's effective tax rate also appears stable, increasing from 10% to 10.7% in the year. However, given the significant movement in the deferred tax liability there should be a corresponding change in the tax expense, assuming that the additional deferred tax should be charged to profit or loss. Currently, it is unclear how this increase in the deferred tax liability has been recorded. The deferred tax liability itself creates a risk of material misstatement, which will be discussed separately, and the audit plan must contain detailed responses to ensure that sufficient and appropriate evidence is obtained in respect of both the current and deferred tax recognised.

BPP
LEARNING

The current ratio has increased sharply in the year from 4.3 to 7.5. This could indicate that current assets are overstated or current liabilities understated and the reasons for the significant change must be discussed with the client as part of audit planning, in order to identify any specific risks such as potential overstatement of inventory included in current assets, for example, if any Chico inventory is not yet written down in value.

Additional information to help with this analysis would be:

- A breakdown of current assets so the individual figures for inventories, receivables and cash (and any other current assets recognised in the statement of financial position) can be identified and trends established.

- A breakdown of current liabilities to establish the reasons for the decrease of 24% on the prior year.

Gearing has increased due to the $20m loan taken out. It is noted that the Group is going to take out another significant loan of $130m should the acquisition of Azalea Co go ahead as planned in early June. Recognition of this loan as a liability will result in the gearing ratio increasing significantly to 50.1% (230/230 + 229). Several risks arise in respect of this additional loan. First, the timing of its receipt is important. If the deal is to take place in early June, the finance would need to be in place in advance, and therefore it is likely that the loan is taken out just prior to the year end on 31 May. In this case it would need to be recognised and disclosed in accordance with IFRS 9 *Financial Instruments* and IFRS 7 *Financial Instruments: Disclosures*, and there is a risk that the liability is not measured appropriately or that disclosure is incomplete. Given the potential materiality of the loan, at 36.3% of existing total assets, this is a significant risk.

There is also a risk that the increase in gearing will breach any existing loan covenants. While this is a business risk rather than an audit risk, the matter may require disclosure in the financial statements, leading to a risk of material misstatement if necessary disclosures are not made.

Additional information which will help with the assessment of this risk includes:

- Copies of any agreements with the bank so that terms can be verified, in particular the anticipated date of the receipt of the funds, and the impact on the financial statements and on analytical review procedures confirmed.

According to note 3 to the forecast financial statements, the $20m loan was used to finance a specific new product development project. However, development costs recognised as an intangible asset have increased by only $15m. The difference of $5m is not explained by analytical review on the draft financial statements, and there is a risk that not all the amount spent on development costs has been capitalised, meaning that the intangible asset could be understated. Conversely, it could be the case that that $5m of the amount spent was not eligible for capitalisation under the recognition rules of IAS 38 *Intangible Assets*, however, as discussed above the movement in operating expenses does not suggest that $5m of research costs has been expensed. It may also be that the company continues to hold the $5m in cash and this may be supported by the significant increase in current assets in the year.

Additional information is required to explain how the $20m raised from the loan has been utilised, whether it was all spent on research and development, and the nature of the development costs which were funded from the loan.

Finally, retained earnings has increased by $8m. Projected profit for the year is $25m, therefore there is an unexplained reconciling item between retained earnings brought forward and carried forward. The difference could be due to a dividend paid in the financial year, but additional information including a statement of changes in equity is required in order to plan an appropriate audit response.

Property, plant and equipment

The change to the estimated useful lives of property, plant and equipment has increased profit by $5m, which represents 17.9% of profit before tax and is therefore material to the financial statements. This change in accounting estimate is permitted, but the audit team should be sceptical and carefully consider whether the change is justified. If the change were found to be inappropriate it would need to be corrected, increasing operating expenses by $5m, reducing operating profit to $30m and the operating margin would fall to only 13.6%. This would be a significant reduction in profit and it could be that management bias is a risk factor, especially given the sizeable loan which is about to be agreed meaning that the projected financial statements may have already been scrutinised by the Group's bank.

Chico brand name and associated issues

The Group finance director states that the Chico brand name has been impaired by $30m. However, the brand name intangible asset has fallen by $35m in the year, so there is an unexplained reduction of $5m. This may have been caused by the impairment or sale of another brand, and additional information should be sought to explain the movement in the year.

The audit team will need to verify whether the $30m impairment recognised in relation to the Chico brand name is a full impairment of the amount recognised in relation to that specific brand within intangible assets. Given that the branded products have been withdrawn from sale, it should be fully written off, and if any amount remains recognised, then intangible assets and operating profit will be overstated. The amount written off amounts to 8.4% of Group assets and 107% of profit before tax. It is a highly material issue which may warrant separate disclosure under IAS 1 *Presentation of Financial Statements*. It is a risk that the necessary disclosures are not made in relation to the discontinuance and/or the impairment of assets.

There is also a risk that other brands could be impaired, for example, if the harmful ingredients used in the Chico brand are used in other perfume ranges. The impairment recognised in the financial statements could therefore be understated, if management has not considered the wider implications on other product ranges.

There is also a risk that inventories are overstated if there are any Chico items included in the amount recognised within current assets. Any Chico products should be written down to the lower of cost and net realisable value in accordance with IAS 2 *Inventories*, and presumably the net realisable value would be zero.

There is a possibility that some non-current assets used in the production of the Chico fragrance may need to be measured and disclosed in accordance with IAS 36 *Impairment of Assets* and/or IFRS 5 *Assets Held for Sale and Discontinued Operations*. This would depend on whether the assets are impaired or meet the criteria to be classified as held for sale, for example, whether they constitute a separate major line of business.

There may also be an issue relating to the health issues caused by use of the Chico products. It is likely that customers may have already brought legal claims against the Group if they have suffered skin problems after using the products. If claims have not yet arisen, they may occur in the future. There is a risk that necessary provisions have not been made, or that contingent liabilities have not been disclosed in the notes to the financial statements in accordance with IAS 37 *Provisions, Contingent Liabilities and Contingent Assets*. This would mean that liabilities are potentially understated and operating profit is overstated, or that disclosures are incomplete.

Goodwill

Goodwill has not been impaired this year; we shall need to carry out a review of management's annual impairment test to assess its appropriateness and whether any of the goodwill has been impaired by the media coverage of the Chico product allegations. This means that goodwill and operating profit could be overstated if any necessary impairment has not been recognised.

Deferred tax liability

The finance director states that the change in the deferred tax liability relates to the changes in estimated useful lives of assets and associated accelerated tax depreciation (capital allowances). However, the impact on profit of the change to estimated useful lives amounts to $5m, so the $8m increase in deferred tax seems inappropriate and it is likely that the liability is overstated.

The deferred tax liability has increased by five times, and the $10m recognised in the year-end projection is material at 2.8% of total assets. The changes in deferred tax and the related property, plant and equipment therefore do not appear to be proportionate and the amounts recognised could be incorrect.

Machine hire

The payments are 3.5% of profit before tax (= $1m / $28m), and are thus not material by themselves. They may of course become material once aggregated with any other misstatements.

The contracts may qualify as leases in line with IFRS 16 *Leases*, if the Group has the right to control the use of specific identified assets. If this is the case then the machines should be recognised as right-of-use assets within non-current assets, along with a lease liability for the present value of lease payments. The assets should then be treated in line with IAS 16 *Property, Plant and Equipment*. Not recognising these leases may mean that both non-current assets and liabilities are understated.

IFRS 16 does allow an exemption from recognition for low-value assets that are held on short-term leases. If the machines met these criteria then the Group could elect merely to recognise the lease payments as an expense on a straight-line basis over the lease term. This does not apply in this case, because payments of $200,000 per machine (=$1m ÷ 5) indicate that the machines are not low-value assets.

Additional information needed would be the contracts, so that the present value of any lease liability can be determined. This could have an effect on the preliminary analytical review. Although the payments recognised this year are not material, it is quite possible that any right-of-use assets (and lease liabilities) not recognised would be material.

Acquisition of Azalea Co

The acquisition is planned to take place in early June and assuming it takes place, it will be a significant event to be disclosed in accordance with IAS 10 *Events after the Reporting Period*. Details of the acquisition will also need to be disclosed to comply with IFRS 3 *Business Combinations* which requires disclosure of information about a business combination whose acquisition date is after the end of the reporting period but before the financial statements are authorised for issue. There is a risk that the necessary disclosures are not made which would be a significant risk of material misstatement given the materiality of the acquisition.

> **Tutorial note.** Credit will be awarded for evaluation of other relevant risks of material misstatement including management bias due to the loan of $130m being provided, and the complex and acquisitive nature of the Group, which leads to inherent risk of misstatement in relation to business combinations.

(c) ### Audit procedures

(i) #### Impairment of Chico brand

- Obtain management's calculations relevant to the impairment and review to understand methodology – for example, whether the brand has been entirely or partly written off

- Evaluate the assumptions used by management in their impairment review and consider their reasonableness

- Confirm the carrying value of the Chico brand pre-impairment to prior year financial statements or management accounts

- From management accounts, obtain a breakdown of total revenue by brand, to evaluate the significance of the Chico brand to financial performance and whether it constitutes a separate line of business for disclosure as a discontinued operation

- If the brand is not fully written off, discuss with management the reasons for this treatment given that the brand is now discontinued

- Obtain a breakdown of operating expenses to confirm that the impairment is included

- Review the presentation of the statement of profit or loss, considering whether separate disclosure of the impairment is necessary given its materiality

(ii) **Acquisition of Azalea Co**

- Read board minutes to understand the rationale for the acquisition, and to see that the acquisition is approved.

- Discuss with Group management the way that control will be exercised over Azalea Co, enquiring as to whether the Group can determine the board members of Azalea Co.

- Review the minutes of relevant meetings held between management of the Group and Azalea Co to confirm matters such as:

    - That the deal is likely to go ahead
    - The likely timescale
    - The amount and nature of consideration to be paid
    - The shareholding to be acquired and whether equity or non-equity shares
    - The planned operational integration (if any) of Azalea Co into the Group

- Obtain any due diligence reports which have been obtained by the Group and review for matters which may need to be disclosed in accordance with IAS 10 or IFRS 3.

- Obtain copies of the finance agreement for the funds used to purchase Azalea Co.

- After the reporting date, agree the cash consideration paid to bank records.

Conclusion

These briefing notes indicate that there are many potentially significant risks of material misstatement to be considered in planning the Group audit. The Group should provide the additional information requested to enable a more thorough analytical review to be performed as part of our audit planning. A range of audit procedures has been recommended, which should reduce our detection risk in relation to the impaired brand and the planned acquisition of Azalea Co after the year end.

(d) In relation to a recurring audit engagement such as this, Holly & Co needs to assess whether there have been any changes in circumstances which could require the terms of the engagement to be revised (ISA 210: para. 13). This could include any significant changes in the nature or size of an entity's business, changes in legal requirements, or changes in the financial reporting framework adopted (ISA 210: para. A30).

Although Bulldog Co has recently expanded overseas (and has set up a treasury management function), this is unlikely to constitute a significant change in the nature of its business.

Holly & Co should also consider whether Bulldog Co needs to be reminded of the existing engagement terms (ISA 210: para. 13). This might be needed where there are indications that the entity misunderstands the objective and scope of the audit (ISA 210: para. A30), but there are no such indications here.

(e) **Audit of financial instruments**

Financial instruments themselves may be difficult to understand. Management themselves may fail to understand the risks involved with them, which may expose the entity to substantial risks.

Financial reporting requirements in this area can be complex, which increases the risk of misstatement. It is possible that neither management nor the auditor will properly understand how the instruments should be accounted for.

Accounting for financial instruments may also involve an element of subjectivity, eg in determining fair values. Fair values may be estimated with the use of models which will involve making assumptions. Therefore is therefore a risk that the assumptions made by management are not reasonable.

Given the presence of subjectivity, it is all the more important that the auditor is professionally sceptical in this area, although this is likely to be difficult.

Alternatively, some financial instruments may be fairly simple to audit, eg where there is an active market, it may be possible to agree fair values to a broker's report. This would of course be subject to the requirements of ISA 500 *Audit Evidence* in relation to the use of a management's expert.

It may be necessary to make use of an auditor's expert, in which case the auditor must ensure that the expert is independent and competent, and must evaluate the suitability of the expert's work as audit evidence. This may not be straightforward to do, given the complexity of the subject matter. Using an auditor's expert may also have the effect of increasing the audit fee, which should be explained to and discussed with the client.

Matters to consider

The company's treasury management function has only been set up recently, so it is possible that there may be teething problems in an area such as this. Internal controls may not be well established, so the auditor will need to spend time obtaining an understanding of them. This increases audit risk in this area.

Consideration should be given to the level of competence of staff in the new department. If they are skilled in this area then they may be new to the company, in which case there may be difficulties integrating the department with the rest of Bulldog's finance function. Alternatively, there is a risk that staff do not have adequate knowledge or experience in this area.

It will be necessary to obtain an understanding of the kinds of financial instruments Bulldog uses to hedge transactions, including Bulldog's reasons for entering into them and the kinds of risks it may be exposed to thereby.

The materiality of the instruments should be considered, bearing in mind especially the possibility that transactions with either no, or very little, initial value may turn out to have effects on the financial statements that are material. Some types of derivative financial instruments may fall into this category.

Management's method for valuing financial instruments should be considered, and the auditor must choose whether to audit management's valuation model, or whether to construct a model of its own. This would depend on the assessed reliability of internal controls in this area.

35 Dasset

Workbook references. Chapters 1 and 8.

Top tips. This was an optional question in the real exam, and it is likely that those who chose to tackle it did so because of part (a). Be sure to calculate materiality for some easy marks, both on the mine as a whole and on the possible impairment. You may have been tempted to write about the risk to the company's operations – this is relevant in this case, but only insofar as it casts doubt over the going concern assumption. There are no marks for discussing business risk as such.

As is often the case, you can score well by thinking of audit evidence in (a)(ii). Don't go overboard on this because marks are likely to be capped, but it is important to spend time on this part of the requirement. Note that the question does not ask for the impact on the auditor's report, so there are no marks available for comments on this.

Part (b) may have been trickier than (a). You needed to know your auditing standards here (ISA 250), and provided you did then you should have been able to pass this part of the question.

There is an article on the subject of NOCLAR on the ACCA website, which is relevant to this question.

Easy marks. Calculating materiality is simple in part (a).

Marking scheme

Marks

(a) (i) **Matters to consider**
Generally 1 mark for each point made:
- Materiality of the mine to total assets
- Impairment review should have been performed
- Materiality of the potential write-off to profit
- No impairment write-off means overstated assets and profit
- Potentially all of the mine may be closed down and therefore impaired
- Improvements to health and safety should be capitalised
- Costs of abandoning/sealing up collapsed tunnels should be expensed
- Separate presentation of material impairment costs in financial statements
- Provision to be recognised for damaged properties/relocation costs of local residents
- Further claims may be made leading to provisions or contingent liabilities
- The authority may impose fine/penalty – provision or contingent liability
- Going concern disclosure if accident creates significant doubt
- Break-up basis if authority withdraw company's operating licence

(ii) **Evidence**

– Operating licence, reviewed for conditions relating to health and safety and for potential fines and penalties

– A written representation from management on their intention (or not) to bring the non-compliance to the attention of the National Coal Mining Authority

– A copy of board minutes where the accident has been discussed to identify the rationale behind the non-disclosure

– A copy of reports issued by engineers or other mining specialists confirming the extent of the damage caused to the mine by the accident

– Any quotes obtained for work to be performed to make the mine safe and for blocking off entrances to abandoned tunnels

– Confirmation, possibly by physical inspection, that the undamaged portion of the mine is operational

– A copy of the surveyor's report on the residential properties, reviewed for the expert's opinion as to whether they should be demolished

– A review of correspondence entered into with the local residents who have been relocated, to confirm the obligation the company has committed to in respect of their relocation

– Copies of legal correspondence, reviewed for any further claims made by local residents

– A review of the Ledge Hill Mine accident book, for confirmation that no one was injured in the accident

– A copy of management's impairment review, if any, evaluated to ensure that assumptions are reasonable and in line with auditor's understanding of the situation

– Confirmation that impairment losses have been recognised as an operating expense

– A review of draft disclosure notes to the financial statements where provisions and contingent liabilities have been discussed

– A review of cash flow and profit forecasts, forming a view on the overall going concern status of the company

Maximum   14

(b) **Responsibilities, actions and reporting**

Generally 1 mark for each point discussed:

– Management responsible for compliance with laws and regulations

– Auditor responsible for understanding applicable laws and regulations

– There is suspected non-compliance with laws and regulations and further procedures are necessary

– Matter should be discussed with those charged with governance

– Need to understand reason for non-disclosure/encourage management to disclose

– The need for external reporting should be evaluated

– Legal advice may be sought

– Confidentiality may be overridden in some circumstances

Maximum   6

Total   **20**

(a)   (i)   The mine is recognised at $10m, which is 5.7% of total assets and is therefore material.

Impairment

The closure of a third of the mine is an indicator that the asset may be impaired. Management should therefore already have conducted an impairment review in line with IAS 36 *Impairment of Assets*.

At a minimum it would appear that no future economic benefit can be derived from one third of the mine. At $3.3m, this is approximately 18.5% of Dasset's profit before tax and is highly material.

It is possible, however, that the situation is far worse than this. If the whole mine were unusable, then an impairment loss of $10m would need to be recognised, which at 56% of profit before tax is very material indeed.

IAS 1 *Presentation of Financial Statements* requires separate disclosure of individual items of income or expense (IAS 1: para. 32), so it is possible that such an impairment loss should be disclosed in this way. Inadequate disclosure would be a material misstatement.

Withdrawal of licence

It is possible that the National Coal Mining Authority ('NCMA') may withdraw Dasset's licence in relation to the Ledge Hill mine. This would result in a $10m impairment loss.

Fines could also be imposed in relation both to the accident and to Dasset's failure to report it. These would need to be either provided for or disclosed in line with IAS 37 *Provisions, Contingent Liabilities and Contingent Assets*. This would further reduce profit before tax, and failure to make the required provisions or disclosures would constitute a material misstatement.

Expenditure on mine

If the mine were to stay open then the monies spent improving the mine should be treated as capital expenditure. Clearly the amounts should be expensed if the mine cannot stay open. Any sums spent restoring the mine to its previous working condition should be treated as expenses, as should any expenditure required to make safe the unusable tunnels (which will not provide future economic benefits).

Provisions

IAS 37 requires provisions to be recognised for liabilities where there is a present obligation as a result of a past event (IAS 37: para. 14). These criteria appear to have been met in the case of the residential properties because the accident took place before the year end, and the fact that the company is meeting the residents' expenses implies that it acknowledges its liability to them.

Provision should therefore be made for:

- Any future costs of rental properties for which Dasset may be liable

- Costs relating to repairs or rebuilding of properties in the village for which Dasset may be liable

- Other future outflows, such as claims for compensation by affected residents.

These costs may be difficult to measure, so consideration should be given to whether these costs meet the IAS 37 criterion regarding an outflow being measured reliably.

The surveyor, a management's expert, should be able to provide a reliable estimate for the first two categories of cost above.

Management integrity

Management's decision not to report the accident to the authorities casts doubt over its integrity, in which case any written representations received from management should be reviewed and treated with professional scepticism.

There does not appear to be any liability to Dasset's employees because nobody was injured in the accident, but given the doubts over management's integrity this claim should be questioned. Procedures need to be performed to determine whether liabilities and disclosures in the financial statements are complete.

Going concern

In addition to withdrawing the licence for the Ledge Hill mine, the NCMA could withdraw the licence for the totality of Dasset's operations. This is unlikely, but not impossible, and its effects would be devastating for Dasset. The financial statements would then need to be prepared on the liquidation basis.

A further risk to going concern arises from the effect of any bad publicity about the accident on Dasset's future sales.

(ii) **Evidence**

- Copy of operating licence, reviewed for health and safety conditions and for potential penalties for non-compliance

- Written representation on management's intention (or not) to inform NCMA of non-compliance

- Board minutes discussing the accident, to identify the rationale behind non-disclosure

- Engineer's reports confirming extent of the damage caused to the mine

- Quotes obtained for work to be performed to make the mine safe

- Confirmation that the undamaged portion of the mine is operational, eg from reviewing engineer's report

- Surveyor's report on the residential properties, reviewed for opinion on whether they should be demolished

- Correspondence with relocated local residents, to confirm the obligation the company has committed to in respect of their relocation

- Copies of legal correspondence, reviewed for any further claims made by local residents

- Review of the Ledge Hill Mine accident book, for confirmation that no one was injured in the accident

- Copy of management's impairment review, if any, evaluated to ensure reasonableness of assumptions

- Confirmation that impairment losses have been recognised as expenses

- Review of draft disclosure relating to provisions and contingent liabilities

- Review of cash flow and profit forecasts with respect to going concern

(b) In line with ISA 250 *Consideration of Laws and Regulations in an Audit of Financial Statements* Dasset's management is responsible for ensuring that its operations comply with relevant law and regulations, in respect of which the auditor has no responsibility as such. The auditor must obtain a general understanding of the legal and regulatory framework and of the entity's compliance with it. The auditor must obtain evidence in relation to laws and regulations that have a direct effect on the financial statements. They must undertake

procedures in relation to those which do not have a direct effect, but which may still have an indirect material effect.

Dasset's management appears in this case not to have complied with NCMA regulations, and has not informed the NCMA of this. The decision not to inform the authority may be a legitimate one, or it could signal a belief on the part of management that it needs to hide the accident from the NCMA.

Burton & Co must obtain an understanding of the nature of the non-compliance with laws and regulations ('NOCLAR') and the surrounding circumstances, evaluating the possible effect on the financial statements and conducting further audit procedures where necessary. Burton & Co should consider the appropriateness of management's response to the NOCLAR, which in this case would include whether it was reasonable not to disclose the incident to the NCMA.

Burton & Co should discuss the NOCLAR with those charged with governance, and should obtain a written representation regarding the reason for the non-disclosure. The auditor should suggest that management reports the incident to the NCMA.

Burton & Co owes Dasset a duty of confidentiality and should therefore not disclose the accident without Dasset's prior consent. This duty may, however, be overridden where disclosure is in the public interest or is required by legislation. The auditor should consult with legal counsel to determine whether it has any legal duty to disclose, or whether disclosure would be appropriate here on public interest grounds.

36 Soprano

Workbook references. Chapters 2, 8, 12 and 14.

Top tips. Part (a) was a knowledge-based discussion on professional scepticism, which is a current issue in the profession. If you had chosen this question in the real exam, it was probably because of this requirement – but take heed of the examining team's warning at the end of the examining team's comments here!

The requirement here is actually quite broad and flexible, and you could have come up with all sorts of things to say. The definition of professional scepticism is a good place to start, allowing you to connect it to other aspects of the auditor's mind, such as the ability to exercise professional judgement and to be objective.

The requirement does include 'planning and performing the audit', so if you could develop one point well in relation to each then you would be on course to pass this part of the question. Fraud comes in at the planning stage, where the sceptical auditor tries to think of ways that fraud might have taken place. This then continues throughout the audit, with the audit team using professional scepticism to sniff out any fraud that might be occurring beneath their noses.

Part (b)(i) was an exercise in criticising the client, trying to think of what might be wrong. This is a little bit like some questions on quality control, where you have the satisfaction of pointing out all of the errors. Almost everything in the paragraph-long quotation from Silvio can be criticised, so this should be the starting point for your answer.

You may have found it difficult in (b)(ii) to think of enough procedures to warrant 5 marks. It is important here that you did not fall back on writing things that would not get you any marks at all, eg procedures on goodwill on acquisition, or explanations of what goodwill is from an accounting point of view. Perhaps the key point here is just realising what an impairment review of goodwill is about: goodwill relates to the value of the subsidiaries. An impairment review tries to see whether the asset (goodwill) is impaired, ie whether it's worth as much as it says it is in the financial statements. This means trying to find out how much the subsidiaries are worth, which is done in terms of their cash inflows. This is clearly a complex task, which will involve lots of judgements (eg which methodology to use), and lots of scope for error, eg calculation errors, not including all of the subsidiaries, and so on. Review the answer here for a flavour of what might go wrong, and what the auditor needs to look for.

Part (c) was not really difficult, but you may have been pressed for time and may have struggled to think of things to write. Try to make your points as specific as possible. For example, it is a good idea to interview the members of the sales team, but you would get more marks if you stated what you were probably thinking anyway: that the aim of the interview would be to determine what had happened and what the payments were for. You could then find evidence for what they say. It is possible that they are innocent – we only have Silvio's word for their guilt – so the auditor needs to have an open mind here. You might want to find out, for example, who was actually responsible for the payments, and whether there might be a business rationale for them.

Easy marks. Part (a) featured a lot of knowledge marks in an area that you should be familiar with – professional scepticism has been well signposted as a topical area.

ACCA examining team's comments. Regarding part (a), it was clear that many candidates had read and understood the contents of a recent *Student Accountant* article on the topic of professional scepticism. **Most answers** provided an appropriate definition of professional scepticism and went on to discuss how it links to audit quality. **Stronger candidates** also discussed how the auditor should apply professional scepticism when considering the risk of material misstatement associated with fraud and areas of the financial statements that rely on the application of judgment. Few candidates however, discussed the recent activities of the regulatory bodies in respect of professional scepticism.

In requirement (b)(i), many candidates were able to explain that the Group finance director was intimidating the audit firm, that his workings were not sufficient as a source of evidence, and that he may have something to hide. It was disappointing that few candidates appreciated that the Group's profit before tax had fallen significantly, and therefore the small impairment to goodwill suggested by the finance director was unlikely to be sufficient in the circumstances, and probably influenced by management bias. Most candidates did however realise that the audit firm should perform their own workings and not place complete reliance on the procedures that had been performed by the head of internal audit.

Requirement (b)(ii) relating to procedures on goodwill impairment was **poorly attempted**. The evidence points provided by candidates for this requirement tended to revolve around recalculation or a discussion with management. Very few suggested specific procedures that would allow the auditor to develop their own expectation in terms of the impairment necessary, which could then be compared with the finance director's workings. This was disappointing, as impairment has featured in several AAA exams as an audit issue and is a topic that candidates should be better prepared to tackle. Many candidates did not answer the question, and simply described the accounting treatment for goodwill, or suggested procedures that were relevant to the calculation of goodwill at acquisition but not relevant to a review of its impairment.

Answers to requirement (c) were **weak**. Many candidates gave no procedures at all, therefore not answering the question set, and instead described agreeing the scope of the work or whether the investigation could be performed for ethical reasons. Other candidates gave broad statements instead of procedures, such as 'quantify the loss' without explaining how this could be done, or 'interview the suspects' without saying what the purpose of this interview would be.

To comment generally on the performance on this optional question, it was quite clear that many candidates had read the relevant article on professional scepticism, but that they had very limited knowledge on either impairment audit issues or on forensic investigation procedures. To improve **exam technique**, candidates should ensure that they have a good attempt at all requirements of a question.

Marking scheme

Marks

(a) **Professional scepticism discussion**
Generally up to 1½ marks for each point discussed, including:
–   Definition of professional scepticism (1 mark for definition)
–   Explaining professional scepticism – alert throughout audit, alert to contradictory evidence, challenge assumptions, reliability of evidence
–   Link between professional scepticism and ethics/objectivity
–   Importance of professional scepticism in relation to complex and subjective areas of the audit, eg fair values
–   Importance of professional scepticism in relation to the audit of going concern
–   Discussion of regulatory bodies actions in relation to professional scepticism

Maximum   5

(b) (i) **Applying professional scepticism**
Generally up to 1½ marks for each point discussed, and 1 mark for calculation of materiality:
–   Risk that impairment loss understated due to Group's fall in profit
–   The determination of the impairment loss is judgemental and subject to management bias
–   Auditor should question the reasons for finance director's insistence that no other audit work is needed
–   Evidence provided by the finance director is not reliable (client-generated)
–   Assumptions are unlikely to have stayed the same since last year
–   Audit team should remain alert for other instances where professional scepticism is needed
–   Possible threat of intimidation by the finance director

Maximum   6

(ii) **Procedures on impairment**
Generally 1 mark for each procedure explained:
–   Review all assumptions, eg used in preparing projected cash flows, to ensure in line with auditor's current business understanding
–   Confirm that the impairment review includes the goodwill relating to all business combinations
–   Consider impact of auditor's assessment of the Group's going concern status
–   Consider operating effectiveness of any controls in place
–   Confirm whether management has performed the impairment test or used an expert
–   Reperform calculations based on auditor-generated inputs
–   Develop an independent estimate of the impairment loss and compare to that prepared by management
–   Confirm that the impairment calculations exclude cash flows relating to tax and finance items

BPP
LEARNING

  –   Perform sensitivity analysis
  –   Check the arithmetic accuracy of the calculations used in
      the impairment calculations

Maximum   5

(c) **Procedures on alleged bribery payments**
     Generally 1 mark for each procedure explained:
  –   Interview the two suspects and question them regarding the
      nature of the cash payments made to the customers prior to the
      signing of the contracts
  –   Using computer-assisted audit techniques to identify all new
      customers in the year and any payments made to these
      customers, and total the amounts
  –   Review the terms of contracts with customers for any such details
      of payments included in the contract, and understand the
      business rationale for any such payments
  –   Review the email and other correspondence entered into by the
      two suspects for any further information about the cash
      payments, eg specifically who the payments were discussed
      with
  –   Perform tests of control on the authorisation of cash payments to
      find out if these payments were known to anyone operating in a
      supervisory capacity

Maximum   4

Total
20

(a) Professional scepticism is defined in ISA 200 *Overall Objectives of the Independent Auditor and the Conduct of an Audit in Accordance with International Standards on Auditing* as an attitude that includes a questioning mind, being alert to conditions which may indicate possible misstatement due to error or fraud and a critical assessment of audit evidence.

ISA 200 requires the auditor to plan and perform an audit with professional scepticism, recognising that circumstances may exist which cause the financial statements to be materially misstated. It is important to use professional scepticism at all stages of the audit.

Professional scepticism includes being alert to the existence of contradictory audit evidence and being able to assess assumptions and judgements critically and without bias, and being ready to challenge management where necessary. It is also important that the auditor considers the reliability of information provided by management during the audit.

ISA 240 *The Auditor's Responsibilities Relating to Fraud in an Audit of Financial Statements* also refers specifically to professional scepticism, stating that the auditor shall maintain professional scepticism throughout the audit, recognising the possibility that a material misstatement due to fraud could exist. The auditor is therefore expected to be alert to indicators of potential fraud.

Recently, regulatory bodies such as the IAASB have stressed the importance of the auditor's use of professional scepticism. The increased use of principles-based financial reporting frameworks such as IFRS, and the prevalence of fair value accounting which introduces subjectivity and judgement into financial reporting, are examples of the reasons why the use of professional scepticism by auditors is increasingly important. It is imperative that professional scepticism is applied to areas of financial reporting which are complex or highly judgemental.

Going concern assessments and related party transactions are also examples of areas where management must exercise judgement in determining the appropriate accounting treatment,

and where the potential for management bias is high. Therefore these areas need to approached with professional scepticism.

The application of professional scepticism is closely aligned with maintaining objectivity, and it is difficult to remain sufficiently sceptical when certain threats to objectivity are present. Ultimately, the exercise of professional scepticism should work to reduce audit risk by ensuring that the auditor has sufficient and appropriate evidence to support the audit opinion, and that all evidence obtained, especially in relation to areas of high risk of material misstatement, has been critically evaluated and is based on reliable information.

(b) (i) The finance director seems to be dictating the audit work to be performed. The audit manager should decide the extent of audit procedures in response to the risk of material misstatement identified. The manager should consider why the finance director seems so insistent that his file is used as the main source of audit evidence; he may be hiding something relevant to the impairment which would be revealed if the auditor looked at other sources of evidence.

The Group's profit before tax has fallen by 33.3%, indicating that a significant impairment loss amounting to more than the $50,000 calculated by the finance director may need to be recognised. There is a risk of material misstatement in that the impairment loss is understated, and there is a risk that management bias has resulted in an inappropriate determination of the loss. The auditor therefore needs to be sceptical and alert for factors indicating that the loss is greater than that calculated by the finance director. Impairment testing is a complex and subjective area, and could easily be manipulated by management wishing to reduce the size of the loss recognised.

The audit manager should obtain corroborating evidence regarding the assumptions used and not just confirm that the assumptions are in line with management's risk assessment or the prior year audit file. The reliability of this source of evidence is not strong as it is prepared by management. An important part of professional scepticism is challenging management's assumptions, especially in an area of high judgement such as impairment testing.

The internal auditor checking the figures is also not a reliable source of evidence, as it is client-generated. The internal auditor may have been pressured to confirm the finance director's calculations.

Professional scepticism should also be applied to the comment that the assumptions are the same as in previous years. New factors impacting on impairment may have arisen during this year, affecting the determination of the impairment loss and up-to-date evidence on the assumptions used in this year's calculation should be sought.

The audit team should also remain alert when auditing balances and transactions other than goodwill in case there are other areas where Silvio does not appear to be providing all evidence required or where he is suggesting the audit approach to be taken.

While his comment does not seem to be intimidating in nature, the audit team should recognise that if Silvio does have something to hide in relation to the goodwill impairment, he may become more aggressive, in which case the matter should be brought to the attention of the firm's ethics partner and discussed with those charged with governance of the Group.

(ii) **Audit procedures – impairment of goodwill**

The auditor should perform the following procedures:

- The assumptions used in the impairment test should be confirmed as agreeing with the auditor's understanding of the business based on the current year's risk assessment procedures, eg assess the reasonableness of assumptions on cash flow projections

BPP
LEARNING

- Confirm that the impairment review includes the goodwill relating to all business combinations

- Consider the impact of the auditor's assessment of going concern on the impairment review, eg the impact on the assumption relating to growth rates which have been used as part of the impairment calculations

- Obtain an understanding of the controls over the management's process of performing the impairment test including tests of the operating effectiveness of any controls in place, for example, over the review and approval of assumptions or inputs by appropriate levels of management and, where appropriate, those charged with governance

- Confirm whether management has performed the impairment test or has used an expert

- The methodology applied to the impairment review should be checked by the auditor, with inputs to calculations, eg discount rates, agreed to auditor-obtained information

- Develop an independent estimate of the impairment loss and compare it to that prepared by management

- Confirm that the impairment calculations exclude cash flows relating to tax and finance items

- Perform sensitivity analysis to consider whether, and if so how, management has considered alternative assumptions and the impact of any alternative assumptions on the impairment calculations

- Check the arithmetic accuracy of the calculations used in the impairment calculations

Note. Credit will be awarded for other relevant audit procedures recommended.

(c) **Forensic investigation**

- Interview the two suspects and question them regarding the nature of the cash payments made to the customers prior to the signing of the contracts.

- Use computer-assisted audit techniques to identify all new customers in the year and any payments made to these customers, and total the amounts.

- Review the terms of the contracts with customers for any details of payments included in the contract, and understand the business rationale for any such payments.

Note. It would be unusual for the Group to be making any payments to customers, so these terms would need to be viewed with professional scepticism.

- Review the email and other correspondence entered into by the two suspects for any further information about the cash payments, eg specifically who the payments were discussed with.

- Perform tests of control on the authorisation of cash payments to find out if these payments were known to anyone operating in a supervisory capacity.

37 Willow

Workbook references. Chapters 8 and 11.

Top tips. In part (a) you were given three situations. Make sure you read the requirement carefully here, as there were a number of things to consider – you might have missed, for example, the requirement to recommend any further procedures. The trick with each of these issues is to take on a sceptical frame of mind. The audit work on inventory, for instance, appears to be complete as long as a written representation is obtained. But even if you did not remember the detailed requirements of ISA 580, you should have been able to question whether such a representation would be reliable,

and to point out that it needs to be backed up by evidence. The further procedures are then just ways of obtaining this evidence.

Part (b) was deceptively difficult. On the face of it there should be two easy marks for each of the four issues, but in reality the first issue in particular was not easy. You should, however, have been able to gather together enough marks to pass the question.

Easy marks. There were relatively easy marks in part (b) in relation to the ethics of accepting gifts and hospitality.

Marking scheme

Marks

(a) **Audit implications**
Generally up to 1 ½ marks for each implication assessed, 1 mark for each impact on the financial statements identified, and 1 mark for each effect on auditor's report:
Inventory
– Comment on individual materiality
– Value at lower of cost and NRV and impact on profit
– Written representation not sufficient evidence
– Recommend procedures (1 mark each)
Legal claim
– Immaterial individually but material to profit when combined with inventory adjustment
– Financial statements materially misstated when two issues combined – implication for opinion
– Suitability of verbal representation as source of evidence
– Recommended procedures (1 mark each)
Current assets
– Material by nature but not material in monetary terms
– Identification of related party transaction
– Disclosure in notes to financial statements inadequate – implication for opinion
– Interest should have been accrued
– Recommended procedures (1 mark each)

Maximum   17

(b) **Issues for attention of audit committee**
Generally up to 2 marks for each matter discussed:
– Property revaluations
– Delay in receiving non-current asset register affects audit efficiency
– Weak controls in procurement department
– Lack of approved supplier list on integrity of supply chain
– Threat to objectivity from financial controller's actions

Maximum   8

Total   **25**

(a) **Matters raised by senior**

(i) **Inventory**

This area is not material to net assets or to income and expenses, but could become so in combination with any other immaterial misstatements detected. Unless this is the case, there would be no effect on the auditor's report.

IAS 2 *Inventories* requires inventory to be measured at the lower of cost and net realisable value (NRV) (IAS 2: para. 9). If the NRV is zero, then an expense of $130,000 will be incurred, reducing both and assets by the same amount.

ISA 580 *Written Representations* states that a written representation is not of itself sufficient appropriate audit evidence. Therefore further evidence must be obtained.

The assertion that must be tested here is that NRV is not less than $130,000. The finance director's claim that the inventory can be recycled would therefore need to be supported by evidence that the NRV of this recycled inventory would not be less than $130,000.

Further procedures include:

- Making enquiries with the operations director to ascertain whether or not the materials could be recycled
- Obtaining documentary evidence of the costs of recycling together with the potential selling price of recycled materials
- Reviewing invoices raised after the period end for evidence that the materials have in fact been recycled and sold on

(ii) **Provisions**

This area is not material to net assets or to income and expenses, but could become so in combination with any other immaterial misstatements detected.

IAS 37 *Provisions, Contingent Liabilities and Contingent Assets* requires that a provision be recognised where it is probable that there would be an outflow of resources embodying economic benefits (IAS 37: para. 14), as is the case here. If this adjustment is not made then liabilities and expenses are both understated. There is also unlikely to be adequate disclosure of the circumstances surrounding the case.

When combined with the inventory misstatement, the result is a total misstatement of $255,000, which is material to income and expenses. If neither adjustment is made then the audit opinion should be qualified.

The verbal confirmation that the case will probably be paid is not sufficient, and written confirmation from the lawyers is required. The finance director's refusal to provide this evidence may constitute a limitation on the scope of the audit if the evidence cannot be obtained elsewhere, and throws into question management's integrity. This should trigger a reassessment of any written representations from management relied on elsewhere in the audit, for example in relation to inventory.

Further procedures include:

- Review correspondence with lawyers for evidence regarding the outcome of the legal claim
- Review board minutes for evidence about the claim

(iii) **Current assets**

A loan to a director is material by nature, irrespective of its monetary value. In line with IAS 24 *Related Party Disclosures* Cherry is key management personnel and thus a related party. The financial statements must therefore disclose the loan principal amount, the amount outstanding at the year end, together with the terms of the loan including details of any security offered.

As the loan is not disclosed in the financial statements, there is a material misstatement in respect of IAS 24. If no adjustment is made then the audit opinion should be qualified.

It is possible that the interest payment has not been made or accrued for. If not, then interest of $4\% \times \$6{,}000 \times {}^2/_{12} = \$40$ should be accrued (the adjustment is immaterial).

Further procedures include:

- Review the written terms of the loan to confirm the interest rate and any other conditions

- Review list of accruals to see whether interest has been accrued

(b) **Property**

A move from recognising properties at cost to at fair value would be acceptable in line with IAS 16 *Property, Plant and Equipment*, as long as it is applied across an entire class of assets (IAS 16: para. 36). The Committee should be aware of the benefits and drawbacks of such a change. Benefits include more relevant information on the values of properties, and quicker recognition of fair value gains in the financial statements. But the drawbacks include the need to remeasure fair value at each period end. It may also be necessary to employ an external expert to estimate fair values, which could be costly.

Asset register

The delay in receiving the non-current asset register would have impaired audit efficiency, and potentially resulted in greater audit costs and therefore fees.

The fact that the issue was discussed with the committee last year but then recurred, suggests some sort of controls failure; either the last year's discussion was not acted upon by the committee, or at some other point. In both cases the reason for this needs to be ascertained.

The fact the financial controller has been on holiday at the start of the audit for two years running is not just unhelpful, but may be indicative of something deeper awry, such as fraud.

Procurement

No explanation is actually given for why invoices are not matched to goods received notes; there is no reason why this cannot be done if suppliers are changed frequently, for example. Without this control, it is possible that invoices are paid without goods ever being received. There is also a risk of fraud if this is done intentionally, either delivering goods to another address or using dummy invoices. The committee should seek to improve controls in this area as a matter of some urgency.

Frequently switching suppliers is not itself a problem, but again this would not seem to totally preclude maintaining a list of approved suppliers – it only means that such a list would be a long one. If totally new suppliers really are being used so frequently, then there may be issues with quality rather than price.

Financial controller

There are a number of ethical issues here. First, the offer of three weeks' use of her holiday home needs to be considered in light of the IESBA's *Code of Ethics'* requirements on gifts and hospitality. In this case the value of the offer is likely to mean that no safeguards could prevent the auditors' independence being impaired, so the offer should be declined. If the team considers that Mia Fern intends to influence the outcome of the audit by making the offer, then this casts doubt on her integrity. The audit committee should be notified of this situation.

The gifts of lunches are unlikely to impair independence as they are likely to be of an insignificant monetary value. Provided that this is the case, they may be accepted.

38 Jovi

Workbook references. Chapters 9 and 10.

Top tips. You may have found part (a)(i) difficult, and therefore struggled to write enough for four marks here. You would have score well if you knew ISA 320 *Materiality in Planning and Performing an Audit* well, but if you did not then there was no need to panic. The basic issue here can be worked out using common sense: the auditor would change materiality if they become aware of something that affects materiality. The requirement here is to 'explain', so giving examples is always going to be helpful. If you could think of just one good example, then you could get 50% on this part of the question.

In part (a)(ii), you could have worked out that there were nine notes (audit findings) and 18 marks available, which equates to two marks per note. This was not an easy question. Your approach should be to work through each issue in turn, trying to think of what the problem might be, and not forgetting to think about whether the audit evidence was adequate. Note the importance of reading the question here (and remembering the requirement as you are writing), as candidates who recommended specific audit procedures would have wasted their time.

Part (b) should not have been too difficult. To score six marks you should have looked to make two to three points both for and against. To score well here you need to apply your knowledge to the scenario. Although joint audits are a current issue, you are not being asked for your opinion on the issue generally; you are being asked about a joint audit of the financial statements of May Co. You therefore need to think about the specific scenario. The examining team tends to like students who make points like 'the small local firm will probably offer a cheaper audit service than Sambora & Co', as this is something that can only really be said about this specific situation.

Easy marks. There were easy marks in part (b) for some of the pros and cons of the joint audit, but all in all this was a difficult question.

ACCA examining team's comments. Answers to requirement (a)(i) were usually limited here to a definition of materiality and a suggestion of how an appropriate materiality figure is determined, and few answers actually answered the question requirement. Those that did tended to focus on risk assessment and the auditor uncovering new information about the client as the audit progresses. These points are both valid, but very few answers discussed them, or any other relevant points, in sufficient detail.

Requirement (a)(ii) is a good example of a question requirement where candidates were expected to think on their feet and not rely on rote learnt facts. The candidates that did as the question instructed and took time to think about the information in the scenario scored well, and there were some sound answers. However, the majority of candidates could not apply their knowledge to this scenario, leading to unfocused answers that did not actually answer the question requirement. Answers were on the whole unsatisfactory. Candidates tended to approach the key audit findings in a logical way, working through them in the order presented in the question. However, for each key audit finding most answers simply stated that audit evidence was not adequate without explaining why, and then gave a list of audit procedures, which was specifically not asked for.

On requirement (b), some answers seemed to confuse a joint audit with an audit involving component auditors, and some used the fact that the foreign audit firm was a small firm to argue that it could not possibly be competent enough to perform an audit or have a good ethical standing. Most answers identified the cost implications for the client, and the advantage of involving a local firm who would have knowledge of the local law and regulations.

Marking scheme

Marks

(a) (i) **Materiality**

Up to 1 mark for each comment:
- Recognise materiality is subjective
- Auditor's business understanding may change during the audit, making some balances and transactions material
- Client's circumstances may change during the audit, making some balances and transactions more material
- Adjustments to the accounts mean materiality has to be revised
- Recognise the high-risk status of the client

Maximum   4

(ii) **Audit completion issues**

Up to 2 marks for each audit completion issue assessed:
- Property disposal/sale and leaseback
- Property revaluation
- Actuarial loss
- Goodwill impairment
- Goodwill classification into assets held for sale
- Associate
- Presentation of assets held for sale (separate and not netted off)
- Measurement of assets held for sale
- Lack of disclosure of discontinued operation
- Non-controlling interest
- Finance cost and loan

Maximum   18

(b) **Joint audit**

Up to 1 mark for each advantage/disadvantage discussed:
- Retain local auditors' knowledge of May Co
- Retain local auditors' knowledge of local regulations
- Sambora & Co can provide additional skills and resources
- Cost effective – reduce travel expenses, local firm likely to be cheaper
- Enhanced audit quality
- But employing two audit firms could be more expensive
- Problems in allocating work

Maximum   6

Total   **28**

(a) (i) **Revising materiality**

Auditors must reassess materiality if they become aware of new information that would have resulted in a different materiality level being set at the planning stage.

Planning materiality is likely to have been based on draft financial statements, but during the course of the audit it could become clear that the final financial statements will be substantially different. For example, the carrying amount of assets held at fair value could be much lower than originally expected, which would affect the amounts in

BPP
LEARNING

the statement of financial position. In that case, the auditor would need to set materiality again, on the basis of the actual results and position.

Alternatively, something could happen during the audit, eg the client could decide to dispose of a subsidiary. This could change the appropriate materiality level, as well as performance materiality. The auditor should take this into account and revise materiality.

(ii) **Statement of profit or loss and other comprehensive income**

1 **Copeland revenue**

Copeland's 25% drop in revenue indicates that goodwill relating to this subsidiary may be impaired. There is a risk that this goodwill has not been impaired when it should have been (see section on goodwill impairment below).

2 **Property disposal**

At $2m, the property disposal is material.

The option to repurchase the property in five years' time points to the possibility that this could not be a genuine sale, but a finance arrangement whose economic substance is that of a secured loan. In this case the audit evidence obtained is inadequate, and further evidence needs to be obtained to determine the substance of the transaction.

If this is indeed a secured loan (in substance), then the asset will be recognised in the statement of financial position, and the cash receipt will be recognised as a loan (liability). Finance costs will be accrued over the period of the loan – five years.

If this is the case, then profit has been materially overstated, and liabilities understated.

3 **Property revaluation**

The gain of $800,000 was just below initial materiality of $900,000, but above the current materiality level of $700,000. Audit procedures must now be performed in this area, as it is possible that there could be a material misstatement here.

4 **Actuarial loss**

The actuarial losses are material, at $1.1m, as is the defined benefit liability of $10.82m.

Axle Co is a service organisation, and ISA 402 *Audit Considerations Relating to an Entity Using a Service Organisation* requires the auditor to obtain an understanding of this organisation. This can be obtained:

- From the Group itself, we should gain an understanding of how Axle Co arrives at its valuation, its systems and its controls

- By obtaining a report from the auditor of Axle Co (the service auditor), which contains an opinion on the description of Axle Co's systems and controls

This has not been done, and we have no information about how the plan assets and liabilities were valued, or how reliable their valuation might be. The audit team must therefore obtain this information before the service organisation's representation can be relied upon.

5   **Goodwill impairment**

There is an indicator that goodwill relating to the Copeland subsidiary is impaired, but this does not appear to have been considered by the audit team. Audit procedures must be performed on the assumptions used by management in conducting this review. The reasons why the 25% fall in revenue has not resulted in impairment must be specifically addressed.

6   **Associate**

The statement of profit or loss includes $1.01m share of profit of associate. The figure in the statement of financial position should include (at a minimum) the amount brought forward, plus any profit attributable, less any dividends received. It is thus highly unlikely that this figure would not have changed since last year.

7   **Trading division held for sale**

The division held for sale is part of a subsidiary. Therefore, some of the goodwill relating to this subsidiary may need to be reclassified as part of the disposal group of assets held for sale. Although it is possible that no goodwill will need to be reclassified, evidence needs to be obtained that this is the case.

The statement of financial position contains one line within non-current assets for 'assets classified as held for sale'. This presentation is incorrect: the assets held for sale should be a separate section in the statement of financial position.

It appears that this $7.8m could be a net figure, which again is incorrect – there should also be a separate section within 'liabilities' showing the liabilities from the disposal group. Audit procedures should be performed to ascertain whether this in fact a net figure, in order to get the classification right.

Although there are assets held for sale from a trading division, the statement or profit or loss shows no discontinued operations. IFRS 5 *Non-current Assets Held for Sale and Discontinued Operations* requires the post-tax profit or loss of discontinued operations to be shown as a single line on the face of the statement of profit or loss. This appears to be a material misstatement, and audit procedures should be performed to determine whether it is or not, and whether there are any discontinued operations.

8   **Non-controlling interest**

There is no disclosure in relation to the non-controlling interest in the statement of profit or loss and other comprehensive income. Both profit for the year and total comprehensive income attributable to the non-controlling interest should be disclosed.

9   **New loan**

Finance costs should be included of $8m \times 2\% \times {}^{9}/_{12} = \$120,000$. However, finance costs have only risen by $40,000. No loans appear to have been paid off during the year, as long-term borrowings have increased by exactly the $8m received for the new loan. Therefore, finance costs appear to be understated.

The amount is not material of itself, but should be accumulated together with any other misstatements that are discovered as they could become material in aggregate.

Work should be performed to understand the components of the finance charge recognised, as other finance costs may have ceased during the year. The notes to the financial statements should also be reviewed to ensure there is adequate disclosure of the loan taken out.

BPP
LEARNING

(b)   **Advantages of joint audit**

In the case of May Co, Sambora & Co would not currently have much understanding of May Co's business. It would therefore make sense to continue to make use of Moore & Co's accumulated understanding of the client's business.

The fact that May Co is located in Farland means that it could be subject to accounting, legal and professional regulations that are different from those under which Sambora & Co are accustomed to operating. It makes sense to continue to use the local auditors' knowledge of this potentially very different regulatory framework.

There may be some cost savings in using Moore & Co, as a result of the fact that Sambora & Co would no longer need to send the whole audit team out of Farland to conduct the audit procedures. It is also possible that Moore & Co might charge lower fees than Sambora & Co, so using Moore & Co's staff to perform procedures could work out cheaper.

Audit quality should increase as a result of a joint audit. As new auditors, Sambora & Co will be approaching the audit with a fresh outlook, unprejudiced by previous events and may be able to spot new issues or offer different solutions from those previously identified by Moore & Co.

Disadvantages of joint audit

A key disadvantage is the uplift in costs that results from the unavoidable duplication of work between the two auditors.

Moore & Co may use a different audit approach and methodology from Sambora & Co, leading to disagreements throughout the audit about which is the correct way to proceed. This could result in a loss of efficiencies, as time is spent agreeing on the best audit approach rather than carrying out actual audit work. If either audit firm's approach is followed exclusively, some of the benefits of a joint audit will be lost.

39 Jolie

Workbook references. Chapters 2, 6 and 7.

Top tips. This question on planning an audit is typical of the kind of question you should expect to have to tackle in Section A of this exam. The question is tough but fair, and if you were well-prepared and well-practised at identifying a variety of risks in scenarios, you should have been able to achieve reasonable marks on it. To tackle questions like this, you have to devise a strategy along these lines:

*   Make sure you understand the requirement and answer it.
*   Look for key words and themes in the scenario that indicate audit risk.
*   Ensure you explain **why** things are risks and **why** you would use a particular strategy.
*   Do not spend too long on the question to the detriment of others.

Part (d), on ethics, should have been relatively straightforward, provided that you are familiar with the technical content. But even if you were struggling technically you could have picked up quite a few marks just by working through the material given in the question.

Easy marks. You should be able to score good marks on part (b). Make sure you get at least two or three of the professional marks.

ACCA examining team's comments. On the whole, candidates seemed to like this question, especially the business risk evaluation. However, many candidates failed to answer the specific question requirements, thereby denying themselves marks.

Answers to requirement (a) tended to display reasonable application skills, with some candidates prioritising the risks identified, and reaching an overall conclusion. There was much less evidence here of 'knowledge-dumping' than in answers to other requirements. However, common weaknesses included:

- Repeating large chunks of text from the scenario with no explanation provided
- Not actually explaining or evaluating a risk identified – just saying 'this is a risk'
- Providing detailed definitions of business risk, which was not asked for
- Providing audit procedures for risks, again not asked for
- Providing recommendations for mitigating the risk, not asked for

In addition, it is worth noting that very few candidates used the figures provided in the scenario to identify risk exposure. The client's revenue and profit had fallen from the previous year, and some simple financial analysis could have revealed falling profit margins and worsening interest cover. This type of analysis is not difficult or time consuming, and is something that demonstrates mark-generating application skills.

Finally, some candidates simply failed to answer the question requirement. A minority of candidates took the opportunity to provide many pages of answer which just described how you would plan an audit in general. All of this was totally irrelevant, and failed to generate any marks.

The quality of answers to requirement (b) was unsatisfactory. Some answers, which were by far the majority, tended to just outline an accounting treatment with no mention of the actual risk itself. Another common weakness was to discuss the detection risk which may arise with a new audit client, which is not a risk of material misstatement.

Requirement (c) was better answered, and some candidates scored well, providing well written procedures specific to the valuation of an intangible asset. Many of those that did not score well had misread the scenario.

Candidates are reminded that audit procedures must be tailored to the facts of the scenario provided and must be sufficiently detailed to make sense. 'Get management rep', 'discuss with management' and 'review cost' are examples of meaningless 'procedures' which earn no credit without further development. In addition there were many instances where candidates were obviously trying to generate procedures using a list of words as a prompt. For example 'observe the asset' or 'inquire about the asset'. Candidates must think carefully and not just use words as a prompt if they make no sense.

The few unsatisfactory answers to part (d)(i) tended to simply repeat extracts from the advertisement and say 'this is unprofessional'.

Requirement (d)(ii) was not well answered. While most candidates could state obvious issues, like whether one person would be enough to provide the service, unfortunately very few clearly distinguished between audit and non-audit clients, which was a key issue, as the scenario clearly stated that only one third of the audit firm's clients were audit clients. Few dealt with the issue of the contingent fee in enough detail, with answers usually saying that it was 'unprofessional' but not elaborating further.

Marks

(a) **Evaluate business risks**

½ mark for each risk identified (to max 4 marks) and up to 1½ further marks for explanation.

Up to 2 marks for calculation of margins, trends, etc:

- High fashion items/high staff turnover in design team
- Obsolete inventory and pressure on margins
- Widespread geographical business model hard to control
- Volume of e-commerce sales – ability of systems to cope
- Security of e-commerce operations
- Tax and regulatory issues on e-commerce
- Foreign exchange risk on new overseas transactions
- Outsourcing of phone operations – quality issues
- Outsourcing of phone operations – unpopular with customers
- Long-term sustainability of outsourced function
- Ethical Trading Initiative – supply chain issues
- Potential restrictions on operation of distribution centres
- Financial performance – general comments on revenue/profitability/margins   16

(b) **Risks of material misstatement**

Up to 3 marks for discussion of each risk.

- Inventory valuation (IAS 2)
- Inventory existence (IAS 2)
- New inventory system
- Unrecorded revenue
- Capitalisation of IT/website costs (IAS 38)
- Valuation of brand name (IAS 38)
- Valuation of properties (IAS 36)   14

(c) **Audit procedures: brand name**

1 mark per specific procedure:

- Agree cost to supporting documentation/prior year accounts
- Review assumptions used in management impairment review
- Perform independent impairment review
- Review planned level of expenditure to support the brand
- Review results of any marketing/customer satisfaction surveys
- Consider whether non-amortisation is GAAP for this industry
- Discuss reasons for non-amortisation with management   5

(d) (i) **Evaluation of advertisement**

Generally 1 mark per comment:

- Advertising not prohibited but must follow ACCA guidelines
- Cannot be misleading/exaggerated claims
- Exaggerated claim re size
- Unprofessional claim re 'most professional'
- Cannot guarantee improvements/tax saving
- Second opinions
- Introductory fee
- Audit and non-audit services

Marks

–	Fees not approved by ACCA	
–	Improper reference to ACCA	7

(ii) **Corporate finance**

Generally 1 mark per comment explained:

–	Partner is competent	
–	Advocacy threat	
–	Self-review threat	
–	Identify contingent fee	
–	Contingent fee not appropriate for audit clients	
–	Contingent fee allowed for non-audit client with safeguards	
–	Safeguards should be in place (examples)	4

Professional marks   4

Total   **50**

(a) **Briefing notes**

Subject: Business risks facing Jolie Co

Introduction

These briefing notes evaluate the business risks facing the new client Jolie Co, which has a financial year ending 30 November 20Y0.

Continuing quality of product

Jolie operates in a dynamic and volatile business environment, with new ranges being introduced every eight weeks. There is a constant need for talented designers to develop product ranges, and given the high staff turnover it may be difficult to retain talented staff. The risk is that if Jolie fails to recruit the right designers the quality of the product could be reduced, which could lead to a fall in revenue. Lower-quality products could potentially tarnish the JLC brand, which is so crucial to Jolie's success.

Obsolete inventory

New ranges are introduced every eight weeks, so there is a risk of inventory becoming obsolete if it is not sold during this short period. Any older inventory may be marked down, which would affect margins. Margins fell from 17.9% in 20X9 to 16.8% in 20Y0, which could be related to this.

E-commerce – sales volume

Online sales now account for $255 million ($250 per order × 1,020,000 orders). In the previous year, online sales accounted for $158 million ($300 per order × 526,667 orders). This represents an increase of 61.4% ((255 – 158) / 158 × 100%).

The risk is that the system may be overwhelmed by the increase in sales volume, which could lead to difficulties fulfilling orders and potential damage to the all-important JLC brand.

E-commerce – new systems

There is a risk of system failure associated with any new system, which could result in unfulfilled orders and hence brand damage.

E-commerce – security

There is a risk that customers' details held on the system are not kept sufficiently securely. There is a risk that data protection laws could be breached. If security were to be breached then the brand would be very likely to suffer.

BPP
LEARNING

E-commerce – overseas sales

Making sales overseas exposes Jolie to several new risks. If sales are made in foreign currencies then there is a risk that the computer system may not be able to handle these sales (eg it could miscalculate foreign currency prices).

Overseas sales expose Jolie to potential tax complications, eg extra sales tax to be paid on exported goods, and additional documentation to comply with foreign regulations.

Jolie may also now be exposed to foreign exchange risks, and may find its profit margins affected by currency fluctuations.

Outsourced phone ordering

Jolie outsourced its phone ordering system to the cheapest provider. If the phone ordering system is not of a good quality then this may be incongruent with the differentiated, high-quality nature of Jolie's products. If many errors occur with orders then this may lead to customer dissatisfaction and damage to the brand.

The location of the call centre overseas, which presumably reflects the low cost, may be a source of frustration to customers, and may ultimately lead to a fall in revenue.

However, the risks associated with phone ordering may to some extent be mitigated by the expansion of e-commerce, which customers may prefer to use.

Ethical trading initiative

The fact that Jolie has spent a significant amount of money advertising its fair trade credentials leads to a risk of bad publicity if these credentials were to be undermined. Any ethical failings in the supply chain may be subjected to public scrutiny, which would again damage the JLC brand.

Distribution centres

There is a real risk of local authorities revoking distribution centres' licences if conditions are breached (eg in relation to noise levels). This could pose Jolie significant operational difficulties if any of the centres are closed, as with its short inventory turnover period Jolie is especially reliant on its ability to deliver inventory on time.

Financial performance

Overall revenue has decreased by $80 million, or 5.2% (80 / 1,535 × 100). Operating profit has also fallen, by $30 million, or 10.9% (30 / 275 × 100). Average spend per order has fallen from $300 to $250, and average revenue per store has fallen by 10.5%.

This may give cause for concern, but operating expenses for 20Y0 are likely to include one-off items, eg the costs of the new sales system. The fall in spend per customer could be a symptom of general economic difficulties. The company has increased the volume of online transactions significantly.

On balance the overall reduction in profit and margins is unlikely to be a significant risk at this year end, though if the trend were to continue it may become a more pressing issue.

Jolie Co's finance costs have increased by $3 million, contributing to a fall in profit before tax of 13%. The company has sufficient interest cover to mean that this is not an immediate concern, but the company should ensure that finance costs do not escalate.

Conclusion

Perhaps the most significant risk for Jolie is that it fails to produce products of sufficient quality, which relates to its ability to make use of talented designers. The risk of inventory obsolescence is also significant. The downward trend in Jolie's financial performance needs to be monitored carefully in the future.

(b)   **Inventory valuation**

IAS 2 *Inventories* states that inventory must be valued at the lower of cost and net realisable value (NRV) (IAS 2: para. 9). The high rate of inventory turnover leads to a risk of inventory becoming obsolete and to a fall in its NRV, and if NRV falls below cost then it will need to be written down. This may be the case with any inventory that is being sold at a reduced price, or which is slow-moving and may not be sold at all. Jolie's declining overall revenue may indicate falling NRVs and hence that inventory is impaired.

Inventory completeness and existence

It will be difficult to count inventory accurately across all of Jolie's 210 stores, and there may be a large number of goods in transit to keep track of. All of this means that the auditor will find it difficult to obtain sufficient evidence over the existence of inventory. There is a risk of fraudulent financial reporting in this area as it is difficult to verify the levels of inventory actually held.

New systems

The existence of a new sales system poses the risk of teething problems if the system did not function properly at first. As a result sales could be recorded incorrectly in the nominal ledger, either as a result of the new system not providing correct information, or because of problems with the integration of the system and the nominal ledger.

There may also be a different system in place for the newly outsourced phone sales, and there is a risk of sales being misstated if the systems are not properly integrated.

Website costs

The expenditure on the new IT systems may have been capitalised in line with IAS 38 *Intangible Assets*, according to which only expenditure in the development phase may be capitalised, with costs before (eg planning) and after (eg operational) being expensed. The risk is the overstatement of intangible assets and understatement of operating expenses if these have not been expensed.

New inventory system

The auditor is likely to be ambivalent about the introduction of a new inventory management system; the new system may introduce better controls, but as a result of the system being new, the controls around it may not yet be fully developed or understood. The new system allows management to keep track of cost inputs into inventory, but with this greater complexity comes a risk that a new, relatively untested system may be prone to error. This suggests a control risk, and a risk of error in relation to inventories.

Jolie's inventory management appears to be complex, being held at multiple sites. Controls will need to be very robust to track the movement of inventory accurately, and to ensure reliable inventory counting across all of Jolie's locations. There is a risk of under- or over-statement of inventory as a result of this.

Brand name

An intangible asset has been recognised in respect of the JLC brand name, as this was purchased and not internally generated. This appears to be in line with IAS 38 *Intangible Assets*. At 12% of total assets this amount is likely to material to the financial statements.

IAS 38 requires an impairment review to be conducted at the end of each reporting period (IAS 38: para. 111). If this is not conducted, the asset could be overvalued. The decline in revenue could be an indicator of impairment.

The significant advertising expenditure during the year should be expensed, and there is a risk of overstatement of assets and non-occurrence of expenses if this expenditure has been capitalised.

Property valuation

Jolie owns numerous distribution centres (rather than leasing them), and there is a risk of these assets being impaired if their licences are revoked. Additionally, there has been a fall in revenue per store, which is an indicator of impairment per IAS 36 *Impairment of Assets*.

Division assets held for sale

The factory represents 0.8% of total assets (=$14m/$1,675m) and the office represents 0.5% (=$8m/$1,675m) of total assets. Individually these are not material, but taken together they may be considered material at 1.3% of total assets (=$22m/$1,675m).

The Nearland division factory and office buildings have been treated as 'held for sale' in the financial statements, but no mention is made of how the items of plant and equipment have been treated. It is possible that they will be sold together with the factory, but this is by no means certain and would need to be confirmed. Another possibility is that the plant and equipment no longer has a value in use to Jolie Co (if the factory is sold), and should therefore be subject to an impairment review. In this case there is a risk that assets are overstated if a required impairment is not recognised.

The assets held for sale may be material, so it is important that evidence is obtained regarding their classification in line with IFRS 5 *Non-current Assets Held for Sale and Discontinued Operations*. The IFRS 5 criteria for this classification appear to have been met for the factory and office because offers have been received. It should be confirmed whether these offers have been accepted, whether contracts have been signed and when the sale is likely to be completed.

It should be ascertained how the values of the assets held for sale were arrived at. They should be held at the lower of their carrying amount, and their fair value less any costs to sell. There is a risk that the assets may be overstated if, for example, costs to sell are not taken into account.

The gain recognised on revaluation should be calculated as the difference between fair value less costs to sell, and their carrying amount. The gain should be recognised in other comprehensive income, and not in profit or loss. There is a risk that profit may be overstated if the gain is recognised directly in profit.

(c) **Audit procedures on JLC brand**

- Agree cost of brand to supporting documentation, eg purchase invoice (if still available).

- Agree cost of brand to prior year audited financial statements.

- Review monthly income streams generated by brand, for indication of any decline in sales.

- Review results of impairment reviews by management, establishing the validity of any assumptions used in the review (eg discount rate used to discount future cash flows; growth rates used to predict cash inflows).

- Perform independent impairment review on the brand, and compare with management's impairment review.

- Review level of planned expenditure on marketing and advertising to support the brand name, and consider its adequacy to maintain the image of the brand.

- Inquire as to the results of any customer satisfaction surveys, to gain an understanding of the public perception of JLC as a high-fashion brand.

- Consider whether non-amortisation of brand names is a generally accepted accounting practice in the fashion retail industry by reviewing the published financial statements of competitors.

- Discuss with management the reasons why they feel that non-amortisation is a justifiable accounting treatment.

> **Tutorial note.** As this is a first-year audit, no marks will be awarded for procedures relating to prior year working papers of the audit firm.

(d) (i)   Neither the ACCA *Code of Ethics and Conduct* nor the IESBA *Code of Ethics for Professional Accountants* prohibits advertising. However, a professional accountant must not bring the profession into disrepute, and adverts must be both honest and truthful. There are a number of question marks over whether this is the case with the draft advert here.

           The advert claims that Jen & Co is the largest accountancy and audit firm in the country, yet the firm has only three offices and 12 partners. This is neither honest nor truthful. Moreover, the claim that the firm is the most professional cannot be proven, and could imply that other firms are not professional, bringing the profession into disrepute.

           The advert claims that a range of services are guaranteed to improve efficiency, which is not something that can be guaranteed, particularly given that the advert does not specify which services would do this.

           The advert guarantees that tax would be saved, but again this cannot be guaranteed as it depends on the application of tax law in the specific circumstances of each client. To guarantee savings in this way may create a self-interest threat to the objectivity of tax work done by the firm, as rules may not be properly applied in order to save tax.

           There is a risk of future litigation from clients who do not see improved efficiency or tax savings as a result of Jen & Co's work.

           It is possible for an audit firm to give a second opinion on another firm's report, but this is unusual. The advert may imply that Jen & Co's opinion would be superior to another firms, which brings the profession into disrepute. Moreover, it may compromise the firm's independence in such cases by creating an expectation that Jen & Co would not modify its auditor's report if it were necessary to do so.

           The 25% 'introductory offer' is effectively lowballing. Although this is not prohibited as such, there is a risk that if fees are too low then this may result in poor quality work being done. For example, staff may be assigned to audits who do not have appropriate levels of skill and experience.

           A reduction is offered where both audit and tax services are provided. Non-audit services should only be provided to an audit client where any threats to auditor objectivity can be reduced to an acceptable level. Offering such a reduction may create self-review and advocacy threats.

           Finally, the advert claims that rates are approved by the ACCA. This is false, because the ACCA does not approve specific firms' rates, and in view of the ethical concerns raised above over fees is disingenuous and dishonest in its intention too.

  (ii)   The new partner has experience of the banking sector and therefore appears to be competent in this area. However, there are a number of problems with the proposed service.

           Negotiating financing arrangements on behalf of an audit client creates an advocacy threat to audit objectivity, as the firm is representing the client's interests to a third party. There may be self-review threats if the partner has been in any way involved with the accounting treatment of these arrangements.

           Safeguards should be applied to reduce these threats to an acceptable level. These would include ensuring that the partner and any other staff members involved in giving advice are not involved in the audit. If an auditor's expert is required in relation to financing arrangements then the partner should not be used in this capacity.

           A contingent fee is proposed, which the IESBA *Code* prohibits outright for audit engagements. For non-audit services such as this, the contingent fee creates a self-interest threat to audit objectivity. Safeguards must be applied to reduce this threat to an acceptable level. Safeguards may include ensuring that the partner is not involved with the audit.

However, if the fee relates to a matter that is material to the financial statements, or is material to the firm, then the threat cannot be reduced to an acceptable level. In this case Jen & Co must not take on, or withdraw from, either the audit or the non-audit service.

40 Vancouver

Workbook references. Chapters 2, 6, and 9.

Top tips. This was quite numerical as AAA questions go. In order to pass the question, you needed to spend some time using your calculator! There is a ½ mark for each correct trend (eg a % change), but these are capped at five marks. That means you should calculate five trends, for both the current year and the comparative. Alternatively, you could calculate some ratios instead of some of these trends, but try not to exceed six or seven in total otherwise you'll be wasting your time. Candidates who don't do any calculations at all are unlikely to pass this question – and on the flipside, candidates who struggle elsewhere will benefit from these easy marks.

It may be sensible to do your calculations on a separate sheet of paper, which you can label 'Appendix' and refer to in your answer as needed. This is easier to do, and will be easier to mark (you always want to please the marker!).

Part (a) was unusually knowledge-based, but it was not easy; in order to pass you needed three points. The key here is thinking about how analytical procedures are used at the planning stage. You could think about it like this: analytical procedures help the auditor to spot something that looks wrong. There are two possibilities: it may be correct, but looks wrong to the auditor because the auditor doesn't **understand** something. In this case, the auditor needs to **obtain an understanding** of the issue – so analytical procedures have helped the auditor to obtain an understanding of the entity. Alternatively, it might be that the figure looks wrong because something is going on, ie there is an audit **risk**. There could be a misstatement, so audit work needs to be focused on that area to see if this is the case. Knowing which areas are risky helps the auditor to **plan** the audit work.

Part (b) was a fairly normal audit risk question, for 25 marks. This part of the question hinges on your ability to spot risks, and to eek marks out of each risk (up to a maximum of 2 marks per risk). There was not a great deal of written information in this scenario – unlike other examples of Q1 – so your performance depended on your analytical procedures.

Your approach here is to read through both the question and the results of your analytical procedures, making a note of the risks. If a risk relates to an accounting treatment, you should **briefly** summarise the accounting requirement, and then say what could have gone wrong.

There are marks available for stating whether an issue is material, and these are easy marks. Every risk you discuss should therefore begin with a calculation of the item as a % of the relevant figure (eg x% of total assets), and then either 'this is material' or 'this is not material'.

It should not need pointing out that there are no marks available for generic discussions of audit risk. If you do this then you will not get any marks for it! Also there is no need to classify risks into inherent risks / control risks / detection risks. You simply need to explore what the risk itself is. Lastly, do not mention business risks unless they're asked for in the requirement, as this is something the examining team has written about again and again.

Part (c) should have been straightforward; if you had revised the audit procedures on the consolidation then most of this was just knowledge.

For part (d), on ethics, you needed first to spot the two ethical issues in the scenario. It's important that you state the **ethical threat** that's present (eg 'this presents an advocacy threat'), together with any **safeguards** that might help reduce it. Finally, conclude on whether the threat can be reduced to an acceptable level (after safeguards are applied).

Finally, be sure to get at least 2–3 of the professional marks. Write a 'briefing notes' heading, an introduction and a conclusion, and use subheadings throughout your answer.

Easy marks. The presentation marks, the marks for assessing materiality for each issue, and the marks for analytical procedures. Most of part (c) was easy, if you knew it. If not, then there is a very easy mark available for suggesting checking the 'arithmetical accuracy' of the consolidation schedule.

ACCA examining team's comments. The question was set at the planning stage of the audit and candidates were presented with several requirements, which covered the use of analytical procedures at planning, identifying audit risks, procedures on the consolidation, and ethics.

The **best answers** demonstrated that a methodical approach had been applied to the information in the scenario, and strong candidates had clearly worked through the information logically, calculating the key ratios and trends from the information provided, identifying the risk factors from the calculations and the remaining information, assessing materiality before going on to explain the risk fully and specifically in terms of how the risk could impact the financial statements. Candidates are reminded that **when discussing risk** relating to a specific accounting treatment, well explained answers will include an **evaluation of the potential impact** of the risk factor on the financial statements [**BPP note.** ie calculate materiality!].

A disappointing number of candidates failed to calculate any ratios or trends from the information supplied and thus provided weak answers and were unable to identify an appropriate number of audit risks for the marks available. Conversely some candidates calculated every trend or ratio possible, which was excessive and demonstrated poor time management; for example there was insufficient information in the question to calculate inventory or trade payable days so these ratios did not add to their answer.

Audit risk continues to be an area that candidates find difficult and particularly it continues to be noted that many candidates fail to engage with the information provided in enough depth, specifically when provided with extracts from financial statements. Candidates are again reminded that in order to provide a full answer in relation to audit risk they should utilise and analyse all the information that is provided.

In relation to requirement (c), many candidates clearly knew the consolidation process very well, but had trouble expressing this knowledge in terms of audit procedures. Many answers simply described what should happen in a consolidation, and thought that by including the words 'check' or 'ensure' every so often that would be enough eg 'check goodwill calculation', 'ensure all subsidiaries included' but didn't actually say how these things should be done. However, despite these problems most answers were satisfactory.

Finally, candidates were required to discuss the ethical issues relevant to the audit firm and to recommend any necessary actions. Performance in this area was mixed and it was clear that many candidates did not know the requirements of the IESBA *Code of Ethics*. For example a sizeable number of candidates advised that the audit engagement partner could simultaneously become a non-executive director on the audit committee of the entity under audit and failed to identify that the *Code* expressly prohibits this due to the extent of the self-review and self-interest threats which would be created. This demonstrates a lack of knowledge of the ethical requirements and a lack of professional judgment. Candidates are reminded that they must revise and be comfortable with the content of the *Code of Ethics*. Most candidates were however, able to highlight that there was a potential advocacy and self-review risk from representing the client in a tax enquiry but did not condition this on either grounds of materiality or that the firm had not been previously involved in the client's tax affairs.

BPP LEARNING

There were four professional marks available and most candidates were able to earn the presentation marks by providing a clear introduction and conclusion and using headings to create an appropriate structure for their answer. Many candidates did not articulate their points in a clear or logical order and therefore many missed out on the logical flow and clarity marks.

Marking scheme

Marks

(a) **Analytical procedures and risk assessment**

Generally up to 1½ marks for each point explained:

- Definition/examples of analytical procedure
- Helps to identify risk of material misstatement
- Helps to develop business understanding
- Helps in developing the audit strategy and audit plan

Maximum   5

(b) **Audit risk evaluation**

Generally 1 mark for each ratio (including comparative) calculated, and ½ mark for relevant trends calculated, up to a maximum of 5 marks.

In addition, up to 2 mark for discussion of audit risks, including the assessment of materiality. Risks in relation to ratio analysis could include:

- Overstatement of operating expenses
- Overstatement of revenue due to finance director's comments
- Interest cover and risk relating to disclosure
- Change in effective tax rates and risk tax expense incorrect
- Ongoing investigation and risk of fines and penalties which need to be provided for
- Liquidity issues and risk relating to disclosure
- Increase in receivables days and overstatement of trade receivables
- Onerous lease provision has halved in value, risk of understatement of liability

Other audit risks – up to 2 marks for each risk identified and explained:

- Allow 1 mark for each correct calculation and comment on materiality
- Whether capital and revenue expenditure appropriately accounted for in respect of the modernisation programme
- Whether revenue recognition policies are in line with IFRS 15
- Whether assets have been accounted for using the concept of significant components
- Treatment of borrowing costs and whether eligible for capitalisation
- The gain on disposal of shares in Calgary Co is incorrectly recognised in profit for the year

Marks

- Non-controlling interest has not been disclosed in respect of profit for the year
- Risk of inadequate disclosure regarding the rationale for, and consequences of, the share disposal
- Management bias due to sale of shares to institutional investor
- Deferred tax – risk of overstatement if the amount is not a recoverable asset
- Lack of financial reporting expert on the Group audit committee increases the risk of incorrect
- Cyber attack – non-compliance with laws and regulations, possible legal case

Maximum   25

(c) **Principal procedures on consolidation**
Generally 1 mark per procedure explained:
- Test controls
- Review group instructions
- Recalculate adjustments
- Reconcile inter-company balances
- Review fair values/consider need for expert
- Consider consistency of accounting policies
- Recalculate deferred tax implications
- Agreement to component financial statements
- Consider treatment of non-controlling interests
- Arithmetical accuracy of consolidation schedule

Maximum   8

(d) **Ethical issues**
Generally up to 1 mark for each relevant matter discussed:

- Assisting in the tax investigation creates advocacy threat (1 mark where risk is explained)
- Assisting in the tax investigation creates self-review threat (1 mark where risk is explained)
- Extent of threat lessened because another firm provided the tax planning
- Need to consider the materiality of the matter to the financial statements
- If matter is immaterial, then the service can be provided as long as safeguards in place (1 mark for each safeguard suggested)
- Where matter is material, the service should not be provided
- Appointment of audit partner to audit committee creates objectivity threat
- The *Code* prohibits appointment of audit firm member as director of audit client
- Matters to be discussed with client's audit committee and the audit firm's ethical partner

Maximum   8

Professional marks

Generally 1 mark for heading, 1 mark for introduction, 1 mark for use of headings within the briefing notes, 1 mark for clarity of comments made.

Maximum   4

Total   **50**

BPP
LEARNING

Briefing notes

To: Albert Franks, audit engagement partner

From: Audit manager

Subject: Vancouver Group audit planning

Introduction

These briefing notes are prepared for use in the audit team briefing for the Vancouver Group (the Group). Following a meeting between the audit partner and the Group finance director and a member of the Group audit committee, and using information provided, audit risks have been identified and explained. Analytical procedures have been used to identify several audit risks, and the briefing notes also explain why analytical procedures are required as part of risk assessment. A recommendation is made of the procedures which should be performed on the consolidation process. Finally, the briefing notes discuss the ethical implications of suggestions made by the Group audit committee.

(a)   **Analytical procedures and risk assessment**

According to ISA 520 *Analytical Procedures*, analytical procedures are the evaluation of financial information through analysis of plausible relationships between both financial and non-financial data. Analytical procedures can involve comparisons of financial data including trend analysis and the calculation and comparison of ratios. Analytical procedures include comparisons of the Group's financial information with, for example:

- Comparable information for prior periods;
- Anticipated results of the Group, such as budgets or forecasts;
- Expectations of the auditor; or
- Comparable information from competitors.   (ISA 520)

Analytical procedures performed at the planning stage help the auditor to identify and respond appropriately to risk, and to assist the auditor in obtaining an understanding of the audited companies within the Group.

ISA 315 *Identifying and Assessing the Risks of Material Misstatement Through Understanding the Entity and its Environment* requires the auditor to perform analytical procedures as part of risk assessment procedures at the planning stage of the audit to provide a basis for the identification and assessment of risks of material misstatement at the financial statement and assertion levels.

An example of how analytical procedures assist the auditor is that performing analytical procedures may alert the auditor to a transaction or event of which they were previously unaware, therefore prompting the auditor to investigate the matter, obtain understanding of the matter and plan appropriate audit procedures to obtain sufficient appropriate audit evidence. Therefore analytical procedures are an essential part of developing the audit strategy and audit plan.

Analytical procedures may also help the auditor to identify the existence of unusual transactions or events, such as significant one-off events. Unusual amounts, ratios, and trends might also indicate matters which indicate risk. Unusual or unexpected relationships which are identified by these procedures may assist the auditor in identifying risks of material misstatement, especially risks of material misstatement due to fraud.

Without performing analytical procedures, the auditor would be unable to identify risks of material misstatement and respond accordingly. This would increase detection risk, making it more likely that an inappropriate audit opinion could be issued.

(b) **Audit risk evaluation including analytical procedures**

Selected analytical procedures and associated audit risk evaluation

	20X6	20X5
Operating margin	$27/375 \times 100 = 7.2\%$	$38/315 \times 100 = 12.1\%$
Return on capital employed	$27/66 + 181 = 10.9\%$	$38/67 + 153 = 17.3\%$
Interest cover	$27/4 = 6.8$	$38/3 = 12.7$
Effective tax rate	$10/33 \times 100 = 30.3\%$	$15/35 \times 100 = 42.9\%$
Receivables days	$62/375 \times 365 = 60$ days	$45/315 \times 365 = 52$ days
Current ratio	$97/120 = 0.8$	$83/95 = 0.9$

Analytical procedures reveals that the Group's revenue has increased by 19%, but that operating expenses have disproportionately increased by 25.6%, resulting in the fall in operating margin from 12.1% in 20X5 to 7.2% in 20X6. This is a significant change, and while the higher costs incurred could be due to valid business reasons, the trend could indicate operating costs are overstated or sales are understated. There is a risk that some of the costs involved in modernising the Group's warehousing facilities have been incorrectly treated as expenses when this should have been capitalised. The trend in operating margin is consistent with the change in return on capital employed which has also fallen. The treatment of the costs involved in the modernisation of the Group's warehouse facilities will need detailed investigation to ensure that costs have been classified appropriately.

However, given the finance director's comment that operations have not changed significantly during the year, the increase in revenue of 19% seems surprising, given that this is a significant increase, and there is therefore also a risk that revenue could be overstated. The Group's revenue recognition policy is to recognise revenue at the point of shipping. This must be assessed in relation to the requirements of IFRS 15 *Revenue from Contracts with Customers*, which requires revenue to be recognised when control passes to the customer. If, for example, it is Group policy to compensate customers for loss or damage during shipping then this could indicate that revenue should be recognised at the point of delivery instead. Alternatively, it could mean that part of the transaction price needs to be allocated to a separate service covering this performance obligation. Audit work will need to be concentrated in this area to determine whether revenue is appropriately stated and recorded in the correct period.

The Group's interest cover has declined sharply, and finance costs have increased by 33%. This could indicate that finance costs are overstated, however, given that the Group has taken out additional debenture finance during the year, and also now has an overdraft, an increase in finance costs is to be expected and is more likely to simply reflect the significant drop which the Group has experienced in its operating profit levels. The debenture may contain a covenant in relation to interest cover, and if so, there is a risk that the covenant may have been breached. While this is a business risk rather than an audit risk, the matter may require disclosure in the financial statements, leading to a risk of material misstatement if necessary disclosures are not made.

The comparison of effective tax rates shows that the effective tax rate is much lower in 20X6. This could be due to the utilisation of Toronto Co's tax losses which seems to have taken place due to the reduction in the Group's deferred tax asset this year. However, this is a complex issue and there is a risk that the tax expense is understated in comparison with the previous year. Given the ongoing tax investigation regarding potential underpayment of tax, this is a significant audit risk.

Depending on the possible outcome of the tax investigation, there may be a need to provide for additional tax liabilities and any penalties which may be imposed by the tax authorities. Details of the investigation and its findings so far will need to be considered and the probability of the tax authorities finding against the Group should be considered as part of our detailed audit testing to verify that liabilities are complete or that disclosures for contingent liabilities are complete.

BPP
LEARNING
MEDIA

The Group appears to be experiencing cash flow problems in the current year with its cash reserves being eradicated during the year and the Group now relying on an overdraft. Its current ratio has fallen from 0.9 to 0.8, indicating that liquidity is a problem. The receivables days figure has increased from 52 days in 20X5 to 60 days in 20X6. This could be due to poor credit control, and if this is a significant risk to the Group the issues involved may need to be disclosed according to IFRS 7 *Financial Instruments: Disclosure*, hence there is a risk of inadequate disclosure. The increase in receivables days may also indicate an overstatement of receivables balances.

The provisions balance has halved in value from $12 million in 20X5 to $6 million in 20X6. This could indicate that the provisions balance is understated and operating profit overstated, if there is not a valid reason for the reduction in value of the liability. Possibly if the onerous lease contracts have now expired, then that could justify the change in value, but this will need to be confirmed. In addition, provisions may be required in respect of dilapidation costs for leased properties, and there is a risk of understated liabilities if any such provisions have not been recognised.

The results of the analytical review should be reconsidered once any necessary adjustments are made to the financial statements in light of potential misstatements identified below.

Modernisation of warehousing facilities

Overall, property, plant and equipment has increased by $43 million or 23% which is a significant movement, representing 11.7% of total assets. A total amount of $25 million has been spent on modernising the warehousing facilities which is material, representing 6.8% of total assets. The modernisation programme explains part of the increase in property, plant and equipment but given that depreciation would have been charged, the reasons for the large increase must be carefully considered. As part of our audit work we will need to ensure that we understand how all of this movement has occurred as there are several risks of material misstatement associated with the expenditure.

First, there is a risk that the amounts capitalised into non-current assets are not correct in that capital and revenue expenditure may not have been correctly identified and accounted for separately. According to IAS 16 *Property, Plant and Equipment*, modernisation costs which give rise to enhanced future economic benefit should be capitalised where the costs are directly attributable, whereas costs which do not create future economic benefit should be expensed. It would seem that costs such as replacing electrical systems should be capitalised, but other incidental costs which may have been incurred such as repairing items within the warehouses should be expensed.

In addition, there is a risk that the various components of each warehouse have not been treated as separate components and depreciated over a specific useful life. IAS 16 requires that each part of an item of property, plant and equipment with a cost which is significant in relation to the total cost of the item must be depreciated separately (IAS 16: para. 43). Items such as computer systems are likely to be significant components of the warehouses and as such should be accounted for as discrete assets in their own right. Failure to correctly determine the significant components of the capital expenditure could lead to misstatement of the assets' carrying values and depreciation expenses.

There is also an issue with the finance costs in respect of the $5 million debenture taken out to finance the modernisation programme. If the criteria of IAS 23 *Borrowing Costs* are met, in particular if the modernisation of the warehouses meets the definition of a qualifying asset, then borrowing costs should be capitalised during the period of modernisation. A qualifying asset is an asset which takes a substantial period of time to get ready for its intended use or sale, so depending on the length of time that the modernisation programme has taken, it may meet the definition so borrowing costs would need to be capitalised. There is therefore a risk that borrowing costs have not been capitalised if the qualifying asset definition has been met, and equally a risk that borrowing costs may have been capitalised incorrectly if the definition has not been met. The borrowing costs, however, may not be material in isolation.

If any accounting errors have occurred in the amounts capitalised into property, plant and equipment, then non-current assets may be over or understated, as would be the depreciation charge calculated on the carrying value of those assets.

Disposal of shares in Calgary Co

A comparison of the statement of profit or loss for both years shows that the profit made on the disposal of shares in Calgary Co has been separately disclosed as part of profit in the year ending 31 July 20X6. The profit recognised is material at 30.3% of profit before tax. Several errors seem to have been made in accounting for the disposal and in respect of its disclosure.

First, it is not correct that this profit on disposal is recognised in the statement of profit or loss. According to IFRS 10 *Consolidated Financial Statements*, changes in a parent's ownership interest in a subsidiary which does not result in the parent losing control of the subsidiary are treated as equity transactions. Any difference between the amount by which the non-controlling interests are adjusted and the fair value of the consideration paid or received is recognised directly in equity, and attributed to the owners of the parent; this appears to have been incorrectly accounted for as there should not be a profit on disposal within the statement of profit or loss. Therefore profit before tax is overstated by $10 million. The tax charge may be overstated if it has been calculated based on profit including the gain made on the share disposal.

Second, while the non-controlling interest has been recognised in equity, the Group's profit for the year has not been attributed and disclosed between the Group and the non-controlling interest. There is also a risk that the disclosure requirements of IFRS 12 *Disclosure of Interests in Other Entities* are not followed, in particular in relation to the change in group structure which has taken place during the year, as IFRS 12 specifically requires disclosure relating to the consequences of changes in a group's ownership interest in a subsidiary which does not result in a loss of control.

Management bias

The sale of shares to an institutional investor creates an inherent risk of management bias as management may feel under pressure to return favourable results. This could explain the positive trends in revenue shown by the analytical review and could also explain the incorrect presentation of the profit on disposal which has incorrectly inflated profit by $10m.

Deferred tax asset

There is a risk that the deferred tax asset is overstated. According to IAS 12 *Income Taxes*, a deferred tax asset is recognised for an unused tax loss carry-forward or unused tax credit if, and only if, it is considered probable that there will be sufficient future taxable profit against which the loss or credit carry-forward can be utilised. While it appears that some of the deferred tax asset has been utilised this year, there remains a risk that if it is no longer recoverable, then the amount would need to be written off. Audit work should be planned to confirm the recoverability of the amount recognised.

Audit committee – lack of financial reporting expert

Guidance on the composition of audit committees suggests that a financial reporting expert should be included in the committee. This is to ensure that the functions of the audit committee in relation to financial reporting are carried out effectively, for example, in ensuring that accounting policies are appropriate. The lack of an expert increases the risk that incorrect accounting treatments will occur, and is effectively a control risk.

Cyber attack

The attack did not adversely affect operations, but this appears to have been merely fortunate. The attack demonstrates the vulnerability of the Group's IT systems, and there is a risk that further information could have been lost, unbeknown to the Group. Procedures should be performed to determine whether this was the case, and what effect this may have had on the Group's accounting records.

The Group may be subject to jurisdictional laws concerning information privacy, such as the *Data Protection Act* 1998 in the UK. This Act gives individuals, including employees, the right to control information about themselves. If the Group has failed to take appropriate measures to protect this data then it may be in breach of the Act.

In line with ISA 250 *Consideration of Laws and Regulations in an Audit of Financial Statements*, the auditor must obtain an understanding of any non-compliance. In this case, it is possible that there may be fines as a result of a breach, which should be reported in the financial statements. The auditor should discuss the non-compliance with the appropriate level of management, and should consider whether disclosure is needed in the public interest.

It is possible that the employees affected by the loss of data could bring legal proceedings against the Group for failing to protect their data. IAS 37 *Provisions, Contingent Liabilities and Contingent Assets* requires the Group to provide for any liabilities that are certain or probable, but not those that are remote. IAS 37 also requires the obligating event to have taken place in the past, which is the case here. There is a risk that any provisions that should be made have not been made.

(c)   The audited accounts of each subsidiary should be agreed to the schedules used in the consolidation process, as figures may not have been transposed correctly. Verify that all subsidiaries are included on the schedule, and that the consolidation schedule agrees to the group financial statements. The consolidation schedule should be arithmetically checked by casting and cross-casting.

All consolidation adjustments should be reviewed and recalculated, for example pre-acquisition reserves and goodwill for subsidiaries, along with any fair value adjustments. It will be necessary to agree adjustments to underlying documents, eg some of the figures making up goodwill may be agreed to prior year financial statements.

All intercompany balances should be reconciled, and a schedule obtained of intercompany transactions to ensure that they are eliminated from profit or loss.

Procedures should be performed to verify that subsidiary items that should be carried in the group accounts at fair value have been, where they may be measured in the subsidiaries' financial statements on a different basis, eg properties which must be carried at fair value in the group, but which may be at depreciated cost in the subsidiary.

The auditor should verify that accounting policies have been applied consistently across the group, and that where adjustments need to be made for the group accounts these have been made correctly (eg because of foreign subsidiaries which operate under different financial reporting requirements).

The deferred tax consequences of consolidation and fair value adjustments should be reviewed for completeness, and calculations reperformed for accuracy.

(d)   **Ethical matters to be considered by our firm**

Tax investigation

There are two key issues to be considered by Montreal & Co. The first relates to the tax investigation by the tax authorities, and the request for the audit firm to look into the Group's tax position and to liaise with the authorities. The IESBA's *Code of Ethics for Professional Accountants* contains guidance on situations where an audited entity is involved in a tax dispute and has requested assistance from the audit firm. The *Code* states that an advocacy or self-review threat may be created when the firm represents an audit client in the resolution of a tax dispute, for example, before a tribunal or court.

The advocacy threat arises because the audit firm will take a position to promote the client's interests at the tribunal, leading to a threat to objectivity. The self-review threat arises where the matter which is the subject of the investigation and tribunal will have an impact on the financial statements on which the audit firm will express an opinion.

The existence and significance of any threat will depend on a number of factors including:

- Whether the firm has provided the advice which is the subject of the tax dispute

- The extent to which the outcome of the dispute will have a material effect on the financial statements on which the firm will express an opinion

In this case the threat is lessened by the fact that it was another firm of accountants, Victoria & Co, which provided the tax planning advice to the Group, but the materiality of the matter will need to be carefully considered by Montreal & Co before they agree to take on the engagement to provide the necessary support to the Group.

The significance of any threat created shall be evaluated and safeguards applied when necessary to eliminate the threat or reduce it to an acceptable level. Examples of such safeguards include:

- Using professionals who are not members of the audit team to perform the service

- Having a tax professional provide advice to the audit team on the Group's tax position, and review the financial statement treatment

The *Code* states that where the taxation services involve acting as an advocate for an audit client before a public tribunal or court in the resolution of a tax matter and the amounts involved are material to the financial statements on which the firm will express an opinion, the advocacy threat created would be so significant that no safeguards could eliminate or reduce the threat to an acceptable level. Therefore, the firm shall not perform this type of service for an audit client. What constitutes a 'public tribunal or court' shall be determined according to how tax proceedings are heard in the particular jurisdiction.

Partner on audit committee

The second ethical issue relates to the request for one of Montreal & Co's audit partners to be appointed as a non-executive director of the Group and to serve on the Group's audit committee. This would seem inappropriate as one of the functions of the audit committee is to oversee the external audit function, and it would not be possible for an audit partner of the firm to remain objective when evaluating matters such as determining the audit fee.

The *Code* specifically states that if a partner or employee of the firm serves as a director or officer of an audit client, the self-review and self-interest threats created would be so significant that no safeguards could reduce the threats to an acceptable level. Accordingly, no partner or employee shall serve as a director or officer of an audit client.

Hence, Montreal & Co must explain to the Vancouver Group that unfortunately it will not be possible for an audit partner to be appointed to serve as a non-executive director of the Group. The provision of the tax investigation service should also be discussed, and the audit committee's approval for Montreal & Co to provide the service should be obtained, depending on the materiality of the matter to the financial statements and the deployment of safeguards to reduce threats to an acceptable level.

Conclusion

These briefing notes have provided an assessment of the audit risks to be considered in planning the audit of the Vancouver Group, including analytical procedures and an explanation of the need for these procedures to be performed. The notes have recommended the principal audit procedures that should be performed on the consolidation process. There are several significant threats to our firm's objectivity which need to be discussed with the client prior to the audit fieldwork commencing.

41 Bluebell

Marking scheme

Marks

(a) **Risks of material misstatement**
Maximum 2 marks for materiality calculations
Up to maximum marks for significant issue explained as below:
- Revenue recognition (2 marks + 1 mark for providing trend/calculation) IFRS 15
- Share-based payment (3 marks) IFRS 2
- Provision for repairs (2 marks) IAS 37
- Insurance reimbursement (1 mark)
- Understatement of operating expenses (2 marks)
- Impairment of properties (1 mark) IAS 36
- Property disposals (3½ marks)
- Property revaluation (1½ marks) IAS 16
- Deferred tax on property revaluation (1½ marks) IAS 12

Marks

- Deferred tax asset (2 marks + 1 mark for recalculating profit for any suggested changes) IAS 12
- Going concern (1 mark)

Maximum   14

(b)   (i)   **Audit procedures**

Generally 1 mark per procedure:
- Agree components of calculation to scheme documentation (½ mark per item agreed max 2)
- Recalculate + check vesting period
- Agreement of grant date, fair values, etc to specialist report
- Review of forecast staffing levels
- Written representation
- Discussion with HR re assumptions used

Maximum   6

(ii)   **Audit procedures**

Generally 1 mark per procedure:
- Obtain client tax comp + deferred tax schedules, recalculate
- Form independent estimate of amount
- Profitability forecasts – assumptions
- Profitability forecast – time period for losses to be utilised
- Tax authority agreement on c/f of losses

Maximum   4

(c)   **Social and environmental KPIs**

Generally ½ mark per KPI, ½ mark per evidence point. Can increase to 1 mark (for either) if the point is very specific to a hotel business.

Ideas list

Employees:
- Training spend
- Absenteeism rates
- Employee engagement index

Customers:
- Customer satisfaction rate
- Number of complaints
- Number of accidents
- Repeat business rates

Community:
- Charitable donations
- Free use of hotel facilities

Environment:
- Waste recycling
- Energy-efficient items purchased
- Carbon footprint

Maximum   8

Up to four professional marks for format, logical structure and use of language appropriate to internal auditor ie free from jargon, all comments clearly explained.

Maximum   <u>4</u>

Total   <u>**36**</u>

(a) **Risks of material misstatement**

Revenue recognition

Bluebell Co recognises income when a room is occupied in line with IFRS 15 *Revenue from Contracts with Customers*. A deposit of 20% is taken when the room is booked and this revenue should be deferred and shown as a liability on the statement of financial position. There is a risk of material misstatement that deposit revenue is recognised immediately leading to an overstatement of revenue and an understatement of liabilities. It is worth noting that revenue has increased by 24.8% at Bluebell Co. This is above the industry average of 10% and could be a result of deposit revenue being recognised in the incorrect period.

Share-based payment expense

The calculation of the share-based payment expense is complex and any inaccuracies or incorrect assumptions may cause it to be over- or understated in the financial statements. In particular, the assumption of 0% staff turnover in three years sounds dubious and this needs to be investigated in order to judge the accuracy of the expense.

The model used to assess the fair value of the share options must comply with IFRS 2 *Share-based Payment*. If a prohibited model is used, then the financial statements will not comply with accounting standards. Fair value must also be measured at the grant date in order to calculate the expense or the financial statements will be inaccurate.

Damaged property repair expenses

A provision of $100m has been made for flood damage to three hotels. However, since flood damage to hotels is already covered by insurance, it appears this provision was made in error. Hence there is a risk that operating expenses are overstated in the financial statements.

Additionally, under IAS 37 *Provisions, Contingent Liabilities and Contingent Assets*, a provision can only be recognised if an entity has a legal or constructive present obligation as a result of a past event (IAS 37: para. 14). Bluebell Co may be intending to repair the damaged properties but it would be difficult to argue this is because of a legal or constructive obligation, rather than a desire to obtain future operating profits. Therefore, a risk that the financial statements do not fully comply with the requirements of IAS 37 exists.

Impairment of properties

The properties must be written down to their recoverable amount. It is not stated whether the damaged properties have been tested for impairment. However it seems likely that some impairment loss should be recognised during the year, given the level of flood damage.

Other operating expenses

If the two new items included in operating expenses are excluded, other operating expenses have fallen from $690m in 20X7 to $597m in 20X8. This does not seem in line with the increase in revenue in the business. If sales of rooms have increased it would be expected that the associated costs would also increase, for example the costs of cleaning the rooms. This could highlight a possible understatement of other operating expenses in the statement of profit or loss. However, it may be that the decrease is reasonable and due to the hotels being able to increase their rates rather than increases in occupancy that would lead to increased costs.

Profit on property disposal

The statement of profit or loss includes $125m profit on the disposal of hotels where Bluebell Co is retaining a hotel management contract. Bluebell Co has an option to repurchase the hotels in fifteen years and this purchase seems likely. The transaction will need to be investigated in more detail during the audit. The substance of the transaction could be a sale and repurchase, rather than merely a sale, in which case the properties should remain on the statement of financial position. Thus, there is a risk that property and assets are understated and operating income is overstated.

If evidence proves the hotels should have remained on the statement of financial position, depreciation and operating expenses will also be understated. Bluebell Co will have stopped depreciating the hotels in March 20X8 when they were sold, eight months before the year end.

Additionally, finance charges should be accrued for any sale and repurchase agreement and allocated over the period of the agreement. If the hotel sale and repurchase have not been correctly shown, then it is unlikely that finance charges have been included and are possibly understated.

Property revaluation

Property has been revalued during the year and a revaluation gain of $250m has been made. Since Bluebell Co are known to be seeking long-term funding to solve their liquidity problems, there is a risk that the properties have been overvalued in order to strengthen their net assets and make the company a more attractive lending prospect. The basis of the valuation will need to be examined during the audit to ensure that any revaluations comply with IAS 16 *Property, Plant and Equipment*.

As per IAS 12 *Income Taxes*, a deferred tax provision should be recognised on the revaluation of a property for which the debit is charged to equity. If any properties are found to have been overvalued, then the related deferred tax provision and equity charge will also be overstated.

Deferred tax asset

Under IAS 12 *Income Taxes*, deferred tax assets can only be recognised where the recoverability of the asset can be demonstrated (IAS 12: para. 24). Bluebell Co will therefore need to show that future profits will be generated for the unutilised tax losses to be offset against. If this is not possible, the deferred tax asset should be limited to the amount of profits that can be measured with reasonable certainty.

The statement of profit or loss currently shows a profit of $145m before tax, the first profit after several years of losses. However, this profit may need to be adjusted to take into account the items discussed previously and could turn out to be a loss. If so, it may be difficult for Bluebell Co to demonstrate a flow of future profits and the deferred tax asset is more likely to be overstated.

Going concern

Bluebell Co has suffered several years of losses, has poor liquidity and is trying to raise long-term finance to secure its future. The going concern of the company may be a problem and if so, will require disclosure in the financial statements. There is a risk of material misstatement that the incorrect disclosure requirements are made.

(b) **Procedures**

(i) **Share-based payment expense**

- Review contractual documentation for the share-based payment scheme and agree the following to the management calculation of the $138m expense.
    - Number of employees and executives in scheme
    - Number of options per employee
    - Length of vesting period
    - Grant date of the share options
    - Any performance conditions attached to the options

- Reperform the management calculation of the share-based payment expense, ensuring fair value is spread correctly over the vesting period.

- Agree the fair value of the options to a specialist report calculating their fair value.

- Assess whether the specialist report is reliable and objective evidence.

- Check that fair value is calculated at the grant date.

BPP
LEARNING

- Enquire of directors as to why the forecast staff turnover is 0% during the three year vesting period and evaluate the assumptions used in making this forecast.

- Perform sensitivity analysis to assess the effect on the expense for changes in the assumptions used, especially 0% staff turnover.

- Discuss the reasonableness of the 0% staff turnover assumption with human resources at Bluebell Co.

- Obtain written representations from management confirming that the assumptions used in measuring the expense are reasonable and there are no share-based payment schemes in existence that have not been disclosed to the auditors.

(ii) Recoverability of deferred tax asset

- Check the arithmetical accuracy of Bluebell Co's deferred tax and corporation tax computations.

- Agree the figures used to any tax correspondence and the financial statements.

- Calculate an independent estimate of the deferred tax asset and compare this to management's estimate.

- Obtain profitability forecasts and ensure there are enough forecast taxable profits for the losses to be offset against.

- Evaluate the reasonableness of the assumptions used in the profitability forecast.

- Assess the length of time it will take to generate enough profits to offset the tax losses and judge whether recognition of the asset should be restricted.

- Check tax correspondence to ensure that Bluebell Co can carry the losses forward and offset these against taxable profits.

(c) Key performance indicators

Briefing notes

For: Audit partner

By: Audit manager

Date: December 20X8

Subject: Notes for meeting with Daisy Rosepetal, internal auditor Bluebell Co

Guidance on social and environmental key performance indicators (KPIs)

Introduction

These notes detail social and environmental KPIs that could be used at Bluebell Co and the evidence that would be necessary for each.

KPIs

Social

KPI	Nature of evidence
Percentage female employees	Human resources permanent files
Number of customer accidents at a hotel	Hotel log of accidents which should include a description of incident and whether the emergency services needed to be called

KPI	Nature of evidence
Customer satisfaction scores – for example scores out of ten for cleanliness of room or efficiency of staff	Customer satisfaction surveys
Number of customer complaints	Hotel log of complaints Number of refunds issued via sales system

Environmental

KPI	Nature of evidence
Percentage of waste recycled at hotel	Amount invested in recycling facilities at hotel for both guests and staff
Amount spent on environmentally friendly products such as energy efficient light bulbs or rubbish bins with separate sections for recycling in all rooms	Preferred suppliers list will contain suppliers stocking these products Products visible throughout hotels
Percentage change in utilities usage since prior year	Supplier bills for gas, water and electricity to compare the cost and volume supplied versus the previous year Comparison of actual to budgeted use of utilities with explanations for unexpected variances
Percentage of sustainable or recycled materials used in building new hotels or when undertaking refurbishment	Project plans for new hotels or refurbishment details Invoices from suppliers detailing sustainable or recycled materials

Conclusion

The KPIs listed are just some of the possible measures which could be used at Bluebell Co. The company should ensure the environmental and social targets it sets are quantifiable and that evidence is available for each. The exact KPIs chosen will need to fit in with the overall priorities of the hotel chain.

BPP
LEARNING
MEDIA

42 Robster

Marking scheme

Marks

(a) (i) **Leases**

Generally 1 mark per matter/evidence point:

Matters
- Correct calculation and assessment of materiality
- Classification of lease
- IFRS 16 indicators of lease
- Asset recognised at cost
- Finance charge
- Depreciation

Evidence
- Lease clauses re substantially all benefits, control of use
- Recalculate lease liability
- Recalculate depreciation and finance charge
- Cash book for payments
- Review of disclosures
- Split current/non-current payable

Marks

(ii) **Financial assets**

Generally 1 mark per matter/evidence point:

Matters

– Correct calculation and assessment of materiality
– Classification as held for trading
– Assets shown at fair value – could be subjective

Evidence

– Agree purchase price

– Agree fair value

– Recalculate gain

– Review of disclosures in notes

– Review of disclosure in OFR/other information published with financial statements

(iii) **Consignment inventory**

Generally 1 mark for each matter/evidence point:

Matters

– Control not transferred to external vendor
– Robster Co retains managerial involvement
– Revenue recognised too early
– Materiality
– Implication for auditor's opinion
– Opening balances could be misstated

Evidence

– Confirm terms of arrangement by review of signed contract

– Consider whether terms of contract mean that revenue should be recognised

– Confirmation of inventories held by external vendors

– Determine amount of returns normally made under the contract

– Attendance at external vendors inventory count

	Maximum	21

(b) **ISA 260 significant findings from audit**

Generally 1 mark per comment.

– Circumstances affecting form and content of modified reports
– Auditor's views of significant areas of subjectivity
– Significant issues
– Significant difficulties

	Maximum	4
Total		**25**

(a) (i) **Matters to consider**

Materiality

Both the non-current assets recognised and the total lease liability are material at 8% and 7.1% of total assets respectively (breaching the 2–5% threshold).

Accounting treatment

We need to consider whether the contracts have been classified correctly as leases in line with IFRS 16 *Leases*.

For a contract to give rise to a lease in line with IFRS 16, there must be an **identified asset**. This must be explicitly specified in the contract. Robster Co ('Robster') must be able to control (direct) the use of the asset, eg it should be able to use the building in whatever way it chooses.

The right-of-use asset must give Robster 'substantially all' the economic benefits from use of the asset, for the whole period of use.

The right-of-use asset is initially measured at cost, ie the same as the initial measurement of the lease liability. Robster, however, has recognised the two at differing amounts. This appears to be incorrect. Further information is needed regarding why Robster has done this, and where the other $0.4m has been accounted for.

The lease liability should be measured at the present value of the lease payments, discounted using the implicit interest rate. If this rate cannot be determined, then Robster can use its incremental borrowing rate instead.

This interest is accounted for as a finance cost against profit and loss.

The right-of-use asset is accounted for under the cost model of IAS 16 *Property, Plant and Equipment*, unless Robster uses the revaluation model for assets of the same class.

Audit evidence

- A copy of Robster's workings in relation to the lease liabilities, which the auditor should have recalculated

- Further information regarding the recognition of the asset and the liability at differing amounts.

- To verify that the contracts are classified correctly as leases, review the lease contracts for indicators that Robster has substantially all the economic benefits of the asset, and has the right to control the asset's use

- Recalculation of the finance charges charged against profit and loss

- Agreement of interest rates used in calculations to lease agreements

- Recalculation of depreciation charges applied to non-current assets

(ii) **Matters to consider**

Materiality

The financial assets of $1.26m are material at 2.8% of total assets. The gain of $350,000 is material at 10.9% of profit before tax.

Accounting treatment

IFRS 9 *Financial Instruments* sets out the categories that financial instruments must fall into, along with the appropriate accounting treatment for each. The initial classification of the financial assets as 'held for trading investments' is therefore a crucial area of judgement as it determines the accounting treatment – in this case, at fair value. This means measuring the fair value at the year end, and recognising any gains or losses directly in profit or loss.

The assets should therefore have been purchased in order to sell them in the short term, and must be part of a whole portfolio of instruments that are managed together with a view to short-term profit.

Audit evidence

- A schedule showing all the investments held in this category and the fair values of each

- Agreement of the fair values to external evidence such as year-end market price (current bid price)

- Recalculation of the total gain or loss as the overall movement in fair value over the course of the year

- Review of the internal controls and procedures followed by the trading department. Testing to confirm that details (quantities, dates, etc) shown on the schedule can be relied upon

- Analytical procedures to confirm that there is a portfolio of investments that are traded frequently with a view to short-term profit. Corroboration by a review of events after the year end

(iii) **Matters to consider**

IFRS 15 requires revenue to be recognised when the performance obligations contained in the contract are met, as control of goods is transferred to the purchaser.

Robster retains legal title to the goods while they are with the vendor, and when they are sold, this title passes straight to the customer. Thus Robster still legally owns the jewellery when it is with the vendor.

Robster retains the ability to change the selling price of the jewellery when it is with the vendor. This constitutes managerial involvement. Robster is also exposed to the risk of inventory not being sold, as unsold inventory must be returned back to it after nine months. Hence in addition to retaining legal title, Robster also retains control.

This would suggest that Robster should only recognise revenue once the vendor has sold an item on to a customer. However, Robster currently recognises revenue as soon as the item is delivered to the vendor. This appears to be incorrect.

The required adjustments would derecognise revenue of $1.25m, recognise inventory of $1m, and reduce retained earnings by $0.25m. Profit before tax would be reduced by $0.25m or 7.8%, which is material. The understatement of inventory by $1m is also highly material at 2.2% of total assets. If these adjustments are not made, then the audit opinion should be qualified 'except for' a material misstatement.

Audit evidence

- Copies of sales contracts with key vendors and confirmation of their terms

- Review of contract terms to determine if Robster retains risks and rewards relating to, and managerial involvement with, the goods

- Enquiries into the proportion of goods usually returned from vendors, to form an understanding of potential levels of obsolete goods

- Results of auditor's test counts of inventory at a selection of vendors' premises to ensure the existence of goods held on consignment

(b) ISA 260 *Communication with Those Charged with Governance* requires that any circumstances affecting the form and content of the auditor's report should be communicated. It is possible that the auditor's opinion will be modified in respect of any of the three matters; if this is the case then it would need to be communicated with those charged with governance. The communication should include the circumstances that led to the expected modification, together with the wording of the modification (ISA 705: para. 30).

The auditor would communicate their views about any significant qualitative aspects of Robster's accounting treatments. For example, it may be that the auditor concludes that the treatment of the financial assets 'held for trading' is acceptable in line with IFRS 9. In this case there would still be an element of subjectivity involved in the measurement and classification of these assets. Robster's treatment could be acceptable and not incorrect, but the auditor may still have a different view of it. Those charged with governance could benefit from hearing this view as part of their responsibility for overseeing the financial reporting process (ISA 260: para. A20).

The auditor would communicate any significant difficulties encountered during the audit, as well as significant matters discussed. All of the issues in question were material and are therefore likely to be significant matters, and each may have given rise to significant difficulties. Other matters that should be communicated here would include any delays by management, unreasonably short timescales or unexpected levels of audit effort required to obtain evidence (ISA 260: para. A21).

43 Connolly

Workbook references. Chapters 2, 6 and 8.

Top tips. This was a challenging question which featured both business risks with risks of material misstatement. To score well you needed to keep the two separate; any discussion of risks of material misstatement within your section on business risks will not get any marks.

In part (a), try to be as specific as you can in what you write, avoiding repetition from the scenario and being as clear as possible about what the business risk is. Including a sentence starting with 'the business risk is' when you discuss each issue might help here.

Note that there are no marks given in the marking scheme for theoretical discussions of the nature of business risk in general, nor are there marks available for categorising business risks as operational, compliance or financial.

There is often a temptation to talk about going concern wherever there is a hint of it in the scenario. In this question, the company's ability to trade in the future may possibly have been at risk, but this was not a major issue and the marks available for mentioning it were limited (no marks are specifically given for going concern on the marking scheme). Going concern certainly was not enough of a problem for you to include it as a risk of material misstatement.

In part (b), pay attention to the number of marks (and thus time) available; there may be more risks in the scenario than you will have time to address in your answer, so there is a risk of going over your time allocation for this part of the question. There are plenty of easier marks for calculating materiality (and saying that a balance is material), and for stating the main aspects of the accounting treatment of the item in question.

Note that the new loan (of $10m) has not yet been taken out, so risks related to this are not relevant to this question. In relation to the accounting and management information system, the question is very clear that 'this is not considered to create any significant control deficiencies' – this is a signal from the examining team that you should include this as a risk of material misstatement.

In part (c), try to say two things for each procedure: which specific procedure to perform, and why it should be performed. For example, 'Obtain the purchase agreement (½ mark) to confirm that Connolly Co has the right to operate the brand (½ mark).' Note that the brand has been acquired by itself, not as a subsidiary company, so any procedures here relating to groups or goodwill are not relevant.

In part (d), candidates sometimes misunderstand the question as referring to ethical issues that might come up as part of doing the audit, eg confidentiality. This will get no marks. The ethical issues are threats to the fundamental principles, and should be reasonably clear in the scenario (the loan guarantee and the systems advice). Your approach should be to state each type of threat (eg advocacy threat), explain why it is a threat, and then to recommend actions (eg accept with safeguards, or do not accept and communicate to management).

BPP
LEARNING
MEDIA

The ACCA's guidance on professional marks changes frequently, and here they are available for the heading, the introduction, the use of headings within your answer, and the clarity of your language – so no marks for a conclusion. BPP's advice is to continue to write a conclusion as this is still a part of the briefing notes format, and it is possible that you will miss out on marks if you don't write one in future sittings.

Easy marks. The marks for audit procedures in relation to the brand are relatively simple. Make sure you maximise your professional marks.

ACCA examining team's comments. The first requirement asked candidates to evaluate the business risks faced by Connolly Co. This requirement was generally well attempted, and in fact for many candidates this was the best attempted out of all of the question requirements. Most candidates proved able to identify and discuss many of the relevant business risks within their briefing notes and the risks surrounding non-compliance with stringent regulations, the risk of losing the licences necessary to produce pharmaceutical products, the lack of cash to support on-going product development, the risks attached to diversifying into a new market, and reputational risks associated with the court case against the company were generally well discussed.

The **best answers** made full use of the information provided and performed analysis of the financial information, allowing for identification of the less obvious but often pertinent risks, such as that without the revenue derived from the new market entered into during the year the company's total revenue would have fallen by a significant amount. Furthermore strong candidates, as well as providing detailed analysis and explanation of the risks, also attempted to prioritise the various risks identified thus demonstrating appropriate judgment and an understanding that the audit partner would want to know about the most significant risks first.

The **key weakness** present in many answers continues to be the poor quality of explanations. Weaker answers tended to just repeat facts given in the scenario with little attempt to discuss or evaluate them. Some answers began with a lengthy discussion of the definition of business risk and its components which was not necessary and demonstrates a lack of judgment when the briefing notes are being requested by an audit partner. Further many answers were very repetitive and did not consider the number of distinct business risks that would be required for the marks available. Many candidates discussed at length risks over going concern that were tenuous or lacked appropriate explanation. Many candidates also confused business risk and audit risk and therefore provided responses that were not relevant to the question.

The second requirement asked candidates to identify and explain the risks of material misstatement to be considered in planning the audit and performance in this area was very mixed. There were some excellent answers to this requirement, with many candidates achieving close to full marks. Most candidates were able to identify the risks surrounding inappropriate accounting treatment which could lead to material misstatements, and were also able to quantify the materiality of the matters discussed. The risks that were most commonly discussed related to provisions, recognition of research and development costs, the valuation of potentially obsolete inventory, and the segmental reporting that would be likely required in relation to the new market entered into during the year.

The **best answers** were well structured in how they explained the potential misstatement and included in their evaluation of each risk an identification of the risk factor from the scenario (eg the court case ongoing against the company), a determination of materiality where possible given the information in the question, a clear comment on the appropriateness of the accounting treatment where relevant, and the impact on the financial statements (eg non-recognition of a provision in relation to the court case could lead to an understatement of liabilities and an overstatement of operating profit). Only the better candidates identified that requesting additional finance from the bank to cover the damages from the court case implied that the outcome was probable rather than possible and should be provided for.

Weaker answers discussed a risk of material misstatement relating to accounting for the loan that had been applied for, but given that this had not yet been received it would not give rise to a risk of this nature in this reporting period. Other candidates discussed at length the issue of going concern and that the company's financial statements should be prepared on a break-up basis but there was certainly not enough evidence in the scenario to justify this as a risk of material misstatement.

The third requirement asked candidates to recommend the principal audit procedures to be performed in respect of a brand name that had been acquired during the year. Answers to this requirement were very mixed, as is typical for requirements relating to audit procedures. The **best answers** provided well explained procedures that clearly set out how the test would be performed and where appropriate the documentation that would be used. **Weaker answers** contained vague or very brief lists that were not specific enough to constitute an audit procedure and therefore did not earn marks. Examples of weaker answer points include 'assess value of the brand' (this is not an audit procedure – how should the assessment take place?), 'discuss accounting treatment with management' (what specifically should be discussed?), 'look at the purchase contract' (what information should the auditor be looking for within the contract?). Candidates should ensure that procedures contain an actual instruction describing an action to be performed to satisfy a specific objective.

A minority of candidates thought that rather than acquiring a specific asset ie the brand, as stated in the question, a company had been purchased. This led to candidates providing irrelevant audit procedures and wrongly discussing the accounting treatment for goodwill. Candidates are reminded to read the question extremely carefully.

The final requirement asked candidates to discuss the ethical issues arising from the engagement and to recommend appropriate actions. There were two matters present in the scenario that were appropriate to discuss – the fact that Connolly Co's bank had asked the audit firm to guarantee the loan extension that had been requested, and that the audit firm had been asked to give advice on the new management information system planned to be introduced the following year.

This requirement was generally well attempted with the majority of candidates correctly identifying the two issues and providing some relevant discussion for each. Most candidates were able to explain the ethical threats associated with the issues and recognised that the significance of the threats would need to be determined. Many candidates appreciated that due to Connolly Co's listed status it qualified as a public interest entity, and therefore the threats to objectivity were heightened. Many candidates demonstrated sound judgment by concluding that the services should not be provided to the audit client as it would be unlikely that safeguards could reduce the threats to an acceptable level. However, credit was awarded where candidates mentioned the types of safeguards that could be considered.

Weaker answers for this requirement identified the wrong ethical threats or failed to identify the significance of the company's listed status, concluding that it would be acceptable to provide the services. Other answers digressed into discussions on the general ethical issues surrounding the testing of medicines on animals or humans, which was not relevant to the question requirement.

Marks

(a) **Evaluation of business risks**
Generally up to 2 marks for each business risk evaluated. In addition,
1 mark for relevant trends calculated and used as part of the risk
valuation:
  – Regulatory risk – licensing of products
  – Regulatory risk – patent infringement
  – Regulatory risk – advertising
  – Skilled workforce

Marks

- Risk of diversification
- Cash flow issues – negative trend/cash management issues
- Cash flow issues – reliance on further bank finance (allow up to 3 marks here if several points covered)
- Cash flow issues – timing of cash flows
- Court case – bad publicity and further scrutiny
- Risk of overtrading

Maximum   11

(b) **Risks of material misstatement**

Up to 2 marks for each risk identified and explained. Also allow up to 1 mark for appropriate and correct materiality calculations:

- Management bias
- Development costs – recognition
- Development costs – amortisation
- Patent costs
- Court case – provision or contingent liability
- Segmental reporting

Maximum   8

(c) **Procedures in relation to purchased brand name**

Generally 1 mark for each relevant, well described audit procedure:

- Review board minutes for evidence of discussion of the purchase, and for its approval
- Agree the cost of $5m to the company's cash book and bank statement
- Obtain the purchase agreement and confirm the rights of Connolly Co
- Discuss with management the estimated useful life of the brand of 15 years and obtain an understanding of how 15 years has been determined as appropriate
- If the 15-year useful life is a period stipulated in the purchase document, confirm to the terms of the agreement
- If the 15-year useful life is based on the life expectancy of the product, review a cash flow forecast of sales of the product
- Obtain any market research or customer satisfaction surveys
- Consider whether there are any indicators of potential impairment
- Recalculate the amortisation expense for the year and confirm adequacy of disclosure in notes to the financial statements

Maximum   5

(d) **Ethical matters**

Generally up to 1 mark for each point discussed:

- Loan guarantee is a financial self-interest threat
- The loan is material and guarantee should not be given
- The advice on systems would be a non-audit service
- Self-review threat created
- Threat of assuming management responsibility
- Service can only be provided if systems unrelated to financial reporting

- In this case the advice relating to accounting systems must not be given
- Advisable not to provide the advice on management information systems
- Discuss both matters with management/those charged with governance

Maximum   7

Professional marks

Generally 1 mark for heading, 1 mark for introduction, 1 mark for use of headings within the briefing notes, 1 mark for clarity of comments made.

Maximum   4

Total   <u>**35**</u>

Briefing notes

To: Partner

From: Manager

Subject: Audit of Connolly Co, y/e 31 Dec 20X4

Introduction

These briefing notes will evaluate the business risks facing our client, identify and explain four risks of material misstatement, recommend audit procedures in relation to a new brand acquired during the year, and finally explain ethical threats to our firm.

(a)   **Business risks**

(Calculations of some key trends are included in an appendix to part (a) below.)

Licensing

There is a risk that Connolly Co (Connolly)'s products in development are not licensed. Any costs incurred developing such products will therefore be wasted.

Research and development costs are significant, with the research and development cash outflow representing 7.5% of revenue ($3m / $40m). Failure to obtain licences is a major threat to achieving business objectives.

Patent infringements

If Connolly breaches a competitor's patent, it will incur legal costs in defending its position. Time must be spent on monitoring to ensure this does not happen, which is a drain on precious resources.

If a competitor breaches one of Connolly's patents then the costs of bringing legal action may also be substantial.

Advertising

Inappropriate advertising campaigns may breach local regulations, for example in countries where television advertising is not allowed. This may result in fines and damage to Connolly's reputation.

Moreover, the fact that television advertising is not allowed will reduce Connolly's ability to earn crucial revenue in those countries. Other forms of advertising may be used instead, but these may be more costly and less effective.

Court case

The court case against the company will result in an outflow of resources which the company can scarcely afford. Increased scrutiny of Connolly by regulators may follow, which brings with it the risk of further problems in future.

It may also result in bad publicity, which is particularly damaging to Connolly given the importance of advertising and branding to its operations.

Skilled staff

Connolly needs a skilled workforce to be able to develop new drugs. There is thus a risk of losing key personnel, perhaps to competitors. This could delay or halt drug development.

It may also be difficult to attract talented staff if Connolly's reputation is damaged by the pending court case.

New products

The growth of the new animal products market is certainly a boon, but brings risks. Since this is a new area, management may not be familiar with regulations and may therefore incur fines or penalties. There could be brand confusion between human and animal products.

Revenue in this area may continue to grow as it has done, but management needs to manage risks here carefully.

Revenue

Connolly has a prima facie growth in revenue of 5.2% in 20X4. However, the new veterinary products contribute about $6m revenue (15% × $40m), which is significant. Without them, Connolly's revenue for 20X4 would have been $34m (= $40m – $6m). This is a reduction of 10.5% (= ($38m – $34m) / $38m).

Cash flow

The net cash outflow of $1.2m may be a cause for concern, however we do not know what Connolly's cash position is. The outflow may be related to the acquisition of the 'Cold Comforts' brand, expenditure to launch the new animal products range, or expenditure on research and development (up 7.1%). Many of these are one-off expenditures, so the cash outflow may not be as concerning as it might first appear to be.

The falling core revenues, however, will have an effect on cash. Connolly has been able to offset this with its new product range, but 85% of its revenue still comes from its traditional business so it needs to continue investing cash in product development.

The fact that Connolly has approached the bank for two new loans, which are very material at 6.5% of assets combined (= $13m / $200m), indicates that it is experiencing cash difficulties. If the bank refuses this, then it may be unable to develop the new products which it sorely needs.

If the loan is accepted, then Connolly's gearing ratio will worsen, and it may struggle to make interest payments to service its debts. On the other hand, if the loan application is refused, then it will need to raise alternative finance for development. Given the fall in its EPS and its high gearing in 20X4, a share issue may not be successful.

If Connolly fails to raise finance, then it may struggle to fund product development in the short-term and thus to generate cash in the longer term. This could become a going concern risk in the future, but this risk does not appear to be pressing at this year end.

Appendix – key trends (figures in $000)

Revenue – up by 5.2% ($2,000 / $38,000)

Operating profit – down by 10.8% ($985 / $9,085)

BPP
LEARNING
MEDIA

Operating margin – down by 16.7% (4% / 24%)

Net cash flow – down by 120% ($7,200 / $6,000)

Research & development ('R&D') cash outflow – up by 7.1% ($200 / $2,800)

(b) **Risks of material misstatement**

    (i) **Management bias**

Connolly is trying to raise finance, and the bank will use the financial statements as part of its lending decision. Management is therefore under pressure to present a favourable position, which may result in bias in relation to any judgemental balances and transactions.

Management may use earnings management techniques to overstate revenue and understate expenses. Estimates included in the financial statements may also be at a higher risk of misstatement, since these by nature involve an element of management judgement.

    (ii) **R&D costs**

IAS 38 *Intangible Assets* requires research costs to be expensed and development costs to be capitalised. Criteria for capitalisation include: the technical feasibility of the developed product; the intention to complete the product development; the ability to sell the asset; that resources are available to complete the development (IAS 38: para. 57).

The R&D cash outflow is material at 1.5% of total assets (= $3m / $200m).

There is a risk that research costs have been capitalised inappropriately as development costs. This is exacerbated by the possible management bias (above).

Connolly's liquidity position means that resources may not be available to complete the development. There is a risk that costs have been capitalised in spite of this.

Overall, the risk relates to the overstatement of assets and the understatement of expenses.

    (iii) **Court case**

IAS 37 *Provisions, Contingent Liabilities and Contingent Assets* requires a provision to be recognised where there is a present obligation as a result of a past event, there is a probable outflow of economic benefits and this can be measured reliably (IAS 37: para. 14).

The amount of $3m is material to total assets at 1.5% (= $3m / $200m).

The clinical trial was in 20X3, so the present obligation relates to a past event. The fact that Connolly is requesting funds from the bank indicates that the event may be probable, and it appears to be measurable at $3m. Hence provision should be made for these costs.

There is a risk that provision is not made, and that liabilities and expenses are both understated.

    (iv) **Segment reporting**

The new product area may require separate disclosure under IFRS 8 *Operating Segments*. This requires listed companies to disclose the performance of the company disaggregated over its operating or geographical segments, as the information is viewed by management (IFRS 8). Since the new area contributes 15% of revenue, it could be seen as a reportable segment. Disclosure of its revenue, profit and other figures may be required. The risk is non-disclosure or incomplete disclosure of the necessary information.

(c)   **Audit procedures**

- Review board minutes for discussion of purchase, and to verify that purchase was authorised.

- Agree the cost of $5m to the bank statement.

- Obtain purchase agreement to confirm both the cost and the rights of Connolly Co in respect of the brand.

- Discuss with management the estimated useful life of the brand of 15 years to assess whether the underlying assumptions are appropriate.

- If useful life is stipulated in the purchase document, confirm the terms of the agreement.

- If useful life is based on the life expectancy of the product, obtain an understanding of the basis for this, eg by reviewing a cash flow forecast of sales of the product.

- Obtain any market research or customer satisfaction surveys to confirm the existence of a revenue stream.

- Consider whether there are any indicators of potential impairment at the year end by obtaining pre year end sales information and reviewing terms of contracts to supply the products to pharmacies.

- Recalculate the amortisation expense and agree the figure to the financial statements for accuracy.

(d)   **Ethical issues**

Loan guarantee

Guaranteeing a loan creates a financial interest in Connolly. If Connolly defaults on loan payments then Davies & Co may become liable for them. This is a self-interest threat because Davies & Co would then have an incentive to express a better audit opinion than it should do, in order to not become liable for the loan. It is also unlikely to be a sound commercial move, since its potential liability may outweigh the audit fee received from Connolly.

The IESBA *Code of Ethics for Professional Accountants* states that where the loan guaranteed is material, then no safeguards can reduce the threat to an acceptable level. The loan is 5% of total assets here and is therefore material.

There is also an advocacy threat here because the firm may find itself acting on Connolly's behalf before the bank.

Davies & Co should therefore communicate to the bank that it cannot provide such a guarantee.

Systems advice

Advice on the systems would be a non-assurance service. As a listed company, Connolly is a public interest entity.

A self-review threat may arise here in future if the auditor relies on systems it has itself developed. There is a risk of taking on a management role.

Since Connolly is a public interest entity, according to the *Code* Davies & Co cannot be involved with the design or implementation of systems relating to internal controls over financial reporting. If the proposed advisory work relates to these systems, the request must be declined.

If the engagement does not relate to financial reporting systems, then it may be possible to accept it. Safeguards may be applied in order to reduce the threat to an acceptable level, such as the use of separate teams for the two engagements.

Conclusion

Connolly faces a variety of business risks. A number of risks of material misstatement have been discussed, and the audit planning must design procedures to mitigate these risks. Detailed tests will need to be performed in relation the acquired brand. Two ethical matters have been identified, both of which create significant threats to independence and objectivity.

44 Osier

Workbook references. Chapters 8 and 15.

Top tips. Part (a) asked about audit evidence in a way that is typical of what you should expect from your exam. Financial reporting knowledge is at the core of questions like this, so you need to remember what you learned in SBR (formerly Paper P2).

Part (a)(i) was probably deceptively simple. If you were comfortable with IAS 2 *Inventories* then you would have recognised that what the entity is doing is essentially OK, and that you really needed to focus on how to audit it. The matters to consider then become some simple points about subjectivity, estimates and bias.

Part (a)(ii) may have been easier. This is a core accounting standard and one that you should be comfortable with – you only really needed to know its outlines to answer this question well.

The hard part throughout (a) would have been thinking of enough pieces of evidence. There are a few points here. Firstly, evidence can be the results of audit procedures – so if you describe the evidence that a completed procedure would give, then this is acceptable. Secondly, it's really important that you say **why** a piece of evidence is needed, as this can double your marks for each point. You don't necessarily have to identify which financial statement assertion you're testing; if you review the model answer with this in mind you'll see that it's good on this point.

Part (b) was knowledge, but this was a slightly tricky point. If you didn't know the answer, then review the answer here as it's an important point. Areas where candidates do badly are often examined again, so you don't want to get caught out.

Part (c) should have been within your reach, as this aspect of auditing performance information is really not dissimilar from thinking of audit procedures.

Easy marks. The marks for calculating materiality and assessing it against a benchmark (in part (a)).

ACCA examining team's comments. In part (a) there were two scenarios where candidates were asked to describe the key matters and audit evidence that would be expected in each. Overall there appeared to be a poor understanding of the accounting issues raised by the scenarios. Part (a)(i) concerned the audit of manufactured inventory and the appropriate inclusion of overhead and labour costs. Most identified the need to check the components back to source documentation and review the reasonableness of the process but many candidates concentrated on discussing auditing and accounting standards rather than detailing the evidence that should have been gathered. However this was the best answered of the two sections.

Part (a)(ii) related to a topical subject – an impairment review of a retailer's property portfolio caused by diminishing shop sales countered by growing internet sales. Many candidates simply discussed whether or not an impairment review should be carried out as there were indicators of impairment (falling retail sales) but this was a given from the question as the review had already been undertaken. Few questioned whether it was reasonable to base the value in use on the assumption that sales would grow by 1% a year when in reality they were falling. Candidates appeared unwilling to challenge this underlying assumption which actually lacked commercial justification.

Part (b) was generally not well answered. It asked candidates to distinguish between a performance audit and audit of performance information and answers were universally poor.

In part (c) candidates were required to explain how to audit some performance KPIs, and although some good points were made a number of candidates stretched their imagination as to how these could be verified and were simply impractical in the nature of their procedures.

Marking scheme

Marks

Osier Co

Generally up to 1½ marks for each well explained matter and 1 mark for each well explained piece of evidence recommended.

Note. Marks will be awarded for explanations of why calculations and balances are complex or subjective and how this affects their accuracy. Simple statements that calculations and balances are complex or subjective will be awarded a maximum of ½ mark each, where relevant.

(a) (i) **Inventory**

Matters
- Materiality
- Complexity of calculation
- Subjectivity in calculation

Evidence
- Documentation of systems and controls
- Summary of purchase costs and matching to purchase invoices
- Calculation of forecast wages matched to underlying HR and payroll records
- Confirmations of wage increments/rises
- Calculation of forecast production units reviewed in comparison to prior year
- Calculation of forecast overheads corroborated to new agreements

Maximum 7

(ii) **Impairment**

Matters
- Materiality
- Uncertainty relating to estimates
- Growth rate assumption in relation to value in use
- Allocation of impairment does not seem to be correct

Evidence
- Copies of offers for retail outlets
- Copy of forecast cash flows relating to retail outlets
- Recalculation of forecasts using management's predictions
- Analytical review by unit/geographical region to assess appropriateness of general growth rate
- Notes re discussion about retail prospects by area
- Schedule of goodwill analysed by division
- Recalculation of allocation of impairment
- Copies of previous forecasts

Maximum 7

BPP
LEARNING
MEDIA

Moosewood Hospital

Generally up to 1½ marks for each well explained point and
1 mark for each well explained procedure recommended.

(b)   **'Performance audit' v 'audit of performance information'**
   –   Performance audit: assurance on effectiveness of operations
   –   Audit of performance information: assurance on accuracy of
       KPIs.

Maximum   3

(c)   **Procedures in relation to performance information**
   General
   –   Document systems and test controls
   –   Identify level of senior management scrutiny of KPIs
   –   Recalculate KPIs to confirm mathematical accuracy
   –   Analytical review to historic performance
   Patient/nurse ratio
   –   Obtain definition of 'average' for patient/nurse ratio
   –   Identify which patients to include
   –   Confirm patient numbers to patient records
   –   Confirm staff numbers to HR records
   Surgical rooms
   –   Discuss normal levels of room usage
   –   Obtain hospital plans to identify number of surgical rooms
   –   Recalculate number of surgical hours available
   –   Confirm surgical times to underlying surgery/treatment records
   Admissions for previously treated conditions
   –   Enquire how a previously treated condition is identified.
   –   Inspect patient admission records to identify readmissions
       within 28 days
   –   Inspect underlying patient records to identify if conditions match

Maximum   8

Total   **25**

(a)   (i)   **Osier Co**

   Cost of inventory

   Matters

   Materiality

   Inventory costs represent 1.1% of total assets and 19.6% of profit. Inventory is
   therefore material to both the statement of financial position and the statement of profit
   or loss.

   Risk of material misstatement

   The calculation of the cost of inventory is complex. This complexity increases the risk of
   error in the calculation, which increases the risk of misstatement.

   The calculation is also subject to a number of estimates; the average production time
   per unit, the forecast annual wage cost, the scheduled hours of production and the

forecast units of production are all estimates. These estimates increase the risk of both error and manipulation of the calculation to suit management's bias.

Given both the complexity and subjectivity involved in the calculation there is a significant risk that the inventory cost may be misstated.

Evidence expected to be on file:

- Documentation of the system for obtaining the data used in the costing exercise and calculating the final cost. This should identify the key controls that operate in this system and there should be evidence on file that these controls have been appropriately tested.

- A copy of the summary of inventory purchase costs. A sample of the purchase costs, including the additional costs of transport and handling, should have been confirmed through inspection of original purchase invoices, copies of which should also be on file.

- Documentation of the results of a discussion with the production manager to ascertain how they estimate the average production time per unit of inventory. Any calculations referred to by management should have been reperformed by the audit team to confirm their mathematical accuracy and agreed to corroborating documentation.

- A copy of the calculation of the forecast annual wage cost. The initial staffing levels should have been confirmed through inspection of current human resource records and for a sample of the staff their initial wages should have been confirmed through inspection of payroll records.

- Forecast wage increments should have been agreed to either post year end confirmation issued by human resources, or minutes of board meetings approving pay rises.

- Documentation of the results of a discussion with management regarding how the forecast is made and who is ultimately responsible for reviewing and approving the forecast.

- A copy of the calculation of forecast units of production. This should have been analytically reviewed in comparison to the previous year's production levels. Where there are significant differences explanations should have been sought from management.

- A copy of the calculation of forecast production overheads. This should have been analytically reviewed by category of overhead in relation to the previous year to identify any significant variances. Corroborating evidence, such as rental and utilities agreements, should have been obtained where possible.

- There should be evidence on all management's schedules that the figures have been recalculated by the audit team to confirm the mathematical accuracy of management's calculations.

(ii) **Impairment**

Matters

Materiality

The impairment of $9 million represents 0.47% of total assets and 8.41% of profit. While it is not material to the statement of financial position it is material to the statement of profit or loss.

BPP
LEARNING
MEDIA

Calculation of recoverable amount

The fair value of the retail outlets, the disposal costs and the value in use are all management estimates. This increases the risk of material misstatement through both error and management manipulation of the reported figures.

In particular, while the estimate for the fair value appears to have a reasonable basis, the estimate of value in use appears to be too basic. The assumption that the cash flows attributable to the whole of the retail division will grow at 1% per annum is too simplistic and appears to lack commercial justification. It is likely that each retail outlet will be subject to regional variations in growth and growth rates will also be subject to annual fluctuations based upon economic variables. There is also no justification as to why 1% growth has been selected to represent 'poor performance', at the very least this should be benchmarked to more widespread and reliable growth forecasts, eg national forecasts of economic growth.

Allocation of the impairment

The impairment has been allocated against all of the tangible assets in the cash generating unit. This is incorrect; as a cash-generating unit the impairment should firstly be allocated against any goodwill relating to the cash-generating unit in accordance with IAS 36 *Impairment of Assets*. It should then be allocated against the remaining assets on a pro-rata basis bearing in mind that an asset should not be impaired below the highest of either its fair value less costs of disposal or its value in use.

Evidence expected to be on file

- Copies of the offers received to purchase the retail outlets, confirming the amounts offered. These should have been used to recalculate the average used for the estimate of fair value.

- Documentation of enquiries with management with regard to how they estimated the disposal costs and what experience they have had with the sale of similar operations.

- A copy of the forecast cash flows attributable to the retail outlets. This should contain evidence of analytical review in comparison to the year ended 31 March 20X7 to confirm the accuracy of the base cash flows.

- There should then be evidence of a recalculation of the future cash flows using management's estimates of 1% growth to confirm the mathematical accuracy of management's calculation.

- There should be evidence of a recalculation of the value in use using a range of growth rates to assess the sensitivity of management's calculations to economic variables. The differences between these valuations and management's valuation should have been reviewed to assess the likelihood of a material under or overvaluation.

- Evidence of an analytical review of performance by retail outlet or geographical area of operations, referenced to sales and cash flow records where available, to confirm whether growth rates are consistent across the brand or whether there are variances.

- Documentation of enquiries with management relating to their expectations for specific retail outlets or areas of operations and whether there are any specific matters which they are aware of which may affect regional performance, eg the opening of new out-of-town shopping facilities or competitors setting up in the same location.

- A schedule of any goodwill included in the statement of financial position with analysis of its various components to assess whether any part is attributable to the retail outlets as a cash generating unit. This is specifically relevant to any acquired brands which may be sold through the retail stores or any retail brands acquired by Osier Co.

- A recalculation of the allocation of the impairment by the auditor, firstly against any goodwill determined to be attributable to the cash generating unit, then against the remaining assets pro rata.

- Copies of previous forecasts. Where the retail outlets forecast performance exceeds the 1% currently predicted by management there should be evidence of discussion with management to ascertain the reasons for changing their outlook.

(b) **Difference between 'performance audit' and 'audit of performance information'**

Performance audit

A performance audit refers to when the practitioner provides assurance to management with regard to the effective functioning of operational activity or an agreed component of operations.

Audit of performance information

In contrast, an audit of performance information refers to when the practitioner provides assurance with regard to specific performance measures published by the reporting entity. The specific assurance objectives may differ between engagements but will normally be in relation to the accuracy of the reported measures.

(c) **Procedures**

General

Document the systems that are in place for recording the information relevant to the performance measures, noting the key controls that should operate to ensure the accuracy of the information that is captured, recorded and reported. Evidence of the operating effectiveness of these controls throughout the period should be obtained.

In particular, the auditor should obtain an understanding of the level of scrutiny of the performance measures by senior management, including: the frequency of their reviews; the level of detail that is provided; and their responses should the reported performance measures differ from their expectations.

Each of the calculations of the performance measures should be obtained. Using the figures supplied by management these should be recalculated by the audit team to ensure mathematical accuracy.

The performance measures should be analytically reviewed against historic performance levels, on a monthly basis if such information is available, to identify any significant fluctuations in reported performance levels. Where fluctuations occur reasons should be sought through management enquiry, which should then be corroborated with evidence wherever possible.

> **Tutorial note.** Other, relevant general procedures will also be awarded credit but will only be awarded credit once, ie candidates will not be given credit for repeating the same general procedure for each performance measure.

Patient/nurse ratio

Obtain copies of the original document in which the basis for calculating the performance measures were agreed; this may be in the form of a strategic document agreed with health service agencies or it may even be the minutes of the executive board. From this, identify whether any specific definition is provided of the term 'average' or whether a specific formula is provided. In particular, it is important to ascertain over what period the average must be calculated.

From the same document ascertain which patients must be included in the calculation, ie should this include emergency patients or just patients admitted for treatment by appointment.

Confirm the calculation of the number of patients treated through inspection of underlying treatment and appointment records. Confirm the calculation of the number of nurses through inspection of underlying staff rotas and records of hours worked supplied to human resources and payroll departments.

Surgical room usage

Enquire of the manager responsible for planning and co-ordinating surgical operations what the 'normal' period of time (ie excluding emergencies) is during which surgical procedures may be performed, ie which hours during the day and whether there are any days where scheduled procedures would not be performed.

Obtain and inspect the hospital plans to identify the total number of surgical rooms available.

Using the information above calculate the total number of surgical hours available to the hospital. Compare the figure calculated to the figure used in management's calculation to identify any significant variances.

Obtain a schedule of the total hours of surgery performed during the year. Confirm a sample of the times recorded to underlying hospital records to confirm the accuracy of the figures used in this calculation.

Admissions for previously treated conditions

Enquire of management how they define a 'previously treated condition'. For example, does this depend upon the underlying symptoms or the diagnosis of the medical practitioner?

Obtain a copy of the patient admissions records. Use computer assisted audit techniques (CAATs) to identify patients admitted to the hospital within 28 days of a previous admission. If possible, inspect the underlying patient records to identify whether the patient was treated for either the same or a similar condition. If not enquire of the medical practitioners responsible for their care during their admission.

Where the above procedure identifies patients admitted for the same condition ensure that these patients are recorded in management's calculation of the performance measure to ensure the completeness of the information used in the calculation.

45 Macau

Workbook references. Chapters 4, 6, 8 and 10.

Top tips. Part (a) was quite a nice question on audit quality control. If you worked through the scenario you should have found plenty of problems to comment on. It was important here that you did not get too carried away and go over your timing – you should have allocated 25 minutes to this question part (13 × 1.95), so don't go over it.

One tip on these questions is not to repeat too much from the question. Spend as little time as you can repeating the question, and as much time as you can saying what was wrong and what should have been done.

Part (b) combined audit evidence with quality control. The audit evidence on the WIP was a little bit tricky, as the treatment involved considering the recoverability of costs as well as subsequent events. Even if you didn't get quite the right answer here, you could have scored marks if you identified the general issue and stated what the standards say, eg that IAS 10 distinguishes adjusting from non-adjusting events (IAS 10: para. 3), or that IFRS 15 allows costs to be recognised as an asset only if they can be recovered.

The second issue – about other information – was slightly hidden but should have been quite straightforward.

Do not overlook part (b)(ii), requiring you to state what evidence is needed. These tend to be relatively easy marks, provided that you are very specific about the evidence required, and you **state why it is needed**. Do not put 'written representation' too many times – it may seem like an easy win, but the examining team is wary of candidates writing this without really understanding the issue, so there may not be any marks for it.

Lastly, the bit at the end of the scenario – saying that going concern is not an issue – might look open to question, but really this is just the examining team's way of saying not to worry about going concern. It is important that you learn to identify things like this in scenarios, as you would have wasted a lot of time if your answer had focused on going concern.

Easy marks. The marks in part (b) for calculating materiality were very easy.

ACCA examining team's comments. In part (a), there was tendency to rewrite statements of fact from the question which scored no marks but stronger candidates discussed the issues and explained why the firm's actions were clearly inappropriate.

Very few candidates were able to discuss the need for materiality to be constantly reviewed throughout the audit in light of changing circumstances. However, most candidates picked up that a significant addition to property, plant and equipment sited at a supplier's premises needed to be physically verified and that reliance on third party evidence for existence was inappropriate in the circumstances. The inventory count had been poorly performed but few candidates developed this to consider where the real audit risks may lie and the need to inform management of the weakness in internal controls and for the auditors to investigate the discrepancies and extend their testing. Improper manager/partner review was highlighted by the majority of candidates but the implications of the partner's cursory review were not always followed through to a logical conclusion.

In relation to the matters to consider, candidates were faced with a situation where the client had encountered a cancelled manufacturing contract. Most candidates scored the materiality marks for both the value of WIP and deferred income. A significant number of candidates discussed how WIP should have been calculated and its composition without realising that this was irrelevant as it needed to be recognised at nil unless a further use for it could be validly identified. Stronger candidates identified that the client may be able to levy a compensation claim for breach of contract.

A worrying number of candidates also believed that writing off a deferred income creditor was a cost rather than a credit to the statement of profit or loss which shows a more fundamental lack of accounting knowledge. Likewise, many candidates confused WIP with R&D contracts and raised irrelevancies such as depreciation.

The question stated that going concern was not an issue yet many candidates discussed this in depth as part of their answer. Candidates must realise that if the question makes a statement of this nature then marks will not be awarded for discussion, regardless of the quality of their answer and are again reminded to read the question scenario carefully.

Audit evidence required was generally well-answered and there were some straightforward marks achieved by a majority of candidates, specifically the needs to obtain the relevant contract, board minutes, the cancellation letter and evidence of funds received. Some candidates were over-reliant on written representations from management, which are never as compelling as third-party evidence.

 BPP LEARNING MEDIA

(a) **Quality control, ethical and other professional issues**
Generally up to 1 mark for each point explained:
- Materiality should be reviewed as the audit progresses
- Insufficient audit evidence obtained in relation to packing machine:
  1 mark for comment on materiality
  1 mark for comment on physical verification
  1 mark for comment on external confirmation
  1 mark for comment on whether the distribution company is a related party
  1 mark for comment on assertions/inappropriate audit conclusion
- Lack of organisation at inventory count should have been discussed with management
- Test count discrepancies should be extrapolated over the population
- Audit staff may need training on inventory count attendance
- Misstatements should be accumulated and discussed with management
- The inaccuracy of the client's test counts should be reported to management as a control deficiency
- Insufficient review performed by audit manager
- Review left too late and should be ongoing during the audit
- Potential self-interest threat regarding audit engagement partner's brother
- Matter should be investigated and notified to audit firm's ethical partner
- The audit partner lacks integrity, maybe has something to hide
- The partner may need to be removed from the audit and his work reviewed

Maximum   13

(b) (i) **Matters and actions to take**
Generally 1 mark per comment/recommended action explained:
- Calculation and determination of materiality (1 mark for each of the work in progress and the deferred income)
- Contract cancellation is an adjusting event after the reporting period
- The work in progress should be written off and charged to profit or loss, unless it can be used on a different contract
- The deferred income may be repayable, if not it should be released to profit
- Auditor's report implications if necessary adjustments not made
- Integrated report may be inconsistent with financial statements or contain a misstatement of fact
- Auditor's responsibility to read the integrated report to identify inconsistencies/misstatements
- Matters to be discussed with management/those charged with governance

Maximum   7

Marks

(ii)   **Evidence**

Generally 1 mark for a well explained audit evidence point:

–   A copy of the contract between Kowloon Co and BMC reviewed for terms, in particular on whether the cancellation of the contract triggers a repayment of the payment in advance and in relation to ownership of the rights to the development which has so far taken place

–   Copies of correspondence between Kowloon and Co and BMC reviewed for implications of the cancellation of the contract

–   Written confirmation from BMC that the contract has been cancelled and the date of the cancellation

–   Written representation from the project manager confirming that BMC contacted him regarding their financial difficulties in December 20X5

–   Notes of a discussion with the project manager to confirm if the work in progress could be used for an different contract or the feasibility of the design work leading to a new type of product which could be produced by Kowloon Co

–   Correspondence with legal counsel regarding legal implications of selling to alternative customer

–   Review of orders/board minutes to identify if course of action has been determined and alternative customer identified

–   Extracts from the financial statements and journals to confirm that the necessary adjustments have been made

–   A copy of the integrated report, reviewed to confirm whether the cancellation of the contract has been discussed

Maximum   5

Total   **25**

(a)   **Quality control, ethical and professional matters**

The audit of Stanley Co does not seem to have been performed with a high regard for the quality of the audit and there appear to be several ways in which the ISA requirements have been breached.

Materiality

First, it is not appropriate that the materiality level was determined at the planning stage of the audit but has not been reviewed or adjusted since. ISA 320 *Materiality in Planning and Performing an Audit* requires the auditor to determine materiality for the financial statements as a whole at the planning stage of the audit, and to revise it as the audit progresses as necessary where new facts and information become available which impact on materiality. It may be the case that no revision to the materiality which was initially determined is necessary, but a review should have taken place and this should be clearly documented in the audit working papers.

BPP
LEARNING

Audit of property, plant and equipment

The audit of the packing machine has not been properly carried out, and there seems to be a lack of sufficient, appropriate audit evidence to support the audit conclusion. The cost of the asset is material, based on the initial materiality, therefore there is a risk of material misstatement if sufficient and appropriate evidence is not obtained. By the year end the asset's carrying value is less than materiality, presumably due to depreciation being charged, but this does not negate the need for obtaining robust audit evidence for the cost and subsequent measurement of the asset.

The packing machine should have been physically verified. Obtaining the order and invoice does not confirm the existence of the machine, or that it is in working order. In addition, without a physical verification, the audit team would be unaware of problems such as physical damage to the machine or obsolescence, which could indicate impairment of the asset.

Relying on the distribution company to provide evidence on the existence and use of the asset is not appropriate. ISA 500 *Audit Evidence* states that audit evidence obtained directly by the auditor is more reliable than audit evidence obtained indirectly or by inference. External confirmations can be used to provide audit evidence but in this case the external confirmation should corroborate evidence obtained directly by the auditor, rather than be the only source of evidence. The relationship between Stanley Co and Aberdeen Co should also be understood by the auditor, and evidence should be obtained to confirm whether or not the two companies are related parties, as this would impact on the extent to which the external confirmation can be relied upon as a source of evidence.

Inventory count

In respect of the inventory count attendance, the audit team should have discussed the discrepancies with management as they could indicate more widespread problems with the inventory count. Given the comment that the inventory count appeared disorganised, it is possible that count instructions were not being followed or that some items had not been included in the count. One of the requirements of ISA 501 *Audit Evidence – Specific Considerations for Selected Items* is that while attending an inventory count, the auditor shall evaluate management's instructions and procedures for recording and controlling the results of the entity's physical inventory counting. It is not clear from the conclusion of the audit work whether the problems noted at the inventory count have been discussed with management. The auditor attending the inventory count should have raised the issues at the time and assessed whether a recount of all of the inventory was required. Training may need to be provided to audit staff to ensure that they understand the auditor's role at an inventory count and can deal with problems which may arise in the appropriate manner.

The discrepancies noted at the inventory count should be subject to further audit work. The results of the test counts should be extrapolated over the population in order to evaluate the potential misstatement of inventory as a whole. The results should then be evaluated in accordance with ISA 450 *Evaluation of Misstatements Identified During the Audit* which requires that the auditor shall accumulate misstatements identified during the audit, other than those which are clearly trivial, and that misstatements should be discussed with management. The issues raised by the way in which the inventory count was performed could represent a significant control deficiency and should be raised with those charged with governance in accordance with ISA 265 *Communicating Deficiencies in Internal Control to Those Charged with Governance and Management*.

Working paper review

The audit senior's comments in relation to the review by the manager and partner indicate that elements of ISA 220 *Quality Control for an Audit of Financial Statements* have been breached. ISA 220 requires that the engagement partner shall, through a review of the audit documentation and discussion with the engagement team, be satisfied that sufficient appropriate audit evidence has been obtained to support the conclusions reached and for the

auditor's report to be issued. It appears that in this case the partner has not properly reviewed the working papers, instead relying on the audit senior's comment that there were no problems in the audit work. ISA 220 does state that the audit partner need not review all audit documentation, but only a 'quick look' at the working papers could indicate that areas of risk or critical judgement have not been reviewed in sufficient detail.

There is also an issue in that the manager and partner reviews took place at the same time and near the completion of the audit fieldwork. Reviews should happen on a timely basis throughout the audit to enable problems to be resolved at an appropriate time. Reviews should also be hierarchical and it appears that the audit partner has not reviewed the work of the audit manager.

Ethical considerations

Finally, there appears to be a potential threat to objectivity due to the audit engagement partner's brother providing a management consultancy service to the audit client. This amounts to a self-interest threat in that the partner's brother receives income from the audit client. The audit partner's objectivity is therefore threatened, and this is a significant risk due to his position of influence over the audit. He may even receive an introducer's commission from his brother.

The matter should be investigated further, and a senior member of the audit firm or the firm's partner responsible for ethics should discuss the comments made in Stanley Co's board minutes with Joe Lantau in order to evaluate the ethical threat and determine any necessary actions. The amount which is being paid to Mick Lantau should be made known, as well as whether the amount is a market rate, and whether other providers of management advice were considered by the company.

The partner's comments to the audit junior indicate a lack of integrity, and indicate that the partner may have something to hide, which increases the threat to objectivity. The audit partner may need to be removed from the audit and his work reviewed.

(b)   (i)   **Matters to consider and actions to take**

The work in progress represents 4.7% of total assets and is therefore material to the statement of financial position. The deferred income is also material at 2.7% of total assets.

Even though the correspondence with BMC is dated after the end of the reporting period, BMC was suffering from financial problems during the year ending 31 December 20X5 which was notified to Kowloon Co before the year end. Therefore the cancellation of the contract appears to meet the definition of an adjusting event under IAS 10 *Events after the Reporting Period* because it confirms conditions which existed at the year end.

Management must consider whether it is still appropriate to recognise the work in progress as an asset. According to IFRS 15 *Revenue from Contracts with Customers*, costs incurred to fulfil a contract are recognised as an asset if and only if all of the following criteria are met:

- The costs relate directly to a contract (or a specific anticipated contract);

- The costs generate or enhance resources of the entity which will be used in satisfying performance obligations in the future; and

- The costs are expected to be recovered.

The cancellation of the contract indicates that the costs of the work in progress are not recoverable from BMC, in which case the balance should be written off. Management is not planning to amend the balances recognised at the year end, and the audit team should investigate the reasons for this. Possibly management is asserting that the machine design costs could be utilised for a different contract, despite the fact that the machine was developed specifically for BMC. Audit work should focus on the contractual arrangements between Kowloon Co and BMC, particularly in relation to the ownership of the rights to the design work which has taken place. If the design work has been based on an innovation by BMC, then it needs to be determined if this information can still be used.

If the design work which has been undertaken to date can be used by Kowloon and results in an ability to develop a new type of product for other customers, there is the possibility that the costs (excluding any research costs) could be capitalised in line with IAS 38 *Intangible Assets*. This should be discussed with the project manager and finance director to assess if this has been considered and if the capitalisation criteria of IAS 38 can be satisfied.

The accounting treatment of the deferred income also needs to be considered. Depending on the terms of the contract with BMC, the amount could be repayable, though this may not be the case given that it is BMC which has cancelled the contract. If part or all of the amount is repayable, it can remain recognised as a current liability. If it is not repayable, it should be released to the statement of profit or loss.

If the costs cannot be capitalised, then there is a loss which needs to be recognised. Assuming that the advance payment is non-refundable, the net position of the development cost and the deferred income balances result in a loss of $150,000. This represents 15.8% of profit for the year and is material. If any necessary adjustments are not made there will be implications for the auditor's report, which would contain a modified opinion due to material misstatement.

Due to the significance of the matter to the financial statements, the contract cancellation and loss of BMC as a customer should be discussed in the other information to be issued with the financial statements, in this case in the integrated report. The audit firm must consider its responsibilities in respect of ISA 720 *The Auditor's Responsibilities Relating to Other Information*. ISA 720 requires the auditor to read the other information to identify material inconsistencies, if any, with the audited financial statements. Depending on the wording used in the integrated report when referring to the company's activities during the year and its financial performance, omitting to mention the cancellation of the contract could constitute a material misstatement of fact or a material inconsistency.

The matter should be discussed with management, who should be encouraged not only to amend the financial statements but also to discuss the cancellation of the contract in the integrated report. If management refuses to make the necessary amendments and disclosures, the matter should be discussed with those charged with governance and/or the company's legal counsel.

(ii)   **Evidence**

- A copy of the contract between Kowloon Co and BMC reviewed for terms, in particular on whether the cancellation of the contract triggers a repayment of the payment in advance and in relation to ownership of the rights to the development which has so far taken place.

- Copies of correspondence between Kowloon Co and BMC reviewed for implications of the cancellation of the contract.

- Written confirmation from BMC that the contract has been cancelled and the date of the cancellation.

- Written representation from the project manager confirming that BMC contacted him regarding their financial difficulties in December 20X5.

- Notes of a discussion with the project manager to confirm if the work in progress could be used for a different contract or the feasibility of the design work leading to a new type of product which could be produced by Kowloon Co.

- Correspondence with legal counsel regarding the ownership of the machine and whether there are any legal implications following the contract cancellation and potential proposal to sell the machine to a different customer.

- Review of post year end orders/board minutes to assess if any conclusion regarding completion of the machine has been made and if it can be sold to an alternative customer, whether any potential customer has been identified.

- Extracts from the financial statements and journals to confirm that the necessary adjustments have been made.

- A copy of the integrated report, reviewed to confirm whether the cancellation of the contract and loss of BMC as a customer has been discussed.

46 Northwest

Workbook references. Chapters 2, 9, 10 and 11.

Top tips. This is a demanding question set in the context of a group audit which requires some thought and planning. The requirement for part (a) is reasonably straightforward, provided you were familiar with ISA 600.

Part (b) might have frightened you by mentioning professional scepticism, but in reality it was just a normal audit evidence question in disguise. Professional scepticism has been a topical issue for a while now, and this scenario is full of statements that you should be sceptical of. The whole thing is a bit difficult, though, because it's all **inconclusive** – we don't have enough information to really find out what is happening. What we do know, however, is **what evidence we *should* be able to obtain** as auditors, even if it doesn't look like we'll be able to. The auditor has to think in the dark here a little bit, which is difficult.

Part (c)(i) was an oddly phrased requirement, and seemed to be trying to restrict you to commenting on ethical and professional issues. Then, however, there was the mention of 'implications for the completion of the audit', which effectively brings the audit work back in – you have to consider the work required in order to say how it affects audit completion.

Part (c)(ii) was similar in the sense of mixing up ethics with audit evidence. One thing to note is that the model answer states that 'transferring the debt to the parent' would not work, because it would simply leave a liability to the parent. This is a valid reading of the scenario, but the group auditor's offer might also be read as saying that the debt could be transferred by the lender, ie so that it did not refer to Northwest Co at all.

Easy marks. This was a tough question, but the easiest marks were probably the ones for applying professional scepticism in part (b).

ACCA examining team's comments. Part (b) of this question examined the concept of scepticism in the context of a group audit where the parent company was reluctant to provide more than verbal assurances that they would support the loss making subsidiary. The parent company was facing a law suit that they may lose and hence good candidates could explain and apply the concept of professional scepticism by questioning why the parent company would not put the support in writing and whether this might reflect uncertainty of the parent company's going concern status given the law suit.

Part (c) required the implications for the audit of the subsidiary in terms of evidence, reporting and pressure from the parent company auditor to refrain from modifying the audit opinion despite insufficient evidence being available.

BPP
LEARNING

The structure of the requirements led candidates to conclude the parent company might not be able to provide support; that a lack of evidence had been obtained in this regard; there was an ethical threat of intimidation; and then discuss the auditor's report and the modification required. Disappointingly candidates often stated correctly that there was inability to collect sufficient appropriate evidence but then incorrectly proposed an adverse opinion.

Marking scheme

Marks

(a) **Current guidance for auditing group accounts**
Generally 1–1½ marks each well-explained point to a maximum of   6

(b) **Professional scepticism**
Generally 1 mark for each well-discussed point made:
– Risk of misstatement in relation to a material matter
– Reliability of confirmation of internally generated evidence
– Judgement required in relation ability to provide support
– Material uncertainty facing parent company
– Unusual behaviour of group engagement partner
– Need to remain alert for other factors affecting going concern
– Need to remain sceptical of all other matters requiring management judgement

Maximum   5

(c) **Ethical and professional matters**
Generally 1 mark for each well-explained point and recommendation made:

(i) **Support offered by Valerian Co**
– Northwest Co would not be a going concern without support of parent
– Verbal confirmation not sufficient evidence
– Additional evidence that Valerian Co is capable of providing support
– Examples of further evidence required (½ mark each, maximum of 2 marks)
– Suspicious conduct of parent and group auditor
– Need for professional due care and potential reappraisal of fraud risk
– Communication with those charged with governance
– Possible modification of auditor's report if additional evidence not received

(ii) **Request not to modify report**
– Intimidation threat
– Responsibility for audit opinion remains with Thornhill & Co
– Transfer of debt to Valerian Co would not resolve the problem
– Possible suggestion of inappropriate accounting treatment

Marks

    –   Potential lack of integrity of group audit partner and
           potential fraud
    –   Matter should be discussed with senior audit staff
    –   Possible resignation as auditor

	Maximum	14
Total		**25**

(a) Current guidance on the audit of groups is provided by ISA 600 *Special Considerations – Audits of Group Financial Statements (Including the Work of Component Auditors)*. ISA 600 introduces the concept of a component as 'An entity or business activity for which group or component management prepares financial information that should be included in the group financial statements' (ISA 600: para. 9).

The standard distinguishes between the group engagement team and the component auditors. The **group engagement partner** is responsible for reporting on the group accounts and has sole responsibility for the audit opinion. **Component auditors** are auditors who are responsible for reporting on the financial information of a component included within the financial statements audited by the group engagement team.

Prior to accepting the engagement, the Group auditor should have obtained an understanding of the group. Where component auditors are involved in the work of significant components, the Group auditor would have evaluated whether they can be sufficiently involved in the component auditor's work to be able obtain sufficient appropriate audit evidence (ISA 600: para. 12).

The Group auditor should thus have determined whether Northwest Co is a significant component of the Group. This would be the case if it is either (i) financially significant to the Group, or (ii) likely to include significant risks of material misstatement to the Group, due its specific nature or circumstances (ISA 600: para. 9). ISA 600 suggests the use of an appropriate benchmark to help determine significance, such as 15% of Group total assets.

If Northwest Co is significant then the Group auditor (or the component auditor, Thornhill & Co, on its behalf) would need to perform an audit using component materiality (ISA 600: para. 26).

The Group auditor should have obtained an understanding of:

• Whether Thornhill & Co is independent in the context of the group audit

• Thornhill & Co's professional competence

• Whether the Group audit engagement team can be sufficiently involved in the work of Thornhill & Co Whether Thornhill & Co operates in an environment with sufficient regulatory oversight.   (ISA 600: para. 19)

If Northwest Co is significant due to its specific nature (rather than in sheer financial terms), then either the Group or component auditor must perform at least one of the following.

• An audit using component materiality

• An audit of one or more account balances, classes of transactions or disclosures relating to the likely significant risks of material misstatement to the Group

• Specified audit procedures relating to the significant risks of material misstatement to the Group   (ISA 600: para. 27)

In effect what this means is that if the component is significant by nature, then a full audit is not necessarily required – only the area of risk to the group needs to be audited.

 BPP LEARNING

(b) **Application of professional scepticism**

Potential for material misstatement

Without support from the parent, it is unlikely that Northwest Co would be considered a going concern. There is therefore a risk in relation to the going concern status of Northwest Co and a risk of material misstatement in the financial statements if an incorrect basis of preparing the accounts is selected. Professional scepticism requires the auditor to remain alert for any circumstances which may cause the financial statements to be materially misstated especially in relation to going concern matters.

Internally generated evidence

In order to reach a satisfactory conclusion in this matter, it would be essential to receive formal confirmation of support from Valerian Co. The auditor must be sceptical of this form of evidence because it is prepared by management and this sort of internally generated evidence is, generally, not as reliable as other forms of externally generated evidence.

Use of judgement

The ability to provide support to Northwest Co is also a matter of judgement. The management of Valerian Co would need to forecast their own cash flows and make a judgement as to whether they will have sufficient capacity to meet Northwest Co's obligations in the event that the subsidiary cannot. Clearly, such forecasts are prone to uncertainty and management bias.

In this case Valerian Co is itself facing a material uncertainty regarding the outcome of the legal case. It is plausible that this could affect their ability to provide full support. The failure to supply a formal letter of support adds weight to this concern. The auditor must therefore remain sceptical when considering management's pledge of support to Northwest Co.

Suspicious behaviour

The group engagement partner's request not to modify the audit opinion should also promote scepticism. This is an unusual request and appears to be based on pressure by the directors of Valerian Co. This reinforces the suspicion that both the group auditor and the directors of Valerian Co may be trying to conceal some sort of problem. It is possible that the outcome of the legal case is less favourable than is currently suggested and this may require some form of modification to the group accounts. This may, in turn, trigger further repercussions which Valerian Co is seeking to avoid.

Heightened scepticism

Based upon these concerns, the auditor needs to remain sceptical and alert for other factors which raise concerns in relation to the going concern status of Northwest Co. They should also be sceptical of all judgements made by management, particularly in relation to the forecasts prepared to assist with the assessment of going concern. It is possible that they are being over-optimistic in their estimates in order to make forecasts appear better than is reasonable to expect.

(c) (i) **Offer of support by Valerian Co**

Insufficient evidence

Without the financial support of its parent company, Northwest Co would not be considered a going concern. A verbal pledge of support from Valerian Co would not be considered sufficient, reliable evidence in regard to this matter.

Ability to provide parental support

In addition to a letter of support, the auditor of Northwest Co would need to obtain sufficient appropriate evidence that Valerian Co can provide the support which they promise.

The statement by the group auditor that they have received adequate representations from the directors and legal advisers of the company does not constitute sufficient appropriate evidence. At the very least, the auditor of Northwest Co would need copies of those representations. While the representations from management would suffer from the same lack of reliability, representations from the legal advisers would represent third-party evidence and, as such, be more reliable.

Uncertainty surrounding legal case

Given the uncertainty surrounding the court case and the gravity of preparing the financial statements on an incorrect basis, Thornhill & Co may seek further documentary evidence before concluding on the going concern status of the company. This could include correspondence between Valerian Co and their legal advisers, minutes of board meetings, copies of Valerian Co's assessments of going concern and their current statement of financial position.

Conduct of client and group auditor

The suspicious behaviour of both the directors and auditors of Valerian Co suggests that they are not being entirely honest with Thornhill & Co. If their statements regarding the likely outcome of the legal case are appropriate and there are no other concerns, then there is no reason why they would not be able to provide copies of the representations and a written letter of support to the auditor of Northwest Co.

This increases the need for professional due care during the audit process, particularly in relation to the reappraisal of fraud risk and the potential for material misstatement in relation to the going concern status of the company and associated disclosures in the financial statements.

Further procedures

The auditor should communicate with those charged with governance of Northwest Co and explain the requirements to obtain sufficient appropriate evidence in this matter. The auditor should also explain the consequences of not receiving this information in terms of the impact this will have on the going concern status of the company and the adjustments they would be required to make to the financial statements.

Finally, the auditor should explain that if the additional evidence is not received and the recommended adjustments are not made, then this will lead to a modification of the auditor's report. The fact that necessary audit evidence is being withheld would constitute a limitation in the scope of the audit, which may result in a qualified opinion or a disclaimer of opinion being issued.

(ii) **The request not to modify the auditor's report**

Intimidation

By trying to influence the decisions in relation to the audit of Northwest Co, the group auditor is creating an intimidation threat to objectivity. The IESBA's *Code of Ethics* defines this as the threat that a professional accountant will be deterred from acting objectively because of actual or perceived pressures.

Responsibility for the opinion

As the auditor of Northwest Co, the responsibility for determining the final audit opinion and wording of the auditor's report remains with Thornhill & Co. If, based upon the evidence obtained, the engagement partner believes that a modification to the auditor's report is necessary, then they should follow this through, regardless of the opinion of the group auditor and the board of the parent company. The group partner's 'oversight' of the whole audit is irrelevant to the audit of Northwest Co; as a company in its own right, it must be audited in accordance with International Standards on Auditing.

BPP
LEARNING

Transferring the debt to the parent

The suggestion to transfer the debts into the parent company would not resolve the problem; if the debt obligations were 'transferred' to the parent using an appropriate journal, they would be replaced by a matching liability to the parent company in the financial statements of Northwest Co, and the same problem would exist and while this would be eliminated in the consolidated accounts, this does not allow the auditor of Northwest Co to gather sufficient appropriate evidence in relation to the going concern status of the company.

Possible manipulation of the financial statements

It is possible that the group engagement partner is recommending some form of inappropriate accounting treatment to transfer the debt into the parent company without any matching liability in Northwest's accounts, for example, by transferring the debts and then consequently cancelling any obligations from Northwest Co due to Valerian Co. This form of accounting manipulation could be used to disguise the true financial position of the group and may constitute fraud. Any suggestion to pursue this line of action should be firmly refused.

Integrity of the group auditor

The overall integrity of the group engagement partner must be questioned. His aggressive attitude towards the audit of Northwest Co and his reluctance to cooperate by providing evidence in relation to the lawsuit indicate some form of inappropriate conduct in the audit of the parent company and group accounts. This matter should be discussed with the audit engagement partner and possibly with other senior partners, possibly including the firm's designated ethics partner. Further, the suggestion that 'he' would transfer the debt from Northwest Co to the parent company suggests that the auditor is becoming involved in the accounting transactions included in the financial statements and may suggest that the firm's independence is compromised.

Position as auditor of Northwest Co

Given the intimidation threat and the potential concerns relating to the audit of the parent and the group, Thornhill & Co may consider resignation from the audit of Northwest Co, if permitted, or may not seek re-election as auditor for the following year.

47 Rope

Workbook references. Chapters 2, 3, 7, 8 and 10.

Top tips. Time management is critical in this question so work out how much time you can allocate to each part of the question and stick to this. If you miss out whole parts of questions you are at very high risk of failing.

A point of confusion when this area has been examined in the past has been whether the engagement is an audit, or an assurance engagement in relation to PFI. This question is clear on this point: it's an audit.

You might think that this is going to be totally different from normal audit work, which deals with historical information (the financial statements are about things that have already happened). Really it isn't so different – what you're looking into is basically whether management's figures (in the forecast) are reasonable and reliable, whether there is some proper basis for them, and whether they have been produced by a system of controls. You don't need to check that each figure is 100% correct (and in the case of a forecast, you can't). The figures can't be completely accurate, so the auditor only needs to look for as much objective evidence as it's possible for there to be.

Since the question contains lots of numbers, you'll need to be fairly detailed in your examination of them. It is sensible, for instance, to calculate by how much the receipts and payments go up in each period.

Spend time thinking of your audit procedures, as these will be a source of marks. As ever, state both what and why wherever you can.

Part (b) was a short requirement on a related party transaction, and should have been within your capabilities.

Part (c) was again brief. It is common in practice for auditors to produce the financial statements for small entities, but this is prohibited for public interest entities.

Part (d) is a longstanding issue that you should be aware of with auditor's reports.

Easy marks. Audit procedures in part (a) are perhaps the simplest marks in this question.

ACCA examining team's comments. Part (a) required candidates to appraise the forecast and suggest further procedures in assessing the use of the report as part of the going concern review during the audit. This was generally well answered by the majority of candidates attempting the question.

In part (b) candidates were required to discuss a loan from the chief executive to the company. This had been provided during the year being audited and the audit was still ongoing. Stronger candidates appropriately recognised this as a related party transaction and commented on the materiality and disclosure requirements before going on to describe procedures to perform. There were a significant number of candidates who had failed to take in to account the date the loan was provided and assumed it was missed in the prior year audit, so instead focused their answers on a perceived lack of integrity of the directors, inappropriate levels of disclosure in prior year financial statements and audit qualifications.

[Examining team comments not available for parts (c) and (d).]

Marks

Rope Co
Generally up to 1½ marks for each well explained matter and 1 mark for each well-explained procedure recommended:

(a) **Cash flow forecast**
  Matters
  –   Potential overestimation of cash receipts from customers
  –   Lower than forecast sales may lead to net overdraft
  –   Potential underestimation of salary and other operating payments
  –   Simplistic assumption of cost inflation
  –   Investments do not match management's forecast disposal valuation
  –   Assumption of growth in value of investments is very optimistic
  –   Ability to repay loans dependent upon other assumptions
  –   Lack of specific consideration of non-operating cash flows
  Procedures
  –   Review latest interim financial statements
  –   Discuss forecast sales and customer receipts with management
  –   Inspect J Stewart loan agreement
  –   Inspect terms of bank loan

BPP
LEARNING

- Enquire of management whether they have begun renegotiations regarding bank loan facility
- Enquire with management about contingency plans
- Perform analytical review of payroll costs
- Perform analytical review of other operating costs
- Inspect non-current asset registers
- Inspect post year end cash book
- Review outcomes of previous management forecasts
- Obtain written representations from management (maximum ½ mark)

Maximum   14

(b) **J Stewart loan**
Matters
- Provision of the loan represents a related party transaction
- Disclosure requirements of RPT
- Calculation of fair value for an interest-free loan
- Determination of market rates for a similar instrument
- Valuation of loan at end of year using amortised cost method

Maximum   3

(c) **Preparation of financial statements**
Generally 1 mark per comment:
- Typing service not prohibited
- But could be seen as part of preparation of financial statements
- For listed client, service is prohibited
- Refuse if listed, apply safeguards if unlisted

Maximum   3

(d) **Liability disclaimer paragraph**
1 mark for each point:
Content of disclaimer
- Report intended for use by company's members as a whole
- No responsibility accepted to third parties
- Commonly used but not required by standards

Advantages
- Potential to limit liability exposure
- Clarifies extent of auditor's responsibility
- Reduces expectation gap
- Manages audit firm's risk exposure

Disadvantages
- Each legal case assessed individually no evidence that a disclaimer would offer protection in all cases
- May lead to reduction in audit quality

Maximum   <u>5</u>

Total   **<u>25</u>**

(a) **The cash flow forecast of Rope Co**

When a company has prepared a cash flow forecast as part of their assessment of going concern, in accordance with ISA 570 *Going Concern* the auditor needs to evaluate the reliability of the underlying data used to prepare the forecast and to determine whether there is adequate support for the assumptions underlying the forecast. There are a number of issues relating to the forecast which raise concerns about the assessment of Rope Co's going concern status and therefore warrant further investigation.

Receipts from customers

There was little growth in cash receipts in the second half of the year ended 30 September 20X6 (0.8%), yet in each consequent six-month period management predicts a significant rise in receipts of between 1.7% and 3.0%.

This could be based on overly optimistic forecasts in relation to sales growth for the same period. If sales forecasts are too optimistic then this could mean that the forecast small positive cash flows turn cash outflows. This could leave the company in a net overdraft position for the entire two-year period.

The movement in relation to customer receipts is a key assumption underpinning the return to a positive cash position and needs to be scrutinised further.

Salaries and other payments

While annual receipts from customers and payments to suppliers are forecast to rise during the forecast period by 8.5% and 9.4% (from 20X6 to 20X9), respectively, the amounts attributable to salaries and other operating payments are only forecast to rise by 4.1%.

This is based on management's simple assumption of a general 2% annual inflation in these costs. This seems to be overly simplistic and will require further investigation. Salary costs could be forecast using a more sophisticated methodology based on required employee numbers and average wages/salaries.

The significant forecast increase in sales suggests that operating activities will increase over the next two years and it might be expected that staff requirements may increase in line with this. For similar reasons, it is likely that a larger increase in other operating costs would be required to match the increased administrative burden of producing and selling more goods and/or services.

Sale of investments

Management is planning to sell some investments in listed shareholdings for $500,000 to repay a loan to the chief executive. At 30 September 20X6, however, the fair value of the investments was only $350,000. As the fair value of these investments is revalued at the end of each year based upon the current share price, this is assumed to reflect the amount at which the shares were trading at the end of September. Management is therefore expecting the shares to increase in value by $150,000 in the space of two years, which represents a 43% rise. This is an extremely optimistic assumption in comparison to average rates of growth across most stock markets.

It therefore appears likely that there will be a shortfall in the amount raised to repay Mr Stewart. Rope Co will therefore have to supplement the amount received from selling investments with cash from other sources, which will lead to a reduction in the cash position in comparison to the forecasts.

Repayment of the bank loan

The bank loan is due for repayment 15 months after the year end. Management is assuming that they will be able to fund the repayment with a new loan facility from the same finance provider. Without any agreement in place from the provider, this represents a significant assumption.

Without a new facility Rope Co will have no means with which to repay their obligation, which could lead to the lender taking action to recover the loan amount. This could include seizing assets which were provided as security over the loan or commencing insolvency proceedings. In either case, this could have a significant impact on Rope Co's ability to trade into the foreseeable future and, therefore, the loan repayment event represents a material uncertainty which may need to be fully disclosed in the financial statements of Rope Co in accordance with IAS 1 *Presentation of Financial Statements*.

Missing cash flows

There seems to be a lack of consideration of a number of non-operating cash flows which one might expect to see in a two-year forecast. For example, most companies maintain a practice of regular replacement of old, inefficient tangible non-current assets as opposed to making larger, less regular replacements which may create a significant drain on cash resources in one particular year. The forecast currently has no allocation for capital investment. In a similar fashion, there are no cash flows related to tax and dividend payments. It is possible that such transactions have been overlooked in the preparation of the forecast.

Further audit procedures

- Obtain a copy of the latest interim financial statements and compare the actual post year end sales performance with the forecast sales upon which the cash flow forecast is based.

- Discuss with management the rationale for the expected increase in customer receipts and where possible confirm this to customer correspondence, orders or contracts.

- Inspect the documentation detailing the terms of the loan with Mr Stewart to confirm the amount outstanding and the agreed date of repayment.

- Inspect the terms of the bank loan to confirm the final amount due for repayment, the date of repayment and whether any assets have been accepted as security for the loan.

- Enquire of management whether they have entered into any negotiations with their bank, or any other financial institution, to provide a replacement loan in January 20X8. If so, request corroborating evidence such as signed agreements, agreements in principle or correspondence with the financial institutions.

- Enquire of management whether they have any contingency plans in place to repay both loans on time should they not be able to raise the required amount through selling investments and obtaining new loan agreements.

- Perform an analytical review of actual monthly payroll costs incurred obtained from the payroll department. Include any available payment periods after 30 September 20X6 to help ascertain whether management's assumptions regarding salaries are appropriate. Seek corroborating evidence for any fluctuations in cost such as HR records confirming pay awards and changes in staff.

- Perform an analytical review of actual other operational costs and consider the level of other costs as a percentage of sales. Compare this to the levels included in the forecast. Investigate any significant differences.

- Corroborate the lack of investment in new tangible non-current assets by performing an analytical review of the levels of additions and disposals over the last, say, five years to see if this supports the absence of any allocation for this in the short-term future and consider this in light of our understanding of the entity and its production process.

- Compare the cash flow forecasts to any capital expenditure forecasts prepared by Rope Co to ensure that the cash flow forecast is consistent with this. Ask management to explain any differences identified.

- Review the non-current asset register and identify any assets with a zero or negligible carrying value which could indicate that the assets have fulfilled their useful lives and are due for replacement.

- Inspect the cash book post year end to see if there are any significant cash transactions which do not appear to have been included in the forecasts, in particular cash transactions relating to purchases or disposals of assets and dividend payments.

- Review the outcome of previous forecasts prepared by management to assess how effective management has been in the past at preparing accurate forecasts.

- Obtain written representations from management confirming that they have no intention to either purchase or dispose of non-current assets or to pay dividends over the next two years.

(b) **Matters relating to the loan from Mr J Stewart**

Related party transaction

As a key member of staff at Rope Co, the loan from the chief executive represents a related party transaction. As such, the transaction and related outstanding balances must be fully disclosed in the financial statements in accordance with IAS 24 *Related Party Disclosures*.

This means that the nature of the related party relationship, the nature and the amount of the loan, the amounts outstanding at the year end and the terms and conditions of the loan, including a description of the fixed charge, must be disclosed in the notes to the financial statements.

Interest-free loan measurement

The loan was received during the current year ended 30 September 20X6. The loan liability should have been initially recorded at its fair value, which would normally be the transaction price of $500,000. IFRS 9 *Financial Instruments*, however, states that in the case of an interest-free loan, the fair value should be measured as the present value of all future cash flows discounted using the prevailing market rates for similar instruments.

While it will be difficult to identify a similar instrument due to the nature of the relationship between the lender and the company, a similar instrument should be identified based upon the currency used, the loan term and any other similar factors, for example, a three-year, $ loan from a bank.

At the year end, the outstanding loan liability should have been measured using the amortised cost method and the effective interest calculated should be recognised as a finance charge in the statement of profit or loss.

(c) **Preparation of financial statements**

Preparation of financial statements for clients is acceptable, however a **self-review threat** may be created where an audit firm prepares financial statements and then audits them. There is also a risk that the audit firm may undertake, or be perceived to undertake, a **management role**.

Safeguards should be in place to ensure the risk is reduced to an acceptable level in this situation. For example, staff members other than the audit team should be responsible for typing the financial statements.

The IESBA *Code of Ethics for Professional Accountants* prohibits the preparation of accounts or financial statements for clients that are public interest entities. It is not stated whether Rope Co is listed, but if it is then the audit firm should decline Uma Thorton's request to type the financial statements.

(d) **Liability disclaimer paragraph**

The paragraph would state that the report is intended to be used only by the company's members as a body. It would state that the report is not to be relied upon by any third party.

Such a paragraph is not required by any auditing standards, and therefore has no specifically prescribed content.

Appropriateness

The advantage of a liability disclaimer paragraph is that it may reduce the exposure of the audit firm to liability claims from anyone other than the company or the company's body of shareholders. It is not certain, however, that this will be use in all situations. Every legal case is unique, and although a disclaimer might protect the audit firm in one circumstance, it may not offer any protection in another.

The paragraph could be argued to help bridge the 'expectation gap' by clarifying that responsibility of the auditor is to obtain reasonable assurance that the financial statements give a fair presentation, rather than for example to check every transaction.

In an increasingly litigious environment, such paragraphs may help audit firms to manage their risk exposure. There is a danger, however, that the use of such a paragraph could encourage low quality audits if the auditor takes the disclaimer into account when assessing the audit risk. The auditor might consider that the use of a disclaimer means that detection risk can be higher, and may not obtain sufficient appropriate audit evidence. This would be for the auditor to fail in their duty to conduct their audit in line with ISAs, which applies irrespective of any issue of liability. In contrast, there should be no need for a disclaimer if the audit is of a high enough quality.

In conclusion, the ACCA discourages the use of liability disclaimer paragraphs, as these could have the effect of devaluing the auditor's report in the eyes of many (ACCA *Technical factsheet 84*: para. 23).

48 Kandinsky

Workbook references. Chapters 10 and 15.

Top tips. Part (a)(i), on going concern, should have been straightforward as the scenario was absolutely replete with indicators of going concern problems. Marks could be harvested simply by working through the scenario and explaining why virtually every point represented a risk.

Note 3 hints that you need to calculate interest cover and the ratio of the bank loan to operating profit. These should be easy marks (calculations usually score well in AAA), provided that you get it correct – don't forget to take the finance charge out of your profit figure when you're calculating interest cover. This is a bit tricky but it is just the kind of thing that happens in real exams, so you need to pay attention to the small details as well as the big ones.

Part (a)(ii) could be answered by a combination of generic procedures on going concern (such as 'review management accounts after the year end'), and procedures addressed to the scenario. You could approach this question, for example, by taking the indicators of going concern that you identified in part (a)(i) and then thinking of audit procedures to obtain evidence in relation to them. For example, revenue is falling, so you would need to obtain evidence of what has happened to revenue since the year end, and of what is expected to happen for the foreseeable future. This suggests procedures, such as reviewing the company's revenue forecasts or order books.

Part (b) was much more difficult. Part (ii) was probably easier, because its requirement resembles other AAA questions more closely. Your starting point is the four KPIs that are given at the end of the question, so you need to think of one or two procedures for each KPI in order to get the marks.

Part (b)(i) asked you to 'discuss', which indicates that you're being asked to discuss a complex issue. The question is after a discussion of how each performance area might be relevant to the university's stakeholders. One of the problems here is that the question also does not state what the organisation's objectives are, so it is difficult to know what the performance measures are supposed to be relevant to. Whatever the ambiguities of the requirement, however, it is fairly clear that what the examining team was after was a discussion of whether the performance measures given in the question are likely to be useful. On the whole they were fairly useful, so the marks were there for saying why this was the case.

Easy marks. Much of part (a)(i) was easy, but the marks for calculating trends in revenue and operating profit were practically no-brainers.

ACCA examining team's comments. This question was a two-part question and presented information relating to two different clients. Initially candidates were required to identify indicators in the scenario which gave rise to going concern issues and then to state procedures to audit the going concern status of the company. In general, this was well attempted and candidates scored high marks, however those using a columnar approach tended to lack depth in their explanation of the factors identified in the question and overlooked some of the more encompassing audit procedures that did not arise from a specific scenario point.

The second part of the question focused on the audit of performance information, a relatively new topic in the relevant syllabus, and required candidates to discuss the relevance and measurability of key performance indicators (KPIs) in respect of a University and to describe how they might be audited. Well-prepared candidates were able to discuss the issues surrounding measuring and determining relevant performance information and were able to draw on the information included in the recent examining team's article on this topic to the scenario. Some candidates did not focus on the question requirement and attempted to describe the theory of public sector KPIs. Many candidates were unprepared and left this requirement out altogether.

Marking scheme

Marks

(a) (i) **Identify and explain going concern matters**
Up to 2½ marks for matter identified and explained, to include
1 mark for relevant calculations:
- Revenue, operating margins and profitability
- Bank loan
- Trade payables
- Borrowing facility
- Contingent liability

Maximum   9

(ii) **Audit procedures in respect of going concern matters**
Up to 1 mark for each well explained procedure:
- Obtain and review management accounts, perform analytical review to ascertain the trends in profitability and cash flows since the year end
- Read the minutes of the meetings for reference to trading and financing difficulties
- Discuss with management the strategy which is being developed to halt the trend in declining sales and evaluate the reasonableness of the strategies in light of the economic recession and auditor's knowledge of the business

BPP LEARNING

- Review the company's current order book and assess the level of future turnover to level required to break even/make a profit
- Analyse and discuss the cash flow, profit and other relevant forecasts with management and review assumptions are in line with management strategy and auditor's knowledge of the business
- Obtain the bank loan agreement to confirm the amount of the loan, the interest rate and repayment dates and whether the charge over assets is specific or general in nature
- Review the bank loan agreement for any clauses or covenants to determine whether there are any breaches
- Calculate the average payment period for trade payables and consider whether any increase is due to lack of cash or changes in the terms of trade
- Obtain the contract in relation to the borrowing facility to confirm the covenant measures and to see if any further covenants are included in the agreement
- Discuss correspondence with the bank in relation to the loan and the borrowing facility to gauge the bank's level of support for Kandinsky Co and for evidence of deteriorating relationships between the bank and the company's management. Inspect minutes of management meetings where those charged with governance discussed the letter of support and authorised its issuance
- Obtain any further documentation available in relation to the letter of support, for example, legal documentation and correspondence with the supplier, to confirm the extent of Kandinsky Co's involvement with the supplier and that no further amounts could become payable

Maximum   6

(b)   (i)   **The relevance and measurability of the reported performance information**
Generally up to 1 mark for each point explained:
- 1 mark for explaining why each measure would be relevant to an existing or potential student (4 measures in total, so maximum 4 marks)
- Problems in defining the measures
- Problems in quantifying the measures – some are subjective
- Issues in validity of the reported information
- Lack of comparative information

(ii)   **Examination procedures**
Up to 1 mark for well-described procedures:
- Obtain a list detailing all of the University's performance objectives and the basis of measurement for each objective
- Discuss with University the availability of comparative information and requirement to include in current year report

Marks

- For the graduation rate, obtain a list of students awarded degrees in 20X5, and a list of all students who registered on the degree programme and use this information to recalculate the %
- For academic performance, review minutes of meetings where degree results were discussed and approval given for the award of distinction to a number of students
- Agree a sample of students' exam results to supporting documentation, eg information in their student files, notices of exam results sent to the students
- Inspect any documentation issued at events such as degree award ceremonies to confirm the number of students being awarded a distinction
- Obtain supporting documentation from the University for the employability rate and discuss with appropriate personnel, for example, the careers centre, the basis of the determination of the rate
- For the employability rate, a confirmation could be sent to a sample of students asking for the details of their post-graduation employment
- If the University supplies references for students seeking employment, inspect the references issued in 20X5 and contact the relevant company to see if the student was offered employment
- For course satisfaction, inspect the questionnaires or surveys completed by students from which the % was derived, and recalculate
- Enquire if there is any other supporting documentation on course satisfaction, for example, minutes of student and lecturer meetings about the quality of courses

Maximum	10
Total	**25**

(a) (i) **Going concern matters**

Revenue and profitability

The extract financial statements show that revenue has fallen by 38.2%. Based on the information provided, operating profit was $1,150,000 in 20X4 but is only $340,000 in 20X5. Operating margins have fallen from 29.1% to 13.9% during the year and the fall in revenue and margin has caused the company to become loss-making this year.

These changes are highly significant and most likely due to the economic recession which will impact particularly on the sale of luxury, non-essential products such as those sold by Kandinsky Co. The loss-making position does not in itself mean that the company is not a going concern. However, the trend is extremely worrying and if the company does not return to profit in the 20X6 financial year, then this would be a major concern. Few companies can sustain many consecutive loss-making periods.

Bank loan

The bank loan is significant, amounting to 33.7% of total assets this year end, and it has increased by $500,000 during the year. The company appears to be supporting operations using long-term finance, which may be strategically unsound. The loan is secured on the company's properties, so if the company defaults on the payment due in June 20X6, the bank has the right to seize the assets in order to recoup their funds. If this were to happen, Kandinsky Co would be left without operational facilities and it is difficult to see how the company could survive. There is also a risk that there is insufficient cash to meet interest payments due on the loan.

Trade payables

The trade payables balance has increased by 38.5%, probably due in part to the change in terms of trade with its major supplier of raw materials. An extension to the payable payment period indicates that the company is struggling to manage its operating cycle, with the cash being generated from sales being insufficient to meet working capital requirements. Relations with suppliers could be damaged if Kandinsky Co cannot make payments to them within agreed credit terms, with the result that suppliers could stop supplying the company or withdraw credit which would severely damage the company's operations. There is also a risk that suppliers could bring legal action against the company in an attempt to recover the amounts owed.

Borrowing facility

Kandinsky Co has $500,000 available in an undrawn borrowing facility, which does provide a buffer as there is a source of cash which is available, somewhat easing the going concern pressures which the company is facing. However, the availability of the borrowing facility depends on certain covenants being maintained. The calculations below show that the covenants have now been breached, so the bank is within its right to withdraw the facility, leaving Kandinsky Co exposed to cash shortages and possibly unable to make payments as they fall due.

	Covenant	20X5	20X4
Interest cover	2	340/520 = 0.65	1150/500 = 2.3
Borrowings to operating profit	4:1	3,500/340 = 10.3:1	3,000/1,150 = 2.6:1

Contingent liability

The letter of support offered to a supplier of raw materials exposes Kandinsky Co to a possible cash outflow of $120,000, the timing of which cannot be predicted. Given the company's precarious trading position and lack of cash, satisfying the terms of the letter would result in the company utilising 80% of their current cash reserve. Providing such support seems unwise, though it may have been done for a strategic reason, ie to secure the supply of a particular ingredient. If the financial support is called upon, it is not certain that Kandinsky Co would have the means to make the cash available to its supplier, which may create going concern issues for that company and would affect the supply of cane sugar to Kandinsky Co. There may also be legal implications for Kandinsky Co if the cash could not be made available if or when requested by the supplier.

(ii) **Audit procedures in relation to going concern matters identified**

- Obtain and review management accounts for the period after the reporting date and any interim financial accounts which have been prepared. Perform analytical review to ascertain the trends in profitability and cash flows since the year end.

- Read the minutes of the meetings of shareholders, those charged with governance and relevant committees for reference to trading and financing difficulties.

- Discuss with management the strategy which is being developed to halt the trend in declining sales and evaluate the reasonableness of the strategy in light of the economic recession and auditor's knowledge of the business.

- Review the company's current order book and assess the level of future turnover required to break even/make a profit.

- Analyse and discuss the cash flow, profit and other relevant forecasts with management and review assumptions to ensure they are in line with management's strategy and auditor's knowledge of the business.

- Perform sensitivity analysis on the forecast financial information to evaluate the impact of changes in key variables such as interest rates, predictions of sales patterns and the timing of cash receipts from customers.

- Calculate the average payment period for trade payables and consider whether any increase is due to lack of cash or changes in the terms of trade.

- Obtain the contract in relation to the borrowing facility to confirm the covenant measures and to see if any further covenants are included in the agreement.

- Review correspondence with the bank in relation to the loan and the borrowing facility to gauge the bank's level of support for Kandinsky Co and for evidence of deteriorating relationships between the bank and the company's management.

- Obtain the bank loan agreement to confirm the amount of the loan, the interest rate and repayment dates and whether the charge over assets is specific or general in nature.

- Review the bank loan agreement for any clauses or covenants to determine whether there are any breaches.

- Obtain the letter of support in relation to the supplier to confirm the conditions under which Kandinsky Co would become liable for payment of the $120,000.

- Discuss with management the reason for the letter of support being given to the supplier to understand the business rationale and its implications, including why the supplier approached Kandinsky Co for the letter of support.

- Inspect minutes of management meetings where those charged with governance discussed the letter of support and authorised its issuance.

- Obtain any further documentation available in relation to the letter of support, for example, legal documentation and correspondence with the supplier, to confirm the extent of Kandinsky Co's involvement with the supplier and that no further amounts could become payable.

(b) (i) **The relevance and measurability of the reported performance information**

Performance information should be relevant to the users of that information. In the case of Rothko University, there is likely to be a wide range of interested parties including current and potential students who will be interested in the quality of the teaching provided and the likelihood of securing employment on completion of the university course. Other interested parties will include the government body which provides funding to the University, regulatory bodies which oversee higher education and any organisations which support the University's work, for example, graduate employers.

For current and potential students, performance measures such as the graduation rate and employability rate will be relevant as this will provide information on the success of students in completing their degree programmes and subsequently obtaining a job. This is important because students pay tuition fees to attend Rothko University and they will want to know if the investment in education is likely to result in employment. However, some students may be more interested in further study after graduation, so employability measures would be less relevant to them.

Students will be interested in the proportion of graduates who achieve a distinction as this may lead to better job prospects and a better return on the investment (of time and money) in their education. Finally, students will find the performance measure on course satisfaction relevant because it indicates that the majority of students rated the quality of the course as high, an important factor in deciding whether to enrol onto a degree programme. Stakeholders other than current and potential students may find other performance information more relevant to them – for example, potential graduate employers may be interested in the amount of work experience which is provided on the University's degree programme.

The performance measures are most relevant where they can be compared to the measures of other universities. Currently, the University has not provided comparative information and this is likely to make it difficult to assess the performance of the University over time and also makes the current year measures harder to gauge.

In terms of measurability, as with many key performance indicators, it is sometimes difficult to precisely define or measure the performance information. Some of the measures are quite subjective. For example, the rating which a student gives to a course is down to personal opinion and is difficult to substantiate – such as the difference between a course rating of excellent and very good. Similarly, defining 'graduate level employment' could be subjective. Some measures will be easier to quantify – such as the degree completion percentage, which will be based on fact rather than opinion.

There may also be problems in how the information is gathered, affecting the validity of the information. For example, only a sample of students may have completed a course evaluation, and possibly the most satisfied students were selected which will improve the measure.

(ii) **Examination procedures**

- Obtain a list detailing all of the University's performance objectives and the basis of measurement for each objective.

- Enquire of the University whether comparative information is available and if this information needs to be verified as part of the disclosure in the current year.

- For the graduation rate, obtain a list of students awarded degrees in 20X5, and a list of all students who registered on the degree programme and use this information to recalculate the %.

- For academic performance, review minutes of meetings where degree results were discussed and approval given for the award of distinction to a number of students.

- For a sample of students awarded a distinction, confirm each student's exam results with supporting documentation – eg information in their student files, notices of exam results sent to the student – and confirm that the grades achieved qualify for a distinction being awarded.

- Inspect any documentation issued at events such as degree award ceremonies to confirm the number of students being awarded a distinction.

- Obtain supporting documentation from the University for the employability rate and discuss with appropriate personnel – for example, the careers centre – the basis of the determination of the rate.

- For the employability rate, a confirmation could be sent to a sample of students asking for the details of their post-graduation employment.

- If the University supplies references for students seeking employment, inspect the references issued in 20X5 and contact the relevant company to see if the student was offered employment.

- For course satisfaction, inspect the questionnaires or surveys completed by students from which the % was derived, and recalculate.

- Enquire if there is any other supporting documentation on course satisfaction – for example, minutes of student and lecturer meetings about the quality of courses.

49 Butler

Workbook references. Chapters 10 and 11.

Top tips. Part (a)(i) required you to critically review a cash flow forecast and a statement of financial position for 9 marks. This should have been relatively straightforward. Your approach should be to look over the main figures in each statement, and think about whether they have gone up or down, and what their movement (or non-movement) might indicate. Each of the notes provided by the examining team is there for a reason, and will probably give rise to something to write in your answer. The main problem with this part of the question would have been the time constraint (9 marks = 17.5 minutes), so you should make sure you don't waffle, and divide your time logically between the two statements being analysed.

Note that the marks available for just identification (rather than explanation) are capped at 3 marks out of 9. Instead of writing lots of superficial points, you should look to make fewer points but which are better-explained.

Part (a)(ii) should have been OK, as most of the points should arise naturally out of your work on the cash flow forecast in (a)(i). The mark scheme gives one mark per 'specific procedure', and the examining team has commented in the past that candidates are often not specific enough in their answers to get the mark. Make sure that each point you make is specific enough to get ½ – 1 mark.

Part (b) tests an area – auditor's reports – that you should be comfortable with, and on a topic that should be familiar (going concern). You should have scored well here, although to get the top marks would not have been easy, particularly if you had gone over time in part (a).

Easy marks. There are a lot of relatively easy marks throughout part (a); the difficulty here is making enough of them within the time available.

ACCA examining team's comments. The answers to this question were generally unsatisfactory. The majority of candidates seemed to ignore the instruction in requirement (a)(i), providing an answer that did little more than work down the statement of financial position, calculating the materiality of each balance, and discussing the accounting treatment of each item, saying nothing about going concern. Only when turning to the cash flow forecast did these answers say anything about going concern, and then the comments were usually restricted to the likelihood of the company receiving a loan and a subsidy.

For requirement (a)(ii), most candidates could provide at least a few well-explained procedures – the most common focusing on the loan from the parent company and the government grant. Some procedures were not well explained – eg 'check the price of the financial asset' without saying how this could be done. Most candidates identified the extreme optimism of the cash flow forecast and that the closing cash position was negative, but not many candidates could recommend sound procedures to verify the claims of management regarding cash receipts from customers, which was a key issue.

BPP
LEARNING

Requirement (b) dealt with the impact of multiple going concern uncertainties on the auditor's report, for 6 marks. Although some candidates scored well on this requirement, the majority again failed to answer the question as set, and discussed every conceivable auditor's report that could be issued for a client with going concern problems. The question stated that 'the use of the going concern assumption is appropriate', yet many candidates ignored this and spent a lot of time discussing what should happen if the use of the going concern assumption were **not** appropriate. Most candidates earned a few marks by discussing the 'material uncertainty related to going concern' section, but often the description of the section was brief. Only a minority correctly focused their answers on the requirement for management to disclose significant uncertainties in the notes to the financial statements, and that the adequacy of these disclosures would drive the auditor's opinion on the financial statements. Overall, answers were inadequate.

Marking scheme

Marks

(a) (i) **Going concern matters**
Up to 1½ marks per matter identified and explained (maximum 3 marks for identification):
- Negative cash position
- Net liabilities position
- Recurring losses
- Possible adjustment to deferred tax and development intangible asset exacerbate net liabilities position (allow 3 marks max)
- Fixed charge over assets
- Significant short term liabilities
- Potential misclassified provisions
- Forecast to remain in negative cash position
- Assumptions re sales optimistic
- Receipt of loan and subsidy not guaranteed
- Assumption of sale value of financial assets could be optimistic

Maximum   9

(ii) **Procedures on cash flow forecast**
Generally 1 mark per specific procedure:
- Enquire regarding and consider validity of assumption re cash sales
- Inspect any supporting documentation re additional resources for credit control
- Seek written confirmation from Rubery Co re loan
- Review financial statements of Rubery Co re adequacy of resources
- Inspect subsidy application
- Seek third party confirmation that subsidy will be awarded
- Confirm cash outflows for operating expenses and interest appear reasonable
- Enquire about potentially missing cash outflows
- Agree date and amount of short term loan repayment to loan documentation
- Agree opening cash to cash book and bank statements

Maximum   7

Marks

Additional information

Generally ½ mark per specific piece of information. Maximum 3

(b) **Matters to be considered and potential effects on auditor's report**

1 mark each point explained:

- – Disclosure of material uncertainty required by IAS 1
- – Auditor considers adequacy of disclosure
- – If disclosure adequate – opinion unmodified
- – If disclosure adequate – include MU relating to GC paragraph
- – If disclosure inadequate – material misstatement leading to qualification or adverse opinion
- – If disclosure inadequate – basis of opinion paragraph explains material uncertainty
- – If multiple uncertainties – opinion may be disclaimed in rare circumstances

Maximum 6

Total **25**

(a) (i) **Draft SOFP**

Cash

Butler Co has a negative cash balance, with an overdraft of $25m. This will make it difficult for Butler to raise the working capital it will need to operate in the short term, unless this overdraft can be extended. However, this is unlikely to be able to continue indefinitely.

Loan repayment

Butler has a total of $775m in loans repayable during the coming year. It appears unlikely that Butler will have the cash available to make this repayment (especially given the cash outflow forecast for the three months to August 20X1), unless it is able to raise additional finance.

Net liabilities

Butler has negative equity and net liabilities of $225m. It has significant retained losses of $525m, and made a retained loss of $620m in the year ended 20X1.

These are both conditions specified by ISA 570 *Going Concern* as casting doubt over the going concern assumption.

Working capital

Butler is drawing heavily on its working capital to extend its cash operating cycle:

	Cashflow $m
Trade receivables (increase = $2,100 – $1,860)	(240)
Trade payables (increase = $2,500 – $1,800)	700
Total cash inflow	460

Butler has effectively raised $460m through taking more credit from its suppliers, and still has a negative cash balance.

Inventory

The value of inventory held at the year end increased by $500m (= $1,300 – $800). This effectively represents an cash outflow, and may be a sign of weak revenue during the year. Some of this inventory may be obsolete and in need to writing down.

Fixed charge

Fixed charges exist over assets valued at $25 million. If Butler fails to make repayments to the creditor holding this charge, the assets could be seized, disrupting Butler's operations.

Development costs

Development costs of $120m have been capitalised. IAS 38 *Intangible Assets* states that these costs can only be capitalised if the entity has the resources to complete the development (IAS 38: para. 57). As this is arguably not the case here, the costs should be recognised as expenses.

Deferred tax asset

A deferred tax asset of $235m has been recognised. However, such an asset can only be recognised in accordance with IAS 12 *Income Taxes* to the extent that the inflow of future economic benefits is probable. IAS 12 specifically states that the existence of unused tax losses, as here, is evidence that there will be no such inflow (IAS 12: paras. 34–35). The tax asset should not be recognised.

Provisions

Provisions of $185m have been classified as non-current liabilities. However, a portion of warranty payments are very likely to be due within the next year, so at least some of this amount should be within current liabilities.

Parent company

Butler is a subsidiary of a multi-national group, and it is possible that its parent company will support Butler even if it is not a going concern on its own. Were this the case, written representations would need to be obtained from the parent company, along with evidence that it is capable of supporting Butler.

However, the $150m loan expected to be received in July 20X1 is unlikely to be sufficient to ensure Butler's survival.

Cash flow forecast

Overall position

For the three months to August 20X1 Butler expects a cash outflow of $30m (= ($40m) + $65m + ($55m)). This means it is unlikely to be able to repay its short term borrowings in September. Had the forecast covered four months not three, it would probably have shown a significantly gloomier picture.

Cash from customers

The assumption that there will be an economic recovery and that this will lead to increased cash receipts is open to question. There may be little or no economic recovery, and cash receipts still may not improve in any case.

The commitment of extra resources to credit control is a wise move given the cash outflow in this area during 20X1, but any estimate of the improvement in cash receipts resulting from this is very uncertain.

Financial assets

$50m is expected to be received from selling financial assets, which is twice their carrying amount at the year end. This $50m is very optimistic, particularly if they have been measured at their fair value in the SOFP.

Loan from parent

The expected loan receipt of $150m is still being negotiated, and may not actually be agreed or received.

Government subsidy

The application for the government subsidy has not yet been approved, so there is significant doubt over whether this amount will be received.

Operating outflows

Operating cash outflows exceed inflows for all three months of the forecast. This is the underlying basis for the company's ability to continue as a going concern in the long term.

(ii) **Audit procedures for cash flow forecast**

- Discuss with management the reasons for assuming that cash collection from customers will improve due to 'anticipated improvement in economic conditions'. Consider the validity of the reasons in light of business understanding.

- Enquire as to the nature of the additional resources to be devoted to the credit control function, eg details of extra staff recruited.

- For the loan receipt, inspect written documentation relating to the request for finance from Rubery Co.

- Obtain and review the financial statements of Rubery Co, to consider if it has sufficient resources to provide the amount of loan requested.

- For the subsidy, inspect the application made to the subsidy awarding body and confirm the amount of the subsidy.

- Read any correspondence between Butler Co and the subsidy awarding body, specifically looking for confirmation that the subsidy will be granted.

- Regarding operating expenses, verify using previous months' management accounts, that operating cash outflows are approximately $200 million per month.

- Enquire as to the reason for the increase in operating cash outflows in August 20X1.

- Verify, using previous months' management accounts, that interest payments of $40 million per month appear reasonable.

- Confirm, using the loan agreement, the amount of the loan being repaid in August 20X1.

- Enquire whether any tax payments are due in the three month period, such as sales tax.

- Agree the opening cash position to cash book and bank statement/bank reconciliation, and cast the cash flow forecast.

- Ensure that a cash flow forecast for the full financial year is received as three months' forecast is inadequate for the purposes of the audit.

Additional information needed

- Loan agreement from Rubery Co, showing the amount of the loan received, the date it will be received, the repayment schedule, and any terms and conditions

- Rubery Co's audited financial statements and auditor's report

BPP LEARNING

- Copy of subsidy application made to awarding body

- Copy of confirmation that subsidy was awarded, including details of the amount receivable

- Management accounts for January to May 20X1

- Copies of tax returns and any correspondence with the tax authorities

- Accounting records, including cash books, bank statements and any reconciliations

(b) IAS 1 *Presentation of Financial Statements* requires that in this situation the financial statements be prepared using the going concern assumption, but that they contain disclosures regarding the material uncertainty over its appropriateness (IAS 1: para. 25).

The auditor must therefore assess whether these disclosures have been made, and if they are adequate.

Material uncertainty related to going concern

If the disclosures are sufficiently detailed then IAS 1 has been complied with. The auditor will express an unmodified opinion, but the auditor's report will contain a paragraph headed 'Material uncertainty related to going concern' (ISA 570).

This paragraph should highlight the disclosures in the financial statements, and should describe the nature of the material uncertainty. It should state that the auditor's opinion is not modified in respect of this matter. Finally, it should include any relevant financial information, eg the amount of net liabilities at the end of the reporting period.

Modified opinion

If the disclosures are not sufficiently detailed, or if no disclosures are made, then the auditor expresses a modified opinion (usually qualified, not adverse) on the basis of a material misstatement (ISA 705). This is because the disclosure requirements of IAS 1 have not been adhered to.

A qualified or an adverse opinion is accompanied by a paragraph headed either Basis for Qualified Opinion or Basis for Adverse Opinion (as appropriate), in which the material misstatement is described.

Disclaimer of opinion

It is possible, but in practice very rare, that multiple uncertainties might exist, each of which would in itself have led to a modified opinion. In this case, a disclaimer of opinion should be issued.

50 Yew

Workbook references. Chapters 8, 9, 10, 11 and 16.

Top tips. The first part of this question was difficult, and doubtless many candidates would struggle to make up 7 marks here. It is important with discussion questions that you plan your answer before you write. If you don't plan, there is a danger that you will change your mind about what you want to say while you are already writing.

This will only waste time and will be unlikely to score marks. You need to plan your answer, and divide your discussion into clearly structured paragraphs. Within each paragraph, you should aim to have an introduction, a point, and a conclusion.

It is also important that you didn't go over time on this part of the question – perhaps through struggling to write clearly – as there were some easier marks to be had in parts (b) and (c).

Part (b) was a typical question on auditor's reports, this time mixed in with IAS 38 and some issues around audit completion. You should have had plenty to say here; the main difficulty would have been staying within the time limit of 23 minutes for this part of the question.

Part (c) contained just two short situations for 6 marks in total. You should think of each situation as being worth three marks. The situations were fairly straightforward, so how you did came down to your knowledge.

Easy marks. A lot of part (b) was easy – for example, stating that the treatment of the development costs was not in line with IAS 38.

ACCA examining team's comments. Candidates were asked to discuss firstly whether auditors should accept some of the blame when a company on which they have expressed an unmodified opinion subsequently fails, and secondly whether auditors should do more to highlight going concern problems. Very few answers were worthy of more than a few marks, most answers simply listing the auditor's responsibilities from ISA 570 *Going Concern*, with no discussion at all of the statement provided in the question. Those who did refer to the statement provided tended to just state whether or not they agreed with it but provided no discussion at all. Answers were especially poor at discussing whether auditors should disclose more in relation to going concern, with most just describing the various ways that going concern issues may affect the audit opinion. It is inadequate that at this level of examination candidates seem simply unable to express an opinion of their own or base a reasoned discussion around a statement provided to them, especially around such a significant current issue facing the profession.

Marking scheme

Marks

(a) **Discussion**
Up to 2 marks for comments discussed from ideas list:
 – Management responsibility for risk assessment
 – Auditor should be aware of going concern issues
 – Auditor must not take on management role
 – Misunderstanding of roles of management and auditor
 – Auditor may be to blame if overlooked a fraud/other matter
 – Financial statements contain disclosure on risk assessment
 – Users may not be financially literate
 – Auditors could make problems more visible and understandable

Maximum   7

(b) **Yew Co**
Generally up to 1½ marks for each matter discussed/recommended:
 – Calculate and comment on materiality
 – No probable economic benefit – IAS 38 recognition criteria not met
 – Lack of finance – IAS 38 recognition criteria not met
 – Consider whether sufficient appropriate evidence obtained
 – Financial statements contain material misstatement and implication for auditor's report
 – Could indicate fraudulent financial reporting
 – Lack of cash may indicate going concern problems – extend audit procedures
 – Audit work should be subject to second partner review
 – Consider asking for a delay in issuing financial statements if necessary for further evidence to be sought
 – Discuss apparent inconsistency in chairman's statement wording

- Discuss accounting treatment, potential qualification and chairman's statement wording with those charged with governance
- Describe matter in Other Information section of auditor's report if material misstatement of other information persists

Maximum   12

(c)   (i)   **Signing of auditor's report**

Generally 1 mark per point:
- Date report when all necessary evidence received, including written representations
- Especially important with regard to subsequent events
- Contrary to ISA 700 to sign report prior to receiving written representations

(ii)   **Prior year auditor's opinion**

Generally 1 mark per point:
- Generally auditors do not refer to third parties in their report
- But optional to refer to predecessor auditor unless prohibited by law and regulations
- If reference made, should be in Other Matter paragraph
- Describe contents of reference made to predecessor auditor
- If prior year modified, explain this in Other Matter paragraph

Maximum   6

Total   **25**

(a)   The concept of an expectations gap between auditors and the public is a key lens through which assertions such as this one can be viewed. The first part of the statement would appear to assert that the auditor is in some way responsible for the failure of a company. This is not the case: those charged with governance are responsible for risk assessment and risk management. It is not the role of the auditor to become involved with the entity's risk management processes – indeed, this could be deemed to constitute a management role, which would compromise the auditor's independence.

However, it is true that the auditor should gain an understanding of the client's business; this is a crucial requirement of ISAs. Amongst other things, it is necessary for an auditor to audit management's assessment of the appropriateness of the going concern assumption, for which a good understanding of the business risks faced by the client is necessary. The auditor must judge whether the going concern assumption used is appropriate. However, this is never a matter of cut-and-dried logic: it is a judgement, based on an assessment of risk. It is in the nature of risk for there to be uncertainties, and it is in the nature of judgement to contain elements of doubt.

It is therefore to be expected that there will be cases where the auditor has judged the going concern assumption to be appropriate, and yet the company fails within the year. The question is not whether the assumption was proved correct by subsequent events, but whether the auditor's assessment was reasonable and in line with auditing standards.

There is more scope for discussion on the question of whether auditors should do more to highlight problems. This may be the responsibility of management; it would be possible for regulators and setters of accounting standards to require increased disclosure on going

concern. For example, financial statements could be required to provide more narrative detail regarding the risks faced by an entity.

At present, auditors should disclose the presence of material uncertainties over going concern by way of a 'material uncertainties related to going concern' section in the auditor's report, and if they deem the assumption to be inappropriate then the opinion would be modified. It may be possible for these disclosures to be made clearer than they are, or for auditors to use their report to draw users' attention to any parts of the financial statements that are significant to the assessment of going concern.

In conclusion, it is unfair to require auditors to accept the blame for company failures which are the proper responsibility of management, although it may be argued that more could be done by auditors to highlight going concern problems where they exist.

(b)   The intangible asset is material to profit (54% of profit before tax) and to the statement of financial position (6% of total assets).

IAS 38 *Intangible Assets* states that for development costs to be capitalised, the existence of a market – or the entity's ability to use the asset itself – must be demonstrable. The audit team has obtained documentation and a written representation which confirms that this is not the case.

IAS 38 also requires the entity to have the financial resources to bring the asset to the market. As Yew Co is short of cash, this may not be the case.

As a result, the financial statements appear to be materially misstated, and that the $12.5m should be treated as expenses. The matter must be discussed with management, who should be asked to amend the financial statements.

The matter should also be discussed with the chairman, as it is possible that he has different information which could change our assessment of the situation. If this is not the case, and if the financial statements are not amended, then the audit opinion will be qualified 'except for' a material misstatement (but one which is not pervasive).

The fact that Yew Co is finding it difficult to raise finance casts doubt over going concern. Further work may need to be done in this area. If there is significant doubt then disclosures should be included in the financial statements, and a material uncertainty related to going concern paragraph should describe the matter in the auditor's report provided that the auditor finds the level of disclosure to be adequate.

If a modified opinion is expected to be expressed, then it may be necessary to consult externally on the effects of doing this, or at a minimum subjecting the audit work to review by another partner.

Consideration needs to be given to whether the misstatement is an indication of fraudulent financial reporting, and a possible lack of management integrity. The fact that the company is struggling to raise finance provides a motive for it to inflate its results and statement of financial position. If this is the case, then any written representations relied upon elsewhere in the audit must be reconsidered.

If the development costs should not be capitalised and the financial statements are amended, then there will be an inconsistency with the chairman's statement. First, the chairman should be asked to amend his statement. If this is not done, then the reporting requirements in ISA 720 *The Auditor's Responsibilities Relating to Other Information* will apply. ISA 720 states that in these circumstances the matter should be described in the Other Information section of the auditor's report.

(c)　(i)　ISA 700 *Forming an Opinion and Reporting on Financial Statements* requires that the auditor's report only be signed once sufficient appropriate audit evidence has been obtained on financial statements.

Written representations from management are audit evidence, so logically there is not sufficient appropriate audit evidence until these are received.

It is therefore not appropriate to sign the report and date it before these are received.

(ii)　It is not generally appropriate to refer to third parties in an auditor's report, as this may give the impression that someone other than the auditor is responsible for the report.

However, ISA 710 *Comparative Information – Corresponding Figures and Comparative Financial Statements* permits reference to be made to a predecessor auditor's report; this is the auditor's own choice.

This reference should be made in an Other Matter paragraph, included after the Key Audit Matters section (or if there are none, after the Basis for Opinion section). This would which state that the financial statements for the prior period were audited by a predecessor auditor, state the opinion they expressed, and the date of their report.

51 Fern

Workbook references. Chapters 1, 2, 8 and 11.

Top tips. This question covered several different areas, and should have been within your capabilities.

Part (a), on ethics, was a slightly out-of-the-ordinary AAA question, and covered professional issues as much as ethics. Non-compliance with laws and regulations is a topical area, and this scenario combined it with intimidation that threated to limit the scope of the audit. In order to pass this question it was important that your answer covered each of these issues – and that you kept to your time for part (a) as a whole, but also within it.

Part (b) was a normal question part on audit evidence. In many ways this was a simple question, and you may have struggled to discover what it was about. The underlying issue in the question is the difficulty of auditing estimated values, which may fluctuate significantly (as they do here). Past estimates have not been very accurate, which, if we are being sceptical, might suggest that creative accounting has been going on. Tying this together with the company's declining performance was a particularly difficult mark to get.

Part (c) covered auditor reporting, an area which is guaranteed to feature in every exam. The material on IFRS 15 *Revenue from Contracts with Customers* tested your knowledge of the standard but was a fair test. Part (ii) on the auditor's report should have been second nature to you.

Easy marks were to be found in part (b) for calculating materiality. Questions on the auditor's report almost always contain marks (as here) for stating that eg the 'Basis for Qualified Opinion' section is placed immediately below the 'Opinion' section. These are like money for nothing.

ACCA examining team's comments. Part (a) was generally **not well-answered**. Part (a) focused on a potential breach of laws and regulations through the potential use of out-of-date medicines and an intimidating client. Most candidates discussed the implication for inventory valuation reasonably and some suggested highlighting the issues and lack of co-operation from the Finance Director to those changed with governance and the potential for a limitation on the scope of the audit. Disappointingly only a minority of candidates identified that there was a wider issue that using out-of-date medication could have severe or fatal health consequences and were able to discuss the balance between the auditor's duty of confidentiality to the client compared with their wider ethical duty to notify the appropriate regulators and after seeking legal advice.

Part (b) asked candidates to describe the key matters and audit evidence that would be expected. Overall, there appeared to be a poor understanding of the issues raised.

Candidates spent a lot of time discussing IAS 37 with only a minority correctly questioning why the warranty provision was decreasing when the revenues were actually increasing, thus the majority of candidates demonstrated a lack of professional scepticism. Evidence and therefore the procedures to audit the provision were generally sound, such as looking at sales volume and historic claims rates by product group and basing the provision on these. Very few candidates questioned if there was the potential for management bias as there was a substantial release of the provision without explanation when the company's profits were falling despite increasing revenues. Candidates are reminded here that the application of professional scepticism is a key component of the auditor's skillset.

Part (c) concerned revenue recognition. Many candidates gave a good summary of the IFRS 15, conditions that revenue cannot be recognised until the goods have been delivered, control transferred and all performance obligations have been met. However, some candidates demonstrated out-of-date financial reporting knowledge by referencing the superseded IAS 18 *Revenue*. For the most part candidates usually correctly identified that the sale had not actually occurred before year end and should be adjusted for. However, many candidates digressed into visiting and inspecting the goods in a third-party warehouse when it was clear that the performance obligations had not yet been met. Most highlighted that they should ask management to amend the accounts and that the matter should be referred to those charged with governance.

The impact on the auditor's report if no adjustment was made was mostly well-answered with candidates explaining that the accounting treatment was factually incorrect and would result in an 'except for' qualification. Candidates were good at highlighting the sequencing of matters in the auditor's report and it is refreshing to see that this area was clearly understood.

Stronger candidates additionally examined whether the matter was pervasive (which would result in a disclaimer of opinion) based on the fact that the issue focused on the timing of revenue recognition.

Marking scheme

Marks

Generally up to 1½ marks for each well-explained point and 1 mark for each well-explained procedure recommended.

(a) **Ethical and professional issues**
- Compliance with laws and regulations/NOCLAR
- Attempt to obtain more evidence for discussion with management
- Confidentiality threat
- Report to those charged with governance/regulator
- Limitation on scope of audit
- Impact on the financial statements
- Intimidation threat
- Management Integrity
- Withdrawal from engagement

Maximum   9

Generally up to 1½ marks for each well-explained matter and 1 mark for each well explained piece of evidence recommended.

BPP LEARNING

Note. Marks will be awarded for explanations of why calculations and balances are complex or subjective and how this affects their accuracy. Simple statements that calculations and balances are complex or subjective will be awarded a maximum of ½ mark each, where relevant.

(b) **Warranty provision**
Matters
Materiality:

– Uncertainty relating to estimates
– Competence of sales director to make estimates
– Evidence of prior overstatement
– Possible creative accounting/profit smoothing

Evidence:
– Copies of terms of sale
– Notes re basis of forecasting returns levels
– Breakdown of provision calculation
– Schedule listing post year end returns
– Notes re the reason for the unutilised provision
– Notes re known production/quality problems

Maximum 5

Generally up to 1½ marks for each well-explained matter/point and 1 mark for each well explained action recommended.

(c) (i) **Revenue recognition**
Matters

Materiality:
– IFRS 15 – Satisfaction of performance obligations
– Control not yet passed to client
– Revenue recognition and management bias
– Revenue recognised too early and, therefore, misstated

Actions:
– Request adjustment to financial statements
– If refused communicate with those charged with governance
– Obtain written representation

Maximum 6

(ii) **Auditor's report**
– Financial statements materially misstated
– Matter is not pervasive
– Modified auditor's report
– Qualified 'except for' opinion
– Basis of qualified opinion paragraph

Maximum 5

Total 25

(a) **Ethical and professional issues**

Compliance with laws and regulations

It appears that Moosewood Hospital is storing and maybe using medicines that have passed their recommended use by date. This may be illegal, and it may breach the terms of agreement with their suppliers and, most significantly, this may lead to patient harm or ineffective treatment.

ISA 250 *Consideration of Law and Regulations in an Audit of Financial Statements* requires that in the event of a suspected non-compliance with law and regulations (NOCLAR), the auditor should document the findings and discuss them with management. The audit team should attempt to obtain more information about the suspected NOCLAR, though this will be difficult given the actions of the financial controller, who is denying access to the relevant source of information and the attempt to intimidate the audit team by the finance director.

The audit team should seek appropriate legal advice in relation to the use of out of date medicines. If this is a breach of regulations then the auditor may have a statutory duty to report this incident to the relevant regulator.

Reporting non-compliance to those charged with governance

If Fern & Co believes that NOCLAR is taking place, then according to ISA 250, the matter should be reported to those charged with governance of Moosewood Hospital. This communication should happen without delay given that it appears to be deliberate and owing to the potential seriousness of the use of expired medical inventory. At present it is unclear whether those charged with governance are aware of these practices. The auditor should request that those charged with governance make any necessary disclosure to the relevant authorities, clearly state the reasons why Moosewood Hospital should make the disclosure and that if the board fails to comply, that Fern & Co will be compelled to make the disclosure themselves.

If the auditor suspects that members of senior management including the board of directors are involved with the non-compliance, then the auditor should report the matter to the next higher level of authority, such as the audit committee.

Confidentiality

Reporting the incident to a regulator would require the auditor to report information about a client to a third party, which is a breach of client confidentiality. In these circumstances, however, legal/regulatory responsibilities would be considered to outweigh the confidentiality requirement.

Given the potential conflict with the IESBA *Code of Ethics for Professional Accountants*, Fern & Co should seek legal advice before they act to minimise the risk of legal dispute with their client or legal action from the regulator due to inaction.

If Fern & Co concludes that the matter should be reported to a regulator they should first communicate this belief to the board of Moosewood Hospital and request that they make a disclosure. At present it is unclear whether those charged with governance are aware of these practices. They should clearly state the reasons why Moosewood Hospital should make the disclosure and that if the board fails to comply, that Fern & Co will be compelled to make the disclosure themselves.

Impact on the financial statements

It is not correct for management to assert that the issue with out-of-date inventory is not relevant to the audit, because if any of the inventory is obsolete, then it should be written off in the financial statements.

By restricting the audit team's ability to audit inventory, management has imposed a limitation on the scope of the audit. If the auditor is unable to obtain satisfactory evidence relating to inventories then this may lead to a modification of the auditor's report.

Fern & Co should report this matter to those charged with governance and request that they provide access to the necessary evidence. They should also explain what repercussions this will have on the auditor's report if they fail to comply.

If Moosewood Hospital has failed to comply with any legal, regulatory or contractual requirements they may incur fines or other financial penalties. The audit approach should now be modified to include additional procedures aimed at investigating the potential implications of the use of out of date medicines and the potential value of fines and penalties.

Intimidation threat

The aggressive actions of the finance director amount to an intimidation threat to objectivity. The finance director has tried to influence the conduct of the audit with threatening behaviour.

Fern & Co should inform those charged with governance, explaining the significance of the matter and that it cannot be tolerated. Fern & Co should explain the reasons for the enquiries made by the audit team and the significance of being allowed to complete these procedures.

Management integrity

While the intentions of management are not clear it does appear that they are trying to conceal a matter of some significance from the auditor.

The audit team must increase their scepticism of all evidence provided by management, particularly written representations obtained from management as they may be subject to bias and evidence which they could potentially manipulate, such as internal spreadsheets. In particular, if the audit team are given access to the inventory valuation spreadsheet they must remain vigilant for any indication that this has been subsequently altered.

Withdrawal from engagement

If the audit team believes that management is complicit in any significant illegal activity and/or attempt to manipulate the financial statements they may reconsider their position as auditor. If permitted by local regulations they may wish to resign from the engagement to protect their reputation and to protect themselves from being implicated in any ensuing legal case.

Before taking any action the matter should be discussed with the senior partners of the firm and an appropriate legal advisor.

(b) **Warranty provision**

Matters

Materiality

The year-end provision represents 0.36% of total assets and 6.54% of profit. It is not, therefore, material to the statement of financial position but it is material to the statement of profit or loss.

Estimates

The estimate of returns is clearly subject to significant subjectivity. This increases the risk of material misstatement due to both error and manipulation.

The estimate is made by the sales director; while this may be the best person to forecast sales they may not be the best person to predict returns. Returns are likely to be influenced more heavily by product quality, which the production or quality control manager may be better placed to predict. This implies that the forecast amount is based on simplistic, general estimates using sales levels rather than consideration of specific product quality issues.

Evidence of prior overstatement

The risk of misstatement is amplified by the evidence of large overstatements in the past. The reversal of unutilised provisions suggests that previous estimates were too high, which indicates inaccuracy in the forecasting process. The reversal of unutilised provisions represents 2.9% of profit so is not individually material to the financial statements.

Possible creative accounting

Provisions can be used to smooth profits; ie a provision made in a year where profits are high and reversed in future years (ie released back to the statement of profit and loss) when earnings targets are not being met.

The reversal of unutilised provisions in the year has increased Lear Co's profits by $3.1m. While this is not a material amount on its own, with other creative accounting devices, such as the manipulation of estimates of the cost of inventory and impairments, this could lead to a material overstatement of profits.

This should be considered a particular risk for Lear Co as their profits have declined during the year, despite a 5.5% increase in revenue during the year. The decline in performance provides an increased incentive for management to adopt manipulative accounting practices to help achieve targets and smooth profits.

Evidence expected to be on file:

- Copies of the terms of sale offered to customers to confirm the length of the warranty period.

- Notes of a discussion with the sales director confirming the basis of the calculation for forecast returns. These should specifically note any general rates of return applied to the calculation and any specific matters the director has taken into consideration, such as known faults or poor quality.

- A copy of the calculation of the provision. The components of the calculation should have been recalculated and analytically reviewed in comparison to previous years and any fluctuations should have been corroborated to supporting evidence

- A schedule analysing the total returns received following the year end. A sample of these returns should have been matched to the original sales invoice, confirming the date upon which the goods were first sold.

- This schedule should also have been analytically reviewed in comparison to the same period in previous years to identify whether returns levels were consistent. Any significant fluctuations should have been corroborated with evidence or management enquiry.

- A schedule confirming the calculation of the total unutilised provisions reversed during the year. These should be accompanied with the notes of a meeting with management identifying the reasons why these provisions were not needed and, where possible, what time period the original provision related to.

- Notes of a discussion with the production or quality control manager identifying whether there are any known problems with goods sold during the warranty period, and what products were affected. If any such matters exist there should be evidence that these have been traced through to the provision calculation.

BPP
LEARNING

(c) **Rocket Co**

(i) **Matters**

Materiality

The revenue of $17m recognised in relation to the highlighted transactions represents 1.2% of revenue and 12.2% of profit before tax. The sales are, therefore, material to the financial statements.

Bill and hold arrangement

IFRS 15 *Revenue from Contracts with Customers* specifies that an entity shall recognise revenue only when it has satisfied its performance obligations by transferring the goods (or services) to its customer.

Rocket Co believes that it has satisfied its performance obligations by having the goods available for the customers by the specified date. The situation, however, represents a 'bill and hold' arrangement, whereby Rocket Co has billed the customer but has yet to physically transfer the goods to them.

Transfer of control

IFRS 15 specifies that in these circumstances it should be determined when the customer obtains control of the goods. The contracts specify that the goods have to be delivered for inspection and 'acceptance', implying that the customer will not accept control until they have satisfactorily completed their inspections. Rocket Co has, therefore, not fulfilled their performance obligations and should not recognise the revenue in relation to these two contracts.

Revenue recognition

Given Rocket Co's listed status, management may be under pressure to report better results. Revenue has fallen by 3.5% based on the draft financial statements. If the $17m relating to the bill and hold arrangement is excluded from the 20X7 financial statements, then the reduction in revenue is greater, at 4.6%.

Further actions

Fern & Co should request that the client adjusts their financial statements to reverse the revenue recognised in relation to the goods being stored at the third party facility.

If they refuse to adjust the financial statements, Fern & Co should communicate the misstatement to those charged with governance. They should repeat the request to adjust the financial statements and inform them of the modifications that will be made to the auditor's report if the adjustments are not made.

If the client still refuses to amend the financial statements, Fern & Co should request a written representation from the client confirming their intention to proceed without amending the financial statements and that they are aware of the potential repercussions.

(ii) **Auditor's report**

Material but not pervasive misstatement

If management refuses to reverse the $17m of revenue recognised in relation to these transactions the auditor will conclude that the financial statements are materially misstated.

The matter is material to the statement of profit or loss but it is unlikely to be considered pervasive; the required adjustment would not lead to a reported profit being restated as a loss and the only captions of the financial statements affected will be revenue and receivables.

Qualified opinion

In these circumstances the auditor would issue a qualified audit opinion stating that 'except for' these matters the financial statements are fairly presented.

The auditor should also include a Basis for Qualified Opinion section below the opinion section. This should describe and quantify the financial effects of the misstatement.

52 Boston

Workbook references. Chapters 10 and 11.

Top tips.

In part (a) there are marks available for making the general point that uncorrected misstatements should be discussed with management, so that management can correct the accounting records. The auditor also tells management what effect misstatements may have on the audit opinion.

All of this seems obvious but it gets you marks! Talking about communication with management is something that markers almost always like to see.

With each issue it is crucial that you calculate materiality – these are really easy marks so you really must get them. If you calculate it correctly and state whether it's material, this is one mark – so four marks on this question. If you then aim for a further 2+ solid marks on each issue then you should be able to pass this part of the question.

Issue (i) – impairment – was odd because the treatment in the question was correct once the auditor's findings are taken into account. This might have confused you. What is not in the question is a proper discussion of IAS 36. If you do this – as in the answer below – then you're confirming that you know the required treatment.

The requirement asks for 'matters that should be discussed with management', so you can get easy marks for asking why management has adopted the treatment it has adopted – you need to pick **something specific** from the scenario, so eg 'ask management why it has used the company's forecast growth rates' – and also for asking management to adjust the financial statements.

Issue (ii) – interest charges – should have been straightforward. The treatment is not line with IAS 23, so the costs must be capitalised.

Issue (iii) – irrecoverable debt – was another tricky one, because the auditor's change in the amount is correct. Your answer should confirm that this is correct, but also think about something that could be asked of management – eg 'has any further correspondence been received?'

Issue (iv) – investment – was straightforward, and there were marks for recalculating the adjustment given in the scenario.

Part (b) was a standard auditor's report requirement. The main nuance here was that the auditor would have to ask management to adjust for all of the issues, but would also state that the factory impairment is material on its own. Since management is not going to make any changes, we only have to consider the aggregate effect on the auditor's report – qualified opinion due to material misstatement. (Although there are multiple misstatements, the effect is not pervasive.)

As ever, there are marks available for discussing whether the opinion should be adverse, and for talking about the precise format of the auditor's report – ie that the 'qualified opinion' section comes first, followed by a 'basis for qualified opinion' section, and so on.

Part (c) should have been straightforward, provided that you had a good grasp of the material. As usual, a good answer to this part would have a clear structure. The examining team is attuned to the fact that weaker students tend to only be able to make general statements, whereas stronger students make specific, accurate statements that are clear about what they are saying. Make sure that your comments are specific, and avoid rambling!

BPP
LEARNING

Marking scheme

Marks

(a)   **Summary of uncorrected misstatements**
In general up to 1 mark for each point of explanation and up to ½
mark for each appropriate calculation:
–   Obtaining an understanding of management's reasons
–   Encourage management to amend all misstatements
–   Communicate effect of misstatements to those charged with
governance

(i)   **Impairment**
–   Explanation of original calculation
–   Inappropriate estimates used
–   Revised impairments
–   Justification of the proposed adjustment
–   Request further clarification at meeting
–   Matter is material individually

(ii)   **Borrowing costs**
–   Capitalisation rules
–   Qualifying asset
–   Identification of incorrect treatment of interest costs
–   Explanation of adjustment
–   Not material individually

(iii)   **Cleveland**
–   Liquidation is indication of further impairment
–   Adjusting event after the reporting period
–   Need to write off remainder of outstanding balance
–   Request evidence of any further correspondence
–   Not material individually

Marks

    (iv) **Nebraska**

–   Need to revalue investment to fair value at year end

–   Calculation of fair value (½ max) and adjustment (½ max)

–   Gain taken to statement of profit and loss

–   Not material individually

            Maximum   14

(b) **Auditor's report**

–   Aggregate impact on financial statements

–   Material to profit

–   Impairment individually material

–   Modification of opinion due to a material misstatement

–   Discussion of whether it is pervasive

–   Qualified opinion

–   Basis for qualified opinion paragraph

            Maximum   6

(c) **Subsequent event**

Generally 1 mark per comment:

–   Definition of subsequent events

–   Adjusting event

–   Auditor's responsibility depends on whether financial statements issued

–   No active duty, but has been informed

–   Consider materiality

–   Perform extended procedures

            Maximum   <u>5</u>

Total   **<u>25</u>**

(a) **Matters to discuss at meeting**

During the completion stage of the audit, the effect of uncorrected misstatements must be evaluated by the auditor, as required by ISA 450 *Evaluation of Misstatements Identified During the Audit*. This requires that the auditor obtains an understanding of management's reasons for not making recommended adjustments to the financial statements and that they take this into account when evaluating whether the financial statements as a whole are free from material misstatement.

In order to maintain accurate accounting records, management should be encouraged to record all misstatements to ensure that the risk of material misstatements in future periods is reduced due to the cumulative effect of immaterial uncorrected misstatements.

ISA 450 also requires that the auditor communicates with those charged with governance about uncorrected misstatements and the effect that they, individually or in aggregate, may have on the opinion in the auditor's report. Each of the matters included in the summary of uncorrected misstatements will be discussed below and the impact on the auditor's report considered individually and in aggregate.

(i) **Impairment**

When performing an impairment test, in accordance with IAS 36 *Impairment of Assets*, the carrying value of the asset (or cash generating unit) in question is compared with the recoverable amount of the asset (IAS 36: para. 8). If the recoverable amount is lower than the carrying value an impairment loss should be recognised, reducing the asset down from its carrying value to the recoverable amount.

The recoverable amount is calculated as the higher of the fair value less costs to sell and value in use. In relation to the cash generating unit, Boston Co estimated that the greater of these two figures was the value in use at $3.5m. This was compared to the carrying value of $3.6m and the asset has been impaired by $100,000 accordingly.

The findings of audit procedures carried out suggest that an inappropriate estimate was used in the calculation of value in use. Boston Co applied the company's annual growth rates when estimating the cash flows attributable to the cash generating unit. A more relevant estimate for the growth rates, specific to the cash-generating unit, was available and should have been used.

This would have generated a value in use of $3.1m which is still higher than fair value less cost to sell of $3m, and should be used as the recoverable amount. As management already impaired the asset to $3.5m, a further impairment of $400,000 is required to value it appropriately at $3.1m.

At the meeting management should be asked why they used the company's forecast growth rates, rather than the factory's growth rates and whether any matters have arisen since the audit to suggest that the growth rates used by the audit team are now inappropriate.

The adjustment represents 6.25% of profit and 0.4% of total assets. While not material to the statement of financial position, it is material to profit. If management does not adjust for this or provide justifications as to why their valuation is more appropriate, then this will lead to a material misstatement of the financial statements.

(ii) **Borrowing costs**

Interest charges are borrowing costs. The borrowing costs relating to the construction of qualifying assets, such as property and plant, should be capitalised during the construction period, in accordance with IAS 23 *Borrowing Costs* (IAS 23: para. 8).

As the manufacturing plant is not due for completion until November 20X6, it is still a qualifying asset and the interest should have been capitalised. Boston Co has incorrectly expensed the interest as part of the finance charges for the year.

The correcting adjustment is therefore to reduce finance charges and to add the interest to the cost of the asset on the statement of financial position.

The charges of $75,000 represent 1.2% of profit and 0.07% of assets so are not material to either profit or the statement of financial position.

(iii) **Cleveland Co**

At the year end Boston Co would have recognised a net receivable of $95,000 as being due from their customer Cleveland Co. Although $30,000 has been received after the year end, the request to have the company liquidated indicates that any further payment is unlikely to be received. In accordance with IAS 10 *Events after the Reporting Period*, this is an adjusting event indicating that management's assessment of the recoverability of the balance is inaccurate and that the remainder of the outstanding balance should be written off as an irrecoverable debt.

As Boston Co has previously provided for $5,000 management should provide for the remaining $65,000 in the financial statements for the year ended 31 December 20X5. This will reduce trade receivables in the statement of financial position and profit before tax by $65,000.

At the meeting enquiries should be made as to whether any further correspondence has been received from either the management of Cleveland Co or the liquidators offering any form of reimbursement to Boston Co. If not, then the proposed adjustment should be encouraged.

The adjustment represents 1.0% of profit and 0.06% of total assets so is not material individually to either profit or the statement of financial position.

(iv) **Investment in Nebraska**

The investment in Nebraska has been designated as fair value through profit or loss. As such, the value at the year end must be adjusted to reflect the fair value of the investment and any gain or loss recognised in the statement of profit or loss.

The fair value of the investment at the year end is $643,500 (150,000 shares × $4.29). This represents an increase in the fair value of $43,500, which should be taken to the statement of profit or loss as a gain. The carrying value of the investment should also be increased by this amount. $43,500 represents 0.7% of profit and 0.04% of total assets. It is therefore not material individually to either profit or the statement of financial position.

(b) **Impact on the audit opinion and auditor's report**

When considering their opinion, the auditor must conclude whether the financial statements as a whole are free from material misstatement. In order to do this, they must consider whether any remaining uncorrected misstatements are material, either on an individual basis or in aggregate.

The aggregate effect of the misstatements would be to overstate Boston Co's profit by $346,500 ($465,000 – $118,500). Total assets on the statement of financial position would also be overstated by this amount.

This represents 5.4% of profit and 0.3% of total assets. The overstatement would therefore be material to the statement of profit or loss on an aggregate basis but not to the statement of financial position.

However, as the necessary adjustment regarding the impairment of the factory building is individually material, management should be informed that if the valuation calculated by the audit team is more appropriate then failure to incorporate this adjustment will result in the auditor concluding that the financial statements are materially misstated. Based upon this, a modification to the audit opinion in accordance with ISA 705 *Modifications to the Opinion in the Independent Auditor's Report* will be required.

The type of modification depends on the significance of the material misstatement. In this case, the misstatement regarding the impairment is material to the financial statements, but is unlikely to be considered pervasive. This is supported by the fact that the adjustment is not material to the statement of financial position and it is therefore unlikely that the auditor will conclude that the financial statements as a whole are misleading.

Therefore a qualified opinion should be expressed, with the auditor stating in the opinion that the financial statements show a true and fair view 'except for' the effects of the matters described in the basis for qualified opinion paragraph.

A basis for qualified opinion section should be placed immediately after the opinion section. This should include a description of the matter giving rise to the qualification, including quantification of the financial effects of the misstatement.

The remaining uncorrected misstatements are, individually and in aggregate, immaterial to the financial statements and it will be at the discretion of management to amend and will have no impact on the auditor's report. Although as previously mentioned because of the impact on future periods, management should be encouraged to amend for all misstatements. If management intends to leave these as uncorrected misstatements, written confirmation of their immaterial nature should be obtained via a written representation.

The discovery of an ongoing error in the company's payroll is a subsequent event.

A subsequent event is any event occurring after the reporting period of the financial statements being audited. The first question for the auditor is whether these have been accounted for properly in accordance with IAS 10 *Events after the Reporting Period*.

Since the errors were made over a period of several months, it is likely that they were made during the reporting period. This would suggest that this is an adjusting event, and that the financial statements may be materially misstated.

The auditor's duty in relation to adjusting subsequent events depends on the point that has been reached when the event is discovered. It is not stated whether the financial statements have been issued, and it is upon this that the auditor's actions depend.

Financial statements not yet issued

If the financial statements have not yet been issued, then the auditor has no active duty to perform procedures (or make enquiries) during this period.

Facts have come to light, however, that suggest that the financial statements should be amended. In this case, the auditor should enquire how management intends to address the errors in the financial statements that are issued. The auditor should assess the materiality of the misstatements, and should consider whether further audit procedures need to be performed as a result of discovering the misstatements.

If the financial statements are amended, then the auditor should perform extended procedures on the amendments, and issue a new auditor's report on the amended financial statements.

Financial statements have been issued

Although the auditor has no active duty to perform procedures during this period, something has been discovered and the auditor should discuss with management how the misstatements are going to be addressed.

If management then amends the financial statements, then a revised auditor's report should be issued including an Emphasis of Matter paragraph discussing the amendment.

If management does not amend the financial statements but the auditor thinks that they should, then the auditor needs to take legal advice in the relevant national jurisdiction to prevent reliance on the auditor's opinion.

53 Coram

Workbook references. Chapters 2, 8, 10 and 11.

Top tips. The format used in part (a) has cropped up in several recent AAA exams, and appears to be favoured by the examining team for AAA. This time the question did not simply deal with the auditor's report, however, but focused on communicating with management.

The first issue, leases, tested an accounting standard that is relatively new but that you should certainly have been familiar with. It did, however, focus on what might appear to be a finer point of the standard (that the short-term lease exemption must be applied to all assets in a class). If you had not been aware of this then you will need to make sure your financial reporting knowledge is strong enough for this paper.

The second issue related to a legal claim and insurance cover. This is an area that gets tested fairly often, and should have been within your reach. This was probably the easiest part of this question.

The final issue focused on impairment. This is an area that is popular with the AAA examining team, so you should review the financial reporting requirements carefully if you were not comfortable with it.

The auditor reporting aspect of this question was as expected for AAA. This is a core area of the syllabus in which you should have been able to score well.

Part (b) was an ethics requirement that effectively split itself into two sub-parts of four marks each. Neither issue should have been horribly unexpected to you. If you had managed to score, say, three marks on each de facto sub-part then you would have put yourself in a good position for the rest of the exam.

Easy marks. The three marks for assessing materiality in part (a) were very simple indeed. Not getting these would make it significantly harder to pass this question.

Marking scheme

Marks

(a) **Clark Co**
Matters to be discussed and individual impact on financial statements
Generally up to 2 marks for full discussion of each matter and impact on opinion.

(i) **Lease of testing equipment**
   – Lease at largest site is material to SOFP at 2.2% of total assets; leases at other two sites are also material at 2.8% of total assets (max 1 mark)
   – General requirement of IFRS 16 to capitalise all leases on SOFP as right-of-use assets at PV of payments from commencement date (ie date asset is available for use)
   – IFRS 16 exemption (optional) for short-term leases of less than 12 months with no purchase option hence if client elects, no need to recognise lease on SOFP (n.b. no P/L effect yet as commencement date at year end)
   – Short-term lease exemption must be made by class of underlying asset, hence treatment across three sites must be consistent
   – To discuss exemption with FD at meeting: if elects not to take exemption across the three sites, assets and liabilities are materially understated; hence the proposed adjustment is correct and a right-of-use asset and lease liability of $475,000 should be recognised
   – Alternatively, if client does elect to take exemption across all three sites, then assets and liabilities are materially overstated and right-of-use assets and lease liabilities of $625,000 should be derecognised

   Impact on audit opinion:
   – If client makes no adjustment, the statement of financial position is materially misstated and the audit opinion should be qualified on this basis with an 'except for' opinion

                                                                    Maximum   7

(ii) **Legal claim**
  - Claim is material to SOFP at 5.5% of total assets (max 1 mark)
  - Provision should be recognised per IAS 37 as unpaid, probable liability at reporting date
  - Asset should also be recognised as payment by insurance company is virtually certain
  - The asset and liability should be shown separately on the SOFP and not offset; there is no net impact on P/L; as a result both assets and liabilities are materially understated
  - Full details of both provision and contingent asset should be disclosed in notes to financial statements

Impact on audit opinion:
  - If client makes no adjustment, the statement of financial position is materially misstated and the audit opinion should be qualified on this basis with an 'except for' opinion

Maximum 5

(iii) **Asset impairment**
  - Impairment of $85,000 is not material in isolation to either SOFP or P/L (max 1 mark)
  - New competitor is significant change in site's market and therefore impairment indicator; site is CGU and therefore appropriate to conduct impairment test at this level
  - Recoverable amount is higher of value in use and fair value less selling costs; fair value less costs of disposal is $3,515,000 and therefore asset is impaired by $85,000 (client appears to have incorrectly excluded cost of removing assets from calculation but correctly excluded the costs of business reorganisation)

Impact on audit opinion:

  - Assets and profits are both (immaterially) overstated; hence if no adjustment made, there will be no impact on the audit opinion in relation to this issue in isolation

Maximum 5

(b) **Turner Co**
Ethical and professional issues and actions to be taken by audit firm
Generally up to 1 mark for each issue and action.
Loan to member of the audit team
Issues:
  - Potential self-interest threat to auditor independence
  - Key issue is whether 'the very best deal which the bank can offer' is made under normal lending procedures, terms and conditions
  - If not, self-interest threat created would be so significant that no safeguards could reduce it to acceptable level and Janette should be told not to take loan
  - If it is made under bank's normal lending procedures, terms and conditions, the loan does not create a threat to auditor's independence and Janette may accept the loan

Marks

Actions:

–   Discuss terms and conditions of loan with Janette and business manager

–   Obtain draft loan documents and review details in order to establish whether under normal lending procedures, terms and conditions

–   Inform audit engagement partner, who is responsible for ethical compliance

–   Advise Janette on outcome of review and whether she can accept loan and advise business manager of decision explaining rationale/ethical rules

Temporary staff assignment

Issues:

–   Potential self-review threat to auditor independence

–   Must not assume management responsibilities or provide non-assurance services prohibited by the *Code*

–   Cannot provide accounting and bookkeeping services (including payroll) to audit client which is a public interest entity

–   Exception if services relate to matters which are collectively immaterial to financial statements

Actions:

–   Discuss details of proposed role of seconded member of staff with payroll manager/other key client contacts in order to establish significance/materiality of role to financial statements

–   Advise client of outcome of these enquiries/decision; seems likely that will have to decline assignment of staff member as payroll supervisor as role appears to be material/significant to financial statements

–   listed/public interest entity, supervisory/management role requiring qualified member of staff on main payroll system.

Maximum   8

Total   25

(a)   **Clark Co**

(i)   **Matters to be discussed with management in relation to the audit supervisor's proposed adjustments**

Lease of testing equipment

The lease at Clark Co's largest site is material to the statement of financial position at 2.2% of total assets. The leases at the other two sites are also material at 2.8% of total assets.

The general recognition and measurement requirements of IFRS 16 *Leases* require lessees to recognise a right-of-use asset and a lease liability at the commencement date of the lease at the present value of the lease payments. The standard defines the commencement date as the date the asset is available for use by the lessee. Given that the commencement date is 31 May 20X8 therefore, it is appropriate on this basis to recognise the lease on the statement of financial position as at this date.

It is significant, however, that IFRS 16 also contains an optional exemption for short-term leases of less than 12 months' duration with no purchase option. If Clark Co elects to

BPP
LEARNING

427

apply this exemption, it does not recognise the leased assets or lease liabilities on the statement of financial position but rather, it recognises the lease payments associated with those leases as an expense in the statement of profit or loss for the year on either a straight-line basis over the lease term or another systematic basis. However, IFRS 16 also requires that if this exemption is taken, it must be applied consistently by each class of underlying asset. Hence in this case, the client must either capitalise the leases across all three of the sites or apply the exemption consistently and not capitalise the leases across any of the sites. On either of these bases, as the commencement date of the lease coincides with the reporting date, there would not yet be any impact on Clark Co's statement of profit or loss for the year.

The audit manager should discuss the option of taking the short-term lease exemption with the finance director at tomorrow's meeting:

- If the client elects not to take the exemption across the three sites, assets and liabilities will be materially understated.

  Hence the audit supervisor's proposed adjustment is correct and a right-of-use asset and lease liability of $475,000 should be recognised on the statement of financial position.

- Alternatively, if the client does elect to take the exemption across all three sites, then assets and liabilities are materially overstated and right-of-use assets and lease liabilities of $625,000 should be derecognised on the statement of financial position.

Impact on audit opinion:

If the client does not make any adjustment to the financial statements, the statement of financial position is materially misstated on the basis of misapplication of an accounting standard and the audit opinion should be qualified on this basis with an 'except for' opinion.

(ii) **Legal claim**

The legal claim is material to the statement of financial position being 5.5% of Clark Co's total assets.

Following the requirements of IAS 37 *Provisions, Contingent Liabilities and Contingent Assets*, a provision should be recognised when: an entity has a present obligation (legal or constructive) as a result of a past event; it is probable that an outflow of resources embodying economic benefits will be required to settle the obligation; and a reliable estimate can be made of the amount of the obligation. In this case the customer has already won the action against the company, the amount of the claim has been agreed by the courts and settlement is still outstanding at the reporting date. Hence, a provision of $1.2 million should be recognised on the statement of financial position.

IAS 37 also states that contingent assets are not recognised in financial statements since this may result in the recognition of income which may never be realised. However, the standard continues by stating that when the realisation of income is virtually certain, then the related asset is not a contingent asset and its recognition is appropriate. With respect to Clark Co's insurance claim therefore and the verified letter dated 25 May 20X8, the settlement of the claim as at the reporting date is virtually certain and an asset should be recognised separately on the statement of financial position.

The audit supervisor's proposed adjustment is correct and the finance director should therefore be requested to adjust the financial statements to include the separate recognition of the asset and the provision. If the adjustment is not made, both assets and liabilities will be materially misstated. There is no net impact on the statement of profit or loss for the year.

The finance director should also be advised that the financial statements should include full disclosure of the facts and amounts surrounding the provision for the legal claim together with full details of the expected reimbursement from the insurance company recognised as an asset.

Impact on audit opinion:

If the client does not make any adjustment to the financial statements, the statement of financial position is materially misstated and the audit opinion should be qualified on this basis with an 'except for' opinion.

(iii) **Asset impairment**

The asset impairment of $85,000 is not material in isolation to either the statement of financial position (0.4% of total assets) or the statement of profit or loss for the period (3.7% of profit before taxation).

According to IAS 36 *Impairment of Assets*, an entity should assess at the end of each reporting period whether there is any indication that an asset or a cash generating unit may be impaired. If any such indication exists, the entity shall estimate the recoverable amount of the asset. The standard states that potential impairment indicators include external sources of information such as significant changes in the market in which the entity operates. As each of Clark Co's sites is considered a cash generating unit for impairment review purposes it seems appropriate therefore for the company to have conducted an impairment review at this site.

IAS 36 states that an asset or cash generating unit is impaired when the carrying amount exceeds the recoverable amount and it defines recoverable amount as the higher of the fair value less costs of disposal and the value in use. In the case of Clark Co, the auditor has agreed figures for carrying value and value in use and the key issue is the correct calculation of fair value less costs of disposal. Following IAS 36, the costs of disposal should include legal costs, transaction taxes and the costs of removing the assets but should exclude the costs associated with reorganising a business. The correct amount for fair value less costs of disposal is therefore $3,515,000 ($3.9 million − $126,000 − $174,000 − $85,000). Given that this is higher than the value in use of $2.9 million, the recoverable amount of the assets is also $3,515,000 and therefore the assets are impaired by $85,000 ($3.6 million − $3,515,000). The client appears to have incorrectly omitted the costs of removing the assets from its calculation of fair value less costs of disposal and as a result the statement of financial position and the statement of profit or loss for the year are both overstated by $85,000.

The audit supervisor's proposed adjustment is therefore correct and the finance director should be advised of this error at tomorrow's meeting. Even though the amount is immaterial to both the statement of financial position and statement of profit or loss for the year, it is appropriate to request that the adjustment is made to the financial statements.

Impact on audit opinion:

Given that assets and profits are both immaterially overstated, if no adjustment is made to the financial statements, it follows that there will be no impact on the audit opinion in relation to this matter in isolation.

(b)   **Turner Co**

Ethical and professional issues and actions to be taken by the audit firm

Loan to member of the audit team

According to the IESBA *Code of Ethics for Professional Accountants* (the *Code*), a loan to a member of the audit team may create a threat to the auditor's independence. If the loan is not made under normal lending procedures, and terms and conditions, a self-interest threat would be created as a result of Janette Stott's financial interest in the audit client. The self- interest threat arises because of the potential personal benefit derived which may motivate the audit team member to behave in a manner aimed at protecting that benefit. Such a threat would be so significant that no safeguards could reduce the threat to an acceptable level. It follows therefore that the audit team member should not accept such a loan or guarantee. The Code, however, also states that a loan from an audit client which is a bank or similar institution to a member of the audit team which is made under normal lending procedures, is acceptable. Examples of such loans include home mortgages, car loans and credit card balances.

It is possible therefore that the secured loan may be ethically acceptable and the key issue is whether 'the very best terms which the bank can offer' fall within Turner Co's normal lending procedures, and terms and conditions. The bank's standard lending terms and conditions should be obtained and reviewed alongside the documentation for Janette Stott's loan. Ultimately, the audit engagement partner is responsible for ensuring that ethical principles are not breached, so the partner should be involved with the discussions. The matter should be discussed with Janette and the client's business manager in order to establish whether the loan is to be made under the bank's normal lending procedures. Janette should be advised of the outcome of the review and Turner Co's business manager should be advised of this decision, explaining the rationale and ethical rules behind it.

Temporary staff assignment

The *Code* states that the lending of staff to an audit client may create a self-review threat to auditor independence. The self- review threat arises when an auditor reviews work which they themselves have previously performed – for example, if the external auditor is involved in the process of preparing the payroll figures for inclusion in the financial statements and then audits them. As a result, there is a risk that the auditor would not be sufficiently objective in performing the audit and may fail to identify any shortcomings in their own work. In addition, there is a risk of the staff member assuming management responsibilities if they are involved in making judgments and decisions which are the remit of management.

Such assistance can only therefore be given for a short period of time and the audit firm's staff must not assume management responsibilities and must not be involved in any activities specifically prohibited. According to the Code, an audit firm cannot provide accounting and bookkeeping services (including payroll) to an audit client which is a public interest entity unless the services relate to matters which are collectively immaterial to the financial statements.

In this case Turner Co is a listed bank and is therefore a public interest entity. The assignment of a qualified member of staff as a supervisor on the client's main payroll system is likely to be material to the financial statements of a service industry client such as a bank and, in addition, may also involve management responsibilities. The audit manager should therefore discuss details of the proposed role of the seconded member of staff with the payroll manager and other key client contacts in order to establish the significance of the role and its materiality to the financial statements. Assuming that the role is material, the audit manager should decline the proposed staff assignment.

54 Dexter

Workbook reference. Chapter 10.

Top tips. You would have required a good knowledge of going concern to score well in part (a) of this question. Part (b) required you to come up with some practical and commercial reasons why directors would be reluctant to include a note to the financial statements addressing the going concern issues the company was facing. Part (c) demanded a methodical approach, looking at all possible outcomes for the auditor's report. Reporting is a topic which is regularly is examined in this exam so make sure you know and understand the different auditor's reports.

It should be noted that, although it is a past question, it is now not indicative of the standard of the AAA exam.

Easy marks. This was a relatively straightforward question with a strong emphasis on technical knowledge in parts (a) and (c). Provided you knew and could apply the basic principles, these sections were not complicated.

ACCA examining team's comments. Requirement (a) asked candidates to 'compare and contrast the responsibilities of management, and of auditors, in relation to the assessment of going concern'. The main deficiency in answers to this requirement was the lack of any kind of comparison of the responsibilities of management and auditors, despite the fact that the requirement began with 'compare and contrast'. The other problem was that many candidates did not restrict their answer, as requested, to the assessment of going concern, but digressed into issues such as corporate governance and maintaining shareholder value.

Requirement (b) asked candidates to consider why the directors may be reluctant to provide such a note. Many answers were provided here. However, some candidates failed to provide more than a couple of reasons, which is not enough for the mark allocation.

Requirement (c) was rarely well answered, and many candidates obviously do not understand the different types of modifications to auditor's reports at all, let alone the implication for the auditor's report of non-disclosure of going concern issues. There was a tendency in (c)(i) to go straight for an adverse opinion, without any discussion of the level of significance of the non-disclosure. There was also confusion over the use of an adverse opinion and a disclaimer of opinion. Some candidates put down all possible types of auditor's opinion as their answer in the hope that one of them would be correct. In (c)(ii) very few candidates suggested that the auditor should consider the adequacy of the note if the directors agree to provide one. In this advanced audit exam it is inexcusable that students do not know these basic facts about the auditor's report. Candidates should also remember that writing one or two sentences is unlikely to be sufficient to answer an eight mark question requirement.

Marking scheme

Marks

(a) **Compare and contrast management and auditors' responsibilities regarding going concern**

Generally 1 mark per explained point
Maximum marks to be capped at 3 for this section.

Matters to consider and audit evidence

Generally 1 mark per point for matters, 1 mark for evidence suggested.

– Loss of key senior personnel
– New objective to generate cash
– Risk of change in terms from supplier

- Need to apply professional scepticism
- Feasibility of new loan receipt
- Shortage of key material

Maximum   7

(b) **Reluctance to disclose note**
Generally 1 mark per comment:
- Directors fear they will be held accountable for problems
- Trigger further financial distress as necessary finance is withheld
- Trigger operational distress due to reactions of suppliers and customers
- Trigger operational problems if key members of staff leave
- Directors may genuinely feel that the financial and operating problems do not affect going concern status

Maximum   5

(c) (i) **Auditor's report implication – note not provided**
Generally 1 mark per comment:
- Breach of IAS 1 leading to material misstatement
- Opinion could be qualified or adverse
- Judgement needed
- Report to refer to material uncertainty

Maximum   4

(ii) **Auditor's report implication – note provided**
Generally 1 mark per comment:
- Review adequacy of disclosure
- If note is sufficient – no breach of financial reporting standards – unmodified opinion
- MU paragraph to highlight uncertainties
- If note inadequate – qualify 'except for' material misstatement

Maximum   4

Total   **20**

(a) (i) **Responsibilities of management and auditors in relation to going concern**

IAS 1

ISA 570 *Going Concern* discusses the responsibilities of management and auditors in relation to the going concern assumption. It explains management's responsibilities with regards to going concern are detailed in IAS 1 *Presentation of Financial Statements*. This standard requires management to make an assessment of an entity's ability to continue as a going concern (IAS 1: para. 25). If management becomes aware of material uncertainties casting significant doubt on the entity's ability to continue as a going concern, these must be disclosed. Management should also disclose if the financial statements are not prepared on a going concern basis and if so, the basis on which they are prepared and the reason the entity is not regarded as a going concern.

The auditor is responsible for obtaining sufficient, appropriate evidence about the appropriateness of management's use of the going concern assumption in the financial statements. Based on the evidence collected, the auditor must conclude whether there is

a material uncertainty about the entity's ability to continue as a going concern and then determine the implications for the auditor's report.

Therefore, the main responsibility of management is to assess the entity's ability to continue as a going concern, use the correct basis of presentation and make the correct disclosures in the financial statements. The auditor is responsible for providing an opinion on whether management have fulfilled these obligations and collecting enough evidence to support this.

Timing

As per ISA 570, the auditor shall remain alert throughout the audit for audit evidence of events or conditions that may cast significant doubt on the entity's ability to continue as a going concern. Similarly, management should consider going concern in their ongoing management of the business. The auditor covers the same period as management in the evaluation of management's assessment of going concern.

(ii) The audit team should have used a range of indicators to assess whether management is right to prepare the financial statements on the going concern basis. Although Dexter Co has a positive cash balance, there are signs in the information given that all is not well with Dexter Co in this respect. For example, Dexter Co has lost key senior management personnel during the year, which is specifically listed in ISA 570 *Going Concern* as an indicator of potential going concern problems (ISA 570: para. A3), although in this case management has been replaced. The loss of senior management personnel means significant knowledge and experience leaving the company, which has the potential to result in strategic errors being made, which could have ill effects on the company as a whole.

It is therefore encouraging that new appointments have been made to the senior management team. The fact that the new team has instigated a change in focus towards generating cash from operations should not be treated as neutral from the auditor's perspective, rather; this must surely reflect a need for cash, which may be a result of problems being experienced in this area. This is an indicator of going concern difficulties, and should be taken extremely seriously by the audit team. The auditor would need to apply increased professional scepticism to Dexter Co's cash flow forecast in particular, but also to any areas affecting Dexter Co's liquidity.

The move to generate cash from working capital cycles – both the payables payment period and the receivables collection period – appears to be an attempt to stave off immediate illiquidity. The audit team should have exercised professional scepticism about the viability of the proposed changes. If the company's suppliers become aware of its difficulties with liquidity then there is a risk that they could require immediate payment on delivery; this would not only exacerbate Dexter Co's cash flow problem, but depending on Dexter Co's cash position, may not even be possible.

It is encouraging that Dexter Co has applied for a new loan to provide it with a cash boost, and it does appear that Dexter Co is able to generate a profit in the longer term. However, the intention to use the loan to fund investment in a new production facility may be naïve, and under the circumstances could constitute a serious failure of the new management team. This statement should again be subjected to professional scepticism; it is not clear whether management does actually intend to invest in a new product facility, or whether its aim is simply to raise funds to keep its liquidity problems at bay.

Dexter Co appears to have suffered some misfortune in experiencing a shortage of key raw materials. Although this is outside the entity's immediate control, there is a danger that it could combine with Dexter Co's internal cash flow problems to create a position of immediate-term illiquidity. The audit file team should have asked management when the raw materials are expected to be available again, and what impact this is having on Dexter Co's operations and cash position. Even a short-term reduction (or even pause) of production could be devastating in its effects, but it may be possible for a substitute material to be found for the time being.

Audit evidence would include:

- Review of management's assessment of the going concern assumption, applying professional scepticism to any assumptions

- Review of the cash flow forecast for Dexter Co, agreeing all key assumptions to underlying evidence and a considering of their feasibility in the light of the auditor's understanding of Dexter Co's operations

- Copy of Dexter Co's management accounts for the period since the end of the reporting period, which should be agreed to the cash flow forecast

- Assessment of the impact of the shortage of raw materials on Dexter Co's production, and in particular its forecast cash receipts

- Consideration of whether any facts or information which have become available since management's assessment of going concern

- Written representations from management regarding both their future plans for future action, and the feasibility of these plans

- Copy of any correspondence available in relation to the loan application, together with an assessment of the likelihood of funds being made available

(b) **Reasons why directors are reluctant to provide a note to the financial statements**

Directors accountable

The directors at Dexter Co may not want to highlight the difficulties the company is experiencing as they will be held directly responsible by shareholders and other stakeholders. Even if the problems are a result of an external force, such as a new competitor, the directors could still be held accountable and will want to protect their own interests.

Trigger further financial distress

Dexter Co is currently trying to raise finance to cover its operating cash flows. The likelihood of being able to raise this finance is reduced by including the note in the financial statements as potential lenders will be concerned about non-repayment. Additionally, it could cause existing lenders to recall their funds early as they too are worried about the company's ability to pay in the future. The directors may therefore be concerned that the note may only exacerbate any financial difficulties Dexter Co is suffering.

Operational problems – customers and suppliers

The directors could be concerned that including the note in the financial statements would lead to operating problems, worsening the current situation. Suppliers may choose to withdraw business if they are concerned about Dexter Co's ability to pay. Customers may be worried that the company will close leaving them without supplies at short notice and so choose to go elsewhere.

Operational problems – loss of staff

Employees at Dexter Co may decide to find alternative employment rather than risk redundancy. The directors may fear that the inclusion of the note will cause valued employees to leave and have a negative impact on the business.

Directors do not think going concern is impacted

The directors could genuinely feel the going concern status of the company is not impacted by the problems it faces. The directors may believe that they are likely to secure the finance they require to cover their cash flow difficulties and so the future of the company is secure.

(c)   **Implications for the auditor's report**

(i)   **The directors refuse to disclose the note**

As mentioned above in part (a), according to IAS 1, management must disclose any material uncertainties related to events or conditions that may cast significant doubt upon the entity's ability to continue as a going concern (IAS 1: para. 25). Working papers from the audit of Dexter Co indicate there is significant doubt over the going concern status of the company. If the directors refuse to include the note, then IAS 1 has not been adhered to.

The auditor will need to express either a qualified or an adverse opinion, depending on how significant they believe the omission of the note to be. If they believe that the non-inclusion of the note is so material and pervasive that a qualification would not be adequate to disclose the misleading nature of the financial statements, then they should express an adverse opinion. If the auditors believe that the lack of note is not so material or pervasive that an adverse opinion is required, then a qualified 'except for' opinion will be adequate.

A statement that there is a material uncertainty related to going concern that is not properly disclosed will then be included in the 'Basis for Qualified (Adverse) Opinion' section of the report, which is placed immediately after the Opinion section.

(ii)   **The directors agree to disclose the note**

If the directors include the note and the auditor believes that the use of the going concern assumption is appropriate but that a material uncertainty exists, then certain provisions of ISA 570 *Going Concern* will apply. The auditor will need to review the note to ensure that it adequately describes the cash flow difficulties which have cast significant doubt on Dexter Co's ability to continue as a going concern and how management intends to deal with these. He will also need to ensure the note clearly discloses there is a material uncertainty casting significant doubt on Dexter Co's ability to continue as a going concern.

If the auditor finds that adequate disclosure is made in the note, then he should express an unmodified opinion and include a 'Material uncertainty related to going concern' paragraph in the auditor's report. This paragraph should highlight the cash flow difficulties Dexter Co is experiencing and that these cast significant doubt on the entity's ability to continue as a going concern. It should also draw the reader's attention to the disclosure note in the financial statements.

If the auditor finds that the note does not make adequate disclosure in line with IAS 1, then a qualified or adverse opinion should be expressed as in (i).

55 Willis

Workbook reference. Chapters 2 and 11.

Top tips. This question tests your knowledge of the auditor's report. In Part (a) make sure that you are very familiar with the contents of the auditor's report, both unmodified and modified. This area comes up in virtually every sitting, so you just have to be comfortable with it.

Part (b) should have been straightforward. Take note of the examining team's comment (below) about candidates not mentioning ISA 265; the examining team has stated recently that candidates often do not have adequate knowledge of ISAs, so this is an area in which you need to show you can apply your knowledge.

Part (c)(i) offered marks that were virtually all knowledge, and you should have got most of these. Part (c)(ii) was more difficult, and required you to think on your feet. Remember that everybody would have found this question difficult, and that the key is to just get a few clear arguments down on either side, and to draw a conclusion.

Easy marks. Part (a) contained some easy marks for picking apart the more obvious failings of the auditor's report given in the question.

ACCA examining team's comments. This was by far the least popular of the optional questions. Regarding part (a)(i), some answers were sound, and worked through the auditor's report, explaining its deficiencies in a logical manner. Some answers appreciated that the disclaimer of opinion may be an over-reaction, and that a qualification may be more suitable.

Unsatisfactory answers, which were by far the majority, tended not to appraise the auditor's report at all, and instead provided lengthy explanations of the accounting treatment for research and development, but completely missed the point that the auditor was unable to verify if the correct accounting treatment had been applied. Some blamed the audit team, rather than the client, for the lack of evidence, and suggested that the whole audit be reperformed.

Coming to part (a)(ii), most candidates suggested that the limitation in scope and its potential impact on the auditor's report be taken to audit committee or those charged with governance for discussion, and many also raised management integrity as an issue. Some candidates tended to repeat what they had written for (a)(i) without further development.

Part (b) was reasonably well attempted, with most answers referring to management letter points, and making recommendations for improving controls to the client. However, there were very few references to ISA 265, and only a handful of answers discussed the importance of determining whether a deficiency is significant or not.

Requirement (c) dealt with the ethical problems raised by long association of audit firms and their clients. For six marks, candidates were asked to explain the ethical threats, and to evaluate the advantages and disadvantages of compulsory firm rotation. On the whole, this was well answered. Most candidates could identify and explain to some extent the various ethical threats posed by long association, with the familiarity threat being the most common to be discussed. The advantages and disadvantages were often dealt with reasonably well, though a lot of answers were just bullet point lists with no real evaluation provided at all. For many candidates this was the last requirement attempted, so the brevity of answers was probably linked to time management in the exam.

Marking scheme

Marks

(a)   (i)   **Critical appraisal of auditor's report**
Up to 1½ marks per comment applied to the scenario:
- – Incorrect order of paragraphs
- – No explanation of imposed limitation
- – Development costs not specifically referred to
- – No quantification of the asset
- – No reference to potential impact on profit
- – ½ mark calculation materiality
- – Disclaimer or qualification more appropriate (2 marks max)
- – Incorrect headings used
- – Incorrect wording of opinion
- – Unprofessional to refer to management integrity
- – 'We are worried' not professional   Maximum   9

(ii) **Further consequences**

Generally 1 mark per comment:
–   Communicate limitation imposed to those charged with governance
–   Communicate proposed modification to those charged with governance

Marks

–   Consider alternative procedures for development costs
–   Consider integrity of management
–   Consider withdrawal from audit/resignation
–   Audit pre-condition (ISA 210)Maximum   Maximum   5

(b) **Actions/implications of control deficiency identified**

Generally 1 mark per comment:
–   ½ mark ref ISA 265
–   Determine if deficiency is a significant deficiency – extend audit testing
–   If significant report in writing to those charged with governance
–   Communication to include description and recommendation
–   Communication on a timely basis
–   Insignificant deficiency need not be reported – depends on auditor judgement   Maximum   5

(c) (i) **Long association threat**

Generally 1 mark per comment:
–   Familiarity threat (½ mark only)
–   Threat more significant for senior personnel
–   Level of threat depends on various factors
–   Lose scepticism
–   The *Code* requires partner rotation for listed client

(ii) **Compulsory firm rotation**

Generally 1 mark per comment:
–   Eliminates familiarity threat
–   Fresh pair of eyes for audit client
–   Loss of fee income
–   Unwilling to invest – lower quality audit
–   Loss of cumulative knowledge – lower quality audit
–   Increase in cost and audit fee
–   Disruption to client

                                                                         Maximum   6
Total   **25**

(a) (i) **Opinion**

This matter is material to the financial statements; at $4.4m the asset represents 8% of total assets, and if it has been wrongly capitalised then the resulting adjustment would turn the profit of $3.1m into a loss of $1.3m.

Management has not allowed the audit team access to the results of tests which have a bearing on whether or not an asset should be recognised here, in accordance with IAS 38 *Intangible Assets*. The senior is correct to identify this limitation on the audit evidence available, and to recognise that this affects the opinion that should be given.

The draft auditor's report contains a disclaimer of opinion. ISA 705 *Modifications to Opinions in the Independent Auditor's Report* states that such an opinion should be given where the matter in question is both material and **pervasive**, so that the auditor cannot reach an opinion on the financial statements as a whole. This may be overly harsh on this occasion. The matter is certainly material to the statement of financial position. In this case it would be appropriate to qualify the auditor's opinion, on the grounds of an inability to obtain sufficient appropriate audit evidence as a result of a limitation on the scope of the audit.

However, recognising an expense of $4.4m would turn a profit of $3.1m into a loss of $1.3m, so the matter is fundamental to users' understanding of the financial statements. There may be an argument for issuing a disclaimer of opinion as the senior has done.

Contents of report

The 'Basis for Opinion' paragraph should be shown immediately after the 'Opinion' paragraph, not before it as appears to be the case from the extracts given. Furthermore, the paragraph headings are not worded correctly. ISA 705 requires them to be headed 'Basis for Disclaimer of Opinion' and 'Disclaimer of Opinion' respectively.

The 'Basis for Opinion' paragraph should be more precise. It should refer to the relevant accounting standard (IAS 38 *Intangible Assets*), and should explain that a limitation has been imposed by management in respect of development costs. It should explain that management did not allow access to the results of scientific testing relating to these costs, and that the auditor has therefore been unable to determine whether the accounting treatment of the costs is correct.

The paragraph should then quantify the effect on the financial statements, stating that the asset is recognised on the statement of financial position at $4.4m, and that if this were to be treated as an expense, this would turn the profit of $3.1m into a loss of $1.3m.

The paragraph also contains the unprofessional form of words 'we are worried that the asset may be overvalued', which is not appropriate to an auditor's report. A lack of management integrity is referred to, and although the auditor should have considered the possible effects of this, it is inappropriate to refer to this in the auditor's report.

The opinion paragraph itself should use the specific form of words set out in ISA 705, including the statement that the auditor has been unable to obtain sufficient appropriate audit evidence, and that it is therefore unable to express an opinion.

(ii) **Communication with those charged with governance**

ISA 260 *Communication with Those Charged with Governance* requires that significant difficulties encountered during the audit should be communicated, of which this is an example. In addition, where the auditor expects to modify the opinion, the circumstances leading to this should be communicated along with the expected wording.

Alternative procedures

The firm should consider whether evidence can be obtained by any alternative procedures. This may be difficult in this case.

Management integrity

The fact that management have imposed a limitation on the scope of the audit casts doubt over their integrity. The auditor must reconsider any representations made by management in this light. It may be necessary for the audit to be subject to an engagement quality control review.

Withdrawing from engagement

The firm should consider withdrawing from this audit engagement in order to protect its integrity. ISA 210 *Agreeing the Terms of Audit Engagements* effectively requires the auditor not to take on next year's audit, as it is a precondition for an audit that management acknowledges and understands its responsibility to provide the auditor with access to all information relevant to the preparation of the financial statements.

(b)   The errors that have been found are already material to the statement of financial position, but further testing on trade payables is required to see whether they are isolated or whether there are more errors.

ISA 265 *Communicating Deficiencies in Internal Control to Those Charged with Governance and Management* defines internal control deficiencies as misstatements have not been prevented, detected or correctly on a timely basis as a result either of the absence of a control or of the manner in which a control is designed, implemented or operated. Both the absence of some supplier statement reconciliations and the absence of invoice approval before payment meet this definition.

We must consider whether this constitutes just a deficiency or a significant deficiency. A significant deficiency must be communicated to those charged with governance and management on a timely basis during the audit, so that action may be taken by management. If the deficiency is not deemed significant then we must consider whether it is important enough to bring to management's attention.

The written communication of a significant deficiency should include a description of the deficiency, details of its possible effects, and recommendations of how management might seek to correct it.

(c)   (i)   Long association with an audit client may create familiarity and self-interest threats. This depends on a number of factors:

- How long an individual has been involved with the audit
- How senior the individual is
- The structure of the firm
- Whether the client's management has changed
- Whether the type of accounting issues has changed   (IESBA *Code of Ethics*)

The self-interest threat may arise because the firm does not want to jeopardise a continuing source of fee income. The familiarity threat may arise if audit personnel lose their professional scepticism, perhaps as a result of a close relationship with client staff, or because there being few problems in the past might lead the auditor to expect there to be no problems in the future.

The *Code* requires that for public interest entities, the key audit partner should be rotated after seven years, and should not be involved with the audit for two years, including helping with quality control, or giving the audit team advice on technical or industry-specific issues.

(ii)   The key argument in favour of firm rotation is that the familiarity and self-interest threats are more thoroughly safeguarded against by changing the whole audit firm instead of eg the partner alone. This would mean that not only the personnel but the whole infrastructure of the firm would be different. This could improve audit quality by bringing a 'fresh pair of eyes' to the audit.

Alternatively, there are those who argue that an acceptable level of independence can be maintained by applying safeguards within the firm to mitigate the familiarity and self-interest threats.

It may actually be the case that firm rotation would **reduce** audit quality. Audit quality is enhanced by the years of knowledge and experience built up by an auditor in understanding the client entity, and this would be lost.

BPP
LEARNING

There would also be likely to be an increase in the cost of conducting audits, and hence in the fees charged, as a result of work that an incoming auditor needs to do, eg to gain an understanding of the entity and its environment.

Furthermore, audit firms may be unwilling to invest in systems that might enhance audit quality and cost-effectiveness, such as bespoke audit software for a client, if they know that they will lose the audit in a few years' time.

In conclusion, auditor rotation would probably be costly both for clients and auditors, and may not increase audit quality, possibly actually having the opposite effect of **reducing** it.

56 Newman

Workbook references. Chapters 5, 10 and 15.

Top tips. This area has not been examined very frequently in recent years, but the fact that it was examined here is a warning against trying to question-spot. You must be ready to answer questions on any area of the syllabus.

Part (a) may have been intimidating if you had not revised this area thoroughly, but actually a lot of the points in the marking scheme are applicable to most kinds of engagement. You could have thought of general points, and then applied them to the situation given in the question. Note the examining team's comment about application below; AAA tutors never tire of telling students to apply their knowledge to the question.

Part (b) should have been straightforward, but just as in part (a) you need to make sure you applied yourself to the actual question, in part (b) you needed to be as specific as possible in coming up with realistic ways of verifying the KPIs.

Part (c) should also have been straightforward, provided you knew the answer! There is no substitute for knowledge here, especially as this is not a difficult area of the syllabus.

Easy marks. The first few marks in part (b)(i) and (ii) were easy, as you should have been able to think of at least a few procedures without much effort.

ACCA examining team's comments. Candidates responded reasonably well to parts of this question, though many answers did not reach their full potential by not being applied to the question scenario.

Some answers to part (a) were much too brief for the 11 marks available, amounting to little more than a bullet point list of matters to be considered but with no application to the scenario. Without application it was not possible to pass this requirement.

A fair proportion of answers to requirement (b) were sound, with precise procedures recommended. But, many recommended procedures relied too much on observation and enquiry, and ignored the fact that the client was a global company with 300,000 employees which led to some bizarre and meaningless procedures being given, such as 'observe a serious accident', 'inspect the location of a serious accident', 'ask how much is spent on training', and 'look at the training room to see how many chairs are there'. None of these could verify the KPIs and are pointless.

Requirement (c) was inadequately attempted overall. Answers were usually extremely brief, and it was clear that most candidates did not know the requirements of ISA 720. Most answers took a guess that the matter would need to be discussed with management, and that if unresolved there would be some kind of impact on the auditor's report (an 'except for' opinion was the usual recommendation). But few could say more than this about the issue. Some candidates assumed that some kind of money laundering was taking place, leading to irrelevant discussions of reporting the situation to outside authorities. Very few candidates recognised that if uncorrected, the issue should be included in the 'Other information' section of the auditor's report, as required by ISA 720. This could imply a lack of knowledge, or that some candidates are studying from out of date learning materials.

Answer Bank

Marking scheme

Marks

(a) **Matters**

Identify and explain acceptance matters.

½ mark for each matter identified (to max 4 marks) and up to 1½ further marks for explanation:
- Objectivity (up to 3 marks allowed)
- Client's specific requirements
- Competence
- Large scale engagement
- Fee level and profitability
- Time pressure
- Global engagement
- Risk
- Commercial considerations

Maximum 11

(b) (i) **Procedures on number of serious accidents**

1 mark per specific procedure:
- HR records review
- Accident book review
- Determine criteria for serious accident
- Review legal correspondence
- Review board minutes
- Review documentation of health and safety inspections
- Ascertain any convictions for breach of health and safety rules

(ii) **Procedures on average training spend**

1 mark per specific procedure:
- Review approved training budget
- Review components of total spend for misclassified items
- Agree sample of invoices/contracts with training providers
- Agree sample to cash book/bank statement (½ only)
- Recalculate average

Maximum 6

(c) (i) **Auditor's responsibilities regarding other information**

1 mark per comment:
- Definition/examples of other information
- Implication if misstatement in financial statements not resolved (qualification)
- Implication if misstatement in other information
- Material misstatements not relating to financial statements

(ii) **Action by Newman & Co**

1 mark per comment:
- Review audit work on charitable donations
- Discuss inconsistency with management/those charged with governance
- If refuse to change the figure, reconsider reliance on written representations
- Implication for auditor's report

Maximum 8

Total **25**

441

(a) **Matters to consider include:**

Ethical issues

In accordance with the IESBA *Code of Ethics for Professional Accountants*, a non-audit service must only be provided to an audit client after careful consideration of whether the firm's independence and objectivity in respect of the audit may be impaired, and of whether safeguards could be put in place to reduce this threat to an acceptable level or to eliminate it entirely. If such safeguards cannot be put in place, then the audit firm should not accept the non-audit engagement or should withdraw from it.

This assignment would appear to carry particular threats in relation to fee dependence and advocacy.

Fees

Eastwood is a 'major client' of Newman & Co, and there is a risk that the provision of further, non-audit, services to Eastwood could lead to a breach in the acceptable level of recurring fees receivable from one audit client. In the case of a public interest client such as Eastwood, the IESBA *Code* states that the public may perceive an auditor's independence to be impaired where recurring fees are 15% (or more) of total fees.

Advocacy

Newman & Co has been engaged by the client partly in response to the client receiving requests for a Sustainability Report from shareholders and pressure groups. This is a potentially risky context in which to provide such a report, as the report is likely to be scrutinised closely. Furthermore, Newman & Co may be perceived as management's advocate, which would be particularly damaging in the event of any dispute.

Newman & Co's independence would be strengthened by the fact that assurance work would be carried out by a separate team from the audit team.

Level of assurance

Assurance reports may be provided giving varying levels of assurance. It will be necessary to obtain clarification from Eastwood of the level of assurance that it requires, and whether it requires different levels of assurance for different KPIs. Clearly, the level of assurance required would affect the level of evidence required and hence the amount of work that needs to be done, which would in turn affect the fees charged. This should be clarified before accepting the engagement, and a form and wording for the proposed report should be agreed with Eastwood.

Competence

It is possible that Newman & Co may not have staff with the requisite experience available to undertake this engagement. The fundamental principle of professional competence and due care requires that members of an engagement team both possess and apply sufficient skill and knowledge to be able to perform the assignment.

If Newman & Co does not have staff with this skill and experience then it could contract an expert to do some of the work, but this would be likely to increase the costs associated with the engagement.

Resources

A total of 75 KPIs would be reported on, which means that this is likely to be a relatively large engagement. A large number of staff would probably be required to work on the engagement.

It is promising that Newman & Co has a dedicated sustainability reporting assurance team, which should put it in a good position to undertake the work. However, the fact that the team is new means that careful consideration must be given to whether it is capable of doing the work required.

Time pressure

It would be very difficult to gather sufficient evidence to provide an assurance report within the four weeks left until the annual report is published. This may cause staff to be working under significant time pressure, which increases the risk of mistakes being made. Newman & Co must clarify when Eastwood intends for the assurance report to be published.

Profitability

This is a large assignment, probably requiring the team to travel from Oldtown to Fartown to perform the work. This would clearly involve incurring significant costs, and should be reflected in the level of fees charged.

The amount of work that would need to be done, and the short time frame in which to do it, mean that a high fee could be commanded here.

Travel

It is likely that members of the assurance department would need to travel to Fartown, and for the engagement to be accepted they must be willing to do so. It is not clear whether there are any language barriers to working in Fartown, and whether these might be overcome.

Risk

The context of the assignment indicates the presence of risks relating to the degree of scrutiny to which the assurance report would be likely to be subjected. In addition to the presence of interested pressure groups and shareholders, Eastwood is listed on two stock exchanges and is thus fairly high profile. This may increase the level of evidence that Newman & Co would seek to obtain, which would in turn affect the level of fee charged.

Moreover, the inconsistency that has already come to light in respect of the charitable donations figure may indicate management manipulation of the KPIs, which adds to the risk associated with the assignment.

(b) (i) • Review HR records of the number and type of accidents in the workplace.

- • Review accident log books from a sample of locations.

- • Discuss the definition of a 'serious' accident and establish the criteria applied to an accident to determine whether it is serious.

- • Review correspondence with legal advisors which may indicate any legal action being taken against Eastwood.

- • Review minutes of board meetings for discussions of serious accidents and repercussions for the company.

- • Discussion with management/legal advisors, of whether Eastwood has any convictions for health and safety offences during the year.

- • Enquire whether the company has received any health and safety visits. Review documentation from any of these for evidence of serious accidents.

- • Talk to employees to identify any accidents not recorded in the accident book.

(ii) • Review Eastwood's training budget in comparison with previous years to ascertain the overall level of planned spending on training.

- • Obtain breakdown of the total training spend and review for any items misclassified as training costs.

- • Agree significant components of the total training spend to supporting documentation, eg contracts and invoices from training providers.

- Agree the total amount spent on significant training programmes to cash book and/or bank statements.

- Using data on total number of employees provided by the payroll department, recalculate the annual training spend per employee.

(c) **Briefing notes**

To: Trainee Accountant

Subject: Other information – auditor's responsibilities

(i) **Introduction**

These notes explain the responsibility of the auditor in relation to other information published with the financial statements, in the context of Eastwood Co's charitable donations.

Auditor's responsibility

ISA 720 *The Auditor's Responsibilities Relating to Other Information* defines other information as financial and non-financial information included in a document containing audited financial statements and the auditor's report. This would include Eastwood's Sustainability Report.

ISA 720 requires the auditor to read the other information to identify material inconsistencies with the audited financial statements, which may raise doubts over the auditor's opinion. If a material inconsistency is discovered, the auditor must determine whether it is the financial statements or the other information that should be revised. It is also possible that it is just the auditor's understanding of the entity which needs to be updated.

If the financial statements need to be revised but are not, and are therefore materially misstated, then the auditor's opinion should be modified.

If the other information needs to be revised and is not (but the financial statements are unaffected), then the Other Information section of the auditor's report should describe the material misstatement of the other information. The audit opinion would remain unmodified. The auditor should consider requesting those charged with governance to consult its legal counsel. In extreme situations, it may be necessary for the auditor to obtain legal advice itself and to withdraw from the assignment.

Although the auditor is not required to look for misstatements in the other information that are unrelated to the financial statements, they must remain alert for these. If one is discovered then the auditor's response is the same as if it were inconsistent with the financial statements, ie the other information is materially misstated.

(ii) Eastwood's Sustainability Report contains a material inconsistency with the financial statements; charitable donations are stated as $10.5m in the Sustainability Report and $9m in the financial statements. The other information appears to be materially misstated.

Audit evidence has been obtained which supports the $9m figure in the financial statements. This evidence should be reviewed to ensure that it is sufficient and appropriate.

The matter should be discussed with management, who should be asked to change the figure in the Sustainability Report. If management refuse to make this change then the auditor's report should describe the misstatement of other information in the Other Information section of the auditor's report. The matter should also be communicated to those charged with governance.

Eastwood is listed on several stock exchanges, so Newman & Co should consider whether it has any other responsibilities in relation to any Listing Rules.

Finally, if management refuses to change the Sustainability Report then this may indicate a lack of integrity on its part. Any reliance placed on written representations should be reconsidered in this light.

Conclusion

Newman & Co needs to consider carefully how it will meet its responsibilities in relation to Eastwood's other information.

57 Marr

Workbook reference. Chapters 2, 11 and 16.

Top tips. Part (a) was an enjoyable question (!). It featured a draft auditor's report which contained several errors, your approach to which should just be to work through the errors systematically. The material on ISA 701 was probably the most difficult, and provided you with a good test in this area.

Part (b)'s requirement was comprised of three elements – explaining the threats, explaining relevant safeguards, and discussing whether Bobby can act as quality control reviewer. This requirement is mainly knowledge-based, so how well you did depended on how well you knew the material. It should be noted that real AAA exam requirements are likely to be less narrowly focused than this one was.

Part (c) was a difficult discussion of a current issue, but this is something that you do need to be aware of. Passing this question did not require an in-depth knowledge of data analytics.

Easy marks. There were easy marks in part (a) for recognising that an inappropriate opinion had been expressed.

ACCA examining team's comments. Part (a) was for 15 marks, and asked for a critical appraisal of a proposed auditor's report. The report contained many errors of fact and of judgment, and well prepared candidates scored highly here. There were some quite obvious matters that most candidates discussed, for example that the structure of the report was not correct, the wording was not professional, the basis for opinion paragraph lacked sufficient detail, and the nature of the modification was wrong in the circumstances described in the scenario. Most candidates also commented on the incorrect use of the Emphasis of Matter paragraph and correctly determined the materiality of the two issues described in the scenario. Overall, however, **answers to this requirement were often too short for the marks available**, and while most issues had been identified, they were **not always well explained**.

Marking scheme

Marks

(a) **Evaluation of draft auditor's report**
   In general up to 1½ marks for each relevant point of evaluation:
   - Incorrect presentation and combining of Opinion and Basis of Opinion paragraphs
   - Reference to materiality threshold is unnecessary
   - Wording regarding 'proven conclusively' is inappropriate
   - Description of material misstatement should include quantification and impact on financial statements
   - The relevant financial reporting standard should be referred to
   - Unprofessional wording regarding the finance director
   - Inappropriate opinion given – should be modified due to material misstatement not due to disclaimer of opinion
   - Level of modification incorrect – it is material but not pervasive

- Key audit matters (KAMs) – no introductory paragraph
- Appears to give multiple opinions
- Description needed for why the matter is a KAM
- Description needed for how the KAM was addressed
- Description is insufficiently detailed
- Court case not fundamental so not appropriate to include in Emphasis of Matter paragraph
- Emphasis of Matter should only be used for matters appropriately accounted for which is not the case

Maximum	15

(b) **Long association of senior audit personnel**

Generally up to 1½ marks for each point discussed:
- Loss of professional scepticism
- Familiarity and self-interest threats to objectivity
- Assessing the significance of the threat
- Appropriate safeguards (1 mark each where well explained to max of 3 marks)
- Specific rule applicable to public interest entities
- Conclusion on whether partner can perform EQCR role

Maximum	5

(c) **Data analytics**

In general up to 2 marks for each relevant discussion point:
- Definitions
- Manipulate complete data set
- Importance of visual representations of data trends
- Effect on ISAs – fundamental change v fundamental continuity

Maximum	5

Total   **25**

(a)   There are several problems with the draft auditor's report.

Layout

The draft report contains a paragraph entitled 'Basis for opinion and disclaimer of opinion'. ISAs require two separate sections here, headed 'Basis for Opinion' and 'Opinion'.

The 'Basis for Opinion' section should be placed immediately after the 'Opinion' section, and its heading reflects the type of opinion being given – hence 'Basis for Qualified Opinion', 'Basis for Adverse Opinion', and so on.

Wording of report

The paragraph states the materiality level used, which is not required by ISAs. All that is needed here is a description of the scope of the audit.

The paragraph states that 'procedures have proven conclusively that trade receivables are materially misstated'. This is misleading. Audit procedures provide reasonable assurance, which is less than the absolute assurance implied by the words 'proven conclusively'.

The basis for modification paragraph should state the amount of the potential adjustment to receivables, along with its financial impact, referring to the relevant financial reporting standard.

The paragraph names the finance director, which is unnecessary and unprofessional. The statement that she 'refused to make an adjustment' is inflammatory and may leave the auditor open to legal action.

Opinion

An inappropriate auditor's opinion has been given here. At 23% of profit, any write-off of the receivable would be material. The draft report is therefore correct inasmuch as an unmodified opinion would be inappropriate because a material amount of the balance should be written-off.

However, the receivable is unlikely to be judged as pervasive to the financial statements, so the level of modification is wrong. Further, there has been no inability to obtain sufficient appropriate audit evidence, as would be implied by a disclaimer of opinion – as the draft report states, this is a material misstatement.

The opinion should the qualified on the grounds of there being a material misstatement.

Key audit matters (KAMs)

ISA 701 *Communicating Key Audit Matters in the Independent Auditor's* requires the auditor to include specified introductory language at the start of the KAMs section of the report (ISA 701: para. 11). This has not been included here, which constitutes a failure to apply ISA 701. The auditor's responsibilities section of the report would also discuss KAMs; we do not know whether this has been included correctly as this section has not been extracted.

This introduction should have stated that the auditor does 'not provide a separate opinion on these matters'. Instead of this, the draft report states that 'in our opinion revenue is presented fairly', which comes very close to expressing a separate opinion in relation to revenue. It is important that the auditor's opinion relates to the financial statements as a whole, and that KAMs are simply explanations of the matters of most significance to that audit.

ISA 701 requires the description of each KAM to include:

– Why the matter was considered to be a KAM
– How the matter was addressed   (ISA 701: para. 13)

The draft report does attempt to describe why the matter was considered to be a KAM, but the description is insufficiently detailed, and could be construed to be a complaint about the complexity of Marr Co's policies. The description should have stated the factors that led the auditor to conclude that revenue recognition would require significant auditor attention, and should have discussed the risks of material misstatement in this area.

The draft report fails to describe how the matter was addressed in the audit. It could have described how the auditor addressed the assessed risks of material misstatement, perhaps providing an overview of the procedures performed.

Emphasis of Matter (EoM)

The use of an EoM paragraph is inappropriate. An EoM is used to refer to a matter which is already correctly disclosed in the financial statements, but which is in need of extra emphasis by the auditor. By contrast, here the EoM refers to a provision not included in the financial statements. In reality this is a misstatement.

The $50,000 is not material, so the draft report is correct not to modify the opinion in this respect. The correct course of action would be to ask Marr Co to provide for this amount, and if they do not then keep track of it as an uncorrected misstatement. Although it is immaterial on its own, it may become material alongside other uncorrected misstatements.

(b)   Bobby Wellington's long association risks diminishing the professional scepticism which he brings to the Marr Co audit. Over time he may become too accepting of the client's approach to financial reporting, and fails to see problems which a fresh pair of eyes would see.

Familiarity threat

There is a familiarity threat here as a result of the close relationship which may develop between Bobby and Marr's management.

The threat should be evaluated, and will depend on factors such as:

- The seniority of the auditor (Bobby is engagement partner, so is very senior)
- The length of time (seven years is a significant amount of time)
- The nature, frequency and extent of interactions with management (this is not stated in the scenario).

Relevant safeguards which could help to mitigate this threat include:

- Rotating senior personnel
- Review of the senior personnel's work by a professional accountant not involved with the audit
- Regular quality control reviews.   (IESBA *Code of Ethics*)

Public interest entity

Marr Co is a public interest entity. The IESBA *Code of Ethics* requires a key audit partner (such as Bobby) to be rotated after seven years. The individual cannot be involved with the audit at all for a 'cooling-off' period of two years, after which they may become involved again.

In spite of this, the *Code of Ethics* does permit the key audit partner to be involved for a further year if there are unforeseen circumstances beyond the firm's control, and where continuity is important for audit quality. There is no sign that this is the case with Marr Co.

Quality control review

Bobby cannot act as engagement quality control at present, because the *Code of Ethics*' requirement for rotating precludes any contact with the audited entity during the cooling-off period.

(c)   Data analytics is the examination of data to try to identify patterns, trends or correlations. As the quantity of data has increased, it has become more necessary to evolve ways of processing and making sense of it. Data analytics is thus part of the 'Big data' movement, namely the qualitative shift in the amount of data that can be held and analysed by modern computers.

Recent advances in IT make it increasingly possible for auditors to examine and to manipulate a complete data set, ie 100% of the transactions. This has the potential to change the way audit testing works; rather than eg performing controls testing on a sample of items, it is possible to perform risk analysis on a whole population.

In an audit environment so saturated with data about a client, one of the key challenges for auditors is knowing how to make the best use of the data. To help avoid the phenomenon of 'drowning in data', audit data analytics tools allow auditors to visualise trends graphically, and to develop new ways of interrogating data to find trends and relationships.

Current auditing standards, such as ISAs, are based on the technique of risk-based auditing which first became the norm in the 1970s, when it replaced the fully substantive approaches that had preceded it. It has been claimed in some quarters that these techniques will bring about changes of this magnitude to the profession. The sheer scale of the work that can be performed using data analytics techniques makes such a difference to auditors that new auditing standards are needed. Alternatively, others have claimed that auditing standards are fundamentally sound, but are in need of modernisation to reflect these techniques.

58 Pluto

Workbook reference. Chapters 3, 4 and 11.

Top tips. Part (a) was a difficult but fair requirement. Owing to the limited space the examining team has for questions like this, they will not have included much information that is not relevant. You should therefore think carefully about everything in the auditor's report as there is likely to be at least one thing you can criticise about it. Go through it sentence by sentence and think about anything that might be wrong with it. It should go without saying here that you need to have a deep understanding of the different types of modified reports and the circumstances in which they apply.

In part (b) your approach should be to read through the question, noting quality control and ethical problems as you go. Just about every line of the junior's comments contains a quality control risk, so you should have had plenty to talk about in your answer.

Part (c) would have required you to think on your feet a bit, but you should have been able to do enough to at least pass this part – provided that you had not gone over your time in the other parts of the question. The key thing here is to be specific in your matters to be considered, so for instance don't just say that the reviewer needs to be 'independent', but try to think about what the specific threats to their independence might be.

Easy marks. There were some easy marks available in part (a), for example for pointing out that the opinion should not have been adverse.

Some aspects of the scenario in part (b) were flagrantly absurd, such as not performing procedures on directors' emoluments and share capital, or juniors' work not being reviewed. These should have cried out to you, and there were easy marks for saying not just that this was wrong, but why it was wrong.

ACCA examining team's comments. Answers to part (a) were on the whole unsatisfactory. As noted in previous examining teams' reports, candidates seem not to understand the concepts underpinning the modification of an auditor's report, and have even less comprehension of the use of an Emphasis of Matter paragraph. Looking initially at the adverse opinion, most candidates correctly suggested that a material misstatement had indeed occurred, and that an adverse opinion may be too harsh, meaning that an except for qualification would be more suitable. Most candidates did not appraise the wording of the extract, but there were easy marks to be gained here.

The best answers rightly criticised the use of the word 'feel' in an auditor's report, as well as it being inappropriate to put forward the views of the directors in the report. Regarding the Emphasis of Matter paragraph, a significant proportion of candidates did not attempt this part of the requirement. Those that did gained credit for briefly explaining the correct use of such a paragraph, but fewer went on to say why its use in this situation was inappropriate.

Answers to part (b) on the whole were satisfactory, and candidates seemed comfortable with applying their knowledge of quality control requirements and ethical threats to the scenario. Most answers were well structured, working through each piece of information and discussing the matters in a relevant way. There were a number of scripts where the maximum marks were awarded for this requirement.

Requirement (c) asked for an explanation of the matters to be considered in deciding who is eligible to perform an engagement quality control review for a listed client. Answers tended to be very brief, often in a bullet point format. The majority of answers mentioned that it should be a partner with experience who should perform the review. Though most candidates could suggest that the reviewer should be independent of both the audit team, and the audit client, few could suggest why.

Marks

(a) **Critical appraisal of auditor's report**
Up to 1½ marks per issue explained:
Adverse opinion:
- Inadequate explanation of material misstatement
- No financial impact given
- Clearer title needed
- Better to refer to IAS 37 in full
- Clearer reference to note needed
- Explanation of material misstatement should be in separate paragraph
- Should it be except for rather than adverse?
- No reference to impact on statement of financial position

Emphasis of Matter:
- Refers to a breach of financial reporting standards
- Except for material misstatement
- EOM not used for this situation

Maximum   9

(b) **Quality control, ethical and other professional matters**
Up to 2 marks for each matter evaluated
(up to a maximum 3 marks for identification only):
- Time pressure
- Planned procedures ignored on potentially material item
- Sampling method changed – increases sampling risk
- Inappropriate review by juniors
- Inappropriate delegation of tasks
- Deferred tax – management not competent
- Deferred tax – self-review/management responsibility threat
- Tax planning – non-audit service with advocacy threat
- Junior lacks experience for this work regardless of ethical issues
- Junior not supervised/directed appropriately
- Overall conclusion

Maximum   12

(c) **Eligibility to perform an engagement quality control review**
Generally 1 mark per comment:
- Technical expertise
- Experience
- Authority
- Independence from audit team

Maximum   4

Total   **25**

(a) **Adverse opinion paragraph**

The auditor's report does not take the form recommended by ISA 705 *Modifications to the Opinion in the Independent Auditor's Report*. Pluto Co auditor's report contains one section that includes both the reasons for the auditor's opinion and the auditor's opinion itself. ISA 705, however, requires that there be two paragraphs, the first entitled simply 'Adverse opinion', and the second 'Basis for adverse opinion'. The opinion paragraph should not state the reason for the opinion in its title. The presentation offered in the Pluto Co auditor's report could be confusing for readers.

There are also some difficulties with the paragraph itself. It is not appropriate for the auditors to give the argument offered by the directors for not recognising the provision. Details of the directors' view should be available in the note to the accounts referred to. The auditor's report should then be giving the auditor's explanation of why this constitutes a material and pervasive misstatement.

This leads onto another problem. There is an insufficient amount of detail given regarding the misstatement itself. It is not enough simply to refer to a note to the accounts, as this note would give details of the director's judgement. The auditor's report should refer to a specific note in the accounts, and state why this is a misstatement. In this context, the word 'feel' is inappropriate to describe the auditor's judgement in an auditor's report, and may be indicative of a lack of rigour on the part of the auditor. A related point is that the full name of IAS 37 *Provisions, Contingent Liabilities and Contingent Assets* should be given, as omitting it could be confusing to readers.

The paragraph states that the profit for the year is overstated, but it does not say by how much, and does not discuss the effect on the statement of financial position, where liabilities are understated. An estimate should be given of the financial effect of omitting the required provision. After all, it is as a result of their view that such an estimate can indeed be made that the auditor disagrees with Pluto Co's treatment. The auditor's report should then also give further details, such as the timings of the probable cash outflow.

However, perhaps the most important point is that the adverse opinion given may not be correct. An adverse opinion should be given only when a misstatement is so pervasive that the financial statements are rendered meaningless by it, but this misstatement would appear to relate to the specific matter of the omission of a provision. It may be that a modified opinion of the type 'except for' would have been more appropriate.

Emphasis of Matter paragraph

Non-disclosure of the earnings per share figure is a material misstatement, as per IAS 33 *Earnings per Share*, it is material by nature. As a listed company, Pluto Co must disclose both basic and diluted EPS irrespective of whether or not it feels it to be distorted by discontinuing operations. If it feels this to be the case, it should simply say so in its directors' report.

As this is a material misstatement, the auditor's report should be modified in respect of it. An 'except for' qualification would appear to be the most appropriate, as the matter is material but not pervasive. A paragraph discussing this misstatement should be inserted, in which its financial effect would be quantified – which in this case would probably mean disclosing the EPS figures.

(b) Retriever obtained a listing during the year which means that its financial statements will be the subject of particular scrutiny. This raises the overall risk level of this assignment, which means it should be subject to especially stringent quality control. This does not appear to have been the case.

Engagement quality control review

The fact that there is an engagement quality control review taking place is an encouraging sign, as it improves the prospect of some of the more significant failings of quality control being made good before the auditor's report is signed.

Time pressure

The existence of time pressure points to poor planning. The purpose of the audit plan is not only to direct audit work to appropriate areas of the financial statements, but also to decide on the resources and deadlines necessary to complete the audit satisfactorily.

Time pressure increases detection risk. Procedures are likely to be rushed, resulting in a lack of professional scepticism and misstatements going undetected. This seems to be what has happened here.

Directors' emoluments

The audit manager described these as low risk, but they are material by nature. Not only are they related party transactions, they carry a high risk of manipulation as directors may attempt to conceal their remuneration from shareholders and other users of the financial statements.

There will also be additional reporting requirements as this is a listed group, which only increases the risk to the auditor.

Even if they were low risk, planned audit procedures would still need to be performed. The fact they are high risk only heightens this necessity.

Share capital

If the group were not listed, then share capital might be low risk. However, the fact it obtained a listing during the year means that share capital could have changed significantly. This is a highly visible area, and is therefore high risk.

Sampling method

ISA 530 *Audit Sampling* does allow samples to be selected haphazardly, which is effectively the exercise of judgement that the manager appears to be advocating. However, several points can be made against the manager's advocacy of judgmental sampling.

Firstly, the audit plan prescribes statistical sampling. It is possible to deviate from the audit plan, but only if this would provide better evidence. Yet this is not the manager's stated argument, so the suggestion should not have been made.

Secondly, haphazard sampling requires the exercise of judgement which juniors are unlikely to possess in view of the fact that their firm usually samples statistically. There is a risk that juniors will not understand how to select samples in this way, and will simply select eg large balances.

Thirdly, the manager's claim that haphazard sampling is quicker is manifestly false. When done properly, haphazard sampling requires the exercise of judgement and this takes time. Statistical sampling is much quicker to implement as it is relatively mechanical.

In fact the manager's suggestion that this would save time amounts to an incitement to the juniors to select the samples without due care, perhaps only picking the items that are close to hand. This is a serious breach of the IESBA *Code of Ethics*.

Trade payables

It is acceptable for juniors to be involved in the audit of trade payables, however the suggestion appears to be that one junior has been made responsible for the whole of trade payables on a listed company audit. This is clearly unacceptable, as the junior would possess neither the skills nor the time to perform the work to a satisfactory standard.

Going concern

Going concern is a difficult area to audit as it usually involves making judgements about a business's future prospects, which requires substantial experience. Juniors are very unlikely be able to do this and so should not have been assigned going concern.

A more senior member of the audit team should have been assigned going concern, such as the audit manager or partner.

Taken together with trade payables, this reveals a disturbing failure of direction on the audit, which is a key quality control.

Review

It may well be good training for juniors to review each other's work, but this is no substitute for proper supervision and monitoring by more senior members of the audit team. Being at the same level, juniors are unlikely to be able to spot any errors or invalid conclusions drawn, so the reviews are likely to be of little use. Moreover, the juniors are likely to be very familiar with each other and may be unwilling to criticise each other's work. The work should have been reviewed by the audit manager.

Financial controller

The financial controller of a listed company should be able to calculate deferred tax, so the fact that she could not raises issues about Retriever's internal controls. The audit team should therefore revisit the risk assessment done at the audit planning, as deficient internal controls may mean that more substantive testing will be required.

The junior should not have been discussing the tax position with the financial controller in the first place. Given that the time on the audit is so short, what time there is would be better allocated to performing audit procedures. This points to a lack of supervision, and also to a need for further training for the audit junior.

Deferred tax asset

This is a good example of the principle of professional competence and due care, which the junior appears to have breached. Although the junior has studied deferred tax in college, they lack the experience to know than in practice the recognition of deferred tax assets is rare. Given that Retriever's subsidiaries have been suffering losses it is not certain that any such asset will be recoverable; making the judgement over the asset's recoverability requires experience that the junior does not yet possess.

The key ethical issue here is that the auditor must not provide accounting services such as this to listed clients. The self-review threat so created – whereby the firm would then be auditing accounts that it has itself prepared – would be deemed by the *Code* to be insurmountable in this instance.

The audit manager said that this would save time and that the figure would not need to be audited. This is wrong. Now that the junior has calculated the figure it will need to be carefully reviewed and reperformed, and discussed with the management of Retriever. The audit manager's suggestion is indicative of a lack of due care.

Tax planning

The audit junior should not be providing tax planning recommendations. This is a non-audit service, which the junior is providing free of charge and without the required professional skills. There is a self-review threat here because the tax balances calculated on the basis of the junior's advice would be included in the audited financial statements. There is a danger that the junior has been taking management decisions. It would usually be possible for a tax planning service to be provided to a listed client, but the auditor would have to put in place safeguards such as separate engagement teams which clearly do not exist here.

BPP
LEARNING

There is a risk that the firm may be the subject of litigation as well as reputational damage if the client relies on wrong advice given by the junior. Steps should therefore be taken to inform Retriever of the situation and to prevent it from relying on this advice.

(c)   There are four key matters to consider:

Technical knowledge

The reviewer must have a high level of technical knowledge if they are to help identify errors in auditing techniques used, and in the financial reporting in the accounts. They should also have knowledge of any relevant industry-specific regulations, such as stock-exchange listing requirements.

Experience

The review should have a substantial amount of audit experience, ideally in the same industry as the client being audited.

Independence

The reviewer should be independent of the engagement team. The key threat is to their objectivity, so care must be taken to ensure that they are fully independent, for example by limiting the extent to which the reviewer's perspective is influenced by any discussions with the audit engagement partner.

Authority

The review should have sufficient authority within the firm for their criticisms to carry weight, and for them not to be afraid of criticising work done by the engagement team. They would normally need to be at least a senior manager, but for listed clients a partner would be required.

59 Burford

Workbook references. Chapters 10 and 11.

Top tips. This AAA question tests auditor's reports, in this case combined with going concern.

Part (a)(i) was very easy, and you should have passed this part with little difficulty. The only real risk here would be going over your time allocation. Part (a)(ii) was perhaps harder, but the examining team included a nice little list of 'assumptions' in the question for you to base your suggestions for evidence on. Here you needed to make sure that your suggestions were specific – eg you might suggest a source for the evidence, and then state the procedure that would have been performed on it.

Part (b) was a standard auditor's report question for AAA – the technical material on auditor reporting should have been within your grasp. Do not overlook the requirement for 'further actions to be taken by the auditor'.

Easy marks. There are easy marks in part (a) for pointing out the going concern indicators in the question.

Marks

(a)   (i)   **Going concern indicators**
Up to 1½ marks for each going concern indicator discussed, for example:
–   Declining profitability and implication
–   Poor liquidity – inability to pay suppliers/employees/overheads

Marks

- Poor liquidity – breach of loan covenant and implication
- Development of new product is a further drain on cash
- Success of new product is not guaranteed

Maximum   6

(ii) **Procedures on cash flow forecast**

Generally 1 mark for each well-described procedure:

- Agreement of the opening cash position to the audited financial statements and general ledger or bank reconciliation
- Confirmation that casting of the cash flow forecast has been reperformed
- Review of the results of any market research which has been conducted on the GreenFire product
- Discussion of the progress made on GreenFire's development with a technical expert or engineer
- Review of correspondence with existing customers to gauge the level of interest in GreenFire and confirm if any orders have yet been placed
- A review of any sales documentation relating to the planned sale of plant and equipment
- Physical inspection of the plant and equipment to be sold, to gauge its condition and the likelihood of sale
- Review of any announcement made regarding the redundancies
- Sample testing of a selection of those being made redundant, agreeing the amount they are to be paid to HR records
- Correspondence from the government department of the $30,000 grant to be received
- If the grant of $30,000 has been received, agree to cash book and bank statement
- Agreement that the cash flow forecast is consistent with profit and other financial forecasts which have been prepared by management
- Confirmation that any other assumptions used in the cash flow forecast are consistent with auditor's knowledge of the business and with management's intentions regarding the future of the company
- Comparison of the cash flow forecast for the period August–November 20X3 with management accounts for the same period
- Analytical review of the items included in the cash flow forecast, for example, categories of expenses, to look for items which may have been omitted

Maximum   8

(b) **Implications for auditor's report and audit completion**

Generally up to 1½ marks for each point discussed:

- Review adequacy of note
- Evaluate its compliance with applicable financial reporting requirements

If note is adequate:

- No modification of auditor's opinion

BPP
LEARNING

    –   MU paragraph to be included (up to 3 marks for discussion of its
         contents and positioning)

    –   Discuss use of MU paragraph with those charged with
         governance

If note is not adequate:

    –   Non-compliance with financial reporting requirements therefore
         material misstatement

    –   Auditor's judgement as to whether misstatement is material or
         pervasive

    –   Content of Basis of Opinion paragraph

    –   Discuss modification of opinion with those charged with
         governance

                                           Maximum   <u>6</u>

Total   **<u>20</u>**

(a)   (i)   **Performance**

Burford's decline from a healthy profit to a $0.5m loss is a veritable fall from grace. This appears to result from the obsolescence of its QuickFire product and the corresponding disappearance of as much as 45% of its revenue.

Profitability looks set to tumble still further in the coming year as the effect of the QuickFire's absence is felt for the full year.

Although Burford does have a replacement lined up in the form of the GreenFire, any new product will take time to gain market share and it is unlikely that such a product will reverse the declining trend in the immediate future.

Liquidity

Burford's worsening current and quick ratios paint a bleak portrait of declining liquidity. With current liabilities greater than current assets the company may be unable to pay its debts as they fall due, and may therefore be illiquid. If suppliers are not paid then they may restrict supply or refuse to extend credit to Burford, which could make trading impossible.

Moreover, if there are any items of the QuickFire still in inventory then impairment losses may have to be recognised in respect of them, in which case the current ratio will decline even further.

The outlook of declining revenue and increasing costs (for example, marketing costs to help establish the new GreenFire) threatens to heap solvency problems on top of the liquidity problems.

Cash position

Burford's cash balance of $25,000 is very low, at only 0.2% of total assets. It is unlikely that Burford could survive for long with such little cash. It is not known whether Burford has any overdraft facility available to it which might help it survive at least a little longer.

Loan covenant

Given that the current and quick ratios have declined still further since the year end, it is possible that the covenant has been breached already. If the loan is recalled (as seems likely), the cash balance of $25,000 will be insufficient to repay it.

Burford may have to sell assets in order to repay the loan, which could put its future operations in jeopardy.

GreenFire launch

Burford's lack of working capital may make it impossible for it to fund the development and launch of the new product, which would surely be a fatal blow to its going concern.

(ii) **Evidence**

- Agreement of opening cash position to audited financial statements to ensure accuracy of extracted figures

- Re-cast of forecast to check arithmetical accuracy

- A review of results of market research on GreenFire, to ensure the assumption regarding its successful launch is appropriate

- Discussion of progress made on GreenFire's development with a technical expert, to gauge the likelihood of a successful launch

- A review of correspondence with customers to gauge interest in GreenFire and confirm if any orders have been placed

- A review of sales documentation relating to the sale of plant and equipment to confirm that $50,000 is achievable

- Physical inspection of plant and equipment to be sold, to gauge its condition and the likelihood of sale

- A review of any announcement made regarding the redundancies, to confirm the number of employees affected and the timing

- Sample testing of a selection of those being made redundant, agreeing the amount to be paid to HR records, to ensure accuracy of figures in the forecast

- A review of the application made to the government to confirm the amount of the grant. Confirmation to correspondence from government department of the $30,000 to be received

- Agreement that the cash flow forecast is consistent with profit and other financial forecasts prepared by management

- Confirmation that any other assumptions used in the cash flow forecast are consistent with auditor's knowledge of the business and with management's intentions

- Comparison of the cash flow forecast for the period August–November 20X3 with management accounts for the same period, to ensure accuracy of the forecast

- Analytical review of the items included in the cash flow forecast, for example, categories of expenses, to look for items which may have been omitted

(b) IAS 1 *Presentation of Financial Statements* requires detailed disclosures to be made in the situations where there is significant doubt over going concern (IAS 1: para. 25). A brief note is unlikely to suffice, since the note must describe the reasons for the doubt together with management's plans for dealing with them.

The key issue is whether or not the disclosure is adequate.

Adequate disclosure

In this case IAS 1 has been complied with, so the financial statements are not materially misstated. In this case the auditor is nevertheless required to include a 'Material Uncertainty related to Going Concern' paragraph in the auditor's report (ISA 570).

BPP
LEARNING

This would draw users' attention to the disclosure note in the financial statements, and would itself contain a description of the uncertain conditions around going concern. The paragraph should be placed after the Basis for Opinion paragraph, and should state that the auditor's opinion is not modified.

The auditor should communicate with those charged with governance of Burford regarding the modification of the auditor's report.

Inadequate disclosure

In this case there is a material misstatement in respect of IAS 1. The question for the auditor is whether the misstatement is simply material, or both material and pervasive. In the former case, a Qualified Opinion would be expressed, and in the latter case an Adverse Opinion would be expressed (in line with ISA 705).

In both cases the Basis for Qualified/Adverse Opinion paragraph would state the reasons for the modified opinion, and would clearly describe the material uncertainties giving rise to significant doubts about going concern. This paragraph would be placed immediately after the Opinion paragraph itself.

The auditor should discuss the situation with those charged with governance, giving them an opportunity to amend the financial statements in respect of the inadequate disclosure.

60 Basking

Workbook references. Chapters 7, 8 and 11.

Top tips. Part (a) is a good example of the advantages to be conferred by reading ACCA's *Student accountant*. The examining team has stated that topics featured in *Student accountant* articles will be examined soon after the article, which is something that happened here. This is where these articles appear: https://www.accaglobal.com/gb/en/student/exam-support-resources/professional-exams-study-resources/p7/technical-articles.html

This was a knowledge-based question, and would have been very difficult for you if you were not familiar with ISA 450 *Evaluation of Misstatements Identified During the Audit*. The examining team has said in the past that candidates' knowledge of ISAs is sometimes poor, so if you struggled then this is something that you need to work on. It is a good idea, though, to focus your revision time on topics that appear in *Student Accountant*, as these are more likely to be examined.

Part (b) was a fair question on audit evidence. You are given the figures so that you can calculate materiality, so you should do so. The first matter, on depreciation, required you to extrapolate the error if you were to score well on the question. The question gave the information to do this (the carrying amount of the sample and the carrying amount of the whole balance), which you should take as a hint!

The second matter was a loan to a director that you should have recognised as a related party transaction. The third matter dealt with a judgement relating to an accounting estimate, and it should have been within your capabilities to pass this question part.

Easy marks. The marks available for calculating and evaluating materiality are easy, provided that you pick an appropriate benchmark (revenue, profit for the year or total assets). The marks for evaluating the effect on the audit opinion are also relatively easy.

Marking scheme

Marks

In general up to 1½ marks for each relevant and adequate point of explanation. Award ½ mark for identification of a relevant matter and up to a further 1 mark for appropriate discussion. ½ mark should be awarded for relevant points which are either too brief or poorly explained:

(a) **Types of misstatement**
   –   Identification and discussion of types of misstatement (max 1 mark)
   –   Impact on evaluation of impact on financial statements
   –   Subjectivity involved in judgemental matters
   –   Potential inaccuracy of projected misstatements

Maximum   5

(b) In general up to 1 mark for each relevant and adequate point of explanation. ½ mark should be awarded for relevant points which are either too brief or poorly explained:

   (i) **Depreciation**
      –   Error in isolation immaterial (max ½ mark)
      –   Error also immaterial when projected to total population
      –   Client should be requested to amend the error
      –   Auditor should investigate revised non-current asset register
      –   If management refuses, there is still no material misstatement
      –   Unmodified opinion

   (ii) **Loan**

Maximum   5

      –   Related party transaction
      –   Material by nature
      –   Requires full disclosure in the financial statements
      –   Failure to adjust leads to a material but not pervasive misstatement
      –   Qualified opinion

Maximum   5

   (iii) **Provision**
      –   Calculation of potential provision values and value of adjustment
      –   Adjustment is material to statement of profit or loss
      –   Matter of judgement – must be reasoned and supported with evidence
      –   Potential for earnings management
      –   Request management to reinstate full provision
      –   Failure to adjust leads to a material but not pervasive misstatement
      –   Qualified opinion

Maximum   5

Total

20

(a) **Types of misstatement**

ISA 450 *Evaluation of Misstatements Identified During the Audit* identifies three types of misstatement:

1 Factual misstatements
2 Judgemental misstatements
3 Projected misstatements

It is important for the auditor to consider the type of misstatement as the nature of an identified misstatement will have a significant impact on the auditor's evaluation of the misstatement and any consequent further actions necessary in response.

When the auditor discovers a factual misstatement, where there can be no doubt over the error, there is little room for discussion with management. Once a factual misstatement, such as a miscalculation of depreciation, has been established, management should be asked to correct it.

With regard to judgemental misstatements, the validity of the auditor's opinion and any consequent corrections recommended by the auditor are more open to debate. It is therefore vital that in such matters the auditor compiles sufficient evidence to justify why they believe management's judgement is inappropriate in a specific circumstance. Without this weight of evidence to support their position, it is unlikely that management will accept the auditor's view. Even with sufficient evidence, management may still disagree with the auditor's opinion and refuse to accept their judgement in a specific matter. This heightens the risk that the auditor makes an inappropriate conclusion and, ultimately, that they issue an incorrect auditor's report. If material matters of this nature are identified, it is vital that they are considered by a suitably senior member of the audit team.

Projected misstatements assume that an error identified in a sample may be repeated throughout the whole population. The smaller the size of the population originally tested, the lower the validity of this assumption. Clearly the auditor should not recommend the correction of a projected misstatement. These should be used by the audit team to determine the potential for a material misstatement in the wider population being tested and this should guide their decisions as to whether they need to extend their testing.

(b) (i) **Depreciation charge**

Matters

The error identified in the sample represents less than 0.001% of total assets and less than 0.02% of profits. In isolation the error is therefore immaterial.

The error is, however, limited to the sample audited, which represents only 3.6% of total vehicles. If the error is extrapolated to the whole population, it could potentially lead to a total error of $9.7million (0.35m/4.5m × 125m). This represents 0.03% of total assets and 0.4% of profits; and it would seem that the potential error is therefore also not material to the financial statements. The auditor should ensure that they understand how the error has occurred and if the error is isolated, for example, to a certain category of asset, as there is scope for the error to be greater depending on how the miscalculation has occurred.

Regardless of the immateriality of the projected misstatement, there is still a factual, known error in the financial statements. Management should be asked to correct the error in relation to the depreciation of newly acquired assets.

Management should be asked to make the corrected non-current asset register available to the audit team so that they are able to audit the revised register to determine its accuracy.

Furthermore, the auditor should seek evidence that, as well as correcting the error in the financial statements, the relevant system has been corrected to ensure that all new non-current asset purchases are correctly depreciated in the future so that it does not affect subsequent periods.

Opinion

If management refuses to amend the valuation of motor vehicles, then assets and depreciation will both be misstated by an immaterial amount.

As long as the auditor is satisfied that the source of the error has been corrected and this is not an ongoing issue which will effect subsequent periods, the auditor would issue a standard, unmodified audit opinion, stating that the financial statements are fairly presented in all material respects.

(ii) **Loan**

Matters

The loan represents a related party transaction as it is between the company and one of its key management personnel.

The value of the loan may be trivial; it certainly is not material to the financial statements by value. Regardless, related party transactions are material by nature. In these circumstances, the directors of the company may be abusing their position and power for their own personal gain and it is likely that the loan is being provided to Mrs Angel on favourable or non-commercial terms.

For this reason, details relating to the loan must be disclosed in the financial statements, including the amount of the loan, who the loan has been made to and the amount outstanding at the end of the year.

The auditor in this circumstance will disagree with the judgement applied by management in their application of IAS 24 *Related Party Transactions* and the auditor should request that the additional disclosures are added to the financial statements.

Opinion

If management refuses to make the recommended adjustments to the financial statements, then the auditor will conclude that the financial statements are materially misstated due to a lack of appropriate disclosure. While the adjustment is material by nature, a lack of disclosure is unlikely to be considered to be pervasive to the financial statements as a whole.

In these circumstances the auditor should issue a qualified opinion, stating that 'except for' the matters identified the financial statements are fairly presented.

(iii) **Provision**

A provision for 7% of one month's sales would total $328 million ($56,360m/12 × 7%). Reducing it to 4% would create a provision of $188 million ($56,360m/12 × 4%). As a result of the change in calculation, the amount of the provision would be reduced by $140 million.

As well as reducing the provision recognised on the statement of financial position, the release of the provision would also increase the profit reported by $140 million. At 5.5% of profit and 0.37% of total assets, the adjustment is material to the statement of profit or loss but not to the statement of financial position.

This is clearly a matter of judgement. The change must, however, be reasonable and supported by evidence that it is more appropriate to the circumstances of the business. The audit team has found no evidence to support the change made by management.

The risk associated with this is heightened because the release of provisions is a known earnings management technique and Basking Co has suffered a reduction in profits this year. The auditor must apply professional scepticism in these circumstances and be aware that management may be using this as a device to restore profits to help achieve their annual targets.

In these circumstances, it would be appropriate to ask the management team of Basking Co for some form of evidence that the change to their system will lead to a lower rate of refunds. In the absence of any evidence the auditor should explain that the change is purely speculative and as it appears to be unjustified at the present time, that Basking Co should revert back to the original provision until there is evidence of improved effectiveness.

Opinion

If management refuses to amend the provision, it is likely that the auditor will conclude that the financial statements are materially misstated. In isolation it is unlikely that the auditor will conclude that this is a pervasive matter as it has limited impact on the financial statements as a whole.

In these circumstances, the auditor should issue a qualified opinion, stating that 'except for' the matters identified the financial statements are fairly presented.

61 Hopper

Workbook references. Chapters 2, 4, 9, 10 and 11.

Top tips. Part (a) required you to criticise an extract from an auditor's report. The way this question is set out might give you the impression that you're only supposed to be criticising the drafting of the report, not the judgements made by the auditor. If you did think this then notice that there are quite a lot of marks available for eg discussing the actual opinion expressed.

You could think of this question as being about two things: (i) what the auditor has done in response to the issue (in this case, express an adverse opinion and include an Emphasis of Matter paragraph), and (ii) how the report has been written and presented.

It is clearly wrong to express an adverse opinion and include an Emphasis of Matter paragraph, so you should spend time saying why this is wrong and what the auditor should have done instead, ie made a judgement based on the materiality and the pervasiveness of the issue, and then either done nothing, qualified the opinion, or issued an adverse opinion.

The report is vague and waffly, so marks were available for pointing out where it should have been tightened up. Auditor's reports should not contain words like 'feel', which in this example is used because the audit senior is not sure of his/her ground. What the auditor needs are firm statements and relevant facts to back them up with.

In part (b), the bottom line is whether the issue is material to the group, and in this case it clearly isn't. There are effectively 3 marks in the marking scheme for this issue, ie for calculating and stating materiality, and for stating that there is no effect on the group auditor's report. That's 50% of the marks for this part of the question!

Other than that, you really just have to discuss the need for the group auditor to understand the issue by communicating both with the component auditor and with the entity. This is quite a difficult question in a way, because there is not that much more to say!

In part (c) you needed to discuss the quality control procedures. This hinged on realising both that this was a listed company (line 2 of the scenario) and that listed company audits must have engagement quality control reviews. Even if you didn't know this you probably could have guessed, as a quality control review is your go-to quality control for these kinds of question.

Parts (d) was normal AAA ethics scenario, and should not have been unduly difficult. Try to identify the kind of threats that are present, as there are usually half-marks available for correctly stating the type of threat. Once you have done this, try to think of some appropriate safeguards, and then evaluate whether the threat will be reduced to an acceptable level (this is one place where the verb 'evaluate' comes in from the requirement).

Easy marks. The marks for calculating materiality in part (b).

Marking scheme

Marks

(a) **Critical appraisal of auditor's report**
Generally up to 1½ mark for each relevant point of appraisal:
- Heading of 'basis of paragraph' (1 max)
- Vagueness of description of subsidiary
- Quantification of contingent consideration
- Identification of note in financial statements
- Vagueness in relation to correct accounting treatment
- Quantification of the effects on the financial statements
- Vague reference to 'relevant accounting standard' (1 max)
- Opinion paragraph heading & positioning (1 max)
- Reference to materiality
- Pervasiveness of the matter
- Appropriate opinion qualified or unmodified
- Use of Emphasis of Matter paragraph

Maximum 10

(b) **Audit of component**
Generally up to 1 mark for each action and each implication for the Hopper Group explained:
- Consideration of significance to group
- Discuss matter with component auditor
- Discuss matter with management of Seurat Sweeteners Co or the Hopper Group
- Sufficiency of audit evidence
- Calculation of materiality
- Materiality to the Hopper Group
- No modification to the Hopper Group auditor's report
- Potential communication to those charged with governance

Maximum 6

(c) **Quality control procedures**
Up to 1 mark for each procedure explained:
- Appointment of reviewer for listed entities
- Discuss lack of evidence in subsidiary
- Discuss contingent consideration including review of working papers
- Review draft auditor's report wording
- Review of working papers to support judgements in opinion
- Signing of report after review complete

Maximum 4

BPP
LEARNING

Marks

(d) Ethical and professional issues

- Conflict of interest due to auditing both the Hopper Group and Pissarro Co
- Normal to audit firms in the same industry
- Threat to objectivity
- Confidentiality threat
- Full disclosure to both clients
- Possible safeguards (½ each, 1 max)
- Consideration of resources available
- Possible resignation from one audit

Maximum   5

Total   **25**

(a) Critical appraisal of the draft auditor's report

Type of opinion

When an auditor issues an opinion expressing that the financial statements 'do not give a true and fair view', this represents an adverse opinion. The section explaining the modification should, therefore, be titled 'Basis for Adverse Opinion' rather than simply 'Basis for Modified Opinion'.

An adverse opinion means that the auditor considers the misstatement to be material and pervasive to the financial statements of the Hopper Group. According to ISA 705 *Modifications to Opinions in the Independent Auditor's Report*, pervasive matters are those which affect a substantial proportion of the financial statements or fundamentally affect the users' understanding of the financial statements. It is unlikely that the failure to recognise contingent consideration is pervasive; the main effect would be to understate goodwill and liabilities. This would not be considered a substantial proportion of the financial statements, neither would it be fundamental to understanding the Hopper Group's performance and position.

However, there is also some uncertainty as to whether the matter is even material. If the matter is determined to be material but not pervasive, then a qualified opinion would be appropriate on the basis of a material misstatement. If the matter is not material, then no modification would be necessary to the audit opinion.

Wording of opinion/report

The auditor's reference to 'the acquisition of the new subsidiary' is too vague; the Hopper Group may have purchased a number of subsidiaries which this phrase could relate to. It is important that the auditor provides adequate description of the event and in these circumstances it would be appropriate to name the subsidiary referred to.

The auditor has not quantified the amount of the contingent element of the consideration. For the users to understand the potential implications of any necessary adjustments, they need to know how much the contingent consideration will be if it becomes payable. It is a requirement of ISA 705 that the auditor quantifies the financial effects of any misstatements, unless it is impracticable to do so.

In addition to the above point, the auditor should provide more description of the financial effects of the misstatement, including full quantification of the effect of the required adjustment to the assets, liabilities, incomes, revenues and equity of the Hopper Group.

The auditor should identify the note to the financial statements relevant to the contingent liability disclosure rather than just stating 'in the note'. This will improve the understandability and usefulness of the contents of the auditor's report.

The use of the term 'we do not feel that the treatment is correct' is too vague and not professional. While there may be some interpretation necessary when trying to apply financial reporting standards to unique circumstances, the expression used is ambiguous and may be interpreted as some form of disclaimer by the auditor with regard to the correct accounting treatment. The auditor should clearly explain how the treatment applied in the financial statements has departed from the requirements of the relevant standard.

> **Tutorial note.** As an illustration to the above point, an appropriate wording would be: 'Management has not recognised the acquisition-date fair value of contingent consideration as part of the consideration transferred in exchange for the acquiree, which constitutes a departure from International Financial Reporting Standards.'

The ambiguity is compounded by the use of the phrase 'if this is the case, it would be appropriate to adjust the goodwill'. This once again suggests that the correct treatment is uncertain and perhaps open to interpretation.

If the auditor wishes to refer to a specific accounting standard they should refer to its full title. Therefore instead of referring to 'the relevant standard' they should refer to IFRS 3 *Business Combinations*.

The opinion paragraph requires an appropriate heading. In this case the auditors have issued an adverse opinion and the paragraph should be headed 'Adverse Opinion'. The 'Averse opinion' paragraph should be placed before the 'Basis for adverse opinion' paragraph.

As with the basis paragraph, the opinion paragraph lacks authority; suggesting that the required adjustments 'may' materially affect the financial statements implies that there is a degree of uncertainty. This is not the case; the amount of the contingent consideration will be disclosed in the relevant purchase agreement, so the auditor should be able to determine whether the required adjustments are material or not. Regardless, the sentence discussing whether the balance is material or not is not required in the auditor's report as to warrant inclusion in the report the matter must be considered material. The disclosure of the nature and financial effect of the misstatement in the basis paragraph is sufficient.

Finally, the Emphasis of Matter paragraph should not be included in the auditor's report. An Emphasis of Matter paragraph is only used to draw attention to an uncertainty/matter of fundamental importance which is correctly accounted for and disclosed in the financial statements. An Emphasis of Matter is not required in this case for the following reasons:

- Emphasis of Matter is only required to highlight matters which the auditor believes are fundamental to the users' understanding of the business. An example may be where a contingent liability exists which is so significant it could lead to the closure of the reporting entity (but without giving rise to a significant doubt over going concern, which would be dealt with differently). That is not the case with the Hopper Group; the contingent liability does not appear to be fundamental.

- Emphasis of Matter is only used for matters where the auditor has obtained sufficient appropriate evidence that the matter is not materially misstated in the financial statements. If the financial statements are materially misstated, in this regard the matter would be fully disclosed by the auditor in the basis of qualified/adverse opinion paragraph and no Emphasis of Matter is necessary.

BPP
LEARNING
MEDIA

(b) Communication from the component auditor

The qualified opinion due to insufficient evidence may be a significant matter for the Hopper Group audit. While the possible adjustments relating to the current year may not be material to the Hopper Group, the inability to obtain sufficient appropriate evidence with regard to a material matter in Seurat Sweeteners Co's financial statements may indicate a control deficiency which the auditor was not aware of at the planning stage and it could indicate potential problems with regard to the integrity of management, which could also indicate a potential fraud. It could also indicate an unwillingness of management to provide information, which could create problems for future audits, particularly if research and development costs increase in future years. If the group auditor suspects that any of these possibilities are true, they may need to reconsider their risk assessment and whether the audit procedures performed are still appropriate.

If the detail provided in the communication from the component auditor is insufficient, the group auditor should first discuss the matter with the component auditor to see whether any further information can be provided. The group auditor can request further working papers from the component auditor if this is necessary. However, if Seurat Sweeteners has not been able to provide sufficient appropriate evidence, it is unlikely that this will be effective.

If the discussions with the component auditor do not provide satisfactory responses to evaluate the potential impact on the Hopper Group, the group auditor may need to communicate with either the management of Seurat Sweeteners or the Hopper Group to obtain necessary clarification with regard to the matter.

Following these procedures, the group auditor needs to determine whether they have sufficient appropriate evidence to draw reasonable conclusions on the Hopper Group's financial statements. If they believe the lack of information presents a risk of material misstatement in the group financial statements, they can request that further audit procedures be performed, either by the component auditor or by themselves.

Ultimately the group engagement partner has to evaluate the effect of the inability to obtain sufficient appropriate evidence on the audit opinion of the Hopper Group. The matter relates to research expenses totalling $1.2m, which represents 0.2% of the profit for the year and 0.03% of the total assets of the Hopper Group. It is therefore not material to the Hopper Group's financial statements. For this reason no modification to the auditor's report of the Hopper Group would be required as this does not represent a lack of sufficient appropriate evidence with regard to a matter which is material to the Group financial statements.

Although this may not have an impact on the Hopper Group audit opinion, this may be something the group auditor wishes to bring to the attention of those charged with governance. This would be particularly likely if the group auditor believed that this could indicate some form of fraud in Seurat Sweeteners Co, a serious deficiency in financial reporting controls or if this could create problems for accepting future audits due to management's unwillingness to provide access to accounting records.

(c) Quality control procedures prior to issuing the auditor's report

Both ISA 220 *Quality Control for an Audit of Financial Statements* and ISQC 1 *Quality Control for Firms that Perform Audits and Reviews of Historical Financial Information, and Other Assurance and Related Services Agreements, and other assurance and related services agreements* require that an engagement quality control reviewer shall be appointed for audits of financial statements of listed entities. The audit engagement partner then discusses significant matters arising during the audit engagement with the engagement quality control reviewer.

The engagement quality control reviewer and the engagement partner should discuss the failure to recognise the contingent consideration and its impact on the auditor's report. The engagement quality control reviewer must review the financial statements and the proposed

auditor's report, in particular focusing on the conclusions reached in formulating the auditor's report and consideration of whether the proposed auditor's opinion is appropriate. The audit documentation relating to the acquisition of Seurat Sweeteners Co will be carefully reviewed, and the reviewer is likely to consider whether procedures performed in relation to these balances were appropriate.

Given the listed status of the Hopper Group, any modification to the auditor's report will be scrutinised, and the firm must be sure of any decision to modify the report, and the type of modification made. Once the engagement quality control reviewer has considered the necessity of a modification, they should consider whether a qualified or an adverse opinion is appropriate in the circumstances. This is an important issue, given that it requires judgement as to whether the matters would be material or pervasive to the financial statements.

The engagement quality control reviewer should ensure that there is adequate documentation regarding the judgements used in forming the final audit opinion, and that all necessary matters have been brought to the attention of those charged with governance.

The auditor's report must not be signed and dated until the completion of the engagement quality control review.

> **Tutorial note.** In the case of the Hopper Group's audit, the lack of evidence in respect of research costs is unlikely to be discussed unless the audit engagement partner believes that the matter could be significant, for example, if they suspected the lack of evidence is being used to cover up a financial statements fraud.

(d) The acquisition of another audit firm creates a potential conflict of interest because Rockwell & Co will become the auditor of both the Hopper Group and its competitor, Pissarro Co.

There is nothing ethically inappropriate having clients in the same industry; this is actually normal practice and allows firms of accountants to develop industry-specific experience, which allows them to offer high-quality, expert services. It is therefore likely that firms will have clients which compete in the same industry.

Acting for two competing companies may give rise to ethical threats though. It may be perceived that the auditor cannot offer objective services and advice to a company where it also audits a competitor. The clients may also be concerned that commercially sensitive information may be inadvertently, or intentionally, passed on to the competitor via the auditor.

The main safeguard available is to disclose the potential conflict to all parties involved. If both the Hopper Group and Pissarro Co accept the situation, it is appropriate for Rockwell & Co to continue in its capacity as auditor to both as long as appropriate safeguards are put in place. These include:

- The use of separate engagement teams
- Issuing clear guidelines to the teams on issues of security and confidentiality
- The use of confidentiality agreements by audit team members
- Regular review of the safeguards by an independent partner   (IESBA *Code of Ethics*)

Rockwell & Co must also evaluate whether there are sufficient resources available to conduct the audits of both companies using separate teams. If not, the audit firm will not be able to accept the additional work into the department.

If either of Pissarro Co or the Hopper Group does not give its consent, then Rockwell & Co must resign as the auditor of one of the companies.

If this is the case, a number of ethical and commercial considerations should be made before deciding which client should be rejected. Rockwell & Co will need to consider the risk profile of both clients and should conduct appropriate acceptance/continuance procedures for both clients prior to making any final decision. From a commercial perspective, Rockwell & Co may also consider which of the two clients provides the highest audit revenue. The Hopper Group appears to be the larger company currently but Pissarro Co is a rapidly expanding business which could be a more lucrative audit client in the future. In this case Rockwell & Co should also consider if they will be able to offer the range of services required by the rapidly expanding Pissarro Co without creating any self-interest or self-review threats to independence.

Rockwell & Co should also consider if any non-audit services are currently offered to the clients and whether additional services could be offered to either of them in the future. As a rapidly expanding business, it is possible that Pissarro Co will require more services than the established Hopper Group.

62 Darren

Workbook references. Chapters 8, 10, 11 and 15.

Top tips. Part (a) was a relatively straightforward requirement on revenue from a long-term contract. The first thing to do is to calculate materiality. Discuss the accounting treatment and then try to answer the requirement to 'discuss the implications [...] on the completion of the audit'. This is slightly difficult because the question does not state what audit procedures have already been performed (or what evidence has been obtained), so you have to decide what should be done given that these issues have come to light at this stage of the audit. These are the 'actions' that the requirement asks for; the main one is to obtain the audit evidence. It is important that you recommend actions for the auditor – as a general point, AAA exams tend to contain many marks for actions, so this is an easy way to score well.

Part (b) was a tricky question because there isn't a great deal wrong with what the auditor has done, so there are not that many actions. The examining team's answer focuses on the possible threat to going concern as a result of making the possible payment, but given that the payment is only possible this does not seem to qualify as a 'significant doubt leading to a material uncertainty' (ISA 570). Taking into account the examining team's recent advice to candidates not to mention going concern at every opportunity, it would have been difficult for candidates to bring going concern into their answers.

Nonetheless, it is true that there is a going concern risk as a result of the payment (which is greater than Darren Co's profit before tax). Even though it seems to have been taken into account correctly by the auditors in the scenario, there are still marks for stating the required IAS 37 treatment and then comparing this with what has happened. It is only the conclusion that differs from other AAA questions, ie you should conclude that IAS 37 has been applied correctly, whereas you're usually in the position of looking for errors.

Part (c) should have been a nice question on other information. You have the information to calculate the increase in profit before tax in the financial statements, so you can work out that there is an inconsistency here. You then need to decide whether the KPI is wrong, or whether the financial statements are wrong – and further evidence is needed to decide this. You then need to state the effect on the auditor's report – a description in the Other Information section – and state what other actions might be needed, eg discussing the possible modification of the auditor's report with those charged with governance, questioning management's integrity (and its representations), or obtaining legal advice.

Easy marks. There were many easy marks available for calculating/assessing materiality, as well as for describing the effects on the auditor's report – particularly for stating where various sections are positioned in relation to one another.

Recommending actions for the auditor is also a good way of getting marks – if you don't do this, it will be difficult to pass.

ACCA examining team's comments. Part (a) was for 8 marks and described how Darren Co's financial statements recognised all of the profit relating to a long-term construction contract even though it was only part completed at the year end. **Candidates performed well** on this requirement, providing answers which confidently discussed both the inappropriate accounting treatment and the implications for the audit opinion if the material misstatements identified were not corrected by management. Some candidates missed out on marks by not recommending any further actions or by only discussing the impact for the audit opinion itself and not the overall impact on the auditor's report, failing to mention the need for a Basis of Opinion paragraph within the auditor's report. Only the strongest candidates realised that this incorrect accounting treatment may have been applied to other contracts and that opening balances may be incorrect given that this was a new audit client.

Part (b) was for 6 marks and provided information on a completed contract in respect of which Darren Co was facing legal action due to problems that had arisen following completion. Candidates again seemed confident of the accounting rules, yet many suggested that a provision should be made for the damages; this may be because candidates assumed that there 'should' be some implication for the auditor's opinion given the facts of the scenario, but this was not the case. The other significant issue was that Darren Co could not afford to pay the damages given its small cash balance, and this could raise a threat to the going concern status of the company.

Only the strongest candidates made this connection and were able to explain clearly the implications for the auditor's report. In this scenario the issue was that a disclosure would be sufficient, as long as there was only a possibility that the claim would need to be paid, but the crucial aspect was that audit firm would need to audit the disclosure carefully to obtain evidence as to its sufficiency especially given the potential impact on going concern. As in part (a), the further actions were generally not given, other than a generic suggestion to 'discuss with management'.

Part (c) was for 6 marks and briefly outlined that Darren Co had included as a key performance indicator in its integrated report the percentage increase in profit before tax. Candidates were provided with the information to calculate that the indicator was incorrect. It was unfortunate that a **significant minority** of candidates were unable to work out a simple percentage increase despite the information being clearly presented in the question scenario. Despite this, almost all answers identified that the stated key performance indicator was incorrect. The **best answers** explained that management should be asked to amend the figure in the integrated report, and that if it remained uncorrected it would not affect the audit opinion, but be described in the Other Information section of the auditor's report. **Weaker answers** suggested that the opinion should be modified due to material misstatement which is incorrect. Again, there were few suggestions of further action to be taken other than 'discuss with management'.

Marking scheme

Marks

Generally up to 1½ marks for each relevant point explained, with 1 mark for correct determination of materiality:

(a) **Bridge contract**
- Profit recognised is material
- Profit should be recognised by reference to stage of completion at the reporting date
- Profit appears to be overstated/recognised too early
- Further actions (1 mark each):
  - Review company's stated accounting policy
  - Review contract terms for revenue recognition trigger points

BPP
LEARNING

- • Verify stage of completion using surveyor's reports
- • Confirm contract progress through correspondence with customer
  - – Material misstatement leading to qualification of audit opinion
  - – Basis for Qualified Opinion paragraph – position and contents
  - – Other contracts need to be reviewed
  - – Opening balances could also be materially misstated

Maximum   8

(b) **Legal action**
  - – Possible cash payment material by monetary amount and by nature
  - – Going concern implication to be assessed due to size of possible cash outflow
  - – Treatment as a contingent liability appears correct
  - – Further actions (1 mark each):
    - • Review post year end legal correspondence
    - • Confirm financing in place in the event of amount becoming payable
    - • Read note to accounts to ensure complete and accurate
  - – Emphasis of Matter paragraph to highlight the significant uncertainty regarding the outcome of the litigation
  - – Content and position of the Emphasis of Matter paragraph

Maximum   6

(c) **KPI**
  - – KPIs included in integrated report are other information
  - – Auditor must read other information to identify material inconsistencies
  - – The profit increase KPI is not the same as reported in the financial statements giving rise to material inconsistency
  - – Further actions (1 mark each):
    - • Consider whether the financial statements or KPI should be amended
    - • Request amendment of the KPI once audit adjustments are finalised
  - – If material inconsistency remains an Other Information section should be included in auditor's report
  - – Position below Opinion section
  - – Auditor should seek legal advice (1 mark)
  - – All matters should be discussed with those charged with governance (1 mark)

Maximum   6

Total **20**

(a) The total estimated profit of $5m which has been recognised in the statement of profit or loss represents 22.2% of profit for the year and is therefore material.

IFRS 15

The contract should be accounted for in accordance with IFRS 15 *Revenue from Contracts with Customers*. This would be a contract whose performance obligations are satisfied over time. Revenue is accounted for at an amount that approximates the selling price of the goods or services transferred to date. Darren Co must choose an appropriate method for estimating the amount of performance completed to date.

Darren Co has recognised 100% of the contract profit even though the contract is not yet complete. The contract activity period is 15 months, and by the year end the contract activity has been ongoing for seven months only. Therefore the profit which has been recognised appears to be overstated, and it seems to have been recognised too early.

The audit firm should clarify Darren Co's accounting policy on long-term contracts and confirm the method which is used for estimating the amount of performance completed at the end of the reporting period. IFRS 15 allows for either input or output methods to be used, eg based on the proportion of total resources (eg costs) used at the end of the period, or on surveys of work performed.

Effect on audit completion

Further evidence should be obtained to determine the amount of performance completed, to enable the appropriate amount of revenue, costs and profit which should be recognised to be determined.

Further procedures should be performed, including:

–   The contract terms should be scrutinised for any terms relating to the completion of stages of the contract which may trigger the recognition of contract revenue.

–   Surveys of work performed by 31 January 20X5 should be reviewed to estimate the stage of completion at the end of the reporting period.

–   Correspondence with the customer should be read to confirm that the contract is progressing in a satisfactory way.

Materiality and reporting

Further audit evidence is required, but based on the time period in months as a rough guide, it appears that the contract is $^7/_{15}$ complete, and therefore profit in the region of \$2.3m (\$5m $\times$ $^7/_{15}$) can be recognised, and that profit is overstated by \$2.7m. The overstatement would be material at 12% of profit before tax.

If any necessary adjustment is not made, then profit is overstated by a material amount. This gives rise to a material misstatement, and the auditor's opinion should be modified. A qualified 'except for' opinion should be expressed, and the Basis for Qualified Opinion section should explain the reason for the qualification, including a quantification of the misstatement. The Basis for Qualified Opinion section is placed immediately after the Qualified Opinion section.

This is only one contract, and Darren Co typically works on three contracts at a time. Therefore further audit work may be needed in respect of any other contracts which are currently being carried out. If the same accounting treatment has been applied to other contracts, the misstatement may be even greater, and could potentially result in an adverse opinion if the accumulated misstatements were considered by the auditor to be both material and pervasive to the financial statements.

In addition, Darren Co may have been using an inappropriate accounting treatment in previous years, and therefore there may be misstatements in the opening balances. This should be discussed with management to determine how contracts have been accounted for historically. Any errors which may be discovered should be corrected retrospectively, leading to further adjustments to the financial statements.

(b)   **Materiality**

The amount claimed by Newbuild Co is material to the financial statements, representing 10.8% of total assets and 178% of profit before tax. It is also likely to be considered material by nature, as the possible payment is much larger than the amount of cash recognised in the financial statements at the year end.

BPP
LEARNING

Going concern

The implications for the going concern status of Darren Co should be considered. The matter should be discussed with management, in order to obtain an understanding of how Darren Co could meet any necessary cash payment, given that the cash balance at the year end is only $3m. Due to the potential for such a sizeable cash payment, management should confirm that if the amount becomes payable, the company will have adequate resources to fund the cash outflow, for example, through the availability of lending facilities.

IAS 37

The correct accounting treatment seems to have been applied. According to IAS 37 *Provisions, Contingent Liabilities and Contingent Assets*, if an amount is possible, rather than probable to be paid, then it is treated as a contingent liability (IAS 37: para. 10), and a note to the financial statements should be provided to describe the nature of the situation, an estimate of the possible financial effect and an indication of any uncertainties (IAS 37: paras. 84–86).

To ensure that IAS 37 has been complied with, the auditor should review the contents of the note for completeness and accuracy. Events after the reporting period should also be considered, for example, legal correspondence should be reviewed, to confirm that the probability of payment has not changed by the time of the auditor's report being signed.

Auditor's report

Due to the size of the potential cash outflow, the auditor should consider including an Emphasis of Matter paragraph in the auditor's report. The purpose of this paragraph is to communicate a matter which is fundamental to the users' understanding of the financial statements. ISA 706 *Emphasis of Matter Paragraphs and Other Matter Paragraphs in the Independent Auditor's Report* provides examples of situations which may give rise to the inclusion of an Emphasis of Matter paragraph, including uncertainty relating to the future outcome of exceptional litigation or regulatory action.

The Emphasis of Matter paragraph should include a clear reference to the matter being emphasised and to the note to the financial statements where the matter is disclosed. The paragraph should also make it clear that the auditor's opinion is not modified in respect of this matter.

If the auditor thinks that there are material uncertainties over going concern, then they should include a 'Material uncertainties related to going concern' section in the auditor's report, not an Emphasis of Matter paragraph, in line with ISA 570 *Going Concern*. This would be placed immediately below the 'Basis for Opinion' section.

(c) ### ISA 720

The key performance indicators (KPIs) included in an integrated report are by definition 'other information' according to ISA 720 *The Auditor's Responsibilities Relating to Other Information*. Other information is defined as financial and non-financial information which is included in an entity's annual report.

According to ISA 720, the auditor is required to read the other information to identify material inconsistencies, if any, with both the audited financial statements and with the auditor's understanding of the entity. There appears to be an inconsistency because the KPI states that profit before tax has increased by 20%, but the increase shown in the financial statements is 12.5%. The auditor must use professional judgement to determine if this is a material inconsistency.

Further actions – amend KPI or financial statements?

Assuming that this is deemed to be a material inconsistency, the auditor should consider whether the financial statements or the other information should be amended. The audit completion procedures, including final analytical review and review of all working papers will determine whether the profit before tax figures as stated in the financial statements need to be

amended. From the discussion above, it is likely that some adjustment to profit before tax will be needed regardless of the inconsistent KPI.

It is most likely that the KPI included in the integrated report should be changed in agreement with the movement in profit shown in the adjusted financial statements, and management should be asked to make the necessary change to the KPI.

Auditor's report

If management refuses to change the KPI, and the material misstatement of the KPI remains, the auditor should describe the material misstatement of the other information in the Other Information section of the auditor's report.

The auditor may also seek legal advice if management refuses to amend the KPI to remove the material misstatement of other information. All of the matters affecting the auditor's report should be discussed with those charged with governance.

63 Chester & Co

Workbook reference. Chapters 2 and 11.

Top tips. Your approach to ethics requirements such as those contained in parts (a) and (b) should be to work through the scenario with pen in hand, noting the threats as you go. It is important that you try to identify the threats to independence, taking care not to just list the threats that you think might be present. You then need to say why such a threat is present, and suggest safeguards to reduce the threat to an appropriate level. It is a good idea to try to evaluate the seriousness of the threat, and to give a conclusion to each mini-scenario, such as 'if these safeguards cannot be implemented then the auditor must decline to tender for this engagement'.

Practical professional and commercial considerations usually score well. The most straightforward example of this being that the audit firm should consider which of either the non-audit services or the audit will be most profitable for it to continue with.

Be very wary about writing about the risk of % fee thresholds being breached, as your examining team considers these to be general points that indicate a lack of application to the scenario at hand. It is not relevant to any of the mini-scenarios in this question, for example, and you should only mention it in an answer if the scenario specifically hints that this might be problem.

Part (c)(i) was a normal AAA reporting requirement, while (c)(ii) might have confused you as there was nothing wrong as such – except for the absence of an Emphasis of Matter paragraph. This might have led you to try to criticise the statement in the scenario that going concern was not an issue. With a question such as this, it is important to learn to distinguish between when the examining team is trying to tell you **not** to write about something (as here), and when a statement is there in the scenario for you to criticise it.

Finally it should be noted that the format of this question, in which the scenarios are set at different stages of the audit, is unlikely to be used in your real exam – the ACCA has stated that there will be one Section B question set at the completion stage, with the other Section B question set at another stage of the audit.

Easy marks were available for calculating materiality in part (c)(i), as in almost all auditor reporting questions.

ACCA examining team's comments. In parts (a) and (b), two short scenarios were provided, describing a range of situations giving rise to ethical threats and other issues, with the requirement to identify and discuss the ethical and other professional issues raised, and to recommend any actions to be taken by the audit firm for each of the scenarios given. This is a fairly standard type of question for AAA, and many candidates performed well, obviously having practised some past exam questions.

Requirement (a) was for 7 marks, and described a potential new audit client, a small owner-managed company providing financial services. There were several issues that candidates should have spotted in the scenario including a potential lack of integrity of the company's managing director, potential self-interest and self-review threats arising from the provision of non-audit services, threats arising from non-compliance with the regulatory body. The majority of candidates picked up on most of these issues and explained the ethical threats well. There has been a definite improvement in the way that candidates tackle this type of question, and in many cases close to the maximum marks were awarded.

Requirement (b) was for 6 marks, and outlined the situation of an existing client facing going concern problems. The audit engagement partner had been asked to accompany the managing director to a meeting with the bank where additional finance would be sought, and there were intimidation threats in that the client had threatened to put the audit out for tender, and there were also outstanding fees. Again, candidates generally did well on this requirement, identifying and explaining the correct ethical threats, and on the whole recommending appropriate courses of action. The only problem in some scripts was a focus on the lack of integrity of the managing director, rather than discussing specific ethical threats raised.

Part (c) of the question described two issues and candidates were required to discuss the implications for the auditor's report. Unfortunately many candidates deviated from the requirement and spent time discussing the accounting treatment and audit procedures for an area where there was a limitation on the scope the audit. Candidates also lost time discussing audit procedures on going concern, which was flagged as already satisfactorily covered. The understanding of auditor's reports and their usage continues to be a weak area for many candidates despite it being a core part of the syllabus.

Marking scheme

Marks

(a) **Tetbury Co**

Generally 1 mark for each point identified and discussed:

–   Customer due diligence/know your client procedures to be performed
–   Audit firm's competence to audit a financial services client
–   Acceptance decision should also include consideration of ethical threats
–   Management integrity threatened by past investigation by financial services authority
–   Integrity also threatened by possible inappropriate financial reporting
–   Management may have intimidated the previous auditor
–   Contact previous auditor for further information
–   Controls appear weak leading to high audit risk
–   Responses to high risk should be considered, eg use of experienced audit team
–   Confirm client's intention to improve controls
–   Threats to objectivity arise from giving business advice – perceived as assuming management responsibility
–   Self-review and self-interest threats created
–   Safeguards to be put in place, eg management acknowledge responsibility for business decisions

Maximum   7

Marks

(b) **Stratford Co**
- – Advocacy threat created by attending meeting
- – Legal proximity may be created by attending meeting
- – Intimidation threat from threat of removal from office
- – Consider appropriate safeguards
- – Integrity of the managing director questionable
- – Overdue fees may represent self-interest threat
- – But amount may be insignificant and not long overdue

Maximum   6

(c) **Implications for the auditor's report and further actions**

In general up to 1 mark for each well explained point and action point recommended:

Military research
- – Expenses are material (must include relevant calculation)
- – Management imposed limitation on scope
- – Auditor should request that management removes the limitation
- – Communication of potential impact to those charged with governance
- – Impact on continuation of audit engagement
- – If limitation is not removed, audit opinion will be modified
- – Matter is material but, currently, not pervasive; qualified opinion
- – Basis for qualified opinion paragraph

Fire
- – No modification of the audit opinion necessary
- – The major catastrophe will have a significant impact on results and make their interpretation difficult
- – Disclosures by management are of fundamental importance to users
- – Emphasis of matter paragraph required

Maximum   12

Total   **25**

(a) **Tetbury Co**

Professional competence

Tetbury operates in the highly regulated, complex environment of financial services. There is therefore a threat to Chester & Co's ability to conduct an audit in this area in line with the principle of professional competence and due care. This is a self-interest threat as a result of the prospective audit fee.

Customer due diligence

Given the complex and therefore risky nature of Tetbury's business environment, it is of paramount importance that Chester & Co conducts customer due diligence procedures before accepting such a client. The risk of Tetbury being involved in laundering money should be weighed carefully.

Previous auditors

The fact that the previous auditors resigned suggests that Tetbury's management may lack integrity. There is a risk that the problems which led to the previous auditors resigning may persist during the tenure of Chester & Co.

BPP
LEARNING

Chester & Co should ask Tetbury for permission to contact the previous auditors regarding the reasons for their resignation. They should be asked whether there are any matters of which Chester & Co should be made aware of in deciding whether to take on the audit. This is a self-interest threat to professional competence and due care, because Chester & Co may fail to exercise due care in order to secure the audit fee.

If Tetbury refuses permission to contact the previous auditors, then Chester & Co should withdraw from the tender process.

Controls

The fact that the reason given for the previous auditors' resignation points to a poor control environment at Tetbury. This is particularly worrisome given that it is an owner-managed business, in which the risk of management override of controls is perennially present. Bearing in mind also the increased need for robust internal controls in as highly-regulated an area as financial services, the Tetbury audit would surely be considered high-risk.

As a high-risk audit, Chester & Co would likely need to perform more audit procedures in order to reduce audit risk to an appropriate level. This would be costly, and would need to be reflected in a high audit fee. The threat to Chester & Co's professional competence is in this light particularly acute. Chester & Co would need to consider carefully whether the Tetbury audit would be worth such a high risk.

Financial services authority investigation

The investigation suggests either a lack of integrity or a poor control environment, or both. In any event Chester & Co ought to find out more about this, for example by contacting the authority for further details.

Business development advice

There is a self-interest threat here in relation to the fee. There is a self-review threat as it is possible that the advice may need to be audited, for example as part of the assessment of the going concern assumption.

The self-review threat can be mitigated by using separate engagement teams, separated by information barriers, or by an independent review of the audit work by a professional accountant.

It is important that Chester & Co avoids taking on management responsibilities, because were they to do so then the tender must be declined. It can avoid doing so by obtaining written confirmation from Tetbury that it acknowledges responsibility for any decisions taken.

(b) **Stratford Co**

Meeting

The request to attend the meeting with the bank suggests an advocacy threat, as the audit partner may be put in the position of supporting the view that the client will continue as a going concern, and that the bank should therefore offer it a loan.

Legally, there is a risk of creating proximity between Chester & Co and Stratford which could result in the bank taking legal action against the auditor in the event of Stratford defaulting on its loan.

In addition, the financial statements being presented at the meeting are only draft versions and have not been audited. It is crucial that Chester & Co does not allow Stratford to give the bank the impression that these financial statements come with any assurance.

It would probably not be possible to mitigate the advocacy threat with the audit engagement partner attending the meeting. It may be possible for another partner to attend, however, if it was made clear that they were not the audit partner and that no assurance was provided in respect of the draft financial statements.

Threat

The managing director's threat to put the audit out to tender is an intimidation threat, since if the audit partner were to attend the meeting, this may give the bank the false impression that assurance has been provided on the draft financial statements.

This places a question mark over the managing director's integrity. Chester & Co should communicate with those charged with governance on this matter, for example with any other board members or with the audit committee. Chester & Co should consider resigning from the audit if the threat does not abate.

Fees

Overdue fees represent a self-interest threat, as Chester & Co may not obtain sufficient appropriate evidence in relation to the audit opinion it expresses in order to receive the fees owing. There is a risk that this may be perceived to be a loan made to Stratford.

In this case the fee relates to a debt that is likely to be only four months old. The severity of the threat would depend on the significance of the amount outstanding.

Chester & Co should request that the audit fee be paid, and should communicate the matter to those charged with governance. It may also wish to review the efficacy of its own system for credit control.

(c) **Military research project**

The research expenses represent 10.8% of profit for the year so they are material to the financial statements.

Chester & Co is unable to obtain sufficient appropriate evidence relating to the research expenses. Given the limitation imposed by management, the auditor will be unable to form a conclusion about the occurrence, completeness, accuracy or classification of the associated expenses.

ISA 705 *Modifications to the Opinion in the Independent Auditor's Report* requires that when management imposes a limitation on the scope of the audit, the auditor should request that they remove the limitation. If management refuses, the auditor should communicate the matter to those charged with governance, explaining the implications of the matter and the impact on this year's audit opinion. In addition, as this is a matter which is likely to arise again in future audits, the auditor should stress that the compound effect of this and the likelihood that there may be development cost implications to consider in the future may give rise to both a material and pervasive matter, which would give rise to a disclaimer of opinion.

As well as the implications on the auditor's report, those charged with governance should be informed that in accordance with ISA 210 *Agreeing the Terms of Audit Engagements*, the auditor may not be able to accept the audit engagement in the future if management continues to impose the limitation on the scope of the auditor's work and the auditor believes that it may result in them disclaiming their opinion.

In the current year under these circumstances, it will be necessary to issue a modified opinion. Given the claimed value of the expenses, it is likely that the matter will be considered material but not pervasive to the financial statements and a qualified opinion will be issued.

A Basis for Qualified Opinion section should be included immediately after the Auditor's Opinion section, and should describe the matter giving rise to the modification.

Fire

Audit procedures have confirmed that the matter has been satisfactorily reflected in the financial statements. There are therefore no misstatements relevant to this matter and no modification to the audit opinion is necessary.

BPP
LEARNING
MEDIA

However, the accident caused the temporary suspension of operations for a number of months, with a significant impact on the results for the year. Overall, the associated reduction in sales and the expenses relating to the repairs have contributed to a $46 million reduction in profits. This may make interpretation of the current year's results difficult. Crow Co is still unable to operate at full capacity, so the matter will continue to affect performance in the following year.

This represents a major catastrophe which has had and continues to have a significant effect on the company's financial position. The disclosures provided by management in relation to this constitute a matter of fundamental importance to users, and should be referred to in an Emphasis of Matter paragraph by Chester & Co, as described in ISA 706 *Emphasis of Matter Paragraphs and Other Matter Paragraphs in the Independent Auditor's Report*.

The auditor should include the paragraph in a separate section of the auditor's report with an appropriate heading that includes the term 'Emphasis of Matter'. It may be appropriate for the paragraph to be entitled 'Emphasis of Matter – effects of a fire'. The placement of the paragraph depends on the auditor's judgement of the significance and the nature of the matter being described. It is likely that in these circumstances it should be placed directly after the basis for qualified opinion paragraph.

The paragraph should clearly refer to the matter being emphasised, including a reference to where the full description of the matter may be found in the financial statements. The paragraph should make it clear that the audit opinion is not modified in respect of this matter.

64 Leopard

Workbook references. Chapters 2 and 12.

Top tips. Part (a) covered due diligence, and had a slightly unusual requirement that asked you to explain why each matter required further investigation. It is clearly important that your answer is focused on this specific requirement. In spite of this, however, your answer to this question would have covered much of the same material as a normal 'matters to consider' requirement.

The two issues themselves are relatively clear, but a few points can be noted. Firstly, your answer must focus on the issues from the point of view of valuing the business, rather than from a normal auditing or financial reporting perspective. Thus inventory valuation, for example, arises as a matter to consider; this is not from the perspective of IAS 2 *Inventories*, however, but for the purpose of determining the value of Zebra Co's assets.

Secondly, there are many points in the scenario that are not resolved. Much of the model answer consists of speculation about what might happen, which is important because the due diligence is focused on the possible value of the business in the future. This entails a different perspective from that of an external auditor.

Finally, it should be clear from the requirement that no marks are available for general theoretical discussions of the nature of due diligence.

Part (b) was altogether more difficult. This type of situation has been examined before, and you should be able to point out the advocacy and intimidation threats. The point about not assuming a management responsibility is important too, however, as is the self-review threat in relation to the loan application.

Easy marks. There are no particular easy marks in this question, with the possible exception of those available for stating what the ethical threat to independence is, and then explaining why this is a threat.

Marking scheme

Marks

(a) (i) **Due diligence investigation**

Generally up to 1 ½ marks for each matter discussed. Award ½ mark for identification of a relevant point and up to a further 1 mark for appropriate discussion of the relevance of this point to the specific case.

Termination of contract:
- Impact on forecast revenues, costs and cash flows
- Wider implications of a new, cheaper supplier entering the market
- Potential impairment of assets employed specifically for the client

Gifted land:
- Possible restriction on sale to Cheetah Co
- Possible restriction on how land is used if purchased
- Uncertainty regarding how to value the land

Maximum   6

(ii) **Procedures**

Up to 1 mark for each adequately explained procedure. Award ½ mark for relevant procedures which are poorly explained:
- Analytically review historic sales to customer
- Enquire of management about further repercussions
- Analytically review sales by customer to identify other major ones
- Review trade contracts/agreements with other major customers
- Inspect correspondence with major customers
- Identify inventories produced specifically for customer
- Inspect forecasts to ensure adequate adjustment made
- Inspect terms of gifted land
- Enquire of legal adviser re. impact of restrictions
- Seek a valuation from an expert
- Identify potential options for land
- Prepare revised forecast excluding land

Maximum   6

(b) **Enquiries**
Up to 1 mark for each appropriately explained matter and
recommended response. Award ½ mark for relevant
matters/responses which are poorly explained:
–   Advocacy threat
–   Management responsibility
–   Self-review: loan transaction
–   Intimidation threat
–   Purpose/scope of meeting
–   Ascertain purpose of attending meeting
–   Obtain written representation
–   Politely decline to attend
–   Explain that you are unable to review interim engagement
    progress

Maximum   <u>8</u>

Total   <u>**20**</u>

(a) (i) **Why the matters require further investigation**

Termination of contract

Impact on forecasts

The loss of the customer may lead to a reduction in forecast revenue by as much as 5% per year. This may also lead to a reduction in costs specifically relevant to servicing the customer. For example, sales staff specifically allocated to servicing this client.

This is significant because the forecast future cash flows of Zebra Co will be critical in determining the value of the company and the price offered by Cheetah Co. It is therefore vital to establish all of the potential revenue and cost implications of the loss of the customer to ascertain the impact on the purchase price.

Wider implications of new competitor

The customer referred to has switched to a new, cheaper supplier. This may have wider implications if the new supplier is directly targeting the customers of Zebra Co. It is possible that other customers may switch to the new supplier in the future, which would have further implications on future revenue and cost forecasts.

It may not be possible to determine the potential impact of the new supplier at this point, which increases the level of uncertainty associated with the potential acquisition. Cheetah Co may be able to use this uncertainty as a tool for bargaining with the owners of Zebra Co over the final agreed price.

Possible impairment of other assets

The loss of a major customer may be an indication of impairment of the assets of Zebra Co. This will be particularly relevant if Zebra Co holds specific assets for manufacturing the unique furniture products made for this client.

As well as production assets, Zebra Co may also be holding inventories which are specifically relevant to the customer which cannot be re-used elsewhere or sold to other customers. If this is the case, these inventories will almost certainly be impaired.

If not performed at the year end, it may now be appropriate to conduct an impairment review to ensure that the valuation of the assets, as presented in the financial statements, is still appropriate in the circumstances.

Gifted land

Possible restriction on sale

The restriction on the sale of the land may mean that Zebra Co is prohibited from including the land as part of the acquisition by Cheetah Co. It is likely that following acquisition, Cheetah Co will not be able to initiate a sale of the land to an external company or develop or change its current use. This may act as a deal breaker if Cheetah Co is not able to obtain control over the land surrounding the entrance to the production facilities.

If Zebra Co is not permitted to include the land as part of the deal with Cheetah Co, then this may also have an impact on the purchase price as the owners of Zebra Co may have attributed some value to the land in their expectation of the price which they can achieve. If so, it will be important to ascertain the value attributed to the land by the owners to negotiate the reduction of the purchase price.

Possible limitation on future usage

If the land can be included as part of the acquisition deal, the restrictions may also mean that Cheetah Co is not able to use the land for their intended purpose, such as the future expansion of production facilities, resulting in the acquisition of Zebra Co not being an appropriate strategic fit for Cheetah Co if one of the key aims is future expansion. If this is the case, then this will severely limit the value of the land to the company.

If the land can be acquired but cannot be developed, it is likely that there will be ongoing maintenance costs and potentially other requirements and conditions regarding the upkeep of the nature reserve set out by the local authority, which need to be understood as part of the review. The cost of maintenance may result in a net annual cost to the business and this needs to be quantified as part of the due diligence work.

It will be vital to ascertain what restrictions are in place and whether the directors of Cheetah Co believe they can extract any value from the use of the land.

Based upon this, the directors of Cheetah Co may wish to try and negotiate the purchase of Zebra Co without the associated land or they may wish to negotiate a lower price based on the restricted usage.

Uncertainty regarding valuation

It may be difficult to accurately value the piece of land. The value attributed to it in the financial statements is zero, so this may not provide an appropriate basis for estimating the resale value. A land valuation expert may be able to provide an estimation of the current market value of the land without restriction on its use but they may find it difficult to accurately value how much it is worth with the local authority restrictions. It may also be difficult to value the land based on the future cash flows attributable to it if it is not currently in use and its future usage is uncertain.

As a result, the valuation of the land may become a point of significant negotiation between the directors of Cheetah Co and Zebra Co. This may also become a deal breaker if the two parties are unable to reach agreement on the matter.

(ii) **Procedures**

Termination of contract

Analytically review the total historic value of revenue earned from the customer to help determine an appropriate estimate for the potential loss of future revenues and cash inflows.

Enquire of management whether the loss of the customer will have any other repercussions, such as the sale of specific assets or the redundancy of staff and the costs associated with this if such action was required.

Perform an analytical review to identify other major customers by value of revenue contributions to the business. For all major customers identified, review any supply agreements/contracts in place to determine when they expire.

If any contracts with major customers are due to expire within the next few years, enquire of management whether any discussions have taken place with those customers in relation to renegotiating the terms.

Obtain any correspondence available with the identified major customers to identify whether there is any indication that they may attempt to either renegotiate the terms of their agreements or switch them to a new supplier.

Enquire of a relevant manager, such as a production manager or sales manager, whether there is any specific inventory which has been produced in relation to the customer who is not renewing their agreement. If this is the case, obtain a breakdown of the total inventories produced for this client and discuss with management whether they will be able to sell this inventory at full price given the notice to terminate the contract.

Inspect the forecasts prepared by management to ensure that the changes to the revenue and cost streams identified above have been appropriately incorporated.

Gifted land

Review the terms supplied when the land was originally gifted to Zebra Co. Identify the specific restrictions in relation to how the land may be used and who the land may be sold to in the future.

Enquire of a legal adviser whether this will have any impact in relation to the sale of the land to Cheetah Co and their consequent usage of it.

Engage a land valuation expert to provide a valuation of the land. Ask them to consider the implications of the restrictions imposed upon the land in the valuation.

If Zebra Co is not permitted to sell the land, or the restrictions imposed on the usage of the land are too restrictive, seek legal advice in relation to the potential options, including whether the land can be gifted back to the local authority prior to the acquisition.

Inspect the forecasts prepared by the management of Zebra Co to identify the specific forecast costs and revenues associated with the usage of the land. Prepare a revised version of the forecasts which excludes these revenues and costs to identify the potential implications on the forecasts if the deal is conducted excluding the gifted land.

(b) **Ethical and other professional issues**

Advocacy threat

Accompanying the client to a meeting with their bankers will create an advocacy threat to objectivity as Leopard & Co may be perceived to be representatives of Cheetah Co.

This is particularly relevant as the bank may wish to establish a number of facts relating to the suitability of providing finance to Cheetah Co. For example, they may ask for representations that the company will continue as a going concern and that any forecast cash flows presented are accurate. As Cheetah Co's auditor, these questions may be directed at the firm's representatives and the bank may take any response provided to their questions as assurance over these matters.

Management responsibility

Leopard & Co must also be careful that in providing services relating to the potential acquisition of Zebra Co and the associated financing arrangements that the firm is not assuming a management responsibility. Although the terms of the engagement have not yet been confirmed, it is likely that by attending the meeting with the client, the audit firm will give the impression of supporting the acquisition of Zebra Co and therefore give credit to the decision.

The IESBA *Code of Ethics for Professional Accountants* (the *Code*) specifically states that the firm shall not assume a management responsibility for an audit client as the threats created would be so significant that no safeguards could reduce the threats to an acceptable level.

Self-review threat – loan transaction

The *Code* specifically states that providing assistance in finance raising transactions for audit clients also creates a self-review threat to objectivity. A self-review threat arises where the outcome or consequences of a corporate finance service provided by the audit firm may be material to the financial statements under review.

This is a particular problem as the transaction will directly affect the financial statements, which the audit team will be responsible for auditing in consequent financial periods and therefore the audit team is likely to be more accepting of information provided or may not investigate issues as thoroughly, as the team may feel that much of this has been done via the due diligence.

Intimidation threat

The request by Cheetah Co to ensure that the interim review does not impede the application for a loan may be perceived as intimidation by the client. It appears as though they are putting pressure on Leopard & Co to finish the work based on the deadlines imposed by the bank, rather than those originally agreed with the client. This may force the auditor into changing their approach to any remaining procedures which would be considered to be undue influence of the client over the procedures performed.

This appears to be supported by a further threat relating to the upcoming tender for the audit. The management team of Cheetah Co appears to be suggesting that failing to ensure the interim review is completed on time for the loan decision may have an adverse impact on any consequent tender bid.

Purpose of meeting

It is not clear why representatives of Leopard & Co have been invited to attend the meeting with the bank. The purpose of both the due diligence service and the interim review is to report to the directors and owners of Cheetah Co, respectively. The firm has no responsibility to report to any third party, including potential lenders.

There may be an expectation for Leopard & Co to provide assurances to the bank in relation to the accuracy of forecasts presented or the financial position of Cheetah Co. If this is the case, it is outside the scope of any of the current engagements and Leopard & Co would not be in a position to provide this assurance.

Actions

The firm should ascertain the purpose of attending the meeting with the bank; if there is any expectation that it will provide assurances to the bank, then the request should be declined, explaining to Cheetah Co that the firm's responsibilities extend to reporting to the management and the owners of the company and not to any third parties.

If there is no expectation to provide any assurances and the firm is expected to attend the meeting solely in regard to the role of providing due diligence services to Cheetah Co and assisting them in determining a purchase price, then it may be possible for representatives of

BPP
LEARNING

Leopard & Co to attend. It must be made clear, however, that no members of the audit team/interim audit team will be able to attend and the firm will not be permitted to make any representations to the bank. A written representation should be obtained from management clarifying these points. In order to reduce the risk of Leopard & Co assuming a management responsibility, the representation should also state that Cheetah Co has assigned responsibility for the final decisions relating to the acquisition and financing to a suitably experienced individual within the company. Futher, that Cheetah Co's management will provide oversight of the services performed, will evaluate the adequacy of the outcome of the services for the purposes of Cheetah Co, and accept responsibility for the actions to be taken as a result of the services performed by Leopard & Co.

On balance, Leopard & Co may consider that the threats, both real and perceived, are too great and it would be most prudent not to attend the meeting. If this is the case, Leopard & Co should politely decline the invitation, explaining the reasons why it is inappropriate.

Leopard & Co should communicate with the directors of Cheetah Co explaining that the firm is unable to be involved in the interim review or to review any of the working papers. Leopard & Co should explain the reasons to the client. The firm should also explain that, if the client has any concerns, they should communicate with the interim review engagement partner to ascertain a reasonable timeframe for conclusion of this engagement.

65 Apricot and Lychee

Workbook references. Chapters 10 and 13.

Top tips. Part (a) should have been straightforward, provided that you had prepared this area. A good approach might be just to go down the forecast thinking about what procedures you could do to test each row of figures. The additional information given at the bottom of the question is the examining team's attempt to give you some context for the forecast. What you need to do is use this information to think of procedures that use this information to test the forecast. It should be possible to think of a procedure relating to virtually every point of information given – just as you should be able to think of a point for virtually every line in the forecast itself.

Note that our answer to this part of the question gives more points that you could probably have written down in the exam, although it is by no means comprehensive. Your approach should be to make sure that you get enough **good points** down in the time available. You should concentrate on properly developing the points that you do make, rather than taking the familiar 'scatter-gun' approach that so often characterises weaker students. It is also a good idea to try to cover all of the areas of the question (ie of the forecast), as you will probably be able to make stronger points over a number areas (by saying the obvious things that there are to say about each) than you would if you get bogged down in just one area of the question. Make sure you stick to your time!

Part (b) saw the examining team returning to an area that was mentioned in a previous examining team's report as being poorly understood by students. If you had been diligent and had read this report, you would have revised this area carefully if this was your real exam. It would be a good idea for you to do this! The actual content of the question was not difficult, again provided that you had revised it thoroughly.

This time, our answer does represent something that a student could achieve in an exam – see the examining team's answer for something more comprehensive. You will notice that as this is a standalone, knowledge-based requirement, the answer can be based closely on the content of the Workbook – although it must still of course be applied to the scenario.

Part (c)(i) contained some easy marks for knowing the financial reporting implications of a proposed restructuring after the year end. The examining team has previously written an article in which they emphasised the importance of financial reporting knowledge for the AAA exam, so take note! Generally speaking, the financial reporting found in AAA is not going to be as intricate as in SBR, but if you don't revise it then you are depriving yourself of the easy marks to be found in questions like this one.

Although the financial reporting marks here were easy, the audit marks here were not. Many students would have struggled to think of enough procedures to make it up to five marks here. What is important in this situation is making sure that the procedures you suggest are specific. Notice that the marking scheme only awards marks here 'per specific procedure provided'. The examining team frequently complains that most students are able to write things like 'look at the board minutes', but that to get the marks a student would need to be more specific, saying something like 'verify the approval both of the restructuring plan itself and of the announcement of the plan by reviewing board minutes'. Being specific in what you write can help you turn your general ideas of what the audit procedures might be into actual marks.

You should have been able to pass part (c)(ii) easily, as this is a major area of the syllabus and you should know it well. Whenever a question asks you to 'recommend action', the main thing an auditor can do is modify/qualify the auditor's opinion. Marks were therefore available just for identifying the type of modification/qualification, the effect on the opinion, and then the fact that the auditor's report should contain a description of the reason for the modification.

Easy marks. Marks were available in part (a) just for saying 'agree the opening cash balance to the bank statement/reconciliation', and 'cast the forecast'. These are very obvious marks, and would be applicable to virtually any other question relating to the audit of cash flow forecasts. Ignore them at your peril!

There is also an easy ½ mark in part (b) for saying that the report should have a title and an addressee.

The mark in part (c) for just defining subsequent events is easy.

ACCA examining team's comments. This was by far the least popular of the optional questions in Section B, but those that did attempt the question tended to perform well.

Requirement (a) asked candidates to recommend the procedures that should be performed on the cash flow projection. The majority of answers produced many specific procedures, based on the information provided. Candidates that approached the answer logically and worked through each item on the cash flow forecast to derive appropriate procedures performed very well. However, some answers were limited to enquiry with management, which restricted the marks that could be awarded.

Requirement (b) asked for an explanation of the main contents of the assurance report that would be provided. Most candidates could make an attempt at a list of contents, but very few answers provided sufficient explanation of the content identified, eg most could identify that a statement of negative assurance would be provided, but few explained what that meant. Some answers provided a contrast between an audit and an assurance report, which was not asked for. The main problem with answers to this requirement is that they were just too brief for the marks available.

Unfortunately, performance on requirement (c) was on the whole unsatisfactory. In relation to part (c)(i), the main problems were:

- Incorrect or absent materiality calculations

- Identifying the event as both adjusting and non-adjusting according to IAS 10, eg stating that the event is non-adjusting but that a provision should be recognised in the statement of financial position

- Failing to provide any audit procedures at all, other than 'discuss with management'

- Writing at length about going concern issues – though this may be a consideration, the question clearly states that the factory in question is being closed and relocated, so there is no hint that the company is insolvent or that operations are likely to cease

Requirement (c)(ii) asked candidates to recommend the actions to be taken by the auditor if the financial statements were not amended. The approach taken by many candidates here was to list every possible type of modification or qualification to the auditor's report, in the hope that one of them would be a correct answer. This displays a complete lack of understanding of the impact of non-amended financial statements, which is a crucial area of knowledge for this syllabus. It also indicates a lack of professional judgment skills. Marks are not awarded to candidates who attempt to 'hedge their bets' in this manner.

Marking scheme

Marks

(a) **Procedures on cash flow forecast**
Generally 1 mark per specific procedure from ideas list:
– Accuracy checks – recalculation
– Agree opening cash position
– Recalculate patterns of cash in and out for credit sales and purchases
– Agree patterns using aged receivables analysis/working capital ratios
– Agree discounts received and allowed to invoices/contracts/correspondences
– Agree derivation of figures from profit forecast
– Agree monthly salary expense to payroll
– Review content of overheads – check non-cash expenses not included
– Review for missing outflows eg tax and finance charges
– Agree premises costs eg to legal documents
– Discuss timing of fixtures cash flow
– General enquiries with the preparer of the forecast

Maximum   11

(b) **Content of an assurance report**
Up to 1 mark per point if explained:
– Title/addressee (½ mark)
– Identification of PFI
– Management responsibility
– Purpose of PFI
– Restricted use of PFI
– Negative assurance opinion re assumptions
– Opinion on presentation

Maximum   5

(c) (i) **Audit procedures in respect of announcement of restructuring**
1 mark per specific procedure provided:
– Non-adjusting event after the reporting date
– 1 mark for calculation/consideration of materiality which can be awarded in either (b)(i) or (b)(ii)
– IAS 10 requires note to financial statements
– Obtain copy of announcement and review for details
– Confirm date of approval and announcement of restructuring
– Read minutes of board meetings where the restructuring was discussed

Marks

- Agree numerical disclosures to supporting documentation
- Consider completeness of the amount disclosed
- Discuss/review potential note to financial statements

Maximum 5

(ii) **Action to be taken if amendments not made**

Marks to be awarded as follows:

1 mark for each comment:

- Material misstatement
- Except for opinion
- Description of reason for qualification
- Report to those charged with governance
- Raise at AGM

Maximum 4

Total 25

(a) **General procedures**

(i) Check that the forecast casts.

(ii) Check that the opening cash balance agrees to bank reconciliations and statements.

(iii) Enquire as to who prepared the forecast, and verify that they are competent to do so (evidence eg by being a chartered certified accountant).

Operating cash receipts

(i) Enquire as to the basis for the forecast rise in both cash and credit sales receipts.

(ii) Perform analytical procedures on historical information to confirm reasonableness of forecast revenues, taking into account knowledge of the business.

(iii) Confirm split between cash and credit sales to past trends and to knowledge of the business.

(iv) Recalculate cash receipts from credit sales from revenue figures in profit forecast and ageing structure of receivables.

(v) Verify that the 10% discount for cash payment has been taken into account when calculating cash received from cash sales.

(vi) Enquire as to who Apricot's major customers are and confirm that they are to continue trading with Apricot, eg that none are going into administration.

Operating cash payments

(i) Confirm that forecast is prepared on the assumption that all purchases are paid for within 30 days.

(ii) Confirm that 12% supplier discount is received from suppliers' invoices, supplier statements, etc.

(iii) Confirm that forecast is prepared on the assumption of receiving the 12% supplier discount.

(iv) Verify the accuracy of the statement that suppliers are paid within 30 days by reviewing aged payables analyses for historical information.

(v) Agree the salary payments to payroll information.

BPP
LEARNING
MEDIA

(vi)   Review the overheads to ensure that non-cash items such as depreciation are not included.

(vii)   Enquire as to the reason for no outflows for taxation (eg Corporation Tax, VAT).

Other cash flows

(i)   Agree the cost of the licence to supporting information from the health and safety authority, and confirm the cost of $35,000.

(ii)   Enquire as to the likelihood of actually receiving the licence – whether the inspection will be passed. For example: if the inspection has already taken place, ask what the result was; if it has not taken place, consider the use of a health & safety expert.

(iii)   Agree the fixtures outflow of $60,000 to underlying information, eg to supplier quotations.

(iv)   Confirm that the fixtures outflow will take place during March – this seems unlikely given that the premises will only be bought on 30 March. This may cast doubt over the reliability of other information in the forecast.

(v)   Agree the $500,000 to be paid for the premises to documentation and verify that it is complete.

(b)   In accordance with the requirements of ISAE 3400, the report should contain the following:

(i)   Title and addressee

(ii)   Identification of the prospective financial information (PFI) being reported on

(iii)   A reference to the purpose of the PFI, which in this case is to provide assurance to Pik Choi's financial advisor regarding Apricot Co's cash flow forecast

(iv)   A statement of negative assurance as to whether the assumptions provide a reasonable basis for the prospective financial information

(v)   An opinion as to whether the prospective financial information is properly prepared on the basis of the assumptions and is presented in accordance with the relevant financial reporting framework

(vi)   Date of the report, auditor's address and signature

(c)   (i)   The restructuring does not relate to conditions at the reporting date, so under IAS 10 *Events After the Reporting Period* this is not an adjusting event. IAS 10 requires that this event be disclosed in the financial statements, usually by way of a note explaining the event and its financial effect (IAS 10: para. 21).

Audit procedures would include:

- Verifying that management have included a note disclosing this event in the financial statements, and that it is drafted in line with IAS 10

- Agreeing the estimated cost of the closure to underlying calculations and supporting documentation, such as staff employment contracts

- Reviewing the announcement for details, and agree these details to the disclosures made in the financial statements

- Reviewing board minutes for details of the plan and to verify that it has been approved by the board

- Discussing the reasons for the plan with management and consider whether it is consistent with the auditor's knowledge of the business

(ii)   If the financial statements are not amended then they are not in accordance with IAS 10. Considering the materiality of the cost of closure:

Based on revenue: $\dfrac{\$250,000}{\$15m} = 1.67\%$

Based on profit: $\dfrac{\$250,000}{\$3m} = 8.3\%$

Based on assets: $\dfrac{\$250,000}{\$80m} = <1\%$

The cost of closure is material to the statement of profit or loss, so non-disclosure of this event is a material misstatement. In line with ISA 705 *Modifications to the Opinion in the Independent Auditor's Report*, the auditor should express a qualified 'except for' opinion, as the misstatement is material but not so pervasive as to render the statement of profit or loss meaningless.

The auditor's report should contain a paragraph discussing the reasons for the modified opinion, in which the auditor would explain the nature of the costs not disclosed, state the financial effect of the costs and state that this is in breach of IAS 10. It would also be helpful for the auditor to state that this does not affect profit for the year, but is a disclosure only.

66 Mizzen

Workbook reference. Chapter 12.

Top Tips. In part (a) it is crucial that you give only three benefits of due diligence, as any further benefits are unlikely to be marked. Another thing to avoid doing is writing about what a due diligence review is – this is not asked for in the requirement, and again receives no marks, serving only to eat into your time.

Although part (a) could be approached as a simply knowledge-based requirement, there are actually several clues in the scenario which you may have picked up on in your answer. For example, the fact that 'Baltimore Co has not previously acquired another company' suggests that it 'lacks the necessary skills' not just to set up a website, but to do a due diligence too.

Do not overlook the requirement in part (b) to recommend additional information needed. As long as you state not just what you need but also why you need it, you can pick up a lot of marks here with relatively little effort.

Part (c) should have been straightforward, and you may have decided to do this part of the question before part (b). Note that a due diligence review does not give 'negative assurance' but rather 'limited assurance' which is expressed in a negative form of words.

It is also worth noting that although this question features an embedded style of requirement, there are no professional marks available.

Easy marks. The whole of part (c) was easy – you should have been able to score close to full marks here.

ACCA examining team's report. This question focused on due diligence, a topic that had appeared in examinations several times previous to this sitting. The scenario described a due diligence assignment to be performed on the target company Mizzen Co, at the request of Baltimore Co. The history and activities of the target company was described in some detail, and some financial information provided for the last four years. For Baltimore Co this would be their first acquisition, and was being considered as a means to diversify the company's operations.

BPP
LEARNING

Requirement (a) asked candidates to discuss three benefits to Baltimore Co of a due diligence review being performed on Mizzen Co. While some reasonable answers were given, possibly by candidates who had practiced the past exam question containing a similar requirement, on the whole answers were unsatisfactory. The following factors contributed to inadequate performance in relation to this requirement:

- Writing answers that were much too brief for the marks available – it was common to see three sentences given as an answer to this requirement, which cannot be enough for a 6-mark requirement.

- At the other extreme, some very lengthy answers were given that usually failed to answer the question requirement and instead either simply wrote in detail on how a due diligence assignment should be performed, or suggested in some detail the operational benefits to Baltimore Co of acquiring Mizzen Co.

- Many answers failed to limit to three benefits and instead provided a bullet point list of benefits that were not discussed at all.

Requirement (b) was the main part of the question, and asked candidates, for 16 marks, to identify and explain the matters that the due diligence review would focus on, and to recommend the additional information needed. The answers provided to this requirement were extremely mixed in quality. There were some exceptionally sound answers, explaining relevant matters in sufficient depth, and using the financial information provided to come up with reasonable points. These answers also provided relevant requests for additional information.

However, the majority of answers were unsatisfactory. Most candidates picked up at least a few marks by identifying some of the matters that the review would focus on, but as in Question One, many candidates let themselves down by failing to explain the matters that they had identified in any real depth. It was common for answers to simply contain a list of bullet points with very little explanation at all, and only a limited amount of marks can be awarded to answers of this type.

Some points were better dealt with, including the following:

- Most answers picked up on the fact that Mizzen Co used premises owned by the venture capitalist company, and the fact that this arrangement would probably cease on the acquisition.

- Many candidates realised that the two founders of Mizzen Co were crucial to the company's success and that without them the acquisition would probably be pointless.

- Many candidates used the financial information to some extent, though sometimes only in a very limited way, but most picked up on the fact that Mizzen Co was paying finance charges, and so information would be needed to understand what those charges relate to.

- Many answers considered that revenue recognition would be a matter to focus on due to the relatively complex nature of the company's revenue streams.

- Some answers performed a little analytical review on the financial information to reveal that expenses were not increasing in line with revenue, and that this would need to be investigated.

The answers that were unsatisfactory, as well as containing inadequately explained points as mentioned above, also tended to focus too much on financial reporting matters, for example giving very lengthy discussions on the calculation of goodwill. While the accounting treatment of some items certainly was relevant to the answer, just focusing on these matters meant that candidates did not provide a broad enough range of comments to score well.

Another factor leading to poor marks for this requirement was that many candidates simply failed to recommend any additional information at all that would be needed in the review. Many candidates missed out on marks here, for example for recommending that a statement of financial position, management accounts and cash flow forecasts would be needed.

Some candidates supplied a lengthy discussion of matters relating to the acceptance of the due diligence assignment, such as agreeing fees and clarifying deadlines, which was not asked for.

Requirement (c) required candidates to describe the type of conclusion that would be issued for a due diligence report and to compare this to an audit report. This was well answered by most candidates, who compared the type of assurance that could be offered for a due diligence assignment with that given in an audit report, and linked this to the type of work that is carried out. Credit was awarded for different types of answers, as some discussed due diligence as being performed as agreed upon procedures rather than a review engagement, either of which is appropriate.

Marking scheme

Marks

(a) **Benefit of due diligence**
Up to 2 marks for each benefit discussed:
- Identification of assets and liabilities
- Valuation of assets and liabilities
- Review of operational issues
- Examination of financial position and performance
- Added credibility and expertise
- Added value for negotiation of purchase price
- Other advice can be given, eg on obtaining finance

Maximum   6

(b) **Areas to focus on and additional information**
Generally up to 1½ marks for each explanation of area to focus on:
- Equity owners of Mizzen Co and involvement of BizGrow
- Key skills and expertise
- Internally generated intangible assets
- Premises
- Other intangible assets
- Accounting policy on revenue recognition
- Sustainability and relevance of revenue streams
- Operating expenses
- Finance charges
- Cash management

1 mark for each specific additional information recommended:
- Contract or legal documentation dealing with BizGrow's investment in Mizzen Co
- A register of shareholders showing all shareholders of Mizzen Co
- An organisational structure
- A list of employees and their role within the company, obligations and compensation
- A list of freelance web designers used by Mizzen Co, and a description of the work they perform
- The key terms of contracts or agreements with freelance web designers

BPP
LEARNING

- A list of all IT innovations which have been created and developed by Mizzen Co, and details of any patent or copyright agreements relating to them
- Agreements with employees regarding assignment of intellectual property and confidentiality
- Copies of the customer databases
- A list of companies which have contracts with Mizzen Co for website development and maintenance
- A copy of all contracts with customers for review of the period for maintenance
- A breakdown of the revenue that has been generated from making each database available to other companies, and the dates when they were made available
- A summary of the controls which are in place to ensure that the database details are regularly updated
- A copy of the premises rental agreement with BizGrow
- Non-current asset register showing descriptions and values of all assets used in the business
- Copies of any lease agreements
- Details of any capital expenditure budgets for previous accounting periods, and any planned capital expenditure in the future
- Mizzen Co's stated accounting policy on revenue recognition
- Systems and controls documentation over the processing of revenue receipts
- Analysis of expenses included in operating expenses for each year and copies of documentation relating to ongoing expenses such as salaries and other overheads
- Copies of management accounts to agree expenses in the audited accounts are in line and to perform more detailed analytical review
- The full set of financial statements and auditor's reports
- Any agreements with banks or other external providers of finance

| | Maximum | 16 |

(c) **Conclusion on due diligence**
Generally 1 mark for each discussion point:
- Due diligence report to express conclusion using a negative form of words
- Limited assurance due to nature of work performed
- Audit opinion is a positive opinion of reasonable assurance

| | Maximum | 3 |

Total **25**

(a) **Identifying assets**

The review would aim to identify and value the assets and liabilities of the target company. This would include items not recognised on Mizzen Co's financial statements. For example, it is possible that Mizzen may have intangible assets that are not recognised separately, but which may be valued. These could become part of any goodwill acquired on acquisition.

The review would also seek to discover previously hidden liabilities, such as contingent liabilities, which could potentially be very significant to Baltimore Co.

Operational issues

The review would focus on operational issues. This might include, for example, an examination of Mizzen's different revenue streams with a view to assessing how Baltimore might seek to benefit from them after the acquisition. The review may also focus on the strategic fit between Baltimore and Mizzen, attempting to determine the extent to which Mizzen meets Baltimore's needs.

This could involve a review of Mizzen's financial position and performance, focusing in particular on its potential for future growth or profitability.

Credibility

Obtaining an external due diligence review would allow Baltimore's management to focus on its own operational matters and yet still receive a timely review. Such a review would be conducted by an independent expert, with experience and knowledge in this area which Baltimore's management lacks, since it has not previously acquired another company. The review would give the benefit of a sharp, fresh pair of eyes which might spot things that Baltimore's management may have missed.

It is for this reason that an externally provided review would be more credible than an internal one, something which may help persuade Baltimore's bank to lend it the money which it believes itself to need.

(b) **Equity owners**

It is crucial to determine the identity of Mizzen's majority shareholder. It appears likely that this is Bizgrow, but further information is needed.

This is important because if Bizgrow does own the shares then it is with Bizgrow that Baltimore would need to negotiate the purchase of Mizzen. If Bizgrow does not want to sell its shares then Mizzen cannot be bought. However, it is unclear how Baltimore came to identify Mizzen as an acquisition target in the first place, and it is possible that Bizgrow may have had something to do with this.

Funding

It is noted that Vic and Lou secured funds from Bizgrow. The nature of any agreement that was made needs to be ascertained, as it is possible that Mizzen may owe Bizgrow a substantial amount of money. This would be material to any decision Baltimore might make about the acquisition.

The precise nature of the ongoing relationship between Mizzen and Bizgrow is unclear. It is possible that Bizgrow is involved with Mizzen at an operational level. Any agreements between the two parties should be obtained and scrutinised.

Examination of the statement of profit or loss reveals a finance cost of $250,000 which appears to be fixed. It is unlikely that this is interest on a loan because loan interest would change as the balance is repaid. It is therefore possible that this is a management charge from Bizgrow, which would be indicative of ongoing involvement. We would need to understand the nature of any liabilities Mizzen may have in relation to this charge.

Reputation

Mizzen's good reputation, and its having won awards for website design, is key evidence for its expertise in this area. This should be verified to external evidence. Customer satisfaction could be gauged by obtaining the results of any customer satisfaction surveys that may have been conducted.

BPP
LEARNING

Vic and Lou

Vic and Lou appear to be crucial to the success of Mizzen, so Baltimore would want them to be involved in future. It is not certain, however, that they would want to be involved with Baltimore and its website, and they may wish to concentrate on their own more innovative work. The acquisition would be much less attractive to Baltimore were they to leave.

Vic and Lou's intentions post-acquisition should be determined. It may be possible to structure any future deal in such a way that Vic and Lou would be required to continue working at Mizzen for a set period after the acquisition.

Staff

Mizzen is a business with few tangible assets, which relies heavily on the expertise of its staff, who may leave after any acquisition – particularly if Vic and Lou were to leave. It would make little sense to acquire Mizzen for its staff, only to find that they leave on acquisition.

An organisational structure should be obtained in order to identify management and key personnel within Mizzen.

It is also possible that Baltimore may wish to restructure Mizzen after acquisition. In this case it is likely that redundancy payments would need to be made to staff members losing their jobs. The amount of any possible liability in this eventuality should be estimated as part of the review.

Freelancers

Mizzen has been using freelancers recently, which may result in a drop in the quality of work done by comparison with established staff. This should be investigated as it may affect Mizzen's ostensibly impeccable reputation.

Intangible assets

Mizzen has few assets, but is likely to have important intangible assets which would form part of any goodwill paid on acquisition. Vic and Lou have developed new website interfaces, and it should be determined whether any resulting intellectual property belongs to them personally or to Mizzen. Valuing these assets is likely to be difficult.

Customer databases should also be valued, which again is likely to be difficult owing to the absence of any active market for assets of this kind.

Premises

It is apparent that the $1,000 nominal rent paid to Bizgrow would increase after the acquisition, so it should be determined what an equivalent market rent might be for the premises. Alternatively, the premises may no longer be available, in which case the rent should be ascertained for premises meeting Mizzen's needs. It may be possible for Mizzen to operate from Baltimore's premises, in which case any opportunity costs should be considered.

Tangible assets

Mizzen's tangible assets need to be valued, and it should be determined whether they are owned or held under lease, as it is possible that Mizzen may be liable for any future lease payments.

Revenue recognition

The first revenue stream should be split into two components, with the revenue relating to maintenance being recognised as deferred income and spread over the contract period. There is a risk that revenue is recognised too early, inflating Mizzen's profit in the short term.

Relevance of revenue

Baltimore needs Mizzen to develop a website for it, and it should be asked whether Baltimore might be better off simply paying Mizzen $10,000 to develop a website rather than acquiring the whole company.

It is clear that Mizzen would have the expertise to do this because it operates its own subscription-based website. It should therefore be able to create something of a similar nature for Baltimore.

The third revenue stream in particular does not appear relevant to Baltimore, and it should be considered how this revenue stream would be managed after the acquisition.

Revenue increase

Revenue rose 23.7% from 20X2 to 20X3, which is an impressive increase although it is lower than the 60.4% increase from 20X1 to 20X2. The question is whether such a growth rate might feasibly be achieved in the future. It will therefore be necessary to scrutinise Mizzen's forecasts and plans for future growth.

Operating expenses

Operating expenses in 20X2 were 58.3% of revenue, but only 49.6% in 20X3. This is unusual, and may be indicative of efficiencies being achieved as Mizzen grows. It does not, however, tally with the fact that freelancers have been used this year, which would be expected to increase operating expenses in relation to revenue.

A detailed review needs to be performed on operating expenses to ensure that expenses are complete and are recorded accurately.

Cash

Mizzen's cash position should be confirmed to its bank statement. Although the company is not lacking cash, from its statements of profit or loss one would expect it to be in a better cash position than it is in. It is possible that cash has been paid out in dividends to shareholders.

Further information

- Copy of Mizzen's register of shareholders, to determine the identity of the majority shareholder

- Copy of any agreement between Bizgrow and Vic and Lou, to help understand their ongoing relationship as well as Bizgrow's planned exit route

- Agreements of any loans received by Mizzen

- Full audited financial statements of Mizzen

- Details of awards won for website design, including press reports, trade journals, for evidence of Mizzen's good reputation

- Details of any customer satisfaction surveys conducted by Mizzen

- Copies of contracts with Vic and Lou

- Copy of organisational structure

- Copies of contracts with key employees containing details of any redundancy payments that might be due in the future, along with other employee benefits and entitlements that are due to them

- List of freelance designers used by Mizzen, together with copies of contracts

- Details of any copyrights or patents owned by Vic and Lou or Mizzen

- Copy of rental agreement with Bizgrow, to be scrutinised for details of possible rental payments after acquisition

BPP
LEARNING

- Details of tangible non-current assets owned or operated by Mizzen

- Copies of any lease agreements for non-current assets such as computers or fixtures and fittings

- Copies of projected financial information for the next year

- Detailed management accounts, including breakdown of operating expenses to ascertain reasons for rising operating margin

- Details of any dividend payments made over the last three years

(c)   Due diligence is a review report, and as such gives only limited assurance. By contrast an auditor's report gives reasonable assurance, which is a higher level of assurance. This is because a review engagement involves obtaining less evidence than is required for an auditor's report, and conducting procedures which are less thorough.

The conclusion of a review report is expressed negatively, and would begin with the wording, 'Based on our review, nothing has come to our attention...'

The conclusion of an auditor's report is phrased positively, and may state that the financial statements do in fact 'present fairly', or 'give a true and fair view of', the entity's financial position, performance and cash flows.

67 Titian

Workbook references. Chapters 2, 3, 8, 12 and 16.

Top tips. Part (a) was a typical question on the purpose of due diligence. You should have been aiming to score well here because part (c) was considerably harder. There are 6 marks which suggests that you need to make three solid points for each part of the requirement (ie the purpose of due diligence, and comparing this with the external audit). You should read through the model answer here carefully as it gives a good exposition of what a due diligence is, although you should be aware that it is somewhat longer than what you would need to write in the exam.

Part (b) featured ethics and liability, and should have been within your reach provided you knew the material and were able to apply it well.

Part (c) was a difficult test. On the face of it this is a straightforward question about additional information and enquiries to make, but you may have found it difficult to think of things to write here. It is important to realise that although there some very big differences between due diligence and audit, they are still related activities: what you're doing here is a bit like auditing these two areas (intangible assets and the contingent liability). The focus is slightly different because here you are looking to gain assurance over the company's financial operations, ie its costs and revenues, rather than its historical financial statements. But the emphasis is still on finding information to verify the claims that are made in the question, just like any other AAA question.

A starting point for part (c)(i), therefore, might be to go through the two paragraphs that relate to intangibles and look for claims that are being made about the company, and what facts you would want to find out in order to substantiate those claims. From this you can work out what information you would need.

Overall this was not an easy question, but it does provide preparation for future tests in this area so you are lucky to be encountering it now!

Easy marks. Much of part (a) is easy.

ACCA examining team's comments. In part (a), candidates were required to provide a description of the purpose of a due diligence assignment and to demonstrate an understanding of the purpose of due diligence by providing a comparison with a statutory audit of financial statements. The majority of candidates attempting this part of the question scored well demonstrating sound knowledge of this area of the syllabus.

Part (c) focused on the work that may be performed during a due diligence assignment and specifically around the valuation of specific assets and liabilities within a target company. The question here asked for further information that may be required and enquiries that would be made in order to provide assurance on such items. Candidates produced the strongest answers with respect to the valuation of a purchased licence albeit often focusing on initial recording rather than current values/impairment. The valuation of an internally generated database proved harder as many candidates quoted the financial reporting rules and concluded it should not be presented within the financial statements. This was often despite having previously described the purpose of due diligence as a method of identifying assets and liabilities not included in the financial statements which nevertheless would form part of the fair values at acquisition. Candidates would benefit from reviewing the question as a whole in order to consider how the different sections and requirements fit together. More effective planning, prior to writing, would allow candidates to demonstrate a better understanding of these connections.

Part (c)(ii) related to a contingent liability that was presented in the target company's financial statements. Answers to this were of mixed quality but it was disappointing how many candidates again lost sight of the assignment being one of due diligence and made comments regarding the financial statements disclosure requirement. Again, candidates are reminded that more effective reading of the scenario would allow a clearer understanding of what is being asked for and that time should be spent ensuring that answers are tailored to the specifics of the question.

Marking scheme

Marks

(a) Purpose and scope of due diligence

Generally up to 1 mark for each description of the purpose of due diligence and up to 1 mark for each point of comparison with an audit.

Purpose:
- Gathering information to reduce risk of investment decisions
- Verification on management representations
- Identification and valuation of assets and liabilities
- Identification of operational concerns and synergies
- Assistance with acquisition planning

Scope:
- Range of sources used
- Level of assurance/type of engagement
- Types of procedure performed
- Forward looking v mainly historical
- No controls testing

Maximum   6

(b) Ethical issues

Generally up to 1 mark each point explained:
Auditor independence
- Self-review threat
- Explanation re IAS 31
- Threat of management responsibilities

Due diligence
- Possible liability to Calloway Co
- Risk / fees
- Engagement letter
- Independence issues

Maximum   5

BPP
LEARNING

(c)   (i)   **Additional Information**

Up to 1 mark for each piece of information recommended and adequately explained.

Database:

- 30 June 20X5 financial statements (carrying value)
- Original software purchase agreement
- Software maintenance contract
- Historic records of sales by customer
- Sample customer communications
- Sales forecasts

Licence:

- Original purchase agreement (cost)
- Original purchase agreement (incremental/contingent consideration)
- Licence terms and conditions
- Sales figures for new brand
- Forecast sales for new brand

(ii)   **Enquiries**

Up to 1 mark for enquiry recommended and adequately explained.

- Legal advice regarding who bears the liability
- Legal advice regarding likelihood of settlement
- Basis of estimation of liability
- Settlement of claims since year end
- How long faulty parts used for
- New claims since year end
- Risk of further claims
- Quality problems with other parts

Maximum   14

Total   **25**

(a)   **The purpose of due diligence**

Information gathering

Due diligence is the process of fact finding to help reduce the risk involved in investment decisions. It is used when gathering information about a target company, for the purpose of ensuring that the acquirer has full knowledge of the operations, financial performance and position, legal and tax situation, as well as the general commercial background of the target. In particular, due diligence helps to uncover potential problems before a decision regarding the acquisition is made.

Verification of management representations

During a sale, the vendor may make representations to the potential acquirer which it is essential to verify. As an example, the vendor may state that the company has recently had a health and safety or fire safety investigation or that since their last year end they have replaced ageing property, plant and equipment. Due diligence can be used to substantiate such claims.

Identification of assets and liabilities

One of the key reasons for performing due diligence is to identify the assets and liabilities of the target company, which is vital when trying to value the target company. It is particularly important to attempt to identify and value the intangible assets of the target company, including their brands, customer databases and development costs. Internally generated intangibles will not be included on the statement of financial position and are particularly difficult to assess.

The valuation of liabilities is also critical because the acquirer will have to settle these in the future. This must be appropriately planned for and considered during the negotiation of the acquisition price. Contingent liabilities are particularly significant because, by their nature, the amount required to settle them and the likelihood of settlement are uncertain.

Operational issues

As well as the risk associated with the valuation of a business, the acquirer must also consider operational implications which could jeopardise a proposed acquisition, such as high staff turnover, the need to renegotiate supplier or customer contracts or contracts with lenders, and future changes in the product mix of the target company. Any of these could lead to operational problems in the future and could be considered potential 'deal breakers' or, at the very least, be used to negotiate the acquisition price.

Acquisition planning

Due diligence will also assess the potential commercial benefits and drawbacks of the acquisition. For example, it could be used to calculate the potential economies of scale from aligning the supply chains of the buyer and the target company. On the other hand, there are post-acquisition costs to consider, such as the costs of reorganisation and the potential staff turnover which may be experienced.

Scope of a due diligence assignment compared to an audit

With due diligence, the scope is focused primarily on fact finding, which means that the investigation will draw on a much wider range of sources than those connected with the current financial statements. These include:

- Several years' worth of historical financial statements
- Management accounts
- Profit and cash flow forecasts
- Recent business plans and internal strategies/objectives
- Employee contracts, particularly those of management
- All binding contracts, such as supply contracts, lease agreements and loan agreement
- Discussions with management, employees and third parties.

While many of these items may be reviewed during an audit of historical financial statements, it is likely that due diligence will require a much wider range of information.

The objective of an audit is to provide reasonable assurance that the financial statements are free from material misstatement. In contrast, the aim of due diligence is to provide the acquirer with a set of information which has been collated and, most likely, reviewed by the practitioner. Unless requested by the client, the practitioner will not express any opinion with regard to the accuracy of the information provided. In this case, due diligence is performed as an 'agreed upon procedures' assignment.

If the practitioner is requested to provide assurance regarding the accuracy of the information provided, the due diligence service would be performed as a limited assurance review engagement. This is a lower level of assurance than that provided in an audit due to the reduced procedures performed during due diligence.

BPP
LEARNING

The type of work performed during due diligence is quite different to an audit, as a due diligence investigation uses, primarily, analytical procedures and enquiry as a means of gathering information. Very few, if any, substantive procedures are carried out, unless they are specifically requested by the client or there are specific issues which cause concern and therefore need more detailed investigation. This is in contrast to an audit, where a comprehensive range of tests of control and substantive tests are performed.

Due diligence is much more 'forward looking' than an audit. Much of the time during a due diligence investigation will be spent assessing forecasts and predictions. This is in contrast to an audit, where procedures only tend to consider future events if they are directly relevant to the year-end financial statements, for example, contingencies, or going concern problems.

In contrast to an audit, when it is essential to evaluate systems and controls, the due diligence investigation will not conduct detailed testing of the accounting and internal control systems, unless specifically requested to do so.

(b)   Raphael & Co is Sanzio Co's auditor, so the requested due diligence review (DD) would be a non-audit service provided to an audit client. Several ethical issues arise.

Independence

Performing the DD engagement may create threats of self-review and of taking on management responsibilities.

Self-review threat

A self-review threat is created where an auditor does not appropriately evaluate the results of a previous judgement made, or service performed (IESBA *Code of Ethics*: para. 100.12).

If Sanzio Co and Calloway Co do eventually proceed with the planned acquisition, then Sanzio Co would need to account for this in line with IAS 31 *Interests in Joint Ventures*. IAS 31 requires different methods of accounting depending on whether the arrangement gives rise to jointly controlled operations, assets, or an entity. It is possible that the DD report could be used to determine the fair values of assets and liabilities in the joint venture's financial statements, and that Raphael & Co could seek to rely on the report when performing the audit of Sanzio Co.

Raphael & Co should evaluate the existence and significance of the self-review threat. The likely form of the joint venture is not stated, and it is not known whether the DD report would be used to prepare financial statements. Enquiries should be made of Sanzio Co to ascertain the situation.

It is likely, however, that it will be possible to put in place safeguards – such as using separate teams for the DD and for the audit – to reduce this threat to a low enough level for the engagement to be accepted.

Management responsibilities

Management responsibilities involve leading an entity, including making decisions regarding the use of its various resources (see IESBA *Code of Ethics*: para. 290.159). Raphael & Co must not take on any such responsibilities, as the threat so created would be too great to be sufficiently mitigated by safeguards.

Raphael & Co should therefore ensure that Sanzio Co's management makes all judgements and decisions that are the responsibility of management. Raphael & Co should ensure that Sanzio Co:

- Designates a suitably skilled and experienced individual, from among senior management, to be responsible for Sanzio's decisions in relation to the DD report

- Oversees the results of the DD report, and evaluates its adequacy for its own purposes

- Accepts responsibility for any actions taken as a result of the DD report

(IESBA *Code of Ethics*: para. 290.162)

Distribution to Calloway Co

Distributing the DD report to Calloway Co could create sufficient proximity for Raphael & Co to be found liable to Calloway Co (as well as to Sanzio Co), in the event of any negligence in relation to the DD engagement. This increases the engagement risk for Raphael & Co, and could in turn affect the fee that Raphael & Co charges for the service.

Raphael & Co could seek to limit the use of the report to Sanzio Co only, but this is unlikely to be acceptable to Sanzio Co in this situation. Alternatively, Raphael & Co could request that Calloway Co signs an engagement letter. This letter would set out the DD report's terms of use, together with any limitations of its liability, and would seek to communicate to Calloway Co the independence requirements to be applied in the DD engagement.

Ethical issues

If it is not possible to prevent the DD report from being distributed to Calloway Co, and if a separate engagement letter is signed, then Raphael & Co needs to consider whether it is independent of Calloway Co.

Raphael & Co should ascertain whether Calloway Co is already its client, and whether any employees are connected to Calloway Co. If there are any threats to Raphael & Co's independence then it should be considered whether safeguards could be applied to reduce them to an acceptable level. If this is not possible, then Raphael & Co should restrict the distribution of the DD report to Sanzio Co only.

(c)   (i)   **Intangible assets**

Customer database

- A copy of the financial statements for the year ended 30 June 20X5 to identify the current carrying value of any purchased intangibles relating to the database, such as computer software.

- A copy of the original purchase agreement for the software to identify the age of the software and when any product licences expire.

- A copy of the original purchase/ongoing maintenance contracts for the software to identify the continuing costs of maintaining the system at its current level of efficiency.

- Historic records of sales by customer to verify management's statement that repeat customers make up over 60% of annual sales.

- Copies of a sample of recent automated customer communications; these can be traced to customer bookings/sales records to confirm the current efficacy of the system.

- Sales forecasts for the foreseeable future to assess the potential future cash flows attributable to the customer database system to assess its value when determining the potential purchase price.

- Confirmation of the current price of similar database software to assess the market value/fair value of the asset.

Licence

- A copy of the original purchase agreement for the licence to confirm the $5m cost and the exclusivity of the agreement.

- The original purchase agreement can also be used to identify whether any further incremental/contingent considerations or royalties are due in the future.

- A copy of the licence agreement to confirm whether the licence is for a fixed period of time or not and to confirm the exclusivity of the licence.

BPP
LEARNING

- A breakdown of the sales figures relating to the new tyres; these can be used to compare the performance of the new tyres to existing brands.

- Forecasts showing the expected future sales attributable to the new tyres to confirm the continued inflow of economic benefit from the asset.

(ii) **Contingent liabilities**

The following enquiries should be made of the management of Titian Tyres Co:

- Enquire of management and ascertain if any legal advice has been sought to determine who is liable to pay compensation in these cases, Titian Tyres Co or the supplier of the parts.

- Enquire whether management has sought any legal advice with regard to the likelihood of having to settle the claims or not.

- Enquire if management has records showing how many vehicles have been fitted with the faulty parts and whether these have been used in any estimates of the likely settlement costs.

- Discuss with management the level of claims which have been settled since the year end. Compare this with the original estimation to establish how effective management has been in making these estimates.

- Enquire of management for how long the company used the faulty parts and for what portion of this time period the known claims relate to.

- Discuss with management the details of any new claims which have been made since the year end which were not included in any estimations of the cost of settlement included in the contingent liability disclosure in the financial statements.

- Discuss with management their assessment of any risk that further claims will be made which they are currently unaware of.

- Enquire of management if other quality problems have been experienced with other parts from the same supplier.

68 Jacob

Workbook references. Chapters 12 and 13.

Top tips. Part (a) was of around average difficulty. You should have been able to pass this part of the question by making sure that you explain each of your points well.

Part (b) should have been simpler than part (a). It was important here that you didn't go over your time limit, but that you wrote enough (in terms of quality, not quantity!) to gain marks for each thing you say. The key to actually getting marks is to be specific about what information you are asking for, and making sure that everything you say is relevant to the scenario. It is a waste of time asking for information that is relevant to due diligence in general, but not to Locke Co in particular. Also, it is no good just stating what information you need, you have to make sure that you say why you need it.

You might have enjoyed part (c) (relatively speaking), as there was plenty to criticise in the assurance report – it can feel good to be in command of your knowledge. This question part was largely a mark gathering exercise, which meant you should have been careful not to go over your time on it.

Easy marks. There were plenty of easy marks in part (b), for example, saying that more information needs to be obtained regarding the court case against Locke Co.

ACCA examining team's comments. Requirement (a), for 6 marks, required an explanation of the benefits of an externally provided due diligence review to the audit client. This was reasonably well answered, though many answers were not made very specific to the scenario and tended to discuss the benefits of any due diligence review rather than an externally provided one.

Requirement (b), for 11 marks asked for additional information to be made available for the firm's due diligence review. Answers were satisfactory, and the majority of candidates did not struggle to apply their knowledge to the scenario, usually providing some very focused answers dealing well with the specifics of the question scenario.

Part (c) involved reviewing a non-audit assurance report which had been prepared in conjunction with seeking a bank loan. Good answers highlighted that the report had been poorly written (in that it was not correctly addressed, provided positive assurance, was not time-bound and was self-contradictory) and explained how each of these should be remedied. Poorer answers only concentrated on omissions, such as the lack of a date on the report.

Marking scheme

Marks

(a) **Benefits of due diligence**

Up to 2 marks for each benefit explained:
- Identify and value assets and liabilities to be acquired
- Identify and allow planning for operational issues
- Provision by external experts – technically competent and time efficient
- Assessment of potential impact of court case
- Evaluation of the liquidity position of Locke Co
- Enhanced credibility provided by an independent review

Maximum   6

(b) **Information required**

Generally ½ mark for identification and up to 1 further mark for explanation (maximum 3 marks for identification):
- Service contracts of directors
- Organisational structure
- Lease/arrangement regarding head office
- Details of land purchased
- Planning permission for new head office
- Prior year accounts and management accounts
- Forecasts and budgets
- Loan agreement
- Overdraft facility details
- Legal correspondence
- Customer satisfaction surveys
- Details of warranty agreements
- Outsourcing agreement

Maximum   11

(c) **Critique of assurance report**
- Addressee inappropriate
- Type of forecast reviewed
- Period covered by the forecast
- Document forecast is included in and page references
- Assurance standards complied with
- Responsibility for preparation

BPP
LEARNING

– Reference to assumptions	
– Negative statement of assurance	
– International Financial Reporting Standards	
– Inappropriate caveat	
– Reference to purpose and distribution of the report	

Maximum   <u>8</u>

Total   <u>**25**</u>

(a) One benefit of due diligence here is that it will help in assigning a valuation to Locke Co. The review would seek to identify all of Locke Co's potential assets and liabilities and provide a value for them. This valuation may include amounts not included within the financial statements, for example any contingent assets or liabilities that are not required to be recognised or disclosed by IAS 37. Armed with this valuation, management would be in a better position to negotiate a price for the business.

A second benefit is that the review should obtain further information about the company's operations. For example, it may be able to obtain further information about the extent of Locke Co's possible liability relating to its court case. It may also be able to provide an indication of the extent to which Locke Co's reputation may be tarnished by the court case.

A third benefit is that since the due diligence review is prepared externally, the directors' time is freed up to concentrate on operational matters. The review will be prepared time-efficiently, and the independence of the firm providing the review helps contribute to the good governance of Jacob Co.

> **Tutorial note.** The answer above includes three benefits (as required). Credit will be awarded for explanation of any three benefits which are specific to the scenario.

(b) Further information should include:

Employment contracts

Contracts for directors and other key personnel should be obtained. It may be that Jacob will seek to terminate the employment of directors after the acquisition. The contracts should be inspected for any amounts payable on termination.

Organisational structure

It may be that Jacob will want to keep hold of key personnel. In order to identify them, an organisational structure should be obtained.

Lease agreements re building

Jacob may wish to relocate away from the building owned by the family estate, in which case the signed lease agreements should be inspected for any penalty clauses for early termination.

New head office – purchase documentation

Documents relating to the land purchase should be obtained to ascertain its value should Jacob wish to sell it, or to see whether it might be put to an alternative use. Alternatively, it may be possible for the land not to be included in the acquisition.

Details should be obtained of any other commitments made in relation to the new head office. For example, construction contracts may have been entered into; these should be obtained, along with details of any possible penalties for termination.

Audited financial statements

Audited financial statements should be obtained in order to verify that Locke has indeed grown rapidly in the last three years.

These will also provide information helpful for the valuation of assets, the existence of contingent liabilities, etc.

Finally, they will allow an assessment to be made of Locke's liquidity, which may be particularly important in view of its use of an overdraft facility during the winter months.

Management accounts and forecasts

These should be obtained for future periods in order to assess Locke's possible future profitability.

Asset valuations

Any significant non-current assets should be assessed for their market value, if they are held in the accounts at historical cost.

Signed bank loan agreement

This should be obtained in order to ascertain the repayment terms, the interest rate, as well as any charges over the company and/or its assets.

The amount of the loan may be significant, as purchasing a company with high financial gearing may affect Jacob's own exposure to risk.

Overdraft details

Details such as the maximum facility available to Locke, the interest rate, and when it is due for renewal.

It is possible that Locke may be a significant drain on Jacob's cash resources during the winter months, so Jacob will need to assess its own ability to take on such a possible commitment.

Information from legal counsel

This should be obtained regarding the court case with the famous actor. This should ascertain the extent of Locke's probably liability, along with the timescale for the case.

Information on bad publicity

The bad publicity from the legal case may affect Locke's ability to generate revenue in future, so information about the extent of the possible brand damage should be sought.

Information on Locke's 'good reputation'

This claim should be substantiated as far as possible, for example by reference to industry journals, customer satisfaction surveys, levels of customer complaints, etc.

Contract with Austin Co

This should be examined in order to understand exactly what services Austin provides, and what the cost of these services is. Jacob may wish to bring some of these activities back in-house.

(c) **Assurance report on examination of forecast**

Addressee

The report is currently addressed to the shareholders of Tulip Co which is not appropriate. The intended users for the report are more likely to be the board of directors, who wishes to use it in conjunction with a loan application, and the report should be addressed as such.

Type of forecast

The report fails to specify what forecast the assurance relates to. Companies can forecast various elements of financial performance, position and cash flow. It is vital to identify

BPP
LEARNING
MEDIA

specifically which forecast, and which elements of the forecast, are covered by the assurance report.

Period covered

The assurance report fails to specify the period covered by the forecast. This is important because it is plausible that only part of the forecast is covered by the assurance report, particularly if it is a long range forecast.

Specific document and page reference

The assurance report simply refers to the forecast 'contained in the loan proposal'. This is not specific enough. This increases the risk that the same forecast can be reissued with the assurance report in other loan proposals. The assurance report should state the title of the document the forecast is included in and the page numbers upon which assurance is being provided.

Relevant standards

The report simply refers to 'relevant standards'; it should state which standards have been followed during the engagement. Given the nature of the assignment the report should state that it has been conducted in accordance with ISAE 3400 *The Examination of Prospective Financial Information*.

Responsibility for preparation

The content of the report in relation to setting out the respective responsibilities of the practitioner and the responsible party are not in line with the relevant standards. Rather than stating that the practitioner is not responsible for the preparation of the forecast, ISAE 3400 specifies that the assurance report should state that management is responsible for the information provided and the assumptions upon which it is based.

Detail regarding the relevant assumptions

The assurance report should make it clear what assumptions the forecast is based upon and what assumptions the assurance report relates to. To this end the report should refer to the note in the forecast where the underlying assumptions are presented.

Negative statement of assurance needed

The assurance provided in the draft assurance report is worded positively; ISAE 3400 requires that for an examination of prospective financial information a statement of negative assurance is provided.

For an unmodified report, such as that presented in the draft, the wording used should state that 'based upon our examination of the evidence supporting the assumptions, nothing has come to our attention which causes us to believe............'

IFRS

The report should refer to 'International Financial Reporting Standards' rather than 'IFRS'.

Inappropriate caveat

The caveat at the end of the report should be reworded as it somewhat undermines the credibility of the forecast and the assurance provided by stating that the forecast is unlikely to be accurate.

A more appropriate statement would refer to the uncertainty in relation to the nature of a forecast and that the actual results may vary from those anticipated.

Reference to the purpose and distribution of the report

It is common practice for a report on prospective financial information to include a reference to the purpose of the information and on its distribution. Thyme & Co should consider including this reference as a means of limiting the distribution of the report to the intended parties.

69 Crocus

Workbook reference. Chapter 14.

Top tips. This question looks at the topic of forensic audits. Many of the points were covered in an article published by the examining team in *Student Accountant* shortly before the exam, and you would have scored well if you had read this article. It is vital that you keep up to date with relevant articles in *Student Accountant* to do well in this exam.

Easy marks. These are available in parts (a) and (c) of this question as they are both knowledge-based.

ACCA examining team's comments. Requirement (b) was the core of the question. Unfortunately, two common problems detracted from the quality of many answers for this requirement. Firstly, providing tactless and unnecessary comments regarding whether the assignment should be accepted. Such comments show that candidates had failed to read and understand the scenario. Secondly, the procedures suggested where often too vague, or not even procedures at all.

Requirement (c) was not often well answered. This requirement asked for the application of the fundamental ethical principles to the provision of a forensic investigation service. Many answers were just not applied in any way, making little or no reference to forensics.

Marking scheme

			Marks
(a)	Up to 1½ marks per comment:		
	– Consider whether firm has skills		
	– Staff availability		
	– No independence issues		
	– Commercial considerations		
		Maximum	4
(b)	Up to 1½ marks per comment:		
	– Aim – clarify fraud taken place		
	– Aim – discover the perpetrator(s)		
	– Aim – prosecute the perpetrator(s)		
	– Aim – quantify losses		
	– Method – consider type of fraud – ghost employee		
	– Method – understand how it could have taken place – controls override		
	– Method – collect evidence – suffice and relevant – allow up to 3 extra marks here if examples given of procedures that could be performed		
	– Method – interview suspect		
	– Method – produce reports		
	– Expert witness		
	– Advice and recommendations to prevent another fraud		
		Maximum	14

(c)   **Professional ethics – application of fundamental principles**
Up to 1½ marks per comment:
–   Integrity (max 1 mark)
–   Objectivity
–   Professional competence and due care
–   Confidentiality
–   Professional behaviour
1 mark for recognition that principles apply to all professional engagements

Maximum   7

Total   25

(a)   The audit firm should first consider whether it has the required skills and experience to perform the work if the engagement were accepted. Forensic investigations are specialist assignments, requiring a detailed knowledge of fraud investigation techniques and the legal framework; they cannot simply be performed by an external auditor. Investigators must have received training in interview and interrogation techniques, and in maintaining the safe custody of evidence gathered.

The firm does have a dedicated forensic investigation department, which suggests that it does have this expertise. Practical arrangements will therefore need to be made to ensure that the requisite staff are available to perform the investigation.

The fact that Crocus Co is not an audit client means that there are no independence issues to consider before acceptance.

Finally, commercial considerations are important. The negotiated fee should be sufficiently high to compensate for the specialist nature of the work, and the likely involvement of senior and experienced members of the firm in the investigation.

(b)   (i)   **Objectives of a forensic investigation**

When investigating an alleged fraud, such as at Crocus Co, the first objective of a forensic investigation would be to **prove that deliberate fraudulent activity has actually occurred**. The employees may have been left on the payroll in error, rather than a deliberate attempt to misappropriate cash.

Once it has been established that a fraud has taken place, a forensic investigation would then aim to **identify the perpetrator** or perpetrators of the fraud. Evidence would be gathered for use in any potential court proceedings, for example, an interview with the suspected fraudster(s).

Finally, the forensic investigation may try to **quantify the financial loss** suffered as a result of the fraud. Legally, no crime has been committed unless Crocus Co has suffered a financial loss.

(ii)   **Steps involved in a forensic investigation into the payroll fraud**

Establishing the type of fraud that has taken place.

At Crocus Co, redundant employees have not been removed from the payroll. Payments to these fictitious employees (known as 'ghost employees') are now being made to the fraudster.

Determining for how long the fraud has been operating

It is likely that the fraud started on the date of the factory closure, but this will need to be confirmed.

Identifying how the fraud operated and was concealed

The forensic investigation team will determine how the fraud was conducted at Crocus Co and how the perpetrator concealed their actions. It appears there was a problem with internal controls over amendments to payroll data. Somehow an employee has been able to make changes to the payroll data without being detected until after payments have taken place. A control should have been in place to ensure that all amendments to payroll data are approved by a more senior member of staff before any payments are made.

Gathering evidence

Evidence will be collected by the forensic investigation team and must be sufficient to prove the following.

- That a fraud has taken place

- Who has committed the fraud and how

- The amount of financial loss suffered by Crocus Co

The evidence must also be relevant to the alleged case. It is important to use a skilled team to collect the evidence and keep a clear trail of its custody so that it cannot be challenged in court.

At Crocus Co, evidence could be obtained by the following methods.

- Reviewing and testing the authorisation procedures for the monthly payroll

- Using computer assisted audit techniques (CAATs) to look for alteration of payroll details

- Using CAATs to search for employees with no contact details, employees who have not taken holiday or sick pay and bank account details which are the same for more than one employee

- Reconciling employees' details in the payroll database with human resources records

- Interviewing the suspect and ideally acquiring a confession. This interview is generally delayed until there is enough evidence to extract a confession and will form a key part of evidence to be presented in court.

Reporting

Once all the evidence has been collected, the forensic investigator will produce a report to the client. This report will summarise all evidence, detail the amount of financial loss suffered as a result of the fraud and identify the suspected fraudster. It is likely that this report is used as evidence in court.

The report may also include advice to the client to help prevent a reoccurrence of the fraud. Advice given is often in the form of suggested improvements to internal controls and systems.

Court proceedings

The forensic investigation team is likely to be called as an expert witness in any resulting court case. Team members will be asked questions about the investigation and to explain the evidence presented.

(c) **Application of fundamental principles of the IESBA's *Code of Ethics for Professional Accountants* to a forensic investigation**

The fundamental principles of the IESBA's *Code of Ethics* apply to all professional assignments.

Integrity

Forensic accountants are often, by definition, working in an environment dealing with individuals who are dishonest and lack integrity. If there is any risk that their own integrity will be compromised they should decline or withdraw from the assignment.

Objectivity

The report produced by the forensic investigator will be used as evidence in court and must apply an opinion which is independent. A useful test of independence is that the investigator would express the same opinion if given the same instructions by the opposing party. Investigators should not take it upon themselves to promote the point of view of the party instructing them or engage in the role of advocates. Any perceived threats to objectivity will undermine the credibility of the accountant's opinion.

A perceived threat to objectivity may occur when an audit firm asks its auditors to conduct a forensic investigation. In this case there would be three threats to the firm's objectivity:

- **Advocacy.** The audit firm may feel compelled to promote the view of the client in court as they are concerned about losing an audit client and the resulting fees.

- **Management involvement.** The audit firm may be seen as making management decisions about the implication of the fraud.

- **Self-review.** A forensic investigation will require any loss suffered to be quantified. If this amount is material to the financial statements, the audit firm may end up auditing their own estimation.

The IESBA *Code* states that appropriate safeguards should be put in place to minimise these threats. If safeguards cannot reduce the threat to an acceptable level, then the firm cannot provide both services.

Professional competence and due care

Forensic investigations may require very specialised skills which require training. Examples of these skills would include:

- Evidence gathering that requires specific IT skills
- An understanding of the legal framework
- Knowledge of evidence gathering methods and the safe custody of evidence

A firm should consider very carefully whether they have adequate skills and resources before accepting the assignment. Evidence presented in court could be discredited if the team is thought to be incompetent.

Confidentiality

Forensic accountants will often be working for one party to a dispute, and have access to very sensitive information. Subject, of course, to legal rules of disclosures in court cases, it is clearly essential to maintain the strictest confidentiality.

Professional behaviour

Fraud cases and other situations such as takeover disputes can be very much in the public eye. Any lapse in the professionalism of, say, an expert witness could do serious damage to the reputation of the profession as a whole.

70 Jansen

Workbook references. Chapters 13 and 10.

Top tips. This question is made up of two unrelated scenarios; one scenario features a non-assurance engagement on prospective financial information (PFI); the other scenario is an engagement quality control question set at the completion stage of an audit.

Part (a) was quite neat in the sense that the first sub-part (a)(i) focused on the first few paragraphs of the scenario, while the next sub-part (ii) focused on the remaining information.

Part (a)(i) tested the matters to consider before accepting the appointment for the PFI engagement. This was partly a test of knowledge – the IESBA *Code of Ethics* suggests the advocacy threat and the self-review threat – but could also have been answered simply by picking up cues from the scenario.

The next sub-part (ii) might have felt more familiar to you, dealing as it did in examination procedures. Your starting point should have been the notes, which gave you some assumptions that you should have tried to pick holes in.

One important point is that marks were available in this question for actually performing basic analytical procedures using the figures provided. This is unusual, given that the requirement did not ask you to do this – and indeed, asks for procedures to be only 'recommended', not actually performed – but you should bear this in mind when working on similar questions in the future.

Part (b) was on engagement quality control in the context of a share-based payment scheme. IFRS 2 *Share-based Payment* is perhaps not the most difficult of the standards you need to be familiar with, so if your knowledge of this area had been strong then this requirement should have been within reach. That being said, however, even if you had struggled a little with the financial reporting you could still have passed the question by drawing on your auditing knowledge. There are a few points here that crop up regularly, such as qualitative materiality (not just quantitative); the need to update the audit plan as the audit progresses, and; the need for supervision and direction of the audit.

Easy marks. The mark for testing the arithmetic accuracy of the forecast in (a)(ii) was among the easiest on the exam.

Marking scheme

Marks

(a) **Narley Co**

   (i) **Matters to be considered before acceptance of engagement**
Up to 2 marks for each matter explained:
- Auditor independence including potentially significant advocacy threat and possible self-review and self-interest threats
- Intended use of report, eg solely for bank or wider distribution
- Nature of assumptions and time period covered (in this case two years)
- Availability of experienced, competent staff and time frame for assurance work
- Appropriate safeguards to reduce risks to acceptable level
- Details of PFI to be given to bank, eg forecast P/L only

Maximum   6

(ii) **Examination procedures to be performed**

Generally up to 1 mark for each described procedure. Also allow 1 mark for each relevant analytical procedure used to max of 3 marks:

- Check arithmetic accuracy of forecast
- Agree accounting policies consistent with financial statements and comply with IFRS
- Discuss key assumptions with management and assess reasonableness
- Review market research documentation and discuss with management
- Obtain and review customer contracts for new customers to confirm projected growth in revenue
- Obtain written representations from management on reasonableness and completeness of assumptions
- Assess competence and experience of client staff preparing forecasts including accuracy of PFI prepared in previous periods and reasons for any significant variances
- Perform analytical review of key trends; up to 3 marks for analysis of key trends by candidates including:
  - Growth in revenue
  - Cost of sales as % of revenue
  - Declining trend in admin expenses
  - Increase in net profit margin
- Review of capex forecasts and agreement to invoices/supplier quotations
- Recalculate depreciation and ensure correct inclusion of depreciation on new HGVs and warehousing facilities
- Obtain and review breakdown of operating expenses; ensure all items appropriately included, eg advertising/marketing costs; additional staff costs for new drivers including recruitment expenses; any trading tariffs with overseas market and any forex implications
- Inspect recent utility bills and assess reasonableness of forecast utility overheads
- Obtain and review documentation for existing loan agreements with bank and draft documentation for new loan and recalculate finance costs

Maximum   9

Marks

(b) **Watson Co**

Generally up to 1 mark for each issue discussed:

- Inadequate planning/consultation with client re SBP scheme (ISA 220)
- Complex judgemental area, should have been identified as high risk
- Part-qualified supervisor, inadequate skills and expertise for this listed client
- Treatment of SBP is incorrect, valuation should have been updated at year end for cash-based scheme
- Recognition as equity reserve is also incorrect, IFRS 2 requires recognition as liability for cash-based scheme
- SBP is immaterial quantitatively (extra 1 mark for relevant calculation and comment) but scheme is RPT with directors which is material by nature especially for listed entity
- Error should have been calculated and adjustment requested
- The matter should have been included in the related party disclosure notes in accordance with IAS 24
- Inadequate staffing levels – only two-member team and audit manager should have been replaced earlier
- Inadequate briefing meeting, poor quality advice to follow last year's working papers – should always be on look out for new situations and issues
- Insufficient monitoring and supervision by audit manager
- No evidence of partner oversight during course of audit work
- Failure to update and change audit plan as necessary during course of audit (ISA 300); clearance meeting is next week and manager review is only just taking place
- Lack of audit evidence re external valuer – competence, capabilities, objectivity, scope of work; reference to website is inadequate and reflects inexperience and lack of expertise of supervisor (up to 2 marks for development of discussion)

	Maximum	10
Total		**25**

(a) **Narley Co**

(i) **Matters to be considered before acceptance of engagement**

When considering acceptance of the engagement to review Narley Co's prospective financial information (PFI), Jansen & Co must consider whether it is ethically acceptable to perform the review. The review of the PFI represents a non-assurance service and the IESBA *Code of Ethics for Professional Accountants* (the *Code*) states that providing this service in addition to the audit may create an advocacy threat. An advocacy threat arises when the auditor is asked to promote or represent their client in some way. In this situation there is a risk of the auditor being seen to promote the interests of the client with a third party such as a bank. As a result, there is a danger that the auditor will be biased in favour of the client and therefore cannot be fully objective. Accepting the assignment may also create a self-interest threat as a result of the auditor being perceived to have an interest in the outcome of negotiations with a third party and which may motivate the auditor to behave in order to protect that interest. A self-review threat may also arise because the negotiations may result in facts and amounts which

BPP
LEARNING

will form part of the audited financial statements. As a result, the auditor will be auditing financial statements which in part at least represent work which they themselves have performed. It follows that there is a risk that the auditor will not be sufficiently objective in performing the audit and may fail to identify any shortcomings in their own work.

In the case of Narley Co, the advocacy threat appears to be particularly significant as the audit firm could be seen to be promoting the interests of the audit client to the bank. The auditor should therefore only accept the engagement if adequate safeguards can be put in place to manage the threat to independence to an acceptable level. Potential safeguards might include the following:

- The use of separate teams of suitably experienced staff for the audit and the review of the PFI;

- Independent senior review of the PFI working papers;

- Discussion of the potential ethical issues and threats to auditor independence with those charged with governance at Narley Co.

It should be noted, however, that it would not be possible to manage a significant advocacy threat through such safeguards and in such a case the appointment should not be accepted.

ISAE 3400 *The Examination of Prospective Financial Information* provides further guidance on the issues which the auditor should consider before accepting an engagement to examine PFI. According to ISAE 3400, the auditor should consider amongst other things:

- The intended use of the information – for example, whether it will be used solely for the purpose of the proposed loan finance;

- Whether the information will be for general or limited distribution – the auditor needs to consider who will receive the report and potentially rely upon it;

- The nature of the assumptions, that is, whether they are best-estimate or hypothetical assumptions – in this case it seems likely that they will be best estimate assumptions as Narley Co expects to obtain finance in order to fund its planned expansion;

- The elements to be included in the information – Jansen & Co needs to clarify the exact content of the PFI which they are being asked to report on, for example, whether it only includes the forecast statements of profit or loss or whether it also includes forecast statements of financial position and forecast cash flow statements; and

- The period covered by the information – shorter term forecasts are likely to be more reliable than projections over a longer period.

Jansen & Co must also consider whether the firm has sufficient staff available with the appropriate skills and experience to perform the review engagement in line with the client's required reporting deadlines.

Overall, the auditor must assess the risks associated with the review engagement and should not accept an engagement when the assumptions are clearly unrealistic or when the auditor believes that the prospective financial information will be inappropriate for its intended use.

(ii) **Examination procedures to be performed**

The examination procedures which should be performed in respect of Narley Co's forecast statements of profit or loss include the following:

- The arithmetic accuracy of the forecast statements of profit or loss should be confirmed;

- Confirmation that the accounting policies used in the forecast statements are consistent with those used in the audited financial statements and that they comply with IFRS;

- Discuss the key assumptions which have been made by the client in the preparation of the forecast statements with management assessing their reasonableness and consistency with the audit firm's cumulative knowledge and understanding of the client;

- Review of market research documentation in Narley Co's existing markets and the new market and discuss it with management to assess whether the growth patterns being forecast in revenue represent reasonable and realistic expectations;

- Obtain copies of any new customer contracts for existing and new markets to confirm the reasonableness of the projected growth in revenue.

- Obtain a written representation from management confirming the reasonableness and completeness of the assumptions they have made in preparing the forecasts;

- The competence and experience of the client staff who have prepared the forecasts should be assessed; the assessment should include the accuracy of PFI which has been prepared in previous periods and the reasons for any significant variances compared to actual outcomes;

- Recalculation of depreciation to ensure the correct inclusion of depreciation on the new HGVs and warehousing facilities within the forecast statements;

- Obtain and review a breakdown of operating expenses in order to ensure that all items have been appropriately included, for example: advertising and marketing costs for the campaign in the new jurisdiction; additional staff costs for the new drivers including recruitment expenses; any trading tariffs relevant to operating in the new market and any foreign currency and exchange implications;

- Recent utility bills should be inspected and an assessment of the reasonableness of forecast utility overheads should be performed;

- Obtain and review the supporting documentation for Narley Co's existing loan agreements with the bank as well as the draft documentation for the new loan; the forecast finance costs should be recalculated and agreed to the forecast statements;

- Perform analytical review, followed by discussion with management to seek corroborating evidence of key trends and ratios including:

    - Growth in revenue (26% from 20X8 to 20X9; 29% from 20X9 to 20Y0)

    - Cost of sales as a percentage of revenue (75.5% in 20X8; 71.3% in 20X9; 69.7% in 20Y0)

    - The declining trend in administrative expenses (decrease of 4.2% from 20X8 to 20X9; 5.6% from 20X9 to 20Y0)

    - The increase in the net profit margin (6.9% in 20X8; 15.2% in 20X9; 20.4% in 20Y0).

BPP
LEARNING

(b)   **Watson Co**

Quality control issues raised by the audit supervisor's email

ISA 220 *Quality Control for an Audit of Financial Statements* requires the auditor to implement quality control procedures at the engagement level which provide reasonable assurance that the audit complies with professional standards and applicable legal and regulatory requirements and that the auditor's report is appropriate in the circumstances. The overall quality of each audit assignment is the responsibility of the audit engagement partner and effective engagement performance entails adequate direction, consultation, supervision and review. In this case, the conduct of the audit raises a number of quality control issues in relation to the effective performance of the audit of Watson Co's financial statements, including the following:

Share-based payment scheme:

The failure to identify the new cash-settled share-based payment scheme as a potentially high risk area indicates inadequate planning and a lack of consultation with the client. The share-based payment scheme is a complex and judgemental area and given that the scheme was only introduced in the year, it should have been identified as a key area of audit risk.

The assignment of a part-qualified supervisor to the audit of a listed entity is also indicative of poor audit planning. The audit supervisor appears to have inadequate skills and expertise to audit this public interest entity. This is evidenced by the incorrect treatment of the share-based payment scheme and the audit supervisor's comment that basing the expense in the profit or loss account on the valuation at the date of grant is appropriate and that the recognition of an equity reserve on the statement of financial position is correct in the email to the audit manager. According to IFRS 2 *Share-based Payments*, the valuation of the share appreciation rights for a cash-settled scheme should be updated at the reporting date and the standard requires recognition of the cumulative cost of the scheme as a liability, not as an equity reserve.

The audit supervisor also fails to recognise that a share-based payment scheme with the directors of Watson Co constitutes a related party transaction. While the supervisor is correct in saying that the cost of the scheme this year of $195,000 is immaterial on a quantitative basis (it represents only 0.36% of profit before taxation and 0.84% of total assets), as a related party transaction with directors, the scheme should be considered to be material by nature and should be fully disclosed in the notes to the financial statements in accordance with IAS 24 *Related Party Disclosures*. The related party disclosures are particularly important for a listed entity such as Watson Co. In line with ISA 450 *Evaluation of Misstatements Identified During the Audit*, all misstatements should be accumulated and therefore the error should also have been included in the audit working papers and adjustment should have been requested.

Other quality control issues include:

- The staffing levels on the audit also appear to be inadequate given that there are only two audit team members. This is again indicative of poor audit planning.

- In addition, it is clear that the audit manager should have been replaced earlier and that Watson Co has failed to provide adequate direction and supervision of the audit.

- The original audit manager, Rodney Evans, has also provided an inadequate briefing meeting prior to the commencement of the audit work. The advice to follow last year's working papers is inappropriate as the auditor must always be on the look out for new situations and issues such as the new share-based payment scheme.

- Jansen & Co has also failed to monitor the progress of the audit and therefore to update and change the audit plan as necessary during the course of the audit as required by ISA 300 *Planning an Audit of Financial Statements*. This is evidenced by the fact that the audit clearance meeting is scheduled for next week and the initial manager review is only just taking place. In addition, there appears to be no evidence of engagement partner oversight over the course of the audit fieldwork and it is the engagement partner's responsibility to ensure that they have reviewed the documentation to ensure that sufficient appropriate evidence has been obtained and that the auditor's report issued in the circumstances is appropriate.

- There appears to be a lack of audit evidence in relation to the firm of external valuers which has been used to value the share options. ISA 500 *Audit Evidence* requires the auditor to obtain sufficient and appropriate audit evidence that the valuation work performed by the management expert is adequate for the purposes of the audit. The auditor must therefore evaluate whether management's expert possesses the necessary competence, capabilities and objectivity to perform the valuations and whether the scope of their work is satisfactory for audit purposes. The 'checking out' of the expert online with reference to a website is clearly inadequate for audit purposes and this again reflects the inexperience and lack of expertise of the audit supervisor and poor audit planning with respect to the staffing on the audit.

Mock exams

ACCA Strategic Professional

AAA

Advanced Audit and Assurance (International)

Mock Examination 1

Question Paper
Time allowed   3 hours 15 minutes
ALL THREE questions are compulsory and MUST be attempted

DO NOT OPEN THIS PAPER UNTIL YOU ARE READY TO START UNDER EXAMINATION CONDITIONS

BPP
LEARNING
MEDIA

ALL THREE questions are compulsory and MUST be attempted

Question 1

The Zed Communications Group (ZCG) is an audit client of your firm, Tarantino & Co, with a financial year ending 31 December 20X6. You are the manager assigned to the forthcoming audit. ZCG is a listed entity, one of the largest telecommunications providers in the country and is seeking to expand internationally. ZCG also provides broadband and fixed telephone line services.

You have been provided with the following exhibits:

1   An email which you have received from Vincent Vega, the audit engagement partner
2   Notes from a meeting held between ZCG's finance director and Vincent Vega
3   Background information on ZCG's internal audit function and an extract of a report
4   Gull Co information

Required

Respond to the instructions in the audit engagement partner's email.   **(46 marks)**

Professional marks will be awarded for the presentation of the briefing notes and the clarity of the explanations provided.   **(4 marks)**

(Total = 50 marks)

Exhibit 1 – Email from audit engagement partner

To:	Audit engagement manager
From:	Vincent Vega, audit engagement partner
Subject:	ZCG audit planning, and Gull Co

Hello

We need to begin planning the final audit of ZCG, which as you know is one of our largest audit clients. I met with the Group's finance director yesterday and I have provided you with notes from this meeting along with extracts from the latest management accounts. We also discussed the possibility of using the Group's internal audit team to improve audit efficiency. I have provided you with an extract from the latest report of the internal audit department.

Using all of the information provided, you are required to prepare briefing notes for my use in which you:

(a)   Evaluate the audit risks relevant to planning the final audit of ZCG;   **(17 marks)**

(b)   Discuss the matters to be considered in determining the assistance which could be provided by, and the amount of reliance, if any, which can be placed on the work of ZCG's internal audit department;   **(7 marks)**

(c)   Recommend the principal audit procedures to be performed on:

   (i)   The classification of the 50% equity shareholding in WTC as a joint venture; and

                                                                                 (4 marks)

   (ii)   The measurement of the intangible asset recognised in respect of the licence to operate in Farland.   **(6 marks)**

Separately from this work on the ZCG audit, a matter has arisen in relation to another client of ours, Gull Co. The details are provided in Exhibit 4; I would like you to provide me with your comments on:

BPP
LEARNING

<table>
<tr><td>(d)</td><td>(i)</td><td>The ethical and professional matters in relation to the recruitment requests made by Gull Co</td><td>**(6 marks)**</td></tr>
<tr><td></td><td>(ii)</td><td>The implications the governance structure and proposed listing may have on the audit process</td><td>**(6 marks)**</td></tr>
</table>

Your comments on the final situation – with Gull Co – should be presented separately from the briefing notes.

Thank you.

Exhibit 2 – Notes from meeting with finance director

One of ZCG's strategic aims is to expand internationally, either by acquiring existing telecommunications providers in other countries, or by purchasing licences to operate in foreign countries.

In March 20X6, ZCG purchased a 50% equity shareholding in Wallace Telecoms Co (WTC), a company operating in several countries where ZCG previously had no interests. The other 50% is held by Wolf Communications Co. The cost of the 50% equity shareholding was $45 million. ZCG is planning to account for its investment in WTC as a joint venture in the Group financial statements.

On 1 January 20X5, ZCG purchased a licence to operate in Farland, a rapidly expanding economy, at a cost of $65m. The licence lasts for 10 years from the date that it was purchased. Since purchasing the licence, ZCG has established its network coverage in Farland and the network became operational on 1 July 20X6. The licence was recognised as an intangible asset at cost in the Group statement of financial position at 31 December 20X5. Since the network became operational, customer demand has been less than anticipated due to a competitor offering a special deal to its existing customers to encourage them not to change providers.

Most of ZCG's mobile phone customers sign a contract under which they pay a fixed amount each month to use ZCG's mobile network, paying extra if they exceed the agreed data usage and airtime limits. The contract also allows connection to a fixed landline, and for internet access using broadband. Most contracts run for two or three years.

In order to extend its broadband services, ZCG has started to purchase network capacity from third-party companies. ZCG enters a fixed-term contract to use a specified amount of the seller's network capacity, with the seller determining which of its network assets are used by ZCG in supplying network services to its customers. In the first six months of 20X6, ZCG purchased $17.8 million of network capacity from a range of suppliers, with the contract periods varying from twelve months to three years. The cost has been capitalised as an intangible asset.

ZCG makes substantial use of Equimal, a credit rating firm which holds the personal information of all of ZCG's customers for the purpose of providing ZCG with credit ratings for them. During September 20X6 it was reported in the national media that Equimal was the subject of a large-scale hacking attack, and that many of its customers' data may have been lost. It is not known at this stage precisely which data were stolen, but it is certain that at least some of ZCG's customers' data were among them.

In February 20X7, an employment tribunal found that for six months ZCG had not been paying the legal minimum wage to some of the new workers in its customer services call centre. Whenever a worker had been late for work, even by just one minute, ZCG had refused to pay them for the entire shift. This is contrary to the relevant regulations. It is likely that a fine will be levied against ZCG, but the tribunal is yet to determine its amount. In ZCG's jurisdiction, the maximum fine for breaching this legislation is $20,000. In addition to this, the wages that would need to be paid to the workers in question total around $210,000.

Exhibit 3 – Internal audit background and report

ZCG has a well-established internal audit department which is tasked with a range of activities including providing assurance to management over internal controls and assisting the Group's risk management team. The internal audit department is managed by Jules Winfield, a qualified accountant with many years' experience. An extract from the executive summary of the latest internal audit report to the Group finance director is shown below:

'We are pleased to report that ZCG's internal controls are working well and there have been no significant changes to systems and controls during the year. As a result of our testing of controls we uncovered only two financial irregularities which related to:

- Failure to obtain appropriate authorisation and approval of senior management expense claims, such as travel and other reimbursements; the unsubstantiated expense claims amounted to $575,000.

- Inadequate access controls over the Group's IT systems; this resulted in a payroll fraud amounting to $750,000.'

Financial information – extracts from latest management accounts

	8 months to 31 August 20X6 $m	Audited financial statements to 31 December 20X5 $m
Revenue:		
Europe	106	102
Americas	30	68
Southeast Asia	33	30
India	29	20
Total	198	220

	At 31 August 20X6 $m	At 31 December 20X5 $m
Total assets	598	565

Exhibit 4 – Gull Co information

You are also responsible for the audit of Gull Co, a large private company which is currently owned by the Brenner family, who own the majority of the company's shares. Following the completion of the audit this year, the finance director, Jim Brenner, contacted you and told you that the family is considering listing the company on the stock exchange. They would like to recruit one of your audit partners for a six-month period to help prepare for the listing. As the board is concerned that the necessary skills and personnel to support the listing are not currently present within the company, Jim Brenner has also requested that your firm assist them in identifying and recruiting new members to the board.

Currently, most of the executive director roles are performed by family members, except for the directors of operations and human resources, who are both long-serving employees. The board operates no audit committee and there is only one non-executive director, who works elsewhere as an IT consultant. Other than the recruitment of new board members, Gull Co is not planning on making any changes to its governance structure prior to or subsequent to listing.

Gull Co has a financial year ending 31 March 20X7, and audit planning is scheduled to take place in January 20X7.

BPP
LEARNING

Question 2

You are a manager in Monet & Co, a firm of accountants which has 12 offices and 30 partners, 10 of whom are members of ACCA. As an expert in ethics and professional conduct, you have been asked to advise the partners on the following issues, which were raised at a recent meeting.

(a)   An advertisement has been drafted as part of the firm's drive to increase the number of clients. It is suggested that it should be placed in a number of quality national as well as local newspapers:

> Have you had enough of your accountant charging you too much for poor quality services?
>
> Does your business need a kick-start?
>
> Look no further; Monet & Co provides the most comprehensive range of finance and accountancy services in the country as well as having the leading tax team in the country who are just waiting to save you money. We are offering free business advice to all new audit clients.
>
> Drop in and see us at your local office for a free consultation.
>
> Monet & Co, Chartered Certified Accountants.

(7 marks)

(b)   The planning for the audit of Renoir Co's financial statements for the year ending 31 March 20X6 will commence shortly. In preparation the audit partner telephoned Renoir Co's finance director, Jim Cassatt, to set up a planning meeting and to remind him that fees relating to a tax engagement from the previous year were still outstanding. Mr Cassatt raised concerns about the conduct of the previous audit, stating numerous examples of when he and his staff had been interrupted when they were busy. He stated that he wanted guarantees that this year's audit will be more efficient, less intrusive and cheaper, otherwise he will seek an alternative auditor.   **(6 marks)**

Required

Evaluate each of the issues described above, commenting on the ethical and professional issues raised and recommend any actions necessary in response to the issues identified.

(c)   You are also the manager responsible for the audit of Juliet Co, and you are planning the final audit of the financial statements for the year ending 30 June 20X6. Juliet Co is a supplier of components used in the manufacture of vehicle engines. Due to a downturn in the economy, and in the automotive industry particularly, the company has suffered a decline in sales and profitability over the last two years, mainly due to the loss of several key customer contracts. Many of Juliet Co's non-current assets are impaired in value, and a significant number of receivables balances have been written off in the last six months.

In response to the deteriorating market conditions, the management of Juliet Co decided to restructure the business. The main manufacturing facility will be reduced in size by two-thirds, and investment will be made in new technology to make the remaining operations more efficient, and to enable the manufacture of a wider variety of components for use in different types of engines and machinery. In order to fund this restructuring, the management of Juliet Co approached the company's bank with a request for a significant loan. You are aware that without the loan, Juliet Co is unlikely to be able to restructure successfully, which will raise significant doubt over its ability to continue as a going concern.

Your firm has been asked to advise on the necessary forecasts and projections that the bank will need to see in order to make a decision regarding the finance requested. Management has also requested that your firm attend a meeting with the bank at which the forecasts will be discussed.

Required

(i) Identify and explain the matters that should be considered, and the principal audit procedures to be performed, in respect of the additional funding being sought. **(6 marks)**

(ii) Comment on the ethical and other implications of the request for your firm to provide advice on the forecasts and projections, and to attend the meeting with the bank. **(6 marks)**

(Total = 25 marks)

Question 3

You are responsible for performing Engagement Quality Control Reviews on selected audit clients of Crocus & Co, and you are currently performing a review on the audit of the Magnolia Group (the Group). The Group manufactures chemicals which are used in a range of industries, with one of the subsidiaries, Daisy Co, specialising in chemical engineering and developing products to be sold by the other Group companies. The Group's products sell in over 50 countries.

A group structure is shown below, each of the subsidiaries is wholly owned by Magnolia Co, the parent company of the Group:

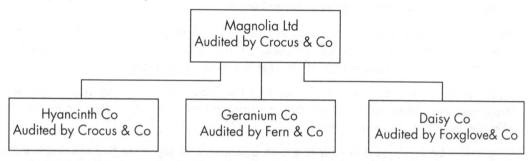

Crocus & Co is engaged to provide the audit of the Group financial statements and also the audit of Hyacinth Co and Magnolia Co. Geranium Co, a new subsidiary, is audited by a local firm of auditors based near the company's head office. Daisy Co is audited by an unconnected audit firm which specialises in the audit of companies involved with chemical engineering.

The Group's financial year ended on 31 December 20X6 and the audit is in the completion stage, with the auditor's report due to be issued in three weeks' time. The Group's draft consolidated financial statements recognise profit before tax of $7.5 million and total assets of $130 million.

The notes from your review of the audit working papers are shown below, summarising the issues relevant to each subsidiary.

(a) **Hyacinth Co – internal controls and results of controls testing**

The Group companies supply each other with various chemical products to be used in the manufacture of chemicals. Audit work performed at the interim stage at Hyacinth Co, including walk through procedures and internal control evaluations, concluded that internal controls over intra-group transactions were not effective, and this was documented in the audit file. At the final audit, tests of controls were performed to confirm this to be the case. The tests of controls confirmed that intra-group transactions are not being separately identified in the Group's accounting system and reconciliations of amounts owed between the subsidiaries are not performed.

The group audit manager has concluded on the audit working papers that 'as intra-group balances are cancelled on consolidation, this issue has no impact on the Group audit and no further work is necessary'.

As part of the audit approach it was determined that extensive testing would be performed over the internal controls for capital expenditure at Hyacinth Co as it was identified during planning that the company had made significant acquisitions of plant and equipment during the year. Following controls testing the internal controls over capital expenditure were evaluated to be effective in Hyacinth Co.

The working papers conclude that 'based on the results of controls testing at Hyacinth Co, it is reasonable to assume that controls are effective across the Group' and substantive procedures on property, plant and equipment in each Group company have been planned and performed in response to this assessment. **(9 marks)**

(b) **Geranium Co – new subsidiary**

This subsidiary was acquired on 30 September 20X6 and is audited by Fern & Co. The Group audit strategy contains the following statement in relation to the audit of Geranium Co: 'Geranium Co will only be consolidated for three months and the post-acquisition profit for that period to be included in the Group financial statements is $150,000. On that basis, Geranium Co is immaterial to the Group financial statements and therefore our audit procedures are based on analytical procedures only.' Other than the analytical procedures performed, there is no documentation in respect of Geranium Co or its audit firm Fern & Co included in the Group audit working papers.

The draft statement of financial position of Geranium Co recognises total assets of $30 million. **(7 marks)**

(c) **Daisy Co – restriction on international trade**

As well as being involved in chemical engineering and supplying chemicals for use by the other Group companies, Daisy Co specialises in producing chemicals which are used in the agricultural sector, and around half of its sales are made internationally.

Daisy Co is audited by Foxglove & Co, and the Group audit working papers contain the necessary evaluations to conclude that an appropriate level of understanding has been obtained in respect of the audit firm.

Foxglove & Co has provided your firm with a summary of key audit findings which includes the following statement: 'During the year new government environmental regulations have imposed restrictions on international trade in chemicals, with sales to many countries now prohibited. Our audit work concludes that this does not create a significant going concern risk to Daisy Co, and we have confirmed that all inventories are measured at the lower of cost and net realisable value.'

The Group audit manager has concluded that 'I am happy that no further work is needed in this area – we can rely on the unmodified audit opinion to be issued by Foxglove & Co. This issue was not identified until it was raised by Foxglove & Co, it has not been mentioned to me by the Group board members, and it has no implications for the consolidated financial statements.'

The draft statement of financial position of Daisy Co recognises total assets of $8 million and the statement of profit or loss recognises profit before tax of $50,000.

The draft consolidated financial statements recognises goodwill in respect of Daisy Co of $3 million (20X5 – $3 million). **(9 marks)**

Required

In respect of each of the matters described above:

(i) Comment on the quality of the planning and performance of the Group audit discussing the quality control and other professional issues raised; and

(ii) Recommend any further actions, including relevant audit procedures, to be taken by your firm, prior to finalising the Group auditor's report.

Note. The split of the mark allocation is shown next to each of the issues above.

(Total = 25 marks)

Answers

**DO NOT TURN THIS PAGE UNTIL YOU HAVE
COMPLETED THE MOCK EXAM**

A PLAN OF ATTACK

If this had been the real Advanced Audit and Assurance exam and you had been told to turn over and begin, what would have been going through your mind?

An important thing to say (while there is still time) is that it is vital to have a good breadth of knowledge of the syllabus because the question requirements for each question will relate to different areas of the AAA syllabus. However, don't panic. Below we provide guidance on how to approach the exam.

Approaching the answer

It is vital that you attempt all the questions in the exam to increase your chances of passing. The best way to do this is to make sure you stick to the time allocation for each question – both in total and for each of the question parts. The worst thing you can do is run over time in one question and then find that you don't have enough time for the remaining questions, leading you to miss out on some of the easier marks in those questions.

Section A consists of one long case-study style question set at the planning stage of the audit. This may contain detailed information such as extracts from financial statements and audit working papers. A range of requirements will be set for this question but will only cover areas from syllabus areas A to D inclusive.

Question 1 is for 50 marks, all set at the planning stage. This is a long question, and as usual covers audit risk, reliance on an internal audit function, audit procedures in some specific areas and then finally a separate requirement on ethics and a change in corporate governance structure.

Section B contains two more compulsory questions, and may be set on any area of the AAA syllabus.

Question 2, for 25 marks, focused on ethical and professional issues in the context of several mini scenarios.

Question 3 featured an engagement quality control review and presented a stiff challenge. All 3 parts of the question related to the same scenario.

Forget about it!

And don't worry if you found the exam difficult. More than likely other candidates will too. If this were the real thing you would need to forget the exam the minute you left the exam hall and think about the next one. Or, if it is the last one, celebrate!

BPP
LEARNING

Question 1

As in previous audit risk questions, there is credit available for calculating and concluding on the materiality of a balance in the financial statements. A majority of candidates are able to correctly select the appropriate benchmark for materiality (eg assessing an asset or liability in the context of total assets rather than on revenue or profits) but frequently answers were presented with materiality based on prior year rather than current year figures. Audit risk continues to be an area that candidates find difficult and particularly it continues to be noted that many candidates fail to engage with the information provided in enough depth, specifically when provided with extracts from financial statements.

Candidates are again reminded that in order to provide a full answer in relation to audit risk they should utilise and analyse all the information that is provided. Candidates were also required to discuss the considerations to be taken into account when assessing whether and how to use internal audit to assist the external auditor. The majority of candidates were able to list the criteria as per ISA 610 *Using the Work of Internal Auditors*, to assess against and relate that back to the scenario, which was an improvement on the last time this standard was examined.

In part (c) candidates were required to provide the principal audit procedures to obtain audit evidence in relation to the classification of a joint venture and the measurement of an intangible asset. The majority of candidates performed satisfactorily in this requirement but again many had not read the requirement carefully enough and described tests covering other FS assertions than those required – for example assessing the cost of the joint venture which was not relevant to the classification risk, or failing to take into account that the intangible had been purchased in the prior year so the cost would have been audited at that point, so audit procedures should have focused on confirming the brought forward figure and any adjustments for amortisation or impairment.

There were four professional marks available, and most candidates secured most of these marks by providing an introduction and using headings to create an appropriate structure for their answer. However, presentation was not always good and candidates are reminded to pay attention to determining an appropriate layout for their answer.

Part (d) had two elements, an ethics part regarding other services which was generally well answered and a second element which required the implications the governance structure and a potential listing may have on the audit process. Many candidates appeared to interpret this as a requirement to comment on how the governance structure of the client fell below best practice and how to improve that structure and did not address the audit implications at all. This is particularly disappointing given the recent examining team's article on the topic and again candidates are reminded to make sure that they read the requirements carefully.

Marking scheme

Marks

(a) **Evaluation of audit risk**
Generally up to 2 marks for each well explained audit risk. In addition, 1 mark for each correct materiality calculation to a maximum of 2 marks and 1 mark for each relevant calculation such as trends.
- Recognition of 50% equity shareholding in WTC
- Amortisation of licence to operate in Farland
- Possible impairment of licence
- Right to use network capacity
- Revenue recognition – max 5 marks if discuss a range of issues specific to IFRS 15 including multiple element contracts, timing of recognition, disclosure requirements, volume of transactions

BPP
LEARNING

    –   Minimum wage – NOCLAR, ISA 250

    –   Cyber attack – use of expert, consideration of IAS 37

    –   Internal controls and fraud risk – up to 4 marks for a detailed discussion of fraud risk

    –   Segmental reporting

Maximum   17

(b) Internal audit

Generally up to 2 marks for discussion of each relevant matter:

– General introduction, comment on prohibition in some jurisdictions

– Objectivity

– Competence

– Disciplined and systematic approach

– Using the internal auditors to provide direct assistance

Maximum   7

(c) Audit procedures

Generally 1 mark for each well explained audit procedure:

(i) Investment in WTC

– Obtain the legal documentation supporting the investment and agree the details of the investment (max 2 marks for details of items to be verified)

– Read board minutes for approval of the investment understanding of the business rationale for the investment

– Read minutes of relevant meetings between ZCG and Wolf Communications to confirm shared control and shared decision-making process

– Confirm that ZCG has successfully appointed members to the board of WTC and that board decisions are made equally

Maximum   4

(ii) Amortisation of licence

– Obtain the licence agreement and confirm the length of the licence period

– Confirm whether the licence can be renewed at the end of the 10-year period

– Reperform management's calculation of the amortisation charged as an expense in 20X6

– Discuss with management the process for determining the method of amortisation

– Review management accounts to confirm that the Farland network became operational on 1 July 20X6 and that Farland is generating a revenue stream from that date

– Review customer contracts to confirm network operational from 1 July 20X6

– Enquire with management on the existence of factors indicating that a shorter useful life is appropriate

Marks

– Review management accounts and cash flow forecasts
   to confirm that Farland is generating an income stream
   and is predicted to continue to generate cash
– Obtain a management representation to confirm that
   there are no indications of impairment of the licence of
   which management is aware

Maximum   6

(d)   (i)   **Ethical and professional matters**
In general up to 1 mark for each well explained point:
Temporary recruitment of audit partner
– Potential self-review threat
– Potential familiarity threat
– Potential management decision making threat
– Recommendations to reduce the potential threats
   described
   (1 mark each to a maximum of 2)
Recruitment services
– Potential self-interest, intimidation and familiarity threat
– Management responsibility in appointing senior
   management
– As listed entity, service cannot be provided
– Decline engagement

Maximum   6

(ii) **Implications for audit process**
In general up to 1 mark for each well explained point:
– Lack of independence and oversight of board
– Ineffective non-executive board
– Need for increased auditor scepticism particularly in
   light of potential listing
– Increased fraud/manipulation risk which will need to
   be reflected in audit approach
– No effective audit committee
– Communication in line with ISA 260 harder with no
   objective audit committee
– Listed company with increased audit risk
– Extended auditor's report requirements

Maximum   6

Professional marks – generally 1 mark each for heading,
introduction, structure and clarity of explanations.   Maximum   4

Total   **50**

Briefing notes

To: Vincent Vega, audit engagement partner

From: Audit engagement manager

Subject: Audit planning – ZCG Introduction

These briefing notes have been prepared to assist in the audit planning of ZCG, and contain an
evaluation of audit risk and a discussion of the matters to be considered in determining whether to
place reliance on the Group's internal audit department. The notes also include the recommended

audit procedures to be performed on the classification of the investment in WTC and on the measurement of a licence acquired on 1 January 20X5.

(a) **Evaluation of audit risks**

Recognition of 50% equity shareholding in WTC

The 50% equity shareholding is likely to give rise to a joint venture under which control of WTC is shared between ZCG and Wolf Communications Co. IFRS 11 *Joint Arrangements* requires that an investor which has joint control over a joint venture should recognise its investment using the equity method of accounting. Audit risk arises in that despite owning 50% of the equity shares of WTC, ZCG may not actually share control with Wolf Communications, for example, if Wolf Communications retains a right to veto decisions or if ZCG cannot appoint an equal number of board members in order to make joint decisions with board members appointed by Wolf Communications. If ZCG does not have joint control, then WTC should not be treated as a joint venture.

Assuming that there is shared control, an audit risk arises in that ZCG may not have correctly applied equity accounting, thereby potentially over or understating ZCG's investment and resulting in incorrect presentation in the consolidated statement of financial position and statement of profit or loss. The cost of the investment in WTC represents 7.5% of ZCG's total assets at 31 August 20X6, thus the investment is material to the Group.

Amortisation of licence to operate in Farland

The licence acquired on 1 January 20X5 should be recognised as an intangible asset and amortised on a systematic basis over its useful life. According to IAS 38 *Intangible Assets*, the amortisation method should reflect the pattern of benefits, or if the pattern cannot be determined reliably, the straight-line method of amortisation should be used. Amortisation should begin when the asset is available for use, meaning when it is in the location and condition necessary for it to be capable of operating in the manner which management intends. ZCG therefore should begin to amortise the licence on 1 July 20X6 and amortise over the remaining licence period of eight and a half years. The audit risk is that amortisation did not commence at the right point in time or that it has been determined using an inappropriate useful life, leading to over or understatement of the amortisation charge to profit as well as the carrying value of the intangible asset.

Assuming that it is appropriate to use the straight-line method, amortisation for the year to 31 December 20X6 should be \$3.8m ($65/8.5 \times {}^{6}/_{12}$). This represents 1.3% of extrapolated revenue for the year of \$297m ($198 \times {}^{12}/_{8}$) and is therefore material, and the amortisation will be more material next year when a full year's charge to profit is made.

Impairment of the Farland licence

IAS 38 does not require an annual impairment review to be conducted for all intangible assets. However, management should consider whether there are indicators of impairment and if necessary perform an impairment review on the licence. The competitor's actions which appear to have reduced customer demand to a level below that anticipated is an indicator of potential impairment, so management must calculate the recoverable amount of the licence and compare to its carrying value in order to determine if the asset is impaired. Therefore there is a risk that the licence is overstated in value, and operating profit also overstated if any necessary impairment has not been recognised.

Revenue recognition

ZCG is supplying customers with a multiple-element contract and is providing access to a mobile phone network and a fixed landline and broadband service. The key audit risk arises in relation to whether ZCG accounts for the elements of the contract separately in accordance with IFRS 15 *Revenue from Contracts with Customers*, which requires the revenue to be derived from the contract to be allocated to each component. ZCG should have robust systems

in place to ensure that contracts can be 'unbundled', enabling the revenue from each part of the contract to be separately determined, otherwise there is a significant risk that the revenue element attributable to each component of the customer contracts will be over or understated.

There is also a risk that the timing of revenue recognition will not be in line with ZCG meeting its performance obligations, also a requirement of IFRS 15. Contracts vary in length, lasting two or three years, and there is an audit risk that the timing of revenue recognition is not appropriate. The fact that total revenue, when extrapolated for the 12-month period, is expected to increase by 35% could indicate that revenue is being recognised too early.

IFRS 15 contains significant disclosure requirements and there is a risk that ZCG fails to provide sufficient disclosure on a range of matters relevant to its contracts with customers, including the significant judgements made in applying IFRS 15 to those contracts and sufficient disaggregation of the necessary disclosures.

Given the significant volume of individual customer contracts and the complexity of the accounting treatment, revenue recognition is a significant audit risk.

Right to use network capacity

The payment of $17.8m to acquire access to network capacity represents 3% of total assets and 6% of extrapolated revenue for the year, thus the amount is material.

It seems that risk and reward does not pass to ZCG in respect of the assets being used and the seller retains control over the use of its network assets. Therefore the network capacity should not be recognised as an intangible asset of ZCG, and the Group is currently adopting an inappropriate accounting treatment which has resulted in intangible assets being overstated.

The accounting treatment for these rights should be discussed with ZCG as soon as possible. The most appropriate accounting treatment would seem to be for ZCG to record the cost of the right to use the network capacity as a prepayment and recognise the cost in profit or loss on a straight-line basis over the term of the agreements and this accounting treatment should be reflected in the financial statements as soon as possible. The audit team will need to be made aware of the risk that prepayments and operating expenses are over or understated if the cost has not been treated as a prepayment and/or is not released to profit or loss over an appropriate period.

A further risk is the payment to the network provider is for a specified amount of access to the network provider's network. There is a risk is that ZCG has exceeded the allocated allowance and that any necessary additional payment due for excess usage is not recognised in the financial statements.

Cyber attack

There is clearly a risk that data protection laws have been breached, so it is imperative that Tarantino & Co obtains an understanding of the relevant legislation in ZCG's jurisdiction – for instance in the UK, this would likely include the Data Protection Act 1998. IAS 37 *Provisions, Contingent Liabilities and Contingent Assets* requires an entity to provide for a future liability where an outflow of resources embodying economic benefits is probable, and the amount can be measured reliably. Audit evidence will need to be obtained regarding whether ZCG is liable to its customers for the loss of their data, and further whether there is a possibility of winning a legal case against Equimal for losing ZCG's data.

It is likely that a legal expert would need to be consulted to help determine the likelihood of both of these outcomes. It should therefore be ascertained whether ZCG has engaged the services of a management's expert, and the significance of any work done by them for the purpose of the audit. Tarantino & Co would need to: evaluate the expert's competence and capabilities; obtain an understanding of the expert's work, and; evaluate the appropriateness of their work as audit evidence (ISA 500 *Audit Evidence*: para. 8). It may be necessary for Tarantino & Co to make use of an auditor's expert if there is no reliable management's expert.

ZCG does not appear to have provided for a possible outflow (or recognised any contingent assets), and this should be confirmed. A contingent asset should only be recognised when a future inflow is virtually certain, and that is not the case here (so no asset should be recognised). Whether a liability is recognised will depend on the outcome of any expert's work, but given that the details of the case are still not certain – it is not known whether all of ZCG's customers' data was stolen, for example – provision cannot be made because the amount of any future outflow cannot be measured reliably.

Minimum wage

The employment tribunal is a subsequent event. IAS 10 *Events After the Period* distinguishes adjusting from non-adjusting events. Adjusting events are those that 'provide further evidence of conditions that existed at the end of the reporting period' (IAS 10: para. 3). The tribunal may be an adjusting event. This is because the condition it relates to (ZCG's failure to pay the legal minimum wage) existed at the end of the reporting period.

This is a case of non-compliance with laws and regulations, or NOCLAR. ISA 250A *Consideration of Laws and Regulations in an Audit of Financial Statements* states that the auditor is not responsible for preventing non-compliance, or detecting non-compliance with all laws and regulations (ISA 250A: para. 4). However, the auditor is responsible for obtaining reasonable assurance that the financial statements are not materially misstated.

In ISA 250A's terms, the legislation that has been breached has a direct effect on the financial statements. Tarantino & Co should obtain an understanding of the non-compliance – together with further information if needed – so that it can evaluate the effect on the financial statements (ISA 250A: para. 19). Tarantino & Co should discuss the matter with the appropriate level of management (ISA 250A: para. 20), and determine the effect that the non-compliance will have on the financial statements. This is likely to include a fine of $20,000, in addition to any unpaid wages that will need to paid to the employees in question. The fine is less than 0.1% of revenue, which is not material. The unpaid wages are estimated to be £210,000, which is 0.1% of revenue and is also not material.

The audit risk is that the fine has not been provided for in the financial statements, together with the effects of the unpaid wages. Tarantino & Co should also consider whether the issue indicates that ZCG's internal controls are not working effectively, which would increase control risk.

Internal controls and fraud risk

The internal audit department has reported that internal controls are 'working well'. This statement will need to be substantiated but gives the impression that control risk is likely to be low. The work of the internal audit department will be discussed in more detail in the next section of the briefing notes.

However, it is worth noting that two frauds have been found to be operating during the year, giving rise to audit risk. Although the total monetary amount attributable to the frauds is less than 1% of revenue, therefore immaterial, the fact that the frauds have occurred indicates that there are significant internal control deficiencies which could mean that other frauds are operating. We will need to carefully plan our audit approach to expenses and payroll in light of the increased fraud risk. This is heightened by the issue of the NOCLAR discussed above.

The lack of approval and authorisation of expenses discovered by internal audit is concerning as this appears to involve higher level management and may call into question management integrity. We should review the work of internal audit to establish if this is an area where controls have been overridden or if there are current gaps within the control framework. We should review and update our systems notes to identify where reliance can potentially be placed on controls and where there are deficiencies.

The issue uncovered by internal audit in relation to payroll suggests that there is inadequate control over the Group's IT system. Access controls, which form part of the Group's general IT controls, are weak which means that other areas of the system may be vulnerable. This significantly increases control risk and as a result presents a significant area of audit risk. We will need to ensure that we carefully plan our approach as this may mean that there are areas of the system where no reliance can be placed on internal controls and appropriate alternative procedures will need to be applied.

Segmental reporting

Being a listed entity, ZCG should provide segmental information in the notes to the financial statements in accordance with IFRS 8 *Operating Segments*. The audit risk is that the segmental information provided is not sufficiently detailed and/or not based on the information reported internally to the Group's chief operating decision maker.

There are some unusual trends in the segmental revenue figures from the management accounts. For example, revenue from Southeast Asia appears to have increased significantly – if the 20X6 revenue figure is extrapolated to a 12-month period, the projected revenue from that segment is $49.5m, an increase of 65% compared to 20X5. There is a risk that revenues have been misallocated between segments, particularly given that revenue from Americas has fallen so much.

IFRS 8 requires disclosure of eg how the entity identified its segments, and any judgements made by management in aggregating segment information. There is a risk that disclosures made are either missing or inadequate.

(b) **Matters which should be considered in determining the amount of reliance, if any, which can be placed on the work of ZCG's internal audit department**

According to ISA 610 *Using the Work of Internal Auditors*, the external auditor may decide to use the work of the audit client's internal audit function to modify the nature or timing, or reduce the extent, of audit procedures to be performed directly by the external auditor. Note that in some jurisdictions the external auditor may be prohibited, or restricted to some extent, by law or regulation from using the work of the internal audit function. Therefore Tarantino & Co should consider whether it is prohibited by the law or regulations which it must adhere to from relying on the work of ZCG's internal audit department or using the internal auditors to provide direct assistance.

Tarantino & Co must evaluate the internal audit department to determine whether its work is suitable by evaluating:

- The extent to which the internal audit function's organisational status and relevant policies and procedures support the objectivity of the internal auditors;

- The level of competence of the internal audit function; and

- Whether the internal audit function applies a systematic and disciplined approach, including quality control.

One of the key issues to be evaluated is objectivity – the internal audit department should be unbiased in their work and be able to report their findings without being subject to the influence of others. The fact that the latest internal audit report is addressed to ZCG's finance director could indicate that there is a conflict of interest, as the internal audit department should report directly to the audit committee or to those charged with governance in order to maintain their independence.

The internal audit team is managed by a qualified accountant who is presumably technically competent, though the nature and status of his qualification should be determined. Tarantino & Co should consider whether the rest of the internal audit department is staffed by professional accountants, whether ZCG has a training programme in place for the internal auditors, for example, to ensure that they are up to date with new IFRS requirements, and whether there are sufficient resources for the internal auditors to carry out their duties in a large multinational organisation.

When assessing competency, consideration must also be given to the overall findings which were reported regarding the deficiencies in the current internal control system. The internal audit department has concluded that controls are working well despite there being two instances of fraud in the year which may have more serious ramifications than first suggested. The scope of work carried out in this area and the resultant recommendations will need to be reviewed. This may further suggest that the internal audit department is not free to investigate or report their findings due to the current reporting chains.

If there are doubts over either the objectivity or the competence of the internal audit department, then Tarantino & Co should not rely on their work.

In order to determine whether the internal audit department works in a systematic and disciplined way, Tarantino & Co should consider matters including the nature of documentation which is produced by the department and whether effective quality control procedures are in place such as direction, supervision and review of work carried out.

If Tarantino & Co wants to use the internal audit function to provide direct assistance, then the firm should:

- Obtain written agreement from an authorised representative of the entity that the internal auditors will be allowed to follow the external auditor's instructions, and that the entity will not intervene in the work the internal auditor performs for the external auditor; and

- Obtain written agreement from the internal auditors that they will keep confidential specific matters as instructed by the external auditor and inform the external auditor of any threat to their objectivity.

If these confirmations cannot be obtained, then the internal auditors should not be used to provide direct assistance.

(c)   (i)   **Audit procedures on the classification of the 50% shareholding in WTC**

- Obtain the legal documentation supporting the investment and agree the details of the investment including:

    - The date of the investment

    - Amount paid

    - Number of shares purchased

    - The voting rights attached to the shares

    - The nature of the profit sharing arrangement between ZCG and Wolf Communications

    - The nature of access to WTC's assets under the terms of the agreement

    - Confirmation that there is no restriction of ZCG's shared control of WTC

- Read board minutes to confirm the approval of the investment and to understand the business rationale for the investment.

- Read minutes of relevant meetings between ZCG and Wolf Communications to confirm that control is shared between the two companies and to understand the nature of the relationship and the decision-making process.

- Obtain documentation such as WTC's organisational structure to confirm that ZCG has successfully appointed members to the board of WTC and that those members have equal power to the members appointed by Wolf Communications.

(ii) **Audit procedures on the measurement of the operating licence to operate in Farland**

- Agree the cost of the licence to the amount included within the opening balances, or the previous year's working papers.

- Obtain the licence agreement and confirm the length of the licence period to be 10 years from the date it was granted.

- Confirm whether the licence can be renewed at the end of the 10-year period, as this may impact on the estimated useful life and amortisation.

- Reperform management's calculation of the amortisation charged as an expense in 20X6.

- Discuss with management the process for identifying an appropriate amortisation method and where relevant, how the pattern of future economic benefits associated with the licence have been determined.

- Confirm with management that the Farland network became operational on 1 July 20X6.

- Review a sample of contracts with customers in Farland to verify that contracts commenced from the operational date of 1 July 20X6.

- Enquire with management on the existence of any factors indicating that a shorter useful life is appropriate, for example, the stability of market demand in Farland or possible restrictions on the network capacity in Farland.

- Review management accounts and cash flow forecasts to confirm that Farland is generating an income stream and is predicted to continue to generate cash.

- Obtain a written representation from management confirming that there are no indications of impairment of the licence of which management is aware.

Conclusion

These briefing notes highlight that there are a number of audit risks to be addressed, in particular revenue recognition, and fraud risks appear to be significant issues requiring a robust response from the audit team. We will need to carefully consider whether it is appropriate to receive direct assistance from the internal audit department.

(d) (i) **Ethical and professional matters**

Temporary recruitment of audit partner

Seconding a member of staff to an audit client may create a self-review threat. This would arise if the member of staff returns to the audit firm and considers matters or documentation which is the result of work which they performed while on assignment to the client.

In this situation, it is likely that the individual would be involved in preparing the financial systems of Gull Co for the flotation. If this is the case, it would create a significant threat to objectivity. This would be reduced if the role was focused on non-financial matters.

Additionally, the member of staff would work alongside employees of the client on a daily basis. This would overstep the normal professional boundary between auditor and client and may compromise the objectivity of the member of staff due to their familiarity with employees of the client.

In order to reduce this threat, the member of staff seconded to Gull Co should not be a current or future member of the audit team.

An additional risk would be if the seconded member of staff assumed managerial responsibilities of the client. This is not permitted. Given that Gull Co has specifically requested a partner, it appears as though they require someone senior, indicating that they may need someone to either make or significantly influence decision making.

In order to reduce this risk, the use of a less senior member of staff with relevant experience of the flotation process could be proposed and make it clear in the contract that they are not able to make decisions for Gull Co and that decision making will always remain their responsibility.

Alternatively, it could be recommended that Gull Co recruit the assistance of either the management or transaction advisory services team to assist them with the flotation as a separate engagement, thus circumventing the ethical threats identified.

Recruitment services

In relation to the request for Tarantino & Co to provide assistance in recruiting new members of the board, this could give rise to self-interest, familiarity or intimidation threats as the firm would essentially be advising on the recruitment of staff who will ultimately be in senior management positions and responsible for the running of and oversight of a listed company. These new members of staff may also go on to be included in any audit committee which the company sets up and will be responsible for assessing the independence of the external auditors. Being involved in any decision on who should be appointed to such a senior position is also likely to involve the firm taking on a management responsibility which is not appropriate. Given that Gull Co is potentially going to be a listed company, Tarantino & Co should not be involved in any activity which involves searching for suitable candidates or undertaking any reference checks of prospective candidates. This request should be turned down by Tarantino & Co due to the potential management responsibility involved.

> **Tutorial note.** Credit will be awarded for relevant comments relating to the professional benefits of accepting the assignment.

(ii) Implications of governance and board structure on audit process

Structure of the board

As a private company with the majority of shares held by the Brenner family, the auditor's report addressed to the shareholders as a body would have been aimed predominantly at the Brenner family. However, the predominance of the Brenner family may undermine the independence of the board. The board may be accustomed to operating in the interests of the family as the majority shareholders. However, once the company is listed, the board will be required to consider the interests of the new shareholders as a group. The executive members of the board are either Brenner family members or long-term employees of the company and potentially loyal to the existing ownership.

With only one non-executive director, the board currently lacks independent oversight and the opinions and decisions of the executive board may not be subject to appropriate levels of challenge and scrutiny.

In addition, non-executive board members are specifically required to scrutinise the performance of management, consider the integrity of the financial statements, determine director remuneration and participate in the appointment and removal of directors. With limited experience outside IT consultancy and limited time, the current non-executive is unlikely to be able to fulfil these roles effectively on their own.

There is no indication that management lacks integrity but Tarantino & Co must remain sceptical of the motivations of the family, particularly leading up to a listing. There will be an incentive to overstate performance and position to inflate the value of the

company. With little effective oversight of the executive board, Tarantino & Co must remain alert for this possibility, particularly when auditing matters involving management judgement in subsequent financial periods.

Audit committee

The lack of any form of audit committee is a significant departure from corporate governance best practice. The audit committee fulfils a number of significant roles, including monitoring the integrity of the financial statements, reviewing internal financial controls, monitoring the independence of the external auditor and communicating with the external auditor on matters relating to the external audit. The audit committee should have a member with relevant financial expertise and this will become of even more importance once the company is listed.

In the absence of an audit committee, Tarantino & Co will have to communicate directly with the board including the requirement to communicate how the auditor has maintained their independence in line with ISA 260 *Communication with Those Charged with Governance*. This may affect the independence of Tarantino & Co, or at least the perception of their independence. It may also reduce the effectiveness of communications between the auditor and the company; the audit committee is responsible for communicating relevant matters, such as deficiencies in internal control, up to the executive board for their consideration. Without an audit committee, matters of significance to the audit may not be given sufficient prominence by the board. Further, the audit committee is responsible for reviewing the integrity of the financial statements and internal controls and currently there is no-one at Gull Co capable of carrying out this role. Overall, this may make it harder for Tarantino & Co to discuss and communicate key findings from the audit including the auditor's qualitative assessment of the company's accounting practices. Also, with the lack of an objective audit committee, it may be harder for Tarantino & Co, to fulfil their responsibilities to communicate any significant difficulties which are encountered during the audit.

Listed status

Further, as a listed company, Gull Co will be subject to increased scrutiny and pressure to achieve performance levels, which may motivate the board to manipulate the financial statements to present an improved picture of performance. For Tarantino & Co, this increases the level of audit risk and is likely to have a significant impact on the firm's assessment of the risk of fraud and management override. This is likely to have a significant impact on the firm's approach to auditing areas of the financial statements subject to judgement, such as management estimates and revenue recognition.

As a listed company, Gull Co may be required to produce more detailed financial statements probably in a shorter time frame and, as mentioned above, the lack of financial expertise and lack of objective scrutiny by an audit committee may result in errors or omissions. This again increases the level of audit risk faced by Tarantino & Co and a lot more detailed testing may need to be performed to ensure compliance with appropriate accounting standards and listing rules.

Further, once listed, the auditor's report issued for Gull Co will be available to a much wider audience and will require additional disclosures in line with ISA 701 *Communicating Key Audit Matters in the Independent Auditor's Report*. This will add another level of work and complexity to the audit of Gull Co.

BPP LEARNING

Question 2

Marking scheme

Marks

(a) **Advertisement**
     Generally 1 mark each per well-explained point:
     -    Advert reflects adversely on other professional accountants
     -    Misleading with regards to size of firm
     -    Misleading comments regarding expertise of tax team
     -    Threat to professional behaviour by guaranteeing to save tax

Marks

- Lowballing – self-interest threat and threat to professional competence and due care
- Potential self-review threat from business advice
- Free consultations permitted
- Remove misleading claims from advert
- Separate teams for audit and other services advertised

Maximum   7

(b) **Renoir Co**

Generally 1 mark each per well-explained point:
- Intimidation threat to objectivity
- Meet senior management and explain the terms of the audit
- Consider integrity of Jim Cassatt and possible implications for audit
- Thorough performance and review of planning
- Early notice of audit requirements and logistics
- Self-interest threat created by overdue fees
- Delay audit until fees paid (1 max)

Maximum   6

(c) (i) **Matters and procedures on funding**

Up to 1 mark each point:

Matters
- Area of critical importance to the audit
- Bank reluctant to confirm arrangements
- Assets impaired
- Have alternative providers been discussed?
- Potential impact on FS and auditor's report if significant doubt remains over going concern

Procedures
- Review assumptions used in forecasts and projections
- Written representation on reasonableness of assumptions used
- Review potential finance for adequacy
- Consider if any previous defaults
- Consider terms of finance – can the company meet repayment terms?
- Written confirmation from bank
- Discuss with bank
- Discuss with management

Maximum   6

(ii) **Ethical and other implications**

Up to 1 mark each point explained:
- Advice is a non-audit service
- Self-review threat
- Advocacy threat
- Safeguards should be used to reduce threats
- Firm may decide that no safeguards can reduce threats to an acceptable level
- Attending meeting could create legal proximity

Maximum   6

Total   25

(a) **Advertisement**

Accountants are permitted to advertise subject to the requirements in the ACCA *Code of Ethics and Conduct* that the advert should 'not reflect adversely on the professional accountant, ACCA or the accounting profession' (ACCA *Code of Ethics*: para. 250A). The advert does not appear to be in keeping with this principle; it suggests that other firms of accountants charge inappropriately high fees and that the quality of their services is questionable. This discredits the services offered by other professional accountants as well as implying that the services offered by Monet & Co are far superior.

The advert states that the firm offers 'the most comprehensive range of finance and accountancy services in the country'. This is misleading; with 12 offices and only 30 partners Monet & Co is unlikely to be one of the largest accountancy firms in the country and is therefore unlikely to offer the most comprehensive range of services. If it is misleading, this statement must be withdrawn from the advertisement.

The advert also implies that they have the country's leading tax team; it is not possible to substantiate this claim as it is not possible to measure the effectiveness of tax teams and even if it were, no such measure currently exists. This is, therefore, also potentially misleading and should be withdrawn from the advert.

The suggestion that the tax experts are waiting to save the client money is inappropriate; no such guarantees can be made because tax professionals must apply relevant tax legislation in an objective manner. This may lead to a reduction in a client's current tax expense or it may not. Any failure to apply these regulations appropriately could raise questions about the professional behaviour of the practitioner.

Guaranteeing to be cheaper than other service providers is often referred to as 'lowballing'. This could create a potential self-interest threat to objectivity, and could also threaten professional competence and due care if the practitioner is unable to apply the appropriate professional standards for that level of fee.

Offering business advice to audit clients creates a potential self-review threat to objectivity. It depends on the sort of advice offered but it is possible that the auditor in subsequent years may have to audit aspects of the business affected by the advice given. This would be particularly relevant if the practitioner provided advice with regard to systems design. It would be possible to offer both services if Monet & Co can use different teams to provide each service. Given that they have 12 offices, it may be possible to keep these services completely separate and they may be able to offer both.

Offering services for free as part of a promotion is not prohibited but, similar to lowballing, this increases the threat to competence and due care if sufficient time and resources are not allocated to the task. This may also devalue the services offered by Monet & Co as they may be perceived as being a promotional tool as opposed to a professional service.

Firms of accountants are permitted to offer free consultations, so this does not create any specific threats. The phrase 'drop in and see us' may cause a problem with potential clients though as it may not always be possible to expect to see senior staff members without an appointment. To avoid damaging the professional profile of the firm, Monet & Co would need to make sure they had a dedicated member of staff available to meet potential customers who is available without prior notice.

Finally, Monet & Co is not permitted to use the term 'Chartered Certified Accountants' because less than 50% of the partners of the firm are ACCA members (ACCA *Code of Ethics*: B4. Para. 15). This reference should be removed.

(b) **Renoir Co**

Mr Cassatt's threat that he will seek an alternative auditor unless the audit is cheaper and less intrusive than the prior year constitutes an intimidation threat to objectivity. This has arisen because Mr Cassatt is trying to unduly influence the conduct of the audit of Renoir Co.

The audit manager or partner should arrange a meeting with the senior management of Renoir Co and the audit committee, if one exists, and they should explain how the audit has to be performed and how the fee is calculated. They should take care to explain the professional standards which they have to comply with and the terms of the engagement which the client agreed to, specifically that management should provide all necessary documents and explanations deemed necessary by the auditor to collect sufficient appropriate evidence. It should be explained that due to the need to comply with these standards, they cannot guarantee to reduce either the volume of procedures or the audit fee.

Monet & Co should also consider the integrity of Mr Cassatt. If the audit firm considers any threat created too significant, then they may wish to resign from the engagement. If not, it may be necessary to use more senior, experienced staff on the assignment who are less likely to be intimidated by Mr Cassatt while performing audit fieldwork.

If the audit proceeds, the planning should be performed by an appropriately experienced member of the audit team. This should be reviewed thoroughly by the audit manager and the partner to ensure that the procedures recommended are appropriate to the risk assessment performed. In this way Monet & Co can ensure that any unnecessary, and potential time wasting, procedures are avoided.

The audit manager should then make sure that Mr Cassatt is given adequate notice of the timing of the audit and provide him with a list of documentation which will be required during the course of the audit so that Renoir Co may prepare for the visit by the audit team. The manager could also recommend that Mr Cassatt and his team make specific time available to meet with the audit team and then request that the audit team use that time to ask all the necessary enquiries of the client. This should minimise any disruption experienced by the client during fieldwork.

The overdue fees create a self-interest threat. IESBA's *Code of Ethics for Professional Accountants* states that a self-interest threat may be created if fees due from an audit client remain unpaid for a long time, especially if not paid before the issue of the auditor's report for the following year. The audit firm should determine the amount of fee which is unpaid, and whether it could be perceived to be a loan made to the client. It may be a relatively insignificant amount, and it may not be long overdue, in which case the threat to objectivity is not significant.

If the self-interest threat is significant, then no audit work should be performed until the fees are paid. This decision, and the reason for it, should be communicated to the management of Renoir Co or their audit committee, if possible.

(c) (i) The central issue here is going concern; there are a number of indications that Juliet Co may not be a going concern. For instance: declining sales and profitability over two years; the loss of key customers; the impairment of assets; debts going bad. Most significant of all is the question of whether the loan will be obtained.

If Juliet Co does not obtain the loan, then the financial statements must contain disclosures regarding the material uncertainty over going concern. The auditor's report should contain a section headed 'Material uncertainty related to going concern', in which the auditor would draw attention to the disclosures, and state that they cast doubt over going concern but that the auditor's opinion is not modified in relation to them. If the financial statements do not contain these disclosures, then the auditor's opinion would need to be either qualified or adverse.

BPP
LEARNING

Procedures in respect of the loan include:

- Obtain and review the forecasts and projections prepared by management and consider if the assumptions used are in line with business understanding.

- Obtain a written representation confirming that the assumptions used in the forecasts and projections are considered achievable in light of the economic recession and state of the automotive industry.

- Obtain and review the terms of the loan that has been requested to see if Juliet Co can make the repayments required.

- Consider the sufficiency of the loan requested to cover the costs of the intended restructuring.

- Review the repayment history of any current loans and overdrafts with the bank, to form an opinion as to whether Juliet Co has any history of defaulting on payments. (Any previous defaults or breach of loan conditions makes it less likely that the new loan would be advanced).

- Discuss the loan request with the company's bankers and attempt to receive confirmation of their intention to provide the finance, and the terms of the finance.

- Discuss the situation with management and those charged with governance, to ascertain if any alternative providers of finance have been considered, and if not, whether any alternative strategies for the company have been discussed.

- Obtain a written representation from management stating management's opinion as to whether the necessary finance is likely to be obtained.

(ii) **Ethical**

These forecasts are crucial for the assessment of whether the company is a going concern. There is a self-review threat if the auditor is both advising on the preparation of the forecasts, and auditing them as part of its work on going concern under ISA 570 *Going Concern*.

The issue is given added weight by ISA 570's insistence that where cash flow is important for the assessment of going concern, particular consideration should be given not only to what the forecasts say, but to their reliability. This exacerbates the potential impact of the self-review threat.

There is potentially an advocacy threat, as the auditor is advising on a matter significant to the company's operational existence, and promoting the company's position to the potential provider of finance.

The auditor must consider whether safeguards can be put in place to reduce these threats to an acceptable level. For instance, a separate team could help prepare the forecasts, and management could be asked to provide representations to the effect that they alone are responsible for the forecasts.

If the firm decides that the threat is still not reduced to an acceptable level, then either, or both, of the services should not be provided.

Other

A further issue is that if the auditor does attend the meeting with the bank, it must be careful not to create the impression that it is responsible for the forecasts, or is in any way guaranteeing the future existence of the company. In legal terms, attending the meeting and promoting the interests of the client could create legal 'proximity', which increases the risk of legal action against the auditor in the event of Juliet Co defaulting on the loan.

Question 3

Workbook reference. Chapters 1, 4, 8, and 9.

Top tips. This was a difficult question, but it should not have been impossible. Questions on quality control reviews of individual engagements are just like any other AAA question, in that your approach should be to begin by looking for what is wrong in the scenario. The requirement asks for quality issues and actions to take; the actions should flow naturally from the issues.

Some students may have written out theoretical discussions of eg what an engagement quality control review is. This was not asked for and would not get any marks!

Part (a) was a relatively straightforward scenario. The misconception, expressed by the audit manager, that since intra-group transactions are eliminated from group accounts they do not need to be audited, has been tested before and was one that you should have been able to debunk (there are several issues with it, eg the need to know what the transactions are if they are to be eliminated on consolidation).

The invalid generalisation from testing controls in one subsidiary to controls across the Group should also have been simple to criticise.

ISA 600 seems to be a bit of a favourite of the examining team, as it contains specific requirements that many candidates are not aware of. If you're not very familiar with it, make sure you review the answer to this question carefully.

Part (b) featured a highly dubious assertion regarding the immateriality of a new subsidiary. You should have been able to criticise this and then say what should now be done. You may have struggled with this second part (ii) if your knowledge of ISA 600 was sketchy.

Part (c) was probably more difficult. Reading the question carefully, the first two paragraphs mainly provide background information. Each of the following 4 paragraphs gives you something that you can criticise – and just about everything that the auditors have done is open to criticism and further recommendations, including the sneaky final paragraph which mentions goodwill.

Easy marks. Up to 1½ marks are available for commenting on the competence of the audit manager and the need for further training – these are easy pickings, so make sure that you say this but do not go overboard and write too much on it.

The marks for calculating a component's materiality were also easy (included as part of the determining whether a component is significant in (b) and (c)).

ACCA examining team's comments. This question focused on a group audit with component auditors and audit issues in each of the subsidiaries. This question was not well answered overall with many candidates appearing not to understand the concept of the level of control required by the group auditor and the amount of instruction and interaction required with component auditors.

Part (a) considered a poorly planned audit where the audit manager had concluded at the interim audit that intercompany balances which were not being properly accounted for did not matter 'as they were eliminated on consolidation' yet he repeated the same tests and reliance on controls at the final audit. Candidates seemed unable to grasp that, because of the control failures, substantive work (such as reconciliations) was required and that this control failure should be highlighted to management at the interim stage so they could take steps to resolve these issues in advance of the final audit.

Additionally, the manager tested capital expenditure controls in only one subsidiary and concluded that those results could be applied to the rest of the group without further testing. Many candidates discussed generically how to audit capital expenditure and did not consider the relevant issues raised in the scenario and that it would be necessary to evaluate the work of the component auditors and identify what additional procedures might be required.

Part (b) concerned a subsidiary acquired during the year which had a different auditor. Candidates generally failed to recognise that the role of the component auditor is firstly to audit the subsidiary for its whole financial year, regardless of the change of ownership. Most did not appreciate that the group auditor needs to issue instructions to the component auditor, assess their competence and independence and review and document their work as part of the group audit. Incorrectly blaming the component auditor for a poorly-planned group audit showed a lack of knowledge of the fundamentals of how a group audit works.

Requirement (c) presented another subsidiary which had a potential going concern issue but the component auditors had concluded that there was not a significant risk. Strong answers proposed a more detailed review of the component auditor's work and conclusions along with an assessment of their competence and then considered the impact on the group as a whole. It is evident that there is poor understanding that goodwill arising in the consolidated accounts is held in the consolidated statement of financial position and not in the financial statements of the subsidiary and that assessing any potential impairment is the role of the group auditor, not the component auditor. Candidates are advised to make sure that they are knowledgeable of the requirements of the ISAs in this area.

Marking scheme

Marks

Generally up to 1½ marks for each relevant point identified and explained. Allow maximum 1½ marks for comments on the competence of the Group audit manager and the need for additional training. These marks can be awarded in any section of the question.

(a) **Internal controls**

    (i) **Quality of audit work**

        – Performing tests of controls not an appropriate response where controls are deficient

        – Intra-group balances and transactions should be audited even if cancelled on consolidation

        – If not performed then the cancellation and determination of provisions for unrealised profit may not be correct

        – Inappropriate assumption on the strength of group-wide controls. The work of component auditors on capex controls should have been evaluated

        – Audit evidence may be lacking on capex and property, plant and equipment

    (ii) **Further actions or procedures**

        – Communicate with those charged with governance on the control deficiency

        – Review working papers on components for evidence on intra-group balances

        – Perform additional audit procedures on intra-group balances (max 3 marks for specific procedures)

        – Perform additional procedures on capex (max 2 marks for specific procedures)

Maximum   9

Marks

(b) **Geranium Co**
  (i) **Quality of audit work**
- Determine that Geranium Co is a significant component
- Not sufficient to perform analytical review only for a significant component
- Audit evidence is insufficient to support group audit opinion
- Understanding of the component auditor should have been obtained

  (ii) **Further actions or procedures**
- Obtain understanding of independence, competence and regulatory framework of Fern & Co
- Liaise with Fern & Co in order to:
  - Obtain their working papers for review
  - Understand their risk assessment procedures and responses to risks identified
  - Plan further audit procedures if considered necessary

Maximum   7

(c) **Daisy Co**
  (i) **Quality of audit work**
- Determine that Daisy Co is significant due to special circumstances
- Goodwill relating to Daisy Co likely to be overstated – not identified by audit manager
- Cannot rely solely on component auditor's opinion
- Further work required by ISA 600 including additional work on the balance identified as high risk
- Further impacts may not have been identified – eg impairment of other assets
- Impact on other group components and group going concern should be evaluated
- Lack of audit manager's professional scepticism and increased audit risk

  (ii) **Further actions or procedures**
- Request working papers of Foxglove & Co for review
- Perform additional procedures relating to the regulations and potential impairment in individual financial statements of Daisy Co (max 2 marks for specific procedures)
- Extend audit procedures at group level on goodwill impairment and going concern (max 2 marks for specific procedures)

Maximum   9

Total   25

(a) **Hyacinth Co – internal controls and results of controls testing**

(i) **Audit planning and performance**

Where assessment of internal controls at the initial stage of the audit concludes that controls are ineffective there is no necessity to perform tests of controls, which was an incorrect response in the Group audit. Tests of controls should not be performed in order to confirm that controls are not effective as, in line with ISA 330 *The Auditor's Response to Assessed Risks*, the auditor should only use tests of control as a method of gathering evidence where there is an expectation that controls are operating effectively.

The correct response should have been to increase substantive audit procedures around the area of intra-group transactions. Given that the Group companies supply each other with chemical products to use in their manufacturing processes, the volume and monetary amount of the intra-group transactions could be significant. Related party transactions are often an area of significant risk and intra-group balances can be an easy way to manipulate the individual company accounts.

The comment made by the audit manager that 'no further work is necessary' on the intra-group transactions seems to be based on the concept that intra-group balances are cancelled in the Group financial statements at consolidation. This is true, but audit work should be performed on these transactions because they will still be recognised in the individual financial statements and audit evidence should be obtained to support the value of the transactions and balances. Further, if these balances have not been appropriately reconciled, this could create significant issues on consolidation.

In addition, if no audit work is performed on the intra-group transactions then no assurance can be obtained over the value of adjustments made during the consolidation process to eliminate them. Also audit work should be performed to determine the validity of any provision for unrealised profit recognised in the Group financial statements. There does not appear to be any audit evidence at all to support the necessary consolidation adjustments which is a significant deficiency in the quality of the group audit. It seems that the communications between Group and component auditors is not robust. The instructions given by Crocus & Co to the component auditors seem to lack detail, for example, Crocus & Co should be instructing the component auditors to carry out specific procedures on intra-group balances and transactions.

In relation to controls over capital expenditure, it is not appropriate to conclude that controls will be effective across the Group just because they are effective in one of the Group components. Testing the controls in one component cannot provide assurance that the control risk in the other components is at the same level. This is particularly the case for Geranium Co, which is a recent acquisition, and Crocus & Co has no previous knowledge of its control environment and processes.

It is possible that the audit of capital expenditure in the Group components other than Hyacinth Co is not of acceptable quality due to over-reliance on controls over which no assurance has been obtained. The instructions given to the component auditors may not have been based on an appropriate audit strategy in relation to the audit of capital expenditure. Crocus & Co, in its evaluation of the work performed by the component auditors, should have assessed the level of testing which was performed on Daisy Co and Geranium Co's internal controls over capital expenditure, and the conclusions which were drawn. Sufficient and appropriate audit evidence may not have been obtained, leading to a risk of material misstatement of property, plant and equipment.

(ii) **Further actions to be taken**

The deficiencies in internal control over intra-group transactions should be brought to the attention of Group management. ISA 600 *Special Considerations – Audits of Group Financial Statements (Including the Work of Component Auditors)* requires that the

group engagement team shall determine which identified deficiencies in internal control to communicate to those charged with governance and group management. This should include group-wide controls and controls over the consolidation process.

The audit working papers for the component companies should be reviewed to establish if any audit procedures on intra-group balances and transactions have been performed at the company level.

Further audit procedures should be performed on intra-group transactions including:

- Discuss with the Group finance director the process used to determine the value of intra-group transactions and balances which are adjusted at consolidation

- Using computer assisted audit techniques (CAATs), determine the monetary value of intra-group balances and agree to the finance director's estimate and amounts in the consolidation schedule

- Perform substantive analytical procedures to form an evaluation of the expected level of intra-group sales and purchases

- Obtain copies of the individual company accounts and agree all relevant group balances and disclosures

- Agree a sample of intra-group sales and purchases to source documentation including orders and invoices

- Determine the basis of any provision for unrealised profit recognised through review of the finance director's calculations, and reperform the relevant calculations

In respect of the audit work on capital expenditure, the Group audit team should firstly determine the materiality of capital expenditure in each component and if material ensure that further substantive audit procedures are performed or have been performed by the component auditor, including:

- Agreeing a sample of capital expenditure items to source documentation including capital expenditure budget, supplier invoice and order or requisition form

- Physical verification of a sample of items

- Obtaining relevant insurance documents for significant assets acquired

(b) **Geranium Co – new subsidiary**

(i) **Audit planning and performance**

The audit manager's conclusion that Geranium is immaterial to the Group financial statements is based on the profit to be consolidated, which amounts to 2% of Group profit before tax. However, the assets of Geranium Co amount to 23.1% of Group total assets and therefore the subsidiary is material to the Group on that basis.

The Group audit team should give further consideration to whether Geranium Co is a significant component of the Group. It is likely that representing nearly one quarter of Group assets makes the company a significant component. According to ISA 600, depending on the nature and circumstances of the group, appropriate benchmarks for determining whether a component is a significant component might include a threshold based on group assets, liabilities, cash flows, profit or turnover. For example, the group engagement team may consider that components exceeding 15% of the chosen benchmark are significant components.

Assuming therefore that Geranium Co is a significant component of the group, obtaining audit evidence purely based on analytical procedures is not sufficient.

ISA 600 allows that for components which are not significant components, the group engagement team can perform analytical procedures at group level. However, for a component which is significant due to its individual financial significance to the group, the group engagement team, or a component auditor on its behalf, shall perform an audit of the financial information of the component using component materiality.

The audit evidence obtained by the group audit team in respect of Geranium Co therefore needs to be more robust in order for the Group audit manager to reach a conclusion on its balances which will be consolidated.

The lack of audit working papers indicates that there has been no communication with the component auditors. This is a significant quality control problem and a breach of ISA 600 which requires that the group audit team obtain an understanding of the component auditor, and be involved with the component auditor's risk assessment to identify risks of material misstatement. This is especially the case given that Geranium Co is a new component of the group, and this is Crocus & Co's first experience of working with their auditors.

(ii) Further actions to be taken

The component auditor's independence and competence should be evaluated and procedures should be performed to evaluate whether the component auditor operates in a regulatory environment which actively oversees auditors. These could be achieved through a discussion with the component auditor and requesting them to complete a questionnaire on these matters for evaluation by the group audit team.

The Group audit team should liaise with the component auditor as soon as possible in order to discuss their audit findings, obtain access to their working papers, and ultimately decide on the specific nature of the further procedures to be performed, which should be based on component materiality.

(c) Daisy Co – restriction on international trade

(i) Audit planning and performance

Based on monetary values, Daisy Co does not appear to be a significant component, as its assets represent 6.2% of consolidated assets, and its profit is less than 1% of group profit and immaterial on that basis. As discussed above, a normal threshold for a significant component is 15% of group assets or profit.

However, due to the new government regulations and their potential impact on the operations of Daisy Co, the component could be evaluated as significant due to its specific circumstances which may create a risk of material misstatement at group level.

One risk arises in relation to the goodwill balance, which is material at 2.3% of group assets. The government regulation is an indicator that goodwill could be impaired, but an assessment of goodwill is required regardless of the existence of such indicators. The audit working papers will need to be carefully reviewed to ascertain the extent of work, if any, which has been performed on the goodwill of Daisy Co. The audit manager's comment that the issue has no impact on the consolidated accounts implies that this matter may not have been factored into any goodwill assessment which has taken place as part of audit procedures. Therefore the quality of the audit evidence to support the goodwill balance of $3m is in doubt.

It is not sufficient to rely solely on the audit opinion issued by Foxglove & Co. ISA 600 requires that for a component which is significant because it is likely to include significant risks of material misstatement of the group financial statements due to its specific nature or circumstances, the group engagement team, or a component auditor on its behalf, shall perform one or more of the following:

- An audit of the financial information of the component using component materiality

- An audit of one or more account balances, classes of transactions or disclosures relating to the likely significant risks of material misstatement of the group financial statements

- Specified audit procedures relating to the likely significant risks of material misstatement of the group financial statements

There is a risk that not all of the implications of the government regulations have been addressed by Foxglove & Co during their audit. For example, they should have considered the overall going concern status of the company, and the impact on the valuation of property, plant and equipment as well as inventories.

There is also a risk that does not appear to have been considered by the Group audit manager in that the government regulation may affect other components of the group due to Daisy Co's role in the group of developing and providing products to the other group companies, and therefore any restrictions on Daisy Co's operations may affect all the other components of the group. This issue may also raise concerns over the work which has been conducted in relation to ISA 250 *Consideration of Laws and Regulations in an Audit of Financial Statements* and there is a risk that the Group auditor's assessment of the legal and regulatory framework that affects the Group has not been sufficiently understood or documented.

The fact that the Group's board members have not mentioned the regulation to the Group audit manager could indicate that the Group's management is trying to hide the situation from the auditor. The audit manager should exercise professional scepticism and enquire further into the matter, as discussed below. If the Group's management were genuinely unaware of the new regulations then corporate governance, especially in relation to risk monitoring and assessment would appear to be deficient. This impacts on the audit by increasing the risk of management bias and actions of management which may deliberately mislead the auditor.

In summary, this situation indicated a lack of quality in the group audit due to the over-reliance on the audit findings of the component auditor. In addition, the group audit manager seems not to have considered the wider implications of the government regulation on the risk assessment for the group as a whole.

(ii) **Further actions to be taken**

Request the audit working papers from Foxglove & Co and review the work performed on the government regulation and its impact on the financial statements and going concern. The group audit team should confirm the materiality level which was used in audit procedures is in line with their assessment of an appropriate component materiality, and should ensure that appropriate methods were used to identify and respond to the risks of material misstatement.

The group audit team may decide that additional audit procedures are necessary, for example:

- Obtain the assessment of going concern performed by the management of Daisy Co and review the reasonableness of the assumptions used, especially those relating to future revenue streams and cash inflows

- Obtain a copy of the government regulation to understand the exact nature of the restrictions imposed and implications for the going concern of Daisy Co

In addition, the group assessment of going concern will need to be re-evaluated, taking into account the impact of the government regulation on the other Group companies.

BPP LEARNING MEDIA

Given that the Group sells products in over 50 countries, it is likely that it is not just Daisy Co which is affected by this new regulation, and additional audit work should be performed on evaluating the going concern status of each company and of the Group as a whole.

Additional procedures should be performed on the $3m goodwill balance recognised in respect of Daisy Co, to include a determination of the value in use of Daisy Co, based on future cash flows taking into account the likely impact of the government regulations.

Conclusion

Overall, the problems noted in the Group audit indicate that the Group audit manager lacks competence, and that inappropriate judgements have been made. There are several instances of ISA requirements not being followed and the audit has not been performed with sufficient due care for professional standards. The Group audit manager should receive training on Group accounting and Group audit issues in order to resolve the deficiencies identified in the planning and performance of this audit, and to ensure that future audits are managed appropriately.

ACCA Strategic Professional

AAA

Advanced Audit and Assurance (International)

Mock Examination 2

ACCA 2018 Specimen Exam

Question Paper
Time allowed   3 hours 15 minutes
ALL THREE questions are compulsory and **MUST** be attempted

DO NOT OPEN THIS PAPER UNTIL YOU ARE READY TO START UNDER EXAMINATION CONDITIONS

BPP
LEARNING
MEDIA

ALL THREE questions are compulsory and MUST be attempted

Question 1

You are a manager in Dando & Co, a firm of Chartered Certified Accountants responsible for the audit of the Adams Group, a listed entity. The Group operates in the textile industry, buying cotton, silk and other raw materials to manufacture a range of goods including clothing, linen and soft furnishings. Goods are sold under the Adams brand name, which was acquired by the Group many years ago. Your firm was appointed as auditor in January 20X6.

You have been provided with the following exhibits:

1   An email which you have received from Joss Dylan, the audit engagement partner

2   Information about the Group's general background and activities

3   Extracts from the draft Group financial statements for the year ending 31 May 20X6

4   Notes from a meeting held between Joss Dylan and the Group's finance director and representatives from its audit committee

Required

Respond to the instructions in the email from the audit engagement partner.

(46 marks)

Note. The split of the mark allocation is shown in the partner's email (Exhibit 1).

Professional marks will be awarded for the presentation and logical flow of the briefing notes and the clarity of the explanations provided.   **(4 marks)**

(Total = 50 marks)

Exhibit 1 – Email from audit engagement partner

To: Audit manager

From: Joss Dylan

Subject: Adams Group audit planning

Hello

I need you to begin planning the audit of the Adams Group (the Group) for the year ended 31 May 20X6. As you know, we have been appointed to audit the Group financial statements, and we have also been appointed to audit the financial statements of the parent company and of all subsidiaries of the Group except for a foreign subsidiary, Lynott Co, which is audited by a local firm, Clapton & Co. All components of the Group have the same year end of 31 May, report under IFRS Standards and in the same currency.

Using the information provided, I require you to prepare briefing notes for my use, in which you:

(a)   Evaluate the audit risks to be considered in planning the audit of the Group. Your evaluation should utilise analytical procedures for identifying relevant audit risks.   **(20 marks)**

(b)   Explain the matters to be considered, and the procedures to be performed, in respect of planning to use the work of Clapton & Co.   **(8 marks)**

(c)   Design the principal audit procedures to be performed in respect of the following balances recognised as non-current assets in the Group statement of financial position:

   (i) $12 million recognised as investment in associate; and   **(5 marks)**
   (ii) $8 million recognised as a brand name.   **(5 marks)**

BPP
LEARNING
MEDIA

(d)   Using the information provided in Exhibit 4, identify and evaluate any ethical threats and other professional issues which arise from the requests made by the Group audit committee.

(8 marks)

Thank you.

Exhibit 2 – Background and structure of the Adams Group

The Group structure and information about each of the components of the Group is shown below:

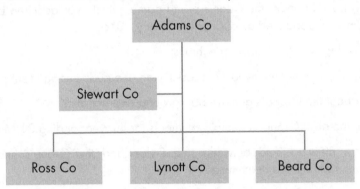

Ross Co, Lynott Co and Beard Co are all wholly owned, acquired subsidiaries which manufacture different textiles. Adams Co also owns 25% of Stewart Co, a company which is classified as an associate in the Group statement of financial position at a value of $12 million at 31 May 20X6. The shares in Stewart Co were acquired in January 20X6 for a consideration of $11.5 million. Other than this recent investment in Stewart Co, the Group structure has remained unchanged for many years.

Information relevant to each of the group companies

Adams Co is the parent company in the group and its main activities relate to holding the investments in its subsidiaries and also the brand name which was purchased many years ago. Adams Co imposes an annual management charge of $800,000 on each of its subsidiaries, with the charge for each financial year payable in the subsequent August.

Ross Co manufactures luxury silk clothing, with almost all of its output sold through approximately 200 department stores. Ross Co's draft statement of financial position recognises assets of $21.5 million at 31 May 20X6. Any silk clothing which has not been sold within 12 months is transferred to Lynott Co, where the silk material is recycled in its manufacturing process.

Lynott Co is located in Farland, where it can benefit from low cost labour in its factories. It produces low price fashion clothing for the mass market. A new inventory system was introduced in December 20X5 in order to introduce stronger controls over the movement of inventory between factories and stores. Lynott Co is audited by Clapton & Co, and its auditor's reports in all previous years have been unmodified. Clapton & Co is a small accounting and audit firm, but is a member of an international network of firms. Lynott Co's draft statement of financial position recognises assets of $24 million at 31 May 20X6.

Beard Co manufactures soft furnishings which it sells through an extensive network of retailers. The company is cash-rich, and surplus cash is invested in a large portfolio of investment properties, which generate rental income. The Group's accounting policy is to measure investment properties at fair value. Beard Co's draft statement of financial position recognises assets of $28 million at 31 May 20X6, of which investment properties represent $10 million.

Exhibit 3 – Extracts from draft Group consolidated financial statements

Draft consolidated statement of profit or loss and other comprehensive income

	Year ended 31 May 20X6 $'000 Draft	Year ended 31 May 20X5 $'000 Actual
Revenue	725,000	650,000
Cost of sales	(463,000)	(417,500)
Gross profit	262,000	232,500
Other income – rental income	200	150
Operating expenses	(250,000)	(225,000)
Operating profit	12,200	7,650
Net finance cost	(1,000)	(1,000)
Profit before tax	11,200	6,650
Income tax expense	(1,500)	(1,000)
Profit for the year	9,700	5,650
Other comprehensive income:		
Gain on investment property revaluation	1,000	3,000
Total comprehensive income	10,700	8,650

Draft consolidated statement of financial position

	31 May 20X6 $'000 Draft	31 May 20X5 $'000 Actual
Non-current assets		
Property, plant and equipment	45,000	45,000
Investment property (recognised at fair value)	10,000	7,500
Intangible asset – brand name (recognised at cost)	8,000	8,000
Investment in associate	12,000	–
	75,000	60,500
Current assets		
Inventory	12,000	6,000
Receivables	10,500	6,000
Cash	10,000	22,000
	32,500	34,600
Total assets	107,500	95,100
Equity and liabilities		
Share capital	35,000	35,000
Retained earnings	34,000	24,600
	69,000	59,600
Non-current liabilities		
Bank loan	20,000	20,000
Current liabilities		
Trade payables	16,000	13,500
Tax payable	2,500	2,000
	18,500	15,500
Total equity and liabilities	107,500	95,100

BPP LEARNING MEDIA

Exhibit 4 – Notes from discussion with Group audit committee and finance director

Recent publicity

During the year, the Group attracted negative publicity when an investigation by a well-known journalist alleged that child-labour was being used by several suppliers of raw materials to Lynott Co. The Group rebutted the allegations, claiming that the suppliers in question had no contract to supply Lynott Co, and that the Group always uses raw materials from ethically responsible suppliers. The media coverage of the issue has now ended. The Group finance director is confident that the negative publicity has not affected sales of the Group's products, saying that in fact sales are buoyant, as indicated by the increase in Group revenue in the year.

Systems and accounting policies

The Group has a policy of non-amortisation of the Adams brand name. The brand name was acquired many years ago and is recognised at its original cost. The previous audit firm accepted the policy due to the strength of the brand name and the fact that the Group spends a significant amount each year on product development and marketing aimed at supporting the brand. The Group has maintained a good market share in the last few years and management is confident that this will continue to be the case.

As part of management's strategy to increase market share, a bonus scheme has been put in place across the Group under which senior managers will receive a bonus based on an increase in revenue.

The Group's accounting and management information systems are out of date, and the Group would like to develop and implement new systems next year. The audit committee would like to obtain advice from Dando & Co on the new systems as they have little specialist in-house knowledge in this area.

Financing

In addition, the audit committee requests that the Group audit engagement partner attends a meeting with the Group's bank, which is planned to be held the week after the auditor's report is issued. The purpose of the meeting is for the Group to renegotiate its existing lending facility and to extend its loan, and will be attended by the Group finance director, a representative of the audit committee, as well as the bank manager. The Group is hoping that the audit partner will be able to confirm the Group's strong financial position at the meeting, and also confirm that the audit included procedures on going concern, specifically the audit of the Group's cash flow forecast for the next two years, which the bank has requested as part of their lending decision.

Question 2

The audit of Bradley Co's financial statements for the year ended 31 August 20X5 is nearly complete, and the auditor's report is due to be issued next week. Bradley Co operates steel processing plants at 20 locations and sells its output to manufacturers and engineering companies. You are performing an engagement quality control review on the audit of Bradley Co, as it is a significant new client of your firm. The financial statements recognise revenue of $2.5 million, and total assets of $35 million.

(a)   One of the audit assistants who has been working on the audit of Bradley Co made the following comments when discussing the completion of the audit with you:

'I was assigned to the audit of provisions. One of the provisions, amounting to $10,000, relates to a legal claim made against the company after an employee was injured in an accident at one of the steel processing plants. I read all of the correspondence relating to this, and tried to speak to Bradley Co's legal advisers, but was told by the finance director that I must not approach them and should only speak to him about the matter. He said that he is confident that only $10,000 needs to be recognised and that the legal advisers had confirmed this amount to him in a discussion of the matter. I noted in the audit working papers that I

could not perform all of the planned audit procedures because I could not speak to the legal advisers. The audit manager told me to conclude that provisions are correctly recognised in the financial statements based on the evidence obtained, and to move on to my next piece of work. He said it didn't matter that I hadn't spoken to the legal advisers because the matter is immaterial to the financial statements.

'We received the final version of the financial statements and the chairman's statement to be published with the financial statements yesterday. I have quickly looked at the financial statements but the audit manager said we need not perform a final detailed analytical review on the financial statements as the audit was relatively low risk. The manager also said that he had discussed the chairman's statement with the finance director, so no further work on it is needed. The audit has been quite time-pressured and I know that the client wants the auditor's report to be issued as soon as possible.'

Required

Explain the quality control and other professional issues raised by the audit assistant's comments, discussing any implications for the completion of the audit. **(10 marks)**

(b) The schedule of uncorrected misstatements included in Bradley Co's audit working papers is shown below, including notes to explain each matter included in the schedule. The audit engagement partner is holding a meeting with management tomorrow, at which the uncorrected misstatements will be discussed.

		Statement of profit or loss		Statement of financial position	
		Debit	Credit	Debit	Credit
		$	$	$	$
1	Share-based payment scheme	300,000			300,000
2	Restructuring provision		50,000	50,000	
3	Estimate of additional allowance required for slow-moving inventory	10,000			10,000
Totals		310,000	50,000	50,000	310,000

Notes

1 A share-based payment scheme was established in January 20X5. Management has not recognised any amount in the financial statements in relation to the scheme, arguing that due to the decline in Bradley Co's share price, the share options granted are unlikely to be exercised. The audit conclusion is that an expense and related equity figure should be included in the financial statements.

2 A provision has been recognised in respect of a restructuring involving the closure of one of the steel processing plants. Management approved the closure at a board meeting in August 20X5, but only announced the closure to employees in September 20X5. The audit conclusion is that the provision should not be recognised.

3 The allowance relates to slow-moving inventory in respect of a particular type of steel alloy for which demand has fallen. Management has already recognised an allowance of $35,000, which is considered insufficient by the audit team.

Required

(i) Explain the matters which should be discussed with management in relation to each of the uncorrected misstatements; and

(ii) Assuming that management does not adjust the misstatements, justify an appropriate audit opinion and explain the impact on the auditor's report.

BPP
LEARNING

The following mark allocation is provided as guidance for this requirement:

(i)   10 marks
(ii) 5 marks

(15 marks)

(Total = 25 marks)

Question 3

(a)   Following recent changes to its *Code of Ethics for Professional Accountants* (the *Code*), in relation to audit firms providing non-assurance services to audit clients, the IESBA commented that:

'The performance of non-assurance services may create threats to independence of the firm or members of the audit team. Such threats include self-review, self-interest and advocacy threats. Further if a firm were to assume a management responsibility for an audit client, the threats created would be so significant that no safeguards could reduce the threats to an acceptable level. However, there are varying views on what constitutes a management responsibility and as such it is in the public interest to enhance the clarity and guidance on this topic in the *Code*.'

Required

Discuss the changes made to the *Code* in relation to non-assurance services and evaluate the arguments for and against auditors providing non-assurance services to audit clients.

(8 marks)

(b)   You are a manager in Hunt & Co, a firm which offers a range of services to audit and non-audit clients. You have been asked to consider a potential engagement to review and provide a report on the prospective financial information of Waters Co, a company which has been an audit client of Hunt & Co for six years. The audit of the financial statements for the year ended 30 April 20X6 has just commenced.

Waters Co operates a chain of cinemas across the country. Currently its cinemas are out of date and use projectors which cannot show films made using new technology, which are becoming more popular. Management is planning to invest in all of its cinemas in order to attract more customers. The company has sufficient cash to fund half of the necessary capital expenditure, but has approached its bank with a loan application of $8 million for the remainder of the funds required. Most of the cash will be used to invest in equipment and fittings, such as new projectors and larger screens, enabling new technology films to be shown in all cinemas. The remaining cash will be used for refurbishment of the cinemas. Prior to finalising the application for the funding from the bank, the finance director has also asked if the audit engagement partner will assist him in presenting the final version of the strategic plan, in relation to the refurbishment, to the board as he knows that Hunt & Co has several clients in the industry and the partner will be able to confirm that the plan is consistent with what others in the industry are doing.

The draft forecast statements of profit or loss for the years ending 30 April 20X7 and 20X8 are shown below, along with the key assumptions which have been used in their preparation. The unaudited statement of profit or loss for the year ended 30 April 20X6 is also shown below. The forecast has been prepared for use by the bank in making its lending decision, and will be accompanied by other prospective financial information including a forecast statement of cash flows.

Forecast statement of profit or loss

	Year ended 30 April 20X6 Unaudited $'000	Note to forecast information	Year ending 30 April 20X7 Forecast $'000	Year ending 30 April 20X8 Forecast $'000
Revenue	35,000	1	43,000	46,000
Operating expenses	(28,250)	2	(31,500)	(32,100)
Operating profit	6,750		11,500	13,900
Finance costs	(1,700)		(2,000)	(1,900)
Profit before tax	5,050		9,500	12,000

Note 1. The forecast increase in revenue is based on the following assumptions:

(i) All cinemas will be fitted with new projectors and larger screens to show new technology films by September 20X6.

(ii) Ticket prices will increase from $7.50 to $10 from 1 September 20X6.

Note 2. Operating expenses include mainly staff costs, depreciation of property and equipment, and repairs and maintenance to the cinemas.

Required

(i) Explain the matters to be considered by Hunt & Co before accepting the engagement to review and report on Waters Co's prospective financial information. **(7 marks)**

(ii) Assuming the engagement is accepted, describe the examination procedures to be used in respect of the forecast statement of profit or loss. **(6 marks)**

(iii) Discuss the content of the report which would be issued on the prospective financial information, explaining the level of assurance which is provided. **(4 marks)**

(Total = 25 marks)

Answers

DO NOT TURN THIS PAGE UNTIL YOU HAVE
COMPLETED THE MOCK EXAM

A PLAN OF ATTACK

If this had been the real Advanced Audit and Assurance exam and you had been told to turn over and begin, what would have been going through your mind?

An important thing to say (while there is still time) is that it is vital to have a good breadth of knowledge of the syllabus because the question requirements for each question will relate to different areas of the AAA syllabus. However, don't panic. Below we provide guidance on how to approach the exam.

Approaching the answer

It is vital that you attempt all the questions in the exam to increase your chances of passing. The best way to do this is to make sure you stick to the time allocation for each question – both in total and for each of the question parts. The worst thing you can do is run over time in one question and then find that you don't have enough time for the remaining questions, leading you to miss out on some of the easier marks in those questions.

Section A consists of one long case-study style question set at the planning stage of the audit. This may contain detailed information such as extracts from financial statements and audit working papers. A range of requirements will be set for this question, but will only cover areas from syllabus areas A to D inclusive.

Question 1 is for 50 marks, all set at the planning stage in the context of a single scenario. As it is a very long question, it is important that you break it down into its component parts as this will make it easier to manage – and enable you to allocate your time to each of them.

Section B contains two more compulsory questions, and may be set on any area of the AAA syllabus.

Question 2, for 25 marks, featured an engagement quality control review. This is in line with ACCA's promise that one question will be set at the completion stage of the audit.

Question 3 offers 25 marks that were made up of an ethics discussion and a comprehensive question on prospective financial information.

Forget about it!

And don't worry if you found the exam difficult. More than likely other candidates will too. If this were the real thing you would need to forget the exam the minute you left the exam hall and think about the next one. Or, if it is the last one, celebrate!

BPP
LEARNING

Question 1

Top tips. Your general approach should be to read the requirement carefully, and then to work through the question noting down issues (audit risks) as they occur to you.

The question includes a set of draft financial statements for the group. Clearly the examining team wants you to look at them, but it is important not to spend too long performing detailed analytical procedures when this is not what the requirement asks you to do.

The requirement asks for 'audit risks', not 'risks of material misstatement' as is often seen in AAA questions. The difference is that audit risk includes detection risk, so this requirement is specifically allowing you to discuss detection risk where this is relevant. As always, there are no marks available for theoretical discussions of the nature of audit risk.

Detection risk is immediately relevant because Adams is a new client, so there is a risk in relation to our relative lack of knowledge of it, and in respect of opening balances and comparatives. Notice, though, that the point about opening balances and comparatives is made quite briefly in our answer. Sometimes candidates like to recite pre-learned material about these two issues, and this is something that your examining team has said it does not like.

With part (b), the procedures should come from each matter to consider. Much of the material here on component auditors is generic, so the trick is in working out which bits of your knowledge are relevant to the scenario and which bits are not.

Part (c) asked for procedures in relation to two areas in the scenario, and was very representative of AAA questions. There shouldn't have been anything untoward here.

Part (d) was effectively a self-contained ethics question featuring a few mini situations. None of these was unusual and there were easy marks available for categorising the kind of threat (eg 'self-review'), stating **why** this was a threat, and then for saying what the auditor should do about it.

Easy marks. The presentation marks here are valuable, and are well worth the time it takes to get them.

ACCA examining team's comments. In terms of **exam technique**, a significant minority of candidates attempted Question One [this question] last. This almost invariably was a flawed exam strategy, as not enough time had been left to attempt the longest and most detailed question in the exam. Candidates are advised to attempt Section A first, to ensure that sufficient time is devoted to these longer scenario-based questions.

This question was based on planning the audit of a new client – the Adams Group. The first requirement asked candidates to evaluate the audit risks to be considered in planning the audit of the Group. **This is a very typical requirement for Question One** in the AAA exam, and while it was encouraging to see that many candidates had clearly revised this part of the syllabus, there were many whose answers were extremely disappointing. The best answers worked through the information provided in the question to identify the various audit risks, and evaluated them by including an assessment of materiality and a discussion of the significance of the risks identified.

Only the better candidates identified the risks arising from the opening balances and comparative information (due to this being a new audit client for the firm), the lack of presentation of income from the associate in the Group statement of profit or loss, the incorrect treatment of the investment property revaluation gains (which should be recognised as part of profit for the year) and the change in the effective tax rate.

The best answers included in their evaluation of each audit risk an **identification of the risk factor** from the scenario (eg the measurement of the investment properties), a **determination of materiality** where possible given the information in the question, a **clear comment** on the appropriateness of the **accounting treatment** where relevant, and the **impact on the financial statements** (eg not cancelling inter-company transactions would lead to overstated revenue, cost of sales, receivables and payables).

The **key weakness** present in many answers was the **poor quality of explanations**. Most candidates could identify a reasonable range of risks but could not develop their answer to demonstrate a **clear evaluation of that risk**, in a suitable structure, like the one discussed above. For example, having identified that the portfolio of investment properties would give rise to some kind of audit risk, many candidates would then attempt to expand their answer with vague comments such as 'there is risk this is not accounted for properly', 'there is risk in the accounting treatment' or 'there is risk that IAS 40 will not be followed'. This type of comment does not represent a detailed evaluation of audit risk and does not earn credit.

Other weaknesses seen in many answers included:

- Incorrect materiality calculations or stating that a balance is material without justification

- Incorrect analysis of the financial statements provided or incorrect trend calculations, the most common of which was stating that inventory had increased by 50% when it had doubled

- Too much emphasis on business risk with no development or discussion of the audit implications

- Not using the draft financial statements at all to identify audit risks

- Not identifying from the scenario that all Group members use IFRS as their financial reporting framework and report in the same currency, leading to sometimes lengthy discussion of irrelevant matters

- Long introductions including definitions of audit risk, showing a lack of appreciation of the fact that the notes are for an audit partner, and general discussions about audit planning

- Lack of understanding of certain accounting treatments such as equity accounting for associates and the correct treatment of investment properties

- Focusing on goodwill – despite the fact that no goodwill was recognised in the Group financial statements many answers discussed at length that it must be tested for impairment annually

- Suggesting that the bonus scheme would lead to manipulation of expenses, when the bonus was based on revenue

Requirement (b), for 8 marks, asked candidates to explain the matters to be considered, and the procedures to be performed, in respect of planning to use the work of the component auditor. **This requirement was relatively well attempted**, with the majority of answers covering a range of relevant matters and associated procedures. It was clear that many candidates had studied this part of the syllabus, and could apply their knowledge to the question scenario. Most candidates identified that the component audit firm was a small firm, so resourcing the audit could be an issue, and that due to its overseas location there may be differences in the ethical code and auditing standards used by the firm. **Weaker answers** incorrectly discussed the problem of the overseas subsidiary not reporting under IFRS (the question clearly stated that it did) and tended to focus on accounting issues rather than answering the question requirement.

BPP note. Examining team comments are not available for all parts of this question. The specimen exam is based on a past exam sitting, so only those parts of it that were in the past exam have comments – the question parts that are new to the specimen exam do not have examining team comments for them.

BPP
LEARNING

(a) **Audit risk evaluation**

In relation to the matters listed below:

Up to 2 marks for each audit risk evaluated

Up to 1 mark for each relevant calculation/trend and ½ mark for relevant materiality calculations:

- New audit client
- Analytical review:
  - Increased revenue and profitability, risk of overstatement
  - Increased current ratio, risk of overstatement of current assets
  - Unusual trend in PPE, risk of over- or understatement
- Brand name – indefinite useful life and lack of amortisation
- Brand name – potential impairment and overstatement if not recognised
- Equity accounting – measurement of associate and possible impairment
- Disclosure of income from associate
- Classification as an associate
- Ross Co's inventory – control issues relating to multi-location of inventory
- Lynott Co's new inventory control system
- Beard Co's investment property – measurement of the gain
- Beard Co's investment property – incorrect classification as other comprehensive income
- Possible error in comparative information and need for scepticism
- Bonus scheme – inherent risk of overstating revenue (linked to analytical review)
- Elimination of management charges
- Inventories – movement in the year and potential overstatement
- Inter-company trading (inventories)
- Goodwill – none recognised
- Reliance on component auditor

Maximum   20

BPP
LEARNING

Marks

(b) **Using the work of a component auditor**

Up to 1½ marks for each matter explained:

– Compliance with ethical requirements

– Professional competence

– Sufficient involvement in component auditor's work/resources

– Existence of a regulated environment

– Assess level of risk in the subsidiary audited by the component auditor

1 mark for each relevant procedure:

– Review the local ethical code (if any) and compare with the IESBA *Code*

– Obtain confirmation from Clapton & Co of adherence to any local ethical code and the IESBA *Code*

– Establish whether Clapton & Co is a member of an auditing regulatory body, and the professional qualifications issued by that body

– Obtain confirmations from the professional body to which Clapton & Co belong, or the authorities by which it is licensed

– Discuss the audit methodology used by Clapton & Co in the audit of Lynott Co, and compare it to those used under ISAs

– A questionnaire or checklist could be used to provide a summary of audit procedures used

– Ascertain the quality control policies and procedures used by Clapton & Co, both firm-wide and those applied to individual audit engagements

– Request any results of monitoring or inspection visits conducted by the regulatory authority under which Clapton & Co operates

Maximum   8

(c) **Procedures to be performed**

Generally 1 mark for each well explained procedure:
(i) **Investment in associate**

– Obtain and review the legal documents for key information

– Agree the cost of investment of $11.5 million to the legal documentation and bank statement and cash book

– Review the minutes of Group management meetings for understanding of the rationale behind the investment and means of exercising significant influence

– Obtain and review management's calculation to determine the $12 million

       –   Obtain the financial statements of Stewart Co to confirm the amount of profit made in the year and confirm that the Group's share of that profit is included in the Group financial statements

       –   Enquire with management as to whether any impairment review of the investment in Stewart Co has taken place, and if so, obtain management's workings and review the assumptions used and the method of calculation

                                                Maximum   5

(ii) **Adams brand name**

       –   Obtain the Group's marketing budget and plans, and review to confirm that there is adequate support of the brand name through advertising

       –   Obtain and review the results of any market research which has been recently carried out

       –   Consider using an expert in brand valuation to provide a fair value for the brand, which can then be compared to the amount recognised in the financial statements

       –   Discuss with management whether in their opinion there are any indicators that the brand name is impaired, in particular discussing the impact of the bad publicity on sales

       –   Obtain written representation from management that in their opinion the brand is not impaired at the year end

                                                  Maximum   5

(d) **Ethical threats**

Generally 1 mark for each relevant point of discussion/explanation:

–   Advice on new systems is a non-assurance service to an audit client

–   Gives rise to a self-review threat and risk of taking on management responsibility (1 mark for each threat explained)

–   Advice on new systems should not be given where systems form significant part of internal control over financial reporting

–   Risk increased because Group is listed entity, service should not be provided

–   Attending meeting with bank is an advocacy threat

–   Legal implication for the firm if partner 'confirms' work performed

–   Partner should not attend meeting with bank

–   Matters and reasons for declining services should be discussed with Group audit committee

                                                  Maximum   8

Marks

Professional marks for the overall presentation, structure and logical flow of the briefing notes, and for the clarity of the evaluation and explanations provided.

	Maximum	4
Total		50

Briefing notes

To: Joss Dylan, Audit engagement partners

From: Audit manager

Regarding: Audit planning for the Adams Group

Introduction

These briefing notes are prepared for use by the audit engagement partner of the Adams Group, and relate to the planning of the audit of the Group for the year ended 31 May 20X6. The notes contain an evaluation of audit risk, and the matters to be considered in respect of using the work of Clapton & Co, and the relevant procedures to be performed. The notes also detail the procedures to be conducted in relation to the investment in Stewart Co, an associate of the group and the Adams brand name. Finally, the notes discuss the ethical and professional issues which need to be addressed as a result of the requests made by the audit committee of the Adams Group.

(a) **Evaluation of audit risk**

New audit client

The Group is a new client of our firm which may create detection risk as we have no previous experience with the client. However, thorough planning procedures which focus on obtaining a detailed knowledge and understanding of the Group and its activities will minimise this risk. We need to obtain a thorough understanding of each of the subsidiaries as they are all significant components of the Group, with Ross Co, Lynott Co and Beard Co's assets representing respectively 20%, 22.3% and 26% of Group assets. There is also a significant risk that comparative information and opening balances are not correct.

Analytical review

Relevant trends and ratio calculations:

- Revenue increased by 11.5%
- Gross profit increased by 12.7%
- Operating profit increased by 59.5%
- Cash fallen by 54.5%
- Inventories increased by 100%
- Receivables increased by 59.1%

	20X6	20X5
Gross margin	36.1%	35.8%
Operating margin	1.7%	1.2%
Interest cover	12.2	7.7
Current ratio	1.8	2.2
Gearing	22.5%	25.1%

The analytical review indicates that the Group's revenue generation and profitability has improved during the year. There could be valid business reasons to explain the trends, however, the audit team should be alert for possible overstatement of revenue and understatement of expenses.

BPP
LEARNING

The risk is increased due to the bonus scheme which gives rise to a risk of material misstatement at the financial statement level. Management will be biased towards accounting treatments which lead to overstatement of revenue, for example, the early recognition of revenue.

There is also a risk of management manipulation of the financial statements due to the renegotiation of the Group's lending facilities, for example, it would be favourable to present a good interest cover to the bank as an analysis of interest cover is likely to feature in their lending decision.

The current ratio has fallen, largely due to the significant reduction in cash of 54.5%. Other changes within current assets could indicate audit risk, as both inventories and trade receivables have increased significantly, by 100% and 59.1% respectively. Given that revenue has increased by only 11.5% in the year, these increases appear very large and could indicate potential overstatement.

The analytical review also reveals that the amount recognised in respect of property, plant and equipment has not changed over the year. This seems unlikely to be reasonable, as the Group would presumably have incurred some capital expenditure in the year, disposed of some assets and charged depreciation. There are implications for operating profit, which, for example, is overstated if any necessary depreciation has not been charged.

Brand name

The brand is material at 7.4% of Group assets. It is recognised in the statement of financial position as an intangible asset which is appropriate given that the brand is a purchased intangible asset. However, the asset is recognised at its original cost and there is risk attached to the policy of non-amortisation of the brand. IAS 38 *Intangible Assets* states that an intangible asset with a finite useful life is amortised, and an intangible asset with an indefinite useful life is not. The risk is that the assumption that the brand has an indefinite life is not correct, and that the asset is overstated and operating expenses understated through the lack of an annual amortisation charge against the asset.

There is also a risk that the brand could be impaired given the bad publicity and allegations made by the journalist against the Group. IAS 36 *Impairment of Assets* requires an impairment review to be carried out when indicators of potential impairment exist. The allegations may have damaged the Group's reputation, with consequential impact on revenue and cash flows, though the increase of 11.5% in the Group's revenue could indicate that this is not the case, as claimed by the Group finance director. However, sales of certain products could be in decline, and the fact that inventories have doubled in value could indicate problems in selling some of the Group's products. The risk is that if any necessary impairment has not been recognised, the asset is overstated and operating expenses understated by the amount of the impairment loss.

Associate

A new associate has been acquired during the year, which gives rise to several risks. It is material at 11.2% of Group assets.

Because this is the first addition to the Group for many years, there is an inherent risk that the Group lacks accounting knowledge on the appropriate accounting treatment. Associates are accounted for under IAS 28 *Investments in Associates and Joint Ventures*, which states that an entity with joint control of, or significant influence over, an investee shall account for its investment in an associate or a joint venture using the equity method. There is a risk that the equity method has not been properly applied. The investment in the associate recognised in the statement of financial position has increased in value since acquisition by $0.5 million, presumably due to the inclusion of the Group's share of profit arising since investment. There is a risk that this has not been calculated correctly, for example, it is not based on the correct share of profit, and the investment may therefore be over- or understated.

Risk also arises in relation to any possible impairment of the investment, which may cause it to be overstated in both the individual financial statements of Adams Co, and the Group financial statements.

There is also a disclosure issue, as the Group's share of post-investment profit of Stewart Co should be recognised in profit or loss, and IAS 1 *Presentation of Financial Statements* requires that the profit or loss section of the statement of profit or loss shall include as a line item the share of the profit or loss of associates accounted for using the equity method. The draft statement of profit or loss and other comprehensive income does not show income from the associate as a separate line item; it may have been omitted or netted against operating expenses, and the risk is inappropriate presentation of the income from investment.

There is also a risk that the investment should not have been classified as an associate. According to IAS 28, if an entity holds, directly or indirectly, 20% or more of the voting power of the investee, it is presumed that the entity has significant influence, unless it can be clearly demonstrated that this is not the case. If the 25% holding does not give rise to significant influence, for example, if the shares do not convey voting rights, it should be classified as an investment rather than an associate. There is a risk of inappropriate classification, recognition and measurement of the investment in Stewart Co.

Ross Co's inventory in multiple locations

A risk arises in relation to inventory, which is held in each of the department stores. There is a risk that controls are not sufficiently strong in respect of the movement of inventory and counting procedures at the year end, as it will be hard for Ross Co to ensure that all locations are subject to robust inventory counting procedures. This control risk leads to potential over- or understatement of inventory and cost of sales.

Systems and controls

The audit committee states that the Group's systems are out of date; this may give rise to control risk across the Group as a whole. In addition, Lynott Co has implemented a new inventory control system. A new system introduced during the year can create control risk. With any new system, there are risks that controls may take time to develop or be properly understood, and the risk of error in relation to inventories is relatively high.

Beard Co's investment properties

The investment properties are material to both Beard Co's individual financial statements, representing 35.7% of its total assets, and also to the Group's financial statements, representing 9.3% of Group assets.

According to IAS 40 *Investment Property*, an entity can use either the fair value model or the cost model to measure investment property. When the fair value model is used the gain is recognised in profit or loss. The draft consolidated statement of profit or loss and other comprehensive income includes the investment property revaluation gain as other comprehensive income rather than as profit or loss, and therefore the gain is not presented in accordance with IAS 40.

An accounting error may have been made in the adjustment made to increase the value of the investment property. The statement of financial position shows an increase in value of investment properties of $2.5 million, however, the gain in the statement of profit or loss and other comprehensive income is stated at $1 million. There is a risk that the gain is understated and part of the gain may have been classified elsewhere in profit or loss. The gain as stated in the statement of profit or loss and other comprehensive income is material at 9.3% of total comprehensive income.

It would be important to obtain information on the type of properties which have been invested in, and whether there have been any additions to the portfolio during the year, as part of the movement in the investment property balance during the year could be explained by

BPP
LEARNING
MEDIA

acquisitions and disposals. Information should also be obtained on any disposals of investment properties during the year, and whether a profit or loss was made on such disposals.

The possible error discussed above in relation to the presentation of the investment property gain is also relevant to the comparative information, which may also be materially misstated. This increases the risk that other balances and transactions in prior years have been incorrectly accounted for. The use of professional scepticism should be stressed during the audit, and further procedures planned on opening balances and comparative information.

Further information should be sought from the previous auditor of the Group in relation to the accounting treatment for the investment properties, and whether it had been identified as an error, in which case the auditor's reports of both Beard Co and the Group should have been modified. A review of prior year auditor's reports is necessary, as well as a review of the previous audit firm's working papers, assuming permission is given for this to take place.

Bonus scheme

It is noticeable from the draft statement of financial position that there is no accrual recognised in respect of the bonus scheme, unless it has been included inappropriately in trade or tax payables. This indicates a potential understatement of liabilities and overstatement of profit if any necessary accrual has not been made for any bonus which is payable.

Management charges

The management charges imposed by the parent company on the subsidiaries represent inter-company transactions. In the individual financial statements of each subsidiary, there should be an accrual of $800,000 for the management charge payable in August 20X5, and Adams Co's individual financial statements should include $2.4 million as a receivable. There is a risk that these payables and the corresponding receivable have not been accrued in the individual financial statements.

At Group level, the inter-company balances should be eliminated on consolidation. If this has not happened, the liabilities and receivables in the Group financial statements will be overstated, though there would be no net effect on Group profit if the balances were not eliminated.

> **Tutorial note.** Credit will also be awarded for comments on relevant issues to do with transfer pricing and relevant tax implications which have not been considered and recognised appropriately in the financial statements.

Inventory

The draft consolidated statement of financial position shows that inventory has doubled in the year. Given that the Group is involved in retail, there could be issues to do with obsolescence of inventory, leading to potentially overstated inventory and overstatement of profit if any necessary write down is not recognised. This may be especially the case for the mass market fashion clothing made by Lynott Co. Inventory is material to the Group, representing 11.2% of Group assets.

Inter-company transfers

Ross Co transfers goods to Lynott Co for recycling when its goods are considered obsolete. There is a risk that at Group level the inter-company trading is not eliminated on consolidation, which would lead to overstated receivables and payables. In addition, if the inventory is transferred at a profit or loss, which is then not realised by the Group at the year end, the Group inventory figure and operating profit could be over- or understated if any necessary provision for unrealised profit or loss is not recognised.

Goodwill

The draft consolidated statement of financial position does not recognise goodwill, which is unusual for a Group with three subsidiaries. It may be that no goodwill arose on the acquisitions, or that the goodwill has been fully written off by impairment. However, there is a risk of understatement of intangible assets at the Group level.

Component auditor

Lynott Co is audited by an overseas firm of auditors. This may introduce audit risk in that Dando & Co will be relying to some extent on their work. Careful planning will be needed to reduce this risk to a minimum, and this is discussed in the next section of the briefing notes.

> **Tutorial note.** Credit will be awarded for relevant calculations which form part of relevant analytical review performed, such as calculations relating to profit margins, liquidity and gearing, and for discussion which is relevant to the evaluation of audit risk. Credit will also be awarded for discussion of other relevant audit risks, for example, risks associated with the lack of a deferred tax figure in the statement of financial position, and the change in effective tax rate.

(b) **Matters to be considered and procedures to be performed in respect of using the work of Clapton & Co**

The requirements in respect of using the work of component auditors are given in ISA 600 *Special Considerations – Audits of Group Financial Statements (Including the Work of Component Auditors)*. ISA 600 requires that if the Group engagement team plans to request a component auditor to perform work on the financial information of a component, the Group engagement team shall obtain an understanding of four matters.

- The Group engagement team should ascertain whether the component auditor understands and will comply with the ethical requirements which are relevant to the group audit and, in particular, is independent. When performing work on the financial information of a component for a group audit, the component auditor is subject to ethical requirements which are relevant to the group audit. Given that Clapton & Co is based overseas, the ethical requirements in that location may be different, possibly less stringent, to those followed by the Group.

- The component auditor's professional competence should also be assessed, including whether the component auditor has the relevant industry specific skills and technical knowledge to adequately obtain evidence on the component. As Lynott Co reports under IFRS, there is less likelihood of Clapton & Co having a knowledge gap in terms of the Group's applicable financial reporting framework than if the company used local accounting rules. The fact that Clapton & Co is a member of an international network means it is likely to have access to regular training programmes and technical updates which adds to the credibility of their audit work.

- The Group audit team should also gain an understanding of Clapton & Co's resource base to ensure it can cope with the work required by the Group. There should also be evaluation of whether the Group engagement team will be able to be involved in the work of the component auditor to the extent it is necessary to obtain sufficient appropriate audit evidence.

- Whether the component auditor operates in a regulatory environment which actively oversees auditors should be understood. The Group audit team should ascertain whether independent oversight bodies have been established in the jurisdiction in which Clapton & Co operates, to oversee the auditing profession and monitor the quality of audit. This allows greater reliance to be placed on their work.

BPP
LEARNING
MEDIA

579

In addition to the matters required to be considered in accordance with ISA 600 discussed above, the risk of material misstatement in the subsidiary being audited by the component auditor must be fully assessed, as areas of high risk may require input from the Group audit team, and not be subject to audit solely by the component auditors. For areas of high risk, such as Lynott Co's inventories, the Group audit team may consider providing instructions to the component auditor on the audit procedures to be performed.

Procedures:

- Review the local ethical code (if any) followed by Clapton & Co, and compare with the IESBA *Code of Ethics for Professional Accountants* for any significant difference in requirements and principles.

- Obtain confirmation from Clapton & Co of adherence to any local ethical code and the IESBA *Code*. Establish through discussion or questionnaire whether Clapton & Co is a member of an auditing regulatory body, and the professional qualifications issued by that body.

- Obtain confirmations of membership from the professional body to which Clapton & Co belongs, or the authorities by which it is licensed.

- Discuss the audit methodology used by Clapton & Co in the audit of Lynott Co, and compare it to those used under ISAs (eg how the risk of material misstatement is assessed, how materiality is calculated, the type of sampling procedures used).

- A questionnaire or checklist could be used to provide a summary of audit procedures used.

- Ascertain the quality control policies and procedures used by Clapton & Co, both firm-wide and those applied to individual audit engagements.

- Request any results of monitoring or inspection visits conducted by the regulatory authority under which Clapton & Co operates.

(c) **Audit procedures to be performed**

(i) **Investment in associate**

- Obtain the legal documents relating to the share acquisition, and review to confirm the terms and conditions including the number of shares purchased and the voting rights attached to each share.

- Agree the cost of investment of $11.5 million to the legal documentation and to Adams Co's bank statement and cash book.

- Review the minutes of Group management meetings to understand the business rationale for the investment, and to confirm that the Group intends to exercise significant influence over Stewart Co, for example, through appointment of board members.

- Obtain management's calculation to determine the $12 million recognised in the Group financial statements, review the method of the calculation for compliance with IAS 28.

- Obtain the financial statements of Stewart Co to confirm the amount of profit made in the year and confirm that the Group's share of that profit is included in the Group financial statements.

- Enquire with management as to whether any impairment review of the investment in Stewart Co has taken place, and if so, obtain management's workings and review the assumptions used and the method of calculation.

(ii) **Adams brand name**

- Obtain the Group's marketing budget and plans, and review to confirm that there is adequate support of the brand name through advertising.

- Obtain the results of any market research which has been recently carried out by the Group and review its conclusions, for example, on the market share of the Group's product lines.

- Given the materiality of the brand name, consider using an expert in brand valuation to provide a fair value for the brand, which can then be compared to the amount recognised in the financial statements.

- Discuss with management whether in their opinion there are any indicators that the brand name is impaired, in particular discussing the impact of the bad publicity on sales.

- Obtain written representation from management that in their opinion the brand is not impaired at the year end.

(d) **Ethical matters**

The first threat relates to the audit committee's request for our firm to provide advice on the new accounting and management information systems to be implemented next year. If the advice were given, it would constitute the provision of a non-assurance service to an audit client. The IESBA's *Code of Ethics for Professional Accountants* has detailed guidance in this area and specific requirements in the case of a public interest entity such as the Group which is a listed entity.

The *Code* states that services related to IT systems including the design or implementation of hardware or software systems may create a self-review threat. This is because when auditing the financial statements the auditor would assess the systems which they had recommended, and an objective assessment would be difficult to achieve. There is also a risk of assuming the responsibility of management, especially as the Group apparently has little experience in this area, so would rely on the auditor's suggestions and be less inclined to make their own decision.

In the case of an audit client which is a public interest entity, the *Code* states that an audit firm shall not provide services involving the design or implementation of IT systems which form a significant part of the internal control over financial reporting or which generate information which is significant to the client's accounting records or financial statements on which the firm will express an opinion.

Therefore the audit firm should not provide a service to give advice on the accounting systems. With further clarification on the nature of the management information systems and the update required to them, it may be possible for the audit firm to provide a service to the Group, as long as those systems are outside the financial reporting system. However, it may be prudent for the audit firm to decline offering any advice on systems to the client especially as Adams Group is a listed entity.

Second, the audit committee has asked the audit engagement partner to attend a meeting with the bank, the objective of the meeting being the renegotiation of the Group's lending facilities. This is an advocacy threat to objectivity, as the audit partner will be supporting the client in its renegotiation.

If the partner were to attend the meeting and confirm the strength of the Group's financial position, or confirm any work performed on the cash flow forecast, there could be legal implications. These actions would potentially expose Dando & Co to liability, it could be perceived that the audit firm is in some way guaranteeing the loan or guaranteeing that the

Group is in a position to service the debt. The partner should not attend the meeting or be seen to be supporting the Group in its attempt to raise further finance.

These ethical issues should be discussed with those charged with governance of the Group, with an explanation provided as to why the audit firm cannot attend the meeting with the bank.

Conclusion

These briefing notes have shown that the audit risk of this engagement is relatively high, largely due to the existence of potential management bias, a change to the group structure in the year and a requirement to place reliance on the work of another audit firm, and the risks associated with the brand. As this is our firm's first audit of the Adams Group, an audit strategy needs to be developed to focus on these areas, as well as dealing with the additional planning issues associated with relying on the component auditor.

Question 2

Workbook references. Chapters 4 and 11.

Top tips. This question focused on the review stage of the audit, encompassing the review of the financial statements and the auditor's report.

Part (a) should have been full of potential marks for you to pluck from the mark tree like low-hanging fruit. You need to work through the scenario and point out the issues.

Part (b) was very practical, and on the whole much more difficult. However, even if you weren't certain of the accounting treatments, marks were available for discussing the audit issues around them. These were not particularly technical accounting points, so you should really have been comfortable with them.

Easy marks. Calculating materiality in part (b) gets you plenty of marks.

ACCA examining team's comments. Requirement (a) provided some information in the form of a comment made by the audit senior, who indicated that there may have been some problems with the performance of the audit. The concerns raised included the lack of a detailed review of the final version of the financial statements and the chairman's statement had been discussed with the finance director but no further work had been conducted. The justification for not carrying out these tasks was the conclusion by the audit manager that the audit was relatively low risk. The requirement was for 10 marks, and asked candidates to explain the quality control and other professional issues raised by the audit senior's comments.

Candidates did not perform well on this requirement, which was somewhat surprising as in the past questions on quality control issues have been well attempted. Only a minority of candidates were able to identify that the audit of a significant new client could not be classified as low risk, and that a final review would be needed on the financial statements at the completion stage of the audit. Very few candidates however mentioned that final analytical review is a requirement of ISA 520 *Analytical Procedures* and even fewer could explain why the final review is so important prior to the issuance of the auditor's report. In respect of the work performed on the chairman's statement, few candidates identified that there was a lack of documentation of the work performed, but most at least understood the auditor's responsibilities in relation to the chairman's statement.

Generally the answers to this requirement were not made relevant to the information given in the scenario and instead mentioned general features of quality control such as the need for supervision and review. This will earn minimal credit, as marks are severely limited when answer points are not related to the scenario. Many answers discussed at length the auditor's report implications of uncorrected inconsistencies in the chairman's statement, but discussing this in a lot of detail was not answering the question requirement.

BPP
LEARNING

Requirements (b)(i) and (b)(ii) dealt with the evaluation of misstatements and their potential implications for the audit opinion and auditor's report. The information was presented as a schedule of proposed adjustments to uncorrected misstatements in relation to three issues – a share-based payment scheme, a restructuring provision, and slow-moving inventory. In each case the auditor's proposed correcting journal was presented, along with an explanation of the audit findings and audit conclusion on the matter.

Requirement (b)(i) asked for an explanation of the matters to be discussed with management in relation to each of the uncorrected misstatements, for ten marks, and requirement (b)(ii) for 5 marks, asked candidates to justify an appropriate audit opinion assuming that management does not make the proposed adjustments.

Both requirement (b)(i) and (b)(ii) **were not well attempted**. Answers were much too brief for the marks available and unfortunately many candidates could not competently demonstrate that they understand the topic of auditor's reports. Firstly in relation to the share-based payment, the required financial reporting requirements were not well understood, with most candidates suggesting that a provision should be created rather than an adjustment made to equity, which was disappointing as this detail was actually given in the question. In relation to the restructuring provision, many candidates did not consider the specific requirements of IAS 37 *Provisions, Contingent Liabilities and Contingent Assets* in relation to restructuring provisions, and instead applied the general recognition criteria for provisions to the scenario. The slow-moving inventory was better dealt with, as most candidates could explain that inventory should be measured at lower of cost and net realisable value. On the whole, the only marks that many candidates were awarded in this requirement were for materiality calculations. There seems to be very little knowledge or understanding of ISA 450 *Evaluation of Misstatements Identified During the Audit* with almost no candidates differentiating between judgmental misstatements and misstatements caused by a breach of IFRS requirement.

The answers in relation to the impact on the auditor's report were also disappointing. Only the very best candidates considered the aggregate effect of the misstatements in discussing the audit opinion. Many attempted to aggregate the misstatements themselves, coming to the wrong total, even though this had been given in the question. Weaker candidates simply stated that each of the material misstatements would result in a qualified 'except for' opinion. Some candidates suggested that the inventory adjustment should be discussed in an Emphasis of Matter or Other Matter paragraph because it was immaterial, clearly demonstrating a complete misunderstanding of when it is appropriate to use these paragraphs. Candidates must learn when an Emphasis of Matter paragraph should be used; it is not a substitute to be used when the candidate cannot decide between a modified and an unmodified audit opinion.

Candidates must appreciate that the process of justifying an audit opinion and explaining the implication for the auditor's report is a core area of the syllabus. It is regularly examined and it should not come as a surprise to see this topic in the exam. The presentation of information in this question was in a new style, but this should not have made the question more difficult, in fact having information presented in the form of journals with totals given should make understanding the question easier. Further the structure of the requirement into two distinct sections should have helped candidates understand that they were being asked to consider the issues first and then to aggregate the effect of the misstatements before assessing the impact on the auditor's report. Candidates are encouraged to practise as many questions as possible on the topic of auditor's reporting to prepare themselves for this exam.

Marks

(a) **Explanation of quality control and other professional issues**

Generally up to 1 mark for each point explained:

- Insufficient audit evidence obtained in relation to legal provision

- Possible limitation on scope imposed by management and intimidation threat

- Matter is immaterial but the issue is potential understatement of provisions

- Further procedures should be performed, necessary to exercise professional scepticism

- Audit manager's instructions are not appropriate and increase detection risk

- Analytical review mandatory at the final review stage

- Objective to ensure that financial statements consistent with auditor's understanding

- A quick look unlikely to be sufficient especially as this is a new audit client

- The fact that it is deemed low risk does not negate the need for analytical review

- Lack of analytical review increases audit risk especially for a new client

- Other information must be read with objective of identifying material inconsistencies

- Manager to be questioned to see what work has been done and what documentation exists

- Likely that chairman's statement needs to be properly read and audit conclusion documented

- Audit manager lacks understanding of ISA requirements or taking short-cuts

- Audit manager may need further training

- Time pressure increased detection risk and impacts on the quality of the audit performed

Maximum   10

Marks

(b) (i) **Explain matters to be considered in forming audit opinion**

Generally 1 mark for each point explained:

– ISAs require auditor to understand management's reason for not adjusting misstatements

– ISAs require auditor to communicate impact of unadjusted misstatement on opinion

Share-based payment:

– Materiality assessment including appropriate calculation

– Fall in share price not valid reason for not recognising expense and credit to equity

– Material misstatement due to breach of financial reporting standards, encourage management to make necessary adjustment

Provision:

– Materiality assessment including appropriate calculation

– Provision recognised too early, obligating event when closure announced

– Material misstatement due to breach of financial reporting standards, encourage management to make necessary adjustment

– Consider if any additional information to explain recognition of provision, eg an announcement before the year end which auditor unaware of

– In the absence of further information, material misstatement exists due to breach of financial reporting standards, encourage management to make necessary adjustment

Inventory provision

– Materiality assessment including appropriate calculation

– Discussion of difference between clearly trivial, immaterial and material items

– Misstatement is a matter of judgement rather than a matter of fact

– Management should still be encouraged to make adjustment but no impact on audit opinion if not done

BPP
LEARNING

(ii) **Impact on auditor's report**

Generally up to 1 mark per point explained:

- – Determination of aggregate impact of adjustments and combined materiality

- – Material misstatement and modified opinion necessary

- – Discussion and conclusion as to whether opinion should be qualified or adverse

- – Basis for qualified opinion paragraph to include a description and quantification of the financial effects of the misstatement

Maximum   <u>15</u>

Total   <u><u>25</u></u>

(a) **Quality control, ethical and other issues**

The first comment made by the audit assistant shows that the audit of the provision in relation to the legal claim has not been properly carried out, and it would seem that there is not sufficient, appropriate audit evidence to conclude that provisions are fairly stated. First, the finance director telling the audit assistant not to approach the company's legal advisers would appear to be placing a limitation on the evidence which can be obtained. Also, the finance director could have used his seniority to intimidate the audit assistant.

The situation indicates that the finance director may be trying to hide something, and professional scepticism should be exercised. Possibly the finance director knows that the amount which should be provided is much larger than the $10,000, and he is reluctant to recognise a larger liability in the financial statements or that the legal advisers are aware of other provisions which should be included with the financial statements which are currently not being recognised. As the key risk for provisions is understatement, the audit team should not so readily accept the finance director's assessment that the amount included is complete. The audit team should challenge his statement regarding the adequacy of the provision and ask for written evidence, for example, confirmation from the legal advisers.

It is also concerning that the audit manager told the audit assistant to conclude on the audit work when the planned procedures had not been performed. This does not provide good direction to the audit team and increases audit risk. There could be a material misstatement if the provision is significantly understated, and there is not sufficient evidence on the audit file to currently support the conclusions drawn.

Regarding the second comment made by the audit assistant, it is a requirement of ISA 520 *Analytical Procedures* that analytical procedures are performed at the overall review stage of the audit. An objective of ISA 520 is that the auditor should design and perform analytical procedures near the end of the audit which assist the auditor when forming their opinion as to whether the financial statements are consistent with the auditor's understanding of the entity.

It is unlikely that the audit senior's 'quick look' at Bradley Co's financial statements is adequate to meet the requirements of ISA 520 and audit documentation would seem to be inadequate. Therefore if the audit manager, or another auditor, does not perform a detailed analytical review on Bradley Co's financial statements as part of the completion of the audit, there is a breach of ISA 520. Failing to perform the final analytical review could mean that further errors are not found, and the auditor will not be able to check that the presentation of the financial statements conforms to the requirements of the applicable financial reporting framework. It is

also doubtful whether a full check on the presentation and disclosure in the financial statements has been made. The firm should evidence this through the use of a disclosure checklist.

The lack of final analytical review increases audit risk. Because Bradley Co is a new audit client, it is particularly important that the analytical review is performed as detection risk is higher than for longer-standing audit engagements where the auditor has developed a cumulative knowledge of the audit client.

The fact that the audit manager suggested that a detailed review was not necessary shows a lack of knowledge and understanding of ISA requirements. An audit client being assessed as low risk does not negate the need for analytical review to be performed, which the audit manager should know. Alternatively, the audit manager may have known that analytical review should have been performed, but regardless of this still instructed the audit assistant not to perform the review, maybe due to time pressure. The audit manager should be asked about the reason for his instruction and given further training if necessary.

The manager is not providing proper direction and supervision of the audit assistant, which goes against the principles of ISA 220 *Quality control for an audit of financial statements*, and ISQC1 *Quality Control for Firms that Perform Audits and Reviews of Financial Statements and Other Assurance and Related Services Engagements*. Both of these discuss the importance of the audit team having proper direction and supervision as part of ensuring a good quality of audit engagement performance.

The final issue relates to the chairman's statement. ISA 720 *The auditor's Responsibilities Relating to Other Information* requires that the auditor shall read the other information to identify material inconsistencies, if any, with the audited financial statements.

The audit manager has discussed the chairman's statement but this does not necessarily mean that the manager has read it for the purpose of identifying potential misstatements, and it might not have been read at all. Even if the manager has read the chairman's statement, there may not be any audit documentation to show that this has been done or the conclusion of the work. The manager needs to be asked exactly what work has been done, and what documentation exists. As the work performed does not comply with the ISA 720 requirements, then the necessary procedures must be performed before the auditor's report is issued. This is especially important as the necessary paragraphs will need to be included within the auditor's report setting out that the other information has been obtained, the responsibility that the auditor has for the other information explained and whether anything needs to be reported in relation to any inconsistencies.

Again, the situation could indicate the audit manager's lack of knowledge of ISA requirements, or that a short-cut is being taken, probably as a result of time pressure. In either case, the quality of the audit is in jeopardy.

(b) (i) **Evaluation of uncorrected misstatements**

During the completion stage of the audit, the effect of uncorrected misstatements must be evaluated by the auditor, as required by ISA 450 *Evaluation of Misstatements Identified During the Audit*. In the event that management refuses to correct some or all of the misstatements communicated by the auditor, ISA 450 requires that the auditor shall obtain an understanding of management's reasons for not making the corrections and shall take that understanding into account when evaluating whether the financial statements as a whole are free from material misstatement. Therefore a discussion with management is essential in helping the auditor to form an audit opinion.

ISA 450 also requires that the auditor shall communicate with those charged with governance about uncorrected misstatements and the effect that they, individually or in aggregate, may have on the opinion in the auditor's report.

 BPP LEARNING

Each of the matters included in the schedule of uncorrected misstatements will be discussed below and the impact on the auditor's report considered individually and in aggregate.

Share-based payment scheme

The adjustment in relation to the share-based payment scheme is material individually to profit, representing 12% of revenue. It represents less than 1% of total assets and is not material to the statement of financial position.

IFRS 2 *Share-based Payment* requires an expense and a corresponding entry to equity to be recognised over the vesting period of a share-based payment scheme, with the amount recognised based on the fair value of equity instruments granted. Management's argument that no expense should be recognised because the options are unlikely to be exercised is not correct. IFRS 2 would classify the fall in Bradley Co's share price as a market condition, and these are not relevant to determining whether an expense is recognised or the amount of it.

Therefore management should be requested to make the necessary adjustment to recognise the expense and entry to equity of $300,000. If this is not recognised, the financial statements will contain a material misstatement, with consequences for the auditor's opinion.

Restructuring provision

The adjustment in relation to the provision is material to profit, representing 2% of revenue. It represents less than 1% of total assets so is not material to the statement of financial position.

The provision appears to have been recognised too early. IAS 37 *Provisions, Contingent Liabilities and Contingent Assets* requires that for a restructuring provision to be recognised, there must be a present obligation as a result of a past event, and that is only when a detailed formal plan is in place and the entity has started to implement the plan, or announced its main features to those affected. A board decision is insufficient to create a present obligation as a result of a past event. The provision should be recognised in September 20X5 when the announcement to employees was made.

Management should be asked to explain why they have included the provision in the financial statements, for example, there may have been an earlier announcement before 31 August 20X5 of which the auditor is unaware.

In the absence of any such further information, management should be informed that the accounting treatment of the provision is a material misstatement, which if it remains unadjusted will have implications for the auditor's opinion.

Inventory provision

The additional slow-moving inventory allowance which the auditor considers necessary is not material on an individual basis to either profit or to the statement of profit or loss or the statement of financial position, as it represents only 0.4% of revenue and less than 1% of total assets.

Despite the amount being immaterial, it should not be disregarded, as the auditor should consider the aggregate effect of misstatements on the financial statements. ISA 450 does state that the auditor need not accumulate balances which are 'clearly trivial', by which it means that the accumulation of such amounts clearly would not have a material effect on the financial statements. However, at 0.4% of revenue the additional provision is not trivial, so should be discussed with management.

This misstatement is a judgemental misstatement as it arises from the judgements of management concerning an accounting estimate over which the auditor has reached a

different conclusion. This is not a breach of financial reporting standards, but a difference in how management and the auditor have estimated an uncertain amount. Management should be asked to confirm the basis on which their estimate was made, and whether they have any reason why the provision should not be increased by the amount recommended by the auditor.

If this amount remains unadjusted by management, it will not on an individual basis impact the auditor's report.

(ii) **Impact on auditor's report**

When considering their opinion, the auditor must conclude whether the financial statements as a whole are free from material misstatement. In order to do this, they must consider whether any remaining uncorrected misstatements are material, either on an individual basis or in aggregate.

Aggregate materiality position

In aggregate, the misstatements have a net effect of $260,000 ($310,000 – $50,000), meaning that if left unadjusted, profit will be overstated by $260,000 and the statement of financial position overstated by the same amount. This is material to profit, at 10.4% of revenue, but is not material to the statement of financial position at less than 1% of total assets.

Impact on auditor's report

The misstatements in relation to the share-based payment scheme and restructuring provision are individually material to the statement of profit or loss and therefore management should be requested to make this adjustment as the statement of profit or loss is materially misstated if the adjustments are not made by management. According to ISA 705 *Modifications to the Opinion in the Independent Auditor's Report*, the auditor shall modify the opinion in the auditor's report when the auditor concludes that, based on the audit evidence obtained, the financial statements as a whole are not free from material misstatement.

The type of modification depends on the significance of the material misstatement. In this case, these misstatements in aggregate are material to the financial statements, but are unlikely to be considered pervasive even though they relate to a number of balances in the financial statements as they do not represent a substantial proportion of the financial statements. This is supported by the fact that the adjustment is not material to the statement of financial position and it is therefore unlikely that the auditor will conclude that the financial statements as a whole are misleading.

Therefore a qualified opinion should be expressed, with the auditor stating in the opinion that except for the effects of the matters described in the basis for qualified opinion paragraph, the financial statements show a true and fair view. The basis for qualified opinion paragraph should be placed immediately after the opinion paragraph, and should contain a description of the matters giving rise to the qualification This should include a description and quantification of the financial effects of the misstatement.

The remaining uncorrected misstatement in relation to the inventory allowance is, individually, immaterial to the financial statements and although management should be encouraged to amend all misstatements, failure to amend the inventory allowance will have no impact on the auditor's report. It should be emphasised to management that failure to correct the allowance will have an impact on future periods. If management intends to leave uncorrected misstatements, written confirmation of their immaterial nature should be obtained via a written representation.

Question 3

Workbook reference. Chapters 1 and 13.

Top tips. Part (a) was a fairly difficult discussion requirement on changes to the *Code of Ethics*. The examining team showed some kindness to candidates by including the quotation from the IESBA, which gave you something to discuss even if you were not aware of the changes. Although you would have lost some marks if you were not aware of these changes, you could still have passed the question with a strong discussion of the issues.

Part (b) was typical of a requirement in this area. Questions on non-audit engagements often include parts on acceptance procedures like (b)(i), many of which are fairly generic. As ever, you need to try to take the generic points from the Workbook and think how they might apply in this situation - the point about ethics, for example, leads on to consideration of the advocacy threat suggested by the fact that the bank will be relying on the report.

Part (b)(ii) on procedures is very practical, and requires you to think through what assumptions there might be behind the forecast and hence what procedures would be necessary.

Part (b)(iii), on an assurance report on PFI, was straightforward. If you hadn't managed your time well, however, you might have run out of time to get the easy marks that are available here.

Easy marks. Part (b)(iii) contained some fairly easy marks for your knowledge of a PFI report.

ACCA examining team's comments. This question was **well attempted** by many candidates, indicating that the relevant syllabus areas had been studied and understood. There was however, **a lack of application to the scenario**, especially in relation to part (b).

Requirement (b)(i) was for seven marks, and asked candidates to explain the matters to be considered by the audit firm before accepting the engagement to review and report on the prospective financial information. The quality of answers here was quite good, with almost all candidates making a reasonable attempt to discuss relevant matters including ethical issues, resource availability, the scope of the engagement and the nature of the assumptions used in the forecast. **Where candidates scored less well** on this requirement it was often due **to lack of application** to the scenario. A minority of answers amounted to little more than a bullet point list, often posed as questions (eg 'are there any ethical matters to consider', 'who is the report for', 'why is the report needed'), and while these are matters to consider the lack of any application to the scenario limits the amount of credit that can be awarded.

Requirement (b)(ii) was also quite well attempted by many candidates, who used the information provided to generate specific and relevant enquiries and other procedures. **Weaker answers** tended to write very vague comments which were not tailored to the scenario or explained, or were just incorrect, such as. 'obtain representations', 'agree forecast to audited financial statements', 'check whether assumptions are realistic', 'perform analytical procedures'.

BPP note. Examining team comments are not available for all parts of this question. The specimen exam is based on a past exam sitting, so only those parts of it that were in the past exam have comments – the question parts that are new to the specimen exam do not have examining team comments for them.

Marking scheme

Marks

(a) **Discussion on non-assurance services**

Generally 1½ marks for each point of discussion:

- The IESBA *Code* has been amended to restrict the provision of non-assurance services especially to public interest entities in emergency situations
- Examples – bookkeeping and tax no longer allowed services
- The *Code* contains enhanced guidance on management responsibilities
- Examples – involvement in recruitment and strategic direction of the company
- Different approaches used in different jurisdictions, eg UK comply or explain approach, US legislative approach
- Arguments against provision are based on threats to objectivity, eg self-review threat, advocacy threat, self-interest threat (1 mark each explained with relevant example)
- Arguments in favour of provision focus on audit firms' enhanced understanding of client, and the firms being in the best position to offer the services to their clients
- Safeguards may be used to reduce threats to an acceptable level in some situations

Maximum   8

(b) (i) **Matters to consider before accepting the review engagement**

Up to 1½ marks for each matter explained:

- Independence – general types of threats raised (self-interest, self-review, advocacy)
- Appropriate safeguards
- Request for assistance with presenting the strategic plan is a management responsibility
- No safeguards can reduce the threat to an acceptable level and the assistance should not be provided
- Competence and time frame
- Elements to be included in the application and intended use
- Key assumptions and time period covered

Maximum   7

(ii)   **Examination procedures**

1 mark for each described procedure. Also allow 1 mark for relevant analytical procedures used in the explanation of procedures.

- Agreement that the accounting policies used in preparing the forecast information are consistent with those used in historical financial information and comply with IFRS
- The forecast should be cast to confirm accuracy
- Review of capital expenditure forecasts
- Quotations received from potential suppliers of the new technology should be reviewed
- The time frame of the work to be carried out needs to be discussed with management
- Review of market research documents and review of prices charged by competitors
- Analytical review followed by discussion with management on the trend in revenue
- Revenue is forecast to increase by 22.9% and 7% in the years to 30 April 20X7 and 20X8 respectively
- Analytical review of the composition of operating expenses
- In 20X6, operating expenses are 80.7% of revenue, but this is forecast to reduce to 73.4% in 20X7 and to 69.8% in 20X8
- Recalculation of depreciation expense and agreement to forecast statement of financial position
- Recalculation of finance cost to ensure that interest payable with confirmation of the rate of interest to bank documentation

Maximum   6

(iii)   **Content of the report**

½ mark for each relevant content element identified (up to 2 marks) and up to 2 marks for discussion of the level of assurance provided.

- Content elements: reference to relevant ISAE or national standards, statement of management responsibility, reference to purpose and distribution of report, opinion on basis of assumptions and application of relevant financial reporting framework, caveats on achievability of results
- Assurance is based on negative assurance
- Assurance limited by future orientation of the subject matter and nature of procedures used

Maximum   <u>4</u>

Total   25

(a)   The issue of auditors providing non-assurance services to audit clients has been topical for many years, and there are many arguments for and against their outright prohibition. IESBA conducted a review of the *Code of Ethics for Professional Accountants* (the *Code*) and made a number of changes to the guidance, tightening the services which can be provided, with a particular focus on public interest entities.

The amendments mean that the *Code* no longer permits the provision of normally prohibited non-assurance services in emergency situations to public interest clients, such as certain bookkeeping and taxation services. The provisions in the *Code* relating to management responsibility were strengthened to ensure better understanding of what constitutes a management responsibility. It continues to be emphasised in the *Code* that auditors must not assume management responsibility when providing non-assurance services to audit clients.

The *Code*, while not providing an exhaustive list, sets out a number of examples of activities which may result in management responsibility. A number of new activities have been explicitly added, including being involved in the strategic direction of the company, hiring of personnel and reporting to those charged with governance on behalf of management, and thus effectively making these activities prohibited in line with the *Code*.

There are varying views on whether it is appropriate for auditors to provide non-assurance services to their clients. For example, governance regulations in some jurisdictions can be relatively lenient. For example, the UK Corporate Governance Code requires the audit committee to review and monitor the external auditor's independence and objectivity. This includes the audit committee evaluating and approving the provision of non-audit services by the audit firm. This assessment would include consideration of whether the audit firm was complying with the relevant ethical guidance. In contrast, the US Sarbanes – Oxley Act takes a stricter approach and prohibits audit firms from providing other services to audit clients.

Those arguing in favour of outright prohibition suggest that this would be a simple way to eliminate the threats to objectivity, which the provision of non-assurance services to audit clients creates. The IESBA quote states that several threats to objectivity are created when performing such services. A self-review threat arises when the auditor, in performing additional services for the client, performs work which impacts on the financial statements, meaning that the auditor is reviewing their own figures, or matters over which they have provided guidance or advice. An example could be where the audit firm performs a valuation service on a matter which is material to the financial statements.

Depending on the nature of the additional service, an advocacy threat may arise, where the audit firm is perceived to be supporting the interests of their client. This could happen, for example, if the audit firm advises their client in relation to a legal dispute or tax tribunal.

In particular, non-audit services can be very lucrative, leading potentially to a self-interest threat. The greater the volume and financial significance of the non-assurance services provided, the greater the risk that the auditor will have relationship and economic reasons not to challenge management's views and positions with the necessary degree of professional scepticism.

It has also been argued that outright prohibition would benefit the market and competition within the audit market, allowing smaller audit firms to provide the services which larger firms would no longer be able to offer to their audit clients or conversely allow smaller firms to ascertain a larger proportion of the external audit market.

However, there are also many arguments which support auditors providing these additional services. By having the same firm provide the audit and the non-assurance service, the client benefits in two ways. The audit firm will already possess a good knowledge and understanding of the client and its operating environment, resulting in deeper insight and a better quality service being provided. This will then lead to cost benefits, as the non-assurance service will be provided in a more efficient way.

Audit firms would also argue that participation in services such as due diligence reviews and forensic investigations allows the audit firm to understand their clients' business and risks better and to obtain insights into management's objectives and capabilities which are useful in an audit context. This may reduce audit risk.

Many non-assurance services can be safely provided as long as steps are taken to assess potential threats to objectivity, and to adequately address those risks, for example, by the use of separate teams to provide audit and non-assurance services. However, in the case of public interest entities, such as listed companies, the IESBA has taken the view that no safeguards are available to reduce the risks to an acceptable level in the case of some non-assurance services and it continues to emphasise that the auditor shall not become involved in activities which result in them assuming any form of management responsibility.

(b) (i)   Before accepting the engagement to review Waters Co's prospective financial information, there are several matters to be considered. A significant matter is whether it is ethically acceptable to perform the review. The review would constitute a non-assurance service provided to an audited entity, and IESBA's *Code of Ethics for Professional Accountants* states that this may create self-interest, self-review and advocacy threats to independence. In this case, the advocacy threat may be deemed particularly significant as Hunt & Co could be perceived as promoting the client's position to the bank. The review engagement should only be provided if safeguards can be used to reduce the threat to an acceptable level, which may include:

- Having a professional accountant who was not involved with the non-assurance service review the non-assurance work performed or otherwise advise as necessary.

- Discussing ethical issues with those charged with governance of the client.

- Using separate teams to work on the audit and on the review engagement.

The request by the finance director to assist him in presenting the final version of the strategic plan to the board also needs to be considered. The request to be involved in confirming that the plan is consistent with competitors suggests that if the board is not satisfied the company may not move forward with the plan or apply for the bank funding. If the engagement partner is involved, this would likely result in the firm taking on a management responsibility as they are essentially supporting the strategic direction suggested by management. Further, by attending the presentation the partner could be seen to be communicating with the board on behalf of management. Both of these activities are now referenced as management activities in the *Code* and therefore the firm should advise the finance director that Hunt & Co may be able to perform the review for the purposes of the bank but the firm will not be able to take part in the presentation.

As well as ethical matters, ISAE 3400 *The Examination of Prospective Information* requires that certain matters are considered before a review engagement is accepted. Hunt & Co must also consider the specific terms of the engagement. For example, the firm will need to clarify whether the bank has requested a review report to be issued, and what exact information will be included in the application to the bank. It is likely that more than just a forecast statement of profit or loss is required, for example, a forecast statement of cash flows and accompanying narrative, including key assumptions is likely to be required for a lending decision to be made.

ISAE 3400 also requires that consideration should be given to the intended use of the information, and whether it is for general or limited distribution. It seems in this case the review engagement and its report will be used solely in connection with raising bank finance, but this should be confirmed before accepting the engagement.

The period covered by the prospective financial information and the key assumptions should also be considered. ISAE 3400 states that the auditor should not accept an engagement when the assumptions used are clearly unrealistic or when the auditor believes that the prospective financial information will be inappropriate for its intended use. For example, the assumption that the necessary capital expenditure can take place by September 20X6 may be overly optimistic.

The firm should also consider whether there are staff available with appropriate skills and experience to perform the review engagement, and the deadline by which the work needs to be completed. If the work on the cinemas is scheduled to be completed by September 20X6, presumably the cash will have to be provided very soon, meaning a tight deadline for the review engagement to be performed.

(ii) **Examination procedures should include the following:**

- Agreement that the accounting policies used in preparing the forecast statement of profit or loss are consistent with those used in historical financial information and comply with IFRS.

- The forecast should be cast to confirm accuracy.

- The time frame of the work to be carried out needs to be discussed with management, with enquiry being made to ascertain how the work can be carried out in such a short period of time, for example, will all cinemas be closed for the period of refurbishment? This will help to confirm the accuracy of the revenue and expenses recognised.

- Review of market research documents and review of prices charged by competitors showing new technology films to support the assumption regarding increase in price and consumer appetite for the films.

- Analytical review followed by discussion with management on the trend in revenue, which is forecast to increase by 22.9% and 7% in the years to 30 April 20X7 and 20X8 respectively.

- Consider the capacity of the cinemas and the number of screenings which can take place to assess the reasonableness of projected revenue.

- Analytical review of the composition of operating expenses to ensure that all expenses are included at a reasonable amount. In 20X6, operating expenses are 80.7% of revenue, but this is forecast to reduce to 73.4% in 20X7 and to 69.8% in 20X8, indicating understatement of forecast expenses.

- Review the list of operating expenses to ensure that any loss to be recognised on the disposal of old equipment has been included, or that profit on disposal has been netted off.

- Quotations received from potential suppliers of the new technology should be reviewed to verify the amount of the capital expenditure and therefore that depreciation included in the forecast statement of profit or loss appears reasonable.

- Recalculation of depreciation expense and confirmation that depreciation on the new technology has been included and correctly calculated and agrees to the forecast statement of financial position.

- Recalculation of finance cost to ensure that interest payable on the new bank loan has been included, with confirmation of the rate of interest to bank documentation.

BPP
LEARNING

- Review of capital expenditure budgets, cash flow forecasts and any other information to accompany the forecast statement of profit or loss for consistency, and confirmation that the amount planned to be spent on the cinemas can be met with the amount of finance applied for as well Waters Co's own cash balance.

(iii) **Report on prospective financial information**

ISAE 3400 contains requirements on the content of a report on prospective financial information, stating that it should contain, in addition to a title, addresses and being appropriately signed and dated:

- Identification of the prospective financial information;

- A reference to the ISAE or relevant national standards or practices applicable to the examination of prospective financial information;

- A statement that management is responsible for the prospective financial information including the assumptions on which it is based;

- When applicable, a reference to the purpose and/or restricted distribution of the prospective financial information;

- An opinion as to whether the prospective financial information is properly prepared on the basis of the assumptions and is presented in accordance with the relevant financial reporting framework;

- Appropriate caveats concerning the achievability of the results indicated by the prospective financial information.

In terms of the assurance level, the report will include a statement of negative assurance as to whether the assumptions provide a reasonable basis for the prospective financial information. This is a lower level of assurance than that given in an audit of historical financial information. The assurance provided is limited due to the future orientation of the information subject to review, and because the nature of the investigative procedures performed are less detailed and substantive in nature.

ACCA Strategic Professional

AAA

Advanced Audit and Assurance (International)

Mock Examination 3

March/June 2018 exam (amended)

Question Paper
Time allowed   3 hours 15 minutes
ALL THREE questions are compulsory and **MUST** be attempted

DO NOT OPEN THIS PAPER UNTIL YOU ARE READY TO START UNDER EXAMINATION CONDITIONS

BPP
LEARNING

ALL THREE questions are compulsory and MUST be attempted

Question 1

You are a manager in the audit department of Bison & Co, a firm of Chartered Certified Accountants, responsible for the audit of the Eagle Group (the Group), which has a financial year ending 31 December 20X8. Your firm is appointed to audit the parent company, Eagle Co, and all of its subsidiaries, with the exception of Lynx Co, a newly acquired subsidiary located in a foreign country which is audited by a local firm of auditors, Vulture Associates.

All companies in the Group report using IFRSR Standards as the applicable financial reporting framework and have the same financial year end.

You are provided with the following exhibits:

1. An email which you have received from Maya Crag, the audit engagement partner.

2. Background information about the Group including a request from the Group finance director in respect of a non-audit engagement.

3. Extracts from the Group financial statements projected to 31 December 20X8 and comparatives, extracted from the management accounts, and accompanying explanatory notes.

4. Management's determination of the goodwill arising on the acquisition of Lynx Co.

5. An extract from the audit strategy document prepared by Vulture Associates relating to Lynx Co.

Required

Respond to the instructions in the email from the audit engagement partner.

(46 marks)

Note. The split of the mark allocation is shown in the partner's email (Exhibit 1).

Professional marks will be awarded for the presentation and logical flow of the briefing notes and the clarity of the explanations provided. **(4 marks)**

(Total = 50 marks)

Exhibit 1 – Email from audit engagement partner

To: Audit manager

From: Maya Crag, Audit engagement partner

Subject: Audit planning for the Eagle Group

Hello

I have provided you with some information in the form of a number of exhibits which you should use in planning the audit of the Eagle Group (the Group). I held a meeting yesterday with the Group finance director and representatives from the Group audit committee, and we discussed a number of issues which will impact on the audit planning.

Using the information provided, I require you to prepare briefing notes for my use in which you:

(a)   Evaluate the audit risks to be considered in planning the Group audit. You should use analytical procedures to assist in identifying audit risks. You are not required to consider audit risks relating to disclosure, as these will be planned for later in the audit process. **(24 marks)**

(b) Design the principal audit procedures to be used in the audit of the goodwill arising on the acquisition of Lynx Co. Management's calculation of the goodwill is shown in Exhibit 4. You do not need to consider the procedures relating to impairment testing, or to foreign currency retranslation, as these will be planned later in the audit. **(6 marks)**

(c) Using the information provided in Exhibit 5, evaluate the extract of the audit strategy prepared by Vulture Associates in respect of their audit of Lynx Co and discuss any implications for the Group audit. **(10 marks)**

(d) After considering the request in Exhibit 2 from the Group finance director in respect of our firm providing advice on the Group's integrated report, discuss the ethical and professional implications of this request, recommending any further actions which should be taken by our firm. **(6 marks)**

Thank you.

Exhibit 2 – Background information about the Group and request from Group finance director

Group operational activities

The Group, which is a listed entity, operates in distribution, supply chain and logistics management. Its operations are worldwide, spanning more than 200 countries. The Group's strategy is to strengthen its market share and grow revenue in a sustainable manner by expansion into emerging markets. There are over 50 subsidiaries in the Group, many of which are international. There are three main business divisions: post and parcel delivery, commercial freight and supply chain management, each of which historically has provided approximately one-third of the Group's revenue.

A fourth business division which focuses purely on providing distribution channels for the oil and coal sector was established two years ago, and in 20X8 began to grow quite rapidly. It is forecast to provide 12% of the Group's revenue this year, growing to 15% in 20X9. This division is performing particularly well in developing economies.

In recent years, revenue has grown steadily, based mainly on growth in some locations where e-commerce is rapidly developing. This year, revenue is projected to decline slightly, which the Group attributes to increased competition, as a new distribution company has taken some of the Group's market share in a number of countries. However, the Group management team is confident that this is a short-term drop in revenue, and forecasts a return to growth in 20X9.

Innovation

The Group has invested in automating its warehousing facilities, and while it still employs more than 250,000 staff, many manual warehouse jobs are now performed by robots. Approximately 5,000 staff were made redundant early in this financial year due to automation of their work. Other innovations include increased use of automated loading and unloading of vehicles, and improvements in the technology used to monitor and manage inventory levels.

Integrated reporting

The Group is proud of this innovation and is keen to highlight these technological developments in its integrated report. The Group finance director has been asked to lead a project tasked with producing the Group's first integrated report.

The finance director has sent the following request to the audit engagement partner:

'We would like your firm to assist us in developing our integrated report, and to provide assurance on it, as we believe this will enhance the credibility of the information it contains. Specifically, we would like your input into the choice of key performance indicators which should be presented, how to present them, and how they should be reconciled, where relevant, to financial information from the audited financial statements.'

The publication of an integrated report is not a requirement in the jurisdiction in which the Group is headquartered, but there is a growing pressure from stakeholders for an integrated report to be produced by listed reporting entities.

If Bison & Co accepts the engagement in relation to the Group's integrated report, the work would be performed by a team separate from the audit team.

Exhibit 3 – Extracts from consolidated financial statements

Statement of financial position

	Note	As at 31 December 20X8 Projected $m	As at 31 December 20X7 Actual $m
Non-current assets			
Goodwill	1	1,100	970
Other intangible assets	2	200	170
Property, plant and equipment		657	600
Other investments		85	100
Total non-current assets		2,042	1,840
Current assets		1,450	1,420
Total assets		3,492	3,260
Equity and liabilities			
Equity			
Share capital	3	1,250	1,150
Retained Earnings		840	780
Other components of equity		130	140
Non-controlling interests		25	23
Total equity		2,245	2,093
Non-current liabilities	4	650	620
Current liabilities		597	547
Total equity and liabilities		3,492	3,260

Statement of profit or loss

	Note	Year to 31 December 20X8 Projected $ million	Year to 31 December 20X7 Actual $ million
Revenue	5	5,770	5,990
Other operating income	6	120	180
Operating expenses	7	(5,540)	(5,800)
Operating profit		350	270
Finance charges		(28)	(30)
Profit before tax		322	240
Tax expense		(64)	(60)
Profit for the year		258	180

BPP
LEARNING
MEDIA

Notes to the extracts from financial statements

Goodwill

1. Goodwill relates to the Group's subsidiaries, and is tested for impairment on an annual basis. Management will

   conduct the annual impairment review in December 20X8, but it is anticipated that no impairment will need to be recognised this year due to anticipated growth in revenue which is forecast for the next two years.

   In March 20X8, the Group acquired an 80% controlling shareholding in Lynx Co, a listed company located in a foreign country, for consideration of $351 million. Management's determination of the goodwill arising on this acquisition is shown in Exhibit 4.

Other intangible assets

2. Other intangible assets relates mostly to software and other technological development costs. During the year $35 million was spent on developing a new IT system for dealing with customer enquiries and processing customer orders. A further $20 million was spent on research and development into robots being used in warehouses, and $5 million on developing new accounting software. These costs have been capitalised as intangible assets and are all being amortised over a 15-year useful life.

Equity and non-current liabilities

3. A share issue in July 20X8 raised cash of $100 million, which was used to fund capital expenditure.

4. Non-current liabilities includes borrowings of $550 million (20X7 – $500 million) and provisions of $100 million (20X7 – $120 million). Changes in financing during the year have impacted on the Group's weighted average cost of capital. Information from the Group's treasury management team suggests that the weighted average cost of capital is currently 10%.

Financial performance

5. Revenue has decreased by 3.7% over the year, due to a new competitor in the market taking some of the Group's market share.

6. Other operating income comprises the following items:

	20X8 $m	20X7 $m
Reversal of provisions	60	40
Reversal of impairment losses on receivables and other assets	30	20
Foreign currency gains	28	23
Profit/(loss) on disposal of non-current assets	2	(3)
Total	120	80

7. Operating expenses includes the following items:

	20X8 $m	20X7 $m
Staff costs	3,650	3,610
Cost of raw materials, consumables and supplies	1,725	1,780
Depreciation, amortisation and impairment	145	140
Other operating expenses	20	270
Total	5,540	5,800

Exhibit 4 – Determination of goodwill on the acquisition of Lynx Co

	Note	$m
Cash consideration – paid 1 March 20X8		80
Contingent consideration	1	271
Total consideration		351
Fair value of non-controlling interest	2	49
		400
Less: Fair value of identifiable net assets	3	(300)
Goodwill		100

Notes

1   The contingent consideration will be payable four years after the acquisition date and is calculated based on a payment of $525 million, only payable if Lynx Co reaches revenue and profit targets outlined in the purchase documentation. The amount included in the goodwill calculation has been discounted to present value using a discount factor based on an 18% interest rate.

2   The non-controlling interest is measured at fair value, the amount being based on Lynx Co's share price on1 March 20X8.

3   The assets and liabilities acquired and their fair values were determined by an independent firm of Chartered Certified Accountants, Sidewinder & Co, who was engaged by the Group to perform due diligence on Lynx Co prior to the acquisition taking place. A fair value uplift of $12 million was made in relation to property, plant and equipment.

Exhibit 5 – Extract from audit strategy – prepared by Vulture Associates in respect of the audit of Lynx Co

The two points below are an extract from the audit strategy. Other sections of the audit strategy, including the audit risk assessment, have been reviewed by the Group audit team and are considered to be satisfactory. Lynx Co is projected to be loss making this year, and the Group audit team is confident that sufficient procedures on going concern have been planned for.

Controls effectiveness

We will place reliance on internal controls, which will reduce the amount of substantive testing which needs to be performed. This is justified on the grounds that in the previous year's audit, controls were tested and found to be highly effective. We do not plan to re-test the controls, as according to management there have been no changes in systems or the control environment during the year.

Internal audit

Lynx Co has offered the services of its internal audit team to help perform audit procedures. We are planning to use the internal auditors to complete the audit work in respect of trade receivables, as they have performed work on this area during the year. It will be efficient for them to perform and conclude on the relevant audit procedures, including the trade receivables circularisation, and evaluation of the allowance for trade receivables, which we will instruct them to carry out.

Question 2

(a)   You are an audit manager in Pointer & Co, a firm of Chartered Certified Accountants which offers a range of assurance services. You are responsible for the audit of Vizsla Co, a company which provides approximately 10% of your firm's practice income each year. The finance director of Vizsla Co has recently contacted you to provide information about another company, Setter Co, which is looking to appoint a provider of assurance services. An extract from the email which the finance director of Vizsla Co has sent to you is shown below:

'One of my friends, Gordon Potts, is the managing director of Setter Co, a small company which is looking to expand in the next few years. I know that Gordon has approached the company's bank for finance of $6 million to fund the expansion. To support this loan application, Gordon needs to appoint a firm to provide a limited assurance review on the company's financial statements. He would also want the appointed firm to provide taxplanning advice and to prepare both the company's and his personal tax computations for submission to the tax authorities. I have asked Gordon to contact you, and I hope that Pointer & Co will be able to provide these services to Setter Co for a low fee. If the fee you suggest is too high, and unacceptable to Gordon, then I will recommend that Gordon approaches Griffon & Co instead, and I would also consider appointing Griffon & Co to provide the audit of Vizsla Co.'

Griffon & Co is a firm of Chartered Certified Accountants which has an office in the same town as Pointer & Co.

You have done some research on both Setter Co and Gordon Potts and have confirmed that the company is small enough to be exempt from audit. The company is owner-managed, with the Potts family owning 90% of the share capital. Gordon Potts is a director and majority shareholder of three other companies. An article in a newspaper from several years ago about Gordon Potts indicated that one of his companies was once fined for breach of employment law and that he had used money from one of the company's pension plans to set up a business abroad, appointing his son as the managing director of that business.

Required

In relation to Pointer & Co's potential acceptance of Setter Co as a client of the firm:

(i)   Explain the ethical issues and other matters which should be considered; and

(ii)   Explain the importance of obtaining customer due diligence and recommend the information which should be obtained. **(16 marks)**

(b)   Pointer & Co has agreed to perform an assurance engagement for Vizsla Co; the engagement will be a review of prospective financial information which is needed to support the company's overdraft facilities. Vizsla Co had a financial year ended 30 September 20X7, and an unmodified opinion was issued on these financial statements last month. Pointer & Co's partner responsible for ethics has agreed that any threats to objectivity will be reduced to an acceptable level through the use of a team separate from the audit team to perform the work. The operating profit forecast for the two years to 31 March 20Y0 prepared by a member of the accounting team of Vizsla Co is shown below, along with some accompanying notes.

	Note	Six months to 30 September 20X8	Six months to 30 March 20X9	Six months to 30 September 20X9	Six months to 30 March 20Y0
	1	$'000	$'000	$'000	$'000
Revenue		12,800	16,900	13,700	18,900
Gross profit %		34%	45%	36%	46%
Operating costs:					
Staff costs		(2,800)	(2,900)	(2,800)	(2,900)
Design costs	2	(1,200)	(1,200)	(1,250)	(1,250)
Marketing		(900)	(1,100)	(1,100)	(1,100)
Interest on overdraft	3	(25)	(10)	–	–
Other expenses	4	(3,840)	(5,070)	(4,110)	(5,670)
Operating profit		4,035	6,720	4,440	7,980

Notes

1   Vizsla Co is a producer of greetings cards and giftware, the demand for which is seasonal in nature.

2   Design costs are mostly payroll costs of the staff working in the company's design team, and the costs relate to the design and development of new product ranges.

3   Vizsla Co has agreed with its bank to clear its overdraft by 1 September 20X9, and the management team is confident that after that point the company will not need an overdraft facility.

4   The total 'Other expenses' is calculated based on 30% of the projected revenue for the six-month period.

Required

Recommend the examination procedures which should be used in the review of the profit forecast.   **(9 marks)**

(Total = 25 marks)

Question 3

(a)   ISA 701 *Communicating Key Audit Matters in the Independent Auditor's Report* states 'The purpose of communicating key audit matters is to enhance the communicative value of the auditor's report by providing greater transparency about the audit that was performed.'

Required

Discuss this statement in relation to the benefits and difficulties of communicating key audit matters to users of the auditor's report and the contribution of ISA 701 in addressing the audit expectation gap.   **(6 marks)**

(b)   You are an audit manager in Gillan & Co, and are responsible for several audit clients.

One of these clients is the Blackmore Group (the Group), a listed manufacturer of high quality musical instruments, for the year ended 31 March 20X8. The draft financial statements of the Group recognise a loss before tax of $2.2 million (20X7 – loss of $1.5 million) and total assets of $14.1 million (20X7 – $18.3 million). The audit is nearing completion and the audit senior has drafted the auditor's report which contains the following extract:

Key audit matters

1.   **Customer liquidation**

Included in receivables shown on the consolidated statement of financial position is an amount of $287,253 from a customer which has ceased trading. On the basis that the Group has no security for this debt, we believe that the Group should make a full provision for impairment of $287,253 thereby reducing profit before taxation for the year and total assets as at 31 March 20X8 by that amount.

Qualified opinion arising from disagreement about accounting treatment

In our opinion, except for the effect on the financial statements of the matter described above, the financial statements have been properly prepared in all material respects in accordance with IFRS Standards.

> **Emphasis of Matter**
>
> We draw attention to the loss before tax of $2.2 million for the year ended 31 March 20X8 and that the Group is in breach of loan covenants with its key finance providers. A material uncertainty therefore exists which may cast doubt on the Group's ability to continue as a going concern. Our opinion is not modified in respect of this matter.

Required

Critically appraise the extract from the auditor's report on the consolidated financial statements of the Blackmore Group for the year ended 31 March 20X8.

Note. You are **NOT** required to re-draft the extract from the auditor's report.   **(7 marks)**

You are also responsible for the audit of the Hughes Group (the Group). You are reviewing the audit working papers for the consolidated financial statements relating to the year ended 31 March 20X8. The Group specialises in the wholesale supply of steel plate and sheet metals. The draft consolidated financial statements recognise revenue of $7,670 million (20X7 – $7,235 million), profit before taxation of $55 million (20X7 – $80 million) and total assets of $1,560 million (20X7 – $1,275 million). Gillan & Co audits all of the individual company financial statements as well as the Group consolidated financial statements. The audit senior has brought the following matters, regarding several of the Group's companies, to your attention:

(c) **Willis Co**

Willis Co is a foreign subsidiary whose functional and presentational currency is the same as Hughes Co and the remainder of the Group. The subsidiary specialises in the production of stainless steel and holds a significant portfolio of forward commodity options to hedge against fluctuations in raw material prices. The local jurisdiction does not mandate the use of IFRS Standards and the audit senior has noted that Willis Co follows local GAAP, whereby derivatives are disclosed in the notes to the financial statements but are not recognised as assets or liabilities in the statement of financial position. The disclosure note includes details of the maturity and exercise terms of the options and a directors' valuation stating that they have a total fair value of $6.1 million as at 31 March 20X8. The disclosure note states that all of the derivative contracts were entered into in the last three months of the reporting period and that they required no initial net investment.   **(6 marks)**

(d) **Knott Co**

Knott Co is a long-standing subsidiary in which the Group parent has a direct holding of 80% of the equity and voting rights. Audit work on revenue and receivables at Knott Co has identified sales of aluminium to its parent company in March 20X8 with a total sales value of $77 million which have been recorded in the subsidiary's financial statements. Audit procedures have identified, however, that the receipt of aluminium was not recorded by the parent company until 2 April 20X8. The group has made no adjustment for this transaction in the draft consolidated financial statements. Knott Co makes a 10% profit margin on all of its sales of aluminium.   **(6 marks)**

Required

Comment on the matters to be considered and explain the audit evidence you should expect to find during your review of the Group audit working papers in respect of each of the issues described above.

Note. The split of the mark allocation is shown against each of the issues above.

(Total = 25 marks)

Answers

DO NOT TURN THIS PAGE UNTIL YOU HAVE COMPLETED THE MOCK EXAM

A PLAN OF ATTACK

If this had been the real Advanced Audit and Assurance exam and you had been told to turn over and begin, what would have been going through your mind?

An important thing to say (while there is still time) is that it is vital to have a good breadth of knowledge of the syllabus because the question requirements for each question will relate to different areas of the AAA syllabus. However, don't panic. Below we provide guidance on how to approach the exam.

Approaching the answer

It is vital that you attempt all the questions in the exam to increase your chances of passing. The best way to do this is to make sure you stick to the time allocation for each question – both in total and for each of the question parts. The worst thing you can do is run over time in one question and then find that you don't have enough time for the remaining questions, leading you to miss out on some of the easier marks in those questions.

Section A consists of one long case-study style question set at the planning stage of the audit. This may contain detailed information such as extracts from financial statements and audit working papers. A range of requirements will be set for this question, but will only cover areas from syllabus areas A to D inclusive.

Question 1 is for 50 marks, all set at the planning stage in the context of a single scenario. As it is a very long question, it is important that you break it down into its component parts as this will make it easier to manage – and enable you to allocate your time to each of them. This question was dominated by a requirement on audit risks, and featured a large number of easy marks (for analytical procedures and materiality).

Section B contains two more compulsory questions, and may be set on any area of the AAA syllabus.

Question 2 offers 25 marks that were made up of an ethics discussion and a comprehensive question on prospective financial information.

Question 3, for 25 marks, was set at the completion stage of the audit and featured a discussion of ISA 701, a critique of an auditor's report, and then two review issues in relation to a Group.

Forget about it!

And don't worry if you found the exam difficult. More than likely other candidates will too. If this were the real thing you would need to forget the exam the minute you left the exam hall and think about the next one. Or, if it is the last one, celebrate!

BPP
LEARNING

Question 1

Marking scheme

Marks

(a) **Audit risk evaluation**

Up to 3 marks for each audit risk identified and explained. Marks may be awarded for other, relevant audit risks not included in the marking guide.

In addition, 1 mark for relevant ratios and ½ mark for relevant trends which form part of analytical review

(max 5 marks).

Materiality calculations should be awarded 1 mark each (max 4 marks).

- Operating margin and ROCE changes – risk understated expenses/overstated revenue

Marks

- Trends within operating expenses and related audit risks, eg misclassification of expenses
- Other operating income – risk of overstatement
- Risk of management bias due to listed status (max 2 marks)
- Current ratio and gearing and related audit risks, eg understated finance costs
- Effective tax rate and risk of tax expense being understated (max 2 marks)
- Consolidation of foreign subsidiaries
- Recognition and measurement of foreign exchange gains and losses
- Goodwill – audit risk regarding measurement, specifically lack of impairment review
- Goodwill on acquisition of Lynx Co (max 4 marks for detailed discussion)
- Intangible assets – audit risks in relation to unexplained movement in year, whether amounts should have been capitalised and amortisation period (max 5 marks)
- Increased detection risk regarding Lynx Co due to being audited by a component auditor

Maximum   24

(b) **Audit procedures on the goodwill recognised on acquisition of Lynx Co**

Up to 1 mark for each well described procedure:

- Obtain and review the legal documentation, in particular, confirm the targets to be used as the basis for payment of the contingent consideration
- Confirm that the Group has obtained an 80% shareholding and that this conveys control
- Agree the $80 million cash paid to the bank statement and cash book of the acquiring company
- Review the board minutes for relevant discussions including the minute of board approval
- Obtain management's calculation of contingent consideration, and evaluate assumptions used
- Discuss the 18% interest rate used in determining the discount factor and evaluate the justification given by management
- Confirm that the fair value of the non-controlling interest has been calculated based on an externally available share price at the date of acquisition by agreeing to stock market records
- Obtain a copy of the due diligence report issued by Sidewinder & Co, review for confirmation of acquired assets and liabilities and their fair values

BPP
LEARNING
MEDIA

- Evaluation of the methods used to determine the fair value of acquired assets, including the property, and liabilities to confirm compliance with IFRS 3 and IFRS 13 *Fair Value Measurement*

- Review the calculation of net assets acquired to confirm that Group accounting policies have been applied

Maximum   6

(c) **Evaluation of Vulture Associate's audit strategy**
Up to 2 marks for each issue evaluated:

- Controls – evidence needs to be obtained to confirm that controls have not changed

- Controls should be tested in a three-year cycle in order to place continued reliance on them

- Group audit team may decide to perform additional tests of control of Vulture Associates do not amend their strategy

- Evaluate status, competence and quality control approach of the internal audit department

- Objectivity should be evaluated where direct assistance is provided

- Consider the type of work – work on inventories and receivables is not appropriate due to subjective nature

- Internal auditors have worked on inventories and receivables so not objective

- Conclusion on audit quality (1 mark)

Maximum   10

(d) **Ethical issues relating to request to assist management in preparing an integrated report**
Up to 2 marks for each relevant point explained, and 1 mark for relevant safeguard or action:

- Explain the threats to objectivity created – self-review, familiarity and management involvement (1 mark each if fully explained)

- Conclusion as to whether service can be provided, following on from justification

- Suggest appropriate safeguards if engagement accepted, eg independent review (1 mark each)

- Explain that audit committee would need to pre-approve the engagement

- Bison & Co to consider competence and resource availability

- Discuss with audit committee (1 mark)

Maximum   6

Marks

Professional marks

Generally 1 mark for heading, 1 mark for introduction, 1 mark for use of headings within the briefing notes, 1 mark for clarity of comments made.

Maximum   <u>4</u>

Total   <u>50</u>

Briefing notes

To: **Maya Crag, Audit engagement partner**

From: **Audit manager**

Subject: **Eagle Group – Audit planning**

Introduction

These briefing notes are prepared to assist with planning the audit of the Eagle Group (the Group) for the financial year ending 31 December 20X8. The notes contain an evaluation of the audit risks which should be considered in planning the Group audit. The notes also recommend the principal audit procedures to be used in the audit of the goodwill which has arisen in respect of a newly acquired subsidiary. The notes then go on to evaluate an extract from the audit strategy which has been prepared by a component auditor. Finally, the Group finance director has requested our firm to provide a non-audit service in relation to the Group's integrated report, and the notes discuss the professional and ethical implications of this request.

(a)   **Evaluation of audit risk**

Selected analytical procedures and associated audit risk evaluation

	20X8	20X7
Operating margin	350/5,770 = 6.1%	270/5,990 = 4.5%
Return on capital employed	350/2,245 + 650 = 12.1%	270/2,093 + 620 = 10%
Current ratio	1,450/597 = 2.4	1,420/547 = 2.6
Debt/equity	550/2,245 = 24.5%	500/2,093 = 23.9%
Interest cover	350/28 = 12.5	270/30 = 9
Effective tax rate	64/322 = 19.9%	60/240 = 25%

Operating margin and operating expenses

The Group's operating margin has increased from 4.5% to 6.1% despite a fall in revenue of 3.7%. This is due to a reduction in operating expenses of 4.5% and increase in other operating income of 50%. Return on capital employed shows a similar positive trend, despite the fall in revenue. There is an audit risk that expenses are understated, with the reduction in expenses being proportionately more than the reduction in revenue.

Within operating expenses the trends for each component are different – cost of raw materials consumables and supplies has decreased by 3.1%, which appears reasonable given the decline in revenue of 3.7%. However, staff costs have increased slightly by 1.1% which seems inconsistent with the revenue trend and with the increased automation of operations which has led to 5,000 staff being made redundant, which presumably means lower payroll costs this year. Expenses could have been misclassified into staff costs in error.

Depreciation, amortisation and impairment has increased by 3.6%, which is not a significant change, but will need to be investigated to consider how each element of the category has changed in the year. The most noticeable trend within operating expenses is that the other operating expenses category has reduced very significantly. The amount recognised this

BPP
LEARNING

613

financial year is only 7.4% of the amount recognised the previous year; this appears totally inconsistent with the other trends noted. It could be that some costs, for example, accrued expenses, have not yet been accounted for, or that the 20X7 figure was unusually high.

Other operating income

There is also an audit risk that other operating income is overstated. According to the information in note 6, during the year a credit of $60 million has been recognised in profit for reversals of provisions, this is 50% greater than the amount recognised in the previous year. In addition, a credit of $30 million has been recognised for reversals of impairment losses. There is a risk that these figures have been manipulated in order to boost profits, as an earnings management technique, in reaction to the fall in revenue in the year.

The risk of management bias is high given the listed status of the Group, hence expectations from shareholders for a positive growth trend. The profit recognised on asset disposal and the increase in foreign currency gains could also be an indication of attempts to boost operating profit this year.

Current ratio and gearing

Looking at the other ratios, the current ratio and gearing ratio do not indicate audit risks; however, more detail is needed to fully conclude on the liquidity and solvency position of the Group, and whether there are any hidden trends which are obscured by the high level analysis which has been performed with the information provided.

The interest cover has increased, due to both an increase in operating profit and a reduction in finance charges. This seems contradictory to the increase in borrowings of $50 million; as a result of this an increase in finance charges would be expected. There is an audit risk that finance charges are understated.

Effective tax rate

The effective tax rate has fallen from 25% to 19.9%. An audit risk arises in that the tax expense and associated liability could be understated. This could indicate management bias as the financial statements suggest that accounting profit has increased, but the profit chargeable to tax used to determine the tax expense for the year appears to have decreased. There could be alternative explanations, for instance a fall in the rate of tax levied by the authorities, which will need to be investigated by the audit team.

Consolidation of foreign subsidiaries

Given that the Group has many foreign subsidiaries, including the recent investment in Lynx Co, audit risks relating to their consolidation are potentially significant. Lynx Co has net assets with a fair value of $300 million according to the goodwill calculation provided by management, representing 8.6% of the Group's total assets and 13.4% of Group net assets. This makes Lynx Co material to the Group and possibly a significant component of the Group. Audit risks relevant to Lynx Co's status as a foreign subsidiary also attach to the Group's other foreign subsidiaries.

According to IAS 21 *The Effects of Changes in Foreign Exchange Rates*, the assets and liabilities of Lynx Co and other foreign subsidiaries should be retranslated using the closing exchange rate. Its income and expenses should be retranslated at the exchange rates at the dates of the transactions. The risk is that incorrect exchange rates are used for the retranslations. This could result in over/understatement of the assets, liabilities, income and expenses which are consolidated, including goodwill. It would also mean that the exchange gains and losses arising on retranslation and to be included in Group other comprehensive income are incorrectly determined.

In addition, Lynx Co was acquired on 1 March 20X8 and its income and expenses should have been consolidated from that date. There is a risk that the full year's income and expenses have been consolidated, leading to a risk of understatement of Group profit given that

Lynx Co is forecast to be loss making this year, according to the audit strategy prepared by Vulture Associates.

Measurement and recognition of exchange gains and losses

The calculation of exchange gains and losses can be complex, and there is a risk that it is not calculated correctly, or that some elements are omitted, for example, the exchange gain or loss on goodwill may be missed out of the calculation.

IAS 21 states that exchange gains and losses arising as a result of the retranslation of the subsidiary's balances are recognised in other comprehensive income. The risk is incorrect classification, for example, the gain or loss could be recognised incorrectly as part of profit for the year, for example, included in the $28 million foreign currency gains which form part of other operating income, which would be incorrect. The amount recognised within other operating income has increased, as only $23 million foreign currency gains were recognised the previous year, indicating a potential risk of overstatement.

Goodwill

The total goodwill recognised in the Group statement of financial position is $1,100 million, making it highly material at 31.5% of total assets.

Analytical review shows that the goodwill figure has increased by $130 million during the year. The goodwill relating to the acquisition of Lynx Co is $100 million according to management's calculations. Therefore there appears to be an unexplained increase in value of goodwill of $30 million during the year and there is an audit risk that the goodwill figure is overstated, unless justified by additional acquisitions or possibly by changes in value on the retranslation of goodwill relating to foreign subsidiaries, though this latter point would seem unlikely given the large size of the unexplained increase in value.

According to IFRS 3 *Business Combinations*, goodwill should be subject to an impairment review on an annual basis. Management has asserted that while they will test goodwill for impairment prior to the financial year end, they do not think that any impairment will be recognised. This view is based on what could be optimistic assumptions about further growth in revenue, and it is likely that the assumptions used in management's impairment review are similarly overoptimistic. Therefore there is a risk that goodwill will be overstated and Group operating expenses understated if impairment losses have not been correctly determined and recognised.

Initial measurement of goodwill arising on acquisition of Lynx Co

In order for goodwill to be calculated, the assets and liabilities of Lynx Co must have been identified and measured at fair value at the date of acquisition. Risks of material misstatement arise because the various components of goodwill each have specific risks attached. The goodwill of $100 million is material to the Group, representing 2.9% of Group assets.

A specific risk arises in relation to the fair value of net assets acquired. Not all assets and liabilities may have been identified, for example, contingent liabilities and contingent assets may be omitted.

A further risk relates to measurement at fair value, which is subjective and based on assumptions which may not be valid. The fair value of Lynx Co's net assets according to the goodwill calculation is $300 million, having been subject to a fair value uplift of $12 million. This was provided by an independent firm of accountants, which provides some comfort on the validity of the figure.

There is also a risk that the cost of investment is not stated correctly, for example, that the contingent consideration has not been determined on an appropriate basis. First, the interest rate used to determine the discount factor is 18% – this seems high given that the Group's weighted average cost of capital is stated to be 10%. Second, the contingent consideration is only payable if Lynx Co reaches certain profit targets. Given that the company, according to

Vulture Associate's audit strategy, is projected to be loss making, it could be that the contingent consideration need not be recognised at all, or determined to be a lower figure than that currently recognised, based on a lower probability of it having to be paid. The results of the analytical review have indicated that the other side of the journal entry for the contingent consideration is not described as a component of the non-current liabilities and the accounting for this will need to be clarified as there is a risk that it has been recorded incorrectly, perhaps as a component of equity.

Intangible assets

In relation to expenditure on intangible assets during the year, which totals $60 million, there are several audit risks. First, there is a question over whether all of this amount should have been capitalised as an intangible asset. Capitalisation is only appropriate where an asset has been created, and specifically in relation to development costs, the criteria from IAS 38 *Intangible Assets* must all be met. There is a risk that if any criteria have not been met, for example, if there is no probable future economic benefit from research into the new technology, then the amount should be expensed. There is a risk that intangible assets are overstated and operating expenses understated.

There is also an unexplained trend, in that intangible assets has only increased by $30 million, yet expenditure on intangible assets, according to management information, is $60 million. More information is needed to reconcile the expenditure as stated by management to the movement in intangible assets recognised in the Group statement of financial position.

Second, there is a risk that the amortisation period is not appropriate. It seems that the same useful life of 15 years has been applied to all of the different categories of intangible assets; this is not likely to be specific enough, for example, the useful life of an accounting system will not be the same as for development of robots. Fifteen years also seems to be a long period – usually technology-related assets are written off over a relatively short period to take account of rapid developments in technology. In respect of amortisation periods being too long, there is a risk that intangible assets are overstated and operating expenses understated.

Detection risk in relation to Lynx Co

Lynx Co is the only subsidiary which is not audited by Bison & Co. This gives rise to a risk that the quality of the audit of Lynx Co may not be to the same standard as Bison & Co, as Vulture Associates may not be used to auditing companies which form part of a listed group and results in increased detection risk at the Group level. The risk is increased by the problems with the audit strategy prepared by Vulture Associates, which will be discussed in part (c) to these briefing notes, which indicate that the audit of Lynx Co has not been appropriately planned in accordance with ISA requirements. Since our firm has not worked with Vulture Associates previously, we are not familiar with their methods and we may have issues with the quality of their work; therefore the detection risk is high in relation to Lynx Co's balances which will form part of the consolidated financial statements.

(b) **Principal audit procedures on the goodwill arising on the acquisition of Lynx Co**

- Obtain the legal documentation pertaining to the acquisition, and review to confirm that the figures included in the goodwill calculation relating to consideration paid and payable are accurate and complete. In particular, confirm the targets to be used as the basis for payment of the contingent consideration in four years' time.

- Also confirm from the purchase documentation that the Group has obtained an 80% shareholding and that this conveys control, ie the shares carry voting rights and there is no restriction on the Group exercising their control over Lynx Co.

- Agree the $80 million cash paid to the bank statement and cash book of the acquiring company (presumably the parent company of the Group).

- Review the board minutes for discussions relating to the acquisition, and for the relevant minute of board approval.

- For the contingent consideration, obtain management's calculation of the present value of $271 million, and evaluate assumptions used in the calculation, in particular to consider the probability of payment by obtaining revenue and profit forecasts for Lynx Co for the next four years.

- Discuss with management the reason for using an 18% interest rate in the calculation, asking them to justify the use of this interest rate when the Group's weighted average cost of capital is stated at 10%.

- Evaluate management's rationale for using the 18% interest rate, concluding as to whether it is appropriate.

- Confirm that the fair value of the non-controlling interest has been calculated based on an externally available share price at the date of acquisition. Agree the share price used in management's calculation to stock market records showing the share price of Lynx Co at the date of acquisition.

- Obtain a copy of the due diligence report issued by Sidewinder & Co, review for confirmation of acquired assets and liabilities and their fair values.

- Evaluate the methods used to determine the fair value of acquired assets, including the property, and liabilities to confirm compliance with IFRS 3 and IFRS 13 *Fair Value Measurement*.

- Review the calculation of net assets acquired to confirm that Group accounting policies have been applied.

(c) **Evaluation of the extract of the audit strategy prepared by Vulture Associates in respect of their audit of Lynx Co**

The extract from the audit strategy covers two areas – reliance on internal controls, and the use of internal audit for external audit work. In each area it appears that ISA requirements have not been followed, meaning that the quality of the audit planned by Vulture Associates is in doubt.

Controls effectiveness

In relation to reliance on internal controls, ISA 330 *The Auditor's Responses to Assessed Risks* contains requirements in relation to relying on work performed during previous audits on internal controls. ISA 330 states that if the auditor plans to use audit evidence from a previous audit about the operating effectiveness of specific controls, the auditor shall establish the continuing relevance of that evidence by obtaining audit evidence about whether significant changes in those controls have occurred subsequent to the previous audit. The auditor shall obtain this evidence by performing inquiry combined with observation or inspection, to confirm the understanding of those specific controls, and if there have been changes which affect the continuing relevance of the audit evidence from the previous audit, the auditor shall test the controls in the current audit. If there have not been such changes, the auditor shall test the controls at least once in every third audit, and shall test some controls each audit to avoid the possibility of testing all the controls on which the auditor intends to rely on a single audit period with no testing of controls in the subsequent two audit periods.

Therefore, in order to comply with ISA 330, Vulture Associates needs to do more than simply accept management's assertion that there have been no changes to controls. There needs to be some observation or inspection of controls, to confirm that there have been no changes, and this work and an appropriate conclusion need to be documented in the audit working papers.

In addition, there should be some testing of internal controls each year, so Vulture Associates should plan to perform some tests of controls each year, so that over a three-year cycle, all controls are tested to confirm that controls are still operating effectively and therefore can continue to be relied upon.

The Group audit team should discuss this issue with Vulture Associates to ensure that adequate controls testing is performed. If, for some reason, Vulture Associates does not amend its audit strategy, then the Group audit team may decide to perform additional testing, given that Lynx Co is material to the Group.

Internal audit

According to ISA 610 *Using the Work of Internal Auditors*, it is acceptable, in some circumstances, for the external audit firm to use the internal audit function of an audited entity to provide direct assistance to the external audit team. However, in some jurisdictions, due to local regulations, the external auditor is prohibited from using internal auditors to provide direct assistance, and therefore the Group auditor team will need to consider whether the prohibition also extends to component auditors and, if so, it would not be appropriate for Vulture Associates to use the internal audit function. Assuming that there is no local restriction, before deciding whether to use the internal audit function, the external auditor must evaluate a number of factors, including:

- The extent to which the internal audit function's organisational status and relevant policies and procedures support the objectivity of the internal auditors.

- The level of competence of the internal audit function.

- Whether the internal audit function applies a systematic and disciplined approach, including quality control.

Vulture Associates must therefore perform this evaluation before making any decision about whether they should instruct the internal audit team to perform audit procedures. For example, if they find that the internal audit function does not have a good quality control procedure, it would not be appropriate to use them in external audit work.

Using the internal audit function to perform audit procedures is direct assistance to the external auditor. ISA 610 requires that where direct assistance is being provided, the external auditor shall evaluate the existence and significance of threats to objectivity and the level of competence of the internal auditors who will be providing such assistance. The external auditor shall not use an internal auditor to provide direct assistance if there are significant threats to the objectivity of the internal auditor or the internal auditor lacks sufficient competence to perform the proposed work. Vulture Associates therefore needs to document and conclude upon their assessment of the internal auditors' objectivity and competence.

There is also an issue with regard to the type of work they are given to perform. Vulture Associates is planning to ask the internal auditors to perform specific audit procedures in relation to trade receivables but this is not likely to be appropriate. ISA 610 states that the external auditor shall make all significant judgements in the audit engagement. Performing a trade receivables circularisation and reviewing the allowance against trade receivables both involve judgements, in relation to sample selection and also in relation to measurement of the receivables. The trade receivables is also likely to be a material balance in the financial statements. Therefore it would not be appropriate for the internal audit team to complete the audit, though they could be used for performing routine procedures not involving the use of judgement.

A further issue is that ISA 610 specifically states that the external auditor shall not use internal auditors to provide direct assistance to perform procedures which relate to work with which the internal auditors have been involved and which has already been, or will be, reported to management or those charged with governance. From the audit strategy, it appears that the internal audit function has worked on trade receivables during the year, so it would not be

appropriate for the internal auditors to provide direct assistance to the external audit firm in relation to this area due to the self-review threat which would be created.

It may be possible for the internal auditors to provide direct assistance on non-judgemental areas of the financial statements if they have not performed internal audit work relating to those areas during the year.

In conclusion, from the evaluation of this extract from the audit strategy, it seems that Vulture Associates is planning to carry out the audit of Lynx Co in a manner which does not comply with ISA requirements. This is a concern, given the materiality of the subsidiary to the Group, and our firm should liaise with Vulture Associates as soon as possible to discuss their audit planning.

(d) **Ethical and professional implications of the request to provide a non-audit service on the Group's integrated report**

There are several issues to consider with regard to providing this service.

A significant issue relates to auditor objectivity. The IESBA *Code of Ethics for Professional Accountants* (the *Code*) provides guidance on situations where the auditor is asked by the client to provide non-assurance services. Bison & Co needs to evaluate the significance of the threat and consider whether any safeguards can reduce the threat to an acceptable level.

While the integrated report is not part of the audited financial statements, the report will contain financial key performance indicators (KPIs), and the Group has asked for input specifically relating to the reconciliations between these KPIs and financial information contained in the financial statements. There is therefore a potential self-review threat to objectivity in that the audit firm has been asked to provide assurance on these KPIs which are related to figures which have been subject to external audit by the firm. The team performing the work will be reluctant to raise queries or highlight errors which have been made during the external audit when assessing the reconciliations of KPIs to audited financial information.

It could also be perceived that Bison & Co is taking on management responsibility by helping to determine content to be included in the integrated report, which is a threat to objectivity. The *Code* states that the audit firm shall not assume management responsibility for an audit client and that the threats created are so significant that safeguards cannot reduce them to an acceptable level. While the Code does not specifically state that helping the client to determine the content of its integrated report is taking on management responsibility, certainly there could be that perception as the auditor will be involved in setting measurements which the company will benchmark itself against. Additionally, working with management on the integrated report could create a familiarity threat to objectivity whereby close working relationships are formed, and the auditor becomes closely aligned with the views of management and is unable to approach the work with an appropriate degree of professional scepticism.

There is a potential problem in terms of compliance with ISA *720 The Auditor's Responsibilities Relating to Other Information*, should Bison & Co accept the engagement. ISA 720 requires that auditors read other information in order to identify any material inconsistencies between the financial statements and information in the other information. ISA 720 applies only to other information in the annual report, and it is not stated whether the Group's integrated report will be included in the annual report, or as a standalone document.

Based on the above, it would seem unlikely that Bison & Co can provide this service to the Group, due to the threats to objectivity created. However, should the firm decide to take on the engagement, safeguards should be used to minimise the threats. For example, a partner who is independent should be involved in reviewing the audit work performed.

Aside from ethical issues, Bison & Co must also consider whether they have the competence to perform the work. Advising on the production of an integrated report is quite a specialist area, and it could be that the audit firm does not have the appropriate levels of expertise and experience to provide a quality service to the Group. The fact that the Group wants to highlight its technological achievements, and presumably will select a range of non-financial KPIs and technological issues to discuss in the integrated report, makes the issue of competence more significant, as the audit firm may not have the necessary technical knowledge to provide advice in this area. Aside from competence, the firm should also consider whether it has resources in terms of staff availability to complete the work to the desired deadline and to perform appropriate reviews of the work which has been completed.

Finally, given that the Group is a listed entity, it should comply with relevant corporate governance requirements. This means that the audit firm may be prohibited from providing services in addition to providing the external audit to the Group. The audit committee should apply the Group's policy on the engagement of the external auditor to supply non-audit services, the objective of which should be to ensure that the provision of such services does not impair the external auditor's independence or objectivity. The Group's audit committee will need to pre-approve the provision of the service, and in making this decision they should consider a number of matters, for instance, the audit committee should consider whether the skills and experience of the audit firm make it the most suitable supplier of the non-audit service, whether there are safeguards in place to eliminate or reduce to an acceptable level any threat to objectivity and the level of fees to be incurred relative to the audit fee.

Conclusion

These briefing notes indicate that there are a large number of audit risks to be considered in planning the audit, and that management needs to supply the audit team with a range of additional information for more thorough audit planning to be carried out. The audit of goodwill, and in particular the goodwill arising on the acquisition of Lynx Co, is an area of significant audit risk, and the notes recommend the principal audit procedures which should be conducted. An evaluation of the audit strategy prepared by Vulture Associates indicates that their audit of Lynx Co might not be a high quality audit. Finally, our firm needs to discuss the request to assist in preparing the Group's integrated report with the Group audit committee, and it seems

Question 2

Marking scheme

Marks

2   (a)   (i)   **Ethical and other matters to be considered before accepting Setter Co as a client of the firm**

Up to 1½ marks for each ethical or other professional issue explained:

–   General requirements of ISQC 1

–   Competence to perform the work – this should not be a problem

–   Intimidation and self-interest threat from Vizsla Co

–   Low fees potentially impair quality of work

–   Pressure on fees from Setter Co indicates lack of integrity

–   Self-review and management threat from performing tax planning for the company

–   Safeguards should be used to reduce threats to an acceptable level, if this is not possible the tax planning should not be performed

–   Providing personal tax advice not ethically wrong but may not want to accept work due to integrity issues

–   Breach of employment law and taking money from pension plan indicates lack of integrity/criminal activity/poor reputation

(ii)   **Customer due diligence – reasons and recommended information**

Up to 1½ marks for each point explained/recommended:

–   Part of anti-money laundering regulations (up to 3 marks for detailed explanation of regulations)

–   Identity of Gordon Potts – passport, recent utility bills or bank statements

–   Identity of other shareholders including the other family members and other 10% shareholders

–   Setter Co – the company certificate of incorporation, to confirm legal status, date and place of incorporation

–   A Companies House search (or equivalent) on Setter Co – confirm the existence of the company, the shareholders and directors, beneficial owners

BPP
LEARNING

–   Other companies controlled by Gordon Potts –
    confirm their existence and the nature of the
    relationship with Setter Co

–   Review of the latest financial statements of Setter
    Co, and the other companies in which Gordon
    Potts has an interest should be reviewed

–   Identify the source of funding, when funding is
    repayable and the existence of any security
    provided by the company or by personal
    guarantee of owners

–   Facts surrounding the breach of employment law
    as reported by the newspaper

                                              Maximum   16

(b)   **Examination procedures**

Up to 1 mark for each procedure explained. In addition, ½
mark for relevant calculations, e.g. trend analysis, up to a
maximum of 2 marks:

General procedures:

–   Identity of the preparer of the operating profit forecast,
    and assess their competence

–   Understanding the procedures/controls which have been
    followed in the preparation of the forecast

–   Confirm the consistency of accounting policies applied

–   Confirm that the assumptions underpinning the forecast
    are in line with knowledge of the business obtained from
    performing the company's audit

–   Re-cast the forecast to ensure it is arithmetically correct

Specific procedures:

–   Ask management to prepare a more detailed profit
    forecast in an appropriate format and to provide forecast
    statement of financial position and statement of cash
    flows

–   Recalculate the gross profit margins and compare with
    gross profit margins from audited financial statements

–   Obtain a break down showing the components of cost of
    sales and other expenses; perform analytical review and
    discuss results

–   Assess whether there are any missing categories of
    expenditure

–   For revenue, consider whether the forecast appears
    overly optimistic – allow credit for calculation of
    appropriate trends from the forecast

Marks

    –   Compare revenue forecast with revenue from prior years' audited financial statements. Investigate any unusual trends through discussion with management

    –   Review any marketing plans and discuss with an appropriate senior member of staff, for example, the sales director

    –   Review design costs, discuss with management and assess if such an increase in revenue can be achieved with such a small increase in design costs

    –   Confirm costs to appropriate supporting documentation, e.g. staff costs to human resources projected costs, marketing costs to advertising budgets

    –   Obtain and review the cash flow forecast prepared for the same period as the operating profit forecast

    –   Discuss with management the rationale for using 30% of revenue as a basis for determining the amount of other expenses

	Maximum	9
Total		25

(a)   (i)   Ethical and other matters to be considered before accepting Setter Co as a client of the firm

Requirements and guidance relevant to accepting and continuing client relationships is contained in ISQC 1 *Quality Control for Firms that Perform Audits and Reviews of Financial Statements and Other Assurance and Related Services Engagements*. The fundamental requirements are that a firm must consider:

- Its competence to perform the engagement and whether the firm has the capabilities, including time and resources to do so,

- Whether the relevant ethical requirements can be complied with; and

- The integrity of the client, and whether there is information which would lead it to conclude that the client lacks integrity.

Competence and resources

Looking at each consideration in turn, there seems no reason why Pointer & Co would not have the competence to carry out the assignment, which is a limited assurance review of historical financial statements. Being a firm of Chartered Certified Accountants, and performing assurance services such as the audit of Vizsla Co, means that the firm has the relevant knowledge and experience to perform a high quality limited assurance review.

BPP
LEARNING

However, the pressure to perform the audit for a low fee could impact on Pointer & Co's ability to perform a high quality limited assurance review if insufficient resources are made available, given the potential restriction on the fee which can be charged to provide the service. ISQC 1 also mentions that where the client is aggressively concerned with maintaining the firm's fees as low as possible, this can indicate a lack of integrity of the client.

Ethical issues

In terms of ethics there are several matters to consider. First, it appears that Vizsla Co is putting pressure on Pointer & Co to accept the engagement. Vizsla Co is a relatively significant client of Pointer & Co, providing 10% of the firm's annual practice income, and there is an intimidation threat in that Vizsla Co has threatened to move to another audit provider if Pointer & Co does not accept Setter Co as a client and perform the work for a low fee. This could also be perceived as a self-interest threat in that Pointer & Co has a financial interest in maintaining a good relationship with Vizsla Co.

A further ethical issue arises from the suggestion that Pointer & Co should provide tax planning advice to Setter Co and prepare its tax submissions. This would give rise to a self-review threat because Pointer & Co would have some input to the tax figures which form part of the financial statements which would then be subject to the limited assurance review. Providing the tax planning advice could also be seen as acting on behalf of management, further impairing the objectivity of the limited assurance provided on the financial statements.

Pointer & Co should consider whether safeguards can be used to reduce any ethical threats to an acceptable level, for example, through the use of separate teams to provide the limited assurance review and the tax services and by having an independent second partner to review the work performed. If safeguards do not reduce the threats to an acceptable level, then the tax service should not be carried out in addition to the limited assurance review.

Client integrity

Preparing the personal tax computations of Gordon Potts is less of an ethical issue in terms of objectivity as his personal tax is a separate issue and not reflected in the company's financial statements, but there may be other issues with providing this advice, linked to integrity, which will be discussed next.

The integrity of Gordon Potts will need to be carefully evaluated. There is nothing wrong with him having business interests in several companies, though information about each of these will need to be obtained. The key issues with integrity relate to the breach of employment law and his taking money from a company pension plan to set up a business which is managed by his son. The breach of employment law indicates that Gordon Potts has a questionable reputation and possibly that he has been involved in criminal activity, depending on what laws have been breached, and the seriousness of the non-compliance. The information comes from a newspaper article, so it may not be very credible and may not even be true, and more information will need to be sought on this issue.

Taking money from the company pension plan is likely to be a breach of the relevant regulations, and it would seem that this was done for the benefit of his son. The fact that this business is located in a foreign country makes the business arrangements complicated, and while it could be completely innocent, it could also mean that there is something more sinister behind the connections between the companies, for example, it could be an arrangement to facilitate money laundering.

Pointer & Co must obtain sufficient information to carefully evaluate the appropriateness of accepting Setter Co as a client, and they must document the acceptance decision in accordance with ISQC 1.

(ii) **The importance of obtaining customer due diligence and the information which should be obtained**

Customer due diligence (CDD), also called know your client procedures, is needed as part of anti-money laundering regulations, which all audit firms should have in place when accepting new clients. It refers to the firm obtaining information to be able to identify who the prospective client is and verify identity by reference to independent and reliable source material. This is a crucial part of risk assessment when taking on a new client and allows the firm to understand not only the identity of the prospective client, but also the nature of the business and its source of funds.

Specifically, the firm should address the following as part of customer due diligence:

*   Identify the customer and verify their identity using documents, data or information obtained from a reliable and independent source.

*   Confirm the identities of all shareholders, including the specific family members who collectively own 90% of the company's share capital, and the other shareholder(s) who own the remaining 10%.

*   Identify any beneficial owner who is not the client. This is the individual (or individuals) behind the client who ultimately own or control the client or on whose behalf a transaction or activity is being conducted.

*   Where a business relationship is established, understand the purpose and intended nature of the relationship, for example, details of the customer's business or the source of the funds.

Businesses must also conduct ongoing monitoring to identify large, unusual or suspicious transactions as part of CDD. All of the documents obtained for the purpose of carrying out CDD checks must be retained for a minimum of five years from the end of the business relationship.

In this scenario, the information which should be obtained includes:

*   To confirm the identity of Gordon Potts, photographic evidence, for example his passport, should be seen and a copy taken, along with other means of identification showing his address, for example, recent utility bills or bank statements.

*   In relation to Setter Co, the company certificate of incorporation should be seen, to confirm its legal status and the date and place of incorporation.

*   A Companies House search (or equivalent) on Setter Co should take place, this will confirm the existence of the company, the shareholders and directors and will provide some financial information. This will confirm that Gordon Potts is the 'beneficial owner' of the entity – ie that he is the person who owns or controls, directly or indirectly, more than 25% of the shares or voting rights or who otherwise exercises control over the directors.

*   The identity of the other companies controlled by Gordon Potts should also be found, and searches on them conducted, to confirm their existence and the nature of the relationship with Setter Co.

- The latest financial statements of Setter Co, and the other companies in which Gordon Potts has an interest should be reviewed. This will help Pointer & Co to understand the businesses and their relationship with each other, identify the sources of income and whether there are significant transactions between the companies.

- Identify the source of funding for the company, whether there are bank loans or other providers of finance, and the nature of the finance provided in terms of when it is repayable, whether any company assets are provided as collateral for the debt, and whether Gordon Potts or other shareholders have made personal guarantees in respect of any sources of company finance.

- While not strictly part of confirming the identity of Gordon or his companies, Pointer & Co would clearly need to obtain further information about the breach of employment law, and confirm the facts surrounding the situation. Currently the only information available is from a newspaper article and this may not be a credible source.

(b) **Examination procedures on the operating profit forecast of Vizsla Co**

General procedures:

- Enquire as to the identity of the preparer of the operating profit forecast, and assess their competence, especially given that interest costs have been included as part of operating profit which is incorrect.

- Obtain an understanding as to the procedures and controls which have been followed in the preparation of the forecast, for example, has the forecast been approved by a senior member of the company's accounting team.

- Confirm that the accounting policies applied in Vizsla Co's financial statements have been consistently applied in the preparation of the operating profit forecast, for example, that design costs are expensed rather than capitalised as a development cost.

- Confirm that the assumptions underpinning the forecast are in line with knowledge of the business obtained from performing the company's audit, for example, the seasonality of the sales can be confirmed by looking at the audit evidence obtained in the audit of revenue.

- Re-cast the forecast to ensure it is arithmetically correct.

Specific procedures:

- Enquire whether a more detailed profit forecast is available, or ask management to prepare one, for example, detailing out cost of sales and other expenses. In addition, request a forecast statement of financial position and statement of cash flows.

> **Tutorial note:** There could be matters which make the profit forecast unachievable revealed through assessment of the statement of financial position and statement of cash flows, eg the timing of the working capital cycle may make achieving the profit forecast unachievable if funds are not available at certain points of time especially given the seasonal nature of the business.

- Request that management prepares a profit forecast in the same format as audited financial statements and in accordance with IFRS Standards, ie the interest cost should be shown below the operating profit line.

- Having obtained the cost of sales figure for each six-month period, recalculate the gross profit figures given in the forecast. Compare this to gross profit margins in the prior year audited financial statements and investigate any anomalies.

- Having obtained a break down showing the components of cost of sales and other expenses, for each significant category of expense, perform analytical review to confirm that the forecast costs appear to be in line with expectations, and discuss any unusually high or low forecast costs with management.

- Based on the above, assess whether there are any missing categories of expenditure which have not been included in the forecast, eg there is no depreciation included in the forecast.

- For revenue, which is forecast to increase by a significant amount (eg 11.8% increase comparing the six months ending 31 March 20X9 and 31 March 20Y0), consider whether the forecast appears overly optimistic. For instance, there is not a corresponding increase in marketing costs to support the forecast increase in revenue.

- Compare revenue in the year forecast to 30 September 20X9 with revenue from prior years' audited financial statements. Investigate any unusual trends through discussion with management.

- Review any marketing plans and discuss with an appropriate senior member of staff, for example, the sales director, to establish the rationale for forecasting a significant increase in revenue, for example, there may be plans to introduce new product lines. Consider this in light of the fact that design costs and marketing are not forecast to increase by a significant amount.

- Review the design costs as they appear to be fairly static with just a small increase to achieve a much bigger % increase in revenue. Discuss with management and assess if such an increase in revenue can be achieved with such a small increase in design costs.

- Confirm costs to appropriate supporting documentation, eg staff costs to human resources projected costs, marketing costs to advertising budgets.

- Assess whether the overdraft is likely to be repaid in September 20X9, for example, by obtaining and reviewing the cash flow forecast prepared for the same period as the operating profit forecast.

- Discuss with management the rationale for using 30% of revenue as a basis for determining the amount of other expenses. In addition, compare this to the results of audit procedures performed on expenses to gauge whether 30% appears to be a reasonable basis.

Question 3

Workbook references. Chapters 2, 3 and 13.

Top tips. Part (a) was a discussion requirement on ISA 701; this type of requirement appears to be increasingly common in the AAA exam, so this should have been good practice for you! The discussion itself was a fairly straightforward matter of the benefits and difficulties, and therefore should not have been too tough.

Part (b) required you to criticise a draft auditor's report, which should have been a straightforward requirement for you.

Parts (c) and (d) shifted the focus to another audit client, this time at the review stage. Part (d) tested intra-group transactions, which is an area that the examining team feels has been answered poorly by candidates in recent sittings. This is therefore an examinable area, so if you struggled here then you may need to brush up your knowledge.

Easy marks. The marks for pointing out the inappropriate use of an Emphasis of Matter paragraph, in the auditor's report in (b), were not difficult to get.

BPP
LEARNING

(a)   In general up to 1 mark for each well explained point:

Benefits:

- Response to users' requests about significant judgements

- Possible increase in confidence in audit process and perception of audit quality

- Improved understanding of financial statements and audit

- Increased focus on management judgement

- Explanation of what expectation gap is

- Role of KAMs in educating public re audit processes

Difficulties:

- Auditor judgement may reduce consistency and comparability of reporting

- Potential increase in volume of reports may obscure most significant matters

- Information provided may lack clarity

- Danger of standardised 'boilerplate' disclosures

Maximum   6

(b)   In general up to 1 mark for each well explained point:

KAM section

- KAM section should include introductory paragraph explaining what KAMs are

- Auditor not forming separate opinion on KAM

Customer liquidation

- Material to profit and assets (with calculation)

- Details of material misstatement should not be included in KAM section at all but should be given in basis for qualified opinion paragraph and should be clearly cross referenced to opinion paragraph

- Wording refers to reducing profit before tax when it should refer to increasing the loss before tax

Opinion paragraph

- Incorrectly positioned, should now be at start of auditor's report and should be clearly cross referenced to basis of opinion paragraph below which details the material misstatement

- Incorrect title, it should be headed simply 'Qualified Opinion'

- Except for qualification appropriate on grounds of material misstatement

Going concern

- Following ISA 570 (revised), use of an EoM paragraph no longer appropriate
- Auditor's report should now include section headed 'Material Uncertainty Related to Going Concern'
- Section should be immediately after basis for opinion but before KAM section
- Should cross reference clearly to disclosure note where directors have given details of uncertainty
- If not adequately disclosed by directors, opinion should be qualified 'except for' lack of disclosure

Maximum   7

(c) **Willis Co**

Matters

- Materiality
- Group accounting policies should be consistent
- Treatment is acceptable in individual entity financial statements but not for Group accounts
- IFRS 9 requires recognition of derivatives on SOFP at fair value with gains and losses in profit or loss for period
- Fair value of derivatives is material to group profit (with supporting calculation)
- Directors may not have expertise required for valuation of the options
- Need for external independent evidence of fair value at reporting date

Evidence

- Fair value based on market prices or if not available, independent expert valuation
- Audit documentation of review of derivative contracts and confirmation of terms and maturity dates
- Notes of discussion with management in relation to the basis of their valuation and the accounting treatment
- Copy of the adjusting journal required to reflect the correct treatment in the financial statements

Generally up to 1½ marks for each matter and up to 1 mark for each evidence point explained.

6

(d)   **Knott Co**

Matters

- Materiality

- Consolidated accounts are prepared from group perspective, inter-company transactions and balances must be eliminated on consolidation

- Details of the transactions need to be verified for individual entity financial statements

- Sales value of $77 million is material to group revenue and assets

- Unrealised profit of $7.7 million is material to group profit before tax

- Group receivables, revenue and profit therefore materially overstate

- Goods in transit: group inventory will be understated by $69.3 million (material to group assets)

- Group retained earnings will be overstated by $6.16 million and NCI by $1.54 million

Evidence

- Transaction agreed to underlying documents – sales invoices, goods despatch notes at Knott Co and goods received notes, purchase invoices at its parent company

- Cost of inventory confirmed to production records

- Confirmation of goods received note at parent dated 2 May 2018 confirming details of inventory in transit

- Workings for the unrealised profit in stock calculation

- Sales invoice traced to sales ledger and details of sales

Maximum	6

Total 25

(a)   Key audit matters ('KAM') are the matters which, in the auditor's judgement, were of most significance in the audit of the financial statements. They were introduced by ISA 701 *Communicating Key Audit Matters in the Independent Auditor's Report*, to enhance the auditor's report issued in respect of listed entities by providing more relevant information to the users of those reports.

Benefits

The principal reason for the disclosure of KAM in the auditor's report was to provide increased transparency in response to requests from users of the financial statements for more information in relation to significant judgements made by both management and the auditor. This should lead to increased focus on the uncertainties created by judgement in the reporting process and help to improve users' understanding of the financial statements. This in turn will serve to increase confidence in the audit process and the perception of audit quality.

BPP
LEARNING

The audit expectation gap is the difference between the actual role of the external auditor and the role which the public believes the auditor performs. In this context, the inclusion of KAM within the auditor's report represents an important step in the process of informing and educating the public about the auditor's role in evaluating areas of high risk, judgements and significant events or transactions which occurred during the period. Furthermore, auditors are expected to discuss how they addressed KAM during the course of the audit and the provision of detail in relation to the procedures performed will also go some way to provide greater transparency on how the audit is performed.

Difficulties

The determination of which audit matters to report as 'key' is subjective and requires auditor judgement. As a result, this may reduce the consistency and comparability of auditor reporting. In order to assist with this, ISA 701 provides a decision making framework to help auditors determine which matters are KAM. This should help reduce ambiguity and promote consistency across audits.

The inclusion of KAM in the auditor's report may lead to a significant increase in the volume of detail contained in the report thereby obscuring which of the matters are of the greatest significance. This increase in volume may deter users from reading the auditor's report in full and therefore undermine its role in closing the audit expectation gap. There are also concerns that the lack of specific guidance may lead to standardised 'boilerplate' disclosures which add little value to the auditor's report.

(b)   There are a number of issues to consider in critically appraising the auditor's report extract which has been drafted by the audit senior. These include the following:

Key audit matters (KAM)

The section should include an introductory paragraph explaining the concept of KAM in order for users of the auditor's report to understand its importance and significance. The introduction should also clearly state that the auditor is not forming a separate opinion on the items identified as KAM.

Customer liquidation

The amount owed by the customer of $287,253 is material to the loss before tax at 13.1% and to assets at 2%. The 'except for' qualification on the grounds of material misstatement is therefore appropriate. However, the details of the material misstatement should not be included in the KAM section at all but should be given in the basis for qualified opinion paragraph. This should also be clearly cross referenced within the opinion paragraph itself. Furthermore, the wording of the report currently references reducing the profit before tax when it should refer to increasing the loss before tax.

Opinion paragraph

This is incorrectly positioned and incorrectly titled. It should be at the start of the auditor's report and should simply be titled 'Qualified Opinion'. The opinion paragraph should be clearly cross referenced to the 'Basis for Qualified Opinion' paragraph which should be placed immediately below the opinion paragraph and should clearly describe the issue which has given rise to a qualified opinion. As above, the 'except for' qualification on the grounds of materiality is appropriate.

Going concern – Emphasis of Matter

Following ISA 570 *Going Concern*, the use of an Emphasis of Matter paragraph to refer to uncertainties in relation to going concern disclosures in the financial statements is not appropriate. The auditor's report should now include a specific section headed 'Material Uncertainty Related to Going Concern' immediately after the basis for opinion paragraph and before the KAM section. The material uncertainty related to going concern should be cross referenced clearly to the disclosure note where the directors have given details of the uncertainty. If the matter has not been adequately disclosed by the directors in the financial statements, the auditor should give full details of the uncertainties in relation to going concern and the audit opinion should be qualified 'except for' the material misstatement in relation to this lack of disclosure.

(c) **Willis Co**

Matters

The fair value of the derivatives of $6.1 million is material to consolidated profit before tax at 11.1% but in isolation, it is immaterial to consolidated assets at 0.4%.

IFRS 9 *Financial Instruments* requires the recognition of derivatives on the statement of financial position at fair value with the associated gains and losses being recognised in profit or loss for the period. The fair value of $6.1 million should therefore be included in current assets on the Group's consolidated statement of financial position and given that the options were entered into in the last three months of the period at no initial net investment, a fair value gain of $6.1 million should also be recorded in the Group's consolidated statement of profit or loss for the year. The treatment of the derivatives under local GAAP is acceptable in Willis Co's individual entity financial statements. For group purposes, however, accounting policies must be consistent and the profit before tax in the draft consolidated financial statements is materially understated.

The auditor must also exercise professional scepticism with regard to whether the directors have the required expertise to value the derivatives and should consider the need for independent, external evidence of the fair value of the options at the reporting date.

Evidence

- Details of the fair value of the options based on prices derived from an active market or if this is not available, an independent expert valuation.

- Audit documentation of the review of derivative contracts and confirmation of the terms and maturity dates.

- Notes of a discussion with management in relation

(d) **Knott Co**

Matters

Consolidated financial statements are prepared from the group perspective and intra-group transactions and balances must be eliminated on consolidation. The sales value of $77 million is material at 1% of consolidated revenue and 4.9% of consolidated assets. The unrealised profit of $7.7 million ($77m × 10%) is also material to consolidated profit before tax for the year at 14% ($7.7m/$55m). Group revenue, receivables and profit before tax are therefore materially overstated. The transactions should be verified in the accounting records of the individual entities to confirm that Knott Co has included the sale in its financial statements and that the parent company has not included the purchase in its financial statements. However, given that the goods are still in transit at the reporting date, group inventory will be understated by $69.3 million ($77m × 90%) which is also material to group assets at 4.4%. Consolidated retained earnings will be overstated by $6.16 million ($7.7 million × 80%) and non-controlling interests will be overstated by $1.54 million ($7.7 million × 20%). The accounting for the transaction within the individual entity financial statements will also be misstated.

The failure to identify and adjust for the intra-group trading transaction indicates a deficiency in internal control within the group and therefore increased control risk for the audit of the consolidated financial statements.

Tutorial note: Credit was also given to candidates who discussed the impact of the inter-company transactions on the financial statements of the individual entities.

Evidence

- Agreement of the transaction details to underlying documents such as sales invoices, goods despatch notes at Knott Co and goods received notes, purchase invoices at its parent company.

- The cost of the inventory in transit should have been confirmed to production records at Knott Co to confirm the 10% profit margin.

- A copy of the goods received note dated 2 April 20X8 raised by the parent company confirming details of the inventory in transit and the transaction being recorded in inventory and the purchase ledger after the year end.

- A copy of the sales invoice traced to Knott Co's sales ledger agreeing details of the sales value.

- The adjustments required to eliminate the transaction should be noted on a schedule of uncorrected misstatements for discussion with the client.

ACCA Strategic Professional

AAA

Advanced Audit and Assurance (International)

Mock Examination 4

December 2018 exam

Question Paper
Time allowed   3 hours 15 minutes
ALL THREE questions are compulsory and MUST be attempted

DO NOT OPEN THIS PAPER UNTIL YOU ARE READY TO START UNDER EXAMINATION CONDITIONS

BPP LEARNING

BPP
LEARNING

ALL THREE questions are compulsory and MUST be attempted

Question 1

You are a manager in the audit department of Huntsman & Co, a firm of Chartered Certified Accountants, responsible for the audit of several companies and for evaluating the acceptance decisions in respect of potential new audit clients.

One of your audit clients is Redback Sports Co, which operates a chain of sport and leisure centres across the country. The company has a financial year ending 28 February 20X9, and you are about to start planning the audit. Stella Cross, the audit engagement partner, met with the company's finance director last week to discuss business developments in the year and recent financial performance.

You are provided with the following exhibits:

1   An email you have received from Stella Cross, in respect of both Redback Sports Co and Emu Gyms Co

2   Notes of a meeting which Stella held recently with the finance director of Redback Sports Co

3   Extracts from the latest management accounts of Redback Sports Co

4   Notes of a telephone conversation which Stella had yesterday with Mick Emu, managing director of Emu Gyms Co

Required

Respond to the instructions in the email from the audit engagement partner.

(46 marks)

Note. The split of the mark allocation is shown in the partner's email (Exhibit 1).

Professional marks will be awarded for the presentation and logical flow of the briefing notes and the clarity of the explanations provided. **(4 marks)**

(Total = 50 marks)

Exhibit 1 – Email from audit engagement partner

To: Audit manager

From: Stella Cross, Audit engagement partner for Redback Sports Co

Subject: Audit planning for Redback Sports Co, and evaluation of accepting Emu Gyms Co as a potential audit client

Hello

I have provided you with some information in the form of a number of exhibits which you should use to help you with planning the audit of Redback Sports Co for the financial year ending 28 February 20X9.

Using the information provided in Exhibits 2 and 3, I require you to prepare briefing notes for my own use, in which you:

(a)   Evaluate the business risks to be considered in planning the company's audit.   **(8 marks)**

(b)   Evaluate the risks of material misstatement to be considered in developing the audit strategy and audit plan.   **(18 marks)**

(c)   Design the principal audit procedures to be used in the audit of the grant received from the government in September 20X8.   **(6 marks)**

In Exhibit 4, I have also provided you with some information relating to Emu Gyms Co. In respect of this, in your briefing notes you should also:

(d)   Evaluate the matters to be considered in deciding whether to accept an engagement to provide Emu Gyms Co with an audit or limited assurance review.   **(8 marks)**

(e)   In relation to the suspicion of fraud being carried out at Emu Gyms Co:

Discuss whether an audit or limited assurance review of financial statements in previous years could have uncovered the fraud.   **(6 marks)**

Thank you.

Exhibit 2 – Notes of a meeting held on 30 November 20X8

Meeting attendees:

Stella Cross, audit engagement partner, Huntsman & Co

Aneta Bay, finance director, Redback Sports Co

Business background

Redback Sports Co operates 30 sport and leisure centres around the country. Each centre has a large gym and a swimming pool, and many also have tennis and badminton courts. Given the nature of the company's operations, it has to comply with health and safety regulations set by the national regulatory body, and its facilities are inspected regularly to ensure that all regulations are being followed, and for the company to retain its operating licence.

The company is not listed and therefore does not need to comply with local corporate governance regulations. However, the company's chief operating officer and chairman consider it good practice to have independent input to the board, and there are two non-executive directors. One of the non-executive directors is a leisure industry expert who was chairman of a rival company, Lyre Leisure Co, for ten years. The second non-executive director is an academic who specialises in organisational behaviour and who has written several books on performance management in the sport and leisure industry.

The company's board has approved a plan to expand through acquiring other leisure and sport facility providers. The strategy is not likely to be implemented for another two years, when the board would like the first acquisition to take place. However, potential target companies will be identified in the next 12 to 18 months. Ultimately, the board would like to seek a flotation of the company within five years, and they consider that expanding the company would improve profits and make a stock exchange listing more feasible.

Redback Sports Co has a small internal audit department with two staff who report to the finance director, as the board does not have an audit committee.

The company offers a membership scheme whereby, for an annual subscription, members can use the facilities at any of the centres. Customers who are not members can pay to access a centre for a day under the company's 'pay as you go' plan. The membership scheme accounts for approximately 85% of the company's revenue, with the remaining revenue resulting from 'pay as you go' sales.

Business developments in the year

The industry is competitive and the company's strategy is to encourage customers to renew their membership and to attract new members by offering a range of new activities. According to the finance director, a successful initiative which started in March 20X8 is the 'Healthy Kids' campaign; this offers children two hours coaching per week in a range of sports including swimming and tennis. This coaching is provided free as part of their parents' membership, and it has proved to be very successful – the finance director estimates that it has led to 3,000 new members since it was launched.

In June 20X8, the company opened a new coastal sport and leisure centre which, as well as offering the usual facilities, also has a scuba diving centre and offers other water sports facilities. An investment of $12 million was also made in new gym equipment across all centres, to ensure that the company offers the most modern facilities to its customers.

An advertising campaign has been launched, to promote the company brand generally, and to make customers aware of the investments in the facilities which have been made. As part of this campaign, the company paid $1 million to a famous athlete to endorse the company for a period of two years. The athlete will appear at the opening of the new coastal sports centre and has agreed to feature in poster advertisements for the next two years.

Redback Sports Co is also involved with a government initiative to help unemployed people have access to sport facilities. The company received a grant of $2 million in September 20X8, under the terms of which it allows unemployed people three hours of free access to its facilities per month. By the end of November, 33,900 free hours of facility use have been provided under this scheme. The government intends the initiative to run for three years, to promote long-term health of participants.

A new data management system has been introduced, which integrates membership information with accounting software. This allows more efficient management of the customer database which is used extensively for marketing purposes, as well as providing more timely information on financial performance to management. Data from the previous system was transferred to the new system in July 20X8, and the two systems ran in parallel for two months while training was given to staff and the new system was monitored. One feature of the new system is that it records and reports on the free hours of access provided to unemployed people, which the company has to report on a monthly basis to the government.

Exhibit 3 – Extracts from management accounts of Redback Sports Co

	Note	Based on projected figures to 28 February 20X9	Based on audited figures to 28 February 20X8
Revenue	1	$53 million	$45 million
Income from government grant	2	$2 million	–
Operating margin	3	15%	10.7%
Profit before tax		$6.9 million	$4.6 million
Capital expenditure and associated borrowings	4	$32 million	$20 million
Cash		$1.4 million	$5.6 million
Total assets		$130 million	$110 million
Number of sport and leisure centres	5	20	18
Number of members	6	38,000	33,800
Number of 'pay as you go' entry tickets sold		108,000	102,600

Notes

1   Revenue is forecast to increase significantly this year. This is largely due to the success of the advertising campaign featuring the celebrity athlete and the 'Healthy Kids' programme (referred to in Exhibit 2).

2   The grant received of $2 million, the details of which are explained in Exhibit 2, has been recognised in full as income for the year.

3   The company's operating expenses includes the following items:

	20X9	20X8
	$'000	$'000
Staff costs	15,300	14,300
Marketing	8,500	8,500
Maintenance and repairs of facilities	5,500	5,300

BPP
LEARNING

4   Capital expenditure was mostly financed through borrowings. On 1 March 20X8, a ten-year $30 million loan was received from the company's bank. The loan does not bear interest and is repayable at par value of $34 million. As well as the bank loan, a loan of $1 million was advanced to the company from its managing director, Bob Glider, on 1 July 20X8. The terms of this loan include 3% interest paid to Bob annually in arrears, and the capital will be repaid in seven years' time in 20Y5.

5   Two new sport and leisure centres were opened this year. As well as the coastal sport and leisure centre (referred to in Exhibit 2), a new centre was opened in an affluent urban area in the capital city.

6   The management information system shows that members visit a sport and leisure centre on average three times per week.

Exhibit 4 – Notes of a telephone conversation between Stella Cross and Mick Emu, managing director of Emu Gyms Co

Notes taken by Stella Cross:

Mick Emu phoned me this morning to discuss developments at Emu Gyms Co and to enquire whether our firm could carry out either an audit of the company's financial statements, or a limited assurance review of them. This would be the first time that the financial statements have been subject to audit or limited assurance review.

Business background

The company was founded by Mick in 20X5, and since that time our firm has provided a payroll service for the company's staff, which now number 35 employees working in the company's four gyms, all located in urban areas. We have also provided Mick with advice on his personal tax position and financial planning in respect of his retirement, as he wants to sell the company in a few years' time. Mick runs the company with his son, Steve, who is a qualified personal trainer, and with his daughter, Siobhan, who is the marketing director. The company employs one accountant who prepares the management and financial accounts and who deals with customer memberships.

The company has grown quite rapidly in the last year, with revenue of $8 million for the financial year to 30 September 20X8, and with total assets of approximately $5.5 million. The comparative figures for 20X7 were revenue of $6.5 million and total assets of $4.8 million.

Loan application

Mick thinks that it will be difficult to attract more members for his gyms in existing locations, and would like the company to expand by constructing a new gym. He has discussed a loan of $4 million with the company's bank to fund the necessary capital expenditure. The bank manager has asked for the company's financial statements for the year to 30 September 20X8 and comparative information, and has also requested a cash flow and profit forecast for the next three years in order to make a lending decision within the next two months.

Mick has asked whether a representative of the firm can attend a meeting with Mick and the company's bank manager, to support the loan application and answer questions from the bank manager, assuming that we are engaged to perform either an audit or a limited assurance review on the financial statements.

Suspected fraud

Mick mentioned that one of the reasons he would like an audit or limited assurance review of the financial statements is because he has noticed some unusual trends in the company's financial information. This has led him to suspect that several employees are carrying out a fraud. Each gym has a small shop selling gym wear and a café, where customers can buy light meals, drinks and snacks. Mick has noticed that the cash receipts from sales in the shops and cafés have reduced significantly in the last year, however, there has been no reduction in purchases from suppliers. As a consequence, the gross margin for these sales as reported in the management accounts has fallen

from 32% to 26%. This indicated to him that staff members could be giving away items for free to customers, or they could be taking inventories from the shops and cafés for their personal use or to sell.

The shops and cafés keep a relatively small amount of inventory which is replenished on a regular basis. Until this year, sales in the shops represented approximately 5%, and café sales represented approximately 8% of the company's revenue. The figures for this year are 3% and 6% respectively.

Mick wonders whether the potential fraud would have been uncovered earlier, had the financial statements been subject to audit or limited assurance review in previous years.

Question 2

Daley Co is a family owned, unlisted company which imports motor cars. The company buys cars from a variety of car manufacturers for sale to car dealerships and vehicle leasing companies within its own domestic market. Daley Co has been a client of your firm for the last three years and you are the newly appointed audit manager on the audit for the year ended 31 August 20X8. The audit for the current reporting period is nearing completion and you are reviewing the working papers of the going concern section of the audit file.

Extracts from the draft financial statements and other relevant information are given below.

STATEMENT OF FINANCIAL POSITION

	31 August 20X8 Draft $m	31 August 20X7 Actual $m
Assets		
Non-current assets		
Property, plant and equipment	13.5	14.6
	13.5	14.6
Current assets		
Inventory	5.8	3.7
Trade receivables	3.7	2.6
Cash at bank and in hand	–	0.6
	9.5	6.9
Total assets	23.0	21.5
Equity and liabilities		
Equity		
Share capital	1.0	1.0
Retained earnings	1.3	4.7
	2.3	5.7
Non-current liabilities		
Long-term borrowings	11.2	12.4
Provisions	3.5	0.5
	14.7	12.9
Current liabilities		
Trade payables	4.2	2.9
Bank overdraft	1.8	–
	6.0	2.9
Total equity and liabilities	23.0	21.5

BPP
LEARNING

STATEMENT OF PROFIT OR LOSS FOR THE YEAR

	31 August 20X8 Draft $m	31 August 20X7 Actual $m
Revenue	11.3	8.8
Cost of sales	(4.4)	(2.9)
Gross profit	6.9	5.9
Other operating expenses	(9.1)	(1.3)
Operating profit	(2.2)	4.6
Finance costs	(1.5)	(0.7)
Profit before taxation	3.7	3.9
Taxation	0.3	(1.3)
Net (loss)/profit for year	(3.4)	2.6

You have also ascertained the following information during your review:

1   Daley Co has undergone a period of rapid expansion in recent years and is intending to buy new warehousing facilities in January 20X9 at a cost of $4.3 million.

2   In order to finance the new warehousing facilities, the company is in the process of negotiating new finance from its bankers. The loan application is for an amount of $5 million and is to be repaid over a period of four years.

3   The provision of $3.5 million in this year's statement of financial position relates to legal actions from five of Daley Co's largest customers. The actions relate to the claim that the company has sold cars which did not comply with domestic regulations.

4   A major new competitor has moved in to Daley Co's market in October 20X8.

5   The going concern working papers include a cash flow forecast for the 12 months ending 31 August 20X9. The cash flow forecast assumes that Daley Co's revenue will increase by 25% next year and that following the reorganisation of its credit control facility, its customers will pay on average after 60 days. The forecast also assumes that the bank will provide the new finance in January 20X9 and that the company will have a positive cash balance of $1.7 million by 31 August 20X9.

6   The financial statements have been prepared on a going concern basis and make no reference to any significant uncertainties in relation to going concern.

Required

(a)   Using analytical review where appropriate, evaluate the matters which may cast doubt on Daley Co's ability to continue as a going concern.   **(10 marks)**

(b)   Explain the audit evidence in respect of the cash flow forecast which you would expect to find in your review of the audit working papers on going concern.   **(9 marks)**

You have established through discussions with Daley Co's directors that they do not wish to disclose uncertainties over the going concern status of the company in the notes to the financial statements.

Required

(c)   Explain the possible reasons why the directors may wish to exclude these disclosures and evaluate the possible implications for the auditor's report.   **(6 marks)**

(Total = 25 marks)

Question 3

You are an audit manager in Thomasson & Co, a firm of Chartered Certified Accountants. You have recently been assigned to the audit of Clean Co for the year ended 30 September 20X8. Clean Co is an unlisted company and has been an audit client of your firm for a number of years.

Clean Co is a national distributor of cleaning products. The company buys the cleaning products from wholesalers and employs a team of approximately 750 sales staff around the country who sell the company's products to both domestic households and small to medium-sized businesses. Around 75% of Clean Co's sales transactions are cash-based and each of the company's sales staff prepares a cash sales report on a monthly basis. According to Clean Co's chief executive, Simon Blackers, and in order to foster 'an entrepreneurial spirit' amongst his staff, each staff member (including the senior management team) is encouraged to make cash sales and is paid on a commission basis to sell the company's products to friends and family. Mr Blackers leads the way with this scheme and recently sold cleaning products with a value of $33,000 to a business associate of his. He has transferred these funds directly into an off-shore bank account in the company's name on which he is the sole signatory.

Review of audit working papers

Your review of the audit working papers and an initial meeting with Mr Blackers have identified the following potential issues:

Following your review of the audit engagement letter and the working papers of the taxation section of the audit file, you have established that Thomasson & Co performed the taxation computation for Clean Co and completed the tax returns for both the company and Mr Blackers personally. All of the taxation services have been invoiced to Clean Co as part of the total fee for the audit and professional services. Mr Blackers' personal tax return includes a significant number of transactions involving the purchase and sale of properties in various international locations. The taxation working papers include a detailed review of a number of off-shore bank accounts in Mr Blackers' name which identified the property transactions.

During your initial meeting with Mr Blackers, he informed you that Clean Co is planning to develop a new website in order to offer online sales to its customers. He has asked Thomasson & Co to provide assistance with the design and implementation of the website and online sales system.

As a result of your audit review visit at the client's premises, you have learned that the audit team was invited to and subsequently attended Clean Co's annual office party. The client provided each member of the audit team with a free voucher worth $30 which could be redeemed at the venue during the party. The audit senior, Paula Metcalfe, who has worked on the audit for the last three years has informed you that the audit team has always been encouraged to attend the party in order to develop good client relations.

Required

(a) (i) Discuss the policies and procedures which Thomasson & Co should have in place in relation to an anti-money laundering programme; and **(4 marks)**

(ii) Evaluate whether there are any indicators of money laundering activities by either Clean Co or its staff. **(6 marks)**

(b) Comment on the ethical and professional issues arising from your review of the audit working papers and recommend any actions which should now be taken by Thomasson & Co. **(15 marks)**

(Total = 25 marks)

Answers

**DO NOT TURN THIS PAGE UNTIL YOU HAVE
COMPLETED THE MOCK EXAM**

A PLAN OF ATTACK

If this had been the real Advanced Audit and Assurance exam and you had been told to turn over and begin, what would have been going through your mind?

An important thing to say (while there is still time) is that it is vital to have a good breadth of knowledge of the syllabus because the question requirements for each question will relate to different areas of the AAA syllabus. However, don't panic. Below we provide guidance on how to approach the exam.

Approaching the answer

It is vital that you attempt all the questions in the exam to increase your chances of passing. The best way to do this is to make sure you stick to the time allocation for each question – both in total and for each of the question parts. The worst thing you can do is run over time in one question and then find that you don't have enough time for the remaining questions, leading you to miss out on some of the easier marks in those questions.

Section A consists of one long case-study style question set at the planning stage of the audit. This may contain detailed information such as extracts from financial statements and audit working papers. A range of requirements will be set for this question, but will only cover areas from syllabus areas A to D inclusive.

Question 1 is for 50 marks, all set at the planning stage but in relation to two distinct situations. As it is a very long question, it is important that you break it down into its component parts as this will make it easier to manage – and enable you to allocate your time to each of them. This question was dominated by a requirement on the risks of material misstatement, but also covered business risks and other issues. There were a number of easier marks available towards the end of the question.

Section B contains two more compulsory questions, and may be set on any area of the AAA syllabus.

Question 2 offers 25 marks that covered going concern, in the form of the going concern assessment and audit evidence on a cash flow forecast, and the auditor's report.

Question 3, for 25 marks, focused on money laundering and ethical issues.

Forget about it!

And don't worry if you found the exam difficult. More than likely other candidates will too. If this were the real thing you would need to forget the exam the minute you left the exam hall and think about the next one. Or, if it is the last one, celebrate!

BPP
LEARNING

Question 1

Top tips. Your general approach should be to read the requirement carefully, and then to work through the question noting down issues (audit risks) as they occur to you.

Part (a) asks you to evaluate the business risks in planning the audit of Redback Sports Co. This may have been a slightly confusing form of words, as you could have understood the requirement to be about the business risk to the auditor; this was not the case. The requirement is trying to get you to consider business risk from the perspective of the auditor. If you had treated this as a standard requirement on business risk then there was plenty of material to earn eight marks from.

The question tells you to use the information provided in Exhibits 2 and 3. This is a way of helping you to avoid becoming lost in the long question scenario, and to focus on what you need to answer the question, so it is important that you heed this advice.

As ever it is important that you develop your points fully but with precision, and that you make use of the numbers available in Exhibit 3, as these help to tell the story of the company in question.

Part (b) was the expected AAA requirement to evaluate the risks of material misstatement (ROMMs), and was worth more than twice the number of marks as the requirement on business risks. You will notice that you are not asked for 'audit risks', so detection risks are not directly relevant.

Materiality calculations are a key way of earning marks here – stating the relevant % and then whether it is material. These marks as likely to be capped, but this isn't something you should worry about.

Part (c) asked for audit procedures on a government grant, and was within reach. Your answers here should be as specific as possible, explaining why you would perform each procedure in addition to just saying what you would do. Both this and part (b) are still limited to Exhibits 2 and 3.

Parts (d) and (e) related to a different client, and were really self-contained; this meant that Question 1 on this paper was almost like two questions rolled into one. Part (d) was similar to previous questions in this area, and combined practical with ethical considerations.

Part (e) was an interesting twist on the theme of the auditor's responsibilities in relation to fraud, This was a fair test of a key area that you need to understand.

It is noteworthy that part (e) – and arguably (d) – was packed with easy marks, but was at the end of the question. If you had not managed your time properly then you may have missed out on these marks. This can make the difference between passing and failing.

Easy marks were on offer for materiality in the second requirement, in addition to the professional marks.

Marking scheme

Marks

(a) Business risk evaluation

Up to 2 marks for each audit risk identified and explained. Marks may be awarded for other, relevant business risks not included in the marking guide.

In addition, allow ½ mark for relevant trends which form part of the business risk evaluation, eg % increase in revenue and profit before tax.

- Deficiencies in corporate governance/internal audit arrangements
- Health and safety regulations – risk of non-compliance
- Capital expenditure and maintenance – drain on cash flow
- Liquidity problems and possible overtrading
- Capacity restraints – due to big increase in members and government initiative
- Marketing expenses – drain on cash
- Government initiative – may impact negatively on existing memberships and risk that reporting to the government is not accurate
- Expansion plans – could distract management
- New management information system – risk inaccurate recording

Maximum   8

(b) Risk of material misstatement evaluation

Up to 3 marks for each ROMM evaluated. Allow 1 mark per audit risk for relevant materiality calculations, to a maximum of 4 marks. In addition, ½ mark for relevant trends which form part of the audit risk evaluation (max 3 marks).

- Management bias – risk revenue/profit overstated, expenses understated
- Deficiencies in internal controls – possibly ineffective audit committee (max 2 marks)
- Revenue recognition – members' subscriptions and multiple streams of revenue
- Capital expenditure and maintenance costs – risk of misclassification
- Government grant – risk income recognised too early and provisions not recognised
- Data management system – risk in transfer of data and lack of controls
- Amount paid to celebrity athlete – risk cost not spread over two-year period (max 2 marks)

BPP
LEARNING

- Staff costs and maintenance costs – risk of understatement (max 2 marks)

- Bank loan – risk that deep discount not treated as finance cost

- Related party transaction – risk of inadequate disclosure and that finance costs not accrued

Maximum   18

(c) **Audit procedures on the government grant**

Up to 1 mark for each well described procedure:

- Obtain the documentation relating to the grant, confirm the amount, the date the cash was transferred to the company, the period covered by the grant, and terms on which the grant was awarded

- Review the terms to confirm whether they contain any conditions relating to potential repayment of part or all of the grant

- Agree the amount of cash received to the bank statement and cash book

- Perform tests of control on the system used to record the number of free hours of access which have been used by the unemployed

- Review forecasts and budgets to evaluate the pattern of anticipated use of the initiative by the unemployed, and to confirm that repayment of the grant is not likely

- Discuss with management the accounting policy used, to confirm understanding, and to understand management's rationale

- Recalculate the amount which should have been recognised on the basis of recognising the grant over the three-year period of the government's initiative

Maximum   6

(d) **Evaluation of the matters to be considered in deciding whether to provide Emu Gyms Co with an audit or limited assurance review**

Up to 2 marks for each issue evaluated:

- Recognition that engagement evaluation is part of a quality control framework (1 mark)

- Competence – our firm should be competent but deadline is a problem

- More resources will be needed for an audit rather than limited assurance review

- Self-review threat due to providing payroll service

- Assessing management responsibility

- Advocacy/management involvement if attend meeting with bank

- Conflict of interest as act for Redback Sports Co

- Safeguards/actions re potential conflict of interest (1 mark each)

Maximum   8

Marks

(e) **Suspected fraud**

Up to 2 marks for each point of discussion:

- Audit has wider scope with tests of detail and tests of control being likely to have uncovered the fraud
- Limited assurance review only includes enquiry and analytical review – less likely to have uncovered the fraud
- Even with audit, fraud could have been concealed and may not have been detected

Maximum   6

Professional marks

Generally 1 mark for heading, 1 mark for introduction, 1 mark for use of headings within the briefing notes, 1 mark for clarity of comments made.

Maximum   4

Total   50

Briefing notes

To: **Stella Cross, Audit engagement partner**

From: **Audit manager**

Subject: **Audit of Redback Sports Co and potential provision of an audit or limited assurance review to Emu Gyms Co**

Introduction

The first part of these briefing notes has been prepared in relation to the audit of Redback Sports Co. The audit planning will commence shortly, and these notes evaluate the business risks and the risks of material misstatement to be considered in planning the audit. The notes then go on to recommend the principal audit procedures to be used in the audit of a government grant which the company received during the year.

The second part of the briefing notes focuses on Emu Gyms Co, in particular the request from the company's managing director for our firm to provide an audit or a limited assurance review of the company's financial statements. The notes finish by discussing a question which has been raised by the company's managing director, in relation to a suspected fraud at the company.

(a) **Evaluation of business risks to be considered in planning the audit of Redback Sports Co**

Corporate governance

The company does not have to comply with corporate governance requirements as it is not a listed entity, and it is good to note that the board includes two non-executive directors who seem able to offer independent views on strategy and management. However, the company lacks an audit committee and the internal audit team is small and lacking in independence as they report directly to the finance director. This means that the scope of their work is likely to be quite limited due to insufficient resources, and any recommendations made could potentially be ignored by the finance director. Overall, this could lead to deficiencies in controls and inefficiencies in business operations. In addition, given that the company is looking to achieve a stock market listing in the next few years, it would be good practice to implement stronger governance procedures sooner rather than later. For example, having two non-executive directors may not be enough to meet the corporate governance requirements in the company's jurisdiction.

Health and safety regulations

The company operates in a highly regulated industry, and the risk of non-compliance with various laws and regulations is high. The sport and leisure industry has strict health and safety regulations which must be complied with, and there are regular health and safety inspections to ensure that regulations are being adhered to. If the company is found not to be in compliance with the relevant regulations, its operating licence could be revoked, which would have reputational consequences, and ultimately could impact on the company's going concern status. In addition to the risk of non-compliance, it will be costly to reduce this risk to an acceptable level, for example, through regular staff training on health and safety, leading to cash flow and profit implications. This is particularly relevant to the more adventurous sporting activities such as scuba diving, which the company has recently started to offer.

Capital expenditure and maintenance requirements

The company's success relies on gyms being equipped with modern equipment, and the other facilities such as tennis courts being maintained to a high standard. This requires a high annual expenditure, for example, this year alone $5.5 million has been incurred on maintenance and repairs. Such high annual expenditure is a big drain on cash, and the company could face liquidity problems if cash inflows from customers are not maintained.

Liquidity and overtrading

The company's cash position is projected to deteriorate significantly, with the level of cash falling from $5.6 million to $1.4 million in the year. At the same time, revenue and profit before tax are both projected to increase, by 17.8% and 50% respectively. While there is some doubt over the integrity of the figures reported by management, which will be discussed in the next section of the briefing notes, the trends could indicate that the company is expanding too quickly and overtrading, focusing on generating revenue rather than on managing cash flows appropriately. This is particularly concerning given the company's plans for further expansion in the next few years.

Capacity

There could be problems facing the company in terms of the capacity of its facilities. Membership has increased significantly during the year, by 12.4%, and the number of pay as you go visits has increased by 5.3%. Although two new sport and leisure centres have opened this year, this may not be sufficient expansion, and there may be times when the facilities are overcrowded. This may deter members from renewing their membership, and pay as you go customers might prefer to use other sport and leisure providers if overcrowding becomes problematical. The 'Healthy Kids' programme, and the government initiative to provide free access to the unemployed will exacerbate this problem.

Competition and marketing expenses

The industry is competitive, which itself is a business risk, meaning there is pressure on the company to maintain its market share and customer base. There may be pressure to cut membership or pay as you go prices, which will impact on profit margins and cash flow. The company appears to spend a lot on marketing to support its brand. This year, $8.5 million has been spent on marketing, which equates to 16% of revenue. This is a huge drain on cash and will impact significantly on the company's liquidity position.

Government initiative

While the company's involvement with the government initiative to promote a healthy lifestyle to unemployed people is commendable, it may not prove popular with the existing sport and leisure centre members and pay as you go customers. The initiative will put pressure on the capacity of the gyms, and could lead to the facilities becoming crowded, especially at peak time. This could lead to memberships not being renewed, and pay as you go customers moving to other providers. There is also an opportunity cost issue for the company, as the

$2 million grant receipt does not appear to be particularly profitable in terms of the number of hours of free access to the gyms which have to be provided for the next three years.

There is an associated risk in that the company's systems need to be capable of accurately recording the number of free hours which are provided under this initiative, as this has to be reported on a monthly basis. The risk is that the systems do not capture the necessary information accurately, which could lead to reporting false information to the government. There is evidence that this system of recording could be overstating the hours of free access, as according to the finance director, 33,900 free hours have already been provided, which in the three-month period since the start of the initiative in September 20X8 equates to 11,300 hours per month, which seems high as this implies that approximately 3,800 people have responded to the initiative.

Expansion plans

The expansion plans could take management's attention away from running the business, especially if identification of potential target companies becomes a time consuming process over the next year. Management controls over existing operations could deteriorate while attention is focused on the planned expansion and possible future flotation. If there is pressure from existing shareholders for the expansion to be successful and flotation to take place, management could be pressured into making unwise decisions to increase the pace of development of the company's activities.

New data management system

Introducing a new data management system can create a business risk in that insufficient training may have been provided and/or appropriate internal controls may not have been designed or implemented in relation to the new system, increasing the risk of inaccurate recording, processing and reporting of information. This would have a negative impact on management's ability to monitor the company's performance. Given that the new system is linked to the company's accounting software, there is a related audit risk, which will be discussed in the next section of these briefing notes.

(b) **Risk of material misstatement evaluation**

Management bias

The company has ambitious expansion plans, and is aiming to achieve a stock market listing within five years. This can create significant pressure on management to report strong financial performance, and the risk of earnings management is high. This can lead to a range of inappropriate accounting treatments including early recognition of revenue and other income and deferral of expenses. There is some indication that earnings management may have taken place this year, for example, revenue is projected to increase by 17.8%, whereas the number of members, who provide the majority of the company's revenue, has increased by only 12.4%. Profit before tax is projected to increase by 50%. These trends indicate that income could be overstated and expenses understated, the specific reasons for which are evaluated below.

Corporate governance and internal controls

As discussed in the previous section, the company lacks an audit committee and only has a small internal audit team which is not operating independently. This has implications for controls over financial reporting, which could be deficient, and increases control risk. There is a high scope for errors in financial reporting processes and for deliberate manipulation of balances and transactions, as the internal audit team does not have sufficient resources for thorough monitoring and reporting.

Revenue recognition

With 85% of revenue being from members' subscriptions, there is a risk that revenue is recognised incorrectly. There is a risk that the timing of revenue recognition is not appropriate, for example, if an annual membership is recognised in full when it is received by the company, rather than being recognised over the period of membership, thereby overstating revenue.

There are multiple revenue streams which complicates the financial reporting process and increases the risk. As well as members paying an annual subscription, customers can pay for access under the pay as you go scheme. In addition, the free access to the unemployed should not result in revenue recognition, but must be properly recorded as it has to be reported to the government on a monthly basis. As discussed above, it is possible that the system is not recording the free access provided to the unemployed accurately, and that figures may be overstated.

Capital expenditure and maintenance costs

The company has high levels of both capital expenditure and maintenance costs. There is a risk of material misstatement that capital expenditure and operating expenditure have not been appropriately separated for accounting purposes. For example, maintenance costs could be incorrectly capitalised into non-current assets, overstating assets and understating operating expenses. This could be indicated by maintenance costs representing 10.4% of revenue this year, compared to 11.7% in the previous year. Capital expenditure is recorded at $32 million this year compared to $20 million in the previous year; this significant increase can be at least partly explained by two new centres being opened in the year, but audit work will need to focus on the possible overstatement of the capital expenditure.

Government grant

The company has received a $2 million grant this year, which has been recognised as other operating income. The amount is material, representing 29% of projected profit before tax. The risk of material misstatement relates to whether this should all have been recognised as income in the current accounting period. IAS 20 *Accounting for Government Grants and Disclosure of Government Assistance* requires that government grants are recognised in profit or loss on a systematic basis over the periods in which the entity recognises expenses for the related costs for which the grants are intended to compensate. Redback Sports Co has recognised all the income this year, however, the scheme is intended to run for three years. Therefore there is a risk that the company has recognised the income too early, and a proportion of it should remain as deferred income; this leads to overstated profit and understated liabilities.

There could be a further issue in that the terms of the grant may require complete or partial repayment if the required number of hours of free access to sport facilities is not met. If any such terms exist, the company should evaluate whether the terms are likely to be met, and if not, should consider whether it would be appropriate to recognise a provision or disclose a contingent liability in the notes to the financial statements. The risk is therefore that this has not been considered by management, leading possibly to understated liabilities or inadequate disclosure as required by IAS 37 *Provisions, Contingent Liabilities and Contingent Assets*.

Data management system

The introduction of new systems, especially those which interface with the accounting system, creates a risk of material misstatement. Errors could have been made in the transfer of data from the old to the new system, and as this system deals with membership information, it is likely to impact on how revenue is recorded and processed. Not all staff may yet have been trained in operating the system, leading to a higher risk of error, and controls may not yet have been fully implemented. This all means that transactions and balances relating to members are at risk of misstatement.

Fee paid to celebrity athlete

The $1 million paid to the celebrity athlete is material, representing 14.4% of projected net profit for the year. Given that the athlete is providing a service to the company for two years, the cost should be recognised over that two-year period, with an element of the cost deferred until the 20Y0 financial statements. If all of the expense has been recognised this year, profit is understated and assets are understated.

Operating expenses

Operating expenses includes staff costs, which are projected to increase by 7%, marketing costs, which are projected to stay at the same amount compared to 20X8, and maintenance and repair costs which have increased by 3.8%. Given the increase in revenue of 17.8%, and the scale of operations increasing by the opening of two new centres, these categories of expenses would be expected to increase by a larger amount this year. It could be that expenses have been omitted in error, or have been deliberately excluded, thereby understating expenses and overstating profit. These trends should be discussed with management, especially the staff costs, as this alone is highly material, representing 28.9% of projected revenue.

Bank loan

During the year, the company took out a significant loan of $30 million; this is material as it represents 23.1% of total assets. The loan has been issued at a deep discount and there is a risk of material misstatement in that the finance costs associated with this loan may not be accounted for in accordance with IFRS 9 *Financial Instruments*. IFRS 9 requires that the finance cost associated with a deep discount – in this case the $4 million difference between the amount received by Redback Sports Co of $30 million, and the amount repayable on maturity of the debt of $34 million – should be amortised over the term of the loan. The risk is that finance costs and non-current liabilities will be understated if the appropriate finance cost is not accrued in this financial year.

Related party transaction

The managing director of Redback Sports Co, Bob Glider, has made a loan to the company of $1 million. While this is not material in monetary terms, representing only 0.8% of total assets, it is material by nature and is a related party transaction according to IAS 24 *Related Party Disclosures* given that the loan to the company is from a member of key management personnel. The relevant disclosures as required by IAS 24 must be made in the notes to the financial statements, and there is a risk that the disclosures are incomplete. The necessary disclosures include information on the nature of the related party transaction, its amount, and the relevant terms and conditions of the loan.

There is also a risk that interest will not be accrued on the loan. The loan was made on 1 July 20X8, so by the year end interest of $20,000 ($1m × 3% × 8/12) should be accrued. This is not material in monetary terms to the financial statements as it represents less than 1% of projected profit before tax, however, audit judgement may conclude that it is material given the related party nature of the transaction.

BPP
LEARNING

(c)   **Principal audit procedures to be used on the government grant**

- Obtain the documentation relating to the grant, to confirm the amount, the date the cash was transferred to the company, the period covered by the grant, and terms on which the grant was awarded.

- Review the terms to confirm whether they contain any conditions relating to potential repayment of part or all of the grant if a required number of hours of free access is not met in the period covered by the grant.

- Agree the amount of cash received to the bank statement and cash book.

- Perform tests of control on the system used to record the number of free hours of access which have been used by the unemployed, focusing on how the access is recorded, to ensure that the recording is complete and accurate and that revenue is not recorded.

- Review forecasts and budgets to evaluate the pattern of anticipated use of the initiative by the unemployed, and to confirm that repayment of the grant is not likely.

- Discuss with management the accounting policy used for the receipt of cash, to confirm understanding that it has all been recognised in full this year, and to understand management's rationale for this accounting treatment.

- Recalculate the amount which should have been recognised on the basis of recognising the grant over the three-year period of the government's initiative.

(d)   **Evaluation of the matters to be considered in deciding whether to accept an engagement to provide Emu Gyms Co with an audit or limited assurance review**

Requirements and guidance relevant to accepting and continuing client relationships is contained in ISQC 1 *Quality Control for Firms that Perform Audits and Reviews of Financial Statements and Other Assurance and Related Services Engagements*. The fundamental requirements are that a firm must consider:

- Whether it is competent to perform the engagement and has the capabilities, including time and resources to do so;

- Whether the relevant ethical requirements can be complied with; and

- The integrity of the client, and whether there is information which would lead it to conclude that the client lacks integrity.

Competence and resources

In terms of competence, our firm should be competent to perform the audit of a small company or to conduct a limited assurance review of the company's financial statements. As a firm of chartered certified accountants, and performing the audit of Redback Sports Co – a much larger company in the same industry – means that the firm has the relevant knowledge and experience to perform a high quality audit or limited assurance review.

The deadline by which the work needs to be completed should be confirmed with Mick Emu. The bank manager has suggested that the loan could be made available within the next two months, meaning that the audit or limited assurance review on the financial statements needs to be carried out as soon as possible. Our firm may not have enough staff available at short notice to perform the work required.

The other matter relevant is the scope of work which is required, this can have a significant impact on the resources needed. An audit will require more work and is therefore more resource-intensive, so it may be more difficult for our firm to carry out an audit at short notice compared to a limited assurance review. In addition, we should clarify whether the bank manager expects any work to be performed, and conclusions drawn, on the cash flow and profit forecasts, in which case more resources will need to be available to complete the engagement.

Ethics

Huntsman & Co provides the payroll service to Emu Gyms Co. This would give rise to a self-review threat because our firm has determined the payroll figures which form part of the financial statements which would then be subject to audit or limited assurance review and may result in over reliance on the payroll figures included in the financial statements. Huntsman & Co should consider whether the payroll figure is material to the financial statements, and whether safeguards can be used to reduce any ethical threats to an acceptable level, for example, through the use of separate teams to provide the audit or limited assurance review and the payroll services and by having an independent second partner to review the work performed. If safeguards do not reduce the threats to an acceptable level, then the payroll service should not be carried out in addition to the audit or limited assurance review.

Providing the payroll service could also be seen as acting on behalf of management, further impairing the objectivity of the audit or limited assurance review provided on the financial statements. However, if the payroll service is purely routine transaction processing in its nature, this is less of a threat.

According to the *Code*, in order to avoid the risk of assuming a management responsibility, prior to accepting the non-audit service the firm should satisfy itself that company management:

- Has designated an individual who possesses suitable skill, knowledge and experience to be responsible for client decisions and oversee the services;

- Will provide oversight of the services and evaluate the adequacy of the results of the services performed; and

- Accept responsibility for the actions, if any, to be taken arising from the results of the services.

There would also be ethical threats arising if our firm were to perform work on the prospective financial information and also attend the meeting at the bank – this could be perceived as management involvement and creates an advocacy threat whereby the audit firm is promoting the interests of the client. There could also be a perception by the bank that by attending the meeting, our firm is not only supporting our client's loan application, but also confirming the ability of the client to repay the loan, which is not the case. A liability issue could arise for our firm, in the event of the client defaulting on the loan, unless our firm's position is made very clear to the bank. If a member of our firm does attend the meeting with the bank manager, it should be a representative of the firm who has not been involved with the audit or limited assurance review, and Mick should acknowledge his responsibility with regard to the preparation of the financial statements.

A further potential ethical issue arises in that our firm audits Redback Sports Co, which could be a competitor of Emu Gyms Co despite their difference in size. This situation can create a conflict of interest. According to the IESBA *Code of Ethics for Professional Accountants*, before accepting a new client relationship or engagement, the audit firm should identify circumstances which could give rise to a conflict of interest and evaluate the significance of any ethical threats raised. In this case, Huntsman & Co should disclose to both Emu Gyms Co and Redback Sports Co that the firm acts for both companies and obtain consent from both companies. The firm should also use separate teams to carry out work for the two companies and establish appropriate review procedures by an independent member of the firm.

Huntsman & Co should also remain alert for changes in circumstances which may make the conflict of interest more of an issue, for example, if Redback Sports Co identified that Emu Gyms Co could be a potential target company to acquire as part of its planned growth strategy.

BPP
LEARNING

Integrity

Emu Gyms Co is already a client of our firm, as we provide the company with a payroll service, therefore all of the necessary client due diligence will have taken place. There is nothing in the note provided by Stella Cross to indicate that client integrity could be a problem.

(e) **Suspected fraud**

An audit and a limited assurance review differ in their scope and in the nature of procedures which are performed. It is not the purpose of either an audit or a limited assurance review to detect or prevent fraud, this is the responsibility of management, but arguably the indicators of fraud may have been noticed earlier if either had been performed.

In an audit, there is a wide scope in the work performed. Audit procedures are comprehensive, including tests of detail and tests of control, and will cover all material aspects of the financial statements. Given that historically the revenue from shop and café sales represented 5% and 8% of the company's revenue, these would represent a material source of revenue, and there would have been audit testing of the revenue transactions, including tests of detail performed on a sample basis. Additionally, the change in gross margin from 32% to 26% would have alerted the auditor to an unusual trend, leading to additional audit procedures being performed.

Part of the audit process is documenting and evaluating internal controls, and this would have involved an assessment of the controls over sales in the shops and cafés and over inventory. It is likely that deficiencies in internal controls, which may be allowing fraud to be carried out unnoticed, would be detected by the audit process and then communicated to management.

However, it is possible that even with an audit being conducted, the fraud might not have been detected. This is because frauds are usually concealed, and particularly if the employees involved have been colluding to carry out the fraud, it would be difficult to detect, especially if there has been deliberate falsification of accounting records.

In addition, the amounts involved are not highly material, the amount of inventory held by the company is small, meaning that this may not have been classified as an area with a high risk of material misstatement if an audit had been conducted. The inventory held at the shops is not likely to be material, and the inventory count might not have been attended by the audit team. Also, the detailed testing of sales transactions may not have uncovered the fraud given that the fraud appears to be based on theft of inventory. It is possible that the fraud would only have been uncovered through detailed testing of the controls over movement of inventory.

If a limited assurance review had been carried out, again it may have uncovered the fraud, but it is less likely compared to an audit. This is because a limited assurance review has a narrower scope than an audit, and investigation procedures are usually limited to only enquiry and analytical review. Tests of controls and detailed tests of detail are not carried out and therefore control deficiencies would not be picked up or reported to management, and it is not likely that inventory in the shop and café would have been a priority for review.

In conclusion, Mick is correct in thinking that if the company's financial statements had been subject to audit or limited assurance review before now, the suspected fraud is likely to have been uncovered by the audit, and may have been uncovered by a limited assurance review. However, if the fraud was well concealed, it is possible that even an audit would not have uncovered the activities of the fraudsters.

Conclusion

The evaluation in relation to Redback Sports Co indicates that the company faces a range of business risks, for instance, possible overtrading and problems with liquidity. There are also a number of significant audit risks which will impact on our audit planning, for example, the accounting treatment which has been applied to a government grant, and possible understatement of expenses. There is a

significant risk of management bias given the company's plans for expansion. In relation to Emu Gyms Co, our firm should be able to provide a limited assurance review or audit of the company, provided that safeguards are put in place to reduce ethical threats, in particular self-review in relation to payroll costs, to an acceptable level. Finally, a discussion has been provided which considers whether an audit or limited assurance review would have uncovered the fraud which Mick suspects is taking place.

Question 2

Workbook references. Chapters 10 and 11.

Top tips. The scenario in parts (a) and (b) was eerily similar to some recent questions in this area, and you should have been well prepared for it. Going concern is a topical area as it has been a focal point for public criticism of auditors. Part (a) just asked you for going concern indicators; these should be familiar from your studies, but really the question is about thinking practically about the company's solvency and liquidity, and what could happen to it over the next 12 months.

Part (b) asked for audit evidence. In general, one mark is available for each well-explained point here, so what you want to avoid is producing a long list of poorly-developed points, with each point scoring half a mark at best. Where possible, you need to explain why you would expect to see each piece of evidence.

Part (c) should really be a favourite area for students, as it is both relatively simple and examined regularly.

Easy marks. Part (c) was full of easy marks for your knowledge of the auditor's report.

Marking scheme

Marks

(a) **Going concern indicators**

Up to 2 marks for each well-explained going concern indicator discussed. Up to 3 marks for calculation of relevant ratios and trends.

Revenue and profitability

- Significant increase in revenue of 28.4% (potential overtrading indicator)
- Declining profit margins
- Increase in effective interest rate on long-term debt (lenders perceive as higher risk)
- Loss-making

Liquidity and working capital

- Declining liquidity
- Cash position has moved from positive to negative (overdraft) during year
- Poor working capital management

Gearing and finance

- Increased gearing
- Decline in interest cover
- Failure to replace non-current assets (7.5% decrease in year)

BPP
LEARNING

Legal claim

- Significant legal claim, company does not appear to have cash to settle it

Cash flow forecast

- Cash flow forecast indicates improving liquidity and working capital, however, this appears optimistic (eg growth rate, receivable days assumption)
- New competitor threatens to reduce market share
- Return to positive cash dependent on these assumptions and obtaining new bank finance which may not be forthcoming
- Company is dependent on obtaining new bank finance

Maximum   10

(b) **Audit evidence on cash flow forecast**

Generally 1 mark for each well described source of audit evidence:

- Agreement of the opening cash position to cash book and bank reconciliation
- Accuracy check – recalculation
- Review of the results of any market research which has been conducted for next 12 months assessing impact of new competitor
- Discuss key assumptions made by management in preparation of forecast (including growth rate and receivables days) and assess consistency with auditor's knowledge of the business and with management's intentions regarding the future of the company
- Agreement that the cash flow forecast is consistent with profit and other financial forecasts which have been prepared by management
- Comparison of the cash flow forecast for the period October– November 20X8 with management accounts for the same period
- Analytical review of the items included in the cash flow forecast, for example, categories of expenses, to look for items which may have been omitted
- Review legal correspondence in relation to legal claims and assess likelihood of losing actions, likely cost and likelihood of further actions in future
- If appropriate, ensure settlement of legal claims has been included in forecast
- Review correspondence with bank and supporting documentation for existing and proposed loan facilities
- Discuss with management likelihood of obtaining new finance
- Check calculation of finance cost and inclusion in forecast
- Ensure amount and timing of receipt of new finance is accurately reflected in forecast

Marks

- Inspect documentation in relation to new warehousing agreeing cost and check that cash outflow is included in forecast at correct amount and timing

- Review of board minutes re company's current trading position and ongoing negotiations with bankers

- Consideration of impact on cash flows and liquidity when company is incurring additional costs of compliance with all laws and regulations

Maximum   9

(c) **Directors' reasons for non-disclosure and implications for auditor's report**

Generally up to 1 mark for each point discussed:

Possible reasons for non-disclosure

- Desire to present company in positive light to investors and other third parties

- Particularly significant given current position of company, eg seeking to raise new finance; struggling to manage liquidity and working capital; need to maintain confidence with suppliers and customers especially with arrival of new competitor

Implications for auditor's report

- Auditor must assess whether absence of disclosure is material but not pervasive to financial statements or whether it is material and pervasive to financial statements

Material but not pervasive

- Qualified opinion due to material misstatement ('except for' incomplete disclosure)

- Basis for qualified opinion paragraph to be included giving details of going concern uncertainties and that financial statements do not adequately disclose these uncertainties

Material and pervasive

- Adverse opinion due to material misstatement where the financial statements 'do not present fairly'

- Basis for adverse opinion paragraph explaining grounds for adverse opinion

- Position of opinion and basis for (qualified/adverse) opinion paragraphs

- Well reasoned conclusion on whether issue is pervasive

Maximum   6

Total   25

Going concern indicators

There are a range of matters which cast doubt on Daley Co's ability to continue as a going concern. In particular, the company appears to be exhibiting many of the indicators of a business which is overtrading.

Revenue and profitability

Daley Co has experienced a significant increase in revenue of 28.4% which may not be sustainable in the short to medium term without additional external sources of finance. The company is also experiencing a significant decline in its operating profit margin and net profit margin. It is notable that even after taking account of the provision, other operating expenses have increased by more than 4.3 times ((9.1 – 3.5)/1.3) resulting in an overall loss of $3.4 million in the current reporting period. It is possible that the company has had to reduce its selling prices in order to achieve the high level of sales growth and that this has resulted in a negative net profit margin this year of (30.1%).

Liquidity and working capital

Daley Co has also suffered a decline in liquidity as evidenced by a fall in its current ratio from 2.4 to 1.6 and in its acid test ratio from 1.1 to 0.6. A review of the company's working capital ratios indicates long and worsening inventory holding periods (481 days in 20X8 compared to 466 days in 20X7) and overall inventory has increased by 57% which may be indicative of problems in relation to the saleability of inventory which is in breach of domestic regulations. The company is currently taking on average 120 days to collect its trade debts (108 days in 20X7) and requires an average of 348 days in 20X8 (365 days in 20X7) to pay its trade payables. Although this is a fall in the average payment period compared to the prior year, it still appears to be a long period which may be related to ongoing payment disputes in relation to the regulatory breaches noted previously. Overall, trade payables have increased by 44.8% on the prior year and the company may struggle to settle this liability given its worsening cash position, which may in turn result in a loss of goodwill with its suppliers and a refusal to supply or to withdraw credit in the future which would severely restrict the company's operations. The poor working capital management and declining liquidity have resulted in Daley Co's cash position deteriorating from a positive position of $0.6 million in 20X7 to an overdraft of $1.8 million in 20X8 which is significant at 7.8% of total assets.

Gearing and finance

In addition to problems with short-term finance and liquidity, Daley Co is also exhibiting a significant increase in gearing as evidenced by the increase in debt to equity from 2.3 in 20X7 to 6.4 in 20X8 and a fall in interest cover from 6.6 times to (1.5) times over the same period, indicating that the business is unable to service its current levels of finance. The company's finance costs as a percentage of long-term borrowings have increased from 5.6% in 20X7 to 13.4% in 20X8. This may be due at least in part to the interest on the overdraft proving to be an expensive way of financing the entity's operations and if the overdraft has not been agreed with the bank, the company may be incurring additional penalties and charges thereby putting additional strain on the company's cash flows. The increasing finance costs may also reflect lenders already perceiving Daley Co to be a high credit risk. It is also notable that non-current assets have decreased by 7.5% this year which suggests that the business is also struggling to replace and renew its existing capital expenditure levels. If this is the case, it may cast further doubt on the feasibility of the planned expansion of its operations.

Legal claim

Given Daley Co's current financial position, it seems unlikely that the business will be able to settle the legal claim of $3.5 million which threatens to place severe demands on the company's cash flow. Indeed, if there is a prospect of more claims arising in the future, the problems with the saleability of inventory and management of working capital as a result of the regulatory breaches discussed earlier may worsen further leading to a greater deterioration in the company's cash flow position.

Cash flow forecast

Overall, Daley Co's ability to continue to trade appears to be dependent on obtaining the new bank finance which it has assumed in its cash flow forecast. The bank financing is needed to meet existing liabilities and it is doubtful whether sufficient funding will be available in order to finance the proposed expansion. Moreover, the forecast itself appears to be unrealistic in its other assumptions. In particular, the assumption that the business's revenue will grow by 25% seems optimistic given the arrival of a major competitor in its market place and the projected trade receivable collection period of 60 days may well be unachievable on the basis of the historic ratios identified above. A return to a positive cash position is dependent on these assumptions and obtaining the new bank finance which may not be forthcoming based on the bank's assessment of the business's current financial position and performance.

(b) **Audit evidence on the cash flow forecast**

The audit working papers should include sufficient evidence that appropriate audit procedures have been conducted in relation to the assumption that Daley Co is a going concern at the reporting date, including the following:

- Evidence of agreement of the opening cash position to the cash book and bank reconciliation

- Reperformance by the audit team of the client's calculations in preparing the forecast in order to check its arithmetic accuracy

- Details of a review of the results of any market research which has been conducted by Daley Co for the next 12 months in order to assess the potential impact of the new competitor

- Notes from meetings with management detailing discussion of the key assumptions made by management in the preparation of the forecast (including the growth rate and receivables days) and an assessment of the consistency of the assumptions with the auditor's knowledge of the business and with management's intentions regarding the future of the company and corroborating evidence of assumptions

- Evaluation by the audit team of previous profit and other financial forecasts and their outcome in order to assess the consistency of the cash flow forecast with other prospective information prepared by management

- A comparison of the cash flow forecast for the period October to November 20X8 with management accounts for the same period in order to assess the accuracy of the forecast compared to actual data to date

- Results of analytical review of the items included in the cash flow forecast including, for example, a detailed review of the breakdown of different categories of expenses in order to identify any items which may have been omitted

- A review of correspondence with Daley Co's lawyers in relation to the legal claims in order to assess the likelihood of losing the actions, the likely cost and the possibility of further claims arising in the future

- Based on the review of legal correspondence, confirmation that the settlement of the legal claims has been appropriately included in the cash flow forecast

- A review of correspondence with Daley Co's bankers and supporting documentation for both the company's existing loan facilities and the proposed new loan

- Minutes of discussions with management in relation to the likelihood of obtaining the new loan

BPP
LEARNING

- Based on these reviews and discussions, a recalculation by the auditor of the finance cost and confirmation that the finance cost and the receipt of the loan have been accurately reflected in the cash flow forecast

- Working paper detailing the review of the documentation in relation to the new warehousing agreeing the cost and checking that the cash outflow is included in the forecast at the correct amount and at the correct date

- A review of board minutes in relation to the company's current trading position and the ongoing negotiations for the proposed new bank finance

- A consideration of the impact on cash flows and liquidity when the company is incurring the additional costs of compliance with all laws and regulations

(c) **Reasons for non-disclosure and implications for the auditor's report**

Motives for directors not wishing to make going concern disclosures

The directors' motives for non-disclosure of uncertainties in relation to going concern seem likely to reflect a desire to present the company in a positive light to investors and other third parties. This is a particularly sensitive issue at a time when the company is planning a major expansion and is seeking to raise significant new finance while struggling to manage its liquidity and working capital.

The disclosure of uncertainties in relation to going concern may well deter the bank from lending the new finance and may lead to a loss of confidence and goodwill with key suppliers and customers. Operational difficulties with suppliers and customers may prove to be particularly problematic with the arrival of the major new competitor in Daley Co's market in October 20X8.

Implications for the auditor's report

ISA 705 *Modifications to the Opinion in the Independent Auditor's Report* requires the auditor to modify the opinion in the auditor's report when they conclude that, based on the audit evidence obtained, the financial statements as a whole are not free from material misstatement. The failure to include disclosures regarding material uncertainties in relation to going concern in Daley Co's financial statements represents a material omission which will therefore require a modification of the auditor's opinion. In this case, the auditor must exercise professional judgement and assess whether the absence of this disclosure is material but not pervasive to the financial statements or whether it is material and pervasive to the financial statements.

Material but not pervasive

If the auditor concludes that the omission of the required disclosures in relation to the going concern uncertainties is material but not pervasive to the financial statements, a qualified audit opinion on the grounds of material misstatement is appropriate, as the directors have failed to include required disclosures. The auditor will include a 'Qualified Opinion' paragraph at the start of the auditor's report which will state that the financial statements are presented fairly in all material respects 'except for' the absence of this disclosure. The qualified opinion paragraph will be followed immediately by a 'Basis for Qualified Opinion' paragraph which will give details of the going concern uncertainties in relation to Daley Co and explain that the financial statements do not adequately disclose these uncertainties.

Material and pervasive

If the auditor concludes that the omission of the required disclosures in relation to the going concern uncertainties is material and pervasive to the financial statements, an adverse qualified audit opinion on the grounds of material misstatement is appropriate as in the auditor's opinion the lack of these disclosures will have a fundamental impact on the users' understanding of the financial statements. The auditor will include an 'Adverse Opinion'

paragraph at the start of the auditor's report which will state that the financial statements are not presented fairly in all material respects. The adverse opinion paragraph will be followed immediately by a 'Basis for Adverse Opinion' paragraph which will give details of the going concern uncertainties in relation to Daley Co and explain that in the opinion of the auditor, the omission of key disclosures in this respect arefundamental and pervasive to the financial statements and therefore require an adverse opinion.

> **Tutorial note.** Key audit matters (KAM) disclosures are not relevant for Daley Co as a result of its unlisted status.

Question 3

Workbook references. Chapters 1 and 2.

Top tips. Part (a) covered money laundering. This is another topical area, and one that is required to be on the AAA syllabus. Part (a)(i) is straight knowledge, so you should be looking to score at least three marks (but of course knowledge is a double-edged sword – if you don't know the material then you are in a difficult position).

Part (a)(ii) is trying to get you to think about how money laundering might appear in the real world, although the fact that you are told in the requirement that there may be indicators of money laundering makes it easier to pick them up *post hoc*.

Part (b) was the second appearance of ethics in this exam, and should again have been reasonable if you had been familiar with the material from Chapter 2 of the Workbook.

Easy marks. The marks for stating anti-money laundering policies, in part (a)(i), were among the easiest on the paper.

Marking scheme

Marks

(a) **Money laundering**

    (i) **Reporting duties and procedures:**

- Suspicions should be reported to nominated person within audit firm (MLRO); MLRO should possess suitable level of experience/seniority

- Audit firm should have established internal reporting lines which should be followed to report any suspicions

- Any individual in audit firm who has suspicions of money laundering activities must disclose them to MLRO; non-disclosure/failure to report constitutes an offence

- MLRO must consider all circumstances, document the process and decide whether to report to appropriate authorities; legal duty to report even though this may conflict with auditor's duty of confidentiality

                                               Maximum   4

BPP
LEARNING

Marks

(ii) **Generally up to 2 marks for each well-explained point of explanation, for example:**

Cash-intensive business:

- High level of cash sales and high volume of individual sales reports; risk illicit cash funds are being passed off as legitimate sales

- Mr Blackers' sale to business associate for $33,000 may be example of placement of illegal funds in order to legitimise them as genuine sales

International property transactions:

- May be example of real estate laundering by Mr Blackers in his personal affairs; may be purchasing international property with illegal funds (placement) and then selling them in order to make funds appear legitimate (integration)

- High volume of transactions and off-shore bank accounts in Mr Blackers' name may be indicative of layering of transactions in attempt to make original source of funds difficult to trace

Maximum 6

(b) **Ethical and professional issues**

Generally 1 mark for each point identified and explained.

Taxation services

- Company tax computation is self-review threat as tax calculation forms basis of tax payable and tax charge in financial statements

- Advocacy threat re acting on client's behalf with tax authorities

- Per IESBA *Code*, completing tax returns does not generally create threat to independence if management takes responsibility for returns including any judgements made

- Tax calculations for purpose of preparing accounting entries – may be acceptable for unlisted audit client; firm should consider safeguards, eg using professionals not members of audit team or independent senior/partner review

- Preparation of Mr Blackers' personal tax return may be taxable benefit which should be included in tax return and fee should be reflected in his director's loan account with the company

- Preparation of personal tax return may result in auditor being associated with criminal activities (ie money laundering as above)

Website and online sales system

- Self-review threat as auditor will audit sales figures generated by system

Marks

- New system appears to be significant to client's financial statements and records

- Risk assume management responsibility relating to design of system and controls

- Threat may be too significant even for unlisted client unless appropriate safeguards put in place

- Examples of possible safeguards include: client acknowledges responsibility for establishing and monitoring system of internal controls; client makes all management decisions re design and implementation process; client is responsible for operating system and data it generates; separate team made up of non-audit staff performs work with independent professional review (max 2 marks for safeguards)

Office party

- Client hospitality (attendance at party) may create familiarity risks as audit staff may be getting too close to client especially given that this happens every year

- Gifts may create self-interest risk as audit staff receiving direct financial benefit from client

- Unless value is trivial and inconsequential, threats would be too significant to mitigate with safeguards and should not be accepted

- Auditor should have internal authorisation procedures to establish whether value is trivial and inconsequential

- In this case, value appears trivial but auditor should consider declining given possible criminal activities by client staff

Maximum   15

Total   25

(a) **Money laundering**

(i) **Policies and procedures for anti-money laundering programme**

Thomasson & Co should have established an anti-money laundering programme within the firm. As part of this programme, the firm should have appointed a money laundering reporting officer (MLRO) with an appropriate level of experience and seniority. The audit firm should also have established internal reporting lines which should be followed to report any suspicions. Thomasson & Co will probably have a standard form which should be used to report suspicions of money laundering to the MLRO.

The typical content of an internal report on suspected money laundering may include the name of the suspect, the amounts potentially involved, and the reasons for the suspicions with supporting evidence if possible, and the whereabouts of the laundered cash. The firm's internal policies should have been set up to ensure that all pertinent information is captured in this standardised report.

BPP
LEARNING

Any individual in the audit firm who has suspicions of money laundering activities is then required to disclose these suspicions to the MLRO. The report must be done as soon as possible as any non-disclosure or failure to report such suspicions will constitute an offence under the money laundering regulations.

On receipt of the internal report, the MLRO must consider all of the circumstances surrounding the suspicions of money laundering activities, document this process and decide whether to report the suspicions to the appropriate external authorities. The audit firm has a legal duty to report even though this may conflict with the auditor's duty of confidentiality.

> **Tutorial note.** Credit will be awarded for other relevant answer points in relation to a firm's anti-money laundering programme.

(ii) **Evaluation of possible indicators of money laundering activities**

Money laundering is the process by which criminals attempt to conceal the true origin and ownership of the proceeds of criminal activity, allowing them to maintain control over the proceeds, and ultimately providing a legitimate cover for their sources of income.

In the case of Clean Co, the circumstances which may be indicative of money laundering activities include the following:

Cash-intensive business

Clean Co has a high level of cash-based sales (75%) and a high volume of individual sales reports. The nature of its business therefore creates a significant risk that illicit cash funds are being passed off as legitimate sales. More specifically Mr Blackers' sale to a business associate for $33,000 may be an example of the placement of illegal funds in order to legitimise them as genuine sales. The size of the transaction in a business selling cleaning products and the round sum amount may be additional grounds for suspicion in relation to this transaction.

International property transactions

The performance of Mr Blackers' personal taxation computation has identified a significant number of transactions involving the purchase and sale of properties in international locations. These transactions may be examples of real estate laundering by Mr Blackers in his personal affairs. It is possible that he may be purchasing these properties with illegal funds ('placement') and then selling them in order to make funds appear legitimate ('integration'). A high volume of such transactions may also be indicative of the 'layering' of transactions in an attempt to make the original source of the funds more difficult to trace.

(b) **Ethical and professional issues**

Taxation services

Company tax computation

The performance of the company tax computation creates a self-review threat. A self-review threat arises when an auditor reviews work which they themselves have previously performed – for example, if the external auditor is involved in the process of preparing the financial statements and then audits them. As a result, there is a risk that the auditor will not be sufficiently objective in performing the audit and may fail to identify any shortcomings in their own work. In this case therefore, a self-review threat to auditor independence arises because the tax calculation forms the basis of the tax payable and the tax charge in the financial statements and as such the audit team may be more likely to accept the tax calculations without adequate testing. There is also a potential advocacy threat. An advocacy threat arises

when the auditor is asked to promote or represent their client in some way. In this situation, there is a risk of the auditor being seen to promote the interests of Clean Co with a third party such as the tax authorities and therefore that the auditor will be biased in favour of the client and cannot be fully objective.

According to the IESBA *Code of Ethics for Professional Accountants* (the Code), however, completing tax returns does not generally create a threat to independence provided management takes responsibility for the returns including any judgements which have been made. Where tax calculations have been prepared by the auditor for the purpose of preparing accounting entries, the Code states that this may be acceptable for an unlisted audit client and that the firm should consider implementing safeguards in order to reduce the self-review threat to an acceptable level. In this case, these safeguards might have included, for example, using professionals who are not members of the audit team to prepare the tax computations together with independent senior or partner review of the work. Therefore, given that Clean Co is an unlisted client, Thomasson & Co should ascertain which members of staff performed the taxation services and should review whether the threat to independence has been adequately assessed before the taxation services were performed and whether adequate safeguards have been applied.

Mr Blackers' personal tax computation

From an ethical perspective, there is no prohibition in the Code on the preparation of personal tax returns for the directors of an audit client such as Clean Co. However, in this case the auditor should consider whether the preparation of Mr Blackers' personal tax return may result in the auditor being associated with criminal activities if the suspicions of money laundering activities noted above prove to be well founded.

The auditor should also consider the appropriateness of personal taxation services being billed to the company. Indeed, the preparation of Mr Blackers' personal tax return may be a taxable benefit which should be included in his tax return and the fee for this service may need to be reflected in his director's loan account with the company.

Website and online sales system

According to the *Code*, providing services to an audit client involving the design or implementation of IT systems which form a significant part of the internal control over financial reporting or generate information which is significant to the accounting records or financial statements on which the firm will express an opinion constitutes a self-review threat. A self-review threat arises when an auditor reviews work which they themselves have previously performed – for example, if the external auditor is involved in the process of preparing the financial statements and then audits them. As a result, there is a risk that the auditor will not be sufficiently objective in performing the audit and may fail to identify any shortcomings in their own work. In this case, the self-review threat arises as the new systems will produce data which will be used directly in the preparation of the financial statements. The audit process will therefore include reviewing and testing of financial data and systems which Thomasson & Co has helped to design and implement. As a result, there is a clear risk that the audit team may too readily place reliance on these systems.

With reference to Clean Co therefore, it is clear that providing assistance with the design and implementation of the website and online sales system will constitute a self-review threat as the auditor will audit sales figures which are generated by the system and there is also a risk that the firm may assume a management responsibility if they become involved in making management decisions. In the case of revenue, this self-review threat may be heightened further by the auditor's reliance on controls testing and on analytical review of the data summaries generated by the new system. It also seems clear that the new online sales system will be significant to the client's financial statements and records. The *Code* states that such a self-review threat may be too significant even for an unlisted client such as Clean Co unless appropriate safeguards are put in place. Examples of possible safeguards which might assist in managing the self-review threat include the following:

- The client should acknowledge its responsibility for establishing and monitoring the system of internal controls and for the operating system and data it generates;

- The respective responsibilities of the audit firm and the client should be clearly defined in a separate engagement letter in order to ensure that the client makes all management decisions in relation to the design and implementation process;

- Thomasson & Co should use a separate team made up of non-audit staff to perform the systems design and implementation assignment and the work performed by this team should be subject to independent professional review.

If the self-review threat cannot be reduced to an acceptable level, or the engagement will result in the firm assuming a management responsibility, the service should not be provided.

Office party

The *Code* states that client hospitality (in this case the attendance at the office party by the audit team) may create a familiarity threat. A familiarity threat occurs when the auditor is too sympathetic or trusting of the client because of a close relationship with them. There is a risk therefore that as a result of attending the client office party, the audit staff may be getting too close to the client staff especially given that according to the audit senior, this practice has occurred every year. This close relationship may result in the audit team becoming less objective and less able to challenge explanations provided by the client.

The *Code* also states that gifts from a client to a member of the audit team may create a self-interest threat. A self-interest threat arises when the auditor derives a potential personal benefit from an audit client which may motivate them to behave in a manner which aims to protect that benefit. With reference to the office party therefore, the audit staff are receiving a direct financial benefit from the client (in this case in the form of vouchers). Unless the value of such gifts is trivial and inconsequential, the self-interest threat would be too significant to mitigate with safeguards and the gifts should not be accepted. The audit firm should consider introducing internal authorisation procedures in order to ensure transparency and to establish whether the value is trivial and inconsequential. In this case, the value of $30 per head does appear to be trivial but the auditor might still consider declining the gifts in order to maintain a visible professional distance from a client which may be involved in criminal activities.